The Writings of St. Augustine Against the Donatists

The Writings of St. Augustine Against the Donatists

Edited by Paul A. Böer, Sr.

VERITATIS SPLENDOR PUBLICATIONS
et cognoscetis veritatem et veritas liberabit vos (Jn 8:32)

MMXIV

Cover Illustration

Title: Saint Augustine
Artist: Philippe de Champaigne (1602–1674)
Date: 1645-1650
Medium: Oil on canvas
Dimensions: 78.7 x 62.2 cm
Current location: Los Angeles County Museum of Art
Los Angeles, CA)

The text of this book is excerpted from:

Nicene and Post-Nicene Fathers, First Series, Vol. 4. Edited by Philip Schaff. (Buffalo, NY: Christian Literature Publishing Co., 1887.)

The text of this work is in the public domain.

Retypeset and republished in 2014 by Veritatis Splendor Publications.

ALL RIGHTS RESERVED.

This typography of this publication is the property of Veritatis Splendor Publications and may not be reproduced, stored in a retrieval system, or transmitted in any form or by any means, in whole or in part, without written permission from the Publisher, except as permitted by United States and International copyright law.

Copyright © 2014. Veritatis Splendor Publications.

Veritatis.splendor.publication@gmail.com

AD MAJOREM DEI GLORIAM

CONTENTS

Introductory Essay By Rev. Chester D. Hartranft, D.D. 27
    Chapter I. 27
    Bibliography. 27
        A. Sources. 27
        B. Literature. 29
    Chapter II. 33
    An Analysis of Augustin's Writings Against the Donatists. 33
Preface 108
THE SEVEN BOOKS OF AUGUSTIN, BISHOP OF HIPPO, ON BAPTISM, AGAINST THE DONATISTS [DE BAPTISIMO CONTRA DONATISTAS.] CIRCA A.D. 400. 115
    Book I. 115
        Chapter 1. 115
        Chapter 2. 119
        Chapter 3. 120
        Chapter 4. 123
        Chapter 5. 125
        Chapter 6. 127
        Chapter 7. 128
        Chapter 8. 130
        Chapter 9. 132
        Chapter 10. 133
        Chapter 11. 136

Chapter 12. 138
Chapter 13. 142
Chapter 14. 143
Chapter 15. 144
Chapter 16. 147
Chapter 17. 148
Chapter 18. 149
Chapter 19. 152
Book II 153
Chapter 1 154
Chapter 2 158
Chapter 3 159
Chapter 4 160
Chapter 5 161
Chapter 6 163
Chapter 7 167
Chapter 8 171
Chapter 9 173
Chapter 10. 175
Chapter 11. 177
Chapter 12. 179
Chapter 13. 180
Chapter 14. 181
Chapter 15. 182

- Book III. 183
  - Chapter 1. 184
  - Chapter 2. 184
  - Chapter 3. 187
  - Chapter 4. 189
  - Chapter 5. 191
  - Chapter 6. 192
  - Chapter 7. 192
  - Chapter 8. 193
  - Chapter 9. 193
  - Chapter 10. 194
  - Chapter 11. 195
  - Chapter 12. 196
  - Chapter 13. 197
  - Chapter 14. 199
  - Chapter 15. 202
  - Chapter 16. 204
  - Chapter 17. 206
  - Chapter 18. 207
  - Chapter 19. 209
- Book IV. 216
  - Chapter 1. 217
  - Chapter 2. 218
  - Chapter 3. 219

Chapter 4 221
Chapter 5 224
Chapter 6 227
Chapter 7 229
Chapter 8 231
Chapter 9 233
Chapter 10. 236
Chapter 11. 239
Chapter 12. 241
Chapter 13. 244
Chapter 14. 246
Chapter 15. 248
Chapter 16. 250
Chapter 17. 251
Chapter 18. 253
Chapter 19. 254
Chapter 20. 256
Chapter 21. 257
Chapter 22. 260
Chapter 23. 261
Chapter 24. 262
Chapter 25. 264
Chapter 26. 265
Book V 265

Chapter 1. 266
Chapter 2. 268
Chapter 4. 271
Chapter 5. 272
Chapter 6. 273
Chapter 7. 275
Chapter 8. 275
Chapter 9. 277
Chapter 10. 280
Chapter 11. 281
Chapter 12. 282
Chapter 13. 283
Chapter 14. 285
Chapter 15. 286
Chapter 16. 288
Chapter 17. 289
Chapter 18. 292
Chapter 19. 293
Chapter 20. 296
Chapter 21. 297
Chapter 22. 300
Chapter 23. 301
Chapter 24. 304
Chapter 25. 305

Chapter 26. 306
Chapter 27. 308
Chapter 28. 310
Book VI. 312
   Chapter 1. 312
   Chapter 2. 315
   Chapter 3. 317
   Chapter 4. 318
   Chapter 5. 319
   Chapter 6. 320
   Chapter 7. 321
   Chapter 8. 324
   Chapter 9. 326
   Chapter 10. 327
   Chapter 11. 328
   Chapter 12. 328
   Chapter 13. 334
   Chapter 14. 334
   Chapter 15. 337
   Chapter 16. 339
   Chapter 17. 340
   Chapter 18. 341
   Chapter 19. 342
   Chapter 20. 343

Chapter 21. 344
Chapter 22. 345
Chapter 23. 347
Chapter 24. 347
Chapter 25. 351
Chapter 26. 354
Chapter 27. 355
Chapter 28. 355
Chapter 29. 356
Chapter 30. 359
Chapter 31. 359
Chapter 32. 361
Chapter 33. 362
Chapter 34. 363
Chapter 35. 366
Chapter 36. 367
Chapter 37. 368
Chapter 38. 369
Chapter 39. 369
Chapter 40. 370
Chapter 41. 372
Chapter 42. 372
Chapter 43. 373
Chapter 44. 374

Book VII. 377
   Chapter 1. 377
   Chapter 2. 379
   Chapter 3. 382
   Chapter 4. 383
   Chapter 5. 385
   Chapter 6. 386
   Chapter 7. 387
   Chapter 8. 388
   Chapter 9. 389
   Chapter 10. 389
   Chapter 11. 390
   Chapter 12. 391
   Chapter 13. 392
   Chapter 14. 393
   Chapter 15. 394
   Chapter 16. 395
   Chapter 17. 396
   Chapter 18. 397
   Chapter 19. 397
   Chapter 20. 398
   Chapter 21. 399
   Chapter 22. 399
   Chapter 23. 400

Chapter 24. 401
Chapter 25. 401
Chapter 26. 403
Chapter 27. 404
Chapter 28. 404
Chapter 29. 405
Chapter 30. 405
Chapter 31. 406
Chapter 32. 406
Chapter 33. 407
Chapter 34. 407
Chapter 35. 408
Chapter 36. 408
Chapter 37. 409
Chapter 38. 410
Chapter 39. 410
Chapter 40. 411
Chapter 41. 412
Chapter 42. 412
Chapter 43. 413
Chapter 44. 413
Chapter 45. 414
Chapter 46. 416
Chapter 47. 417

Chapter 48. 418

Chapter 49. 418

Chapter 50. 420

Chapter 51. 422

Chapter 52. 424

Chapter 53. 425

Chapter 54. 428

THE THREE BOOKS OF AUGUSTIN, BISHOP OF HIPPO, IN ANSWER TO THE LETTERS OF PETILIAN, THE DONATIST [CONTRA LITTERAS PETILIANI DONATISTÆ CORTENSIS, EPISCOPI] CIRCA A.D. 400. 430

Book I. 430

Chapter 1 431

Chapter 2 433

Chapter 3 433

Chapter 4 435

Chapter 5 435

Chapter 6 437

Chapter 7 437

Chapter 8 439

Chapter 9 439

Chapter 10. 441

Chapter 11. 443

Chapter 12. 443

Chapter 13. 444
Chapter 14. 446
Chapter 15. 446
Chapter 16. 447
Chapter 17. 447
Chapter 18. 448
Chapter 19. 450
Chapter 20. 452
Chapter 21. 453
Chapter 22. 454
Chapter 23. 454
Chapter 24. 456
Chapter 25. 457
Chapter 26. 458
Chapter 27. 459
Chapter 28. 459
Chapter 29. 460
Book II. [1967] 461
Chapter 1. 461
Chapter 2. 462
Chapter 3. 463
Chapter 4. 463
Chapter 5. 463
Chapter 6. 465

Chapter 7...466

Chapter 8...469

Chapter 9...475

Chapter 10. 475

Chapter 11. 476

Chapter 12. 478

Chapter 13. 478

Chapter 14. 479

Chapter 15. 484

Chapter 16. 486

Chapter 17. 487

Chapter 18. 487

Chapter 19. 490

Chapter 20. 492

Chapter 21. 495

Chapter 22. 497

Chapter 23. 499

Chapter 24. 506

Chapter 25. 507

Chapter 26. 507

Chapter 27. 509

Chapter 28. 510

Chapter 29. 511

Chapter 30. 511

Chapter 31. 514
Chapter 32. 514
Chapter 33. 521
Chapter 34. 524
Chapter 35. 524
Chapter 36. 526
Chapter 37. 527
Chapter 38. 535
Chapter 39. 536
Chapter 40. 540
Chapter 41. 541
Chapter 42. 541
Chapter 43. 542
Chapter 44. 544
Chapter 45. 545
Chapter 46. 545
Chapter 47. 547
Chapter 48. 550
Chapter 49. 551
Chapter 50. 553
Chapter 51. 553
Chapter 52. 555
Chapter 53. 556
Chapter 54. 557

Chapter 55. 558
Chapter 56. 560
Chapter 57. 560
Chapter 58. 561
Chapter 59. 563
Chapter 60. 564
Chapter 61. 564
Chapter 62. 566
Chapter 63. 567
Chapter 64. 568
Chapter 65. 568
Chapter 66. 569
Chapter 67. 570
Chapter 68. 571
Chapter 69. 571
Chapter 70. 573
Chapter 71. 573
Chapter 72. 574
Chapter 73. 575
Chapter 74. 576
Chapter 75. 579
Chapter 76. 579
Chapter 77. 580
Chapter 78. 581

Chapter 79. 582

Chapter 80. 584

Chapter 81. 585

Chapter 82. 586

Chapter 83. 588

Chapter 84. 589

Chapter 85. 593

Chapter 86. 596

Chapter 87. 596

Chapter 88. 598

Chapter 89. 600

Chapter 90. 602

Chapter 91. 603

Chapter 92. 603

Chapter 93. 604

Chapter 94. 627

Chapter 95. 627

Chapter 96. 628

Chapter 97. 629

Chapter 98. 631

Chapter 99. 634

Chapter 100. 636

Chapter 101. 638

Chapter 102. 639

Chapter 103. 642
Chapter 104. 644
Chapter 105. 647
Chapter 106. 651
Chapter 107. 654
Chapter 108. 655
Chapter 109. 656
Book III. 659
Chapter 1. 659
Chapter 2. 662
Chapter 3. 665
Chapter 4. 667
Chapter 5. 669
Chapter 6. 670
Chapter 7. 672
Chapter 8. 674
Chapter 9. 675
Chapter 10. 675
Chapter 11. 677
Chapter 12. 678
Chapter 13. 680
Chapter 14. 680
Chapter 15. 681
Chapter 16. 683

Chapter 17. 684
Chapter 18. 685
Chapter 19. 686
Chapter 20. 687
Chapter 21. 688
Chapter 22. 692
Chapter 23. 693
Chapter 24. 694
Chapter 25. 695
Chapter 26. 697
Chapter 27. 698
Chapter 28. 700
Chapter 29. 701
Chapter 30. 703
Chapter 32. 706
Chapter 33. 707
Chapter 34. 709
Chapter 35. 710
Chapter 36. 712
Chapter 37. 714
Chapter 38. 715
Chapter 39. 716
Chapter 40. 717
Chapter 41. 720

Chapter 42. 722

Chapter 43. 723

Chapter 44. 725

Chapter 45. 726

Chapter 46. 727

Chapter 47. 730

Chapter 48. 732

Chapter 49. 733

Chapter 50. 735

Chapter 51. 738

Chapter 52. 740

Chapter 53. 743

Chapter 54. 745

Chapter 55. 746

Chapter 56. 748

Chapter 57. 750

Chapter 58. 751

Chapter 59. 754

ST. AUGUSTIN: A TREATISE CONCERNING THE CORRECTION OF THE DONATISTS, OR EPISTLE CLXXXV [DE CORRECTIONE DONATISTARUM, LIBER SEU EPISTOLA CLXXXV.] CIRCA A.D. 417 [2465] 756

Chapter 1 756

Chapter 2 761

Chapter 3. 768
Chapter 4. 772
Chapter 5. 776
Chapter 6. 779
Chapter 7. 784
Chapter 8. 791
Chapter 9. 794
Chapter 10. 801
Chapter 11. 807

A SELECT LIBRARY
OF THE
NICENE AND
POST-NICENE FATHERS
OF
THE CHRISTIAN CHURCH.

EDITED BY
PHILIP SCHAFF, D.D., LL.D.,
PROFESSOR IN THE UNION THEOLOGICAL
SEMINARY, NEW YORK,
IN CONNECTION WITH A NUMBER OF PATRISTIC
SCHOLARS OF EUROPE AND
AMERICA.

VOLUME IV

ST. AUGUSTIN:
THE WRITINGS AGAINST THE MANICHÆANS
AND
AGAINST THE DONATISTS

T&T CLARK
EDINBURGH

WM. B. EERDMANS PUBLISHING COMPANY
GRAND RAPIDS, MICHIGAN

WRITINGS IN CONNECTION WITH THE DONATIST CONTROVERSY

TRANSLATED BY THE REV. J. R. KING, M.A.
VICAR OF ST. PETER'S IN THE EAST, OXFORD, AND LATE FELLOW AND TUTOR OF MERTON COLLEGE, OXFORD.

REVISED, WITH ADDITIONAL NOTES,
BY, THE REV. CHESTER D. HARTRANFT, D.D.
PROFESSOR OF BIBLICAL AND ECCLESIASTICAL HISTORY, IN THE THEOLOGICAL SEMINARY AT HARTFORD, CONN.

Introductory Essay
By Rev. Chester D. Hartranft, D.D.

Chapter I.

Bibliography.

A. Sources.

I. Of course all the Anti-Donatist writings of Augustin are found in the general editions from Amerbach, 1506, to Migne, 1861. A few are also collected in Du Pin's edd. of Optatus Mil. 1. In the Monumenta vetera ad Donatistarum Historiam pertinentia. 2. In the Gesta Collationis Carthagini habitae Honorii Caesaris iussu inter Catholicos et Donatistas. See also the different Collections of Councils, Labbe, Baluze, Harduin, Mansi, etc. Since these works are discussed in Chapter II. it is unnecessary to repeat the titles here. Cp. titles in Retractationes: and Indiculus librorum, tractatuum et epistolarum S. Augustini, ed. cura Possidii, cap. III.

II. Separate editions of Augustin's Anti-Donatist writings. (From Schönemann's Bibliotheca, and other bibliographies.)

1. S. Augustini liber seu Epistola de unitate Ecclesiae contra Petiliani Donat. Epistolam, Argumentis, Notis atque Analysi illustrata, studio Justi Caluini. Moguntiae. 1602.

2. SS. Cypriani et Augustini de unitate Ecclesiae tractatus. Accedit Georgii Calixti, S. Theo. Doct. et in Acad. Julia Prof. primarii, in eorundem librorum lectionem Introductionis fragmentum edente Frid. Ulrico Calixto. Georgii filio. Helmæstadii ex typogr. Calixt. 1657. 8.

3. Aurelii Augustini, Episcopi Hipponensis, Liber de Unitate Ecclesiae contra Donatistas. Ext. cum Commentariis uberrimis et utillisimis in Melchioris Lydeckeri Historia illustrata Ecclesiae Africanae, cujus totum pæne tomum secundum constituit inscriptum:

Tomus secundus ad Librum Augustini de Unitate Ecclesiae contra Donatistas, de principiis Ecclesiae Africanae, illiusque fide in Articulis de Capite Christo et Ecclesia, de Unitate et Schismate, plurimisque Religionis Christianae capitibus agit. Ultrajecti apud viduam Guil. Clerck, 1690. 4.

4. D. Augustini liber de moderate coercendis haereticis ed Bonifacium Comitem. Nic. Bergius Revalensis Holmiae, 1696, in 8.

III. Translations.

1. Epistre ou le Livre de St. Augustin de l'Unité de l'Eglise, contre Petilien, Evesque Donatiste, avec certaines observations pour entendre les lieux plus difficiles par Jac. Tigeou, imprimé à Reims par Jean de Foigny. 1567. 8.

2. L'Epistre à Vincent, Evesque de l'heresie Rogatiane, traduict de latin par Clément Vaillant. A Paris, Mathurin Prevost. 1573. 8.

3. Traité du Baptême trad. par l'abbé Dujat, chapelain d'Étampes. Paris. 1778. 12.

4. Writings in connection with the Donatist controversy, translated by the Rev. J. R. King, M.A. In the Series of Translations of the Works of Augustin. Edinburgh. T. & T. Clark. 1872.

5.Ausgewählte Schriften des heil. Aurelius Augustinus, Kirchenlehrers, nach aem Urtexte ubersetzt. Mit einer kurzen Lebensbeschreibung des Heiligen von J. Motzberger. 1871-1879. In the Bibliothek der Kirchenväter, Kempten, 1869 sqq.

B. Literature.

This is a selected literature of the Donatist controversy so far as Augustin was connected with it.

I. In the Benedictine editions occur:

1.Their Vita S. Aurelii Augustini. Tom. XI. Antw., pp. 1-344. Tom. I. Migne, pp. 65-578.

2.Praefatio of Tom. IX. Antw. s. p. Migne, pp. 9-24.

3.Index opusculorum S. Augustini contra Donatistas. Tom. IX. Antw., pp. 463, 4. Migne, pp. 757-760.

4.Excerpta et scripta vetera ad Donatistarum historiam pertinentia. Tom. IX. Antw., App. pp. 7-50. Migne, pp. 773-842.

5.Epistolarum ordo chronologicus. Tom. II. Antw., s. p. Migne, pp. 13-48.

II.Possidius: Vita S. Aurelii Augustini. Reprinted in Migne Aug. Op. Tom. I., pp. 33-66. Cp. Migne Pat. Lat. L. p. 407.

III.Ecclesiastica Historia. By the Magdeburg Centuriators. 1559-1574. Tom. II. and III., Centuria, IV. and V., contain the Donatist history.

IV.Balduinius, Franc.

1. Delibatio Africanae historiae ecclesticae, s. Optati libri VII. de Schismate Donatistarum, etc. Paris, 1563. A second edition with improved readings. Ib., 1569. In this the prefaces and annotations are of value. Reprinted in Du Pin's ed. of Optatus Mil.

2. Historia Carthaginensis Collationis sive disputationis de ecclesia, olim habitae inter Catholicos et Donatistas. Paris, 1566. 8. Reprinted in Du Pin. ib.

V. Baronius. Annales Ecclesiatici. 1588-1607. Tom. III.-V., contain the Donatist history.

VI. Albaspinæus: Optati Mel. opera cum notis et observationibus Gabrielis Albaspinæi. Paris, 1631. Valuable mainly for the observations; reprinted in Du Pin's ed. of Optatus.

VII. Casaubonus: Optati Mel. de schismate Donatistarum libri VII. In eosd. notae et emendationes Merici Casauboni. Lond. 1631. These notes are of value and are reproduced with those of other editions in the Annotationes Variorum of Du Pin's ed.

VIII. Valesius Henricus: Eusebii Pamph. Historia ecc., libri de Vita Constantini, Panegyricus, Const. Oratio ad Sanctorum coetum, gr. et lat. cum annotatt. Paris, 1659 and often. In this is his dissertation: De schismate Donatistarum.

IX. Long, Thomas, B.D. History of the Donatists. Lond. 1677. 8.

X. Du Pin: Nouvelle Bibliothéque des Auteurs Ecclésiastiques.

1. St. Augustin. Tom. III. première partie, pp. 522-839, 1690. Particularly the review of vol. IX. of Augustin's collected works, pp. 792-811.

2. In Tom. II., Troisième partie, 1701, there are also many allusions to the history and literature.

3. In his ed. of Optatus Mel., Historia Donatistarum.

XI. Ittig, Thomas: de Haeresiarchis oevi apostolici at apostol. prox. Lips. 1690-1703. 4.

XII. Leydecker Melchior; Historia Ecclesiastica Africana. 2 Tom. 4, See above. Traj. 1690. 4.

XIII. Witsius, Hermann: Miscellaneorum Sacrorum libri. 2 vols. Amst. 1692. 4. In vol. I. Dissertatio de schismate Donatistarum.

XIV. Bernino: Historia di tutte l'heresie descritta da Domenico Bernino. Venezia 1711. Tom. I., contains hist. of Donatism.

XV. Storren, J. Ph.: ansführlicher und gründlicher Bericht von den Namen, Ursprung, v.s.w. der Donatisten. Frankf. 1723. 8.

XVI. Norisius, Henricus: Opera omnia nunc prim. collecta et ordinata. Veronae, Tumermani, 1729-32, fol. 4vols. The fourth volume contains his posthumous work on History of Donatism, as finished by Ballerini.

XVII. Tillemont: in his Memoires pour servir a l'histoire Ecclésiastique:

1. Tom. VI. Histoire du schisme des Donatistes, où l'on marque aussi tout ce qui regardé l'Eglise d'Afrique depuis l'an 305, jusques en l'an 391que S. Augustin fut fait Prestre. 1732.

2.Tom. XIII. La Vie de Saint Augustin, dans laquelle on trouvera l'histoire des Donatistes de son temps, et celle des Pelagiens. 1732.

XVIII.Orsi: Della Istoria Ecclesiastica descritta da F. Guiseppe Agostino Orsi. Tom. IV. (1741) and V. (1749) contain the history ot the Donatists.

XIX.Walch, Ch. Wilh. Fr.:Entwurf einer vollständigen Historie der Ketzereien, Spaltungen und Religionsstreitigkeiten, bis auf die Zeiten der Reformation. Leipzig, 1768. Vierter Theil: Von der Spaltung der Donatisten; with its three sections:

a.Von der historie der Donatisten.

b.Von den zwischen den Donatisten und ihren Gegnern geführten Religionsstreitigkeiten.

c.Beurtheilung der Donatistichen Streitigkeiten. This work was the beginning of a new critical estimate of the documents.

XX.Schröckh, Johann Mattheus: Christliche Kirchengeschichte. Sechster Theil: 1784, but particularly Elfter Theil, 1786. A juster estimate of Donatism.

XXI.Morcellii, Steph. Ant.: Africa christiana in tres partes distributa. 3 vols. 4Brixiae, 1816-17. 4. P. II. for Donatism.

XXII.Bindemann, C.: Der heilige Augustinus, 1844-1869. Bdd. II. & III. contain excellent analyses of the works on Donatism, as well as a history during Augustin's life.

XXIII.Roux, Adrianus: Dissertatio de Aurelio Augustino, adversario Donatistarum. Lugduni Batavorum, 1838. A brief summary of the works and doctrine.

XXIV. Ribbeck: Donatus und Augustinus oder der erste entscheidende Kampf zwischen Separatismus und Kirche. Ein Kirchenhistorischer Versuch von Ferdinand Ribbeck. Elberfeld. 1857. 8. An uncritical history; but a vigorous analysis, apologetic and polemic.

XXV. Deutsch: Drei Actenstücke zur Geschichte Donatismus. Neu herausgegeben und erklärt von Martin Deutsch. Berlin, 1875. The first work on the textual and historical criticism of the sources.

XXVI. Voelter: Der Ursprung des Donatismus, nach den Quellen untersucht und dargestellt von Lic Dr. Daniel Voelter. Freiburg i. B. und Tübingen, 1883. This keen writer, at present Prof. Ord. in Univ. of Amsterdam, has gone still further into textual and historical criticism, and gives fair promise of a more impartial hearing for Donatism. It is to be hoped that he will fulfill his qualified promise of further research.

Among the general church histories particular mention may be made of Gieseler, Neander, Lindner, Niedner, Robertson, Ritter, Hergenröther, Schaff. The articles on Augustin, Donatism and related persons and topics in Ceillier, Ersch und Gruber, Herzog, Schaff-Herzog, Smith's Dictionary of Christian Biography, Wetzer and Welte, Lichtenberger, are more or less noteworthy. Mention must also be made of the Patrologies, the biographies, Hefele's Conciliengeschichte, the Analyses Patrum, etc.

Chapter II.

An Analysis of Augustin's Writings Against the Donatists.

The object of this chapter is to present a rudimentary outline and summary of all that Augustin penned or spoke against those traditional North African Christians whom he was pleased to regard as schismatics. It will be arranged, so far as may be, in chronological order, following the dates suggested by the Benedictine edition. The necessary brevity precludes anything but a very meagre treatment of so considerable a theme. The writer takes no responsibility for the ecclesiological tenets of the great Father, nor will he enter here into any criticism of the text and truth of the documents, upon which the historical argument was so laboriously and peremptorily built, to the utter ignoring of the Donatist archives, and the protests of their scholars against the validity and integrity of their opponents' records. Both parties claimed to be the historic Catholic church; both were little apart in doctrine, worship, and polity; both tended toward externalism in piety; both accused one another of fraud in inventing records. Later Romanism in its bright spirit of selection took much spoil from either camp.

The city of Augustin's birth, its neighborhood, indeed the whole ecclesiastical province of Numidia, was a stronghold for this puristic school. Is it not singular, then, that it seems to have made no impression upon his early years? As a child he had witnessed its brief restoration under Julian, and then the severe or lax efforts at suppression under succeeding emperors; the Rogatian schism and the Tychonian reformation were quite familiar to him in his Manichæan period; but the Confessions are silent as to any such stamp or hold upon his mind. His activity begins with his ordination to the presbyterate, a time marked in Donatist annals by the Maximianist separation, and increases as he becomes bishop. From about 392 to near the close of his life, pen and voice were seldom still. In all those years the outlinear thoughts grew in breadth and depth; endless are the forms in which his few and radical conceptions manifest themselves; never does he lose sight of the popular effect, so that he knows when to relax his love of word-play and delight in mysterious inductions, in order to make the chief themes plain to the dullest mind.

How varied the channels through which he struggled for the mastery of his idea of the Church! In the pulpit he made Donatism the occasion of many a polemic, many an appeal; in his correspondence it was an ever-recurrent topic; it was the staple of many a tract and book; verse was not shunned to destroy its fashionableness and popularity; commentaries and manuals for the meditative hour or for the training of the theological student, abounded in warnings against its aggressiveness; no opportunity for debate or conference or epistolary discussion was left unimproved. And no wonder: it was a living thing, of the street, of the market, of the social circle, of the home; it threatened at times to obliterate the transmarine view of the church from North Africa; its spirit of political independence and plea for religious liberty went to the hearts of a people, more and more restive under the decline of the Empire.

The literary creations of Donatism had been somewhat more fertile than that of Cæcilianism. We must not belittle Donatus the Great, Parmenian, Petilian, Gaudentius, and certainly the eminence of Tychonius is confessed by Augustin himself. Up to this time Optatus of Milevis had been the only forcible opponent. But against the great Augustin whom could they bring into the field? And against the great Augustin, backed by the energy of the State, there was little hope of fairness.

Augustin found a new and weighty school. Donatism, with its impossible ideal, already began to despise the culture which seemed to help its defeat and withdrew into its sensitive shell after the manner of all puristic tendencies under persecution.

The two prevalent lines of attack are the historical on the origin of the schism, which involved the dissection of the documents, and the doctrinal, or the discussion of the true notes of the Church from the basis of the Scriptures. This latter Augustin preferred, because final; he bowed to no patristic. One or the other or both may be traced in all his works, great or small, against them. Out of so protracted a controversy there grew up a symmetrical and comprehensive theory of the Church and the Sacraments on either side.

Of three fundamental points of Donatism, as perpetuated practices of North Africa, rebaptism and the encouragement of a martyr spirit with its attendant feasts, the continuance of the Seniores in the government of the Church, we find Augustin aiming mainly at the overthrow of the first two. One of his earliest letters suggests to his bishop some means for checking the drunkenness and great excess connected with the Natalitia. Passing to the specific subject in view:

In the early period of his presbyterate, (possibly about 392, others place it later), Augustin journeyed through Mutugenna, which apparently belonged to his bishop's see. He learned how pacifically disposed Maximin, Donatist bishop of Sinaita, was. The friendly feeling thus kindled toward him was shaken by the rumor that he had rebaptized a defecting Catholic deacon of Mutugenna; not willing to credit the story, he visited the deacon's home. His parents testified to their son's reception into the same office by the Donatists. In the absence of Bishop

Valerius, he writes to Maximin with entreaty, refusing to credit the repetition of the rite, and urging him to remain firm in the convictions which had been imputed to him. He solicits a reply, that both letters may be read in the public service, after the dismission of the military. The prominent points of the letter are: while declining to recognize the validity of Maximin's orders, he does not refuse to salute him as Dominus dulcissimus, and Pater venerabilis. His solicitude as a shepherd to do his duty to all the sheep, constrains him to force himself upon their attention, and to be eager for correspondence or conference with a view to bringing them back to the fold. He is perfectly assured of the absolute and final correctness of his idea of the Church, and of the hopeless error of Donatism, an error so great as to merit eternal destruction. He discriminates, however, between heresy and schism at this time. Rebaptism in any case is a sin, but as applied to apostatizing Catholics, is an immanissimum scelus. There is only one baptism; that of Christ; as there was no double circumcision, so the sacrament of the New Testament should not be repeated. The Church is the owner of the nations which are Christ's inheritance, and of the ends of the earth, which are his possession; hence it is universal; the seamless robe should not be rent. Moreover the Lord's threshing-floor has chaff upon it along with the wheat, and therefore he urged the disuse of imputations through unworthy members on either side, whether Macarius or Circumcelliones. The schism made itself disastrously felt in all domestic and social relations. He engages to avoid anything that would look like using the power of the state for coercing conscience, and begs that on Maximin's side the Circumcelliones may be restrained. [Ep. xxiii.]

A Plenary council of all Africa was convened in Hippo-Regius in 393, before which Augustin preached the sermon. His subject was Faith and the Creed: his handling made such an impression that he was induced to expand it into the treatise: De Fide et Symbolo. In explaining the article credimus et sanctam ecclesiam, utique catholicam, he reflects on heretics and schismatics as claiming the title of churches for their congregations; and distinguishes between these two opponents of the Catholic body, heretics erring in doctrine, schismatics, while similar to the Catholic body in views of truth yet transgressing in the rupture of fraternal love. Neither pertain to the true Church of God. (Cp. Retractt. I. xvii).

Determined if possible to win the ear of all classes, the presbyter next affected a poem, "Psalmus contra Partem Donati," in the art of an Abecedarium, running the letters to U. The line with which it began was to be chanted as a refrain after each group of usually twelve lines connected with each letter, the whole closing with an extended epilogue. A generally vulgar performance it is, and purposely disclaimed all metrical dignity; and yet it contains the germs of his logical and historical opinions on the controverted points. The Church is a net in the sea of the world, enclosing the good and bad, which are not to be separated until the net is drawn to the shore. Those who accuse the Catholics of tradition, were themselves traditors and broke the net. The history is repeated, and all proof of the Donatist charges declared to be wanting. Unity is a note of the Church, and toleration within the net essential to its preservation. Over against Macarius he puts the violent Circumcelliones. The wicked members of the Church do not contaminate the good by a communion which is only outward and not of the heart. The threshing-floor has chaff upon it;

wheat and tares must grow together. The Catholics rear the Elijah altar, the Donatist the Baal altar over against it. Christ endured Judas. Why rebaptize us, he exclaims, when you do not repeat the rite upon your once expelled but now restored Maximianists? Surely it is better to draw life from the real root. The character of him who administers the sacrament has nothing to do with its efficiency; and so he returns to the necessity for toleration within the net, as Judas was forborne in the apostolic company. The epilogue pictures the personified Church expostulating with the Donatists for quarreling with their Mother, and presents a loose summary of the previous arguments.

It is doubtful whether, even in the fashion of the times, so lengthy a poem could become a street theme, or find many repeaters in the markets and inns of Hippo or Carthage, although the refrain for peace and truthful judgment might catch the ear of the more zealous. [Cp. Retractt. I. xx.].

The Bishop of Carthage, Donatus the Great, the sphinx of Donatism, had written a book to vindicate the claim of his church to the only Christian baptism. The work obtained considerable currency, and maintained its authority, even in Augustin's day, so he answered it during the year 393, most probably, in a treatise of one book now no longer extant, but which has been given the title: "Contra Epistolam Donati hæretici," The Retractations (I. xxi.) correct some points which had been held in this work. (1). According to the Ambrosian view, Augustin here identified Peter with the rock, on which the Church was to be built; but afterwards he regarded that rock as Christ, who was the subject of the Petrine confession; on Christ was the Church to be built, and to the Church as thus reared, were given the keys. (2). The Donatus present at the

Roman Synod, he had spoken of as the bishop of Carthage, the author of the book, which error is corrected in the Retractations. (3). He had also charged the writer with falsifying a favorite passage of their side, Ecclus. xxxiv. 30, but afterwards found that some codices read according to the Donatist quotation, and apologizes for his assertions.

Doubtless many of the sermons preached during his presbyterate had reference to the schism, but the chronology of these is too uncertain to allow of any definite arrangement.

We pass to the period of his co-bishopric with the aged Valerius, which dates from 395 A.D.

Evodius, a brother connected with the Church at Hippo Regius, had a chance meeting with Proculeianus, bishop of the Donatist body in that diocese. The two fell into a discussion of their mutual differences. Evodius spoke in rather a lofty and censorious way, after the fashion of his side, and wounded the feelings of the older disputant, for the Donatists, like all kindred bodies, cultivated an undue sensitiveness and were altogether too ready to take offense. Proculeianus, however, expressed a perfect readiness to have a friendly debate with Augustin in the presence of competent men. In view of this suggestion, and in the absence of Valerius, Augustin, always anxious to improve such an opening, addressed a letter to Proculeianus (c. 396), with courteous recognition, and no such sharp denial of the episcopal function as in the case of Maximin. He apologizes for the severe language of his friend, and in every way avoids any expression which might cause the tendrils again to be drawn in. The methods suggested for discussion show the anxiety of Augustin to beat out the fire of Donatism; there is the debate before chosen hearers, all the statements to be written out for use; or there is the private discussion through mutual discourse, to be read to one another and corrected, and so given to the people; or the single correspondence with a view to public lections, or any possible way that the aged bishop himself might prefer. He urges that the dead bury their dead, and the past history be left out of the debate; the present with its burning dissensions affords sufficient topics. As the people seek the bishop to arbitrate in their private litigations, let these worthies cultivate peace in this broader field; to this end he invites to prayer and conference. (Ep. xxxiii.).

Apparently the letter led to nothing practical. A new turn was given to matters. A son had beaten his mother, and threatened her life; to avoid Catholic discipline, he joined the Donatists and was rebaptized by them: as Augustin says, he wounded also his spiritual mother by contemning her sacrament. Public registration of the facts were made by Augustin, all the more because the reported instructions, given by bishop Proculeianus to his presbyter Victor concerning the affair, had already been denied. The case presented an opportunity for getting at some rule for the recognition of one another's discipline. Accordingly Augustin addresses himself to Eusebius, a judicious Donatist of higher rank. He professes that his aim is peace; he emphasizes with impatient vehemence his opposition to coercive measures in matters of conscience: neque me id agere ut ad communionem catholicam quisquam cogatur invitus. He asks Eusebius to find out whether Proculeianus had given the order to his presbyter as recorded; whether the bishop would consent to a collation between themselves and ten selected men on each side, agreeably to the original suggestion so that the whole question might be discussed from the Scriptural grounds, not the historical. Some proposals for a meeting either at the Donatist region of Constantina, or at their projected council at Milevis, he could not accept, because both lay outside of his diocese. If Proculeianus objected to the dialectic and rhetorical skill of his counter bishop, the latter would propose Samsucius, bishop of Turris, an earnest but uncultivated man, as a substitute to lead the Catholic side. (Ep. xxxiv.).

Eusebius declined to interfere on the ground that he could not be a judge, so Augustin replies (Ep. xxxv.) that he had only asked him to make some inquiries, because the bishop refused to have any direct communication. The need for some adjustment concerning discipline had become very pressing; a Catholic subdeacon and some nuns under rebuke had been received into full standing by the Donatists, yet their subsequent career had been even more scandalous. Augustin claimed that the Catholics always respected the penal enactments of their opponents. To show his own hostility to compulsory conversions, he cites the case of a daughter, who against the paternal will had joined the Donatists, and had professed among them; when the father was about to use violence for her recall, he was dissuaded by Augustin, and when a presbyter of Proculeianus had shouted abusive epithets at him, although upon the property of a Catholic woman, he neither replied nor allowed others to resent the insult.

A practical treatise is ascribed by some to this time, called de Agone Christiano. In expounding the faith he warns against different groups of heretics and schismatics. In Chap. xxix. 31, he cautions against listening to the Donatist party, who deny the one holy Catholic church to be diffused throughout the whole world, and claim it to be alone in Africa, and there among themselves, against the plain Scripture teaching of its universality; they affirm that the prophecies of its extension have already been fulfilled, after which the whole church perished outside of their remnant. He alludes to the divisions which have befallen them as a retribution for their separation. If the end shall come after the preaching of the gospel to all nations, how can all nations have lapsed from the faith, when there remain some who are yet to hear and believe? This system robs Christ of His glory, and is to be avoided by all who love the Church. (Cp. Retractt. II. iii.).

In 397 A.D., at the death of Valerius, he became sole bishop. In this year, while on a visit to Tibursi, he had met with Glorius and other Donatists, with whom he held a friendly disputation on the origin and history of the schism, during which some Donatist documents were produced which he declared to be false, and from memory recapitulated the archives current on his side. Augustin pursued his journey to Gelizi, where he attended to some episcopal duties, and brought back with him a copy of the Catholic Gesta, and spent a day with these friends in reading them, but could not quite finish. He subsequently reproduces this story with the arguments in a letter. (Ep. xliii.). The chief burden is a criticism of the Acts, highly important in its place, but it must be passed by here save to remark that in speaking of Bishop Secundus, he suggests that it would have been better to appeal to the principalities of Rome or of some other apostolic church, than to have proceeded as he did; he should have preserved the unity at all hazards; had the case been inexplicable, he should have left it to God; if definable, he should have addressed the transmarine bishops, after finding that his peers at home could not adjust the difficulty; disobedience on the part of Cæcilian to such an order, would have made him the author of the schism; but now the Donatist altar is set up against the Universal Church. It may be well to note that throughout the survey of these acts, there appears a manifest contradiction as to the beginning of the appellations. In the next place, the Donatists are held guilty of schism, rebaptism, and resistance to civil correction; of non-communion with those churches concerning whom they read in their lections; and of the demand for purism against the Lord's parable. The angels of the churches in the apocalypse are ecclesiastical powers, not heavenly messengers. The Church cannot be charged with the crimes of the evil men in it. Toleration is the only practice by which unity can be conserved; Moses bore with murmurers, David with Saul, Samuel with the sons of Eli, Christ with Judas. They themselves forbear with Circumcelliones, with Optatus bishop of Thamugada. The emphasis, however, is not so much upon those matters as upon schism. He would rather leave the archives and elucidate the doctrine, in which he claims to have the book of the world; that the Catholics are the Lord's inheritance; that they stand in fellowship with the churches of the New Testament; they are the light of the world. A divine rebuke has befallen Donatism in all the tenets of its particularity, by the schism and return of the Maximianists.

No open door was passed by. On a journey to Cirta, possibly about the beginning of 398 A.D., he visited with clerical friends the aged Donatist, bishop Fortunius, at Tibursi. A great company gathered who interrupted the debate; all attempts at taking notes were finally given up. In a letter (Ep. xliv.) to the Donatists, Eleusius, Glorius, and the two Felixes, who were of the number of those addressed in the previous epistle, he speaks of their witness to the conciliatory disposition of

Fortunius, and recounts the substance of the interview, with the desire that it may be submitted to that bishop for correction. The discussion had opened with the question of the Church. Fortunius regretted that Augustin was not in it; the latter reversed the wish. What is the Church? Is it diffused throughout the whole world, or is it confined to Africa? Can the Donatists send letters of communion to any of the apostolic churches? Thence they dissected the Donatist claim to be the people of God, on account of their subjection to persecution; in which it appears that they recorded the schism of the whole world from themselves as the true Church as due to sympathy with the Macarian persecution; up to that time they had held fellowship with the whole world, and as proof thereof brought forward a letter of a council of Sardica addressed to them. From the condemnation of Athanasius and Julius by this document, Augustin, to whom it was new, concluded that this was an Arian council, and was only the more damaging to their theory. The note of persecution being resumed, he maintained that there was no approved suffering unless for a just cause, and hence the justice of the cause must first be established. Though Ambrose had endured violence at the hand of the soldiery, they would deny him to be a Christian, for they would rebaptize even him. Maximianists on the other hand were confessed to be just, although they had been dispossessed of their basilicas by the Primianist appeal to the state. As an offset, Fortunius urged the curious fact that before the election of Majorinus, an interventor had been chosen, whom the Cæcilianists put out of the way. On the following day Augustin had to confess that there was no example in the New Testament to justify compulsion in matters of faith. The next topic was Discipline. Augustin pleaded for toleration in order to keep unity. A point as to Johannic baptism sprang up, but was not pressed. From this time the debate became miscellaneous and repetitious; in its progress Fortunius confessed reluctantly that rebaptism was a fixed practice among them, and that even a Catholic bishop so highly esteemed among the Donatists for his non-persecuting spirit as was Genethlius, would have to submit to the rite before he could be recognized by their body. Augustin proposes a further examination of matters, with a view to peace, but the pacific Fortunius doubts whether many of the so-called Catholics really desire concord, to which Augustin replies that he can find ten men who would heartily enter into such a conference.

On the next day the venerable Donatist calls upon his opponent to resume their talk, until an ordination called Augustin away; we also obtain information of the Coelicolæ professing a new sort of baptism, with whose leader he desired to confer. The letter closes with a proposition to meet in the little village of Titia, near Tibursi, where there was no church, and the population pretty equally divided, and where no crowd could disturb the progress of the investigation; thither all documents should be brought and the whole subject canvassed for as long a time as it might take to terminate the discussion.

During the year Augustin issued a weighty work, which stands closely related to these visits to Fortunius. It was in two books named by himself: Contra partem Donati. Unhappily it is lost, but in the Retractations (II. v.), he says, that in the first book he had opposed the use of the secular power for compelling the schismatics to return to the communion of the State Church, a form of discipline which experience afterwards persuaded him was necessary and wholesome.

Possibly it was at the close of the year 398 that a hint from the Donatist bishop Honoratus was brought by Herotes to Augustin, to the effect that they carry on a correspondence on the questions in dispute between them, and avoid the uproar of public debates. Augustin acquiesces heartily, and at once plunges (Ep. xlix.) into the doctrinal aspect of the matter. He begins with the note of Universality, the Church is diffused through the whole world, to establish which he brings forward some of his key passages, Ps. ii. 7, 8, Matt. xxiv. 14, Rom. i. 5. With all the apostolic churches Catholics communicate, Donatists do not. How then can this universality be limited? Why call the Catholic church Macarian, when the name of Macarius or Donatus is not known in any of these gospel regions? It rests with Donatists to prove how the Church is lost from the whole world and is confined to them. Catholics can rely on the Scriptures only for their theory. Correspondence seems to him also the better plan for discussion. Whether this mutual approach went further is not known.

It may have been in 399 A.D. that the Donatist presbyter Crispinus had met Augustin at Carthage; the two joined words, and both seem to have become heated; the former made promise to resume the parley at a later date, to the fulfillment of which the bishop had occasionally urged him. When Crispinus was elevated to the see of Calama, c. 400 A.D., and was not far from Augustin's diocese, the latter addressed him a letter (Ep. li.) rehearsing these facts. A new rumor credited Crispinus with being ready to enter the arena once more. All salutation is avoided in Augustin's letter, because the Donatists had accused him of servility. For the sake of accuracy and instruction he proposes simply to correspond, whether by one interchange of letters or by many. He pleads that present interests alone may be touched upon. Schism according to the Old Testament was more severely punished than idolatry or the burning of the sacred scroll. The charge of traditorship is set off by the acceptance of the Maximianists, whom the council of Bagai had condemned in such severe terms. If a mistake was made with regard to them why not in Cæcilian's case? If these were really guilty, you consulted the wider duties of unity and toleration, and why not carry these principles farther and apply them to communion with the Catholics? As to the charge of persecution, Augustin will not enter into the merits of the matter theoretically, nor stop to plead the mildness of the measures used, but at once asks why the Donatists used the State to dislodge the Maximianists, and to deny the Catholics the possession of genuine baptism is made foolish by the recognition of the rite as existing among the Maximianists who had been cut off, and were restored without a renewal of the ceremony. The whole world had been condemned by the Donatists without an opportunity of being heard, and yet they accept the sacrament of the condemned Felicianus and Prætextatus. While they deny the validity of the symbol as administered by apostolic communions, and by the missionary churches which brought the light to Africa, they maintain that their little fraction alone is its possessor. Summarizing these arguments as a weight for the bishop to stagger under, he invokes the peace of Christ to conquer his heart.

In this same year one of his relatives, Severinus, who was a Donatist, sent a communication to him at Hippo by a special messenger, with a view of reopening friendly intercourse with his kinsman; and Augustin seizes it as a way to reestablish as well the higher kinship in Christ (Ep. lii.). The Church is an unconcealable city set on a hill; it is Catholic, being diffused throughout the whole world. The party of Donatus is cut off from the historic root of the Oriental churches, and therefore cannot bring forth the fruits of peace and love; indeed it suppresses Christ by its rebaptism. Had their charges been genuine the transmarine bishops would have supported them; at any rate they should not have withdrawn from the Unity, but rather have practiced toleration. He hopes that the bonds of custom may be broken by Severinus, and that both may find their truest relationship in Christ, since the state of schism is a despising of the eternal heritage and of perpetual salvation.

Further along in the year, a Donatist presbyter had sent to Generosus an ordo Christianitatis, or episcopal succession of Constantina, his native city, asserting that it had been delivered by an angel from heaven. About nothing were the church externalists of every camp so eager as the preservation of the succession in proof of antiquity. Generosus had only laughed at the man's stupidity, but nevertheless wrote to the bishop of Hippo about it. Fortunatus, Alypius and Augustin combine in a reply, undeniably written by the latter, commending him (Ep. liii.). The ordo Christianitatis of the whole world is theirs, from which the Donatists do not hesitate to separate themselves. This presbyter's fiction would have to be rejected at any rate, even had it come from an angel, since all other gospels than that which teaches the universality of the Church are anathema. That doctrine is in Matt. xxiv. 14, Gen. xii. 3, Gal. iii. 16. The true ordo is the Roman, which he gives from Peter to Anastasius, the cotemporary pope; no Donatist is found in this list; yet as Montenses and Cutzupitæ, they have intruded into Rome. Had there been an actual tradition, or any wicked man in the Church, that would not have vitiated the ordo, or the

Church, for the law of Christ is plain, Matt. xxiii. 3, a passage again and again quoted by Augustin to substantiate this thought. They are separated from the peace of these very churches, concerning which they read in their codices, and sing pax tecum. There follows a very full and notable summary of the acts, as a refutation of the schism. He prefers the Scriptural proofs, which certify to the world-wide reach of Christ's inheritance, and its existence among all nations; from this they are separated by a nefarious schism, and charge upon the Catholics the crimes of the chaff on the threshing-floor, which must be mixed with the grain until the winnowing; these accusations do not affect the wheat which grows with the tares in the field until the end. Their divinely appointed retribution is in the history of the Maximianists, with whom they now commune, and affirm that they are not stained thereby; let them apply that lenity of judgment to the inheritance of Christ. The angel then was either Satan, or the man is Satanic, yet his salvation is desired; the sharp writing concerning him is without odium, and seeks only his correction.

Celer was a Donatist, a man of middle age and of considerable estate and civil position. He afterwards rose to the proconsulship. Augustin expresses (Ep. lvi.) a peculiar respect and affection for him, as a man of integrity and seriousness. He had desired direct instruction from the bishop, both in a matter of Christian culture and in the controversies between the two parties. Weighed down with the cares of visitation, Augustin had to delegate his presbyter Optatus to the reading and explanations of the bishop's works and views in Celer's leisure hours. The superior claims of the life beyond are set before him, together with the overwhelming force of the proofs against the schism, so that the dullest with patience and attention can get correction. The sundering of the bonds of custom and of a perversity that has become familiar, is a matter requiring great strength of character, for which step however, he, under God, would be readily capable.

But Celer was not persuaded to change his church connection by this first endeavor. On the contrary, Augustin thought he saw a laxity in the enforcement of the repressive measure ordered by the government, and so wrote a second time (Ep. lvii.). He affirms that there is no just cause for separation from that Catholic church which prophets and evangelist have declared should be diffused through the whole world. A long retained codex of Augustin, which had been loaned to Celer through Cæcilian, his own son, who seems to have been under the special tutelage of the bishop, was designed to convince the state official on this very point (we do not know which writing it may have been), should inclination or leisure lead him to its perusal, and whatever difficulties might occur, Augustin was ready to answer. He desires him also to stir up his subordinates to greater care in restoring the Catholic unity in the region of Hippo; indeed he cautions him to diligence on his own estates; a friend there, who fears to be strict in the carrying out of the statutes, could have his position alleviated by a word from Celer his patron. From this point we notice a decided sympathy with the effort to break up Donatism by force.

Parmenian, the successor of Donatus the Great in the see of Carthage, was one of the brightest disputants on their side. Against him Optatus of Milevis had directed his review of the schism, full indeed of grave historical blunders, but not lacking in that suavity which those who think they have the keys of heaven sometimes affect. When Tychonius had exposed some of the inconsequences and weaknesses of the Donatist theory of the Church, Parmenian undertook a reply, whose main object was to fortify the propositions, (1) that the evil defile the good in the Church, and must therefore be cut off; and (2) that puristic folly, that the Donatist community was absolutely pure in its membership and priesthood. To this much-esteemed work, Augustin replies (c. 400 A.D.) in three books: Contra Epistolam Parmeniani.

In Book I. the main question is, who really incurred the guilt of schism, and initiated the appeal to the State? He opens with the praise of Tychonius as man and author, but misses the acute drift of that great man's argument. He seeks to answer the data of the origin of the separation as given by Parmenian, who attributes it to the joint movement of Gaul, Spain and Italy in seeking to make their views universal, and to the influence of Hosius over Constantine, in winning him to their opinion; nor does Parmenius cease to deprecate the imperial intervention. Augustin defends this use of the secular arm, but accuses the Donatists by their history of beginning it in the appeal to Constantine, in the treatment of the Rogatists and Maximianists, in the abuses of the Circumcelliones, in their petition to Julian.

Book II. discusses the texts alleged by the Donatists in support of the purity of the Church, the need of discipline, the sole validity of their baptism and ordination, the blamelessness of their members and clergy. While both fail in exegetical principles, Parmenian, after the manner of his school, is aggravatingly guilty of using mere catch-words, without regard to text or context. He quotes indiscriminately whatever sounds favorable to his cause. Some of the passages are: Is. v. 20, Prov. xvii. 15, Is. lix. 1-8, Ecclus. x. 2, Is. lxvi. 3, Prov. xxi. 27, and others. Augustin gives his interpretations, and does not fail to prod his opponent with barbs of Optatus, Maximianists, and Circumcelliones.

Book III. handles further the theory of purism in the light of Scriptural proofs. The first part is mainly an endeavor to give the true significance of I Cor. v. 12, 13. (Compare his correction in the Retractt. II. xvii.). Augustin is constrained to confess the need of some internal discipline, and then enforces with wider range the notes of universality, unity and toleration, especially as illustrated by Cyprian. [Cp. Retractt.. II. xvii.].

In the work against Parmenian, he had promised to write more fully on this subject of baptism, the frequent persuasions of the brethren also moved him so that in this same year (400 A.D.) he issued the seven books De Baptismo: Contra Donatistas. The double purpose is to define that sacrament as the property of Christ, and to overthrow the Donatist appeal to the authority of Cyprian and the famous council of Carthage, with its eighty-seven deliverances in favor of the repetition of the rite. Since this is one of the works translated in the accompanying volume any further analysis may be passed by. [Cp. Retractt. II. xviii.].

In this period of frequent and heated controversy, a Donatist layman, Centurius by name, brought some of their quotations and writings, and supported with Scriptural proofs to the Church in Hippo. It seems to have begun with an exposition of Prov. ix. 17. (N. Afr. version and LXX). Augustin answered them briefly in a tractate, which he entitles: Contra quod attulit Centurius a Donatistis. It is however not extant. In the Retractations (II. xix.) it is placed immediately after the work on Baptism.

Meanwhile, and as the Retractations tell us, before he had finished his work on the Trinity, and his literal commentary on

Genesis, he found it desirable to reply to the pastoral letter of Petilian, Donatist bishop of Constantina; unfortunately only a part of the epistle came into his hand, so strenuous and vigilant were the efforts to hide their literature from the eyes of this ardent foe. He replied with one book to so much as he had received, c. 400 A.D. Some of his clergy subsequently obtained and wrote out a complete copy, so that he composed the second book, c. 401 A.D. Meanwhile Petilian responded to the first issue, and this necessitated a third book, c. 401 or 402 A.D. The three books were collected into one treatise, and are known under the title Contra Litteras Petiliani. The main object of the series is the refutation of Petilian's proposition: "Conscientia namque (sancte) dantis attenditur, quæ (qui) abluat accipientis." "Nam qui fidem (sciens) a perfido sumpserit, non fidem percipit, sed reatum." "What we look for is the conscience of the giver (him who gives in holiness), to cleanse that of the recipient." "For he who (wittingly) receives faith from the faithless receives not faith, but guilt." Since the work is also a part of this volume, we need not dwell on it farther. [Cp. Retractt. II. xxv.]

The civil restraints were applied with vigor on the one side and resented on the other by the retaliatory Circumcelliones. To Pammachius, a man of senatorial rank, Augustin, in 401 A.D., sends a letter [Ep. lviii.] of exuberant congratulations and flatteries, because he had compelled some of his Numidian tenants to return to the mother Church; a converting agency which he condemns unmercifully when practiced by the Donatists. The plan, he says, would have been urged upon other landholders, had the clergy not been afraid of the scornful finger of the Donatists, who were in such favor with the proprietors, that an effort like this might have failed. He desires the senator to circulate this letter wherever there was promise of effect. The bishop, now thoroughly committed to these arbitrary procedures, was in some trepidation lest the plausible arguments which the Donatists were urging, might shake the resolution of Pammachius himself, and so he sends a secret commission of instruction.

The coercive measures yielded fruit, and the question about the status of recedent Donatist clergy now became pressing. Augustin had already met with a certain Theodore on this subject, and in a letter addressed to him [Ep. lxi.] c. 401, recapitulated the proposition then agreed upon, to be used as a basis for treatment with all who wanted to come over. The Catholic church opposed only the schism and the rebaptism among the Donatists; what was good she was ready to acknowledge. Baptism itself, ordination, self-denial, celibacy, doctrinal views, especially as to the Trinity, these were confessedly right, only to reap the profit of them, it was essential for Donatists to be in the unity and in the root.

The Council of Carthage of September 13, 401, adopted this view, Can. 2. There had also been a remarkable scarcity of Catholic clergy, so that application had been made to Rome and Milan for relief; probably this had its influence upon so charitable a view of schismatic ordination.

It was alleged that Crispinus, the bishop of Calama, had bought a state farm at Mappalia, and had rebaptized the tenants. Augustin was roused by this counter-irritant and wrote him a letter, c. 402 A.D. [Ep. lxvi.], wondering what he would do if the authorities were to impose the fine for every offense. He pleads for an answer to Christ, whose was all the world, because bought with his blood, while the Donatist would affirm that Christ had lost all the world save Africa. He urges a public discussion of the mooted points before these converts, which should be reported and done into Punic as a test of their freedom in this conversion, and frankly enough offers to do the same for any case of coercion on his side. Unless Crispinus and his helpers acquiesce, he will hold them guilty.

The uppermost talk of those times was the extraordinary charity of the Donatists toward the Maximianists. One form of apology for such a seeming vacation of all their tenets was to say, e.g., of Felicianus of Musti, that he was ignorantly condemned when innocent and absent, so in his absence, he was reinstated. This statement was made by a Donatis bishop, Clarentius, in reply to the inquiries of Naucelio. Alypius and Augustin, who were made aware of this defense, urged in criticism [Ep. lxx.] that the Council of Bagai was therefore guilty in condemning Felicianus unheard, and all the more in that they afterward found him to be innocent. Either he ought not to have been condemned if he was innocent, or if guilty, he ought not to have been received back. If the council erred, why not apply such a liability to error to the origin of the schism; might not Cæcilian, unheard, have been condemned although innocent? But, as a matter of fact, Felicianus was found guilty while in thorough and declared sympathy with Maximian, and the state was called upon to enforce his ejection. If he was welcomed without rebaptism, why not treat the Church diffused through the whole world with the same consideration?

It was probably in the year 402 that he addressed a general appeal to the Donatist [Ep. lxxvi.], not to endanger their salvation by continuance in schism. If they counted the surrender of the sacred books so great a sin, how much more grievous a transgression ought the refusal to obey the plain commands of these books as to unity be considered. He brings forward the usual array of passages to demonstrate the universality of the Church, and that any limitation of this note, can only be at the end of the world. The attempt to separate the wheat from the tares before the harvest, is only a proof that they are of the tares. A rapid survey of the origin of the schism follows, and all the archives are made to tell against them. He asks how they can hold any theory of purism while they regard Optatus as a martyr and welcome the excommunicated Maximianists? Schism in the Scriptures is punished more severely than the burning of the books. Why complain about traditorship when Maximianists are received? Why abuse the imperial laws directed against them, when they had invoked the same against the Maximianists? If theirs is the only baptism, what is the baptism of these Maximianists, which is without question validated? He challenges the Donatist bishops to discuss these matters with their laity, if they persist in declining to meet the Catholics, and bids the sheep beware of the wolves and their den.

The ad Catholicos Epistola, popularly known as de Unitate Ecclesiæ, is pretty generally attributed to Augustin, and is addressed to the brethren of his charge; it may be taken as a contrast to the previous letter directed to the Donatists, and not unlikely saw the light in 402 A.D. This book is designed as a continuance of the controversy with Petilian, and indeed a further correspondence is proposed, so that the work must have appeared before that bishop's death, which is generally placed in this year. The chief question between the two parties is, Where is the Church? Is it with Catholic or Donatist? The Church is one and Catholic: it is the body of Christ, consisting of Him as its Head and those in Him as members. The historical issue in any of four possibilities of truth or falsity does not justify separation from this body. The point is, What does the Lord say? The Donatist should believe in the books, which he says were delivered up, and put aside all other documents except the divine canons. Do the Scriptures say that the Church is in Africa only, and in the few Cutzupitanæ or Montenses at Rome, and in the house or patrimony of one woman in Spain, or is it in the whole world? A second time does he start out with a definition of the Church, as having for its head the Only Begotten Son, and for its body the members in Him; as bridegroom and bride, two in one flesh. Any divergence from the Head or the body, whether caused by difference in doctrine or government, is per se outside of the Church. He meets the two favorite Donatistic comparisons of the divine institution with the ark and Gideon's fleece, and then enlarges upon the note of universality, with included unity, by Scripture texts from the Law, the Prophets, especially Isaiah, and the Psalms. From the Donatist position these are not fulfilled, because, say they, men are unwilling. Men were created with free will; they believe or disbelieve according to that. When the Church began to increase in the world, men refused to persevere, and the Christian religion was lost from all the nations with the exception of the Donatists. All this, replies Augustin, as if the Spirit of God did not know the future volitions of men. But Christ, after the resurrection, said that the Law, the Prophets and the Psalms testified of Him, and that the fulfillment of his kingdom should begin from Jerusalem. He then follows out the expansion of the Church as given in the Acts, and the foundation of Christian communities as mentioned in the Epistles and the Revelation. The Donatists reply to this theory of development that the Church perished save among them in North Africa. It is among the few: for which they cite a similar state of things under Enoch, Noah, Lot, Abraham, Isaac, and Jacob, and the Kingdom of Judah. The spread of the Church did indeed begin from Jerusalem, but afterwards an apostasy befell it, in the progress of which the communion of the Donatists alone remained faithful. Augustin says the fact that there are evil persons in the Church is simply a proof of the fulfillment of those parables of our Lord, which illustrate the mixed characters in his kingdom. There is indeed a paucity of the good, but within that communion. Then follows a discussion of the geographical limitation, the Donatists maintaining that the Oriental churches and the rest mentioned in the sacred canon had receded from the faith. Especially is their favorite paragraph, a passage from Cant. i. 7, commented upon. He presses the continuous preaching among all nations, after which event the end is to come; there must be such a universal growth to that end. Let us cease drawing from the acts and sayings of men about this great matter, and take the simple testimony of the Scriptures. But the Donatists object: If the Church be among you why do you compel us by force to enter its peace? Or if we are evil why do you desire us? and if we are tares why hinder us from growing until the harvest? Augustin then justifies the system of correction adopted in loving care for their salvation, not failing to remind them of the Circumcelliones and their own action with regard to the Maximianists. Another inquiry of the Donatists was, How will you recognize us if we come to you? Augustin says, as the universally founded Church is wont to receive, put away all hatred and your sacraments are acknowledged. This leads to the discussion of baptism and of that related topic, the effect, of the celebrant's character, upon the recipient. He returns finally to the note of universality as essential to the unity, with the one Head and the one body.

Somewhere about 404 A.D. two official cases of discipline had occurred in Augustin's monasterium, which had grieved the pride of the clergy, because they had boasted of their establishment as really purer than the puristic body gathered about the Donatist bishop Proculeianus. They were more troubled about this than about the sins of the suspected brethren, one of whom, however, seemed to have considerable injustice done him. While discussing this matter [in Ep. lxxviii.] he incidentally mentions the lapse of two Donatists, who had been received into Augustin's communion, and whose conduct the clergy had regarded as a proof of the laxity of discipline under Proculeianus.

A sermon on the 95th Ps. (96) may have been preached in the year 404 or thereabouts, in which he rebukes the Donatists for their pride in claiming either that they, the few in Africa, are the ones bought by Christ, or that they are so great because this large gift was bestowed on them alone. And in commenting on v. 10, dicite in nationibus, Dominus regnavit a ligno, etc., he twits them with seeking this reign by the wood through the cudgels of the Circumcelliones; and enlarges too upon the theme of universality, against their undiscoverable here and there.

Cæcilianus, whose exact civil office, whether vicar or præfectus annonæ is yet undetermined, Augustin addresses as præses in Ep. lxxxvi., which is ascribed to 405 A.D. The severer edicts of Honorius had just been published. This official had carried them out with telling earnestness. His administration in the greater part of Africa is particularly commended; the bishop begs of him to restore the Catholic unity also in Hippo and the frontiers of Numidia. The ill-success of his own work is not due to lack of episcopal duty, and he asks Cæcilianus to inquire of the clergy, or of the bearer, a commissioned presbyter, about the true state of matters; he would have the State begin with monitions in the hope of preventing a resort to severer remedies.

Emeritus, the bishop of Julia Cæsarea, one of the seven Donatist disputants at the later conference, did not shun correspondence or association with his opponents. He is described as a man of parts and character. Augustin had written a letter to him, which is not preserved, and it had received no reply. He once more seeks to win him to a friendly discussion or correspondence [Ep. lxxxvii.], in this time of general return to the mother Church. He would have all men of culture come back to the true fellowship. What Emeritus's particular ground for continuing in separation may be he does not know. He proceeds to discuss universality, purism, the validity of the documents, the heinousness of schism, the paucity of numbers, and the right of coercion.

The enforcement of the civil edicts was followed by violent outbreaks of the Circumcelliones, especially in Augustin's diocese. The clergy united in a protest [Ep. lxxxviii.] addressed to the venerable Bishop Januarius, a Donatist, probably in 406 A.D. They claim (1) that they are receiving evil for good. (2) The appeal to the state was begun by the Majorinists, and two full documents are given in proof. (3) All decrees of the empire since, are the simple execution of the edict of Constantine against the party of Donatus which these had wanted to be issued against Cæcilian. (4) The acts of the Circumcelliones; were the real occasion for sharper efforts at suppression; instances of their cruelty are mentioned. (5) The Catholics have pursued a conciliatory policy by conferences and by desiring a mitigation of the penalties, which were frustrated the one by refusals, the other by a gross assault on the Catholic bishop of Bagai; all who come into the hands of the state clergy, are treated with merciful persuasion. (6) Various proposals for peace are suggested.

Festus, a government official and a landed proprietor apparently in Hippo, had written a letter urging a return of the Donatists to the mother Church. It bore little fruit, and he asks Augustin first to instruct him and also to give him a tractate for general use. Augustin, c. 406. [Ep. lxxxix.], enforces the duty of perseverance in the civil reclamation of the Donatists; their claim of persecution as a note attesting them to be the true people of God is folly, because it is not the mere suffering but the cause for which one suffers that makes a martyr. He exhorts him to read the archives and see how the schismatics initiated the appeal to the secular power, and how all things that have befallen them through that arm would have been the just fate of the Cæcilianists, had the Donatist course been approved. Besides, why this unjust treatment of the Church universal in condemning it unheard, and rebaptizing its members, who have done them no wrong? The theory that baptism alone is valid when administered by the just, is putting a trust in man which the Scriptures condemn; the sacrament is not man's but Christ's; further, one would prefer to be baptized by a bad man, for then he would receive grace from Christ directly, according to their subterfuge. He is vexed with their active and passive opposition; the mother has to correct, although her obstinate child may not like it. They aver that the Catholics accept them without requiring any change in them, but the change required is great, no less a one than from error to truth. The bishop proposes as a substitute for Festus's plan, the sending of an authorized messenger secretly to himself, and they would devise together a method for the correction of the Donatists.

In the second sermon on Ps. cii. (ci.) preached about this time, when enlarging upon the unity he ridicules the Donatist assertion that the Church which was among all the nations had perished, as the impudent voice of those who are not in it declares. So is their affirmation that Scripture prophecies about the spread of the kingdom have been fulfilled; all nations have believed, but this diffused communion apostatized and perished. He rebukes the conceit that the Lord's saying, I am with you, even to the end of the world, was designed for them alone, the Lord foreseeing that the party of Donatus would be in the earth. If emperors have propounded laws against heretics, it is a part of the predictions which foretold how kings would serve the Lord. Thence he expands the notes of universality and perpetuity.

Cresconius, a layman and philologist, read Augustin's first book in answer to Petilian, and wrote a reply, which, however, was circulated among the Donatists only. Augustin at last secured a copy, and wrote (406 A.D., some say as late as 409) Contra Cresconium Grammaticum Partis Donati, libri IV. Three of these books controvert the arguments of Cresconius; part of the third and the fourth entire is a detailed polemic history of the Maximian schism.

In Book I. he alludes to the occasion of the writing, and hesitates between being regarded as contumelious if he declined an answer, and arrogant, should he reply. Cresconius had attacked eloquence, which Augustin defends as simply the art of speaking, and as not to be condemned because it has been abused. You do not condemn military armament for your country because others have taken up arms against the country; the physician does not refuse to use all drugs because some are baneful; because there are sophists one is not to deny the value of eloquence. Cresconius seemed to regard its cultivation as injurious to the simplicity of Christian law and teaching. He also had accused Augustin of persistent arrogance in his pertinacious pursuit of the Donatists. Augustin claims to do a good work with good ends in view, and says its fruit has been a rich harvest for the Church. So the discussion passes on to the use of dialectics, which Cresconius assails, but Augustin defends as nothing else than a demonstration of results, either the true from the true or the false from the false. He justifies not disputatiousness, but the arguments by which truth is built up, for Christ employed it, and St. Paul wielded its weapons not only with the Jews but with Epicureans and Stoics. In all this we have an illustration of that unfortunate tendency to undervalue culture whenever a puristic community passes into the fires. Augustin applies the art to one of the points which Cresconius had discussed, viz., rebaptism. He had endeavored to prove that it was solely among them. Augustin concedes that the rite is there, but not its profit; in order to enjoy its profit, it must be administered lawfully. The oneness of baptism as a ceremony is not dependent on the oneness of the Church, whereas its profit is. A reprobate society of heretics can have a good baptism, but it is not properly and not profitably administered among them; the proper and profitable administration is solely in the Church to salvation; the rite outside is to judgment.

In Book II. after a résumé of the previous book, he notices first the criticism as to the true construction of the name Donatistoe; it should rather be Donatiani as Cresconius claimed. He is ready to concede this, and in his controversy with the philologist will use that form, but on all other occasion he would prefer the more familiar termination. Cresconius also protests against the term heretic as applied to them, which he regards as a divergence of views from the Christian faith; while a schism has sprung up among those for whom the same Christ was born, died and rose again, who have one religion, the same sacraments, and no diversity in Christian observance. Augustin, however, while not particularly dwelling on these agreements, presses upon him the articles of divergence, and asks why they rebaptize? The recognition of Donatist ordination concerning which Cresconius had asked, Augustin declares to be a matter of charity. As to the question of Cresconius, Why, if the Donatists are such heretics and so sacrilegious, if they are indeed guilty of a nefarious and inexpiable crime, some purification is not adopted when they come over to the Catholic church? Augustin answers: We do not regard it as inexpiable, and baptism is not to be repeated, it is Christ's; on coming to us the Donatist receives the Spirit signified by that rite; he begins to have healthfully what he previously had hurtfully and unworthily. The relation of the celebrant to the symbol as presented by Cresconius is a modification of Petilianism. "Regard is had," says he, "to the conscience of the giver, not according to its actuality, which cannot be perceived but according to his reputation, whether that be true or false." Augustin does not fail to crowd him for the change of base. The favorite passages of Ps. cxli. 5, Jer. xv. 18, and Ecclus. xxxiv. 31, are gone over. Then he answers the charge made by Cresconius, as to the right of any sinner to baptize among the Catholics. Finally, he reviews Cyprian's relation to rebaptism, who is not a canonical authority for him; the Scriptures alone are such; but the Donatists ought to consider that decision of his to remain in unity from the fact that the mixed nature of its membership requires toleration.

Book III. Augustin contends that the Donatists by their schism from especially the Eastern churches had violated the principle of toleration, which their boasted leader had so strenuously enforced. There follows then a seriatim consideration of the points made by Cresconius, similar to those maintained by Petilian, as to the importance of the origin and the head and root in baptism, or the character of the celebrant, and the rebaptism by Paul of John's disciples. The case of Optatus and the Maximianists next come under review, as witnesses against their testimonies. Cresconius says he will neither absolve nor condemn Optatus, and as to the Maximianists, he professes to have made special inquiry into the whole history. The Synod had granted a season of delay during which all who returned should be held innocent. Of this very many availed themselves; the baptism of these was valid; those who remained outside lost both baptism and the church. Augustin refutes the statement from its inherent contradictions and from the language of the Synod against the Maximianists. Cresconius also brings forward the Sardican council's letter to Donatus as a proof of sustained fellowship. Augustin declares it to be an Arian council; and he insists on paralleling all Cresconius would say about Cæcilianism with the career of the Maximianists. With reference to persecution, he cites in extenso their own persecutions, the case of Severus, bishop of Thubursicubur; the acts of Optatus; his own treatment at a collation by the Circumcelliones; the case of Crispinus, the Donatist bishop of Calama; their own invocation of the state against the Maximianists. Thence he returns to the doctrine of the unity as universal with many of the familiar Scripture texts, and asserts by the documents that the Donatists were the occasion of the rupture.

Book IV. is a review of Cresconius's work by the light of the Maximianist records. Beginning with a pleasantry as to their eloquence and dialectic spirit, he follows in detail the points of Cresconius whether doctrinal or historical as to Cæcilian, mainly with Maximianist data as offsets. Cresconius charges Augustin with having called Petilian Satan, and so violating the peace he professes. Augustin claims that he only compared the error not the person, to Satan. Nor had Cresconius forgotten to bring out the Manichæism of his opponent. Augustin reminds him both of what he had written against them and also of what sins were forgiven in the return of Maximian, who was an old man when Augustin was but young; these were the sins of his youth. The theories of fellowship, of persecution, of baptism, are all considered in the light of their own council of Bagai and its sequences. [Cp. Retractt. II. xxvi.].

After concluding his work against Cresconius, he issued, probably in this same year, a little treatise he had promised, containing a collection of proofs both for Donatist and Catholic popular use. To the pledge itself an unknown Donatist replied, which led to the production of a second book, whose title Augustin designed to be: Contra nescio quem Donatistam. The original promise was fulfilled in the publication of the Probationes et Testimonia contra Donatistas, embracing all the ecclesiastical and public acts and Scripture proofs bearing on the questions between them. It was designed mainly for public reading in the basilicas. Both were joined in one book, although apparently afterwards separated. In each he confesses to the error of placing the purgation of Felix after instead of before the vindication of Cæcilian. At this writing he still regarded the Donatists as psychics and babes, but in his old age corrects his application of the words to them, since he came to consider them rather as dead and lost. Unfortunately neither treatise has been preserved. [Cp. Retractt. II. xxvii. and xxviii.].

He also conceived the plan of preparing a polemic for the people who had little time for extended reading, by refuting the entire theory of the schism through the story of the excision and restoration of the Maximianists. It appeared c. 406 A.D. under the name of Admonitio Donatistarum de Maximianistis: this too is lost. [Cp. Retractt. II. xxix.].

An acquaintance of earlier days in Carthage, Vincentius, had become bishop of the little Rogatist fragment as the immediate successor of Rogatus himself at Cartenna. He, or some one of that little band, had written a letter to Augustin with a pretty strong plea against persecution. This was not unlikely in c. 408 A.D., and Augustin answers in one of his most weighty epistles (Ep. xciii.), under the supposition that Vincentius was the author, and vindicates the help of the State. Evidently a change had come over Numidia, for he boasts of the multitudes who had been converted, and rejoices in the fruitful use of the secular arm for their salvation. Even Circumcelliones had become steadfast Catholics. Coercion stimulates the thoughtless and those bound by custom, and delivers these held back by fear; it is like a wholesome medicine, or the wounds inflicted by a friend. God chastens in order to better the life and to bring men to repentance. The householder instructs us to compel them to come in. Sarah and Hagar are types; so the mother Church corrects her children. Everything depends on the aim in persecution, whether it be done for oppression or for good; it is the difference between Pharaoh and Moses in their treatment of Israel. The Father gave up the Son, and the Son gave Himself up; while Judas betrayed Him. The righteousness of the end for which one suffers alone constitutes martyrdom. The Rogatist is not suffering for righteousness but for unrighteousness. Augustin is constrained to confess that there are no persecutions recorded in the New Testament as inflicted by Christians, but explains the omission as due to the fact that rulers were not yet members of the Church. He thinks, too, that the moderate and discriminating form of the correction employed, helps to justify a resort thereto. If the Rogatists have nothing to do with the violence of the Circumcelliones, and use no force as the rest of the Donatists do, it is because they are so few and feeble. The Donatists, however, did use the secular arm against the Maximianists, and in the appeal to Julian. He will not allow a distinction between resort to law for the recovery of property and for the coercion of the conscience. He claims that to regain one's own in this way has no apostolic warrant. The Donatists, too, sought imperial aid to coerce Cæcilianus. Why shall not Catholics return in kind? The very edict of confiscation which had hit them they had hoped might fall on the head of Cæcilian and his followers. What Tychonius said describes the very essence of Donatist arbitrariness: quod volumus sanctum est. The sin of separation from the whole world followed; the universal church was condemned unheard, and the toleration which Cyprian urged disregarded. He traces his own change of views from the non-coercive to the coercive policy, the success of the method in hastening conversions won him wholly as an enthusiastic and persistent supporter. He bids Vincentius flee from the wrath to come. What is his little handful compared with the universal Church? This note of universality he develops in extenso against their limitation, and especially their new definition of Catholic, as obedience to all the laws and the sacraments, and to their childish allegory of Cant. i. 7. He hints that in the ancient times there might have been a little schism which anticipated the Rogatists, and which had called itself exclusively the Church. He thinks it is also the duty of the State to suppress idolatry. The passage quoted from Hilary by Vincentius, as to the few who in Asia in his day were believers in spite of the spread of the Church, Augustin softens into an excited picture of the dark times of persecution. Next, he discusses the position of Cyprian. All patristic testimony, however, is of no final value; the only authority is the Word of God. Moreover, if Cyprian be quoted, why not on the side of his love for unity and toleration? The averment that the Church, with the exception of the Rogatists, perished by fellowship with the unbaptized, is met with the fact that in Cyprian's time men had been received without rebaptism into the Church, and therefore the Church, according to their theory, must have perished before their day; if it, however, survived that condition, then there is no excuse left for a schism on that ground. One is not of higher merit than Cyprian simply because he may abhor that father's error, any more than they who did not fall into Peter's mistake are above him in worth on that account. Indeed Cyprian may have rectified his fault before death; and some say that those passages are interpolations. Augustin, however, concedes their authenticity. Cyprian, in his Epistle to Antonianus, shows how the African bishops maintained unity in spite of the corrupt lives of some colleagues; variations of opinion were allowed; neither were they contaminated by such a fellowship, nor was the Church destroyed. Tychonius states the result of a Donatist council which granted fellowship to those in their own body who had been guilty of tradition, and that without rebaptism, in case the restored should oppose such a repetition of the rite. Deuterius, bishop of Macriana, had admitted traditors to his communion without renewing the sacrament, and many witnesses of both facts were living in Tychonius's own day. Parmenian had indeed replied to the arguments, but could not gainsay the facts. Augustin professes in all sincerity his anxiety for the salvation of the jeopardized Donatists; the Church acknowledges the Sacrament which they have administered, and desires them to have the profit thereof. In defence of rebaptism Vincentius had alleged the case of Paul, repeating the ceremony after John. Augustin asks was John then a heretic? If not, it is for you to say why the ordinance was iterated; Christ's baptism is always the same and must not be iterated; it has nothing to do with the merit or demerit of the individual, or else Paul would not have declined its continuous administration. He begs him to put no confidence in the accident of their being a little company, and not to arrogate to themselves the title of Catholic, in the sense of being keepers of the entire law and all the sacraments, nor to peculiar sanctity as the few who were to have faith at the coming of the Son of Man. The Church does not take pleasure in correction, save for conversion; she abhors those who seek Donatist property out of sheer covetousness, yet all property does belong to the true Church. She has also no delight in any who disregard Donatist discipline, by receiving members who have been ejected from that body for sin. The Catholic Church sustains the unity, and recognizes the mixture of chaff and wheat, good and bad fish, the goats and the sheep. He bids him come to that Church into whose fellowship Vincentius had described Augustin as entering. He closes with reflections on the aggravations in the sin of schism and on the need of repentance.

Olympius had recently been elevated to the dignity of magister officiorum. He had written to Augustin soliciting his advice on the best way for the civil authority to help the Church. Augustin, c. 408 [Ep. xcvii.], welcomes his elevation, commends his devotion to the body of Christ, and is glad to have his own timidity relieved by this invitation to lay before the highest official the exacting needs of the hour. These had become grave; the very success of coercion had precipitated new commotions among the Circumcelliones and their clerical abettors. A commission had sailed in mid-winter to solicit imperial help against their fury. The first point he would suggest, but without having had the opportunity of consultation, save probably with bishop Severus, is to declare by proclamation that the imperial edicts were not the invention of Stilicho, as the Donatists and heathen boasted. As to further plans, the episcopal commission would doubtless consult with him on their return from court. He invites Olympius to rejoice with him on the practical benefits of coercion thus far.

It may have been a little later (c. 408 or 409) that Augustin writes to Donatus the proconsul (Ep. c.) regretting indeed that the Church must avail herself of the State, but he is gratified that so devoted a son is wielding the sword for her. The crimes against the Church are greater than all other crimes, but in her discipline he deprecates any spirit of revenge, and pleads most beseechingly against the infliction of capital punishment; that would be a deterrent to the bringing in of any charges against the guilty. He asks for a republication of the repressive laws, since the enemy is boasting of their repeal.

Augustin wrote a general letter to the Donatist people in c. 409 [Ep. cv.], in which he declares that the Catholic effort at their conversion is the work of peacemakers. Some Donatist presbyters had ordered the Catholics to let their people alone, if they did not want to be killed, but Augustin would all the rather ask the people to recede from the schismatics because they were separated from that body for which Christ died. Catholics must seek for the stolen sheep that had on them the mark of Christ. The charge of being traditors, says he, we meet with a like accusation against you, and then you bid us leave. You claim to be the Church on this unproved charge, unmindful of what law, prophecy, Psalms, Apostles and Gospels say as to its universality beginning at Jerusalem. You are not in communion with that universal body, and you prevent the escape of others from a similar perdition. The objection as to persecution he meets with an invitation to look at the deeds of clergy and Circumcelliones, and cites instances of grievous ill-treatment toward voluntary converts: Marcus, presbyter of Casphalia, Restitutus of Victoria, Marcianus of Urga, Maximinus and Possidius, and then protests against their general violence and robberies, and especially against attributing martyrdom to those who had only been punished for their crimes. To all this compulsion we oppose the State, he affirms, and many of your own people rejoice in deliverance from your oppressions. You have filled Africa with false charges as to Cæcilian, Felix, etc., and though we do not place our hope in man, yet we do recognize the State as the servant of the Church. Nebuchadnezzar is an example both of the persecutor and the correctionist. You despise the baptism of Christ; ought this not to be punished? He then reviews the history of the case in the light of the documents; commenting on them as forms of their own appeal to the State. The liberty of error is most deadly to the soul. Christ and the Apostles command unity, and this command the Emperors seek to enforce. Only Julian and the heathen emperors were persecutors; the only martyrs are those who suffer for Catholic truth. The whole imperial legislation against Donatism is the outcome of the original statute of Constantine and sprang after all from their appeal. He next discusses their view of baptism and insists that the rite is independent of the character of the celebrant; were it dependent, then, according to their notion, we should rather desire to be baptized by a bad man, in order to receive the grace directly from Christ. The appeal to unity follows. Make concord with us he urges; we love you and desire to serve you, even by the aid of the temporal laws; we do not want you to perish as aliens from your Catholic mother. Your charges you are unable to substantiate, and yet you avoid all conference with us, as if to shun fellowship with sinners; a false pride, which is rebuked by Paul's conduct, by the Lord's in his treatment of Judas; the Lord held conference even with the devil. This he follows with extended Scriptural proofs of the universality of the Church. He reminds them again of the unproved charges which apply rather to themselves; but he has no desire for the historical argument, rather for the doctrinal. The Catholic aim is their conversion, whether by the persuasion of argument or the correction of laws. They should remember the mixed nature of the Church, and that mere contact with evil does not defile. If you hold to Christ, hold also to His Church; you kill us who seek to tell you the truth, and do not want you to perish in evil. May God vindicate us and his cause by slaying your errors and making you rejoice with us in the truth.

On the death of Proculeianus, Macrobius succeeded to the see of Hippo Regius. Augustin hears that he is about to rebaptize a subdeacon (Rusticianus) who under discipline left the Catholics. Augustin urges him [Ep. cvi.], c. 409, not to do this by his desire to have life in God, and to please God by not making the sacraments vain, and by his hope of not being separated from the body of Christ eternally. The Donatists have admitted the validity of baptism as administered by Felicianus and Primianus, why then rebaptize others? and begs him to search that case as a test of the whole matter.

Maximus and Theodore had been commissioned to deliver the previous letter to Bishop Macrobius. He at first declined to listen to its reading, but was at last persuaded to attend, and in reply said: It was his duty to receive all who came, and to give faith to those who asked it. Into the question about Primian he would not enter, because of his own recent ordination; he was not a judge of his father, and he would remain in what his predecessors had accepted. These replies were conveyed to Augustin in the letter cvii. (c. 409) by the two commissioners.

In still further hope of reaching Bishop Macrobius, Augustin addressed another epistle, (cviii.) c. 409, to him in answer to the objections offered by him at the interview with the commissioners. 1. As to the point that he must receive those who come and give them the faith they ask: Augustin proposes the case of some one who has received the rite in their communion, but had been separated from it for a time, and having returned, conscientiously desires to be rebaptized; Macrobius, according to his objection, could not repeat the rite, but would proceed to instruct him. Why repeat it when Augustin administers it? May be you will quote, "keep thyself from strange water and do not drink from a strange fountain." How then will you explain the reception of Felicianus? 2. As to the second conclusion, that you would remain in the faith of your predecessors: It is a pity for a young man of good parts to say so; nothing compels you to remain in evil; you had better be in the Church which began in Jerusalem and spread thence through the world. 3. And if you will not judge your fathers why judge my fathers? If not Primian, why Cæcilian? Why deny us to be brethren? why rend the body? why extinguish the baptism of Christ, who baptizes with the Spirit, and who gave Himself for the Church? Yet your colleagues in effect do yield to the truth in their recognition of the Maximianists. Judge not the evil but do judge what was good in Primian. That act of his, the reception of the Maximianists, absolves the nations who are ignorant of what you accuse us. He then traces the whole development of that schism and its overthrow, to show that those schismatics were not rebaptized at their return. That history Augustin considers a divinely appointed refutation of all the Donatist tenets. He proceeds to criticise their Scripture proofs, Prov. ix. 18, Jer. xv. 18, Eccl. xxxiv. 30, Ps. cxli. 5, which he turns against them through the story of the schism. He next addresses himself to their theory of fellowship, and discusses their proof texts, I Tim. v. 22, Is. lii. 11, I Cor. v. 6; Ezekiel, Daniel, the Apostles, Christ and Paul all rebuke this purism. Cyprian's authority for rebaptism is reviewed. Augustin repeats the doubts of very many as to the authenticity of those parts of his works which favor this view; but granted that they are valid, Cyprian, nevertheless, maintained unity and toleration, and by martyrdom purged his mistake. There is, however, no martyrdom outside of the unity, as that father also testified. Cyprian acknowledged as well the presence of many evil persons in the ministry and in the Church, but stood to it that unity must not be sacrificed on that account. The Church is a mixed society; this is Christ's law. Had Macrobius's associates remembered the parable of the wheat and tares they would not have separated. This argument is concluded with a sort of summary of the points traversed before. As to the note of persecution: that alone is a martyrdom which surrenders the life for a good cause. The Donatists too used the State in the case of the Maximianists, and to them belong the Circumcelliones. The matter of unity and the connected points of toleration and fellowship are again enlarged upon.

A sermon attributed to Augustin, De Rusticiano subdiacono a Donatistis rebaptizato et in diaconum ordinato, falls in the same year, 409, with the letter to Bishop Macrobius. There is an outburst of deep grief over the act. It would appear that Rusticianus had been a special favorite of Augustin, on whom he had expended much care; but he had become involved in scurrilous deeds, in feasting and intemperance, day and night, and was plunged in debt, and at last was excommunicated by his presbyter, and so fled to the Donatists, by whom he was rebaptized and made a deacon; this defection happened in the diocese of the bishop Valerius (?); so Augustin interposed through Maximius and Theodorus with Bishop Macrobius, but in vain. He deplores the disgrace done to the sacrament, as dishonor done to the sign of the King. The repetition is contradicted by the procedure with regard to the returning Maximianists. He corrects the misinterpretation of Ecclus. xxxiv. 30. He wishes for the Donatists the experience of the prodigal, that they may be forgiven by return to the Church and so attain to the profit of charity.

Great calamities were befalling the Church in all parts of the world. Victorianus, a presbyter, wrote to Augustin for relief from doubts as to the office of such afflictions; in the bishop's reply, [Ep. cxi.] possibly of Nov., 409, he mentions the cruelties of the Donatists at Hippo exceeding those of the Barbarians, especially in the resort to acidified lime, clubbing, robberies, and other destructive measures to compel rebaptism; forty-eight in one place were thus forced to a repetition. The coercion policy, in other words, had stimulated some of the Donatists to retaliation.

Donatus had resigned his proconsulship. Augustin writes [Ep. cxii.] at the end of 409 or beginning of 410 A.D., to express his regrets at not meeting him on his visit to Tibilis; his retirement would now give leisure for a larger development in graces, and would lead him to esteem the superiority of eternal things. He praises him for his official worth, which indeed was in everybody's mouth, but he urges him not to defer to that popularity, but to seek the higher approbation. After reminding him of the duty of Christian progress, he asks for a reply and an exhortation to be addressed to all his dependents at Sinitis and Hippo to return to the Church. Greetings are sent to his father, whom the son had been instrumental in converting to the faith.

Petilian of Constantina had written a treatise, de unico baptismo, which Constantinus had come into possession of through some Donatist presbyter, and then gave it to Augustin while they were in the country, imploring him to answer it. He did so, c. 410, in the book bearing the same title. He scorns those who desire secrecy in such matters; when the deeds are public let the discussion be. Petilian claims that the only true baptism is theirs: and therefore it is not repeated by the sacrilegious theorists. Yes, replies Augustin, baptism is indeed one, but it is Christ's, not yours; yours is only a repetition of the rite. We correct what is yours and recognize what is Christ's. Therefore we do not repeat it. So Christ corrected what was evil and recognized what was good among the Jews. So Paul exposed the sin of the heathen world but acknowledged what truth it had. Moreover you perform the ceremony, but it is to destruction: there is no real advantage in baptism outside of the Church. Petilian pleads for rebaptism because Paul rebaptized John's disciples; but, says Augustin, that is to declare John a heretic. These are two different things, as indeed Petilian himself suggests, some might say, and then gives two irrelevant passages, Matt. xii. 30, and vii. 21-23, as if the Catholics had no fellowship with Christ and were not recognized by Him. Augustin, after considering the import of these passages, avers the readiness of the Church to recognize the baptism of Christ as administered by Donatists when they return to the Church; for to deny Christ's baptism because it is administered by heretics, is to say Christ Himself should be denied, when even demons confess Him. There is a belief in God outside of the Church; the devils believe in Him outside of the Church. So there is one baptism of Christ which may exist also outside of the Church. Petilian's declaration that true baptism is where the true faith is, Augustin disproves by citing the case of the unbelieving and schismatic, yet baptized Corinthians. So all the ages of the kingdom bear witness to a like state of things. The action of Agrippinus and Cyprian on the one side, and of Stephen on the other, as to rebaptism is reviewed; differing in this, they yet maintained unity, especially Cyprian. Further, if the contact of evil men within the fellowship really defiles the good, then the Church perished in Cyprian's time; where could Donatus then have been spiritually born? If there is no such pollution, then there is no occasion to rage for separation. The origin of the schism is then denied from documentary testimony, and the charges declared to be not sustained; on the other hand, these archives prove the schismatics to have been traditors. A summary of the main points concludes his plea for the sole baptism as that of Christ. [Cp. Retractt. II. xxxiv.].

After this book against Petilian just mentioned had been finished, he wrote another work of larger proportions and with more thoroughness, in refutation of their schism, by the data of the Maximian schism, which he considered a full surrender of all their particularism. This has been styled: De Maximianistis contra Donatistas. It is lost, but noticed in the Retractations (II. xxxv.) immediately after de unico Baptismo.

At Carthage, about May 15, 411, he preached in praise of peace (Sermo ccclvii.). After its eulogy, he summons his hearers to the love of that peace; and recalls Donatists as alienated from the unity unto the concord which exists in the Church only. Patience and prayer are better means to their conquest than reproof. After the pentecostal fast he bade them exercise hospitality toward the guests who should attend the Conference.

The two edicts concerning the great Conference had been issued by Marcellinus. The Donatists had sent in their protest to the second, while the Catholic bishops sent in their acquiescence in a letter [Ep. cxxviii.], which is ascribed to Augustin's hand. It was of course written before June 1, 411, the day appointed for the opening. They agree to all the provisions for maintaining an orderly discussion; to the time and place of meeting; to the numbers to be present; to the requirement that all the delegated disputants sign their deliverances; to the countersignatures; to the order prohibiting the people from access to the Conference. If the Donatists prove the Church universal to have been lost and to be solely with them, the Catholic bishops will resign their sees; if, however, the collation prove the universality of the Church, then they suggest the recognition of the ordination and office of the Donatist clergy, and propose details for the succession in case of any jointure. The conciliatory example of Christ persuades them to this step; the peace of Christ in the Church is higher than the episcopate. The Donatist use of the civil authority against the Maximianists, and their gladness in receiving the returning schismatics without rebaptism, and without any diminution of their honors, give hope of a return to the root.

Before the meeting of the Conference, Augustin preached a sermon (No. ccclviii.) in Carthage, on peace and love, of which the main thoughts were the peace to which the Catholics cling and which they love under the persuasion of the divine testimonies; the victory of truth is love. He presents the Scripture proofs of charity and universality; the inheritance should not be divided. Donatus and Cæcilian were but men, but baptism is Christ's and not man's. The charity spread abroad in the heart is a broad commandment. He invites the Donatists to share in the Church's possessions, and to be bishops along with the Catholics, and pleads for a joint fraternal recognition; the Catholics seek peace and want to build up the Church. He finally requests the people to keep aloof from the place of dispute, but invokes their prayers in its behalf.

The objection to the second edict on the part of the Donatists respecting the restriction upon the number to be present at the collation, led the Catholics to write a second letter to Marcellinus, which is most likely also from the pen of Augustin. [Ep. cxxix.]. Solicitude over the opposition is expressed; some seem disposed to present a hindrance to the peaceful progress of the Conference; and yet the writers hope that the thought and suspicion may not prove true, but that the desire of the whole body may after all be to press into the unity of the

Catholic Church. Then they go on, very wrongfully in such a document, to discuss their favorite note of the universality of the Church, as the body of Christ was not stolen, so neither are His members outside of the few in Africa, dead. From Jerusalem outward was to be its progress and thence it filled the whole world. The fact that the Donatists have the very same Scriptures as the Catholics which contain these proofs of universality, fills the complainants with grief for them. The Jews who denied the resurrection rejected also the New Testament; but the Donatists receive it, and yet they deny the note of universality, and accuse the Catholics of being traditors of the sacred books. Now at the collation probably they wish to be in full numbers, in order to search completely the Scriptures; and through their innumerable testimonies they long to come en masse, not to create a tumult, but to put an end to the old discord. It is true that they have found fault with our use of the State; and yet the Scriptures vindicate such a recourse, and the Donatists themselves appealed to Constantine. The Scriptures too show the mixed character of the Church, wheat and chaff, good and bad fish, to the final harvest, the winnowing, and the further shore. Perhaps they see the wrong of their opposition to the Church. The case of the Maximianists has shown their willingness to use the power of the State and to ignore rebaptism; and probably moved by these things, they want to come in such large numbers in the interest not of tumult but of peace. They desire to show that they are not so few as their enemies report them to be. The Catholic numbers exceed in proconsular Africa, and, except in Numidia, are more numerous than in the rest of the African provinces; and most of all when one comes to compare the whole world with the few Donatists. Why, however, could not the number be just as well certified by the subscription? Even though quiet be preserved, yet at such a Conference the murmur of such a crowd will impede the progress of the work. If they all are allowed to be present, the writers, nevertheless, will limit themselves to the delegation suggested by the Judge, and then no blame for disorder can attach to them. If, however, the protest has been made in behalf of unity, they all will be present joyfully to welcome the Donatists as brethren.

The Mandatum Catholicorum, a sort of voucher and letter of instruction for the disputants on the side of the State Church, was undoubtedly the product of Augustin's pen. After a preamble which attests the sufficiency of the Church through her divine proofs against all heretics and schismatics, and the desire of Church and State to settle the long pending controversy in Africa, and the duty to enlighten men as to the eternal salvation, which things had induced them to convene and to select defenders, there follows the note of the universality, which, as the great proposition, is expanded with many proof texts from the Old and the New Testament. This truth is to be defended against the Donatist assertion that the universal Church had perished through contamination with Cæcilian; for the Church is a mixed society of good and evil, and not to be condemned on this account, but its unity is to be preserved by toleration. If they maintain this view, the documents concerning Cæcilian's character must be examined. The contestants must prove that the Church was thus defiled, or else the evil do not defile the good in this unity. The mandate then gives Scriptural and also post-apostolic proofs on this point, especially from Cyprian, and quotes the Donatist action concerning the Maximianists. The next topic is baptism as a sacrament of Christ and not of man, and as independent of the character of the celebrant: the Maximian schism again affords material for the confutation of this Donatistic tenet. They are instructed also to use the archives to show that their opponents initiated civil appellation.

In the session of the second day, Augustin is the speaker, mainly on the matter of delay and adjournment.

In the third session, he appears as the chief disputant on the doctrinal and historical points, and also as answering the letter of the Donatists in reply to the mandate.

In a sermon preached after the close of the Conference, (Sermo ccclix. on Ecclus. xxv. 2), he exhorted all Christians to be brethren; the Catholics desire to have the Donatists unite with them in worship in the universal Church. The history of Cæcilian should not affect the doctrine of the body. He claims a triumph indeed for his side and rejoices over the many who are returning to the mother Church, but candidly confesses that many harden themselves in their opposition. His exordium appeals for a restoration of brotherly harmony.

A little later in the year, probably, Augustin preached from Gal. vi. 2-5 (Sermo clxiv.), in which he rebukes those who say: "We are saints, we do not carry your burdens, therefore we do not communicate with you;" and says: "your ancestors carry burdens of separation, burdens of schism, burdens of heresy, burdens of dissension, burdens of animosity, burdens of false proofs, burdens of calumnious accusations." In your boast of non-participation in other's sins, you desert the flock, the threshing-floor and the net. The traditors who had condemned the absent Cæcilian dissolved connection with the whole world. He reminds them of the Maximianists; he charges them with breaking the parables, and yet inculcates patience. The whole sermon indicates that the effect of the conference had been to embitter both sides.

Another sermon (xcix.) on Luke vii. 36, 50, was also preached about this time, in which he conceives that the Puristic noli me tangere may develop into a system for sin-pardoning, and justification and sanctification; the men of the Gesta Collationis are likely to bring about such a machine religion. Already do they say: if men do not remit sins, then what Christ says is false as to loosing on earth and in heaven. With this conception of the tendency of their tenets he further says against them, that the cleansing in baptism does not depend on the man.

In a fragment of another sermon (ccclx.), preached on the vigils of Maximian, he personates a Donatist, who has returned to the unity, thanking the Lord that the lost is found, and expressing his joy in the vine, the unity, the baptism and peace of Christ.

The authorized acts of the council of 411 were too unwieldy for either general or popular use, and a compendium framed from them was too obscure; so Augustin, about the close of 411, determined to make a digest, called the Breviculus collationis cum Donatistis. It gives the collations of the three days, but it is thoroughly disconnected without the official account, for too many links known to the actors alone are not apparent to the uninitiated; too much of what would throw light on the animus of the parties in power is passed over, and a considerable deal of the minor business necessary to the understanding of the spirit of the debate does not appear. A reader would certainly get a still more one-sided and intolerant idea of the Conference from the digest than from the Gesta. The analysis of the order of business would require a comparison with the Gesta

Collationis, and that lies outside of our present purpose. [Cp. Retractt. II. xxxix.].

The decision of the Conference again stirred up a counter movement by the Circumcelliones, especially in Augustin's diocese, during which some terrible outrages were perpetrated; the presbyter Restitutus was killed; the presbyter Innocentius was clubbed and mutilated. A trial was instituted by Marcellinus and the crimes confessed. Augustin hastens to write to him [Ep. cxxxiii.], somewhere about the opening of 412 A.D., imploring that the punishment be not capital or retaliatory; restraint and labor would be just. He commends the tribune-notary's moderation in the examination, in that he did not resort to torture for extorting evidence, but only to whipping. He commands him, as bishop, not to proceed to extremity, which would be an injury to the Church, or at least to the diocese of Hippo. Since the pronouncing of the sentence presumably belonged to the proconsul, he had also indicted a letter to him.

Apringius, the proconsul, was a brother of Marcellinus. To him Augustin addressed a letter in the same interest, and at the same date. [Ep. cxxxiv.] For the use of his newly gained authority, he was accountable to God; he was also a Christian, so that Augustin felt a greater confidence in petitioning and in warning, and begs that he may regard his interference as a part of a bishop's zeal for the welfare of the Church. He repeats the story of the arrest of the Circumcelliones and Donatist clergy, the trial by Apringius's own brother, the tribune-notary, Marcellinus, and the gentleness of the hearing, in which the accused confessed their crime, especially as to the copresbyters. He now begs for a mild punishment; in the one case it cannot be strictly retaliatory; in that of the homicide he fears it may be capital punishment. Apringius must not only consider the State, but the Church, and respect her clemency. He is not only a ruler of exalted power but a son of Christian piety. Our enemies boast of persecution; we must give them no occasion for it. These acts should be read for the cure of the minds which have been perverted. If the extreme penalty has to fall, spare at least the children. He implores him to imitate the patience and mildness of the Church and of Christ.

Augustin, in 412, writes to Marcellinus [Ep. cxxxix.] expressing his delight that the proceedings connected with the trial are in preparation, and for the intention of having them read in the churches of the city, and, if possible, in all the churches of his diocese. The crimes mentioned are the same as before, with added confessions of many who were in some degree abettors. These are the men who refuse to commune with the Catholic Church for fear of pollution from wicked men, and yet refuse to leave a schism debased by such a fellowship. It was a question in Marcellinus's mind whether the Gesta should be read in the Donatist church of Theoprepia in Carthage. Augustin urges it, and if it be too small then in some other quarter, in that region of the city. Augustin pleads for a mild punishment in imitation of the clemency of the Church; however weak it may seem at the outset, men will afterward regard it with favor, and the reading of the Gesta will be more welcome and more effective by the contrast between Donatist cruelty and Catholic moderation. He speaks of the commission of the bishop Bonifacius and the bearer Peregrinus, who were empowered to treat upon some new measures for the benefit of the Church. The Donatist Bishop Macrobius was busy reopening the churches of his sect, followed by a band of both sexes. In the absence of Celer, a Donatist, his procurator,

Spondeus, a Catholic, had broken their audacity. He is commended to the favorable notice of Marcellinus. While Spondeus was on a visit to Carthage, Macrobius had actually reopened the Donatist churches on the estates of Celer. He was assisted by Donatus, a rebaptized deacon and a leader in the slaughter; from which fact other outrages might be expected. Should the plea for mildness not be granted, Augustin asks that his letters urging clemency [Epp. cxxxiii. and cxxxiv.] be read along with the Gesta. At least let a remission be granted to give time for an appeal to the Emperors, for no martyrs desire their blood to be avenged by death. In apologizing for his inability to complete his work on the baptism of infants, he urges the variety of his labors; among other things he had completed the Breviculus Collationis, as a compend for those who had not the leisure to read the entire proceedings of the Conference; also a letter addressed to the Donatist laity.

The Donatists were charged with circulating the story of the bribery of the cognitor or judge of the Conference. The letter from the council of Zerta, June 14, 412, in refutation of this was written by Augustin, [Ep. cxli.] in which it is said that they had become acquainted with this rumor so easily credited by the common people. The vote of the council was to authorize a refutation of it as a falsehood. The Donatists had been convicted of mendacity in the charge which they had made and signed against the Catholics as traditors; they had also invented stories to account for the signature of an absent bishop. How can they be believed in such a charge against the cognitor? Since the acts of the Collation are so voluminous we present herewith a digest. The meeting, the election of disputants and scribes, the matter of the subscriptions, are then recapitulated.

In the attempt at discussion, the whole aim of the Donatist disputants was to avoid coming to the point to be debated, while the Catholic representatives exerted themselves to reach just that goal and nothing else. When at last the Donatists were forced to the issue, they were vanquished by the clear testimony of the Scriptures to the universality of the Church. Any one separated from this unity has not life; the wrath of God abides upon him. The communion with the wicked does not defile any one by the mere participation in the sacraments, but only by agreement with their deeds. All these truths they had to acknowledge. The Catholics had prevented a confusion between the doctrinal and historical sides of the question. In the discussion of the documents, the chief offset to all the points was found in the case of the Maximianists, although the Donatists plead that a case should not be prejudged by a case, nor a person by a person. All the accusations which had been concentrated against Cæcilian they were unable to meet with proofs. Defeated men are wont to suggest such a defense as the corruption of the judge. Then says the paper in effect: If you will believe us, let us hold fast to the unity which God commands and loves. But if you are unwilling to believe us, read the proceedings themselves, or allow them to be read to you, and do you yourselves test whether what we have written to you be true. If you decline all these, and will still cleave to the Donatists, we are clear from your judgment. If you will renounce the schism, we will welcome you to the peace of Christ, and you will have the profit of that sacrament which was administered among you to judgment.

The Donatist presbyters Saturninus and Eufrates had joined the Catholic Church and maintained their rank. Augustin writes [Ep. cxlii.], c. 412 A.D., to express his joy at their arrival and bids them not to grieve at his absence, for they are now in the one Church whose note of universality he expands as the one Body of the one Head, and as the one house in all the earth; in the unity of this house we rejoice as embracive of those transmarine churches, to whom the appeal had vainly been made by the Donatists. He who lives evilly in this Church eats and drinks condemnation to himself, but whoever lives correctly, another case and another person cannot prejudge him. The Donatists had protested against the parallel proofs drawn from the Maximianists, on the ground that a case should not be prejudged by a case nor a person by a person. On the Lord's threshing-floor the chaff must be tolerated. He exhorts them to a faithful discharge of their clerical duties, especially in mercifulness and also in prayer for the removal of the schism.

The hostility of the Donatists was increased by the Collation. Their clergy charged the judge with bribery, and protested against the unfairness of the trial, the compulsion of the meeting, the unjust decision. Augustin felt compelled to write, c. 412 A.D., to the people in order to stay the fury of their leaders. The treatise is known as Ad Donatistas post Collationem. Why make such a charge? Why does Primian say, it is unworthy for the sons of the martyrs to meet in the same place with the offspring of traditors? Why did they come? Why were they unable to prove the old accusations? And how are they the sons of martyrs? The universality of the Church was demonstrated at the Conference. Donatists do not commune with the churches addressed in those epistles which they read at their services, because they say these perished by communion with the African Cæcilians, and yet they put in the plea that a case should not be prejudged by a case nor a person by a person. He meets the Cæcilian charge by the Maximianists in spite of this caveat. He represents all the New Testament churches and the East as expostulating on the basis of this very plea with the Donatists for separation from them. So the case and the person of the bad does not prejudice the case and the person of the good; they must abide together until the end. He condemns their arrogant pretense to holiness. The wicked must be tolerated in the Church, but their deeds are not to be participated in. Cyprian would not destroy the unity because bad people were in it; frequent are the examples of such forbearance in the Scriptures, and the principle was not changed after the resurrection of Christ; it continued in force in the New Testament Church; the winnowing and severance come at the end of the world. They would perhaps deny their own words as uttered in the Conference were they not written; that was the beauty of requiring subscription. They charge too that the sentence against them was pronounced in the night. Augustin playfully speaks of many good things which have been said and done in the night. He subsequently reminds them of the days in which they tried to prove the origin of heresy, and their defeat at every point of the Cæcilian history. It appears here again that the Donatists had a considerable body of acts of their own. The plea of persecution as a note of the Church and as an experience of the Donatists was one of the points urged at the conference in the Donatist reply to the Catholic mandate, and by Primian, to which we have the usual answer. Another complaint of the Donatists was that they were tried by those who had been condemned by themselves, and were compelled to unite with sinners; to which Augustin gives a little Maximianist parallel and then considers the questions of purism, the paucity of believers, the need of discipline, the fellowship of a mixed community which ought not to degenerate into a participation in the deeds of the wicked therein. These are discussed with considerable detail of quotations from the Old and New Testaments. Some who thought Cæcilian guilty would not break the unity; they imitated Cyprian. He charges their clergy with duplicity. He reminds them of the deception practiced in presenting the signature of a Donatist, who was already dead; so with regard to the show of numbers in attendance and the alleged multitude absent, and also the means adopted for securing delay, the interruptions and turnings of the debate from the true object in view. He vindicates the cognitor's method and rulings. He then renews the discussion concerning the archival origin of the schism. In conclusion he addresses them as brethren and exhorts them to love peace and unity.

The Donatists of Cirta, clergy and people, had returned to the Catholic Church and had written a letter of thanks to Augustin for his preaching, under which they had been persuaded to renounce the schism. Augustin in reply [Ep. cxliv.], probably at end of 412 A.D., says that this is not man's work, but God's. Their allusion to the conversion of the drunken and luxurious Polemo by Xenocrates, draws from him the reflection, that such a change of character, though not a Christian repentance, is, nevertheless, a work of God. So he bids them not to give thanks to himself but to God, for their return to the unity. Those who still are alienated, whether from love or fear, he charges to remember the undeceived scrutiny of God; to weigh Scripture testimony as to the universality of the Church; and the documents as to the origin of the schism. The case has been tried or not been tried by the transmarine churches; if not, then there is no existing ground for the separation; if it has, the defeated ones are the separatists. But alas! the obstacles to their persuasion are well-nigh insuperable. He hopes that the mutual desire for his visit to them may be fulfilled.

About the beginning of the year 413, appeared the book De Fide et Operibus. In Chap. iv. 6, he speaks of the need of coercion against the Donatists as disturbers of the peace of the Church, as separators of the tares from the wheat before the time, as those who have blindly preferred to cut themselves off from the unity; commixture of evil and good is a necessity, and we ought to remain in that fellowship which is not at all destitute of discipline. [Cp. Retractt. II. xxxviii.]

Donatus, a Donatist presbyter, and another person connected with that body, had been arrested by order of Augustin about the beginning of 416 A.D. Mounted upon a beast against his will, he dashed himself to the ground and so received injuries which his less obstinate companion escaped. Augustin writes [Ep. clxxiii.] to vindicate himself as concerned about the salvation of the recusants, and puts the blame of the wounds upon the offender. Donatus urged in opposition to this style of conversion that no one should be compelled to be good. Augustin claims on the other hand that many are compelled to take the good office of a bishop against their will. Donatus argues that God had given us free will, therefore a man should not be compelled even to be good. Augustin replies that the effort of a good will is to restrain and change the evil will, because of the awful results which follow a vitiated will. Why were the Israelites compelled to go to the land of promise? Why was Paul forced to turn from persecution to the embrace of the truth? Why do parents correct children? Why are negligent shepherds blamed? You are an errant sheep, with the Lord's mark upon you, and I as shepherd must save you from perishing. Of your own will you threw yourself into a well, but it would have been wicked to leave you there where you had cast yourself according to your will, and hence the attendants took you out; how much more is it a duty to save you from eternal death. Besides, it is unlawful to inflict death upon yourself. He reminds him that the Scriptures do not allow suicide; and controverts his use of I. Cor. xiii. 3, "though I give my body to be burned." Severed from charity and unity, nothing can profit, not even the surrender of the body to burning. The points of the recent joint Conference are then dwelt upon. Donatus was understood to have criticized the saying of his party as to the Maximianist parallel: do not prejudge a case by a case or a person by a person. Augustin twits him in this wise: If you object to this, then you are deceived concerning it, because you oppose your authority to theirs, and if you say it is not true, the hope of vindicating the great schism falls through entirely. He presses him to weigh all the proceedings. But Donatus objects also that the Lord did not cause the seventy to come back, and did not put a barrier in the way of the twelve when he asked, "Will ye also go away?" Augustin says that was in the beginning of Christianity; kings were not yet converted; now the State helps the Church. Our Lord said prophetically, Compel them to come in. So we hunt you in the hedges; the unwilling sheep is brought to the true pasture.

The series of Tractatus on the Gospel of John, which are ascribed to 416 A.D., contain many reflections on Donatism. We can only notice the passages:

Tractatus IV.in Jo. i. 19-33.

Tractatus V. in Jo. i. 33.

Tractatus VI.in Jo. i. 32, 33. Quite fully.

Tractatus IX. in Jo. ii. 1-11.

Tractatus X. in Jo. ii. 12-21.

Tractatus XI. in Jo. ii. 23-25, and iii. 1-5.

Tractatus XII. in Jo. iii. 6-21.

Tractatus XIII. in Jo. iii. 22-29.

To the same year are ascribed the Tractatus on the I. Ep. of John.

Tractatus I. 1 Jo. i. and ii. 1-11.

Tractatus II. 1 Jo. ii. 12-17.

Tractatus III. 1 Jo. ii. 18-27.

Tractatus IV. 1 Jo. iii. 1-8.

In the Retractations, II. xlvi., we read of a book addressed to Emeritus, the Donatist bishop of Cæsarea, in the province of Mauritania Cæsariensis. [See Ep. lxxxvii.] He speaks of him as the best of the seven Donatist disputants at the Conference. The work marked briefly the lines on which the Donatists were defeated. Its title is: Ad Emeritum Donatistarum Episcopum, post collationem, liber unus. Since the Retractations place it before De Gestis Pelagii, and De Correctione Donatistarum, it was most likely written in the beginning of 417 A.D.

Boniface had requested from Augustin a letter of instructions on the relation of the Donatists to the Arians. The bishop replies, c. 417 [Ep. clxxxv.], which he himself calls a book de Correctione Donatistarum. [Cp. Retractt. II. xlviii.]. Since this is translated in the present volume, we will omit any further notice.

The above-mentioned Emeritus was present at a Synod of the Catholics, near Deuterius, September 20, 418. At a service held two days after, Augustin preached the Sermo ad Cæsariensis Ecclesiæ plebem. Emeritus was present. In the church during a previous colloquy with Augustin he had said: I cannot will what you will, but I can will what I will. Augustin in this sermon (and the writing has all the abruptness and repetition of an extempore address) urges him to will what God wills, viz., peace, and that now, in response to the cry of the people; and if you ask why I, who call you schismatics and heretics, desire to receive you, it is because you are brethren; because you have the baptism of Christ; because I want you to have salvation: one can have everything outside the Church except salvation; he can have honor, he can have the sacraments, he can sing Allelulia, he can respond Amen, he can hold to the gospels, he can have faith in the name of the Father and the Son and the Holy Spirit, and can preach. Persecution after all is rather of you. The failure of the archival evidence as to Cæcilian is alleged as usual, and hence no reason for separation exists. He recites too the story of the seizure, escape, reseizure, compulsory baptism and ordination of Petilian, while at the time a Catholic catechumen. This occurred at Constantina, when that city and region were largely Donatist. He was seized unto death, do we not draw him to salvation? Here or nowhere, says Augustin, repeating the voice of the people, is the place for peace.

There was a gathering of clergy (the bishops Alypius, Augustinus, Possidius, Rusticus Palladius, etc., many presbyters and deacons and a considerable number of people) in the exedra of the larger church at Cæsarea, c. 418 A.D. Emeritus, the Donatist bishop of the city, was also present. Augustin addresses those devoted to the unity, and says that when he came to the city on the day before yesterday he found Emeritus returned from a journey. Augustin met him in the street and invited him to the Church, and Emeritus consented without any demur. The sermon of Augustin is full of the peace, love and related themes of the Church, in hope of winning Emeritus. He alludes to the many conversions in the city and since the collation; if Emeritus has anything new to say in defense of his side, he invites him to state it. Emeritus had been reported as affirming that at the Conference the Donatists were overcome by power rather than by truth. Augustin then addresses inquiries to Emeritus directly: as to why he had come if he was defeated at the council; or if he thought his party had triumphed, then to state the ground for such an opinion. Emeritus said: The acts show whether I am defeated or not, whether I am defeated by truth or oppressed by power. Augustin: Then why do you come? Emeritus: That I might say this very thing which you ask, and so on. Under some taunting and arrogant observations to the brethren, Emeritus keeps quiet. From Augustin's statement it appears that the Acts were read during Lent, at Thagaste, Constantina, Hippo, and all the faithful churches. Part of these Gesta are then read by Alypius, viz, the imperial convocation of the Conference, and comments are made by Augustin. Then follows his application of the lessons afforded by the Maximianist schism, in which he says the Donatists make shipwreck of all their tenets. Emeritus, however, remained a silent hearer. The account of the above meeting is given in the treatise: De Gestis cum Emerito, Cæsariensi Donatistarum Episcopo liber unus. [Cp. Retractt. II. li.]

The book de Patientia is assigned to 418 A.D. In Chapter xiii. he contrasts genuine and false martyrdom.

Dulcitius had been appointed Tribune-notary. The effect of his carrying out of the renewed edicts against the Donatists was signalized by many conversions, but also by many suicides. He had written to Augustin requesting directions about how he ought to proceed against the heretics. Augustin replies [Ep. cciv.], c. 420 A.D., that his work had indeed persuaded many to return to their salvation, but others were stirred either to kill the Catholics or themselves. We indeed do desire the return of all to unity, yet some are doubtless predestinated to perish by an occult yet just decree of God. They perish not only in their own fires but in that of Gehenna. The Church grieves over them as David over his son, although they have met the deserved punishment of rebels. Augustin does not find fault with the notary's edict at Thamugada, only with the phrase: You may know that you are to be given over to the death which you deserve; for that is not contained in the rescripts. In the second edict there is a clearer statement of the notary's aim. Augustin also criticizes his courtesy toward Gaudentius, the Donatist bishop of Thamugada. As to a special reply to that bishop Augustin urges a more diligent refutation of the fallacious doctrines by which the Donatists are accustomed to be seduced. He had already done this in very many works, but adds some points by way of suggestion. He alone is a martyr who dies for a true cause. Man's will is free, but nevertheless amenable to divine and human laws. The State can punish not only adulteries and homicides, but also sacrileges. Many think it strange that we do not rebaptize, but the sacrament once given ought not to be repeated. Suicides are utterly prohibited by the Scriptures. The case of Razius gives the Donatist no pretext, for the deed is simply mentioned but not commended. (II. Mac. xiv. 37-46). In conclusion he intimates that in answer to the united wish of the people of Thamugada, of himself and of Eleusinus, the tribune of that place, that Augustin should answer both epistles of Gaudentius, the Donatist bishop, and especially the latter of the two, which contained Scriptural proofs, he will write such a criticism.

Dulcitius had written a pacific letter to Gaudentius, the Donatist bishop of Thamugada, one of the quieter members of the seven Donatist disputants, concerning the enforcement of the imperial edicts. Gaudentius replied in two epistles, one short, the other longer and fortified by Scripture proofs. Augustin was requested to answer these, which he does (c. 420) in the work Contra Gaudentium Donatistarum Episcopum, Libra duo. In Book I. he makes a change of form from the Petilian cast of personal dialogue, because of the captious fault found with that way as savoring of untruth, and takes a duller formula, "Verba Epistolæ" and "ad hæc responsio," whose dryness and literality the most sensitive Donatist could take no exception to. In the first epistle of Gaudentius, the fairly courteous strain in which he had replied to the tribune-notary, with titles and recognition of character, Augustin rather resents by saying that the Catholic had treated the heretic too kindly and incautiously, and bids Gaudentius consider what he had said at the Collation. Gaudentius proposes to remain in the communion where the name of God and of his Christ is and where the Sacraments are, and pleads for religious liberty against compulsion as to matters of faith; and concludes, by another hand, with wishing him well and desiring his recession from the disquieting of Christians. Augustin objects that Gaudentius had not reproduced the language of Dulcitius correctly, and accuses the Donatists of holding the truth of baptism in the iniquity of human error; he comments on their false eagerness for death; he responds to all the good wishes for the tribune, but not that he should cease from correcting the heretics.

The second epistle of Gaudentius is mainly a protest from Scriptural grounds; against persecution he brings forward the case of Gabinus, who, if bad, should not have been received without correction, that is, baptism; but if innocent, why kill the innocent Donatists from whom he came to you? The false rumor about Emeritus, as having turned Catholic, is another instance of this persecution. The duty of a persecuted pastor is to be a doer of the law and to lay down his life for the sheep; there is no place whither the persecuted may now flee; the divine right of free will is restrained by the arbitrary laws of the emperor; persecution is a note of the Church from the blessings attached to it by Christ and the apostles. The peace of Christ invites the willing but does not compel the unwilling; a thing very different from the war-bearing peace and the bloody unity which their oppressors present. We rejoice in the hatred of the world; there is a martyr host of the apocalypse; Christians may yield up their souls in testimony against sacrilege, as Razius did. He begs Dulcitius to turn to the few who have the solidity and not the semblance of truth. God gave prophets not kings to teach the people: the Saviour sent fishermen not soldiers. God never needs the aid of soldiers. Gaudentius charges the Catholics with coveting the Donatist possessions. The farewell is in another handwriting, in which he wishes Dulcitius well, and advises him to pursue a lenient and temperate course.

The points of Augustin's reply are in no way different save form from those so constantly presented, unless there be an increase of roughness and a more hardened idea of the Church's right to use coercion. As to Gabinus, the Church's course with regard to him is a vindication of the right to receive a convert without rebaptism: in communion with charity and unity he received the profit of that rite which had been administered among the Donatists. In the case of Emeritus, Augustin confesses that the rumor of his having turned Catholic was false; but Emeritus came to Cæsarea of his own will; he came to the Church where a multitude was present; he could say nothing for his or his party's defense; he kept quiet. The argument against suicide from the case of Razius is well made; he died rather in suffering for the state; and besides the narrative does not commend the deed, but only states it; then too the books have not the weight that the Law, the Prophets and the Psalms carry with them. The plea for correction is precisely as usual. The doctrines of universality and unity and charity are incidentally brought forward. Circumcelliones, Secundus and Maximianists furnish the concluding parallels.

Book II. Gaudentius had written a reply to Augustin's first book. He had taken refuge under the example of Cyprian; but Augustin now refers him to the writings of Cyprian on De Simplicitate Prælatorum seu De Catholicæ Ecclesiæ unitate, showing Cyprian's belief in the universality of the Church which Augustin expands by the explanation of the term Catholic. Purgation of the Church is not by separation, but by toleration, as Cyprian too held in his letter to Maximus and others. The explanation of the field not as the Church, but rather as the world outside of the Church, had been supported at the Conference and is repeated by Gaudentius; and also its alternative, that were the field the Church then it must have perished from the tares which were in it. If so, says Augustin, then the ancestors of the Donatists would have perished. The period of separation is at the end, when the Gospel shall have been preached in the whole world. As to their theme of rebaptism, Augustin replies that he had already before referred him to his Maximianist practice, so that the action of Agrippinus and Cyprian are vain for him. And then too, according to Cyprian's own confession, and Stephen's testimony, there were crimes in the Church in their day; did the Church perish then? If so where was Donatus born? If not, then why did the party of Donatus separate? They are guilty of the very schism which Cyprian particularly deprecated as a cure, instead of toleration and discipline, for the ills of the Church. As to baptism: The Catholics recognize the Donatist rite, for the sacrament cannot be lost upon those who receive it among Catholics and then pass over to heretics; they have the truth but in iniquity; the truth is not the property of the Donatists. The apostle recognized such truth as he found among the Gentiles. Gaudentius had vindicated his reference to the tribune's letter, as to the Donatists having the names of God and of his Christ, and quoted the passage in proof. Augustin acknowledges his mistake, which, however, was not intentional, and he apologizes for the tribune's error as that of a military man who was not familiar with theology. Since Gaudentius had called the tribune religious in his first letter, Augustin accuses him of insincerity and berates him as superstitious. He also corrects Gaudentius for saying that God sent Jonah not to the king but only to the people of Nineveh, for the king compelled the humiliation of his subjects. In conclusion he quotes from Cyprian's letter to Maximus in behalf of universality and tolerant unity. His exordium is an earnest appeal to the

Catholics to maintain all the notes of the Church. [Cp. Retractt. II. lix.].

Felicia had been a Donatist originally and was converted by force. She had devoted herself to the virgin life and apparently had become head of a religious house; but by reason of some wicked deeds of the clergy, possibly the extortion and rapacity of Antonius at Fussala, she was much disturbed and seemed inclined to relapse into her earlier puristic notions, if not to return to the body that upheld them. To quiet her doubts Augustin writes Ep. ccviii. c. 423. The Lord had predicted offenses. There are two kinds of shepherds over the flock, and will be to the end: the flock too has the good and the bad in it. The gathering is the present duty, the separation will be the future one; this latter is the Lord's prerogative. To abide in unity under such circumstances is a duty until the winnowing, and one is to believe what these shepherds teach, not what they do. Good and bad are therefore in the world under the widely diffused Catholic Church; the Donatist has no such note of universality. Love Christ and the Church, and then He will not permit you to lose the fruit of your virginity and to perish with the lost. If you go out of this life, separated from the unity of the body of Christ, this preserved integrity of the body will not profit you. You were compelled to come in; be thankful to those who compelled you. Show your devotion to the Lord, as your only hope, by being unmoved with these offenses, and by cleaving to his body, the Church.

A letter addressed to Pope Coelestine is ascribed to Augustin [Ep. ccix. c. 423]; its authenticity has been disputed. The author, in giving an account of the appointment of Antonius as bishop of Fussala, remarks that at Fussala, a castellum about forty miles distant from Hippo, as in all the adjoining region, there had been a Donatist population; in Fussala itself there had not been a solitary Catholic; the Punic was the common language. The coercive measures had converted the whole territory, but the process had also aroused a violent opposition in the form of robbery, beating, blinding, murder. After its conversion, the distance from Hippo and the great numbers to be instructed, required a new bishopric, the history of which and the troubles growing out of it, the author further relates.

In that valuable book De doctrina christiana, (begun in 397, but ended in 426, including the part having reference to our subject III. xxx. 42), Augustin quotes approvingly from the book of Tychonius the De septem regulis, and prefaces a discussion of these rules by an allusion to the treatise of Tychonius, which had refuted some of the narrow and puristic doctrines of the Church, as held by his own party; this we have already seen was answered by Parmenian, whose letter in turn was dissected by Augustin. The first, second, fourth and seventh of these rules bear especially upon the doctrinal points under discussion. [Cp. Retractt. II. iv. and Tychonius de Septem Regulis is reprinted in Migne. Pat. Lat. xviii.]

In his de Hoeresibus [c. 428 A.D.] Chapter lxix. gives a brief account of the Donatiani or Donatistæ: (a) as to origin and progress; (b) Donatus's view of the Trinity; (c) the Montenses at Rome; (d) the Circumcelliones; (e) the schism of Maximian.

This was his parting arrow after the thirty-six years of battle. Catholics and Donatists passed under the persecutions of the Arian Vandals. Two years after this treatise Augustin laid aside his weapons to enter the land of eternal peace and unity.

More or less extended allusions are made to Donatism in the following sermons, arranged in the order of the Benedictine editions; for the years in which they were delivered cannot be determined. Want of space prevents the presentation of any analysis.

Sermo X. 1 Kings iii. 16-28.

Sermo XLV. Is. lvii. 13 and 2 Cor. vii. 1.

Sermo XLVI.Ez. xxxiv. 1-16.

Sermo XLVII. Ez. xxxiv. 17-31.

Sermo LXXI.Matt. xii. 32.

Sermo LXXXVIII. Matt. xx. 30-34.

Sermo XC. Matt. xxii. 1-14.

Sermo CVII.Luc. xii. 13-21.

Sermo CXXIX. Jo. v. 39-47.

Sermo CXXXVII. Jo. x. 1-16.

Sermo CXXXVIII. Jo. x. 11-16.

Sermo CLXXXIII. 1 Jo. iv. 2.

Sermo CCXVIII. Luc. xxiv. 38-47.

Sermo CCXLIX. Jo. xxi. 1-14.

Sermo CCLII. Jo. xxi. 1-14.

Sermo CCLXV. The Ascension.

Sermo CCLXVI. Ps. cxli. (cxl.) 5.

Sermo CCLXVIII. Pentecost.

Sermo CCLXIX. Pentecost.

Sermo CCLXXXV. Anniversary of the martyrs Castus and Æmilus.

Sermo CCXCII. John the Baptist.

Sermo CCCXXV. Anniversary of the Twenty Martyrs.

Similar references are to be found in the expositions and sermons based on the Psalms. The first column is the Hebrew and English order; the second that of LXX. and Vulgate.

Exposition of Psalms XI. (X.)

Exposition of Psalms XXVI. (XXV.) Sermon.

Exposition of Psalms XXXI. (XXX.) Sermons I. and II.

Exposition of Psalms XXXIII. (XXXII.) Sermon II.

Exposition of Psalms XXXIV. (XXXIII.) Sermon II.

Exposition of Psalms XXXVI. (XXXV.) Sermon.

Exposition of Psalms XXXVII. (XXXVI.) Sermons II. (archival) and III.

Exposition of Psalms XL. (XXXIX.) Sermon.

Exposition of Psalms LV. (LIV.) Sermon.

Exposition of Psalms LVIII. (LVII.) Sermon.

Exposition of Psalms LXXXVI. (LXXXV.) Sermon.

Exposition of Psalms XCIX. (XCVIII.) Sermon.

Exposition of Psalms CXX. (CXIX.) Sermon.

Exposition of Psalms CXXV. (CXXIV.) Sermon.

Exposition of Psalms CXXXIII. (CXXXII.) Sermon.

Exposition of Psalms CXLVI. (CXLV.) Sermon.

Exposition of Psalms CXLVII. 12-20 (CXLVII.) Sermon.

Exposition of Psalms CXLIX. Sermon.

The time of writing the de Utilitate Jejunii is unknown. Chapter V. 9, contrasts pagan, heretical and Catholic fasts; heretics claim indeed to fast in order to please God; how can they, when they sever the unity? All heretics perish; they are the dividers of the inheritance of Christ.

In conclusion the reviser desires to commend the fidelity and lucidity of the translation made by the Rev. J. R. King, M.A.

No changes made by the reviser have been indicated, since all could not be without confusion. The translation had taken most of its notes and references from the Benedictines. The citations of Cyprian are according to the numerals in Hartel's edition.

Preface

The schism of the Donatists, with which the treatises in the present volume are concerned, arose indirectly out of the persecution under Diocletian at the beginning of the fourth century. At that time Mensurius, bishop of Carthage, and his archdeacon Cæcilianus, had endeavored to check the fanatical spirit in which many of the Christians courted martyrdom; and consequently, on the death of Mensurius in 311, and the elevation of Cæcilianus to the see of Carthage in his place, the opposing party, alleging that Felix, bishop of Aptunga, by whom Cæcilianus had been consecrated, had been a traditor, and that therefore his consecration was invalid, set up against him Majorinus, who was succeeded in 315 by Donatus. The party had by this time gained strength, through the professions that they made of extreme purity in the discipline which they maintained, and had gone so far, under the advice of another Donatus, bishop of Casæ Nigræ in Numidia, as to accuse Cæcilianus before the Roman Emperor Constantine,--thus setting the first precedent for referring a spiritual cause to the decision of a civil magistrate. Constantine accepted the appeal, and in 313 the matter was laid for decision before Melchiades, bishop of Rome, and three bishops of the province of Gaul. They decided in favor of the validity of the consecration of Cæcilianus; and a similar verdict was given by a council held at Arles, by direction of the Emperor, in the following year. The party of Majorinus then appealed to the personal judgment of the Emperor, which was likewise given against them, not without strong expressions of his anger at their pertinacity. This was followed by severe laws directed against their schism; but so far from crushing them, the attack seemed only to increase their enthusiasm and develop their resources. And, under the leadership of Donatus, the successor of Majorinus, their influence spread widely throughout Africa, and continued to prevail, in spite of various efforts at their forcible suppression, during the whole of the fourth century. They especially brought on themselves the vengeance of the civil powers, by the turbulence of certain fanatical ascetics who embraced their cause, and who, under the name of Circumcelliones, spread terror through the country, seeking martydom for themselves, and offering violence to every one who opposed them.

Towards the close of the century, this schism attracted the attention of Augustin, then a priest of Hippo Regius in Numidia. The controversy seems to have had for him a special attraction, not merely because of its intrinsic importance, but also because of the field which it presented for his unrivalled powers as a dialectician. These the Donatists had recently provoked, by inconsistently receiving back into their body a deacon of Carthage named Maximianus who had separated himself from them, and by recognizing as valid all baptism administered by his followers. Hence they naturally shrank from engaging in a contest with an antagonist who was sure to make the most of such a deviation from the very principles on which they based their schism; and, on the other hand, Augustin was so firmly convinced that his own position was impregnable, that he seems to have thought that if he could only secure a thorough and dispassionate discussion of the matter, the Donatists must necessarily be brought to acknowledge not only their theoretical errors, but also the practical sinfulness of their separation from the Church. Throughout the controversy, however, he appears to have put out of sight two considerations: first, the influence of party spirit and prejudice in blinding men to argument; and, secondly, the necessity of treating his opponents in a logical discussion as on an equal footing with himself. The first was in some degree an unavoidable element of disappointment; but Augustin made concession yet more difficult on the part of his opponents, by expecting them to acknowledge his superior position as a member of the Catholic Church, whose duty it was to expose the error of their views. He practically begs the very point at issue, by assuming that he, and not the Donatists, was in the Catholic communion; and though his argument is conducted independently of this premise, yet it naturally rendered them more unwilling to admit its force.

This dogmatism was of less consequence in the first pamphlet which Augustin published on the subject,--his Alphabetical Psalm, in which he set forth the history and errors of the Donatists in a popular form,--since it was not intended as a controversial treatise, but only as a means of enlightening the less educated as to the Catholic tenets on the question in dispute. His next work, written in answer to a letter of Donatus of Carthage, in which the latter tried to prove that the baptism of Christ existed only in his communion, is unfortunately lost; and we can only gather hints as to the further part which he took in the controversy during the next few years from certain of his letters, especially those to the Donatist Bishops Honoratus and Crispinus. [1142]From the former he claims the admission that the exclusiveness of the Donatists proves that they are not the Church of Christ; and his letter to the latter contains an invitation to discuss the leading points at issue, which Crispinus seems to have declined.

In the year 400 he wrote two books Against the Party of Donatus, which are also lost; and about the same time he published his refutation of the letter of Parmenianus in answer to Tichonius, in which he handles and solves the famous question, whether, while abiding in unity in the communion of the same sacraments, the wicked pollute the good by their society. [1143]

Then followed his seven books On Baptism, included in this volume, in which he shows the emptiness of the arguments of the Donatists for the repetition of baptism; and proves that so far was Cyprian from being on their side, that his letters and conduct are of the highest value as overthrowing their position, and utterly condemning their separation from the Church.

Not long after this, Petilianus, bishop of Cirta or Constantina, the most eminent theologian among the Donatist divines, wrote a letter to his clergy against the Catholics, of which Augustin managed to obtain a copy, though the Donatists used their utmost care to keep it from him; and he replied to it in two books, written at different times,--the first in the year 400, before he was in possession of the whole letter, the remainder in 402. To the first book Petilianus made an answer, of which we gather the main tenor from a third book written by Augustin in reply to it. It appears to have been full of vehement abuse, and to have assumed the question in dispute, that the existence of the true Church, and the catholicity of any branch of it, depended on the purity and orthodoxy of all its ministers; so that the guilt or heresy of any minister would invalidate the whole of his ministerial acts. Hence he argued that Cæcilianus being the spiritual father of the so-called Catholics, and having been a traditor, none of them could possibly have been lawfully baptized, much less rightfully ordained.

Augustin admits neither of his assumptions; but, leaving the guilt or innocence of Cæcilianus as a point which was irrelevant (though practically the case against him utterly broke down), he addresses himself to the other point, and argues most conclusively that all the functions of the clergy in celebrating the rites of the Church being purely ministerial, the efficacy of those rites could in no way depend upon the excellence of the individual minister, but was derived entirely from Christ. Hence there was a certainty of the grace bestowed through the several ordinances, which otherwise there could not possibly have been, had their virtue depended on the character of any man, in whom even an unblemished reputation might have been the fruit of a skilled hypocrisy.

The third treatise in this volume belongs to a later period, being a letter written to Bonifacius, the Roman Count of Africa under Valentinian the Third. He had written to Augustin to consult him as to the best means of dealing with the Donatists; and Augustin in his reply points out to him his mistake in supposing that the Donatists shared in the errors of the Arians, whilst he urges him to use moderation in his coercive measures; though both here and in his answer to Petilianus we find him countenancing the theory that the State has a right to interfere in constraining men to keep within the Church. Starting with a forced interpretation of the words, "Compel them to come in," in Luke xiv. 23, he enunciates principles of coercion which, though in him they were subdued and rendered practically of little moment by the spirit of love which formed so large an element in his character, yet found their natural development in the despotic intolerance of the Papacy, and the horrors of the

Inquisition. It is probable that he was himself in some degree misled by confounding the necessity of repressing the violence of the Circumcelliones, which was a real offense against the State, with the expediency of enforcing spiritual unity by temporal authority.

The Donatist treatises have met with little attention from individual editors. There is a dissertation, De Aur. Augustino adversario Donatistarum, by Adrien Roux, published at Louvain in 1838; [1144] but it is believed that no treatises of this series have ever before been translated into English, nor are they separately edited. They are in themselves a valuable authority for an important scene in the history of the Church, and afford a good example both of the strength and the weakness of Augustin's writing,--its strength, in the exhaustive way in which he tears to pieces his opponent's arguments, and the clearness with which he exposes the fallacies of their reasoning; its weakness, in the persistency with which he pursues a point long after its discussion might fairly have been closed, as though he hardly knew when he had gained the victory; and his tendency to claim, by right of his position, a vantage-ground which did not in reality belong to him till the superiority of his cause was proved.

J. R. King

Oxford, March, 1870.

[1142] Epist. xlix. li.

[1143] Bened. Ed. Vol. ix. pp. 7-52. Migne, Vol. ix. pp. 33-108.

[1144] The other works bearing on this controversy are mentioned in the exhaustive volume of Ferd. Ribbeck, Donatus und Augustinus (Elberfeld, 1858).

Ed.

THE SEVEN BOOKS OF AUGUSTIN, BISHOP OF HIPPO,
ON BAPTISM, AGAINST THE DONATISTS
[DE BAPTISIMO CONTRA DONATISTAS.]
CIRCA A.D. 400.

This treatise was written about 400 A.D. Concerning it Aug. in Retract. Book II. c. xviii., says: I have written seven books on Baptism against the Donatists, who strive to defend themselves by the authority of the most blessed bishop and martyr Cyprian; in which I show that nothing is so effectual for the refutation of the Donatists, and for shutting their mouths directly from upholding their schism against the Catholic Church, as the letters and act of Cyprian.

Book I.

He proves that baptism can be conferred outside the Catholic communion by heretics or schismatics, but that it ought not to be received from them; and that it is of no avail to any while in a state of heresy or schism.

Chapter 1.

1. In the treatise which we wrote against the published epistle of Parmenianus [1145] to Tichonius, [1146] we promised that at some future time we would treat the question of baptism more thoroughly; [1147] and indeed, even if we had not made this promise, we are not unmindful that this is a debt fairly due from us to the prayers of our brethren. Wherefore in this treatise we have undertaken, with the help of God, not only to refute the objections which the Donatists have been wont to

urge against us in this matter, but also to advance what God may enable us to say in respect of the authority of the blessed martyr Cyprian, which they endeavor to use as a prop, to prevent their perversity from falling before the attacks of truth. [1148]And this we propose to do, in order that all whose judgment is not blinded by party spirit may understand that, so far from Cyprian's authority being in their favor, it tends directly to their refutation and discomfiture.

2. In the treatise above mentioned, it has already been said that the grace of baptism can be conferred outside the Catholic communion, just as it can be also there retained. But no one of the Donatists themselves denies that even apostates retain the grace of baptism; for when they return within the pale of the Church, and are converted through repentance, it is never given to them a second time, and so it is ruled that it never could have been lost. So those, too, who in the sacrilege of schism depart from the communion of the Church, certainly retain the grace of baptism, which they received before their departure, seeing that, in case of their return, it is not again conferred on them whence it is proved, that what they had received while within the unity of the Church, they could not have lost in their separation. But if it can be retained outside, why may it not also be given there? If you say, "It is not rightly given without the pale;" we answer, "As it is not rightly retained, and yet is in some sense retained, so it is not indeed rightly given, but yet it is given." But as, by reconciliation to unity, that begins to be profitably possessed which was possessed to no profit in exclusion from unity, so, by the same reconciliation, that begins to be profitable which without it was given to no profit. Yet it cannot be allowed that it should be said that that was not given which was given, nor that any one should reproach a man with

not having given this, while confessing that he had given what he had himself received. For the sacrament of baptism is what the person possesses who is baptized; and the sacrament of conferring baptism is what he possesses who is ordained. And as the baptized person, if he depart from the unity of the Church, does not thereby lose the sacrament of baptism, so also he who is ordained, if he depart from the unity of the Church, does not lose the sacrament of conferring baptism. For neither sacrament may be wronged. If a sacrament necessarily becomes void in the case of the wicked, both must become void; if it remain valid with the wicked, this must be so with both. If, therefore, the baptism be acknowledged which he could not lose who severed himself from the unity of the Church, that baptism must also be acknowledged which was administered by one who by his secession had not lost the sacrament of conferring baptism. For as those who return to the Church, if they had been baptized before their secession, are not rebaptized, so those who return, having been ordained before their secession, are certainly not ordained again; but either they again exercise their former ministry, if the interests of the Church require it, or if they do not exercise it, at any rate they retain the sacrament of their ordination; and hence it is, that when hands are laid on them, [1149] to mark their reconciliation, they are not ranked with the laity. For Felicianus, [1150] when he separated himself from them with Maximianus, was not held by the Donatists themselves to have lost either the sacrament of baptism or the sacrament of conferring baptism. For now he is a recognized member of their own body, in company with those very men whom he baptized while he was separated from them in the schism of Maximianus. And so others could receive from them, whilst they still had not joined our society, what they themselves had not lost by severance from our society. And hence it is clear that they are guilty of impiety who endeavor to rebaptize those who are in Catholic unity; and we act rightly who do not dare to repudiate God's sacraments, even when administered in schism. For in all points in which they think with us, they also are in communion with us, and only are severed from us in those points in which they dissent from us. For contact and disunion are not to be measured by different laws in the case of material or spiritual affinities. For as union of bodies arises from continuity of position, so in the agreement of wills there is a kind of contact between souls. If, therefore, a man who has severed himself from unity wishes to do anything different from that which had been impressed on him while in the state of unity, in this point he does sever himself, and is no longer a part of the united whole; but wherever he desires to conduct himself as is customary in the state of unity, in which he himself learned and received the lessons which he seeks to follow, in these points he remains a member, and is united to the corporate whole.

[1145] Parmenianus was successor to Donatus the Great in the See of Carthage, circ. 350 A.D., and died circ. 392 A.D.

[1146] Tichonius, who flourished circ. 380, was the leader of a reformatory movement in Donatism, which Parmenianus opposed, in the writing here alluded to. The reformer was excommunicated. He had the clearest ideas concerning the church and concerning interpretation of any of the ancients.

[1147] Contra Epist. Parmen. ii. 14, also written circ. 400 A.D.

[1148] Cyprian, in his controversy with Pope Stephen of Rome, denied the validity of heretical or schismatical baptism. The

Donatists denied the validity of Catholic baptism. See Schaff, Church History, vol. ii. 262 sqq.

[1149] Comp. v. 23, and iii. 16, note.

[1150] Felicianus, bishop of Musti, headed the revolt against Primianus, the successor of Parmenianus in the Carthaginian See. Listening to the complaint of the deacon Maximianus, who had been deposed by Primianus, a synod was convened in 393 at Cabarsussis, which ordained Maximianus as bishop of Carthage. Hence the title Maximianistæ. Primianus, in 394, at the council of Bagai, was recognized by 310 bishops. The larger fraction, according to the Catholics, was subsequently forced into reunion. Prætextatus, bp. of Assuris, was also one of the leaders in this separation.

Chapter 2.

3. And so the Donatists in some matters are with us; in some matters have gone out from us. Accordingly, those things wherein they agree with us we do not forbid them to do; but in those things in which they differ from us, we earnestly encourage them to come and receive them from us, or return and recover them, as the case may be; and with whatever means we can, we lovingly busy ourselves, that they, freed from faults and corrected, may choose this course. We do not therefore say to them, "Abstain from giving baptism," but "Abstain from giving it in schism." Nor do we say to those whom we see them on the point of baptizing, "Do not receive the baptism," but "Do not receive it in schism." For if any one were compelled by urgent necessity, being unable to find a Catholic from whom to receive baptism, and so, while preserving Catholic peace in his heart, should receive from one without the pale of Catholic unity the sacrament which he was

intending to receive within its pale, this man, should he forthwith depart this life, we deem to be none other than a Catholic. But if he should be delivered from the death of the body, on his restoring himself in bodily presence to that Catholic congregation from which in heart he had never departed, so far from blaming his conduct, we should praise it with the greatest truth and confidence; because he trusted that God was present to his heart, while he was striving to preserve unity, and was unwilling to depart this life without the sacrament of holy baptism, which he knew to be of God, and not of men; wherever he might find it. But if any one who has it in his power to receive baptism within the Catholic Church prefers, from some perversity of mind, to be baptized in schism, even if he afterwards bethinks himself to come to the Catholic Church, because he is assured that there that sacrament will profit him, which can indeed be received but cannot profit elsewhere, beyond all question he is perverse, and guilty of sin, and that the more flagrant in proportion as it was committed wilfully. For that he entertains no doubt that the sacrament is rightly received in the Church, is proved by his conviction that it is there that he must look for profit even from what he has received elsewhere.

Chapter 3.

4. There are two propositions, moreover, which we affirm,--that baptism exists in the Catholic Church, and that in it alone can it be rightly received,--both of which the Donatists deny. Likewise there are two other propositions which we affirm,--that baptism exists among the Donatists, but that with them it is not rightly received, of which two they strenuously confirm the former, that baptism exists with them; but they are unwilling to allow the latter, that in their Church it cannot be

rightly received. Of these four propositions, three are peculiar to us; in one we both agree. For that baptism exists in the Catholic Church, that it is rightly received there, and that it is not rightly received among the Donatists, are assertions made only by ourselves; but that baptism exists also among the Donatists, is asserted by them and allowed by us. If any one, therefore, is desirous of being baptized, and is already convinced that he ought to choose our Church as a medium for Christian salvation, and that the baptism of Christ is only profitable in it, even when it has been received elsewhere, but yet wishes to be baptized in the schism of Donatus, because not they only, nor we only, but both parties alike say that baptism exists with them, let him pause and look to the other three points. For if he has made up his mind to follow us in the points which they deny, though he prefers what both of us acknowledge, to what only we assert, it is enough for our purpose that he prefers what they do not affirm and we alone assert, to what they alone assert. That baptism exists in the Catholic Church, we assert and they deny. That it is rightly received in the Catholic Church, we assert and they deny. That it is not rightly received in the schism of Donatus, we assert and they deny. As, therefore, he is the more ready to believe what we alone assert should be believed, so let him be the more ready to do what we alone declare should be done. But let him believe more firmly, if he be so disposed, what both parties assert should be believed, than what we alone maintain. For he is inclined to believe more firmly that the baptism of Christ exists in the schism of Donatus, because that is acknowledged by both of us, than that it exists in the Catholic Church, an assertion made alone by the Catholics. But again, he is more ready to believe that the baptism of Christ exists also with us, as we alone assert, than that it does not exist with us, as they alone assert. For he has already determined and is fully convinced, that where we differ, our authority is to be preferred to theirs. So that he is more ready to believe what we alone assert, that baptism is rightly received with us, than that it is not rightly so received, since that rests only on their assertion. And, by the same rule, he is more ready to believe what we alone assert, that it is not rightly received with them, than as they alone assert, that it is rightly so received. He finds, therefore, that his confidence in being baptized among the Donatists is somewhat profitless, seeing that, though we both acknowledge that baptism exists with them, yet we do not both declare that it ought to be received from them. But he has made up his mind to cling rather to us in matters where we disagree. Let him therefore feel confidence in receiving baptism in our communion, where he is assured that it both exists and is rightly received; and let him not receive it in a communion, where those whose opinion he has determined to follow acknowledge indeed that it exists, but say that it cannot rightly be received. Nay, even if he should hold it to be a doubtful question, whether or no it is impossible for that to be rightly received among the Donatists which he is assured can rightly be received in the Catholic Church, he would commit a grievous sin, in matters concerning the salvation of his soul, in the mere fact of preferring uncertainty to certainty. At any rate, he must be quite sure that a man can be rightly baptized in the Catholic Church, from the mere fact that he has determined to come over to it, even if he be baptized elsewhere. But let him at least acknowledge it to be matter of uncertainty whether a man be not improperly baptized among the Donatists, when he finds this asserted by those whose opinion he is convinced should be preferred to theirs; and, preferring certainty to uncertainty, let him be baptized here, where he has good grounds for being assured that it is rightly done, in the fact that when he thought of doing it elsewhere, he had still determined that he ought afterwards to come over to this side.

Chapter 4.

5. Further, if any one fails to understand how it can be that we assert that the sacrament is not rightly conferred among the Donatists, while we confess that it exists among them, let him observe that we also deny that it exists rightly among them, just as they deny that it exists rightly among those who quit their communion. Let him also consider the analogy of the military mark, which, though it can both be retained, as by deserters, and, also be received by those who are not in the army, yet ought not to be either received or retained outside its ranks; and, at the same time, it is not changed or renewed when a man is enlisted or brought back to his service. However, we must distinguish between the case of those who unwittingly join the ranks of these heretics, under the impression that they are entering the true Church of Christ, and those who know that there is no other Catholic Church save that which, according to the promise, is spread abroad throughout the whole world, and extends even to the utmost limits of the earth; which, rising amid tares, and seeking rest in the future from the weariness of offenses, says in the Book of Psalms, "From the end of the earth I cried unto Thee, while my heart was in weariness: Thou didst exalt me on a rock." [1151]But the rock was Christ, in whom the apostle says that we are now raised up, and set together in heavenly places, though not yet actually, but only in hope. [1152]And so the psalm goes on to say, "Thou wast my guide, because Thou art become my hope, a tower of strength from the face of the enemy." [1153]By means of His promises, which are like spears and javelins stored up in a strongly

fortified place, the enemy is not only guarded against, but overthrown, as he clothes his wolves in sheep's clothing, [1154] that they may say, "Lo, here is Christ, or there;" [1155] and that they may separate many from the Catholic city which is built upon a hill, and bring them down to the isolation of their own snares, so as utterly to destroy them. And these men, knowing this, choose to receive the baptism of Christ without the limits of the communion of the unity of Christ's body, though they intend afterwards, with the sacrament which they have received elsewhere, to pass into that very communion. For they propose to receive Christ's baptism in antagonism to the Church of Christ, well knowing that it is so even on the very day on which they receive it. And if this is a sin, who is the man that will say, Grant that for a single day I may commit sin? For if he proposes to pass over to the Catholic Church, I would fain ask why. What other answer can he give, but that it is ill to belong to the party of Donatus, and not to the unity of the Catholic Church? Just so many days, then, as you commit this ill, of so many days' sin are you going to be guilty. And it may be said that there is greater sin in more days' commission of it, and less in fewer; but in no wise can it be said that no sin is committed at all. But what is the need of allowing this accursed wrong for a single day, or a single hour? For the man who wishes this license to be granted him, might as well ask of the Church, or of God Himself, that for a single day he should be permitted to apostatize. For there is no reason why he should fear to be an apostate for a day, if he does not shrink from being for that time a schismatic or a heretic.

[1151] Ps. lxi. 2, 3. Cp. Hieron, and LXX.

[1152] Eph. ii. 6.

[1153] Ps. lxi. 2, 3. Cp. Hieron, and LXX.

[1154] Matt. vii. 15.

[1155] Matt. xxiv. 23.

Chapter 5.

6. I prefer, he says, to receive Christ's baptism where both parties agree that it exists. But those whom you intend to join say that it cannot be received there rightly; and those who say that it can be received there rightly are the party whom you mean to quit. What they say, therefore, whom you yourself consider of inferior authority, in opposition to what those say whom you yourself prefer, is, if not false, at any rate, to use a milder term, at least uncertain. I entreat you, therefore, to prefer what is true to what is false, or what is certain to what is uncertain. For it is not only those whom you are going to join, but you yourself who are going to join them, that confess that what you want can be rightly received in that body which you mean to join when you have received it elsewhere. For if you had any doubts whether it could be rightly received there, you would also have doubts whether you ought to make the change. If, therefore, it is doubtful whether it be not sin to receive baptism from the party of Donatus, who can doubt but that it is certain sin not to prefer receiving it where it is certain that it is not sin? And those who are baptized there through ignorance, thinking that it is the true Church of Christ, are guilty of less sin in comparison than these, though even they are wounded by the impiety of schism; nor do they escape a grievous hurt, because others suffer even more. For when it is said to certain men, "It shall be more tolerable for the land of Sodom in the day of judgment than for you," [1156] it is not

meant that the men of Sodom shall escape torment, but only that the others shall be even more grievously tormented.

7. And yet this point had once, perhaps, been involved in obscurity and doubt. But that which is a source of health to those who give heed and receive correction, is but an aggravation of the sin of those who, when they are no longer suffered to be ignorant, persist in their madness to their own destruction. For the condemnation of the party of Maximianus, and their restoration after they had been condemned, together with those whom they had sacrilegiously, to use the language of their own Council, [1157] baptized in schism, settles the whole question in dispute, and removes all controversy. There is no point at issue between ourselves and those Donatists who hold communion with Primianus, which could give rise to any doubt that the baptism of Christ may not only be retained, but even conferred by those who are severed from the Church. For as they themselves are obliged to confess that those whom Felicianus baptized in schism received true baptism, inasmuch as they now acknowledge them as members of their own body, with no other baptism than that which they received in schism; so we say that that is Christ's baptism, even without the pale of Catholic communion, which they confer who are cut off from that communion, inasmuch as they had not lost it when they were cut off. And what they themselves think that they conferred on those persons whom Felicianus baptized in schism, when they admitted them to reconcilation with themselves, viz., not that they should receive that which they did not as yet possess, but that what they had received to no advantage in schism, and were already in possession of, should be of profit to them, this God really confers and bestows through the Catholic communion on

those who come from any heresy or schism in which they received the baptism of Christ; viz., not that they should begin to receive the sacrament of baptism as not possessing it before, but that what they already possessed should now begin to profit them.

[1156] Matt. xi. 24.

[1157] The Council of 310 Donatist bishops, held at Bagai in Numidia, A.D. April 24, 394. Cp. Contra. Crescon. iii. 52, 56.

Chapter 6.

8. Between us, then, and what we may call the genuine [1158] Donatists, whose bishop is Primianus at Carthage, there is now no controversy on this point. For God willed that it should be ended by means of the followers of Maximianus, that they should be compelled by the precedent of his case to acknowledge what they would not allow at the persuasion of Christian charity. But this brings us to consider next, whether those men do not seem to have something to say for themselves, who refuse communion with the party of Primianus, contending that in their body there remains greater sincerity of Donatism, just in proportion to the paucity of their numbers. And even if these were only the party of Maximianus, we should not be justified in despising their salvation. How much more, then, are we bound to consider it, when we find that this same party of Donatus is split up into many most minute fractions, all which small sections of the body blame the one much larger portion which has Primianus for its head, because they receive the baptism of the followers of Maximianus; while each endeavors to maintain that it is the sole receptacle of true baptism, which exists nowhere else, neither in the whole of the world where the Catholic Church

extends itself, nor in that larger main body of the Donatists, nor even in the other minute sections, but only in itself. Whereas, if all these fragments would listen not to the voice of man, but to the most unmistakable manifestation of the truth, and would be willing to curb the fiery temper of their own perversity, they would return from their own barrenness, not indeed to the main body of Donatus, a mere fragment of which they are a smaller fragment, but to the never-failing fruitfulness of the root of the Catholic Church. For all of them who are not against us are for us; but when they gather not with us, they scatter abroad.

[1158] Quodam modo cardinales Donatistas.

Chapter 7.

9. For, in the next place, that I may not seem to rest on mere human arguments,--since there is so much obscurity in this question, that in earlier ages of the Church, before the schism of Donatus, it has caused men of great weight, and even our fathers, the bishops, whose hearts were full of charity, so to dispute and doubt among themselves, saving always the peace of the Church, that the several statutes of their Councils in their different districts long varied from each other, till at length the most wholesome opinion was established, to the removal of all doubts, by a plenary Council of the whole world: [1159] --I therefore bring forward from the gospel clear proofs, by which I propose, with God's help, to prove how rightly and truly in the sight of God it has been determined, that in the case of every schismatic and heretic, the wound which caused his separation should be cured by the medicine of the Church; but that what remained sound in him should rather be recognized with approbation, than wounded by condemnation. It is indeed

true that the Lord says in the gospel, "He that is not with me is against me; and he that gathereth not with me scattereth abroad." [1160]Yet when the disciples had brought word to Him that they had seen one casting out devils in His name, and had forbidden him, because he followed not them, He said, "Forbid him not: for he that is not against us is for us. For there is no man which shall do a miracle in my name, that can lightly speak evil of me." [1161]If, indeed, there were nothing in this man requiring correction, then any one would be safe who, setting himself outside the communion of the Church, severing himself from all Christian brotherhood, should gather in Christ's name; and so there would be no truth in this, "He that is not with me is against me; and he that gathereth not with me scattereth abroad." But if he required correction in the point where the disciples in their ignorance were anxious to check him, why did our Lord, by saying, "Forbid him not," prevent this check from being given? And how can that be true which He then says, "He that is not against you is for you?" For in this point he was not against, but for them, when he was working miracles of healing in Christ's name. That both, therefore, should be true, as both are true,--both the declaration, that "he that is not with me is against me, and he that gathereth not with me scattereth abroad;" and also the injunction, "Forbid him not; for he that is not against you is for you,"--what must we understand, except that the man was to be confirmed in his veneration for that mighty Name, in respect of which he was not against the Church, but for it; and yet he was to be blamed for separating himself from the Church, whereby his gathering became a scattering; and if it should have so happened that he sought union with the Church, he should not have received what he already possessed, but be made to set right the points wherein he had gone astray?

[1159] See below, on ii. 9.

[1160] Matt. xii. 30.

[1161] Mark ix. 38, 39; Luke ix. 50.

Chapter 8.

10. Nor indeed were the prayers of the Gentile Cornelius unheard, nor did his alms lack acceptance; nay, he was found worthy that an angel should be sent to him, and that he should behold the messenger, through whom he might assuredly have learned everything that was necessary, without requiring that any man should come to him. But since all the good that he had in his prayers and alms could not benefit him unless he were incorporated in the Church by the bond of Christian brotherhood and peace, he was ordered to send to Peter, and through him learned Christ; and, being also baptized by his orders, he was joined by the tie of communion to the fellowship of Christians, to which before he was bound only by the likeness of good works. [1162] And indeed it would have been most fatal to despise what he did not yet possess, vaunting himself in what he had. So too those who, by separating themselves from the society of their fellows, to the overthrow of charity, thus break the bond of unity, if they observe none of the things which they have received in that society, are separated in everything; and so any one whom they have joined to their society, if he afterwards wish to come over to the Church, ought to receive everything which he has not already received. But if they observe some of the same things, in respect of these they have not severed themselves; and so far they are still a part of the framework of the Church, while in all other respects they are cut off from it. Accordingly, any one whom they have associated with themselves is united to the

Church in all those points in which they are not separated from it. And therefore, if he wish to come over to the Church, he is made sound in those points in which he was unsound and went astray; but where he was sound in union with the Church, he is not cured, but recognized,--lest in desiring to cure what is sound we should rather inflict a wound. Therefore those whom they baptize they heal from the wound of idolatry or unbelief; but they injure them more seriously with the wound of schism. For idolaters among the people of the Lord were smitten with the sword; [1163] but schismatics were swallowed up by the earth opening her mouth. [1164] And the apostle says, "Though I have all faith, so that I could remove mountains, and have not charity, I am nothing." [1165]

11. If any one is brought to the surgeon, afflicted with a grievous wound in some vital part of the body, and the surgeon says that unless it is cured it must cause death, the friends who brought him do not, I presume, act so foolishly as to count over to the surgeon all his sound limbs, and, drawing his attention to them, make answer to him, "Can it be that all these sound limbs are of no avail to save his life, and that one wounded limb is enough to cause his death?" They certainly do not say this, but they entrust him to the surgeon to be cured. Nor, again, because they so entrust him, do they ask the surgeon to cure the limbs that are sound as well; but they desire him to apply drugs with all care to the one part from which death is threatening the other sound parts too, with the certainty that it must come, unless the wound be healed. What will it then profit a man that he has sound faith, or perhaps only soundness in the sacrament of faith, when the soundness of his charity is done away with by the fatal wound of schism, so that by the overthrow of it the other points, which were in

themselves sound, are brought into the infection of death? To prevent which, the mercy of God, through the unity of His holy Church, does not cease striving that they may come and be healed by the medicine of reconciliation, through the bond of peace. And let them not think that they are sound because we admit that they have something sound in them; nor let them think, on the other hand, that what is sound must needs be healed, because we show that in some parts there is a wound. So that in the soundness of the sacrament, because they are not against us, they are for us; but in the wound of schism, because they gather not with Christ, they scatter abroad. Let them not be exalted by what they have. Why do they pass the eyes of pride over those parts only which are sound? Let them condescend also to look humbly on their wound, and give heed not only to what they have, but also to what is wanting in them.

[1162] Acts x.

[1163] Ex. xxxii.

[1164] Num. xvi.

[1165] 1 Cor. xiii. 2.

Chapter 9.

12. Let them see how many things, and what important things, are of no avail, if a certain single thing be wanting, and let them see what that one thing is. And herein let them hear not my words, but those of the apostle: "Though I speak with the tongues of men and of angels, and have not charity, I am become as sounding brass, or a tinkling cymbal. And though I have the gift of prophecy, and understand all mysteries, and all knowledge; and though I have all faith, so that I could remove

mountains, and have not charity, I am nothing." [1166]What does it profit them, therefore, if they have both the voice of angels in the sacred mysteries, and the gift of prophecy, as had Caiaphas [1167] and Saul, [1168] that so they may be found prophesying, of whom Holy Scripture testifies that they were worthy of condemnation? If they not only know, but even possess the sacraments, as Simon Magus did; [1169] if they have faith, as the devils confessed Christ (for we must not suppose that they did not believe when they said, "What have we to do with Thee, O Son of God? We know Thee who Thou art" [1170]; if they distribute of themselves their own substance to the poor, as many do, not only in the Catholic Church, but in the different heretical bodies; if, under the pressure of any persecution, they give their bodies with us to be burned for the faith which they like us confess: yet because they do all these things apart from the Church, not "forbearing one another in love," nor "endeavoring to keep the unity of the spirit in the bond of peace," [1171] insomuch as they have not charity, they cannot attain to eternal salvation, even with all those good things which profit them not.

[1166] 1 Cor. xiii. 1, 2.

[1167] John xi. 51.

[1168] 1 Sam. xviii. 10.

[1169] Acts viii. 13.

[1170] Mark i. 24.

[1171] Eph. iv. 2, 3.

Chapter 10.

13. But they think within themselves that they show very great subtlety in asking whether the baptism of Christ in the party of Donatus makes men sons or not; so that, if we allow that it does make them sons, they may assert that theirs is the Church, the mother which could give birth to sons in the baptism of Christ; and since the Church must be one, they may allege that ours is no Church. But if we say that it does not make them sons, "Why then," say they, "do you not cause those who pass from us to you to be born again in baptism, after they have been baptized with us, if they are not thereby born as yet?"

14. Just as though their party gained the power of generation in virtue of what constitutes its division, and not from what causes its union with the Church. For it is severed from the bond of peace and charity, but it is joined in one baptism. And so there is one Church which alone is called Catholic; and whenever it has anything of its own in these communions of different bodies which are separate from itself, it is most certainly in virtue of this which is its own in each of them that it, not they, has the power of generation. For neither is it their separation that generates, but what they have retained of the essence of the Church; and if they were to go on to abandon this, they would lose the power of generation. The generation, then, in each case proceeds from the Church, whose sacraments are retained, from which any such birth can alone in any case proceed,--although not all who receive its birth belong to its unity, which shall save those who persevere even to the end. Nor is it those only that do not belong to it who are openly guilty of the manifest sacrilege of schism, but also those who, being outwardly joined to its unity, are yet separated by a life of sin. For the Church had herself given birth to Simon Magus through the sacrament of baptism; and yet it was

declared to him that he had no part in the inheritance of Christ. [1172]Did he lack anything in respect of baptism, of the gospel, of the sacraments? But in that he wanted charity, he was born in vain; and perhaps it had been well for him that he had never been born at all. Was anything wanting to their birth to whom the apostle says, "I have fed you with milk, and not with meat, even as babes in Christ"? Yet he recalls them from the sacrilege of schism, into which they were rushing, because they were carnal: "I have fed you," he says, "with milk, and not with meat: for hitherto ye were not able to bear it, neither yet now are ye able. For ye are yet carnal: for whereas there is among you envying and strife, are ye not carnal, and walk as men? For while one saith, I am of Paul; and another, I am of Apollos; are ye not men?" [1173]For of these he says above: "Now I beseech you, brethren, by the name of our Lord Jesus Christ, that ye all speak the same thing, and that there be no divisions among you; but that ye be perfectly joined together in the same mind, and in the same judgment. For it hath been declared unto me of you, my brethren, by them which are of the house of Chlöe, that there are contentions among you. Now this I say, that every one of you saith, I am of Paul, and I of Apollos, and I of Cephas, and I of Christ. Is Christ divided? was Paul crucified for you? or were ye baptized in the name of Paul?" [1174]These, therefore, if they continued in the same perverse obstinacy, were doubtless indeed born, but yet would not belong by the bond of peace and unity to the very Church in respect of which they were born. Therefore she herself bears them in her own womb and in the womb of her handmaids, by virtue of the same sacraments, as though by virtue of the seed of her husband. For it is not without meaning that the apostle says that all these things were done by way of figure. [1175]But those who are too proud, and are not joined to their lawful mother, are like Ishmael, of whom it is said, "Cast out this bond-woman and her Son: for the son of the bond-woman shall not be heir with my son, even with Isaac." [1176] But those who peacefully love the lawful wife of their father, whose sons they are by lawful descent, are like the sons of Jacob, born indeed of handmaids, but yet receiving the same inheritance. [1177] But those who are born within the family, of the womb of the mother herself, and then neglect the grace they have received, are like Isaac's son Esau, who was rejected, God Himself bearing witness to it, and saying, "I loved Jacob, and I hated Esau;" [1178] and that though they were twin-brethren, the offspring of the same womb.

[1172] Acts viii. 13, 21.

[1173] 1 Cor. iii. 1-4.

[1174] 1 Cor. i. 10-13.

[1175] 1 Cor. x. 11. In figura; tupikos; A.V., "for ensamples."

[1176] Gen. xxi. 10.

[1177] Gen. xxx. 3.

[1178] Mal. i. 2, 3; Gen xxv. 24.

Chapter 11.

15. They ask also, "Whether sins are remitted in baptism in the party of Donatus:" so that, if we say that they are remitted, they may answer, then the Holy Spirit is there; for when by the breathing of our Lord the Holy Spirit was given to the disciples, He then went on to say, "Baptize all nations in the name of the Father, and of the Son, and of the Holy Ghost." [1179]Whose

soever sins ye remit, they are remitted unto them; and whosesoever sins ye retain, they are retained." [1180]And if it is so, they say, then our communion is the Church of Christ; for the Holy Spirit does not work the remission of sins except in the Church. And if our communion is the Church of Christ, then your communion is not the Church of Christ. For that is one, wherever it is, of which it is said, "My dove is but one; she is the only one of her mother;" [1181] nor can there be just so many churches as there are schisms. But if we should say that sins are not there remitted, then, say they, there is no true baptism there; and therefore ought you to baptize those whom you receive from us. And since you do not do this, you confess that you are not in the Church of Christ.

16. To these we reply, following the Scriptures, by asking them to answer themselves what they ask of us. For I beg them to tell us whether there is any remission of sins where there is not charity; for sins are the darkness of the soul. For we find St. John saying, "He that hateth his brother is still in darkness." [1182]But none would create schisms, if they were not blinded by hatred of their brethren. If, therefore, we say that sins are not remitted there, how is he regenerate who is baptized among them? And what is regeneration in baptism, except the being renovated from the corruption of the old man? And how can he be so renovated whose past sins are not remitted? But if he be not regenerate, neither does he put on Christ; from which it seems to follow that he ought to be baptized again. For the apostle says, "For as many of you as have been baptized into Christ have put on Christ;" [1183] and if he has not so put on Christ, neither should he be considered to have been baptized in Christ. Further, since we say that he has been baptized in Christ, we confess that he has put on Christ; and if we confess

this, we confess that he is regenerate. And if this be so, how does St. John say, "He that hateth his brother remaineth still in darkness," if remission of his sins has already taken place? Can it be that schism does not involve hatred of one's brethren? Who will maintain this, when both the origin of, and perseverance in schism consists in nothing else save hatred of the brethren?

17. They think that they solve this question when they say: "There is then no remission of sins in schism, and therefore no creation of the new man by regeneration, and accordingly neither is there the baptism of Christ." But since we confess that the baptism of Christ exists in schism, we propose this question to them for solution: Was Simon Magus endued with the true baptism of Christ? They will answer, Yes; being compelled to do so by the authority of holy Scripture. I ask them whether they confess that he received remission of his sins. They will certainly acknowledge it. So I ask why Peter said to him that he had no part in the lot of the saints. Because, they say, he sinned afterwards, wishing to buy with money the gift of God, which he believed the apostles were able to sell.

[1179] Matt. xxviii. 19.

[1180] John xx. 23.

[1181] Song of Sol. vi. 9.

[1182] 1 John ii. 11.

[1183] Gal. iii. 27.

Chapter 12.

18. What if he approached baptism itself in deceit? were his sins remitted, or were they not? Let them choose which they will. Whichever they choose will answer our purpose. If they say they were remitted, how then shall "the Holy Spirit of discipline flee deceit," [1184] if in him who was full of deceit He worked remission of sins? If they say they were not remitted, I ask whether, if he should afterwards confess his sin with contrition of heart and true sorrow, it would be judged that he ought to be baptized again. And if it is mere madness to assert this, then let them confess that a man can be baptized with the true baptism of Christ, and that yet his heart, persisting in malice or sacrilege, may not allow remission of sins to be given; and so let them understand that men may be baptized in communions severed from the Church, in which Christ's baptism is given and received in the said celebration of the sacrament, but that it will only then be of avail for the remission of sins, when the recipient, being reconciled to the unity of the Church, is purged from the sacrilege of deceit, by which his sins were retained, and their remission prevented. For, as in the case of him who had approached the sacrament in deceit there is no second baptism, but he is purged by faithful discipline and truthful confession, which he could not be without baptism, so that what was given before becomes then powerful to work his salvation, when the former deceit is done away by the truthful confession; so also in the case of the man who, while an enemy to the peace and love of Christ, received in any heresy or schism the baptism of Christ, which the schismatics in question had not lost from among them, though by his sacrilege his sins were not remitted, yet, when he corrects his error, and comes over to the communion and unity of the Church, he ought not to be again baptized: because by his very reconciliation to the peace of the Church he receives

this benefit, that the sacrament now begins in unity to be of avail for the remission of his sins, which could not so avail him as received in schism.

19. But if they should say that in the man who has approached the sacrament in deceit, his sins are indeed removed by the holy power of so great a sacrament at the moment when he received it, but return immediately in consequence of his deceit: so that the Holy Spirit has both been present with him at his baptism for the removal of his sins, and has also fled before his perseverance in deceit so that they should return: so that both declarations prove true,--both, "As many of you as have been baptized into Christ have put on Christ;" and also, "The holy spirit of discipline will flee deceit;"--that is to say, that both the holiness of baptism clothes him with Christ, and the sinfulness of deceit strips him of Christ; like the case of a man who passes from darkness through light into darkness again, his eyes being always directed towards darkness, though the light cannot but penetrate them as he passes;--if they should say this, let them understand that this is also the case with those who are baptized without the pale of the Church, but yet with the baptism of the Church, which is holy in itself, wherever it may be; and which therefore belongs not to those who separate themselves, but to the body from which they are separated; while yet it avails even among them so far, that they pass through its light back to their own darkness, their sins, which in that moment had been dispelled by the holiness of baptism, returning immediately upon them, as though it were the darkness returning which the light had dispelled while they were passing through it.

20. For that sins which have been remitted do return upon a man, where there is no brotherly love, is most clearly taught by

our Lord, in the case of the servant whom He found owing Him ten thousand talents, and to whom He yet forgave all at his entreaty. But when he refused to have pity on his fellow-servant who owed him a hundred pence, the Lord commanded him to pay what He had forgiven him. The time, then, at which pardon is received through baptism is as it were the time for rendering accounts, so that all the debts which are found to be due may be remitted. Yet it was not afterwards that the servant lent his fellow-servant the money, which he had so pitilessly exacted when the other was unable to pay it; but his fellow-servant already owed him the debt, when he himself, on rendering his accounts to his master, was excused a debt of so vast an amount. He had not first excused his fellow-servant, and so come to receive forgiveness from his Lord. This is proved by the words of the fellow-servant: "Have patience with me, and I will pay thee all." Otherwise he would have said, "You forgave me it before; why do you again demand it?" This is made more clear by the words of the Lord Himself. For He says, "But the same servant went out, and found one of his fellow-servants which was owing [1185] him a hundred pence." [1186]He does not say, "To whom he had already forgiven a debt of a hundred pence." Since then He says, "was owing him," it is clear that he had not forgiven him the debt. And indeed it would have been better, and more in accordance with the position of a man who was going to render an account of so great a debt, and expected forbearance from his lord, that he should first have forgiven his fellow-servant what was due to him, and so have come to render the account when there was such need for imploring the compassion of his lord. Yet the fact that he had not yet forgiven his fellow-servant, did not prevent his lord from forgiving him all his debts on the occasion of receiving his accounts. But what advantage was it to him, since they all immediately returned with redoubled force upon his head, in consequence of his persistent want of charity? So the grace of baptism is not prevented from giving remission of all sins, even if he to whom they are forgiven continues to cherish hatred towards his brother in his heart. For the guilt of yesterday is remitted, and all that was before it, nay, even the guilt of the very hour and moment previous to baptism, and during baptism itself. But then he immediately begins again to be responsible, not only for the days, hours, moments which ensue, but also for the past,--the guilt of all the sins which were remitted returning on him, as happens only too frequently in the Church.

[1184] Wisd. i. 5.

[1185] Debebat. Hieron, debebat, LXX. opheilen.

[1186] Matt. xviii. 23-35.

Chapter 13.

21. For it often happens that a man has an enemy whom he hates most unjustly; although we are commanded to love even our unjust enemies, and to pray for them. But in some sudden danger of death he begins to be uneasy, and desires baptism, which he receives in such haste, that the emergency scarcely admits of the necessary formal examination of a few words, much less of a long conversation, so that this hatred should be driven from his heart, even supposing it to be known to the minister who baptizes him. Certainly cases of this sort are still found to occur not only with us, but also with them. What shall we say then? Are this man's sins forgiven or not? Let them choose just which alternative they prefer. For if they are forgiven, they immediately return: this is the teaching of the

gospel, the authoritative announcement of truth. Whether, therefore, they are forgiven or not, medicine is necessary afterwards; and yet if the man lives, and learns that his fault stands in need of correction, and corrects it, he is not baptized anew, either with them or with us. So in the points in which schismatics and heretics neither entertain different opinions nor observe different practice from ourselves, we do not correct them when they join us, but rather commend what we find in them. For where they do not differ from us, they are not separated from us. But because these things do them no good so long as they are schismatics or heretics, on account of other points in which they differ from us, not to mention the most grievous sin that is involved in separation itself, therefore, whether their sins remain in them, or return again immediately after remission, in either case we exhort them to come to the soundness of peace and Christian charity, not only that they may obtain something which they had not before, but also that what they had may begin to be of use to them.

Chapter 14.

22. It is to no purpose, then, that they say to us, "If you acknowledge our baptism, what do we lack that should make you suppose that we ought to think seriously of joining your communion?" For we reply, We do not acknowledge any baptism of yours; for it is not the baptism of schismatics or heretics, but of God and of the Church, wheresoever it may be found, and whithersoever it may be transferred. But it is in no sense yours, except because you entertain false opinions, and do sacrilegious acts, and have impiously separated yourselves from the Church. For if everything else in your practice and opinions were true, and still you were to persist in this same separation, contrary to the bond of brotherly peace, contrary to

the union of all the brethren, who have been manifest, according to the promise, in all the world; the particulars of whose history, and the secrets of whose hearts, you never could have known or considered in every case, so as to have a right to condemn them; who, moreover, cannot be liable to condemnation for submitting themselves to the judges of the Church rather than to one of the parties to the dispute,--in this one thing, at least, in such a case, you are deficient, in which he is deficient who lacks charity. Why should we go over our argument again? Look and see yourselves in the apostle, how much there is that you lack. For what does it matter to him who lacks charity, whether he be carried away outside the Church at once by some blast of temptation, or remain within the Lord's harvest, so as to be separated only at the final winnowing? And yet even such, if they have once been born in baptism, need not be born again.

Chapter 15.

23. For it is the Church that gives birth to all, either within her pale, of her own womb; or beyond it, of the seed of her bridegroom,--(either of herself, or of her handmaid. [1187]) But Esau, even though born of the lawful wife, was separated from the people of God because he quarrelled with his brother. And Asher, born indeed by the authority of a wife, but yet of a handmaid, was admitted to the land of promise on account of his brotherly good-will. Whence also it was not the being born of a handmaid, but his quarrelling with his brother, that stood in the way of Ishmael, to cause his separation from the people of God; and he received no benefit from the power of the wife, whose son he rather was, inasmuch as it was in virtue of her conjugal rights that he was both conceived in and born of the womb of the handmaid. Just as with the Donatists it is by the

right of the Church, which exists in baptism, that whosoever is born receives his birth; but if they agree with their brethren, through the unity of peace they come to the land of promise, not to be again cast out from the bosom of their true mother, but to be acknowledged in the seed of their father; but if they persevere in discord, they will belong to the line of Ishmael. For Ishmael was first, and then Isaac; and Esau was the elder, Jacob the younger. Not that heresy gives birth before the Church, or that the Church herself gives birth first to those who are carnal or animal, and afterwards to those who are spiritual; but because, in the actual lot of our mortality, in which we are born of the seed of Adam, "that was not first which is spiritual, but that which is natural, and afterward that which is spiritual." [1188]But from mere animal sensation, because "the natural man receiveth not the things of the Spirit of God," [1189] arise all dissensions and schisms. And the apostle says [1190] that all who persevere in this animal sensation belong to the old covenant. that is, to the desire of earthly promises, which are indeed the type of the spiritual; but "the natural man receiveth not the things of the Spirit of God." [1191]

24. At whatever time, therefore, men have begun to be of such a nature in this life, that, although they have partaken of such divine sacraments as were appointed for the dispensation under which they lived, they yet savor of carnal things, and hope for and desire carnal things from God, whether in this life or afterwards, they are yet carnal. But the Church, which is the people of God, is an ancient institution even in the pilgrimage of this life, having a carnal interest in some men, a spiritual interest in others. To the carnal belongs the old covenant, to the spiritual the new. But in the first days both were hidden, from Adam even to Moses. But by Moses the old covenant

was made manifest, and in it was hidden the new covenant, because after a secret fashion it was typified. But so soon as the Lord came in the flesh, the new covenant was revealed; yet, though the sacraments of the old covenant passed away; the dispositions peculiar to it did not pass away. For they still exist in those whom the apostle declares to be already born indeed by the sacrament of the new covenant, but yet capable, as being natural, of receiving the things of the Spirit of God. For, as in the sacraments of the old covenant some persons were already spiritual, belonging secretly to the new covenant, which was then concealed, so now also in the sacrament of the new covenant, which has been by this time revealed, many live who are natural. And if they will not advance to receive the things of the Spirit of God, to which the discourse of the apostle urges them, they will still belong to the old covenant. But if they advance, even before they receive them, yet by their very advance and approach they belong to the new covenant; and if, before becoming spiritual, they are snatched away from this life, yet through the protection of the holiness of the sacrament they are reckoned in the land of the living, where the Lord is our hope and our portion. Nor can I find any truer interpretation of the scripture, "Thine eyes did see my substance, yet being imperfect" [1192] considering what follows, "And in Thy book shall all be written." [1193]

[1187] The words in parenthesis are wanting in the Mss., and seem to have crept from the margin into the text.

[1188] 1 Cor. xv. 46.

[1189] 1 Cor. ii. 14.

[1190] Gal. iv.

[1191] 1 Cor. ii. 14.

[1192] Ps. cxxxix. 16.

[1193] Cf. Hieron, and LXX. A.V. "In Thy book were all my members written."

Chapter 16.

25. But the same mother which brought forth Abel, and Enoch, and Noah, and Abraham, brought forth also Moses and the prophets who succeeded him till the coming of our Lord; and the mother which gave birth to them gave birth also to our apostles and martyrs, and all good Christians. For all these that have appeared have been born indeed at different times, but are included in the society of our people; and it is as citizens of the same state that they have experienced the labors of this pilgrimage, and some of them are experiencing them, and others will experience them even to the end. Again, the mother who brought forth Cain, and Ham, and Ishmael, and Esau, brought forth also Dathan and others like him in the same people; and she who gave birth to them gave birth also to Judas the false apostle, and Simon Magus, and all the other false Christians who up to this time have persisted obstinately in their carnal affections, whether they have been mingled in the unity of the Church, or separated from it in open schism. But when men of this kind have the gospel preached to them, and receive the sacraments at the hand of those who are spiritual, it is as though Rebecca gave birth to them of her own womb, as she did to Esau; but when they are produced in the midst of the people of God through the instrumentality of those who preach the gospel not sincerely, [1194] Sarah is indeed the mother, but through Hagar. So when good spiritual disciples are produced by the preaching or baptism of those who are

carnal, Leah, indeed, or Rachel, gives birth to them in her right as wife, but from the womb of a handmaid. But when good and faithful disciples are born of those who are spiritual in the gospel, and either attain to the development of spiritual age, or do not cease to strive in that direction, or are only deterred from doing so by want of power, these are born like Isaac from the womb of Sarah, or Jacob from the womb of Rebecca, in the new life and the new covenant.

[1194] Non caste; ouch agnos. Phil. i. 16. Hieron. non sincere.

Chapter 17.

26. Therefore, whether they seem to abide within, or are openly outside, whatsoever is flesh is flesh, and what is chaff is chaff, whether they persevere in remaining in their barrenness on the threshing-floor, or, when temptation befalls them, are carried out as it were by the blast of some wind. And even that man is always severed from the unity of the Church which is without spot or wrinkle, [1195] who associates with the congregation of the saints in carnal obstinacy. Yet we ought to despair of no man, whether he be one who shows himself to be of this nature within the pale of the Church, or whether he more openly opposes it from without. But the spiritual, or those who are steadily advancing with pious exertion towards this end, do not stray without the pale; since even when, by some perversity or necessity among men, they seem to be driven forth, they are more approved than if they had remained within, since they are in no degree roused to contend against the Church, but remain rooted in the strongest foundation of Christian charity on the solid rock of unity. For hereunto belongs what is said in the sacrifice of Abraham: "But the birds divided he not." [1196]

[1195] In the Retractations, ii. 18, Augustin notes on this passage, that wherever he uses this quotation from the Epistle to the Ephesians, he means it to be understood of the progress of the Church towards this condition, and not of her success in its attainment; for at present the infirmities and ignorance of her members give ground enough for the whole Church joining daily in the petition, "Forgive us our debts."

[1196] Gen. xv. 10.

Chapter 18.

27. On the question of baptism, then, I think that I have argued at sufficient length; and since this is a most manifest schism which is called by the name of the Donatists, it only remains that on the subject of baptism we should believe with pious faith what the universal Church maintains, apart from the sacrilege of schism. And yet, if within the Church different men still held different opinions on the point, without meanwhile violating peace, then till some one clear and simple decree should have been passed by an universal Council, it would have been right for the charity which seeks for unity to throw a veil over the error of human infirmity, as it is written "For charity shall cover the multitude of sins." [1197]For, seeing that its absence causes the presence of all other things to be of no avail, we may well suppose that in its presence there is found pardon for the absence of some missing things.

28. There are great proofs of this existing on the part of the blessed martyr Cyprian, in his letters,--to come at last to him of whose authority they carnally flatter themselves they are possessed, whilst by his love they are spiritually overthrown. For at that time, before the consent of the whole Church had declared authoritatively, by the decree of a plenary Council,

[1198] what practice should be followed in this matter, it seemed to him, in common with about eighty of his fellow bishops of the African churches, that every man who had been baptized outside the communion of the Catholic Church should, on joining the Church, be baptized anew. And I take it, that the reason why the Lord did not reveal the error in this to a man of such eminence, was, that his pious humility and charity in guarding the peace and health of the Church might be made manifest, and might be noticed, so as to serve as an example of healing power, so to speak, not only to Christians of that age, but also to those who should come after. For when a bishop of so important a Church, himself a man of so great merit and virtue, endowed with such excellence of heart and power of eloquence, entertained an opinion about baptism different from that which was to be confirmed by a more diligent searching into the truth; though many of his colleagues held what was not yet made manifest by authority, but was sanctioned by the past custom of the Church, and afterwards embraced by the whole Catholic world; yet under these circumstances he did not sever himself, by refusal of communion, from the others who thought differently, and indeed never ceased to urge on the others that they should "forbear one another in love, endeavoring to keep the unity of the Spirit in the bond of peace." [1199] For so, while the framework of the body remained whole, if any infirmity occurred in certain of its members, it might rather regain its health from their general soundness, than be deprived of the chance of any healing care by their death in severance from the body. And if he had severed himself, how many were there to follow! what a name was he likely to make for himself among men! how much more widely would the name of Cyprianist have spread than that of Donatist! But he was not a son of perdition, one of those of whom it is said, "Thou castedst them down while they were elevated;" [1200] but he was the son of the peace of the Church, who in the clear illumination of his mind failed to see one thing, only that through him another thing might be more excellently seen. "And yet," says the apostle, "show I unto you a more excellent way: though I speak with the tongues of men and of angels, and have not charity, I am become as sounding brass, or a tinkling cymbal." [1201]He had therefore imperfect insight into the hidden mystery of the sacrament. But if he had known the mysteries of all sacraments, without having charity, it would have been nothing. But as he, with imperfect insight into the mystery, was careful to preserve charity with all courage and humility and faith, he deserved to come to the crown of martyrdom; so that, if any cloud had crept over the clearness of his intellect from his infirmity as man, it might be dispelled by the glorious brightness of his blood. For it was not in vain that our Lord Jesus Christ, when He declared Himself to be the vine, and His disciples, as it were, the branches in the vine, gave command that those which bare no fruit should be cut off, and removed from the vine as useless branches. [1202]But what is really fruit, save that new offspring, of which He further says, "A new commandment I give unto you, that ye love one another?" [1203]This is that very charity, without which the rest profiteth nothing. The apostle also says: "But the fruit of the Spirit is love, joy, peace, long-suffering, gentleness, goodness, faith, meekness, temperance;" [1204] which all begin with charity, and with the rest of the combination forms one unity in a kind of wondrous cluster. [1205]Nor is it again in vain that our Lord added, "And every branch that beareth fruit, my Father purgeth it, that it may bring forth more fruit," [1206] but because those who are strong in the fruit of charity may yet have something which requires purging, which the Husbandman will not leave untended. Whilst then, that holy man entertained on the subject of baptism an opinion at variance with the true view, which was afterwards thoroughly examined and confirmed after most diligent consideration, his error was compensated by his remaining in catholic unity, and by the abundance of his charity; and finally it was cleared away by the pruning-hook of martyrdom.

[1197] 1 Pet. iv. 8.

[1198] See below, ii. 9.

[1199] Eph. iv. 2, 3.

[1200] Ps. lxxiii. 18; cp. Hieron.

[1201] 1 Cor. xii. 31, xiii. 1.

[1202] John xv. 1, 2.

[1203] John xiii. 34.

[1204] Gal. v. 22, 23.

[1205] Botrum.

[1206] John xv. 2.

Chapter 19.

29. But that I may not seem to be uttering these praises of the blessed martyr (which, indeed, are not his, but rather those of Him by whose grace he showed himself what he was), in order to escape the burden of proof, let us now bring forward from his letters the testimony by which the mouths of the Donatists

may most of all be stopped. For they advance his authority before the unlearned, to show that in a manner they do well when they baptize afresh the faithful who come to them. Too wretched are they--and, unless they correct themselves, even by themselves are they utterly condemned--who choose in the example set them by so great a man to imitate just that fault, which only did not injure him, because he walked with constant steps even to the end in that from which they have strayed who "have not known the way of peace." [1207]It is true that Christ's baptism is holy; and although it may exist among heretics or schismatics, yet it does not belong to the heresy or schism; and therefore even those who come from thence to the Catholic Church herself ought not to be baptized afresh. Yet to err on this point is one thing; it is another thing that those who are straying from the peace of the Church, and have fallen headlong into the pit of schism, should go on to decide that any who join them ought to be baptized again. For the former is a speck on the brightness of a holy soul which abundance of charity [1208] would fain have covered; the latter is a stain in their nether foulness which the hatred of peace in their countenance ostentatiously brings to light. But the subject for our further consideration, relating to the authority of the blessed Cyprian, we will commence from a fresh beginning.

[1207] Rom. iii. 17; from which it has been introduced into the Alexandrine Ms. of the Septuagint at Ps. xiv. 3, cf. Hieron.; it is also found in the English Prayer-book version of the Psalms.

[1208] Charitatis ubera.

Book II.

In which Augustin proves that it is to no purpose that the Donatists bring forward the authority of Cyprian, bishop and martyr, since it is really more opposed to them than to the Catholics. For that he held that the view of his predecessor Agrippinus, on the subject of baptizing heretics in the Catholic Church when they join its communion, should only be received on condition that peace should be maintained with those who entertained the opposite view, and that the unity of the Church should never be broken by any kind of schism.

Chapter 1.

1. How much the arguments make for us, that is, for catholic peace, which the party of Donatus profess to bring forward against us from the authority of the blessed Cyprian, and how much they prove against those who bring them forward, it is my intention, with the help of God, to show in the ensuing book. If, therefore, in the course of my argument, I am obliged to repeat what I have already said in other treatises (although I will do so as little as I can,) yet this ought not to be objected to by those who have already read them and agree with them; since it is not only right that those things which are necessary for instruction should be frequently instilled into men of dull intelligence, but even in the case of those who are endowed with larger understanding, it contributes very much both to make their learning easier and their powers of teaching readier, where the same points are handled and discussed in many various ways. For I know how much it discourages a reader, when he comes upon any knotty question in the book which he has in hand, to find himself presently referred for its solution to another which he happens not to have. Wherefore, if I am compelled, by the urgency of the present questions, to repeat what I have already said in other books, I would seek forgiveness from those who know those books already, that those who are ignorant may have their difficulties removed; for

it is better to give to one who has already, than to abstain from satisfying any one who is in want.

2. What, then, do they venture to say, when their mouth is closed [1209] by the force of truth, with which they will not agree? "Cyprian," say they, "whose great merits and vast learning we all know, decreed in a Council, [1210] with many of his fellow-bishops contributing their several opinions, that all heretics and schismatics, that is, all who are severed from the communion of the one Church, are without baptism; and therefore, whosoever has joined the communion of the Church after being baptized by them must be baptized in the Church." The authority of Cyprian does not alarm me, because I am reassured by his humility. We know, indeed, the great merit of the bishop and martyr Cyprian; but is it in any way greater than that of the apostle and martyr Peter, of whom the said Cyprian speaks as follows in his epistle to Quintus? "For neither did Peter, whom the Lord chose first, and on whom He built His Church, [1211] when Paul afterwards disputed with him about circumcision, claim or assume anything insolently and arrogantly to himself, so as to say that he held the primacy, and should rather be obeyed of those who were late and newly come. Nor did he despise Paul because he had before been a persecutor of the Church, but he admitted the counsel of truth, and readily assented to the legitimate grounds which Paul maintained; giving us thereby a pattern of concord and patience, that we should not pertinaciously love our own opinions, but should rather account as our own any true and rightful suggestions of our brethren and colleagues for the common health and weal." [1212]Here is a passage in which Cyprian records what we also learn in holy Scripture, that the Apostle Peter, in whom the primacy of the apostles shines with

such exceeding grace, was corrected by the later Apostle Paul, when he adopted a custom in the matter of circumcision at variance with the demands of truth. If it was therefore possible for Peter in some point to walk not uprightly according to the truth of the gospel, so as to compel the Gentiles to judaize, as Paul writes in that epistle in which he calls God to witness that he does not lie; for he says, "Now the things which I write unto you, behold, before God, I lie not;" [1213] and, after this sacred and awful calling of God to witness, he told the whole tale, saying in the course of it, "But when I saw that they walked not uprightly, according to the truth of the gospel, I said unto Peter before them all, If thou, being a Jew, livest after the manner of the Gentiles, and not as do the Jews, why compellest thou the Gentiles to live as do the Jews?" [1214] --if Peter, I say, could compel the Gentiles to live after the manner of the Jews, contrary to the rule of truth which the Church afterwards held, why might not Cyprian, in opposition to the rule of faith which the whole Church afterwards held, compel heretics and schismatics to be baptized afresh? I suppose that there is no slight to Cyprian in comparing him with Peter in respect to his crown of martyrdom; rather I ought to be afraid lest I am showing disrespect towards Peter. For who can be ignorant that the primacy of his apostleship is to be preferred to any episcopate whatever? But, granting the difference in the dignity of their sees, yet they have the same glory in their martyrdom. And whether it may be the case that the hearts of those who confess and die for the true faith in the unity of charity take precedence of each other in different points, the Lord Himself will know, by the hidden and wondrous dispensation of whose grace the thief hanging on the cross once for all confesses Him, and is sent on the selfsame day to paradise, [1215] while Peter, the follower of our Lord, denies Him thrice, and has his crown postponed: [1216] for us it were rash to form a judgment from the evidence. But if any one were now found compelling a man to be circumcised after the Jewish fashion, as a necessary preliminary for baptism, this would meet with much more general repudiation by mankind, than if a man should be compelled to be baptized again. Wherefore, if Peter, on doing this, is corrected by his later colleague Paul, and is yet preserved by the bond of peace and unity till he is promoted to martyrdom, how much more readily and constantly should we prefer, either to the authority of a single bishop, or to the Council of a single province, the rule that has been established by the statutes of the universal Church? For this same Cyprian, in urging his view of the question, was still anxious to remain in the unity of peace even with those who differed from him on this point, as is shown by his own opening address at the beginning of the very Council which is quoted by the Donatists. For it is as follows:

[1209] Præfocantur.

[1210] The Council of Carthage, A.D. 256, in which eighty-seven African bishops declared in favor of rebaptizing heretics. The opinions of the bishops are quoted and answered by Augustin, one by one, in Books vi and vii.

[1211] Matt. xvi. 18.

[1212] Cypr. Ep. lxxi.

[1213] Gal. i. 20.

[1214] Gal. ii. 14.

[1215] Luke xxiii. 40-43.

[1216] Matt. xxvi. 69-75.

Chapter 2.

3. "When, on the calends of September, very many bishops from the provinces of Africa, [1217] Numidia, and Mauritania, with their presbyters and deacons, had met together at Carthage, a great part of the laity also being present; and when the letter addressed by Jubaianus [1218] to Cyprian, as also the answer of Cyprian to Jubaianus, on the subject of baptizing heretics, had been read, Cyprian said: Ye have heard, most beloved colleagues, what Jubaianus, our fellow-bishop, has written to me, consulting my moderate ability concerning the unlawful and profane baptism of heretics, and what answer I gave him,--giving a judgment which we have once and again and often given, that heretics coming to the Church ought to be baptized, and sanctified with the baptism of the Church. Another letter of Jubaianus has likewise been read to you, in which, agreeably to his sincere and religious devotion, in answer to our epistle, he not only expressed his assent, but returned thanks also, acknowledging that he had received instruction. It remains that we severally declare our opinion on this subject, judging no one, nor depriving any one of the right of communion if he differ from us. For no one of us sets himself up as a bishop of bishops, or, by tyrannical terror, forces his colleagues to a necessity of obeying, inasmuch as every bishop, in the free use of his liberty and power, has the right of forming his own judgment, and can no more be judged by another than he can himself judge another. But we must all await the judgment of our Lord Jesus Christ, who alone has the power both of setting us in the government of His Church, and of judging of our acts therein.'"

[1217] That is, the proconsular province of Africa, or Africa Zeugitana, answering to the northern part of the territory of Tunis.

[1218] The letters of Jubaianas, Mauritanian bishop, are not extant.

Chapter 3.

4. Now let the proud and swelling necks of the heretics raise themselves, if they dare, against the holy humility of this address. Ye mad Donatists, whom we desire earnestly to return to the peace and unity of the holy Church, that ye may receive health therein, what have ye to say in answer to this? You are wont, indeed, to bring up against us the letters of Cyprian, his opinion, his Council; why do ye claim the authority of Cyprian for your schism, and reject his example when it makes for the peace of the Church? But who can fail to be aware that the sacred canon of Scripture, both of the Old and New Testament, is confined within its own limits, and that it stands so absolutely in a superior position to all later letters of the bishops, that about it we can hold no manner of doubt or disputation whether what is confessedly contained in it is right and true; but that all the letters of bishops which have been written, or are being written, since the closing of the canon, are liable to be refuted if there be anything contained in them which strays from the truth, either by the discourse of some one who happens to be wiser in the matter than themselves, or by the weightier authority and more learned experience of other bishops, by the authority of Councils; and further, that the Councils themselves, which are held in the several districts and provinces, must yield, beyond all possibility of doubt, to the authority of plenary Councils which are formed for the whole

Christian world; and that even of the plenary Councils, the earlier are often corrected by those which follow them, when, by some actual experiment, things are brought to light which were before concealed, and that is known which previously lay hid, and this without any whirlwind of sacrilegious pride, without any puffing of the neck through arrogance, without any strife of envious hatred, simply with holy humility, catholic peace, and Christian charity?

Chapter 4.

5. Wherefore the holy Cyprian, whose dignity is only increased by his humility, who so loved the pattern set by Peter as to use the words, "Giving us thereby a pattern of concord and patience, that we should not pertinaciously love our own opinions, but should rather account as our own any true and rightful suggestions of our brethren and colleagues, for the common health and weal," [1219] --he, I say, abundantly shows that he was most willing to correct his own opinion, if any one should prove to him that it is as certain that the baptism of Christ can be given by those who have strayed from the fold, as that it could not be lost when they strayed; on which subject we have already said much. Nor should we ourselves venture to assert anything of the kind, were we not supported by the unanimous authority of the whole Church, to which he himself would unquestionably have yielded, if at that time the truth of this question had been placed beyond dispute by the investigation and decree of a plenary Council. For if he quotes Peter as an example for his allowing himself quietly and peacefully to be corrected by one junior colleague, how much more readily would he himself, with the Council of his province, have yielded to the authority of the whole world, when the truth had been thus brought to light? For, indeed, so

holy and peaceful a soul would have been most ready to assent to the arguments of any single person who could prove to him the truth; and perhaps he even did so, [1220] though we have no knowledge of the fact. For it was neither possible that all the proceedings which took place between the bishops at that time should have been committed to writing, nor are we acquainted with all that was so committed. For how could a matter which was involved in such mists of disputation even have been brought to the full illumination and authoritative decision of a plenary Council, had it not first been known to be discussed for some considerable time in the various districts of the world, with many discussions and comparisons of the views of the bishop on every side? But this is one effect of the soundness of peace, that when any doubtful points are long under investigation, and when, on account of the difficulty of arriving at the truth, they produce difference of opinion in the course of brotherly disputation, till men at last arrive at the unalloyed truth; yet the bond of unity remains, lest in the part that is cut away there should be found the incurable wound of deadly error.

[1219] See above, c. i. 2.

[1220] Bede asserts that this was the case. Book VIII. qu. 5.

Chapter 5.

6. And so it is that often something is imperfectly revealed to the more learned, that their patient and humble charity, from which proceeds the greater fruit, may be proved, either in the way in which they preserve unity, when they hold different opinions on matters of comparative obscurity, or in the temper with which they receive the truth, when they learn that it has been declared to be contrary to what they thought. And of

these two we have a manifestation in the blessed Cyprian of the one, viz., of the way in which he preserved unity with those from whom he differed in opinion. For he says, "Judging no one nor depriving any one of the right of communion if he differ from us." [1221] And the other, viz., in what temper he could receive the truth when found to be different from what he thought it, though his letters are silent on the point, is yet proclaimed by his merits. If there is no letter extant to prove it, it is witnessed by his crown of martyrdom; if the Council of bishops declare it not, it is declared by the host of angels. For it is no small proof of a most peaceful soul, that he won the crown of martyrdom in that unity from which he would not separate, even though he differed from it. For we are but men; and it is therefore a temptation incident to men that we should hold views at variance with the truth on any point. But to come through too great love for our own opinion, or through jealousy of our betters, even to the sacrilege of dividing the communion of the Church, and of founding heresy or schism, is a presumption worthy of the devil. But never in any point to entertain an opinion at variance with the truth is perfection found only in the angels. Since then we are men, yet forasmuch as in hope we are angels, whose equals we shall be in the resurrection, [1222] at any rate, so long as we are wanting in the perfection of angels, let us at least be without the presumption of the devil. Accordingly the apostle says, "There hath no temptation taken you but such as is common to man." [1223] It is therefore part of man's nature to be sometimes wrong. Wherefore he says in another place, "Let us therefore, as many as be perfect, be thus minded: and if in anything ye be otherwise minded, God shall reveal even this unto you." [1224] But to whom does He reveal it when it is His will (be it in this life or in the life to come), save to those who walk in the way of peace, and stray not aside into any schism? Not to such as those who have not known the way of peace, [1225] or for some other cause have broken the bond of unity. And so, when the apostle said, "And if in anything ye be otherwise minded, God shall reveal even this unto you," lest they should think that besides the way of peace their own wrong views might be revealed to them, he immediately added, "Nevertheless, whereto we have already attained, let us walk by the same rule." [1226]And Cyprian, walking by this rule, by the most persistent tolerance, not simply by the shedding of his blood, but because it was shed in unity (for if he gave his body to be burned, and had not charity, it would profit him nothing [1227]), came by the confession of martyrdom to the light of the angels, and if not before, at least then, acknowledged the revelation of the truth on that point on which, while yet in error, he did not prefer the maintenance of a wrong opinion to the bond of unity.

[1221] See above, c. ii. 3.

[1222] Matt. xxii. 30.

[1223] 1 Cor x. 13.

[1224] Phil. iii. 15.

[1225] Rom. iii. 17; see on i. 19, 29.

[1226] Phil. iii. 16.

[1227] 1 Cor. xiii. 3.

Chapter 6.

7. What then, ye Donatists, what have ye to say to this? If our opinion about baptism is true, yet all who thought differently in the time of Cyprian were not cut off from the unity of the Church, till God revealed to them the truth of the point on which they were in error, why then have ye by your sacrilegious separation broken the bond of peace? But if yours is the true opinion about baptism, Cyprian and the others, in conjunction with whom ye set forth that he held such a Council, remained in unity with those who thought otherwise; why, therefore, have ye broken the bond of peace? Choose which alternative ye will, ye are compelled to pronounce an opinion against your schism. Answer me, wherefore have ye separated yourselves? Wherefore have ye erected an altar in opposition to the whole world? Wherefore do ye not communicate with the Churches to which apostolic epistles have been sent, which you yourselves read and acknowledge, in accordance with whose tenor you say that you order your lives? Answer me, wherefore have ye separated yourselves? I suppose in order that ye might not perish by communion with wicked men. How then was it that Cyprian, and so many of his colleagues, did not perish? For though they believed that heretics and schismatics did not possess baptism, yet they chose rather to hold communion with them when they had been received into the Church without baptism, although they believed that their flagrant and sacrilegious sins were yet upon their heads, than to be separated from the unity of the Church, according to the words of Cyprian, "Judging no one, nor depriving any one of the right of communion if he differ from us."

8. If, therefore, by such communion with the wicked the just cannot but perish, the Church had already perished in the time of Cyprian. Whence then sprang the origin of Donatus? where

was he taught, where was he baptized, where was he ordained, since the Church had been already destroyed by the contagion of communion with the wicked? But if the Church still existed, the wicked could do no harm to the good in one communion with them. Wherefore did ye separate yourselves? Behold, I see in unity Cyprian and others, his colleagues, who, on holding a council, decided that those who have been baptized without the communion of the Church have no true baptism, and that therefore it must be given them when they join the Church. But again, behold I see in the same unity that certain men think differently in this matter, and that, recognizing in those who come from heretics and schismatics the baptism of Christ, they do not venture to baptize them afresh. All of these catholic unity embraces in her motherly breast, bearing each other's burdens by turns, and endeavoring to keep the unity of the Spirit in the bond of peace, [1228] till God should reveal to one or other of them any error in their views. If the one party held the truth, were they infected by the others, or no? If the others held the truth, were they infected by the first, or no? Choose which ye will. If there was contamination, the Church even then ceased to exist; answer me, therefore, whence came ye forth hither? But if the Church remained, the good are in no wise contaminated by the bad in such communion; answer me, therefore, why did ye break the bond?

9. Or is it perhaps that schismatics, when received without baptism, bring no infection, but that it is brought by those who deliver up the sacred books? [1229]For that there were traditors of your number is proved by the clearest testimony of history. And if you had then brought true evidence against those whom you were accusing, you would have proved your cause before the unity of the whole world, so that you would have been

retained whilst they were shut out. And if you endeavored to do this, and did not succeed, the world is not to blame, which trusted the judges of the Church rather than the beaten parties in the suit; whilst, if you would not urge your suit, the world again is not to blame, which could not condemn men without their cause being heard. Why, then, did you separate yourselves from the innocent? You cannot defend the sacrilege of your schism. But this I pass over. But so much I say, that if the traditors could have defiled you, who were not convicted by you, and by whom, on the contrary, you were beaten, much more could the sacrilege of schismatics and heretics, received into the Church, as you maintain, without baptism, have defiled Cyprian. Yet he did not separate himself. And inasmuch as the Church continued to exist, it is clear that it could not be defiled. Wherefore, then, did you separate yourselves, I do not say from the innocent, as the facts proved them, but from the traditors, as they were never proved to be? Are the sins of traditors, as I began to say, heavier than those of schismatics? Let us not bring in deceitful balances, to which we may hang what weights we will and how we will, saying to suit ourselves, "This is heavy and this is light;" but let us bring forward the sacred balance out of holy Scripture, as out of the Lord's treasure-house, and let us weigh them by it, to see which is the heavier; or rather, let us not weigh them for ourselves, but read the weights as declared by the Lord. At the time when the Lord showed, by the example of recent punishment, that there was need to guard against the sins of olden days, and an idol was made and worshipped, and the prophetic book was burned by the wrath of a scoffing king, and schism was attempted, the idolatry was punished with the sword, [1230] the burning of the book by slaughter in war and captivity in a foreign land, [1231] schism by the earth opening, and swallowing up alive the leaders of the schism while the rest were consumed with fire from heaven. [1232]Who will now doubt that that was the worse crime which received the heavier punishment? If men coming from such sacrilegious company, without baptism, as you maintain, could not defile Cyprian, how could those defile you who were not convicted but supposed betrayers of the sacred books? [1233]For if they had not only given up the books to be burned, but had actually burned them with their own hands, they would have been guilty of a less sin than if they had committed schism; for schism is visited with the heavier, the other with the lighter punishment, not at man's discretion, but by the judgment of God.

[1228] Eph. iv. 3.

[1229] Traditores sanctorum librorum.

[1230] Ex. xxxii.

[1231] Jer. xxxvi.

[1232] Num. xvi.

[1233] Non convicti sed conficti traditores.

Chapter 7.

10. Wherefore, then, have ye severed yourselves? If there is any sense left in you, you must surely see that you can find no possible answer to these arguments. "We are not left," they say, "so utterly without resource, but that we can still answer, It is our will. Who art thou that judgest another man's servant? to his own master he standeth or falleth.'" [1234]They do not understand that this was said to men who were wishing to judge, not of open facts, but of the hearts of other men. For

how does the apostle himself come to say so much about the sins of schisms and heresies? Or how comes that verse in the Psalms, "If of a truth ye love justice, judge uprightly, O ye sons of men?" [1235] But why does the Lord Himself say, "Judge not according to the appearance, but judge righteous judgment," [1236] if we may not judge any man? Lastly, why, in the case of those traditors, whom they have judged unrighteously, have they themselves ventured to pass any judgments at all on another man's servants? To their own master they were standing or falling. Or why, in the case of the recent followers of Maximianus, have they not hesitated to bring forward the judgment delivered with the infallible voice, as they aver, of a plenary Council, in such terms as to compare them with those first schismatics whom the earth swallowed up alive? And yet some of them, as they cannot deny, they either condemned though innocent, or received back again in their guilt. But when a truth is urged which they cannot gainsay, they mutter a truly wholesome murmuring: "It is our will: Who art thou that judgest another man's servant? to his own master he standeth or falleth.'" But when a weak sheep is espied in the desert, and the pastor who should reclaim it to the fold is nowhere to be seen, then there is setting of teeth, and breaking of the weak neck: "Thou wouldst be a good man, wert thou not a traditor. Consult the welfare of thy soul; be a Christian." What unconscionable madness! When it is said to a Christian, "Be a Christian," what other lesson is taught, save a denial that he is a Christian? Was it not the same lesson which those persecutors of the Christians wished to teach, by resisting whom the crown of martyrdom was gained? Or must we even look on crime as lighter when committed with threatening of the sword than with treachery of the tongue?

11. Answer me this, ye ravening wolves, who, seeking to be clad in sheep's clothing, [1237] think that the letters of the blessed Cyprian are in your favor. Did the sacrilege of schismatics defile Cyprian, or did it not? If it did, the Church perished from that instant, and there remained no source from which ye might spring. If it did not, then by what offense on the part of others can the guiltless possibly be defiled, if the sacrilege of schism cannot defile them? Wherefore, then, have ye severed yourselves? Wherefore, while shunning the lighter offenses, which are inventions of your own, have ye committed the heaviest offense of all, the sacrilege of schism? Will ye now perchance confess that those men were no longer schismatics or heretics who had been baptized without the communion of the Church, or in some heresy or schism, because by coming over to the Church, and renouncing their former errors, they had ceased to be what formerly they were? How then was it, that though they were not baptized, their sins remained not on their heads? Was it that the baptism was Christ's, but that it could not profit them without the communion of the Church; yet when they came over, and, renouncing their past error, were received into the communion of the Church by the laying on of hands, then, being now rooted and founded in charity, without which all other things are profitless, they began to receive profit for the remission of sins and the sanctification of their lives from that sacrament, which, while without the pale of the Church, they possessed in vain?

12. Cease, then, to bring forward against us the authority of Cyprian in favor of repeating baptism, but cling with us to the example of Cyprian for the preservation of unity. For this question of baptism had not been as yet completely worked out, but yet the Church observed the most wholesome custom

of correcting what was wrong, not repeating what was already given, even in the case of schismatics and heretics: she healed the wounded part, but did not meddle with what was whole. And this custom, coming, I suppose, from apostolical tradition (like many other things which are held to have been handed down under their actual sanction, because they are preserved throughout the whole Church, though they are not found either in their letters, or in the Councils of their successors),--this most wholesome custom, I say, according to the holy Cyprian, began to be what is called amended by his predecessor Agrippinus. [1238]But, according to the teaching which springs from a more careful investigation into the truth, which, after great doubt and fluctuation, was brought at last to the decision of a plenary Council, we ought to believe that it rather began to be corrupted than to receive correction at the hands of Agrippinus. Accordingly, when so great a question forced itself upon him, and it was difficult to decide the point, whether remission of sins and man's spiritual regeneration could take place among heretics or schismatics, and the authority of Agrippinus was there to guide him, with that of some few men who shared in his misapprehension of this question, having preferred attempting something new to maintaining a custom which they did not understand how to defend; under these circumstances considerations of probability forced themselves into the eyes of his soul, and barred the way to the thorough investigation of the truth.

[1234] Rom. xiv. 4.

[1235] Ps. lviii. 1. Aug.: Si vere justitiam diligitis, recte judicate filii hominum. Cp. Hieron.: Si vere utique justitiam loquimini, recta judicate filii hominum.

[1236] John vii. 24.

[1237] Matt. vii. 15.

[1238] Agrippinus was probably the second (some place him still earlier) bishop before Cyprian. He convened the council of 70 (disputed date), who were the first to take action in favor of rebaptism. Cp. Cypr. Ep. lxxi. 4, bonæ memoriæ vir. Cp. lxxiii. 3.

Chapter 8.

13. Nor do I think that the blessed Cyprian had any other motive in the free expression and earlier utterance of what he thought in opposition to the custom of the Church, save that he should thankfully receive any one that could be found with a fuller revelation of the truth, and that he should show forth a pattern for imitation, not only of diligence in teaching, but also of modesty in learning; but that, if no one should be found to bring forward any argument by which those considerations of probability should be refuted, then he should abide by his opinion, with the full consciousness that he had neither concealed what he conceived to be the truth, nor violated the unity which he loved. For so he understood the words of the apostle: "Let the prophets speak two or three, and let the other judge. If anything be revealed to another that sitteth by, let the first hold his peace." [1239]"In which passage he has taught and shown, that many things are revealed to individuals for the better, and that we ought not each to strive pertinaciously for what he has once imbibed and held, but if anything has appeared better and more useful, he should willingly embrace it." [1240]At any rate, in these words he not only advised those to agree with him who saw no better course, but also exhorted any who could to bring forward arguments by which the

maintenance of the former custom might rather be established; that if they should be of such a nature as not to admit of refutation, he might show in his own person with what sincerity he said "that we ought not each to strive pertinaciously for what he has once imbibed and held, but that, if anything has appeared better and more useful, he should willingly embrace it." [1241]But inasmuch as none appeared, except such as simply urged the custom against him, and the arguments which they produced in its favor were not of a kind to bring conviction to a soul like his, this mighty reasoner was not content to give up his opinions, which, though they were not true, as he was himself unable to see, were at any rate not confuted, in favor of a custom which had truth on its side, but had not yet been confirmed. And yet, had not his predecessor Agrippinus, and some of his fellow-bishops throughout Africa, first tempted him to desert this custom, even by the decision of a Council, he certainly would not have dared to argue against it. But, amid the perplexities of so obscure a question, and seeing everywhere around him a strong universal custom, he would rather have put restraint upon himself by prayer and stretching forth his mind towards God, so as to have perceived or taught that for truth which was afterwards decided by a plenary Council. But when he had found relief amid his weariness in the authority of the former Council [1242] which was held by Agrippinus, he preferred maintaining what was in a manner the discovery of his predecessors, to expending further toil in investigation. For, at the end of his letter to Quintus, he thus shows how he has sought repose, if one may use the expression, for his weariness, in what might be termed the resting-place of authority. [1243]

[1239] 1 Cor. xiv. 29, 30.

[1240] Cypr. Ep. lxxi.

[1241] Cypr. Ep. lxxi.

[1242] The former Council of Carthage was held by Agrippinus early in the third century, the ordinary date given being 215-7 A.D.; others 186-7.

[1243] Tanquam lectulo auctoritatis.

Chapter 9.

14. "This, moreover," says he, "Agrippinus, a man of excellent memory, with the rest, bishops with him, who at that time governed the Church of the Lord in the province of Africa and Numidia, did establish and, after the investigation of a mutual Council had weighed it, confirm; whose sentence, being both religious and legitimate and salutary in accordance with the Catholic faith and Church, we also have followed." [1244]By this witness he gives sufficient proof how much more ready he would have been to bear his testimony, had any Council been held to discuss this matter which either embraced the whole Church, or at least represented our brethren beyond the sea. [1245]But such a Council had not yet been held, because the whole world was bound together by the powerful bond of custom; and this was deemed sufficient to oppose to those who wished to introduce what was new, because they could not comprehend the truth. Afterwards, however, while the question became matter for discussion and investigation amongst many on either side, the new practice was not only invented, but even submitted to the authority and power of a plenary Council,-- after the martyrdom of Cyprian, it is true, but before we were born. [1246]But that this was indeed the custom of the Church, which afterwards was confirmed by a plenary Council, in which

the truth was brought to light, and many difficulties cleared away, is plain enough from the words of the blessed Cyprian himself in that same letter to Jubaianus, which was quoted as being read in the Council. [1247]For he says, "But some one asks, What then will be done in the case of those who, coming out of heresy to the Church, have already been admitted without baptism?" where certainly he shows plainly enough what was usually done, though he would have wished it otherwise; and in the very fact of his quoting the Council of Agrippinus, he clearly proves that the custom of the Church was different. Nor indeed was it requisite that he should seek to establish the practice by this Council, if it was already sanctioned by custom; and in the Council itself some of the speakers expressly declare, in giving their opinion, that they went against the custom of the Church in deciding what they thought was right. Wherefore let the Donatists consider this one point, which surely none can fail to see, that if the authority of Cyprian is to be followed, it is to be followed rather in maintaining unity than in altering the custom of the Church; but if respect is paid to his Council, it must at any rate yield place to the later Council of the universal Church, of which he rejoiced to be a member, often warning his associates that they should all follow his example in upholding the coherence of the whole body. For both later Councils are preferred among later generations to those of earlier date; and the whole is always, with good reason, looked upon as superior to the parts.

[1244] Cypr. Ep. lxxi. 4.

[1245] Transmarinum vel universale Concilium.

[1246] The plenary Council, on whose authority Augustin relies in many places in this work, was either that of Arles, in 314

A.D., or of Nicæa, in 325 A.D., both of them being before his birth, in 354 A.D. He quotes the decision of the same council, contra Parmenianum, ii. 13, 30; de Hæresibus 69: Ep. xliii. 7, 19. Contra Parmenianum, iii. 4, 21: "They condemned," he says, "some few in Africa, by whom they were in turn vanquished by the judgment of the whole world;" and he adds, that "the Catholics trusted ecclesiastical judges like these in preference to the defeated parties in the suit." Ib. 6, 30: He says that the Donatists, "having made a schism in the unity of the Church, were refuted, not by the authority of 310 African bishops, but by that of the whole world." And in the sixth chapter of the first book of the same treatise, he says that the Donatists, after the decision at Arles, came again to Constantine, and there were defeated "by a final decision," i.e. at Milan, as is seen from Ep. xliii. 7, 20, in the year 316 A.D. Substance of note in Benedictine ed. reproduced in Migne.

[1247] See above, ch. ii. 3.

Chapter 10.

15. But what attitude do they assume, when it is shown that the holy Cyprian, though he did not himself admit as members of the Church those who had been baptized in heresy or schism, yet held communion with those who did admit them, according to his express declaration, "Judging no one, nor depriving any one of the right of communion if he differ from us?" [1248]If he was polluted by communion with persons of this kind, why do they follow his authority in the question of baptism? But if he was not polluted by communion with them, why do they not follow his example in maintaining unity? Have they anything to urge in their defense except the plea, "We choose to have it so?" What other answer have any sinful or

wicked men to the discourse of truth or justice,--the voluptuous, for instance, the drunkards, adulterers, and those who are impure in any way, thieves, robbers, murderers, plunderers, evil-doers, idolaters,--what other answer can they make when convicted by the voice of truth, except "I choose to do it;" "It is my pleasure so"? And if they have in them a tinge of Christianity, they say further, "Who art thou that judgest another man's servant?" [1249]Yet these have so much more remains of modesty, that when, in accordance with divine and human law, they meet with punishment for their abandoned life and deeds, they do not style themselves martyrs; while the Donatists wish at once to lead a sacrilegious life and enjoy a blameless reputation, to suffer no punishment for their wicked deeds, and to gain a martyr's glory in their just punishment. As if they were not experiencing the greater mercy and patience of God, in proportion as "executing His judgments upon them by little and little, He giveth them place of repentance," [1250] and ceases not to redouble His scourgings in this life; that, considering what they suffer, and why they suffer it, they may in time grow wise; and that those who have received the baptism of the party of Maximianus in order to preserve the unity of Donatus, may the more readily embrace the baptism of the whole world in order to preserve the peace of Christ; that they may be restored to the root, may be reconciled to the unity of the Church, may see that they have nothing left for them to say, though something yet remains for them to do; that for their former deeds the sacrifice of loving-kindness may be offered to a long-suffering God, whose unity they have broken by their wicked sin, on whose sacraments they have inflicted such a lasting wrong. For "the Lord is merciful and gracious, slow to anger, plenteous in mercy and truth." [1251]Let them embrace His mercy and long-suffering in this life, and fear His truth in the next. For He willeth not the death of a sinner, but rather that he should turn from his way and live; [1252] because He bends His judgment against the wrongs that have been inflicted on Him. This is our exhortation.

[1248] Ib.

[1249] Rom. xiv. 4.

[1250] Wisd. xii. 10.

[1251] Not Ps. ciii. 8, but lxxxvi. 15.

[1252] Ezek. xxiii. 11.

Chapter 11.

16. For this reason, then, we hold them to be enemies, because we speak the truth, because we are afraid to be silent, because we fear to shrink from pressing our point with all the force that lies within our power, because we obey the apostle when he says, "Preach the word; be instant in season out of season; reprove, rebuke, exhort." [1253]But, as the gospel says, "They love the praise of men more than the praise of God;" [1254] and while they fear to incur blame for a time, they do not fear to incur damnation for ever. They see, too, themselves what wrong they are doing; they see that they have no answer which they can make, but they overspread the inexperienced with mists, whilst they themselves are being swallowed up alive,-- that is, are perishing knowingly and willfully. They see that men are amazed, and look with abhorrence on the fact that they have divided themselves into many schisms, especially in Carthage, [1255] the capital and most noted city of all Africa; they have endeavored to patch up the disgrace of their rags. Thinking that they could annihilate the followers of

Maximianus, they pressed heavily on them through the agency of Optatus the Gildonian; [1256] they inflicted on them many wrongs amid the cruellest of persecutions. Then they received back some, thinking that all could be converted under the influence of the same terror; but they were unwilling to do those whom they received the wrong of baptizing afresh those who had been baptized by them in their schism, or rather of causing them to be baptized again within their communion by the very same men by whom they had been baptized outside, and thus they at once made an exception to their own impious custom. They feel how wickedly they are acting in assailing the baptism of the whole world, when they have received the baptism of the followers of Maximianus. But they fear those whom they have themselves rebaptized, lest they should receive no mercy from them, when they have shown it to others; lest these should call them to account for their souls when they have ceased to destroy those of other men.

[1253] 2 Tim. iv. 2.

[1254] John xii. 43.

[1255] He is alluding to that chief schism among the Donatists, which occurred when Maximianus was consecrated bishop of Carthage, in opposition to Primianus, probably immediately after the Synod of Cabarsussum, 393.

[1256] Optatus, a Donatist bishop of Thamogade in Numidia, was called Gildonianus from his adherence to Gildo, Count of Africa, and generalissimo of the province under the elder Theodosius. On his death, in 395 A.D., Gildo usurped supreme authority, and by his aid Optatus was enabled to oppress the Catholics in the province, till, in 398 A.D., Gildo was defeated by his brother Mascezel, and destroyed himself, and Optatus was put in prison, where he died soon afterwards. He is not to be confounded with Optatus, Bishop of Milevis, the strenuous opponent of the Donatists.

Chapter 12.

17. What answer they can give about the followers of Maximianus whom they have received, they cannot divine. If they say, "Those we received were innocent," the answer is obvious, "Then you had condemned the innocent." If they say, "We did it in ignorance," then you judged rashly (just as you passed a rash judgment on the traditors), and your declaration was false that "you must know that they were condemned by the truthful voice of a plenary Council." [1257] For indeed the innocent could never be condemned by a voice of truth. If they say, "We did not condemn them," it is only necessary to cite the Council, to cite the names of bishops and states alike. If they say, "The Council itself is none of ours," then we cite the records of the proconsular province, where more than once they quoted the same Council to justify the exclusion of the followers of Maximianus from the basilicas, and to confound them by the din of the judges and the force of their allies. If they say that Felicianus of Musti, and Prætextatus of Assavæ, whom they afterwards received, were not of the party of Maximianus, then we cite the records in which they demanded, in the courts of law, that these persons should be excluded from the Council which they held against the party of Maximianus. If they say, "They were received for the sake of peace," our answer is, "Why then do ye not acknowledge the only true and full peace? Who urged you, who compelled you to receive a schismatic whom you had condemned, to preserve the peace of Donatus, and to condemn the world unheard, in violation of the peace of Christ?" Truth hems them in on every

side. They see that there is no answer left for them to make, and they think that there is nothing left for them to do; they cannot find out what to say. They are not allowed to be silent. They had rather strive with perverse utterance against truth, than be restored to peace by a confession of their faults.

[1257] The Council of Bagai. See above, I. v. 7.

Chapter 13.

18. But who can fail to understand what they may be saying in their hearts? "What then are we to do," say they, "with those whom we have already rebaptized?" Return with them to the Church. Bring those whom you have wounded to be healed by the medicine of peace: bring those whom you have slain to be brought to life again by the life of charity. Brotherly union has great power in propitiating God. "If two of you," says our Lord, "shall agree on earth as touching anything that they shall ask, it shall be done for them." [1258]If for two men who agree, how much more for two communities? Let us throw ourselves together on our knees before the Lord. Do you share with us our unity; let us share with you your contrition and let charity cover the multitude of sins. [1259]Seek counsel from the blessed Cyprian himself. See how much he considered to depend upon the blessing of unity, from which he did not sever himself to avoid the communion of those who disagreed with him; how, though he considered that those who were baptized outside the communion of the Church had no true baptism, he was yet willing to believe that, by simple admission into the Church, they might, merely in virtue of the bond of unity, be admitted to a share in pardon. For thus he solved the question which he proposed to himself in writing as follows to Jubaianus: "But some will say, What then will become of those

who, in times past, coming to the Church from heresy, were admitted without baptism?' The Lord is able of His mercy to grant pardon, and not to sever from the gifts of His Church those who, being out of simplicity admitted to the Church, have in the Church fallen asleep." [1260]

[1258] Matt. xviii. 19.

[1259] 1 Pet. iv. 8.

[1260] Cypr. Ep. lxxiii. 23 to Jubaianus.

Chapter 14.

19. But which is the worse, not to be baptized at all, or to be twice baptized, it is difficult to decide. I see, indeed, which is more repugnant and abhorrent to men's feelings; but when I have recourse to that divine balance, in which the weight of things is determined, not by man's feelings, but by the authority of God, I find a statement by our Lord on either side. For He said to Peter, "He who is washed has no need of washing a second time;" [1261] and to Nicodemus, "Except a man be born of water and of the Spirit, he cannot enter into the kingdom of God." [1262] What is the purport of the more secret determination of God, it is perhaps difficult for men like us to learn; but as far as the mere words are concerned, any one may see what a difference there is between "has no need of washing," and "cannot enter into the kingdom of heaven." The Church, lastly, herself holds as her tradition, that without baptism she cannot admit a man to her altar at all; but since it is allowed that one who has been rebaptized may be admitted after penance, surely this plainly proves that his baptism is considered valid. If, therefore, Cyprian thought that those whom he considered to be unbaptized yet had some share in

pardon, in virtue of the bond of unity, the Lord has power to be reconciled even to the rebaptized by means of the simple bond of unity and peace, and by this same compensating power of peace to mitigate His displeasure against those by whom they were rebaptized, and to pardon all the errors which they had committed while in error, on their offering the sacrifice of charity, which covereth the multitude of sins; so that He looks not to the number of those who have been wounded by their separation, but to the greater number who have been delivered from bondage by their return. For in the same bond of peace in which Cyprian conceived that, through the mercy of God, those whom he considered to have been admitted to the Church without baptism, were yet not severed from the gifts of the Church, we also believe that through the same mercy of God the rebaptized can earn their pardon at His hands.

[1261] John xiii. 10. "Qui lotus est, non habet necessitatem iterum lavandi." The Latin, with the A.V., loses the distinction between ho leloumenos, "he that has bathed," and niptein, "to wash:" and further wrongfully introduces the idea of repetition.

[1262] John iii. 5.

Chapter 15.

20. Since the Catholic Church, both in the time of the blessed Cyprian and in the older time before him, contained within her bosom either some that were rebaptized or some that were unbaptized, either the one section or the other must have won their salvation only by the force of simple unity. For if those who came over from the heretics were not baptized, as Cyprian asserts, they were not rightly admitted into the Church; and yet he himself did not despair of their obtaining pardon from the mercy of God in virtue of the unity of the Church. So again, if

they were already baptized, it was not right to rebaptize them. What, therefore, was there to aid the other section, save the same charity that delighted in unity, so that what was hidden from man's weakness, in the consideration of the sacrament, might not be reckoned, by the mercy of God, as a fault in those who were lovers of peace? Why, then, while ye fear those whom ye have rebaptized, do ye grudge yourselves and them the entrance to salvation? There was at one time a doubt upon the subject of baptism; those who held different opinions yet remained in unity. In course of time, owing to the certain discovery of the truth, that doubt was taken away. The question which, unsolved, did not frighten Cyprian into separation from the Church, invites you, now that it is solved, to return once more within the fold. Come to the Catholic Church in its agreement, which Cyprian did not desert while yet disturbed with doubt; or if now you are dissatisfied with the example of Cyprian, who held communion with those who were received with the baptism of heretics, declaring openly that we should "neither judge any one, nor deprive any one of the right of communion if he differ from us," [1263] whither are ye going, ye wretched men? What are ye doing? You are bound to fly even from yourselves, because you have advanced beyond the position where he abode. But if neither his own sins nor those of others could stand in his way, on account of the abundance of his charity and his love of brotherly kindness and the bond of peace, do you return to us, where you will find much less hindrance in the way of either us or you from the fictions which your party have invented.

[1263] See above, cii. 3.

Book III.

Augustin undertakes the refutation of the arguments which might be derived from the epistle of Cyprian to Jubaianus, to give color to the view that the baptism of Christ could not be conferred by heretics.

Chapter 1.

1. I think that it may now be considered clear to every one, that the authority of the blessed Cyprian for the maintenance of the bond of peace, and the avoiding of any violation of that most wholesome charity which preserves unity in the Church, may be urged on our side rather than on the side of the Donatists. For if they have chosen to act upon his example in rebaptizing Catholics, because he thought that heretics ought to be baptized on joining the Catholic Church, shall not we rather follow his example, whereby he laid down a manifest rule that one ought in no wise, by the establishment of a separate communion, to secede from the Catholic communion, that is, from the body of Christians dispersed throughout the world, even on the admission of evil and sacrilegious men, since he was unwilling even to remove from the right of communion those whom he considered to have received sacrilegious men without baptism into the Catholic communion, saying, "Judging no one, nor depriving any of the right of communion if he differ from us?" [1264]

[1264] See above, II. ii. 3.

Chapter 2.

2. Nevertheless, I see what may still be required of me, viz., that I should answer those plausible arguments, by which, in even earlier times, Agrippinus, or Cyprian himself, or those in Africa who agreed with them, or any others in far distant lands

beyond the sea, were moved, not indeed by the authority of any plenary or even regionary Council, but by a mere epistolary correspondence, to think that they ought to adopt a custom which had no sanction from the ancient custom of the Church, and which was expressly forbidden by the most unanimous resolution of the Catholic world in order that an error which had begun to creep into the minds of some men, through discussions of this kind, might be cured by the more powerful truth and universal healing power of unity coming on the side of safety. And so they may see with what security I approach this discourse. If I am unable to gain my point, and show how those arguments may be refuted which they bring forward from the Council and the epistles of Cyprian, to the effect that Christ's baptism may not be given by the hands of heretics, I shall still remain safely in the Church, in whose communion Cyprian himself remained with those who differed from him.

3. But if they say that the Catholic Church existed then, because there were a few, or, if they prefer it, even a considerable number, who denied the validity of any baptism conferred in an heretical body, and baptized all who came from thence, what then? Did the Church not exist at all before Agrippinus, with whom that new kind of system began, at variance with all previous custom? Or how, again after the time of Agrippinus, when, unless there had been a return to the primitive custom, there would have been no need for Cyprian to set on foot another Council? Was there no Church then, because such a custom as this prevailed everywhere, that the baptism of Christ should be considered nothing but the baptism of Christ, even though it were proved to have been conferred in a body of heretics or schismatics? But if the Church existed even then, and had not perished through a

breach of its continuity, but was, on the contrary, holding its ground, and receiving increase in every nation, surely it is the safest plan to abide by this same custom, which then embraced good and bad alike in unity. But if there was then no Church in existence, because sacrilegious heretics were received without baptism, and this prevailed by universal custom, whence has Donatus made his appearance? From what land did he spring? or from what sea did he emerge? or from what sky did he fall? And so we, as I had begun to say, are safe in the communion of that Church, throughout the whole extent of which the custom now prevails, which prevailed in like manner through its whole extent before the time of Agrippinus, and in the interval between Agrippinus and Cyprian, and whose unity neither Agrippinus nor Cyprian ever deserted, nor those who agreed with them, although they entertained different views from the rest of their brethren--all of them remaining in the same communion of unity with the very men from whom they differed in opinion. But let the Donatists themselves consider what their true position is, if they neither can say whence they derived their origin, if the Church had already been destroyed by the plague-spot of communion with heretics and schismatics received into her bosom without baptism; nor again agree with Cyprian himself, for he declared that he remained in communion with those who received heretics and schismatics, and so also with those who were received as well: while they have separated themselves from the communion of the whole world, on account of the charge of having delivered up the sacred books, which they brought against the men whom they maligned in Africa, but failed to convict when brought to trial beyond the sea; although, even had the crimes which they alleged been true, they were much less heinous than the sins of heresy and schism; and yet these could not defile Cyprian in the persons of those who came from them without baptism, as he conceived, and were admitted without baptism into the Catholic communion. Nor, in the very point in which they say that they imitate Cyprian, can they find any answer to make about acknowledging the baptism of the followers of Maximianus, together with those whom, though they belonged to the party that they had first condemned in their own plenary Council, and then gone on to prosecute even at the tribunal of the secular power, they yet received back into their communion, in the episcopate of the very same bishop under whom they had been condemned. Wherefore, if the communion of wicked men destroyed the Church in the time of Cyprian, they have no source from which they can derive their own communion; and if the Church was not destroyed, they have no excuse for their separation from it. Moreover, they are neither following the example of Cyprian, since they have burst the bond of unity, nor abiding by their own Council, since they have recognized the baptism of the followers of Maximianus.

Chapter 3.

4. Let us therefore, seeing that we adhere to the example of Cyprian, go on now to consider Cyprian's Council. What says Cyprian? "Ye have heard," he says, "most beloved colleagues, what Jubaianus our fellow-bishop has written to me, consulting my moderate ability concerning the unlawful and profane baptism of heretics, and what answer I gave him,--giving a judgment which we have once and again and often given, that heretics coming to the Church ought to be baptized and sanctified with the baptism of the Church. Another letter of Jubaianus has likewise been read to you, in which, agreeably to his sincere and religious devotion, in answer to our epistle, he

not only expressed his assent, but returned thanks also, acknowledging that he had received instruction." [1265]In these words of the blessed Cyprian, we find that he had been consulted by Jubaianus, and what answer he had given to his questions, and how Jubaianus acknowledged with gratitude that he had received instruction. Ought we then to be thought unreasonably persistent if we desire to consider this same epistle by which Jubaianus was convinced? For till such time as we are also convinced (if there are any arguments of truth whereby this can be done), Cyprian himself has established our security by the right of Catholic communion.

5. For he goes on to say: "It remains that we severally declare our opinion on this same subject, judging no one, nor depriving any one of the right of communion if he differ from us." [1266]He allows me, therefore, without losing the right of communion, not only to continue inquiring into the truth, but even to hold opinions differing from his own. "For no one of us," he says, "setteth himself up as a bishop of bishops, or by tyrannical terror forces his colleagues to a necessity of obeying." What could be more kind? what more humble? Surely there is here no authority restraining us from inquiry into what is truth. "Inasmuch as every bishop," he says, "in the free use of his liberty and power, has the right of forming his own judgment, and can no more be judged by another than he can himself judge another,"--that is, I suppose, in those questions which have not yet been brought to perfect clearness of solution; for he knew what a deep question about the sacrament was then occupying the whole Church with every kind of disputation, and gave free liberty of inquiry to every man, that the truth might be made known by investigation. For he was surely not uttering what was false, and trying to catch his simpler

colleagues in their speech, so that, when they should have betrayed that they held opinions at variance with his, he might then propose, in violation of his promise, that they should be excommunicated. Far be it from a soul so holy to entertain such accursed treachery; indeed, they who hold such a view about such a man, thinking that it conduces to his praise, do but show that it would be in accordance with their own nature. I for my part will in no wise believe that Cyprian, a Catholic bishop, a Catholic martyr, whose greatness only made him proportionately humble in all things, so as to find favor before the Lord, [1267] should ever, especially in the sacred Council of his colleagues, have uttered with his mouth what was not echoed in his heart, especially as he further adds, "But we must all await the judgment of our Lord Jesus Christ, who alone has the power both of setting us in the government of His Church, and of judging of our acts therein." [1268]When, then, he called to their remembrance so solemn a judgment, hoping to hear the truth from his colleagues, would he first set them the example of lying? May God avert such madness from every Christian man, and how much more from Cyprian! We have therefore the free liberty of inquiry granted to us by the most moderate and most truthful speech of Cyprian.

[1265] See above, II. ii. 3.

[1266] See above, II. ii. 3.

[1267] Ecclus. iii. 18.

[1268] See above, II. ii. 3.

Chapter 4.

6. Next his colleagues proceed to deliver their several opinions. But first they listened to the letter written to Jubaianus; for it was read, as was mentioned in the preamble. Let it therefore be read among ourselves also, that we too, with the help of God, may discover from it what we ought to think. "What!" I think I hear some one saying, "do you proceed to tell us what Cyprian wrote to Jubaianus?" I have read the letter, I confess, and should certainly have been a convert to his views, had I not been induced to consider the matter more carefully by the vast weight of authority, originating in those whom the Church, distributed throughout the world amid so many nations, of Latins, Greeks, barbarians, not to mention the Jewish race itself, has been able to produce,--that same Church which gave birth to Cyprian himself,--men whom I could in no wise bring myself to think had been unwilling without reason to hold this view,--not because it was impossible that in so difficult a question the opinion of one or of a few might not have been more near the truth than that of more, but because one must not lightly, without full consideration and investigation of the matter to the best of his abilities, decide in favor of a single individual, or even of a few, against the decision of so very many men of the same religion and communion, all endowed with great talent and abundant learning. And so how much was suggested to me on more diligent inquiry, even by the letter of Cyprian himself, in favor of the view which is now held by the Catholic Church, that the baptism of Christ is to be recognized and approved, not by the standard of their merits by whom it is administered, but by His alone of whom it is said, "The same is He which baptizeth," [1269] will be shown naturally in the course of our argument. Let us therefore suppose that the letter which was written by Cyprian to Jubaianus has been read among us, as it was read in the Council. [1270]And I would

have every one read it who means to read what I am going to say, lest he might possibly think that I have suppressed some things of consequence. For it would take too much time, and be irrelevant to the elucidation of the matter in hand, were we at this moment to quote all the words of this epistle.

[1269] John i. 33.

[1270] The Council of Carthage.

Chapter 5.

7. But if any one should ask what I hold in the meantime, while discussing this question, I answer that, in the first place, the letter of Cyprian suggested to me what I should hold till I should see clearly the nature of the question which next begins to be discussed. For Cyprian himself says: "But some will say, What then will become of those who in times past, coming to the Church from heresy, were admitted without baptism?" [1271]Whether they were really without baptism, or whether they were admitted because those who admitted them conceived that they had partaken of baptism, is a matter for our future consideration. At any rate, Cyprian himself shows plainly enough what was the ordinary custom of the Church, when he says that in past time those who came to the Church from heresy were admitted without baptism.

8. For in the Council itself Castus of Sicca says: "He who, despising truth, presumes to follow custom, is either envious or evil-disposed towards the brethren to whom the truth is revealed, or is ungrateful towards God, by whose inspiration His Church is instructed." [1272] Whether the truth had been revealed, we shall investigate hereafter; at any rate, he acknowledges that the custom of the Church was different.

[1271] Epist. lxxiii. 23, to Jubianus.

[1272] Seventh Conc. Carth. under Cyprian, the third which dealt with baptism, A.D. 256, sec. 28. These opinions are quoted again in Books VI. and VII.

Chapter 6.

9. Libosus also of Vaga says: "The Lord says in the gospel, I am the Truth.' [1273]He does not say, I am custom.' Therefore, when the truth is made manifest, custom must give way to truth." [1274]Clearly, no one could doubt that custom must give way to truth where it is made manifest. But we shall see presently about the manifestation of the truth. Meanwhile he also makes it clear that custom was on the other side.

[1273] John xiv. 6.

[1274] Conc. Carth. sec. 30.

Chapter 7.

10. Zosimus also of Tharassa said: "When a revelation of the truth has been made, error must give way to truth; for even Peter, who at the first circumcised, afterwards gave way to Paul when he declared the truth." [1275]He indeed chose to say error, not custom; but in saying "for even Peter, who at the first circumcised, afterwards gave way to Paul when he declared the truth," he shows plainly enough that there was a custom also on the subject of baptism at variance with his views. At the same time, also, he warns us that it was not impossible that Cyprian might have held an opinion about baptism at variance with that required by the truth, as held by the Church both before and after him, if even Peter could hold a view at variance with the truth as taught us by the Apostle Paul. [1276]

[1275] Ib. sec. 56.

[1276] Gal. ii. 11-14.

Chapter 8.

11. Likewise Felix of Buslacene said: "In admitting heretics without the baptism of the Church, let no one prefer custom to reason and truth; because reason and truth always prevail to the exclusion of custom." [1277]Nothing could be better, if it be reason, and if it be truth; but this we shall see presently. Meanwhile, it is clear from the words of this man also that the custom was the other way.

[1277] Conc. Carth. sec. 63.

Chapter 9.

12. Likewise Honoratus of Tucca [1278] said: "Since Christ is the Truth, we ought to follow truth rather than custom." [1279]By all these declarations it is proved that we are not excluded from the communion of the Church, till it shall have been clearly shown what is the nature of the truth, which they say must be preferred to our custom. But if the truth has made it clear that the very regulation ought to be maintained which the said custom had prescribed, then it is evident both that this custom was not established or confirmed in vain, and also that, in consequence of the discussions in question, the most wholesome observance of so great a sacrament, which could never, indeed, have been changed in the Catholic Church, was even more watchfully guarded with the most scrupulous caution, when it had received the further corroboration of Councils.

[1278] Thucca.

[1279] Conc. Carth. sec. 77.

Chapter 10.

13. Therefore Cyprian writes to Jubaianus as follows, "concerning the baptism of heretics, who, being placed without, and set down out of the Church," seem to him to "claim to themselves a matter over which they have neither right nor power. Which we," he says, "cannot account valid or lawful, since it is clear that among them it is unlawful." [1280]Neither, indeed, do we deny that a man who is baptized among heretics, or in any schism outside the Church, derives no profit from it so far as he is partner in the perverseness of the heretics and schismatics; nor do we hold that those who baptize, although they confer the real true sacrament of baptism, are yet acting rightly, in gathering adherents outside the Church, and entertaining opinions contrary to the Church. But it is one thing to be without a sacrament, another thing to be in possession of it wrongly, and to usurp it unlawfully. Therefore they do not cease to be sacraments of Christ and the Church, merely because they are unlawfully used, not only by heretics, but by all kinds of wicked and impious persons. These, indeed, ought to be corrected and punished, but the sacraments should be acknowledged and revered.

14. Cyprian, indeed, says that on this subject not one, but two or more Councils were held; always, however, in Africa. For indeed in one he mentions that seventy-one bishops had been assembled, [1281] --to all whose authority we do not hesitate, with all due deference to Cyprian, to prefer the authority, supported by many more bishops, of the whole Church spread throughout the whole world, of which Cyprian himself rejoiced that he was an inseparable member.

15. Nor is the water "profane and adulterous" [1282] over which the name of God is invoked, even though it be invoked by profane and adulterous persons; because neither the creature itself of water, nor the name invoked, is adulterous. But the baptism of Christ, consecrated by the words of the gospel, is necessarily holy, however polluted and unclean its ministers may be; because its inherent sanctity cannot be polluted, and the divine excellence abides in its sacrament, whether to the salvation of those who use it aright, or to the destruction of those who use it wrong. Would you indeed maintain that, while the light of the sun or of a candle, diffused through unclean places, contracts no foulness in itself therefrom, yet the baptism of Christ can be defiled by the sins of any man, whatsoever he may be? For if we turn our thoughts to the visible materials themselves, which are to us the medium of the sacraments, every one must know that they admit of corruption. But if we think on that which they convey to us, who can fail to see that it is incorruptible, however much the men through whose ministry it is conveyed are either being rewarded or punished for the character of their lives?

[1280] Ctpr. Ep. lxxiii. 1.

[1281] Ctpr. Ep. lxxiii. 1.

[1282] Ctpr. Ep. lxxiii. 1.

Chapter 11.

16. But Cyprian was right in not being moved by what Jubaianus wrote, that "the followers of Novatian [1283] rebaptize those who come to them from the Catholic Church." [1284]For, in the first place, it does not follow that whatever heretics have done in a perverse spirit of mimicry, Catholics are

therefore to abstain from doing, because the heretics do the same. And again, the reasons are different for which heretics and the Catholic Church ought respectively to abstain from rebaptizing. For it would not be right for heretics to do so, even if it were fitting in the Catholic Church; because their argument is, that among the Catholics is wanting that which they themselves received whilst still within the pale, and took away with them when they departed. Whereas the reason why the Catholic Church should not administer again the baptism which was given among heretics, is that it may not seem to decide that a power which is Christ's alone belongs to its members, or to pronounce that to be wanting in the heretics which they have received within her pale, and certainly could not lose by straying outside. For thus much Cyprian himself, with all the rest, established, that if any should return from heresy to the Church, they should be received back, not by baptism, but by the discipline of penitence; whence it is clear that they cannot be held to lose by their secession what is not restored to them when they return. Nor ought it for a moment to be said that, as their heresy is their own, as their error is their own, as the sacrilege of disunion is their own, so also the baptism is their own, which is really Christ's. Accordingly, while the evils which are their own are corrected when they return, so in that which is not theirs His presence should be recognised, from whom it is.

[1283] The Novatian bishop, Acesius, was invited by Constantine to attend the Council of Nicaea. Soc., H.E.I. 10.

[1284] Cypr. Ep. lxxiii. 2.

Chapter 12.

17. But the blessed Cyprian shows that it was no new or sudden thing that he decided, because the practice had already begun under Agrippinus. "Many years," he says, "and much time has passed away since, under Agrippinus of honored memory, a large assembly of bishops determined this point." Accordingly, under Agrippinus, at any rate, the thing was new. But I cannot understand what Cyprian means by saying, "And thenceforward to the present day, so many thousand heretics in our provinces, having been converted to our Church, showed no hesitation or dislike, but rather with full consent of reason and will, have embraced the opportunity of the grace of the laver of life and the baptism unto salvation," [1285] unless indeed he says, "thenceforward to the present day," because from the time when they were baptized in the Church, in accordance with the Council of Agrippinus, no question of excommunication had arisen in the case of any of the rebaptized. Yet if the custom of baptizing those who came over from heretics remained in force from the time of Agrippinus to that of Cyprian, why should new Councils have been held by Cyprian on this point? Why does he say to this same Jubaianus that he is not doing anything new or sudden, but only what had been established by Agrippinus? For why should Jubaianus be disturbed by the question of novelty, so as to require to be satisfied by the authority of Agrippinus, if this was the continuous practice of the Church from Agrippinus till Cyprian? Why, lastly, did so many of his colleagues urge that reason and truth must be preferred to custom, instead of saying that those who wished to act otherwise were acting contrary to truth and custom alike?

[1285] Cypr. Ep. lxxiii. 3.

Chapter 13.

18. But as regards the remission of sins, whether it is granted through baptism at the hands of the heretics, I have already expressed my opinion on this point in a former book; [1286] but I will shortly recapitulate it here. If remission of sins is there conferred by the sacredness of baptism, the sins return again through obstinate perseverance in heresy or schism; and therefore such men must needs return to the peace of the Catholic Church, that they may cease to be heretics and schismatics, and deserve that those sins which had returned on them should be cleansed away by love working in the bond of unity. But if, although among heretics and schismatics it be still the same baptism of Christ, it yet cannot work remission of sins owing to this same foulness of discord and wickedness of dissent, then the same baptism begins to be of avail for the remission of sins when they come to the peace of the Church,--[not] [1287] that what has been already truly remitted should not be retained; nor that heretical baptism should be repudiated as belonging to a different religion, or as being different from our own, so that a second baptism should be administered; but that the very same baptism, which was working death by reason of discord outside the Church, may work salvation by reason of the peace within. It was, in fact, the same savor of which the apostle says, "We are a sweet savor of Christ in every place;" and yet, says he, "both in them that are saved and in them that perish. To the one we are the savor of life unto life; and to the other the savor of death unto death." [1288]And although he used these words with reference to another subject, I have applied them to this, that men may understand that what is good may not only work life to those who use it aright, but also death to those who use it wrong.

[1286] Above, Book I. c. xi. sqq.

[1287] Non ut jam vere dimissa non retineantur. One of the negatives here appears to be superfluous, and the former is omitted in Amerbach's edition, and in many of the Mss., which continue the sentence, "non ut ille baptismus," instead of "neque ut ille," etc. If the latter negative were omitted, the sense would be improved, and "neque" would appropriately remain.

[1288] 2 Cor. ii. 15, 16.

Chapter 14.

19. Nor is it material, when we are considering the question of the genuineness and holiness of the sacrament, "what the recipient of the sacrament believes, and with what faith he is imbued." It is of the very highest consequence as regards the entrance into salvation, but is wholly immaterial as regards the question of the sacrament. For it is quite possible that a man may be possessed of the genuine sacrament and a corrupted faith, as it is possible that he may hold the words of the creed in their integrity, and yet entertain an erroneous belief about the Trinity, or the resurrection, or any other point. For it is no slight matter, even within the Catholic Church itself, to hold a faith entirely consistent with the truth about even God Himself, to say nothing of any of His creatures. Is it then to be maintained, that if any one who has been baptized within the Catholic Church itself should afterwards, in the course of reading, or by listening to instruction, or by quiet argument, find out, through God's own revelation, that he had before believed otherwise than he ought, it is requisite that he should therefore be baptized afresh? But what carnal and natural man is there who does not stray through the vain conceits [1289] of his own heart, and picture God's nature to himself to be such

as he has imagined out of his carnal sense, and differ from the true conception of God as far as vanity from truth? Most truly, indeed, speaks the apostle, filled with the light of truth: "The natural man," says he, "receiveth not the things of the Spirit of God." [1290]And yet herein he was speaking of men whom he himself shows to have been baptized. For he says to them, "Was Paul crucified for you? or were ye baptized in the name of Paul?" [1291]These men had therefore the sacrament of baptism; and yet, inasmuch as their wisdom was of the flesh, what could they believe about God otherwise than according to the perception of their flesh, according to which "the natural man receiveth not the things of the Spirit of God?" To such he says: "I could not speak unto you as unto spiritual, but as unto carnal, even as unto babes in Christ. I have fed you with milk, and not with meat: for hitherto ye were not able to bear it, neither yet now are ye able. For ye are yet carnal." [1292]For such are carried about with every wind of doctrine, of which kind he says, "That we be no more children, tossed to and fro, and carried about with every wind of doctrine." [1293]It is then true that, if these men shall have advanced even to the spiritual age of the inner man, and in the integrity of understanding shall have learned how far different from the requirements of the truth has been the belief which they have been led by the fallacious character of their conceits to entertain of God, they are therefore to be baptized again? For, on this principle, it would be possible for a Catholic catechumen to light upon the writings of some heretic, and, not having the knowledge requisite for discerning truth from error, he might entertain some belief contrary to the Catholic faith, yet not condemned by the words of the creed, just as, under color of the same words, innumerable heretical errors have sprung up. Supposing, then, that the catechumen was under the impression that he was studying the work of some great and learned Catholic, and was baptized with that belief in the Catholic Church, and by subsequent research should discover what he ought to believe, so that, embracing the Catholic faith, he should reject his former error, ought he, on confessing this, to be baptized again? Or supposing that, before learning and confessing this for himself, he should be found to entertain such an opinion, and should be taught what he ought to reject and what he should believe, and it were to become clear that he had held this false belief when he was baptized, ought he therefore to be baptized again? Why should we maintain the contrary? Because the sanctity of the sacrament, consecrated in the words of the gospel, remains upon him in its integrity, just as he received it from the hands of the minister, although he, being firmly rooted in the vanity of his carnal mind entertained a belief other than was right at the time when he was baptized. Wherefore it is manifest that it is possible that, with defective faith, the sacrament of baptism may yet remain without defect in any man; and therefore all that is said about the diversity of the several heretics is beside the question. For in each person that is to be corrected which is found to be amiss by the man who undertakes his correction. That is to be made whole which is unsound; that is to be given which is wanting, and, above all, the peace of Christian charity, without which the rest is profitless. Yet, as the rest is there, we must not administer it as though it were wanting, only take care that its possession be to the profit, not the hurt of him who has it, through the very bond of peace and excellence of charity.

[1289] Phantasmata.

[1290] 1 Cor ii. 14.

[1291] 1 Cor. i. 13.

[1292] 1 Cor iii. 1-3.

[1293] Eph. iv. 14.

Chapter 15.

20. Accordingly, if Marcion consecrated the sacrament of baptism with the words of the gospel, "In the name of the Father, and of the Son, and of the Holy Ghost," [1294] the sacrament was complete, although his faith expressed under the same words, seeing that he held opinions not taught by the Catholic truth, was not complete, but stained with the falsity of fables. [1295]For under these same words, "In the name of the Father, and of the Son, and of the Holy Ghost," not Marcion only, or Valentinus, or Arius, or Eunomius, but the carnal babes of the Church themselves (to whom the apostle said, "I could not speak unto you as unto spiritual, but as unto carnal"), if they could be individually asked for an accurate exposition of their opinions, would probably show a diversity of opinions as numerous as the persons who held them, "for the natural man receiveth not the things of the Spirit of God." Can it, however, be said on this account that they do not receive the complete sacrament? or that, if they shall advance, and correct the vanity of their carnal opinions, they must seek again what they had received? Each man receives after the fashion of his own faith; yet how much does he obtain under the guidance of that mercy of God, in the confident assurance of which the same apostle says, "If in anything ye be otherwise minded, God shall reveal even this unto you"? [1296]Yet the snares of heretics and schismatics prove for this reason only too pernicious to the carnally-minded, because their very progress is intercepted when their vain opinions are confirmed in opposition to the

Catholic truth, and the perversity of their dissension is strengthened against the Catholic peace. Yet if the sacraments are the same, they are everywhere complete, even when they are wrongly understood, and perverted to be instruments of discord, just as the very writings of the gospel, if they are only the same, are everywhere complete, even though quoted with a boundless variety of false opinions. For as to what Jeremiah says:--"Why do those who grieve me prevail against me? My wound is stubborn, whence shall I be healed? In its origin it became unto me as lying water, having no certainty," [1297] --if the term "water" were never used figuratively and in the allegorical language of prophecy except to signify baptism, we should have trouble in discovering what these words of Jeremiah meant; but as it is, when "waters" are expressly used in the Apocalypse [1298] to signify "peoples," I do not see why, by "lying water having no certainty," I should not understand, a "lying people, whom I cannot trust."

[1294] Matt. xxviii. 19.

[1295] Cp. Concilium Arelatense, A.D. 314, can. 8. "De Afris, quod propria lege utuntur ut rebaptizent; placuit ut si ad ecclesiam aliquis de hæresi venerit, interrogent eum symbolum; et si perviderint eum in Patre, et Filio, et Spiritu sancto esse baptizatum, manus ei tantum imponatur, ut accipiat Spiritum sanctum. Quod si interrogatus non responderit hanc Trinitatem, baptizetur."

[1296] Phil. iii. 15.

[1297] Jer. xv. 18, cp. LXX.

[1298] Rev. xvii. 15.

Chapter 16.

21. But when it is said that "the Holy Spirit is given by the imposition of hands in the Catholic Church only, I suppose that our ancestors meant that we should understand thereby what the apostle says, "Because the love of God is shed abroad in our hearts by the Holy Ghost which is given unto us." [1299]For this is that very love which is wanting in all who are cut off from the communion of the Catholic Church; and for lack of this, "though they speak with the tongues of men and of angels, though they understand all mysteries and all knowledge, and though they have the gift of prophecy, and all faith, so that they could remove mountains, and though they bestow all their goods to feed the poor, and though they give their bodies to be burned, it profiteth them nothing." [1300]But those are wanting in God's love who do not care for the unity of the Church; and consequently we are right in understanding that the Holy Spirit may be said not to be received except in the Catholic Church. For the Holy Spirit is not only given by the laying on of hands amid the testimony of temporal sensible miracles, as He was given in former days to be the credentials of a rudimentary faith, and for the extension of the first beginnings of the Church. For who expects in these days that those on whom hands are laid that they may receive the Holy Spirit should forthwith begin to speak with tongues? but it is understood that invisibly and imperceptibly, on account of the bond of peace, divine love is breathed into their hearts, so that they may be able to say, "Because the love of God is shed abroad in our hearts by the Holy Ghost which is given unto us." But there are many operations of the Holy Spirit, which the same apostle commemorates in a certain passage at such length as he thinks sufficient, and then concludes: "But all these worketh that one

and the selfsame Spirit, dividing to every man severally as He will." [1301]Since, then, the sacrament is one thing, which even Simon Magus could have; [1302] and the operation of the Spirit is another thing, which is even often found in wicked men, as Saul had the gift of prophecy; [1303] and that operation of the same Spirit is a third thing, which only the good can have, as "the end of the commandment is charity out of a pure heart, and of a good conscience, and of faith unfeigned:" [1304]whatever, therefore, may be received by heretics and schismatics, the charity which covereth the multitude of sins is the especial gift of Catholic unity and peace; nor is it found in all that are within that bond, since not all that are within it are of it, as we shall see in the proper place. At any rate, outside the bond that love cannot exist, without which all the other requisites, even if they can be recognized and approved, cannot profit or release from sin. But the laying on of hands in reconciliation to the Church is not, like baptism, incapable of repetition; for what is it more than a prayer offered over a man? [1305]

[1299] Rom. v. 5.

[1300] 1 Cor. xiii. 1-3.

[1301] 1 Cor. xii. 11.

[1302] Acts viii. 13.

[1303] 1 Sam. x. 6, 10.

[1304] 1 Tim. i. 5.

[1305] He refers to laying on of hands such as he mentions below, Book V. c. xxiii.: "If the laying on of hands were not applied to one coming from heresy, he would be, as it were, judged to be wholly blameless."

Chapter 17.

22. "For as regards the fact that to preserve the figure of unity the Lord gave the power to Peter that whatsoever he should loose on earth should be loosed," [1306] it is clear that that unity is also described as one dove without fault. [1307] Can it be said, then, that to this same dove belong all those greedy ones, whose existence in the same Catholic Church Cyprian himself so grievously bewailed? For birds of prey, I believe, cannot be called doves, but rather hawks. How then did they baptize those who used to plunder estates by treacherous deceit, and increase their profits by compound usury, [1308] if baptism is only given by that indivisible and chaste and perfect dove, that unity which can only be understood as existing among the good? Is it possible that, by the prayers of the saints who are spiritual within the Church, as though by the frequent lamentations of the dove, a great sacrament is dispensed, with a secret administration of the mercy of God, so that their sins also are loosed who are baptized, not by the dove but by the hawk, if they come to that sacrament in the peace of Catholic unity? But if this be so, why should it not also be the case that, as each man comes from heresy or schism to the Catholic peace, his sins should be loosed through their prayers? But the integrity of the sacrament is everywhere recognized, though it will not avail for the irrevocable remission of sins outside the unity of the Church. Nor will the prayers of the saints, or, in other words, the groanings of that one dove, be able to help one who is set in heresy or schism; just as they are not able to help one who is placed within the Church, if by a wicked life he himself retain the debts of his sins against himself, and that

though he be baptized, not by this hawk, but by the pious ministry of the dove herself.

[1306] Matt. xvi. 19.

[1307] Song of Sol. vi. 9.

[1308] Cypr. de Lapsis c vi.

Chapter 18.

23. "As my Father hath sent me," says our Lord, "even so send I you. And what He had said this, He breathed on them, and saith unto them, Receive ye the Holy Ghost. Whose soever sins ye remit, they are remitted unto them; and whose soever sins ye retain, they are retained." [1309]Therefore, if they represented the Church, and this was said to them as to the Church herself, it follows that the peace of the Church looses sins, and estrangement from the Church retains them, not according to the will of men, but according to the will of God and the prayers of the saints who are spiritual, who "judge all things, but themselves are judged of no man." [1310]For the rock retains, the rock remits; the dove retains, the dove remits; unity retains, unity remits. But the peace of this unity exists only in the good, in those who are either already spiritual, or are advancing by the obedience of concord to spiritual things; it exists not in the bad, whether they make disturbances abroad, or are endured within the Church with lamentations, baptizing and being baptized. But just as those who are tolerated with groanings within the Church, although they do not belong to the same unity of the dove, and to that "glorious Church, not having spot or wrinkle, or any such thing," [1311] yet if they are corrected, and confess that they approached to baptism most unworthily, are not baptized again, but begin to belong to the

dove, through whose groans those sins are remitted which were retained in them who were estranged from her peace; so those also who are more openly without the Church, if they have received the same sacraments, are not freed from their sins on coming, after correction, to the unity of the Church, by a repetition of baptism, but by the same law of charity and bond of unity. For if "those only may baptize who are set over the Church, and established by the law of the gospel and ordination as appointed by the Lord," were they in any wise of this kind who seized on estates by treacherous frauds, and increased their gains by compound interest? I trow not, since those are established by ordination as appointed of the Lord, of whom the apostle, in giving them a standard, says, "Not greedy, not given to filthy lucre." [1312] Yet men of this kind used to baptize in the time of Cyprian himself; and he confesses with many lamentations that they were his fellow-bishops, and endures them with the great reward of tolerance. Yet did they not confer remission of sins, which is granted through the prayers of the saints, that is, the groans of the dove, whoever it be that baptizes, if those to whom it is given belong to her peace. For the Lord would not say to robbers and usurers, "Whose soever sins ye remit, they shall be remitted to him; and whose soever sins ye retain, they shall be retained." "Outside the Church, indeed, nothing can be either bound or loosed, since there there is no one who can either bind or loose;" but he is loosed who has made peace with the dove, and he is bound who is not at peace with the dove, whether he is openly without, or appears to be within.

24. But we know that Dathan, Korah, and Abiram, [1313] who tried to usurp to themselves the right of sacrificing, contrary to the unity of the people of God, and also the sons of Aaron who

offered strange fire upon the altar, [1314] did not escape punishment. Nor do we say that such offenses remain unpunished, unless those guilty of them correct themselves, if the patience of God leading them to repentance [1315] give them time for correction.

[1309] John xx. 21-23.

[1310] 1 Cor. ii. 15.

[1311] Eph. v. 27. Cp. Retract. ii. 18, quoted above on I. xvii.

[1312] Tit. i. 7.

[1313] Num. xvi.

[1314] Lev. x. 1, 2.

[1315] Rom. ii. 4.

Chapter 19.

25. They indeed who say that baptism is not to be repeated, because only hands were laid on those whom Philip the deacon had baptized, [1316] are saying what is quite beside the point; and far be it from us, in seeking the truth, to use such arguments as this. Wherefore we are all the further from "yielding to heretics," [1317] if we deny that what they possess of Christ's Church is their own property, and do not refuse to acknowledge the standard of our General because of the crimes of deserters; nay, all the more because "the Lord our God is a jealous God," [1318] let us refuse, whenever we see anything of His with an alien, to allow him to consider it his own. For of a truth the jealous God Himself rebukes the woman who commits fornication against Him, as the type of an erring

people, and says that she gave to her lovers what belonged to Him, and again received from them what was not theirs but His. In the hands of the adulterous woman and the adulterous lovers, God in His wrath, as a jealous God, recognizes His gifts; and do we say that baptism, consecrated in the words of the gospel, belongs to heretics? and are we willing, from consideration of their deeds, to attribute to them even what belongs to God, as though they had the power to pollute it, or as though they could make what is God's to be their own, because they themselves have refused to belong to God?

26. Who is that adulterous woman whom the prophet Hosea points out, who said, "I will go after my lovers, that give me my bread and my water, my wool and my flax, and everything that befits me?" [1319] Let us grant that we may understand this also of the people of the Jews that went astray; yet whom else are the false Christians (such as are all heretics and schismatics) wont to imitate, except false Israelites? For there were also true Israelites, as the Lord Himself bears witness to Nathanael, "Behold an Israelite indeed, in whom is no guile." [1320] But who are true Christians, save those of whom the same Lord said, "He that hath my commandments, and keepeth them, he it is that loveth me?" [1321] But what is it to keep His commandments, except to abide in love? Whence also He says, "A new commandment I give unto you, that ye love one another;" and again, "By this shall all men know that ye are my disciples, if ye have love one to another." [1322] But who can doubt that this was spoken not only to those who heard His words with their fleshly ears when He was present with them, but also to those who learn His words through the gospel, when He is sitting on His throne in heaven? For He came not to destroy the law, but to fulfill. [1323] But the fulfilling of the

law is love. [1324]   And in this Cyprian abounded greatly, insomuch that though he held a different view concerning baptism, he yet did not forsake the unity of the Church, and was in the Lord's vine a branch firmly rooted, bearing fruit, which the heavenly Husbandman purged with the knife of suffering, that it should bear more fruit. [1325]But the enemies of this brotherly love, whether they are openly without, or appear to be within, are false Christians, and antichrists. For when they have found an opportunity, they go out, as it is written: "A man wishing to separate himself from his friends, seeketh opportunities." [1326]But even if occasions are wanting, while they seem to be within, they are severed from that invisible bond of love. Whence St. John says, "They went out from us, but they were not of us; for had they been of us, they would no doubt have continued with us." [1327]He does not say that they ceased to be of us by going out, but that they went out because they were not of us. The Apostle Paul also speaks of certain men who had erred concerning the truth, and were overthrowing the faith of some; whose word was eating as a canker. Yet in saying that they should be avoided, he nevertheless intimates that they were all in one great house, but as vessels to dishonor,--I suppose because they had not as yet gone out. Or if they had already gone out, how can he say that they were in the same great house with the honorable vessels, unless it was in virtue of the sacraments themselves, which even in the severed meetings of heretics are not changed, that he speaks of all as belonging to the same great house, though in different degrees of esteem, some to honor and some to dishonor? For thus he speaks in his Epistle to Timothy: "But shun profane and vain babblings; for they will increase unto more ungodliness. And their word will eat as doth a canker; of whom is Hymenæus and Philetus; who concerning the truth have erred, saying that the resurrection is past already; and overthrow the faith of some. Nevertheless the foundation of God standeth firm, having this seal, The Lord knoweth them that are His. And, Let every one that nameth the name of Christ depart from iniquity. But in a great house there are not only vessels of gold and of silver, but also of wood and of earth; and some to honor, and some to dishonor. If a man therefore purge himself from these, he shall be a vessel unto honor, sanctified, and meet for the master's use, and prepared unto every good work." [1328]But what is it to purge oneself from such as these, except what he said just before, "Let every one that nameth the name of Christ depart from iniquity." And lest any one should think that, as being in one great house with them, he might perish with such as these, he has most carefully forewarned them, "The Lord knoweth them that are His,"-- those, namely, who, by departing from iniquity, purge themselves from the vessels made to dishonor, lest they should perish with them whom they are compelled to tolerate in the great house.

27. They, therefore, who are wicked, evildoers, carnal, fleshly, devilish, think that they receive at the hands of their seducers what are the gifts of God alone, whether sacraments, or any spiritual workings about present salvation. But these men have not love towards God, but are busied about those by whose pride they are led astray, and are compared to the adulterous woman, whom the prophet introduces as saying, "I will go after my lovers, that give me my bread and my water, my wool and my flax, and my oil, and everything that befits me." For thus arise heresies and schisms, when the fleshly people which is not founded on the love of God says, "I will go after my lovers," with whom, either by corruption of her faith, or by the puffing

up of her pride, she shamefully commits adultery. But for the sake of those who, having undergone the difficulties, and straits, and barriers of the empty reasoning of those by whom they are led astray, afterwards feel the prickings of fear, and return to the way of peace, to seeking God in all sincerity,--for their sake He goes on to say, "Therefore, behold, I will hedge up thy way with thorns, and make a wall, that she shall not find her paths. And she shall follow after her lovers, but she shall not overtake them: and she shall seek them, but she shall not find them: then shall she say, I will go and return to my first husband; for then was it better with me than now." Then, that they may not attribute to their seducers what they have that is sound, and derived from the doctrine of truth, by which they lead them astray to the falseness of their own dogmas and dissensions; that they may not think that what is sound in them belongs to them, he immediately added, "And she did not know that I gave her corn, and wine, and oil, and multiplied her money; but she made vessels of gold and silver for Baal." [1329]For she had said above, "I will go after my lovers, that give me my bread," etc., not at all understanding that all this, which was held soundly and lawfully by her seducers, was of God, and not of men. Nor would even they themselves claim these things for themselves, and as it were assert a right in them, had not they in turn been led astray by a people which had gone astray, when faith is reposed in them, and such honors are paid to them, that they should be enabled thereby to say such things, and claim such things for themselves, that their error should be called truth, and their iniquity be thought righteousness, in virtue of the sacraments and Scriptures, which they hold, not for salvation, but only in appearance. Accordingly, the same adulterous woman is addressed by the mouth of Ezekiel: "Thou hast also taken thy fair jewels of my gold and of my silver, which I had given thee, and madest to thyself images of men, and didst commit whoredom with them; and tookest my [1330] broidered garments, and coveredst them: and thou hast set mine oil and mine incense before them. My meat also which I gave thee, fine flour, and oil, and honey, wherewith I fed thee, thou hast even set it before thine idols for a sweet savor: and this thou hast done." [1331]For she turns all the sacraments, and the words of the sacred books, to the images of her own idols, with which her carnal mind delights to wallow. Nor yet, because those images are false, and the doctrines of devils, speaking lies in hypocrisy, [1332] are those sacraments and divine utterances therefore so to lose their due honor, as to be thought to belong to such as these; seeing that the Lord says," Of my gold, and my silver, and my broidered garments, and mine oil, and mine incense, and my meat," and so forth. Ought we, because those erring ones think that these things belong to their seducers, therefore not to recognize whose they really are, when He Himself says, "And she did not know that I gave her corn, and wine, and oil, and multiplied her money"? For He did not say that she did not have these things because she was an adulteress; but she is said to have had them, and that not as belonging to herself or her lovers, but to God, whose alone they are. Although, therefore, she had her fornication, yet those things wherewith she adorned it, whether as seduced or in her turn seducing, belonged not to her, but to God. If these things were spoken in a figure of the Jewish nation, when the scribes and Pharisees were rejecting the commandment of God in order to set up their own traditions, so that they were in a manner committing whoredom with a people which was abandoning their God; and yet for all that, whoredom at that time among the people, such as the Lord brought to light by convicting it, did not cause that the mysteries should belong to them, which were not theirs but God's, who, in speaking to the adulteress, says that all these things were His; whence the Lord Himself also sent those whom He cleansed from leprosy to the same mysteries, that they should offer sacrifice for themselves before the priests, because that sacrifice had not become efficacious for them, which He Himself afterwards wished to be commemorated in the Church for all of them, because He Himself proclaimed the tidings to them all;--if this be so, how much the more ought we, when we find the sacraments of the New Testament among certain heretics or schismatics, not to attribute them to these men, nor to condemn them, as though we could not recognize them? We ought to recognize the gifts of the true husband, though in the possession of an adulteress, and to amend, by the word of truth, that whoredom which is the true possession of the unchaste woman, instead of finding fault with the gifts, which belong entirely to the pitying Lord.

28. From these considerations, and such as these, our forefathers, not only before the time of Cyprian and Agrippinus, but even afterwards, maintained a most wholesome custom, that whenever they found anything divine and lawful remaining in its integrity even in the midst of any heresy or schism, they approved rather than repudiated it; but whatever they found that was alien, and peculiar to that false doctrine or division, this they convicted in the light of the truth, and healed. The points, however, which remain to be considered in the letter written by Jubaianus, must, I think, when looking at the size of this book, be taken in hand and treated with a fresh beginning.

[1316] Acts viii. 5-17.

[1317] Because Cyprian, in his letter to Jubaianus (Ep. lxxiii. 10), had urged as following from this, that "there is no reason, dearest brother, why we should think it right to yield to heretics that baptism which was granted to the one and only Church."

[1318] Deut. iv. 24.

[1319] Hos. ii. 5, cp. LXX.

[1320] John i. 47.

[1321] John xiv. 21.

[1322] John xiii. 34, 35.

[1323] Matt. v. 17.

[1324] Rom. xiii. 10.

[1325] John xv. 1-5.

[1326] Prov. xviii. 1, cp. Hieron, and LXX.

[1327] 1 John ii. 19.

[1328] 2 Tim. ii. 16-21.

[1329] Hos. ii. 5-8, cp. LXX.

[1330] In Hieron, and LXX., as well as in the English version, this is in the second person, vestimenta tua multicolaria; ton himatismon ton poikilon sou.

[1331] Ezek. xvi. 17-19.

[1332] 1 Tim. iv. 1, 2.

Book IV.

In which he treats of what follows in the same epistle of Cyprian to Jubaianus.

Chapter 1.

1. The comparison of the Church with Paradise [1333] shows us that men may indeed receive her baptism outside her pale, but that no one outside can either receive or retain the salvation of eternal happiness. For, as the words of Scripture testify, the streams from the fountain of Paradise flowed copiously even beyond its bounds. Record indeed is made of their names; and through what countries they flow, and that they are situated beyond the limits of Paradise, is known to all; [1334] and yet in Mesopotamia, and in Egypt, to which countries those rivers extended, there is not found that blessedness of life which is recorded in Paradise. Accordingly, though the waters of Paradise are found beyond its boundaries, yet its happiness is in Paradise alone. So, therefore, the baptism of the Church may exist outside, but the gift of the life of happiness is found alone within the Church, which has been founded on a rock, which has received the keys of binding and loosing. [1335]"She it is alone who holds as her privilege the whole power of her Bridegroom and Lord;" [1336] by virtue of which power as bride, she can bring forth sons even of handmaids. And these, if they be not high-minded, shall be called into the lot of the inheritance; but if they be high-minded, they shall remain outside.

[1333] Cypr. Ep. lxxiii. ad Jubaian. 10.

[1334] Gen. ii. 8-14.

[1335] Matt. xvi. 18, 19.

[1336] Cypr. Ep. lxxiii. 11.

Chapter 2.

2. All the more, then, because "we are fighting [1337] for the honor and unity" of the Church, let us beware of giving to heretics the credit of whatever we acknowledged among them as belonging to the Church; but let us teach them by argument, that what they possess that is derived from unity is of no efficacy to their salvation, unless they shall return to that same unity. For "the water of the Church is full of faith, and salvation, and holiness" [1338] to those who use it rightly. No one, however, can use it well outside the Church. But to those who use it perversely, whether within or without the Church, it is employed to work punishment, and does not conduce to their reward. And so baptism "cannot be corrupted and polluted," though it be handled by the corrupt or by adulterers, just as also "the Church herself is uncorrupt, and pure, and chaste." [1339]And so no share in it belongs to the avaricious, or thieves, or usurers,--many of whom, by the testimony of Cyprian himself in many places of his letters, exist not only without, but actually within the Church,--and yet they both are baptized and do baptize, with no change in their hearts.

3. For this, too, he says, in one of his epistles [1340] to the clergy on the subject of prayer toGod, in which, after the fashion of the holy Daniel, he represents the sins of his people as falling upon himself. For among many other evils of which he makes mention, he speaks of them also as "renouncing the world in words only and not in deeds;" as the apostle says of certain men, "They profess that they know God, but in works they deny Him." [1341]These, therefore, the blessed Cyprian shows to be contained within the Church herself, who are

baptized without their hearts being changed for the better, seeing that they renounce the world in words and not in deeds, as the Apostle Peter says, "The like figure whereunto even baptism doth also now save us, (not the putting away of the filth of the flesh, but the answer of a good conscience)," [1342] which certainly they had not of whom it is said that they "renounced the world in words only, and not in deeds;" and yet he does his utmost, by chiding and convincing them, to make them at length walk in the way of Christ, and be His friends rather than friends of the world.

[1337] Ib.

[1338] Ib.

[1339] Cypr. Ep. lxxiii. 11.

[1340] Cypr. Ep. xi. 1.

[1341] Tit. i. 16.

[1342] 1 Pet. iii. 21.

Chapter 3.

4. And if they would have obeyed him, and begun to live rightly, not as false but as true Christians, would he have ordered them to be baptized anew? Surely not; but their true conversion would have gained this for them, that the sacrament which availed for their destruction while they were yet unchanged, should begin when they changed to avail for their salvation.

5. For neither are they "devoted to the Church" [1343] who seem to be within and live contrary to Christ, that is, act against

His commandments; nor can they be considered in any way to belong to that Church, which He so purifies by the washing of water, "that He may present to Himself a glorious Church, not having spot or wrinkle, or any such thing." [1344] But if they are not in that Church to whose members they do not belong, they are not in the Church of which it is said, "My dove is but one; she is the only one of her mother;" [1345] for she herself is without spot or wrinkle. Or else let him who can assert that those are members of this dove who renounce the world in words but not in deeds. Meantime there is one thing which we see, from which I think it was said, "He that regardeth the day, regardeth it unto the Lord," [1346] for God judgeth every day. For, according to His foreknowledge, who knows whom He has foreordained before the foundation of the world to be made like to the image of His Son, many who are even openly outside, and are called heretics, are better than many good Catholics. For we see what they are to-day, what they shall be to-morrow we know not. And with God, with whom the future is already present, they already are what they shall hereafter be. But we, according to what each man is at present, inquire whether they are to be to-day reckoned among the members of the Church which is called the one dove, and the Bride of Christ without a spot or wrinkle, [1347] of whom Cyprian says in the letter which I have quoted above, that "they did not keep in the way of the Lord, nor observe the commandments given unto them for their salvation; that they did not fulfill the will of their Lord, being eager about their property and gains, following the dictates of pride, giving way to envy and dissension, careless about single-mindedness and faith, renouncing the world in words only and not in deeds, pleasing each himself, and displeasing all men." [1348] But if the dove does not acknowledge them among her members, and if the Lord shall say to them, supposing that they continue in the same perversity, "I never knew you: depart from me, ye that work iniquity;" [1349] then they seem indeed to be in the Church, but are not; "nay, they even act against the Church. How then can they baptize with the baptism of the Church," [1350] which is of avail neither to themselves, nor to those who receive it from them, unless they are changed in heart with a true conversion, so that the sacrament itself, which did not avail them when they received it whilst they were renouncing the world in words and not in deeds, may begin to profit them when they shall begin to renounce it in deeds also? And so too in the case of those whose separation from the Church is open; for neither these nor those are as yet among the members of the dove, but some of them perhaps will be at some future time.

[1343] Cypr. Ep. lxxiii. 11.

[1344] Eph. v. 26, 27.

[1345] Song of Sol. vi. 9.

[1346] Rom. xiv. 6.

[1347] Retract. ii. 18, quoted on I. 17.

[1348] Cypr. Ep. xi. I, first part loosely quoted.

[1349] Matt. vii. 23.

[1350] Cypr. Ep. lxxiii. 11.

Chapter 4.

6. We do not, therefore, "acknowledge the baptism of heretics," [1351] when we refuse to baptize after them; but

because we acknowledge the ordinance to be of Christ even among evil men, whether openly separated from us, or secretly severed whilst within our body, we receive it with due respect, having corrected those who were wrong in the points wherein they went astray. However as I seem to be hard pressed when it is said to me, "Does then a heretic confer remission of sins?" so I in turn press hard when I say, Does then he who violates the commands of Heaven, the avaricious man, the robber, the usurer, the envious man, does he who renounces the world in words and not in deeds, confer such remission? If you mean by the force of God's sacrament, then both the one and the other; if by his own merit, neither of them. For that sacrament, even in the hands of wicked men, is known to be of Christ; but neither the one nor the other of these men is found in the body of the one uncorrupt, holy, chaste dove, which has neither spot nor wrinkle. And just as baptism is of no profit to the man who renounces the world in words and not in deeds, so it is of no profit to him who is baptized in heresy or schism; but each of them, when he amends his ways, begins to receive profit from that which before was not profitable, but was yet already in him.

7. "He therefore that is baptized in heresy does not become the temple of God; [1352] but does it therefore follow that he is not to be considered as baptized? For neither does the avaricious man, baptized within the Church, become the temple of God unless he depart from his avarice; for they who become the temple of God certainly inherit the kingdom of God. But the apostle says, among many other things, "Neither the covetous, nor extortioners, shall inherit the kingdom of God." [1353]For in another place the same apostle compares covetousness to the worship of idols: "Nor covetous man," he

says, "who is an idolater;" [1354] which meaning the same Cyprian has so far extended in a letter to Antonianus, that he did not hesitate to compare the sin of covetousness with that of men who in time of persecution had declared in writing that they would offer incense. [1355]The man, then, who is baptized in heresy in the name of the Holy Trinity, yet does not become the temple of God unless he abandons his heresy, just as the covetous man who has been baptized in the same name does not become the temple of God unless he abandons his covetousness, which is idolatry. For this, too, the same apostle says: "What agreement hath the temple of God with idols?" [1356]Let it not, then, be asked of us "of what God he is made the temple" [1357] when we say that he is not made the temple of God at all. Yet he is not therefore unbaptized, nor does his foul error cause that what he has received, consecrated in the words of the gospel, should not be the holy sacrament; just as the other man's covetousness (which is idolatry) and great uncleanness cannot prevent what he receives from being holy baptism, even though he be baptized with the same words of the gospel by another man covetous like himself.

[1351] Ib., lxiii. 12, quando a nobis baptisma eorum in acceptum refertur.

[1352] Cypr. Ep. lxxvii. 12.

[1353] 1 Cor. vi. 10.

[1354] Eph. v. 5.

[1355] Cypr. Ep. lv. 26.

[1356] 2 Cor. vi. 16.

[1357] Cypr. Ep. lxxvii. 12.

Chapter 5.

8. "Further," Cyprian goes on to say, "in vain do some, who are overcome by reason, oppose to us custom, as though custom were superior to truth, or that were not to be followed in spiritual things which has been revealed by the Holy Spirit, as the better way." [1358] This is clearly true, since reason and truth are to be preferred to custom. But when truth supports custom, nothing should be more strongly maintained. Then he proceeds as follows: "For one may pardon a man who merely errs, as the Apostle Paul says of himself, Who was before a blasphemer, a persecutor, and injurious; but I obtained mercy, because I did it ignorantly;' [1359] but he who, after inspiration and revelation given, perseveres advisedly and knowingly in his former error, sins without hope of pardon on the ground of ignorance. For he rests on a kind of presumption and obstinacy, when he is overcome by reason." This is most true, that his sin is much more grievous who has sinned wittingly than his who has sinned through ignorance. And so in the case of the holy Cyprian, who was not only learned, but also patient of instruction, which he so fully himself understood to be a part of the praise of the bishop whom the apostle describes, [1360] that he said, "This also should be approved in a bishop, that he not only teach with knowledge, but also learn with patience." [1361]I do not doubt that if he had had the opportunity of discussing this question, which has been so long and so much disputed in the Church, with the pious and learned men to whom we owe it that subsequently that ancient custom was confirmed by the authority of a plenary Council, he would have shown, without hesitation, not only how learned he was in those things which he had grasped with all the security of truth, but also how ready he was to receive instruction in what he had

failed to perceive. And yet, since it is so clear that it is much more grievous to sin wittingly than in ignorance, I should be glad if any one would tell me which is the worse,--the man who falls into heresy, not knowing how great a sin it is, or the man who refuses to abandon his covetousness, knowing its enormity? I might even put the question thus: If one man unwittingly fall into heresy, and another knowingly refuse to depart from idolatry, since the apostle himself says, "The covetous man, which is an idolater;" and Cyprian too understood the same passage in just the same way, when he says, in his letter to Antonianus, "Nor let the new heretics flatter themselves in this, that they say they do not communicate with idolaters, whereas there are amongst them both adulterers and covetous persons, who are held guilty of the sin of idolatry; for know this, and understand, that no whoremonger, nor unclean person, nor covetous man, who is an idolater, hath any inheritance in the kingdom of Christ and of God;' [1362] and again, Mortify therefore your members which are upon the earth; fornication, uncleanness, inordinate affection, evil concupiscence, and covetousness, which is idolatry.'" [1363]I ask, therefore, which sins more deeply,--he who ignorantly has fallen into heresy, or he who wittingly has refused to abandon covetousness, that is idolatry? According to that rule by which the sins of those who sin wittingly are placed before those of the ignorant, the man who is covetous with knowledge takes the first place in sin. But as it is possible that the greatness of the actual sin should produce the same effect in the case of heresy that the witting commission of the sin produces in that of covetousness, let us suppose the ignorant heretic to be on a par in guilt with the consciously covetous man, although the evidence which Cyprian himself has advanced from the apostle does not seem to prove this. For what is it that we abominate in heretics except their blasphemies? But when he wished to show that ignorance of the sin may conduce to ease in obtaining pardon, he advanced a proof from the case of the apostle, when he says, "Who was before a blasphemer, and a persecutor, and injurious; but I obtained mercy, because I did it ignorantly." [1364]But if possible, as I said before, let the sins of the two men--the blasphemy of the unconscious, and the idolatry of the conscious sinner--be esteemed of equal weight; and let them be judged by the same sentence,--he who, in seeking for Christ, falls into a truth-like setting forth of what is false, and he who wittingly resists Christ speaking through His apostle, "seeing that no whoremonger, nor unclean person, nor covetous man, which is an idolater, hath any inheritance in the kingdom of Christ and of God," [1365] --and then I would ask why baptism and the words of the gospel are held as naught in the former case, and accounted valid in the latter, when each is alike found to be estranged from the members of the dove. Is it because the former is an open combatant outside, that he should not be admitted, the latter a cunning assenter within the fold, that he may not be expelled?

[1358] Cypr. Ep. lxxiii. 13.

[1359] 1 Tim. i. 13.

[1360] 2 Tim. ii. 24.

[1361] Cypr. Ep. lxxiv. 10.

[1362] Eph. v. 5.

[1363] Col. iii. 5. Cypr. Ep. lv. 27.

[1364] 1 Tim. i. 13.

[1365] Eph. v. 5.

Chapter 6.

9. But as regards his saying, "Nor let any one affirm that what they have received from the apostles, that they follow; for the apostles handed down only one Church and one baptism, and that appointed only in the same Church:" [1366]this does not so much move me to venture to condemn the baptism of Christ when found amongst heretics (just as it is necessary to recognize the gospel itself when I find it with them, though I abominate their error), as it warns me that there were some even in the times of the holy Cyprian who traced to the authority of the apostles that custom against which the African Councils were held, and in respect of which he himself said a little above, "In vain do those who are beaten by reason oppose to us the authority of custom." Nor do I find the reason why the same Cyprian found this very custom, which after his time was confirmed by nothing less than a plenary Council of the whole world, already so strong before his time, that when with all his learning he sought an authority worth following for changing it, he found nothing but a Council of Agrippinus held in Africa a very few years before his own time. And seeing that this was not enough for him, as against the custom of the whole world, he laid hold on these reasons which we just now, considering them with great care, and being confirmed by the antiquity of the custom itself, and by the subsequent authority of a plenary Council, found to be truth-like rather than true; which, however, seemed to him true, as he toiled in a question of the greatest obscurity, and was in doubt about the remission of sins,--whether it could fail to be given in the baptism of Christ, and whether it could be given among heretics. In which matter, if an imperfect revelation of the truth was given to

Cyprian, that the greatness of his love in not deserting the unity of the Church might be made manifest, there is yet not any reason why any one should venture to claim superiority over the strong defenses and excellence of his virtues, and the abundance of graces which were found in him, merely because, with the instruction derived from the strength of a general Council, he sees something which Cyprian did not see, because the Church had not yet held a plenary Council on the matter. Just as no one is so insane as to set himself up as surpassing the merits of the Apostle Peter, because, taught by the epistles of the Apostle Paul, and confirmed by the custom of the Church herself, he does not compel the Gentiles to judaize, as Peter once had done. [1367]

10. We do not then "find that any one, after being baptized among heretics, was afterwards admitted by the apostles with the same baptism, and communicated;" [1368] but neither do we find this, that any one coming from the society of heretics, who had been baptized among them, was baptized anew by the apostles. But this custom, which even then those who looked back to past ages could not find to have been invented by men of a later time, is rightly believed to have been handed down from the apostles. And there are many other things of the same kind, which it would be tedious to recount. Wherefore, if they had something to say for themselves to whom Cyprian, wishing to persuade them of the truth of his own view, says, "Let no one say, What we have received from the apostles, that we follow," with how much more force we now say, What the custom of the Church has always held, what this argument has failed to prove false, and what a plenary Council has confirmed, this we follow! To this we may add that it may also be said, after a careful inquiry into the reasoning on both sides of the

discussion, and into the evidence of Scripture, What truth has declared, that we follow.

[1366] Cypr. Ep. lxxiii. 13.

[1367] Gal. ii. 14.

[1368] Cypr. Ep. lxxiii. 13.

Chapter 7.

11. For in fact, as to what some opposed to the reasoning of Cyprian, that the apostle says, "Notwithstanding every way, whether in pretence or in truth, let Christ be preached;" [1369] Cyprian rightly exposed their error, showing that it has nothing to do with the case of heretics, since the apostle was speaking of those who were acting within the Church, with malicious envy seeking their own profit. They announced Christ, indeed, according to the truth whereby we believe in Christ, but not in the spirit in which He was announced by the good evangelists to the sons of the dove. "For Paul," he says, "in his epistle was not speaking of heretics, or of their baptism, so that it could be shown that he had laid down anything concerning this matter. He was speaking of brethren, whether as walking disorderly and contrary to the discipline of the Church, or as keeping the discipline of the Church in the fear of God. And he declared that some of them spoke the word of God steadfastly and fearlessly, but that some were acting in envy and strife; that some had kept themselves encompassed with kindly Christian love, but that others entertained malice and strife: but yet that he patiently endured all things, with the view that, whether in truth or in pretence, the name of Christ, which Paul preached, might come to the knowledge of the greatest number, and that the sowing of the word, which was as yet a new and

unaccustomed work, might spread more widely by the preaching of those that spoke. Furthermore, it is one thing for those who are within the Church to speak in the name of Christ, another thing for those who are without, acting against the Church, to baptize in the name of Christ." [1370] These words of Cyprian seem to warn us that we must distinguish between those who are bad outside, and those who are bad within the Church. And those whom he says that the apostle represents as preaching the gospel impurely and of envy, he says truly were within. This much, however, I think I may say without rashness, if no one outside can have anything which is of Christ, neither can any one within have anything which is of the devil. For if that closed garden can contain the thorns of the devil, why cannot the fountain of Christ equally flow beyond the garden's bounds? But if it cannot contain them, whence, even in the time of the Apostle Paul himself, did there arise amongst those who were within so great an evil of envy and malicious strife? For these are the words of Cyprian. Can it be that envy and malicious strife are a small evil? How then were those in unity who were not at peace? For it is not my voice, nor that of any man, but of the Lord Himself; nor did the sound go forth from men, but from angels, at the birth of Christ, "Glory to God in the highest, and on earth peace to men of good will." [1371]And this certainly would not have been proclaimed by the voice of angels when Christ was born upon the earth, unless God wished this to be understood, that those are in the unity of the body of Christ who are united in the peace of Christ, and those are in the peace of Christ who are of good will. Furthermore, as good will is shown in kindliness, so is bad will shown in malice.

[1369] Phil. i. 18. Hieron. "annuntietur."

[1370] Cypr. Ep. lxxiii. 14.

[1371] Luke ii. 14. "Hominibus bonæ voluntatis;" and so the Vulgate, following the reading en anthropois eudokias.

Chapter 8.

12. In short, we may see how great an evil in itself is envy, which cannot be other than malicious. Let us not look for other testimony. Cyprian himself is sufficient for us, through whose mouth the Lord poured forth so many thunders in most perfect truth, and uttered so many useful precepts about envy and malignity. Let us therefore read the letter of Cyprian about envy and malignity, and see how great an evil it is to envy those better than ourselves,--an evil whose origin he shows in memorable words to have sprung from the devil himself. "To feel jealousy," he says, "of what you regard as good, and to envy those who are better than yourselves, to some, dearest brethren, seems a light and minute offense." [1372]And again a little later, when he was inquiring into the source and origin of the evil, he says, "From this the devil, in the very beginning of the world, perished first himself, and led others to destruction." [1373] And further on in the same chapter: "What an evil, dearest brethren, is that by which an angel fell! by which that exalted and illustrious loftiness was able to be deceived and overthrown! by which he was deceived who was the deceiver! From that time envy stalks upon the earth, when man, about to perish through malignity, submits himself to the teacher of perdition,--when he who envies imitates the devil, as it is written, Through envy of the devil came death into the world, and they that do hold of his side do find it.'" [1374]How true, how forcible are these words of Cyprian, in an epistle known throughout the world, we cannot fail to recognize. It was truly

fitting for Cyprian to argue and warn most forcibly about envy and malignity, from which most deadly evil he proved his own heart to be so far removed by the abundance of his Christian love; by carefully guarding which he remained in the unity of communion with his colleagues, who without ill-feeling entertained different views about baptism, whilst he himself differed in opinion from them, not through any contention of ill will, but through human infirmity, erring in a point which God, in His own good time, would reveal to him by reason of his perseverance in love. For he says openly, "Judging no one, nor depriving any of the right of communion if he differ from us. For no one of us setteth himself up as a bishop of bishops, or by tyrannical terror forces his colleagues to a necessity of obeying." [1375]And in the end of the epistle before us he says, "These things I have written to you briefly, dearest brother, according to my poor ability, prescribing to or prejudging no one, so as to prevent each bishop from doing what he thinks right in the free exercise of his own judgment. We, so far as in us lies, do not strive on behalf of heretics with our colleges and fellow-bishops, with whom we hold the harmony that God enjoins, and the peace of our Lord, especially as the apostle says, If any man seem to be contentious, we have no such custom, neither the churches of God.' [1376]Christian love in our souls, the honor of our fraternity, the bond of faith, the harmony of the priesthood, all these are maintained by us with patience and gentleness. For this cause we have also, so far as our poor ability admitted, by the permission and inspiration of the Lord, written now a treatise on the benefit of patience, [1377] which we have sent to you in consideration of our mutual affection." [1378]

[1372] Cypr. de Zel. et Liv. c. 1.

[1373] Ib. c. 4.

[1374] Wisd. ii. 24, 25.

[1375] Conc. Carth. sub in.

[1376] 1 Cor. xi. 16.

[1377] This treatise is still extant. See Trans. in Ante-Nicene Fathers, vol. V. 484-490.

[1378] Cypr. Ep. lxxiii. 26.

Chapter 9.

13. By this patience of Christian love he not only endured the difference of opinion manifested in all kindliness by his good colleagues on an obscure point, as he also himself received toleration, till, in process of time, when it so pleased God, what had always been a most wholesome custom was further confirmed by a declaration of the truth in a plenary Council, but he even put up with those who were manifestly bad, as was very well known to himself, who did not entertain a different view in consequence of the obscurity of the question, but acted contrary to their preaching in the evil practices of an abandoned life, as the apostle says of them, "Thou that preachest a man should not steal, dost thou steal?" [1379]For Cyprian says in his letter of such bishops of his own time, his own colleagues, and remaining in communion with him, "While they had brethren starving in the Church, they tried to amass large sums of money, they took possession of estates by fraudulent proceedings, they multiplied their gains by accumulated usuries." [1380]For here there is no obscure question. Scripture declares openly, "Neither covetous nor extortioners shall inherit the kingdom of God;" [1381] and "He

that putteth out his money to usury," [1382] and "No whoremonger, nor unclean person, nor covetous man, who is an idolater, hath any inheritance in the kingdom of Christ and of God." [1383]He therefore certainly would not, without knowledge, have brought accusations of such covetousness, that men not only greedily treasured up their own goods, but also fraudulently appropriated the goods of others, or of idolatry existing in such enormity as he understands and proves it to exist; nor assuredly would he bear false witness against his fellow-bishops. And yet with the bowels of fatherly and motherly love he endured them, lest that, by rooting out the tares before their time, the wheat should also have been rooted up, [1384] imitating assuredly the Apostle Paul, who, with the same love towards the Church, endured those who were ill-disposed and envious towards him. [1385]

14. But yet because "by the envy of the devil death entered into the world, and they that do hold of his side do find it," [1386] not because they are created by God, but because they go astray of themselves, as Cyprian also says himself, seeing that the devil, before he was a devil, was an angel, and good, how can it be that they who are of the devil's side are in the unity of Christ? Beyond all doubt, as the Lord Himself says, "an enemy hath done this," who "sowed tares among the wheat." [1387]As therefore what is of the devil within the fold must be convicted, so what is of Christ without must be recognized. Has the devil what is his within the unity of the Church, and shall Christ not have what is His without? This, perhaps, might be said of individual men, that as the devil has none that are his among the holy angels, so God has none that are His outside the communion of the Church. But though it may be allowed to the devil to mingle tares, that is, wicked men,

with this Church which still wears the mortal nature of flesh, so long as it is wandering far from God, he being allowed this just because of the pilgrimage of the Church herself, that men may desire more ardently the rest of that country which the angels enjoy, yet this cannot be said of the sacraments. For, as the tares within the Church can have and handle them, though not for salvation, but for the destruction to which they are destined in the fire, so also can the tares without, which received them from seceders from within; for they did not lose them by seceding. This, indeed, is made plain from the fact that baptism is not conferred again on their return, when any of the very men who seceded happen to come back again. And let not any one say, Why, what fruit hath the tares? For if this be so, their condition is the same, so far as this goes, both inside and without. For it surely cannot be that grains of corn are found in the tares inside, and not in those without. But when the question is of the sacrament, we do not consider whether the tares bear any fruit, but whether they have any share of heaven; for the tares, both within and without, share the rain with the wheat itself, which rain is in itself heavenly and sweet, even though under its influence the tares grow up in barrenness. And so the sacrament, according to the gospel of Christ, is divine and pleasant; nor is it to be esteemed as naught because of the barrenness of those on whom its dew falls even without.

[1379] Rom. ii. 21.

[1380] Cypr. de Lapsis. c. vi.

[1381] 1 Cor. vi. 10.

[1382] Ps. xv. 5.

[1383] Eph. v. 5.

[1384] Matt. xiii. 29.

[1385] Phil. i. 15-18.

[1386] Wisd. ii. 24, 25.

[1387] Matt. xiii. 28, 25.

Chapter 10.

15. But some one may say that the tares within may more easily be converted into wheat. I grant that it is so; but what has this to do with the question of repeating baptism? You surely do not maintain that if a man converted from heresy, through the occasion and opportunity given by his conversion, should bear fruit before another who, being within the Church, is more slow to be washed from his iniquity, and so corrected and changed, the former therefore needs not to be baptized again, but the churchman to be baptized again, who was outstripped by him who came from the heretics, because of the greater slowness of his amendment. It has nothing, therefore, to do with the question now at issue who is later or slower in being converted from his especial waywardness to the straight path of faith, or hope, or charity. For although the bad within the fold are more easily made good yet it will sometimes happen that certain of the number of those outside will outstrip in their conversion certain of those within; and while these remain in barrenness, the former, being restored to unity and communion, will bear fruit with patience, thirty-fold, or sixty-fold, or a hundred-fold. [1388]Or if those only are to be called tares who remain in perverse error to the end, there are many ears of corn outside, and many tares within.

16. But it will be urged that the bad outside are worse than those within. It is indeed a weighty question, whether Nicolaus, being already severed from the Church, [1389] or Simon, who was still within it, [1390] was the worse,--the one being a heretic, the other a sorcerer. But if the mere fact of division, as being the clearest token of violated charity, is held to be the worse evil, I grant that it is so. Yet many, though they have lost all feelings of charity, yet do not secede from considerations of worldly profit; and as they seek their own, not the things which are Jesus Christ's, [1391] what they are unwilling to secede from is not the unity of Christ, but their own temporal advantage. Whence it is said in praise of charity, that she "seeketh not her own." [1392]

17. Now, therefore, the question is, how could men of the party of the devil belong to the Church, which has no spot, or wrinkle, or any such thing, [1393] of which also it is said, "My dove is one?" [1394]But if they cannot, it is clear that she groans among those who are not of her, some treacherously laying wait within, some barking at her gate without. Such men, however, even within, both receive baptism, and possess it, and transmit it holy in itself; nor is it in any way defiled by their wickedness, in which they persevere even to the end. Wherefore the same blessed Cyprian teaches us that baptism is to be considered as consecrated in itself by the words of the gospel, as the Church has received, without joining to it or mingling with it any consideration of waywardness and wickedness on the part of either minister or recipients; since he himself points out to us both truths,--both that there have been some within the Church who did not cherish kindly Christian love, but practised envy and unkind dissension, of whom the Apostle Paul spoke; and also that the envious belong to the

devil's party, as he testifies in the most open way in the epistle which he wrote about envy and malignity. Wherefore, since it is clearly possible that in those who belong to the devil's party, Christ's sacrament may yet be holy,--not, indeed, to their salvation, but to their condemnation, and that not only if they are led astray after they have been baptized, but even if they were such in heart when they received the sacrament, renouncing the world (as the same Cyprian shows) in words only and not in deeds; [1395] and since even if afterwards they be brought into the right way, the sacrament is not to be again administered which they received when they were astray; so far as I can see, the case is already clear and evident, that in the question of baptism we have to consider, not who gives, but what he gives; not who receives, but what he receives; not who has, but what he has. For if men of the party of the devil, and therefore in no way belonging to the one dove, can yet receive, and have, and give baptism in all its holiness, in no way defiled by their waywardness, as we are taught by the letters of Cyprian himself, how are we ascribing to heretics what does not belong to them? how are we saying that what is really Christ's is theirs, and not rather recognizing in them the signs of our Sovereign, and correcting the deeds of deserters from Him? Wherefore it is one thing, as the holy Cyprian says, "for those within in the Church, to speak in the name of Christ, another thing for those without, who are acting against the Church, to baptize in His name." [1396]But both many who are within act against the Church by evil living, and by enticing weak souls to copy their lives; and some who are without speak in Christ's name, and are not forbidden to work the works of Christ, but only to be without, since for the healing of their souls we grasp at them, or reason with them, or exhort them. For he, too, was without who did not follow Christ with His disciples, and yet in Christ's name was casting out devils, which the Lord enjoined that he should not be prevented from doing; [1397] although, certainly, in the point where he was imperfect he was to be made whole, in accordance with the words of the Lord, in which He says, "He that is not with me is against me; and he that gathereth not with me scattereth abroad." [1398]Therefore both some things are done outside in the name of Christ not against the Church, and some things are done inside on the devil's part which are against the Church.

[1388] Matt. xiii. 23; Luke viii. 15.

[1389] Rev. ii. 6.

[1390] Acts viii. 9-24.

[1391] Phil. ii. 21.

[1392] 1 Cor. xiii. 5.

[1393] Eph. v. 27; Retract. ii. 18.

[1394] Song of Sol. vi. 9.

[1395] Cypr. Ep. xi. i.

[1396] Cypr. Ep. lxxiii. 14.

[1397] Luke ix. 49, 50.

[1398] Matt. xii. 30.

Chapter 11.

18. What shall we say of what is also wonderful, that he who carefully observes may find that it is possible that certain persons, without violating Christian charity, may yet teach what

is useless, as Peter wished to compel the Gentiles to observe Jewish customs, [1399] as Cyprian himself would force heretics to be baptized anew? whence the apostle says to such good members, who are rooted in charity, and yet walk not rightly in some points, "If in anything ye be otherwise minded, God shall reveal even this unto you;" [1400] and that some again, though devoid of charity, may teach something wholesome? of whom the Lord says, "The scribes and the Pharisees sit in Moses' seat: all therefore whatsoever they bid you observe, that observe and do; but do not ye after their works: for they say and do not." [1401]Whence the apostle also says of those envious and malicious ones who yet preach salvation through Christ, "Whether in pretense, or in truth, let Christ be preached." [1402]Wherefore, both within and without, the waywardness of man is to be corrected, but the divine sacraments and utterances are not to be attributed to men. He is not, therefore, a "patron of heretics" who refuses to attribute to them what he knows not to belong to them, even though it be found among them. We do not grant baptism to be theirs; but we recognize His baptism of whom it is said, "The same is He which baptizeth," [1403] wheresoever we find it. But if "the treacherous and blasphemous man" continue in his treachery and blasphemy, he receives no "remission of sins either without" or within the Church; or if, by the power of the sacrament, he receives it for the moment, the same force operates both without and within, as the power of the name of Christ used to work the expulsion of devils even without the Church.

[1399] Gal. ii. 14.

[1400] Phil. iii. 15.

[1401] Matt. xxiii. 2, 3.

[1402] Phil. i. 18; see on ch. 7. 10.

[1403] John i. 33.

Chapter 12.

19. But he urges that "we find that the apostles, in all their epistles, execrated and abhorred the sacrilegious wickedness of heretics, so as to say that their word does spread as a canker.'" [1404]What then? Does not Paul also show that those who said, "Let us eat and drink, for to-morrow we die," were corrupters of good manners by their evil communications, adding immediately afterwards, "Evil communications corrupt good manners;" and yet he intimated that these were within the Church when he says, "How say some among you that there is no resurrection of the dead?" [1405]But when does he fail to express his abhorrence of the covetous? Or could anything be said in stronger terms, than that covetousness should be called idolatry, as the same apostle declared? [1406]Nor did Cyprian understand his language otherwise, inserting it when need required in his letters; though he confesses that in his time there were in the Church not covetous men of an ordinary type, but robbers and usurers, and these found not among the masses, but among the bishops. And yet I should be willing to understand that those of whom the apostle says, "Their word does spread as a canker," were without the Church, but Cyprian himself will not allow me. For, when showing, in his letter to Antonianus, [1407] that no man ought to sever himself from the unity of the Church before the time of the final separation of the just and unjust, merely because of the admixture of evil men in the Church, when he makes it manifest how holy he was, and deserving of the illustrious martyrdom which he won,

he says, "What swelling of arrogance it is, what forgetfulness of humility and gentleness, that any one should dare or believe that he can do what the Lord did not grant even to the apostles,--to think that he can distinguish the tares from the wheat, or, as if it were granted to him to carry the fan and purge the floor, to endeavor to separate the chaff from the grain! And whereas the apostle says, But in a great house there are not only vessels of gold and of silver, but also of wood and of earth,' [1408] that he should seem to choose those of gold and of silver, and despise and cast away and condemn those of wood and of earth, when really the vessels of wood are only to be burned in the day of the Lord by the burning of the divine conflagration, and those of earth are to be broken by Him to whom the rod of iron [1409] has been given.'" [1410]By this argument, therefore, against those who, under the pretext of avoiding the society of wicked men, had severed themselves from the unity of the Church, Cyprian shows that by the great house of which the apostle spoke, in which there were not only vessels of gold and of silver, but also of wood and of earth, he understood nothing else but the Church, in which there should be good and bad, till at the last day it should be cleansed as a threshing-floor by the winnowing-fan. And if this be so, in the Church herself, that is, in the great house itself, there were vessels to dishonor, whose word did spread like a canker. For the apostle, speaking of them, taught as follows: "And their word," he says, "will spread as doth a canker; of whom is Hymenæus and Philetus; who concerning the truth have erred, saying that the resurrection is past already; and overthrow the faith of some. Nevertheless the foundation of God standeth sure, having this seal, The Lord knoweth them that are His. And, Let every one that nameth the name of Christ depart from iniquity. But in a great house there are not only vessels of gold and of silver, but also of wood and of earth." [1411]If, therefore, they whose words did spread as doth a canker were as it were vessels to dishonor in the great house, and by that "great house" Cyprian understands the unity of the Church itself, surely it cannot be that their canker polluted the baptism of Christ. Accordingly, neither without, any more than within, can any one who is of the devil's party, either in himself or in any other person, stain the sacrament which is of Christ. It is not, therefore, the case that "the word which spreads as a canker to the ears of those who hear it gives remission of sins;" [1412] but when baptism is given in the words of the gospel, however great be the perverseness of understanding on the part either of him through whom, or of him to whom it is given, the sacrament itself is holy in itself on account of Him whose sacrament it is. And if any one, receiving it at the hands of a misguided man, yet does not receive the perversity of the minister, but only the holiness of the mystery, being closely bound to the unity of the Church in good faith and hope and charity, he receives remission of his sins,--not by the words which do eat as doth a canker, but by the sacraments of the gospel flowing from a heavenly source. But if the recipient himself be misguided, on the one hand, what is given is of no avail for the salvation of the misguided man; and yet, on the other hand, that which is received remains holy in the recipient, and is not renewed to him if he be brought to the right way.

[1404] Cypr. Ep. lxxiii. 15; 2 Tim. ii. 17.

[1405] 1 Cor. xv. 32, 33, 12.

[1406] Eph. v. 5.

[1407] Antonianus, a bishop of Numidia, wrote 252 A.D., to Cyprian, favoring his milder view in opposition to the purism of Novatian: subsequently Novatian wrote to him, advocating the purist movement and impugning the laxity of Cornelius, bp. of Rome. To overthrow the effect upon A. of this letter, Cyprian wrote Epistle LV. In Ep LXX., A. is of the number of those Numidian bishops whom Cyprian addresses.

[1408] 2 Tim. ii. 20.

[1409] Ps. ii. 9.

[1410] Cypr. Ep. lv. 25.

[1411] 2 Tim. ii. 17-20.

[1412] Cypr. Ep. lxxiii. 15.

Chapter 13.

20. There is therefore "no fellowship between righteousness and unrighteousness," [1413] not only without, but also within the Church; for "the Lord knoweth them that are His," and "Let every one that nameth the name of Christ depart from iniquity." There is also "no communion between light and darkness," [1414] not only without, but also within the Church; for "he that hateth his brother is still in darkness." [1415] And they at any rate hated Paul, who, preaching Christ of envy and malicious strife, supposed that they added affliction to his bonds; [1416] and yet the same Cyprian understands these still to have been within the Church. Since, therefore, "neither darkness can enlighten, nor unrighteousness justify," [1417] as Cyprian again says, I ask, how could those men baptize within the very Church herself? I ask, how could those vessels which the large house contains not to honor, but to dishonor, administer what is holy for the sanctifying of men within the great house itself, unless because that holiness of the sacrament

cannot be polluted even by the unclean, either when it is given at their hands, or when it is received by those who in heart and life are not changed for the better? of whom, as situated within the Church, Cyprian himself says, "Renouncing the world in word only, and not in deed." [1418]

21. There are therefore also within the Church "enemies of God, whose hearts the spirit of Antichrist has possessed;" and yet they, "deal with spiritual and divine things," [1419] which cannot profit for their salvation so long as they remain such as they are; and yet neither can they pollute them by their own uncleanness. With regard to what he says, therefore, "that they have no part given them in the saving grace of the Church, who, scattering and fighting against the Church of Christ, are called adversaries by Christ Himself, and antichrists by His apostles, [1420] this must be received under the consideration that there are men of this kind both within and without. But the separation of those that are within from the perfection and unity of the dove is not only known in the case of some men to God, but even in the case of some to their fellow-men; for, by regarding their openly abandoned life and confirmed wickedness, and comparing it with the rules of God's commandments, they understand to what a multitude of tares and chaff, situated now some within and some without, but destined to be most manifestly separated at the last day, the Lord will then say, "Depart from me, ye that work iniquity," [1421] and "Depart into everlasting fire, prepared for the devil and his angels." [1422]

[1413] Cypr. Ep. lxxiii. 15; 2 Cor. vi. 14.

[1414] Ib.

[1415] 1 John ii. 9.

[1416] Phil. i. 15, 16.

[1417] Cypr l.c.

[1418] Cypr Ep. xi. 1.

[1419] Cypr. Ep. lxxiii. 15.

[1420] Cypr. Ep. lxxiii. 15.

[1421] Matt. vii. 23.

[1422] Matt. xxv. 41.

Chapter 14.

22. But we must not despair of the conversion of any man, whether situated within or without, so long as "the goodness of God leadeth him to repentance," [1423] and "visits their transgressions with the rod, and their inquiry with stripes." For in this way "He does not utterly take from them His loving-kindness," [1424] if they will themselves sometimes "love their own soul, pleasing God." [1425] But as the good man "that shall endure unto the end, the same shall be saved," [1426] so the bad man, whether within or without, who shall persevere in his wickedness to the end, shall not be saved. Nor do we say that "all, wheresoever and howsoever baptized, obtain the grace of baptism," [1427] if by the grace of baptism is understood the actual salvation which is conferred by the celebration of the sacrament; but many fail to obtain this salvation even within the Church, although it is clear that they possess the sacrament, which is holy in itself. Well, therefore, does the Lord warn us in the gospel that we should not company with ill-advisers, [1428] who walk under the pretence of Christ's name; but these are found both within and without, as, in fact, they do not proceed

without unless they have first been ill-disposed within. And we know that the apostle said of the vessels placed in the great house, "If a man therefore purge himself from these, he shall be a vessel unto honor, sanctified, and meet for the Master's use, and prepared unto every good work." [1429] But in what manner each man ought to purge himself from these he shows a little above, saying, "Let every one that nameth the name of Christ depart from iniquity," [1430] that he may not in the last day, with the chaff, whether with that which has already been driven from the threshing-floor, or with that which is to be separated at the last, hear the command, "Depart from me, ye that work iniquity." [1431] Whence it appears, indeed, as Cyprian says, that "we are not at once to admit and adopt whatsoever is professed in the name of Christ, but only what is done in the truth of Christ." [1432] But it is not an action done in the truth of Christ that men should "seize on estates by fraudulent pretenses, and increase their gains by accumulated usury," [1433] or that they should "renounce the world in word only;" [1434] and yet, that all this is done within the Church, Cyprian himself bears sufficient testimony.

[1423] Rom. ii. 4.

[1424] Ps. lxxxix. 32, 33.

[1425] Ecclus. xxx. 23. The words, "placentes Deo" are derived from the Latin version only.

[1426] Matt. xxiv. 13.

[1427] From a letter of Pope Stephen's, quoted Cypr. Ep. lxxiii. 16.

[1428] Mark xiii. 21.

[1429] 2 Tim. ii. 21.

[1430] 2 Tim. ii. 19.

[1431] Matt. vii. 23.

[1432] Cypr. Ep. lxxiii. 16.

[1433] Ib. de Laps. c. vi.

[1434] Ib. Ep. xi. 1.

Chapter 15.

23. To go on to the point which he pursues at great length, that "they who blaspheme the Father of Christ cannot be baptized in Christ," [1435] since it is clear that they blaspheme through error (for he who comes to the baptism of Christ will not openly blaspheme the Father of Christ, but he is led to blaspheme by holding a view contrary to the teaching of the truth about the Father of Christ), we have already shown at sufficient length that baptism, consecrated in the words of the gospel, is not affected by the error of any man, whether ministrant or recipient, whether he hold views contrary to the revelation of divine teaching on the subject of the Father, or the Son, or the Holy Ghost. For many carnal and natural men are baptized even within the Church, as the apostle expressly says: "The natural man receiveth not the things of the Spirit of God;" [1436] and after they had received baptism, he says that they "are yet carnal." [1437]But according to it carnal sense, a soul given up to fleshly appetites cannot entertain but fleshly wisdom about God. Wherefore many, progressing after baptism, and especially those who have been baptized in infancy or early youth, in proportion as their intellect becomes clearer and brighter, while "the inward man is renewed day by

day," [1438] throw away their former opinions which they held about God while they were mocked with vain imaginings, with scorn and horror and confession of their mistake. And yet they are not therefore considered not to have received baptism, or to have received baptism of a kind corresponding to their error; but in them both the perfection of the sacrament is honored and the delusion of their mind is corrected, even though it had become inveterate through long confirmation, or been, perhaps, maintained in many controversies. Wherefore even the heretic, who is manifestly without, if he has there received baptism as ordained in the gospel, has certainly not received baptism of a kind corresponding to the error which blinds him. And therefore, in returning into the way of wisdom he perceives that he ought to relinquish what he has held amiss, he must not at the same time give up the good which he had received; nor because his error is to be condemned, is the baptism of Christ in him to be therefore extinguished. For it is already sufficiently clear, from the case of those who happen to be baptized within the Church with false views about God, that the truth of the sacrament is to be distinguished from the error of him who believes amiss, although both may be found in the same man. And therefore, when any one grounded in any error, even outside the Church, has yet been baptized with the true sacrament, when he is restored to the unity of the Church, a true baptism cannot take the place of a true baptism, as a true faith takes the place of a false one, because a thing cannot take the place of itself, since neither can it give place. Heretics therefore join the Catholic Church to this end, that what they have evil of themselves may be corrected, not that what they have good of God should be repeated.

[1435] Ib. Ep. lxxiii. 17.

[1436] 1 Cor. ii. 14.

[1437] 1 Cor. iii. 3.

[1438] 2 Cor. iv. 16.

Chapter 16.

24. Some one says, Does it then make no difference, if two men, rooted in like error and wickedness, be baptized without change of life or heart, one without, the other within the Church? I acknowledge that there is a difference. For he is worse who is baptized without, in addition to his other sin,--not because of his baptism, however, but because he is without; for the evil of division is in itself far from insignificant or trivial. Yet the difference exists only if he who is baptized within has desired to be within not for the sake of any earthly or temporal advantage, but because he has preferred the unity of the Church spread throughout the world to the divisions of schism; otherwise he too must be considered among those who are without. Let us therefore put the two cases in this way. Let us suppose that the one, for the sake of argument, held the same opinions as Photinus [1439] about Christ, and was baptized in his heresy outside the communion of the Catholic Church; and that another held the same opinion but was baptized in the Catholic Church, believing that his view was really the Catholic faith. I consider him as not yet a heretic, unless, when the doctrine of the Catholic faith is made clear to him, he chooses to resist it, and prefers that which he already holds; and till this is the case, it is clear that he who was baptized outside is the worse. And so in the one case erroneous opinion alone, in the other the sin of schism also, requires correction; but in neither of them is the truth of the sacrament to be repeated. But if any one holds the same view as the first, and knows that it is only in

heresy severed from the Church that such a view is taught or learned, but yet for the sake of some temporal emolument has desired to be baptized in the Catholic unity, or, having been already baptized in it, is unwilling on account of the said emolument to secede from it, he is not only to be considered as seceding, but his offense is aggravated, in so far as to the error of heresy and the division of unity he adds the deceit of hypocrisy. Wherefore the depravity of each man, in proportion as it is more dangerous and wanting in straightforwardness, must be corrected with the more earnestness and energy; and yet, if he has anything that is good in him, especially if it be not of himself, but from God, we ought not to think it of no value because of his depravity, or to be blamed like it, or to be ascribed to it, rather than to His bountiful goodness, who even to a soul that plays the harlot, and goes after her lovers, yet gives His bread, and His wine, and His oil, and other food or ornaments, which are neither from herself nor from her lovers, but from Him who in compassion for her is even desirous to warn her to whom she should return. [1440]

[1439] Various Synods from 345 on anathematized Photinus, the bishop of Sirmium. The two of Sirmium, 351 and 357, accused him of constituting two Gods.

[1440] Hos. ii. 5-8.

Chapter 17.

25. "Can the power of baptism," says Cyprian, "be greater or better than confession? than martyrdom? that a man should confess Christ before men, and be baptized in his own blood? And yet," he goes on to say, "neither does this baptism profit the heretic, even though for confessing Christ he be put to death outside the Church." [1441] This is most true; for, by

being put to death outside the Church, he is proved not to have had charity, of which the apostle says, "Though I give my body to be burned, and have not charity, it profiteth me nothing." [1442]But if martyrdom is of no avail for this reason, because it has not charity, neither does it profit those who, as Paul says, and Cyprian further sets forth, are living within the Church without charity in envy and malice; and yet they can both receive and transmit true baptism. "Salvation," he says, "is not without the Church." [1443]Who says that it is? And therefore, whatever men have that belongs to the Church, it profits them nothing towards salvation outside the Church. But it is one thing not to have, another to have so as to be of no use. He who has not must be baptized that he may have; but he who has to no avail must be corrected, that what he has may profit him. Nor is the water in the baptism of heretics "adulterous," [1444] because neither is the creature itself which God made evil, nor is fault to be found with the words of the gospel in the mouths of any who are astray; but the fault is theirs in whom there is an adulterous spirit, even though it may receive the adornment of the sacrament from a lawful spouse. Baptism therefore can "be common to us, and the heretics," [1445] just as the gospel can be common to us, whatever difference there may be between our faith and their error,--whether they think otherwise than the truth about the Father, or the Son, or the Holy Spirit; or, being cut away from unity, do not gather with Christ, but scatter abroad, [1446] --seeing that the sacrament of baptism can be common to us, if we are the wheat of the Lord, with the covetous within the Church, and with robbers, and drunkards, and other pestilent persons of the same sort, of whom it is said, "They shall not inherit the kingdom of God," [1447] and yet the vices by which they are separated from the kingdom of God are not shared by us.

[1441] Cypr. Ep. lxxiii. 21.

[1442] 1 Cor. xiii. 3.

[1443] Cyp. l.c.

[1444] Cyp. l.c.

[1445] Cyp. l.c.

[1446] Matt. xii. 30.

[1447] 1 Cor. vi. 10.

Chapter 18.

26. Nor indeed, is it of heresies alone that the apostle says "that they which do such things shall not inherit the kingdom of God." But it may be worth while to look for a moment at the things which he groups together. "The works of the flesh," he says "are manifest, which are these; fornication, uncleanness, lasciviousness, idolatry, witchcraft, hatred, variance, emulations, wrath, strife, seditions, heresies, envyings, murders, drunkenness, revellings, and such like: of the which I tell you before, as I have also told you in time past, that they which do such things shall not inherit the kingdom of God." [1448]Let us suppose some one, therefore, chaste, continent, free from covetousness, no idolater, hospitable, charitable to the needy, no man's enemy, not contentious, patient, quiet, jealous of none, envying none, sober, frugal, but a heretic; it is of course clear to all that for this one fault only, that he is a heretic, he will fail to inherit the kingdom of God. Let us suppose another, a fornicator, unclean, lascivious, covetous, or even more openly given to idolatry, a student of witchcraft, a lover of strife and contention, envious, hot-tempered, seditious,

jealous, drunken, and a reveller, but a Catholic; can it be that for this sole merit, that he is a Catholic, he will inherit the kingdom of God, though his deeds are of the kind of which the apostle thus concludes: "Of the which I tell you before, as I have also told you in time past, that they which do such things shall not inherit the kingdom of God?" If we say this, we lead ourselves astray. For the word of God does not lead us astray, which is neither silent, nor lenient, nor deceptive through any flattery. Indeed, it speaks to the same effect elsewhere: "For this ye know, that no whoremonger, nor unclean person, nor covetous man, which is an idolater, hath any inheritance in the kingdom of Christ and of God. Let no man deceive you with vain words." [1449]We have no reason, therefore, to complain of the word of God. It certainly says, and says openly and freely, that those who live a wicked life have no part in the kingdom of God.

[1448] Gal. v. 19-21.

[1449] Eph. v. 5, 6.

Chapter 19.

27. Let us therefore not flatter the Catholic who is hemmed in with all these vices, nor venture, merely because he is a Catholic Christian, to promise him the impunity which holy Scripture does not promise him; nor, if he has any one of the faults above mentioned, ought we to promise him a partnership in that heavenly land. For, in writing to the Corinthians, the apostle enumerates the several sins, under each of which it is implicitly understood that it shall not inherit the kingdom of God: "Be not deceived," he says: "neither fornicators, nor idolaters, nor adulterers, nor effeminate, nor abusers of themselves with mankind, nor thieves, nor covetous, nor

drunkards, nor revilers, nor extortioners, shall inherit the kingdom of God." [1450]He does not say, those who possess all these vices together shall not inherit the kingdom of God; but neither these nor those: so that, as each is named, you may understand that no one of them shall inherit the kingdom of God. As, therefore, heretics shall not possess the kingdom of God, so the covetous shall not inherit the kingdom of God. Nor can we indeed doubt that the punishments themselves, with which they shall be tortured who do not inherit the kingdom of God, will vary in proportion to the difference of their offences, and that some will be more severe than others; so that in the eternal fire itself there will be different tortures in the punishments, corresponding to the different weights of guilt. For indeed it was not idly that the Lord said, "It shall be more tolerable for the land of Sodom in the day of judgment than for thee." [1451] But yet, so far as failing to inherit the kingdom of God is concerned, it is just as certain, if you choose any one of the less heinous of these vices, as if you choose more than one, or some one which you saw was more atrocious; and because those will inherit the kingdom of God whom the Judge shall set on His right hand, and for those who shall not be found worthy to be set at the right hand nothing will remain but to be at the left, no other announcement is left for them to hear like goats from the mouth of the Shepherd, except, "Depart into everlasting fire, prepared for the devil and his angels;" [1452] though in that fire, as I said before, it may be that different punishments will be awarded corresponding to the difference of the sins.

[1450] 1 Cor. vi. 9, 10.

[1451] Matt. xi. 24.

[1452] Matt. xxv. 41.

Chapter 20.

28. But on the question whether we ought to prefer a Catholic of the most abandoned character to a heretic in whose life, except that he is a heretic, men can find nothing to blame, I do not venture to give a hasty judgment. But if any one says, because he is a heretic, he cannot be this only without other vices also following,--for he is carnal and natural, and therefore must be also envious, and hot-tempered, and jealous, and hostile to truth itself, and utterly estranged from it,--let him fairly understand, that of those other faults of which he is supposed to have chosen some one less flagrant, a single one cannot exist by itself in any man, because he in turn is carnal and natural; as, to take the case of drunkenness, which people have now become accustomed to talk of not only without horror, but with some degree of merriment, can it possibly exist alone in any one in whom it is found? For what drunkard is not also contentious, and hot-tempered, and jealous, and at variance with all soundness of counsel, and at grievous enmity with those who rebuke him? Further, it is not easy for him to avoid being a fornicator and adulterer, though he may be no heretic; just as a heretic may be no drunkard, nor adulterer, nor fornicator, nor lascivious, nor a lover of money, or given to witchcraft, and cannot well be all these together. Nor indeed is any one vice followed by all the rest. Supposing, therefore, two men,--one a Catholic with all these vices, the other a heretic free from all from which a heretic can be free,--although they do not both contend against the faith, and yet each lives contrary to the faith, and each is deceived by a vain hope, and each is far removed from charity of spirit, and therefore each is severed from connection with the body of the one dove; why

do we recognise in one of them the sacrament of Christ, and not in the other, as though it belonged to this or that man, whilst really it is the same in both, and belongs to God alone, and is good even in the worst of men? And if of the men who have it, one is worse than another, it does not follow that the sacrament which they have is worse in the one than in the other, seeing that neither in the case of two bad Catholics, if one be worse than the other, does he possess a worse baptism, nor, if one of them be good and another bad, is baptism bad in the bad one and good in the good one; but it is good in both. Just as the light of the sun, or even of a lamp, is certainly not less brilliant when displayed to bad eyes than when seen by better ones; but it is the same in the case of both, although it either cheers or hurts them differently according to the difference of their powers.

Chapter 21.

29. With regard to the objection brought against Cyprian, that the catechumens who were seized in martyrdom, and slain for Christ's name's sake, received a crown even without baptism, I do not quite see what it has to do with the matter, unless, indeed, they urged that heretics could much more be admitted with baptism to Christ's kingdom, to which catechumens were admitted without it, since He Himself has said, "Except a man be born of water and of the Spirit, he cannot enter into the kingdom of God." [1453]Now, in this matter I do not hesitate for a moment to place the Catholic catechumen, who is burning with love for God, before the baptized heretic; nor yet do we thereby do dishonor to the sacrament of baptism which the latter has already received, the former not as yet; nor do we consider that the sacrament of the catechumen [1454] is to be preferred to the sacrament of baptism, when we acknowledge

that some catechumens are better and more faithful than some baptized persons. For the centurion Cornelius, before baptism, was better than Simon, who had been baptized. For Cornelius, even before his baptism, was filled with the Holy Spirit; [1455] Simon, even after baptism, was puffed up with an unclean spirit. [1456]Cornelius, however, would have been convicted of contempt for so holy a sacrament, if, even after he had received the Holy Ghost, he had refused to be baptized. But when he was baptized, he received in no wise a better sacrament than Simon; but the different merits of the men were made manifest under the equal holiness of the same sacrament--so true is it that the good or ill deserving of the recipient does not increase or diminish the holiness of baptism. But as baptism is wanting to a good catechumen to his receiving the kingdom of heaven, so true conversion is wanting to a bad man though baptized. For He who said, "Except a man be born of water and of the Spirit, he cannot enter into the kingdom of God," said also Himself, "except your righteousness shall exceed the righteousness of the scribes and Pharisees, ye shall in no case enter into the kingdom of heaven." [1457]For that the righteousness of the catechumens might not feel secure, it is written, "Except a man be born again of water and of the Spirit, he cannot enter into the kingdom of God." And again, that the unrighteousness of the baptized might not feel secure because they had received baptism, it is written, "Except your righteousness shall exceed the righteousness of the scribes and Pharisees, ye shall in no case enter into the kingdom of heaven." The one were too little without the other; the two make perfect the heir of that inheritance. As, then, we ought not to depreciate a man's righteousness, which begins to exist before he is joined to the Church, as the righteousness of Cornelius began to exist before he was in the body of Christian men,--which righteousness was not thought worthless, or the angel would not have said to him, "Thy prayers and thine alms are come up as a memorial before God;" nor did it yet suffice for his obtaining the kingdom of heaven, or he would not have been told to send to Peter, [1458] --so neither ought we to depreciate the sacrament of baptism, even though it has been received outside the Church. But since it is of no avail for salvation unless he who has baptism indeed in full perfection be incorporated into the Church, correcting also his own depravity, let us therefore correct the error of the heretics, that we may recognize what in them is not their own but Christ's.

[1453] John iii. 5.

[1454] Another reading, of less authority, is, "Aut catechumeno sacramentum baptismi præferendum putamus." This does not suit the sense of the passage, and probably sprung from want of knowledge of the meaning of the "catechumen's sacrament." It is mentioned in the Council of Carthage, A.D. 397, as "the sacrament of salt" (cap. 5). Augustin (de Peccat. Meritis, ii. c. 26), says that "what the catechumens receive, though it be not the body of Christ, yet is holy, more holy than the food whereby our bodies are sustained, because it is a sacrament."-- Cp. de Catech. Rudibus, c. 26 [Bened.]. It appears to have been only a taste of salt, given them as the emblem of purity and incorruption. See Bingham, Orig. Eccles. Book x. c. ii. 16.

[1455] Acts x. 44.

[1456] Acts viii. 13, 18, 19.

[1457] Matt. v. 20.

[1458] Acts x. 4, 5.

Chapter 22.

30. That the place of baptism is sometimes supplied by martyrdom is supported by an argument by no means trivial, which the blessed Cyprian adduces [1459] from the thief, to whom, though he was not baptized, it was yet said, "To-day shall thou be with me in Paradise." [1460]On considering which, again and again, I find that not only martyrdom for the sake of Christ may supply what was wanting of baptism, but also faith and conversion of heart, if recourse may not be had to the celebration of the mystery of baptism for want of time. [1461]For neither was that thief crucified for the name of Christ, but as the reward of his own deeds; nor did he suffer because he believed, but he believed while suffering. It was shown, therefore, in the case of that thief, how great is the power, even without the visible sacrament of baptism, of what the apostle says, "With the heart man believeth unto righteousness, and with the mouth confession is made unto salvation." [1462]But the want is supplied invisibly only when the administration of baptism is prevented, not by contempt for religion, but by the necessity of the moment. For much more in the case of Cornelius and his friends, than in the case of that robber, might it seem superfluous that they should also be baptized with water, seeing that in them the gift of the Holy Spirit, which, according to the testimony of holy Scripture, was received by other men only after baptism, had made itself manifest by every unmistakable sign appropriate to those times when they spoke with tongues. Yet they were baptized, and for this action we have the authority of an apostle as the warrant. So far ought all of us to be from being induced by any imperfection in the inner man, if it so happen that before baptism a person has advanced, through the workings of a

pious heart, to spiritual understanding, to despise a sacrament which is applied to the body by the hands of the minister, but which is God's own means for working spiritually a man's dedication to Himself. Nor do I conceive that the function of baptizing was assigned to John, so that it should be called John's baptism, for any other reason except that the Lord Himself, who had appointed it, in not disdaining to receive the baptism of His servant, [1463] might consecrate the path of humility, and show most plainly by such an action how high a value was to be placed on His own baptism, with which He Himself was afterwards to baptize. For He saw, like an excellent physician of eternal salvation, that overweening pride would be found in some, who, having made such progress in the understanding of the truth and in uprightness of character that they would not hesitate to place themselves, both in life and knowledge, above many that were baptized, would think it was unnecessary for them to be baptized, since they felt that they had attained a frame of mind to which many that were baptized were still only endeavoring to raise themselves.

[1459] Cypr. Ep. lxxiii. 22.

[1460] Luke xxiii. 43.

[1461] In Retract. ii. 18, Augustin expresses a doubt whether the thief may not have been baptized.

[1462] Rom. x. 10.

[1463] Matt. iii. 6, 13.

Chapter 23.

31. But what is the precise value of the sanctification of the sacrament (which that thief did not receive, not from any want

of will on his part, but because it was unavoidably omitted) and what is the effect on a man of its material application, it is not easy to say. Still, had it not been of the greatest value, the Lord would not have received the baptism of a servant. But since we must look at it in itself, without entering upon the question of the salvation of the recipient, which it is intended to work, it shows clearly enough that both in the bad, and in those who renounce the world in word and not in deed, it is itself complete, though they cannot receive salvation unless they amend their lives. But as in the thief, to whom the material administration of the sacrament was necessarily wanting, the salvation was complete, because it was spiritually present through his piety, so, when the sacrament itself is present, salvation is complete, if what the thief possessed be unavoidably wanting. And this is the firm tradition of the universal Church, in respect of the baptism of infants, who certainly are as yet unable "with the heart to believe unto righteousness, and with the mouth to make confession unto salvation," as the thief could do; nay, who even, by crying and moaning when the mystery is performed upon them, raise their voices in opposition to the mysterious words, and yet no Christian will say that they are baptized to no purpose.

Chapter 24.

32. And if any one seek for divine authority in this matter, though what is held by the whole Church, and that not as instituted by Councils, but as a matter of invariable custom, is rightly held to have been handed down by apostolical authority, still we can form a true conjecture of the value of the sacrament of baptism in the case of infants, from the parallel of circumcision, which was received by God's earlier people, and before receiving which Abraham was justified, as Cornelius also

was enriched with the gift of the Holy Spirit before he was baptized. Yet the apostle says of Abraham himself, that "he received the sign of circumcision, a seal of the righteousness of the faith," having already believed in his heart, so that "it was counted unto him for righteousness." [1464]Why, therefore, was it commanded him that he should circumcise every male child in order on the eighth day, [1465] though it could not yet believe with the heart, that it should be counted unto it for righteousness, because the sacrament in itself was of great avail? And this was made manifest by the message of an angel in the case of Moses' son; for when he was carried by his mother, being yet uncircumcised, it was required, by manifest present peril, that he should be circumcised, [1466] and when this was done, the danger of death was removed. As therefore in Abraham the justification of faith came first, and circumcision was added afterwards as the seal of faith; so in Cornelius the spiritual sanctification came first in the gift of the Holy Spirit, and the sacrament of regeneration was added afterwards in the laver of baptism. And as in Isaac, who was circumcised on the eighth day after his birth, the seal of this righteousness of faith was given first, and afterwards, as he imitated the faith of his father, the righteousness itself followed as he grew up, of which the seal had been given before when he was an infant; so in infants, who are baptized, the sacrament of regeneration is given first, and if they maintain a Christian piety, conversion also in the heart will follow, of which the mysterious sign had gone before in the outward body. And as in the thief the gracious goodness of the Almighty supplied what had been wanting in the sacrament of baptism, because it had been missing not from pride or contempt, but from want of opportunity; so in infants who die baptized, we must believe that the same grace of the Almighty supplies the want, that, not from perversity of will, but from insufficiency of age, they can neither believe with the heart unto righteousness, nor make confession with the mouth unto salvation. Therefore, when others take the vows for them, that the celebration of the sacrament may be complete in their behalf, it is unquestionably of avail for their dedication to God, because they cannot answer for themselves. But if another were to answer for one who could answer for himself, it would not be of the same avail. In accordance with which rule, we find in the gospel what strikes every one as natural when he reads it, "He is of age, he shall speak for himself." [1467]

[1464] Rom. iv. 11, 3.

[1465] Gen. xvii. 9-14.

[1466] Ex. iv. 24-26.

[1467] John ix. 21.

Chapter 25.

33. By all these considerations it is proved that the sacrament of baptism is one thing, the conversion of the heart another; but that man's salvation is made complete through the two together. Nor are we to suppose that, if one of these be wanting, it necessarily follows that the other is wanting also; because the sacrament may exist in the infant without the conversion of the heart; and this was found to be possible without the sacrament in the case of the thief, God in either case filling up what was involuntarily wanting. But when either of these requisites is wanting intentionally, then the man is responsible for the omission. And baptism may exist when the conversion of the heart is wanting; but, with respect to such

conversion, it may indeed be found when baptism has not been received, but never when it has been despised. Nor can there be said in any way to be a turning of the heart to God when the sacrament of God is treated with contempt. Therefore we are right in censuring, anathematizing, abhorring, and abominating the perversity of heart shown by heretics; yet it does not follow that they have not the sacrament of the gospel, because they have not what makes it of avail. Wherefore, when they come to the true faith, and by penitence seek remission of their sins, we are not flattering or deceiving them, when we instruct them by heavenly discipline for the kingdom of heaven, correcting and reforming in them their errors and perverseness, to the intent that we may by no means do violence to what is sound in them, nor, because of man's fault, declare that anything which he may have in him from God is either valueless or faulty.

Chapter 26.

34. A few things still remain to be noticed in the epistle to Jubaianus; but since these will raise the question both of the past custom of the Church and of the baptism of John, which is wont to excite no small doubt in those who pay slight attention to a matter which is sufficiently obvious, seeing that those who had received the baptism of John were commanded by the apostle to be baptized again [1468] they are not to be treated in a hasty manner, and had better be reserved for another book, that the dimensions of this may not be inconveniently large.

[1468] Acts xix. 3-5.

Book V.

He examines the last part of the epistle of Cyprian to Jubaianus, together with his epistle to Quintus, the letter of the African synod to the Numidian bishops, and Cyprian's epistle to Pompeius.

Chapter 1.

1. We have the testimony of the blessed Cyprian, that the custom of the Catholic Church is at present retained, when men coming from the side of heretics or schismatics, if they have received baptism as consecrated in the words of the gospel, are not baptized afresh. For he himself proposed to himself the question, and that as coming from the mouth of brethren either seeking the truth or contending for the truth. For in the course of the arguments by which he wished to show that heretics should be baptized again, which we have sufficiently considered for our present purpose in the former books, he says: "But some will say, What then will become of those who in times past, coming to the Church from heresy, were admitted without baptism?" [1469]In this question is involved the shipwreck of the whole cause of the Donatists, with whom our contest is on this point. For if those had not really baptism who were thus received on coming from heretics, and their sins were still upon them, then, when such men were admitted to communion, either by those who came before Cyprian or by Cyprian himself, we must acknowledge that one of two things occurred,--either that the Church perished then and there from the pollution of communion with such men, or that any one abiding in unity is not injured by even the notorious sins of other men. But since they cannot say that the Church then perished through the contamination arising from communion with those who, as Cyprian says, were admitted into it without baptism--for otherwise they cannot

maintain the validity of their own origin if the Church then perished, seeing that the list of consuls proves that more than forty years elapsed between the martyrdom of Cyprian and the burning of the sacred books, [1470] from which they took occasion to make a schism, spreading abroad the smoke of their calumnies,--it therefore is left for them to acknowledge that the unity of Christ is not polluted by any such communion, even with known offenders. And, after this confession, they will be unable to discover any reason which will justify them in maintaining that they were bound to separate from the churches of the whole world, which, as we read, were equally founded by the apostles, seeing that, while the others could not have perished from any admixture of offenders, of whatsoever kind, they, though they would not have perished if they had remained in unity with them, brought destruction on themselves in schism, by separating themselves from their brethren, and breaking the bond of peace. For the sacrilege of schism is most clearly evident in them, if they had no sufficient cause for separation. And it is clear that there was no sufficient cause for separation, if even the presence of notorious offenders cannot pollute the good while they abide in unity. But that the good, abiding in unity, are not polluted even by notorious offenders, we teach on the testimony of Cyprian, who says that "men in past times, coming to the Church from heresy, were admitted without baptism;" and yet, if the wickedness of their sacrilege, which was still upon them, seeing it had not been purged away by baptism, could not pollute and destroy the holiness of the Church, it cannot perish by any infection from wicked men. Wherefore, if they allow that Cyprian spoke the truth, they are convicted of schism on his testimony; if they maintain that he does not speak truth, let them not use his testimony on the question of baptism.

[1469] Cypr. Ep. lxxiii. ad Jubaian. 23.

[1470] See below, Book VII. c. 2, 3.

Chapter 2.

2. But now that we have begun a disputation with a man of peace like Cyprian, let us go on. For when he had brought an objection against himself, which he knew was urged by his brethren, "What then will become of those who in times past, coming to the Church from heresy, were admitted without baptism? The Lord," he answers, "is able of His mercy to grant indulgence, and not to separate from the gifts of His Church those who, being admitted in all honesty to His Church, have fallen asleep within the Church." [1471]Well indeed has he assumed that charity can cover the multitude of sins. But if they really had baptism, and this were not rightly perceived by those who thought that they should be baptized again, that error was covered by the charity of unity so long as it contained, not the discord and spirit of the devil, but merely human infirmity, until, as the apostle says, "if they were otherwise minded, the Lord should reveal it to them." [1472]But woe unto those who, being torn asunder from unity by a sacrilegious rupture, either rebaptize, if baptism exists with both us and them, or do not baptize at all, if baptism exist in the Catholic Church only. Whether, therefore, they rebaptize, or fail to baptize, they are not in the bond of peace; wherefore let them apply a remedy to which they please of these two wounds. But if we admit to the Church without baptism, we are of the number of those who, as Cyprian has assumed, may receive pardon because they preserved unity. But if (as is, I think, already clear from what has been said in the earlier books) Christian baptism can preserve its integrity even amid

the perversity of heretics, then even though any in those times did rebaptize, yet without departing from the bond of unity, they might still attain to pardon in virtue of that same love of peace, through which Cyprian bears witness that those admitted even without baptism might obtain that they should not be separated from the gifts of the Church. Further, if it is true that with heretics and schismatics the baptism of Christ does not exist, how much less could the sins of others hurt those who were fixed in unity, if even men's own sins were forgiven when they came to it even without baptism! For if, according to Cyprian, the bond of unity is of such efficacy, how could they be hurt by other men's sins, who were unwilling to separate themselves from unity, if even the unbaptized, who wished to come to it from heresy, thereby escaped the destruction due to their own sins?

[1471] Cypr. Ep. lxxiii. 23.

[1472] Phil. iii. 15.

Chapter. 3.

3. But in what Cyprian adds, saying, "Nor yet because men once have erred must there be always error, since it rather befits wise and God-fearing men gladly and unhesitatingly to follow truth, when it is clearly laid before their eyes, than obstinately and persistently to fight for heretics against their brethren and their fellow-priests," [1473] he is uttering the most perfect truth; and the man who resists the manifest truth is opposing himself rather than his neighbors. But, so far as I can judge, it is perfectly clear and certain, from the many arguments which I have already adduced, that the baptism of Christ cannot be invalidated even by the perversity of heretics, when it is given or received among them. But, granting that it is not yet certain,

at any rate no one who has considered what has been said, even from a hostile point of view, will assert that the question has been decided the other way. Therefore we are not striving against manifest truth, but either, as I think, we are striving in behalf of what is clearly true, or, at any rate, as those may hold who think that the question has not yet been solved, we are seeking for the truth. And therefore, if the truth be other than we think, yet we are receiving those baptized by heretics with the same honesty of heart with which those received them whom, Cyprian supposed, in virtue of their cleaving to the unity of the Church, to be capable of pardon. But if the baptism of Christ, as is indicated by the many arguments used above, can retain its integrity amid any defect either of life or faith, whether on the part of those who seem to be within, and yet do not belong to the members of the one dove or on the part of those whose severance from her extends to being openly without, then those who sought its repetition in those former days deserved the same pardon for their charity in clinging to unity, which Cyprian thought that those deserved for charity of the same kind whom he believed to have been admitted without baptism. They therefore who, without any cause (since, as Cyprian himself shows, the bad cannot hurt the good in the unity of the Church), have cut themselves off from the charity which is shown in this unity, have lost all place of pardon, and whilst they would incur destruction by the very crime of schism, even though they did not rebaptize those who had been baptized in the Catholic Church, of how bitter punishment are they deserving, who are either endeavoring to give to the Catholics who have it what Cyprian affirms that they themselves have not, or, as is clear from the facts of the case, are bringing as a charge against the Catholic Church that she has not what even they themselves possess?

[1473] Cypr. Ep. lxxiii. 23.

Chapter 4.

4. But since now, as I said before, we have begun a disputation with the epistles of Cyprian, I think that I should not seem even to him, if he were present, "to be contending obstinately and persistently in defense of heretics against my brethren and my fellow-priests," when he learned the powerful reasons which move us to believe that even among heretics, who are perversely obstinate in their malignant error, the baptism of Christ is yet in itself most holy, and most highly to be reverenced. And seeing that he himself, whose testimony has such weight with us, bears witness that they were wont in past times to be admitted without a second baptism, I would have any one, who is induced by Cyprian's arguments to hold it as certain that heretics ought to be baptized afresh, yet consider that those who, on account of weight of the arguments on the other side, are not as yet persuaded that this should be so, hold the same place as those in past time, who in all honesty admitted men who were baptized in heresy on the simple correction of their individual error, and who were capable of salvation with them in virtue of the bond of unity. And let any one, who is led by the past custom of the Church, and by the subsequent authority of a plenary Council, and by so many powerful proofs from holy Scripture, and by much evidence from Cyprian himself, and by the clear reasoning of truth, to understand that the baptism of Christ, consecrated in the words of the gospel, cannot be perverted by the error of any man on earth,--let such an one understand, that they who then thought otherwise, but yet preserved their charity, can be saved by the same bond of unity. And herein he should also understand of those who, in the society of the Church dispersed throughout

the world, could not have been defiled by any tares, by any chaff, so long as they themselves desired to be fruitful corn, and who therefore severed themselves from the same bond of unity without any cause for the divorce, that at any rate, whichever of the two opinions be true,--that which Cyprian then held, or that which was maintained by the universal voice of the Catholic Church, which Cyprian did not abandon,--in either case they, having most openly placed themselves outside in the plain sacrilege of schism, cannot possibly be saved, and all that they possess of the holy sacraments, and of the free gifts of the one legitimate Bridegroom, is of avail, while they continue what they are, for their confusion rather than the salvation of their souls.

Chapter 5.

5. Wherefore, even if heretics should be truly anxious to correct their error and come to the Church, for the very reason that they believed that they had no baptism unless they received it in the Church, even under these circumstances we should not be bound to yield to their desire for the repetition of baptism; but rather they should be taught, on the one hand, that baptism, though perfect in itself, could in no way profit their perversity if they would not submit to be corrected; and, on the other hand, that the perfection of baptism could not be impaired by their perversity, while refusing to be corrected: and again, that no further perfection is added to baptism in them because they are submitting to correction; but that, while they themselves are quitting their iniquity, that which was before within them to their destruction is now beginning to be of profit for salvation. For, learning this, they will both recognize the need of salvation in Catholic unity, and will cease to claim as their own what is really Christ's, and will not confound the

sacrament of truth, although existing in themselves, with their own individual error.

6. To this we may add a further reason, that men, by a sort of hidden inspiration from heaven, shrink from any one who for the second time receives baptism which he had already received in any quarter whatsoever, insomuch that the very heretics themselves, when their arguments start with that subject, rub their forehead in perplexity, and almost all their laity, even those who have grown old in their body, and have conceived an obstinate animosity against the Catholic Church, confess that this one point in their system displeases them; and many who, for the sake of gaining some secular advantage, or avoiding some disadvantage, wish to secede to them, strive with many secret efforts that they may have granted to them, as a peculiar and individual privilege, that they should not be rebaptized; and some, who are led to place credence in their other vain delusions and false accusations against the Catholic Church, are recalled to unity by this one consideration, that they are unwilling to associate with them lest they should be compelled to be rebaptized. And the Donatists, through fear of this feeling, which has so thorough possession of all men's hearts, have consented to acknowledge the baptism which was conferred among the followers of Maximianus, whom they had condemned, and so to cut short their own tongues and close their mouths, in preference to baptizing again so many men of the people of Musti, and Assuræ, and other districts, whom they received with Felicianus and Prætextatus, and the others who had been condemned by them and afterwards returned to them.

Chapter 6.

7. For when this is done occasionally in the case of individuals, at great intervals of time and space, the enormity of the deed is not equally felt; but if all were suddenly to be brought together who had been baptized in course of time by the aforesaid followers of Maximianus, either under pressure of the peril of death or at their Easter solemnities, and it were told them that they must be baptized again, because what they had already received in the sacrilege of schism was null and void, they might indeed say what obstinate perseverance in their error would compel them to say, that they might hide the rigor and iciness of their hardness under any kind of false shade of consistency against the warmth of truth. But in fact, because the party of Maximianus could not bear this, and because the very men who would have to enforce it could not endure what must needs have been done in the case of so many men at once, especially as those very men would be rebaptizing them in the party of Primianus who had already baptized them in the party of Maximianus, for these reasons their baptism was received, and the pride of the Donatists was cut short. And this course they would certainly not have chosen to adopt, had they not thought that more harm would have been done to their cause by the offense men would have taken at the repetition of the baptism, than by the reputation lost in abandoning their defense. And this I would not say with any idea that we ought to be restrained by consideration of human feelings, if the truth compelled those who came from heretics to be baptized afresh. But because the holy Cyprian says, "that heretics might have been all the more impelled to the necessity of coming over, if only they were to be rebaptized in the Catholic Church," [1474] on this account I have wished to place on record the intensity of the repugnance to this act which is seated deeply in the heart of nearly every one,--a repugnance which I can believe was

inspired by God Himself, that the Church might be fortified by the instinct of repugnance against any possible arguments which the weak cannot dispel.

[1474] Cypr. Ep. lxxiii. 24.

Chapter 7.

8. Truly, when I look at the actual words of Cyprian, I am warned to say some things which are very necessary for the solution of this question. "For if they were to see," he says, "that it was settled and established by our formal decision and vote, that the baptism with which they are baptized in heresy is considered just and lawful, they will think that they are in just and lawful possession of the Church also, and all its other gifts." [1475]He does not say "that they will think they are in possession," but "in just and lawful possession of the gifts of the Church." But we say that we cannot allow that they are in just and lawful possession of baptism. That they are in possession of it we cannot deny, when we recognize the sacrament of the Lord in the words of the gospel. They have therefore lawful baptism, but they do not have it lawfully. For whosoever has it both in Catholic unity, and living worthily of it, both has lawful baptism and has it lawfully; but whosoever has it either within the Catholic Church itself, as chaff mixed with the wheat, or outside, as chaff carried away by the wind, has indeed lawful baptism, but not lawfully. For he has it as he uses it. But the man does not use it lawfully who uses it against the law,--which every one does, who, being baptized, yet leads an abandoned life, whether inside or without the Church.

[1475] Ib.

Chapter 8.

9. Wherefore, as the apostle said of the law, "The law is good, if a man use it lawfully," [1476] so we may fairly say of baptism, Baptism is good, if a man use it lawfully. And as they who used the law unlawfully could not in that case cause that it should not be in itself good, or make it null and void, so any one who uses baptism unlawfully, either because he lives in heresy, or because he lives the worst of lives, yet cannot cause that the baptism should be otherwise than good, or altogether null and void. And so, when he is converted either to Catholic unity, or to a mode of living worthy of so great a sacrament, he begins to have not another and a lawful baptism, but that same baptism in a lawful manner. Nor does the remission of irrevocable sins follow on baptism, unless a man not only have lawful baptism, but have it lawfully; and yet it does not follow that if a man have it not lawfully, so that his sins are either not remitted, or, being remitted, are brought on him again, therefore the sacrament of baptism should be in the baptized person either bad or null and void. For as Judas, to whom the Lord gave a morsel, gave a place within himself of the devil, not by receiving what was bad, but by receiving it badly, [1477] so each person, on receiving the sacrament of the Lord, does not cause that it is bad because he is bad himself, or that he has received nothing because he has not received it to salvation. For it was none the less the body of the Lord and the blood of the Lord, even in those to whom the apostle said, "He that eateth unworthily, eateth and drinketh damnation to himself." [1478] ^ Let the heretics therefore seek in the Catholic Church not what they have, but what they have not,--that is, the end of the commandment, without which many holy things may be possessed, but they cannot profit. "Now, the end of the commandment is charity out of a pure heart, and of a good conscience, and of faith unfeigned." [1479] Let them therefore

hasten to the unity and truth of the Catholic Church, not that they may have the sacrament of washing, if they have been already bathed in it, although in heresy, but that they may have it to their health.

[1476] 1 Tim. i. 8.

[1477] John xiii. 27.

[1478] 1 Cor. xi. 29.

[1479] 1 Tim. i. 5.

Chapter 9.

10. Now we must see what is said of the baptism of John. For "we read in the Acts of the Apostles, that those who had already been baptized with the baptism of John were yet baptized by Paul," [1480] simply because the baptism of John was not the baptism of Christ, but a baptism allowed by Christ to John, so as to be called especially John's baptism; as the same John says, "A man can receive nothing, except it be given him from heaven." [1481]And that he might not possibly seem to receive this from God the Father in such wise as not to receive it from the Son, speaking presently of Christ Himself, he says, "Of His fullness have all we received." [1482]But by the grace of a certain dispensation John received this, which was to last not for long, but only long enough to prepare for the Lord the way in which he must needs be the forerunner. And as our Lord was presently to enter on this way with all humility, and to lead those who humbly followed Him to perfection, as He washed the feet of His servants, [1483] so was He willing to be baptized with the baptism of a servant. [1484]For as He set Himself to minister to the feet of those whose guide He was

Himself, so He submitted Himself to the gift of John which He Himself had given, that all might understand what sacrilegious arrogance they would show in despising the baptism which they ought each of them to receive from the Lord, when the Lord Himself accepted what He Himself had bestowed upon a servant, that he might give it as his own; and that when John, than whom no greater had arisen among them that are born of women, [1485] bore such testimony to Christ, as to confess that he was not worthy to unloose the latchet of His shoe, [1486] Christ might both, by receiving his baptism, be found to be the humblest among men, and, by taking away the place for the baptism of John, be believed to be the most high God, at once the teacher of humility and the giver of exaltation.

11. For to none of the prophets, to no one at all in holy Scripture, do we read that it was granted to baptize in the water of repentance for the remission of sins, as it was granted to John; that, causing the hearts of the people to hang upon him through this marvellous grace, he might prepare in them the way for Him whom he declared to be so infinitely greater than himself. But the Lord Jesus Christ cleanses His Church by such a baptism that on receiving it no other is required; while John gave a first washing with such a baptism that on receiving it there was further need of the baptism of the Lord,--not that the first baptism should be repeated, but that the baptism of Christ, for whom he was preparing the way, might be further bestowed on those who had received the baptism of John. For if Christ's humility were not to be commended to our notice, neither would there be any need of the baptism of John; again, if the end were in John, after his baptism there would be no need of the baptism of Christ. But because "Christ is the end of the law for righteousness to every one that believeth," [1487]

it was shown by John to whom men should go, and in whom, when they had reached Him, they should rest. The same, John, therefore, set forth both the exalted nature of the Lord, when he placed Him far before himself, and His humility, when he baptized Him as the lowest of the people. But if John had baptized Christ alone, he would be thought to have been the dispenser of a better baptism, in that with which Christ alone was baptized, than the baptism of Christ with which Christians are baptized; and again, if all ought to be baptized first with the baptism of John, and then with that of Christ, the baptism of Christ would deservedly seem to be lacking in fullness and perfection, as not sufficing for salvation. Wherefore the Lord was baptized with the baptism of John, that He might bend the proud necks of men to His own health-giving baptism; and He was not alone baptized with it, lest He should show His own to be inferior to this, with which none but He Himself had deserved to be baptized; and He did not allow it to continue longer, lest the one baptism with which He baptizes might seem to need the other to precede it.

[1480] Cypr. Ep. lxxiii. 24; Acts xix. 3-5.

[1481] John iii. 27.

[1482] John i. 16.

[1483] John xiii. 4, 5.

[1484] Matt. iii. 13.

[1485] Matt. xi. 11.

[1486] John i. 27.

[1487] Rom. x. 4.

Chapter 10.

12. I ask, therefore, if sins were remitted by the baptism of John, what more could the baptism of Christ confer on those whom the Apostle Paul desired to be baptized with the baptism of Christ after they had received the baptism of John? But if sins were not remitted by the baptism of John, were those men in the days of Cyprian better than John, of whom he says himself that they "used to seize on estates by treacherous frauds, and increase their gains by accumulated usuries," [1488] through whose, administration of baptism the remission of sins was yet conferred? Or was it because they were contained within the unity of the Church? What then? Was John not contained within that unity, the friend of the Bridegroom, the preparer of the way of the Lord, the baptizer of the Lord Himself? Who will be mad enough to assert this? Wherefore, although my belief is that John so baptized with the water of repentance for the remission of sins, that those who were baptized by him received the expectation of the remission of their sins, the actual remission taking place in the baptism of the Lord,--just as the resurrection which is expected at the last day is fulfilled in hope in us, as the apostle says, that "He hath raised us up together, and made us sit together in heavenly places in Christ Jesus;" [1489] and again, "For we are saved by hope;" [1490] or as again John himself, while he says, "I indeed baptize you with water unto repentance, for the remission of your sins," [1491] yet says, on seeing our Lord, "Behold the Lamb of God, which taketh away the sin of the world," [1492] --nevertheless I am not disposed to contend vehemently against any one who maintains that sins were remitted even in the baptism of John, but that some fuller sanctification was

conferred by the baptism of Christ on those whom Paul ordered to be baptized anew. [1493]

[1488] Cypr. Serm. de Lapsis, c. vi.

[1489] Eph. ii. 6.

[1490] Rom. viii. 24.

[1491] Matt. iii. 11.

[1492] John i. 29.

[1493] Acts xix. 3-5.

Chapter 11.

13. For we must look at the point which especially concerns the matter before us (whatever be the nature of the baptism of John, since it is clear that he belongs to the unity of Christ), viz., what is the reason for which it was right that men should be baptized again after receiving the baptism of the holy John, and why they ought not to be baptized again after receiving the baptism of the covetous bishops. For no one denies that in the Lord's field John was as wheat, bearing an hundred-fold, if that be the highest rate of increase; also no one doubts that covetousness, which is idolatry, is reckoned in the Lord's harvest among the chaff. Why then is a man baptized again after receiving baptism from the wheat, and not after receiving it from the chaff? If it was because he was better than John that Paul baptized after John, why did not also Cyprian baptize after his usurious colleagues, than whom he was better beyond all comparison? If it was because they were in unity with him that he did not baptize after such colleagues, neither ought Paul to have baptized after John, because they were joined together

in the same unity. Can it be that defrauders and extortioners belong to the members of that one dove, and that he does not belong to it to whom the full power of the Lord Jesus Christ was shown by the appearance of the Holy Spirit in the form of a dove? [1494]Truly he belongs most closely to it; but the others, who must be separated from it either by the occasion of some scandal, or by the winnowing at the last day, do not by any means belong to it, and yet baptism was repeated after John and not after them. What then is the cause, except that the baptism which Paul ordered them to receive was not the same as that which was given at the hands of John? And so in the same unity of the Church, the baptism of Christ cannot be repeated though it be given by an usurious minister; but those who receive the baptism of John, even from the hands of John Himself, ought to be afterwards baptized with the baptism of Christ.

[1494] Matt. iii. 16; John i. 33.

Chapter 12.

14. Accordingly, I too might use the words of the blessed Cyprian to turn the hearts of those that hear me to the consideration of something truly marvellous, if I were to say "that John, who was accounted greater among the prophets,-- he who was filled with divine grace while yet in his mother's womb; he who was upheld in the spirit and power of Elias; who was not the adversary, but a forerunner and herald of the Lord: who not only foretold our Lord in words, but also showed Him to the sight; who baptized Christ Himself, through whom all others are baptized," [1495] --he was not worthy to baptize in such wise that those who were baptized by him should not be baptized again after him; and shall no one

think that a man should be baptized in the Church after he had been baptized by the covetous, by defrauders, by extortioners, by usurers? Is not the answer ready to this invidious question, Why do you think this unmeet, as though either John were dishonored, or the covetous man honored? But His baptism ought not to be repeated, of whom John says, "The same is He which baptizeth with the Holy Ghost." [1496]For whoever be the minister by whose hands it is given, it is His baptism of whom it was said, "The same is He which baptizeth." But neither was the baptism of John himself repeated, when the Apostle Paul commanded those who had been baptized by him to be baptized in Christ. For what they had not received from the friend of the Bridegroom, this it was right that they should receive from the Bridegroom Himself, of whom that friend had said, "The same is He which baptizeth with the Holy Ghost."

[1495] Cypr. Ep. lxxiii. 25.

[1496] John i. 33.

Chapter 13.

15. For the Lord Jesus might, if He had so thought fit, have given the power of His baptism to some one or more of His chief servants, whom He had already made His friends, such as those to whom He says, "Henceforth I call you not servants, but friends;" [1497] that, as Aaron was shown to be the priest by the rod that budded, [1498] so in His Church, when more and greater miracles are performed, the ministers of more excellent holiness, and the dispensers of His mysteries, might be made manifest by some sign, as those who alone ought to baptize. But if this had been done, then though the power of baptizing were given them by the Lord, yet it would necessarily be called their own baptism, as in the case of the baptism of

John. And so Paul gives thanks to God that he baptized none of those men who, as though forgetting in whose name they had been baptized, were for dividing themselves into factions under the names of different individuals. [1499]For when baptism is as valid at the hands of a contemptible man as it was when given by an apostle, it is recognized as the baptism neither of this man nor of that, but of Christ; as John bears witness that he learned, in the case of the Lord Himself, through the appearance of the dove. For in what other respect he said, "And I knew Him not," I cannot clearly see. For if he had not known Him in any sense, he could not have said to Him when He came to his baptism, "I have need to be baptized of Thee." [1500]What is it, therefore, that he says, "I saw the Spirit descending from heaven like a dove, and it abode upon Him. And I knew Him not: but He that sent me to baptizewith water, the same said unto me, Upon whom thou shall see the Spirit descending, and remaining on Him, the same is He which baptizeth with the Holy Ghost?" [1501]The dove clearly descended on Him after He was baptized. But while He was yet coming to be baptized, John had said, "I have need to be baptized of Thee." He therefore already knew Him. What does he therefore mean by the words, "I knew Him not: but He that sent me to baptize with water, the same said unto me, Upon whom thou shalt see the Spirit descending, and remaining on Him, the same is He which baptizeth with the Holy Ghost," since this took place after He was baptized, unless it were that he knew Him in respect of certain attributes, and in respect of others knew Him not? He knew Him, indeed, as the Son of God, the Bridegroom, of whose fullness all should receive; but whereas of His fullness he himself had so received the power of baptizing that it should be called the baptism of John, he did not know whether He would so give it to others also, or whether He would have His own baptism in such wise, that at whosesoever hands it was given, whether by a man that brought forth fruit a hundredfold, or sixtyfold, or thirtyfold, whether by the wheat or by the chaff, it should be known to be of Him alone; and this he learned through the Spirit descending like a dove, and abiding on Him.

[1497] John xv. 15.

[1498] Num. xvii. 8.

[1499] 1 Cor. i. 12-15.

[1500] Matt. iii. 14.

[1501] John i. 32, 33.

Chapter 14.

16. Accordingly we find the apostles using the expressions, "My glorying," [1502] though it was certainly in the Lord; and "Mine office," [1503] and "My knowledge," [1504] and "My gospel," [1505] although it was confessedly bestowed and given by the Lord; but no one of them ever once said, "My baptism." For neither is the glorying of all of them equal, nor do they all minister with equal powers, nor are they all endowed with equal knowledge, and in preaching the gospel one works more forcibly than another, and so one may be said to be more learned than another in the doctrine of salvation itself; but one cannot be said to be more or less baptized than another, whether he be baptized by a greater or a less worthy minister. So when "the works of the flesh are manifest, which are these, fornication, uncleanness, lasciviousnness, idolatry, witchcraft, hatred, variance, emulations, strife, seditions, heresies, envyings, drunkenness, revellings, and such like;" [1506] if it be strange

that it should be said, "Men were baptized after John, and are not baptized after heretics," why is it not equally strange that it should be said, "Men were baptized after John, and are not baptized after the envious," seeing that Cyprian himself bears witness in his epistle concerning envy and malignity that the covetous are of the party of the devil, and Cyprian himself makes it manifest from the words of the Apostle Paul, as we have shown above, that in the time of the apostles themselves there were envious persons in the Church of Christ among the very preachers of the name of Christ?

[1502] 1 Cor. ix. 15.

[1503] Rom. xi. 13.

[1504] Eph. iii. 4.

[1505] 2 Tim. ii. 8.

[1506] Gal. v. 19-21.

Chapter 15.

17. That therefore the baptism of John was not the same as the baptism of Christ, has, I think, been shown with sufficient clearness; and therefore no argument can be drawn from it that baptism should be repeated after heretics because it was repeated after John: since John was not a heretic, and could have a baptism, which, though granted by Christ, was yet not the very baptism of Christ, seeing that he had the love of Christ; while a heretic can have at once the baptism of Christ and the perversity of the devil, as another within the Church may have at once the baptism of Christ and the envy of the devil.

18. But it will be urged that baptism after a heretic is much more required, because John was not a heretic, and yet baptism was repeated after him. On this principle, a man may say, much more must we rebaptize after a drunkard, because John was sober, and yet baptism was repeated after him. And we shall have no answer to make to such a man, save that the baptism of Christ was given to those who were baptized by John, because they had it not; but where men have the baptism of Christ, no iniquity on their part can possibly effect that the baptism of Christ should fail to be in them.

19. It is not therefore true that "by baptizing first, the heretic obtains the right of baptism;" [1507] but because he did not baptize with his own baptism, and though he did not possess the right of baptizing, yet that which he gave is Christ's, and he who received it is Christ's. For many things are given wrongfully and yet they are not therefore said to be non-existent or not given at all. For neither does he who renounces the world in word only and not in deed receive baptism lawfully, and yet he does receive it. For both Cyprian records that there were such men in the Church in his day, and we ourselves experience and lament the fact.

20. But it is strange in what sense it can be said that "baptism and the Church cannot in any way be separated and detached from one another." [1508] For if baptism remains inseparably in him who is baptized, how can it be that he can be separated from the Church, and baptism cannot? But it is clear that baptism does remain inseparably in the baptized person; because into whatever depth of evil, and into whatever fearful whirlpool of sin the baptized person may fall, even to the ruin of apostasy, he yet is not bereft of his baptism. And therefore, if through repentance he returns, it is not given again, because

it is judged that he could not have been bereft of it. But who can ever doubt that a baptized person can be separated from the Church? For hence all the heresies have proceeded which deceive by the use of Christian terms.

[1507] Cypr. Ep. lxxiii. 25.

[1508] Ib.

Chapter 16.

Wherefore, since it is manifest that the baptism remains in the baptized person when he is separated from the Church, the baptism which is in him is certainly separated with him. And therefore not all who retain the baptism retain the Church, just as not all who retain the Church retain eternal life. Or if we say that only those retain the Church who observe the commandments of God, we at once concede that there are many who retain baptism, and do not retain the Church.

21. Therefore the heretic is not "the first to seize baptism," since he has received it from the Church. Nor, though he seceded, could baptism have been lost by him whom we assert no longer to retain the Church, and yet allow to retain baptism. Nor does any one "yield his birthright, and give it to a heretic," [1509] because he says that he took away with him what he could not give lawfully, but what would yet be according to law when given; or that he no longer has lawfully what yet is in accordance with law in his possession. But the birthright rests only in a holy conversation and good life, to which all belong of whom that bride consists as her members which has no spot or wrinkle, [1510] or that dove that groans amid the wickedness of the many crows,--unless it be that, while Esau lost his birthright from his lust after a mess of pottage, [1511] we are yet to hold

that it is retained by defrauders, robbers, usurers, envious persons, drunkards and the like, over whose existence in the Church of his time Cyprian groaned in his epistles. Wherefore, either it is not the same thing to retain the Church and to retain the birthright in divine things, or, if every one who retains the Church also retains the birthright, then all those wicked ones do not retain the Church who yet both seem and are allowed by every one of us to give baptism within the Church; for no one, save the man who is wholly ignorant of sacred things, would say that they retain the birthright in sacred things.

[1509] Cypr. Ep. lxxiii. 25.

[1510] Eph. v. 27. Cp. Aug. Retract. ii. 18, quoted above, I. 17, 26.

[1511] Gen. xxv. 29-34.

Chapter 17.

22. But, having considered and handled all these points, we have now come to that peaceful utterance of Cyprian at the end of the epistle, with which I am never sated, though I read and re-read it again and again,--so great is the pleasantness of brotherly love which breathes forth from it, so great the sweetness of charity in which it abounds. "These things," he says, "we have written unto you, dearest brother, shortly, according to our poor ability, prescribing to or prejudging no one, lest each bishop should not do what he thinks right, in the free exercise of his own will. We, so far as in us lies, do not contend on the subject of heretics with our colleagues and fellow-bishops, with whom we maintain concord and peace in the Lord; especially as the apostle also says, If any man seem to be contentious, we have no such custom, neither the churches

of God.' [1512]We observe patiently and gently charity of spirit, the honor of our brotherhood, the bond of faith, the harmony of the priesthood. For this reason also, to the best of our poor ability, by the permission and the inspiration of God we have written this treatise on The Good of Patience,' which we have sent to you in consideration of our mutual love." [1513]

23. There are many things to be considered in these words, wherein the brightness of Christian charity shines forth in this man, who "loved the beauty of the Lord's house, and the place of the tabernacle of His habitation." [1514]First, that he did not conceal what he felt; then, that he set it forth so gently and peacefully, in that he maintained the peace of the Church with those who thought otherwise, because he understood how great healthfulness was bound up in the bond of peace, loving it so much, and maintaining it with sobriety, seeing and feeling that even men who think differently may entertain their several sentiments with saving charity. For he would not say that he could maintain divine concord or the peace of the Lord with evil men; for the good man can observe peace towards wicked men, but he cannot be united with them in the peace which they have not. Lastly, that prescribing to no one, and prejudging no one, lest each bishop should not do what he thinks right in the free exercise of his own will, he has left for us also, whatsoever we may be, a place for treating peacefully of those things with him. For he is present, not only in his letters, but by that very charity which existed in so extraordinary a degree in him, and which can never die. Longing, therefore, with the aid of his prayers, to cling to and be in union with him, if I be not hindered by the unmeetness of my sins, I will learn if I can through his letters with how great peace and comfort the Lord administered His Church through him; and, putting on

the bowels of humility through the moving influence of his discourse, if, in common with the Church at large, I entertain any doctrine more true than his, I will not prefer my heart to his, even in the point in which he, though holding different views, was yet not severed from the Church throughout the world. For in that, when that question was yet undecided for want of full discussion, though his sentiments differed from those of many of his colleagues, yet he observed so great moderation, that he would not mutilate the sacred fellowship of the Church of God by any stain of schism, a greater strength of excellence appeared in him than would have been shown if, without that virtue, he had held views on every point not only true, but coinciding with their own. Nor should I be acting as he would wish, if I were to pretend to prefer his talent and his fluency of discourse and copiousness of learning to the holy Council of all nations, whereat he was assuredly present through the unity of his spirit, especially as he is now placed in such full light of truth as to see with perfect certainty what he was here seeking in the spirit of perfect peace. For out of that rich abundance he smiles at all that here seems eloquence in us, as though it were the first essay of infancy; there he sees by what rule of piety he acted here, that nothing should be dearer in the Church to him than unity. There, too, with unspeakable delight he beholds with what prescient and most merciful providence the Lord, that He might heal our swellings, "chose the foolish things of the world to confound the wise," [1515] and, in the ordering of the members of His Church, placed all things in such a healthful way, that men should not say that they were chosen to the help of the gospel for their own talent or learning, of whose source they yet were ignorant, and so be puffed up with deadly pride. Oh, how Cyprian rejoices! With how much more perfect calmness does he behold how greatly it conduces to the health of the human race, that in the writings even of Christian and pious orators there should be found what merits blame, and in the writings of the fishermen there should nothing of the sort be found! And so I, being fully assured of this joy of that holy soul, neither in any way venture to think or say that my writings are free from every kind of error, nor, in opposing that opinion of his, wherein it seemed to him that those who came from among heretics were to be received otherwise than either they had been in former days, as he himself bears witness, or are now received, as is the reasonable custom, confirmed by a plenary Council of the whole Christian world, do I set against him my own view, but that of the holy Catholic Church, which he so loved and loves, in which he brought forth such abundant fruit with tolerance, whose entirety he himself was not, but in whose entirety he remained; whose root he never left, but, though he already brought forth fruit from its root, he was purged by the heavenly Husbandman that he should bring forth more fruit; [1516] for whose peace and safety, that the wheat might not be rooted out together with the tares, he both reproved with the freedom of truth, and endured with the grace of charity, so many evils on the part of men who were placed in unity with himself.

[1512] 1 Cor. xi. 16.

[1513] Cypr. Ep. lxxiii. 26.

[1514] Ps. xxvi. 8.

[1515] 1 Cor. i. 27.

[1516] John xv. 2.

Chapter 18.

24. Whence Cyprian himself [1517] again admonishes us with the greatest fullness, that many who were dead in their trespasses and sins, although they did not belong to the body of Christ, and the members of that innocent and guileless dove (so that if she alone baptized, they certainly could not baptize), yet to all appearance seemed both to be baptized and to baptize within the Church. And among them, however dead they are, their baptism nevertheless lives, which is not dead, and death shall have no more dominion over it. Since, therefore, there be dead men within the Church, nor are they concealed, for else Cyprian would not have spoken of them so much, who either do not belong at all to that living dove, or at least do not as yet belong to her; and since there be dead men without, who yet more clearly do not belong to her at all, or not as yet; and since it is true that "another man cannot be quickened by one who himself liveth not,"--it is therefore clear that those who within are baptized by such persons, if they approach the sacrament with true conversion of heart, are quickened by Him whose baptism it is. But if they renounce the world in word and not in deed, as Cyprian declares to be the case with some who are within, it is then manifest that they are not themselves quickened unless they be converted, and yet that they have true baptism even though they be not converted. Whence also it is likewise clear that those who are dead without, although they neither "live themselves, nor quicken others," yet have the living baptism, which would profit them unto life so soon as they should be converted unto peace.

[1517] In this and the following chapter, Augustin is examining the seventy-first epistle of Cyprian to his brother Quintas, bishop in Mauritania. Here LXXI. 1.

Chapter 19.

25. Wherefore, as regards those who received the persons who came from heresy in the same baptism of Christ with which they had been baptized outside the Church, and said "that they followed ancient custom," as indeed the Church now receives such, it is in vain urged against them "that among the ancients there were as yet only the first beginning of heresy and schisms, [1518] so that those were involved in them who were seceders from the Church, and had originally been baptized within the Church, so that it was not necessary that they should be baptized again when they returned and did penance." For so soon as each several heresy existed, and departed from the communion of the Catholic Church, it was possible that, I will not even say the next day, but even on that very day, its votaries might have baptized some who flocked to them. And therefore if this was the old custom, that they should be so received into the Church (as could not be denied even by those who maintained the contrary part in the discussion), there can be no doubt in the mind of any one who pays careful attention to the matter, that those also were so received who had been baptized without in heresy.

26. But I cannot see what show of reason there is in this, that the name of "erring sheep" [1519] should be denied to one whose lot it has been that, while seeking the salvation which is in Christ, he has fallen into the error of heretics, and been baptized in their body; while he is held to have become a sheep already within the body of the Catholic Church herself, who has renounced the world in words and not in deeds, and has received baptism in such falseness of heart as this. Or if such an one also does not become a sheep unless after turning to God with a true heart, then, as he is not baptized at the time when he becomes a sheep, if he had been already baptized, but was

not yet a sheep; so he too, who comes from the heretics that he may become a sheep, is not then to be baptized if he had been already baptized with the same baptism, though he was not yet a sheep. Wherefore, since even all the bad that are within--the covetous, the envious, the drunkards, and those that live contrary to the discipline of Christ--may be deservedly called liars, and in darkness, and dead, and antichrists, do they yet therefore not baptize, on the ground that "there can be nothing common between truth and falsehood, between light and darkness, between death and immortality, between Antichrist and Christ?" [1520]

27. He makes an assumption, then, not "of mere custom," but "of the reason of truth itself," [1521] when he says that the sacrament of God cannot be turned to error by the error of any men, since it is declared to exist even in those who have erred. Assuredly the Apostle John says most plainly, "He that hateth his brother is in darkness even until now;" [1522] and again, "Whosoever hateth his brother is a murderer;" [1523] and why, therefore, do they baptize those within the Church whom Cyprian himself declares to be in the envy of malice? [1524]

[1518] Apud veteres hæreses et schismata prima adhuc fuisse initia; that among the ancients heresies and schisms were yet in their very infancy. Benedictines suggest: "hæresis et schismatum." Hartel reads: apud veteres hæreseos et schismatum prima adhuc fuerint initia.

[1519] Cypr. Ep. lxxi. 2.

[1520] Cypr. Ep. lxxi. 2.

[1521] Cypr. Ep. lxxi. 3.

[1522] 1 John ii. 9.

[1523] 1 John iii. 15.

[1524] Cypr. Ep. lxxiii. 14.

Chapter 20.

How does a murderer cleanse and sanctify the water? [1525] How can darkness bless the oil? But if God is present in His sacraments to confirm His words by whomsoever the sacraments may be administered, then both the sacraments of God are everywhere valid, and evil men whom they profit not are everywhere perverse.

28. But what kind of argument is this, that "a heretic must be considered not to have baptism, because he has not the Church?" And it must be acknowledged that "when he is baptized, he is questioned about the Church." [1526] Just as though the same question about the Church were not put in baptism to him who within the Church renounces the world in word and not in deed. As therefore his false answer does not prevent what he receives from being baptism, so also the false reply of the other about the holy Church does not prevent what he receives from being baptism; and as the former, if he afterwards fulfill with truth what he promised in falsehood, does not receive a second baptism, but only an amended life, so also in the case of the latter, if he come afterwards to the Church about which he gave a false answer to the question put to him, thinking that he had it when he had it not, the Church herself which he did not possess is given him, but what he had received is not repeated. But I cannot tell why it should be, that while God can "sanctify the oil" in answer to the words which proceed out of the mouth of a murderer, "He yet cannot

sanctify it on the altar reared by a heretic," unless it be that He who is not hindered by the false conversion of the heart of man within the Church is hindered by the false erection of some wood without from deigning to be present in His sacraments, though no falseness on the part of men can hinder Him. If, therefore, what is said in the gospel, that "God heareth not sinners," [1527] extends so far that the sacraments cannot be celebrated by a sinner, how then does He hear a murderer praying, either over the water of baptism, or over the oil, or over the eucharist, or over the heads of those on whom his hand is laid? All which things are nevertheless done, and are valid, even at the hands of murderers, that is, at the hands of those who hate their brethren, even within, in the Church itself. Since "no one can give what he does not possess himself," [1528] how does a murderer give the Holy Spirit? And yet such an one even baptizeth within the Church. It is God, therefore, that gives the Holy Spirit even when a man of this kind is baptizing.

[1525] In this and the next two chapters Augustin is examining the seventieth epistle of Cyprian, from himself and thirty other bishops (text of Hartel), to Januarius, Saturninus, Maximus, and fifteen others.

[1526] In the question, "Dost thou believe in eternal life and remission of sins through the holy Church?" Cyp. l.c. 2.

[1527] John ix. 31.

[1528] Cypr. Ep. lxx. 2.

Chapter 21.

29. But as to what he says, that "he who comes to the Church is to be baptized and renewed, that within he may be hallowed through the holy," [1529] what will he do, if within also he meets with those who are not holy? Or can it be that the murderer is holy? And if the reason for his being baptized in the Church is that "he should put off this very thing also that he, being a man that sought to come to God, fell, through the deceit of error, on one profane," [1530] where is he afterwards to put off this, that he may chance, while seeking a man of God within the Church itself, to have fallen, through the deceit of error, on a murderer? If "there cannot be in a man something that is void and something that is valid," [1531] why is it possible that in a murderer the sacrament should be holy and his heart unholy? If "whosoever cannot give the Holy Spirit cannot baptize," [1532] why does the murderer baptize within the Church? Or how has the murderer the Holy Spirit, when every one that has the Holy Spirit is filled with light, but "he who hates his brother is still in darkness?" [1533]If because "there is one baptism, and one Spirit," [1534] therefore they cannot have the one baptism who have not the one Spirit, why do the innocent man and the murderer within the Church have the one baptism and not have the one Spirit? So therefore the heretic and the Catholic may have the one baptism, and yet not have the one Church, as in the Catholic Church the innocent man and the murderer may have the one baptism, though they have not the one Spirit; for as there is one baptism, so there is one Spirit and one Church. And so the result is, that in each person we must acknowledge what he already has, and to each person we must give what he has not. If "nothing can be confirmed and ratified with God which has been done by those whom God calls His enemies and foes," [1535] why is the baptism confirmed which is given by murderers? Are we not to

call murderers the enemies and foes of the Lord? But "he that hateth his brother is a murderer." How then did they baptize who hated Paul, the servant of Jesus Christ, and thereby hated Jesus Himself, since He Himself said to Saul, "Why persecutest thou me?" [1536] when he was persecuting His servants, and since at the last He Himself shall say, "Inasmuch as ye did it not to one of the least of these that are mine, ye did it not to me?" [1537]Wherefore all who go out from us are not of us, but not all who are with us are of us; just as when men thresh, all that flies from the threshing-floor is shown not to be corn, but not all that remains there is therefore corn. And so John too says, "They went out from us, but they were not of us; for if they had been of us, they would no doubt have continued with us." [1538]Wherefore God gives the sacrament of grace even through the hands of wicked men, but the grace itself only by Himself or through His saints. And therefore He gives remission of sins either of Himself, or through the members of that dove to whom He says, "Whosoever sins ye remit, they are remitted unto them; and whosoever sins ye retain, they are retained." [1539]But since no one can doubt that baptism, which is the sacrament of the remission of sins, is possessed even by murderers, who are yet in darkness because the hatred of their brethren is not excluded from their hearts, therefore either no remission of sins is given to them if their baptism is accompanied by no change of heart for the better, or if the sins are remitted, they at once return on them again. And we learn that the baptism is holy in itself, because it is of God; and whether it be given or whether it be received by men of such like character, it cannot be polluted by any perversity of theirs, either within, or yet outside the Church.

[1529] Cypr. Ep. lxx. 2.

[1530] Cypr. Ep. lxx. 2.

[1531] Cypr. Ep. lxx. 3.

[1532] Cypr. Ep. lxx. 3.

[1533] 1 John ii. 9.

[1534] Cypr. Ep. lxx. 3.

[1535] Cypr. Ep. lxx. 3.

[1536] Acts ix. 4.

[1537] Matt. xxv. 45.

[1538] 1 John ii. 19.

[1539] John xx. 23.

Chapter 22.

30. Accordingly we agree with Cyprian that "heretics cannot give remission of sins;" [1540] but we maintain that they can give baptism,--which indeed in them, both when they give and when they receive it, is profitable only to their destruction, as misusing so great a gift of God; just as also the malicious and envious, whom Cyprian himself acknowledges to be within the Church, cannot give remission of sins, while we all confess that they can give baptism. For if it was said of those who have sinned against us, "If ye forgive not men their trespasses, neither will your Father forgive your trespasses," [1541] how much more impossible is it that their sins should be forgiven who hate the brethren by whom they are loved, and are baptized in that very hatred; and yet when they are brought to the right way, baptism is not given them anew, but that very

pardon which they did not then deserve is granted them in their true conversion? And so even what Cyprian wrote to Quintus, and what, in conjunction with his colleagues Liberalis, Caldonius, Junius, and the rest, he wrote to Saturninus, Maximus, and others, is all found, on due consideration, to be in no wise meet to be preferred as against the agreement of the whole Catholic Church, of which they rejoiced that they were members, and from which they neither cut themselves away nor allowed others to be cut away who held a contrary opinion, until at length, by the will of the Lord, it was made manifest, by a plenary Council many years afterwards, what was the more perfect way, and that not by the institution of any novelty, but by confirming what was old.

[1540] Cypr. Ep. lxx. 3.

[1541] Matt. vi. 15.

Chapter 23.

31. Cyprian writes also to Pompeius [1542] about this selfsame matter, and clearly shows in that letter that Stephen, who, as we learn, was then bishop of the Roman Church, not only did not agree with him upon the points before us, but even wrote and taught the opposite views. But Stephen certainly did not "communicate with heretics," [1543] merely because he did not dare to impugn the baptism of Christ, which he knew remained perfect in the midst of their perversity. For if none have baptism who entertain false views about God, it has been proved sufficiently, in my opinion, that this may happen even within the Church. "The apostles," indeed, "gave no injunctions on the point;" [1544] but the custom, which is opposed to Cyprian, may be supposed to have had its origin in apostolic tradition, just as there are many things which are

observed by the whole Church, and therefore are fairly held to have been enjoined by the apostles, which yet are not mentioned in their writings.

32. But it will be urged that it is written of heretics that "they are condemned of themselves." [1545] What then? are they not also condemned of themselves to whom it was said, "For wherein thou judgest another, thou condemnest thyself?" [1546] But to these the apostle says, "Thou that preachest a man should not steal, dost thou steal?" [1547] and so forth. And such truly were they who, being bishops and established in Catholic unity with Cyprian himself, used to plunder estates by treacherous frauds, preaching all the time to the people the words of the apostle, who says, "Nor shall extortioners inherit the kingdom of God." [1548]

33. Wherefore I will do no more than run shortly through the other sentiments founded on the same rules, which are in the aforesaid letter written to Pompeius. By what authority of holy Scripture is it shown that "it is against the commandment of God that persons coming from the society of heretics, if they have already there received the baptism of Christ, are not baptized again?" [1549] But it is clearly shown that many pretended Christians, though they are not joined in the same bond of charity with the saints, without which anything holy that they may have been able to possess is of no profit to them, yet have baptism in common with the saints, as has been already sufficiently proved with the greatest fullness. He says "that the Church, and the Spirit, and baptism, are mutually incapable of separation from each other, and therefore" he wishes that "those who are separated from the Church and the Holy Spirit should be understood to be separated also from baptism." [1550] But if this is the case, then when any one has

received baptism in the Catholic Church, it remains so long in him as he himself remains in the Church, which is not so. For it is not restored to him when he returns, just because he did not lose it when he seceded. But as the disaffected sons have not the Holy Spirit in the same manner as the beloved sons, and yet they have baptism; so heretics also have not the Church as Catholics have, and yet they have baptism. "For the Holy Spirit of discipline will flee deceit," [1551] and yet baptism will not flee from it. And so, as baptism can continue in one from whom the Holy Spirit withdraws Himself, so can baptism continue where the Church is not. But if "the laying on of hands" were not "applied to one coming from heresy," [1552] he would be as it were judged to be wholly blameless; but for the uniting of love, which is the greatest gift of the Holy Spirit, without which any other holy thing that there may be in a man is profitless to his salvation, hands are laid on heretics when they are brought to a knowledge of the truth. [1553]

[1542] Cypr. Ep. lxxiv., which is examined by Augustin in the remaining chapters of this book.

[1543] Cypr. Ep.lxxiv. 2.

[1544] Cypr. Ep.lxxiv. 2.

[1545] Tit. iii. 11.

[1546] Rom. ii. 1.

[1547] Rom. ii. 21.

[1548] 1 Cor. vi. 10.

[1549] Cypr. Ep. lxxiv. 4.

[1550] Cypr. Ep. lxxiv. 4.

[1551] Wisd. i. 5.

[1552] Cypr. Ep. lxxiv. 5.

[1553] Cyprian, in the laying on of hands, appears to refer to confirmation, but Augustin interprets it of the restoration of penitents. Cp. III. 16, 21.

Chapter 24.

34. I remember that I have already discussed at sufficient length the question of "the temple of God," and how this saying is to be taken, "As many of you as have been baptized into Christ have put on Christ." [1554]For neither are the covetous the temple of God, since it is written, "What agreement hath the temple of God with idols?" [1555]And Cyprian has adduced the testimony of Paul to the fact that covetousness is idolatry. But men put on Christ, sometimes so far as to receive the sacrament, sometimes so much further as to receive holiness of life. And the first of these is common to good and bad alike; the second, peculiar to the good and pious. Wherefore, if "baptism cannot be without the Spirit," then heretics have the Spirit also,--but to destruction, not to salvation, just as was the case with Saul. [1556]For in the Holy Spirit devils are cast out through the name of Christ, which even he was able to do who was without the Church, which called forth a suggestion from the disciples to their Lord. [1557]Just as the covetous have the Holy Spirit, who yet are not the temple of God. For "what agreement hath the temple of God with idols?" If therefore the covetous have not the Spirit of God, and yet have baptism, it is possible for baptism to exist without the Spirit of God.

35. If therefore heresy is rendered "unable to engender sons to God through Christ, because it is not the bride of Christ," [1558] neither can that crowd of evil men established within the Church, since it is also not the bride of Christ; for the bride of Christ is described as being without spot or wrinkle. [1559]Therefore either not all baptized persons are the sons of God, or even that which is not the bride can engender the sons of God. But as it is asked whether "he is spiritually born who has received the baptism of Christ in the midst of heretics," [1560] so it may be asked whether he is spiritually born who has received the baptism of Christ in the Catholic Church, without being turned to God in a true heart, of whom it cannot be said that he has not received baptism.

[1554] Gal. iii. 27.

[1555] 2 Cor. vi. 16.

[1556] 1 Sam. xix. 23.

[1557] Mark ix. 38.

[1558] Cypr. Ep. lxxiv. 6.

[1559] Eph. v. 27. Cp. Aug. Retract. ii. 18, quoted above, I. 17, 26.

[1560] Cypr. Ep. lxxiv. 7.

Chapter 25.

36. I am unwilling to go on to handle again what Cyprian poured forth with signs of irritation against Stephen, as it is, moreover, quite unnecessary. For they are but the selfsame arguments which have already been sufficiently discussed; and

it is better to pass over those points which involved the danger of baneful dissension. But Stephen thought that we should even hold aloof from those who endeavored to destroy the primitive custom in the matter of receiving heretics; whereas Cyprian, moved by the difficulty of the question itself, and being most largely endowed with the holy bowels of Christian charity, thought that we ought to remain at unity with those who differed in opinion from ourselves. Therefore, although he was not without excitement, though of a truly brotherly kind, in his indignation, yet the peace of Christ prevailed in their hearts, that in such a dispute no evil of schism should arise between them. But it was not found that "hence grew more abundant heresies and schisms," [1561] because what is of Christ in them is approved, and what is of themselves is condemned; for all the more those who hold this law of rebaptizing were cut into smaller fragments.

[1561] Ib.

Chapter 26.

37. To go on to what he says, "that a bishop should be teachable,'" [1562] adding, "But he is teachable who is gentle and meek to learn; for a bishop ought not only to teach, but to learn as well, since he is indeed the better teacher who daily grows and advances by learning better things;" [1563] --in these words assuredly the holy man, endowed with pious charity, sufficiently points out that we should not hesitate to read his letters in such a sense, that we should feel no difficulty if the Church should afterwards confirm what had been discovered by further and longer discussions; because, as there were many things which the learned Cyprian might teach, so there was still something which the teachable Cyprian might learn. But the

admonition that he gives us, "that we should go back to the fountain, that is, to apostolic tradition, and thence turn the channel of truth to our times," [1564] is most excellent, and should be followed without hesitation. It is handed down to us, therefore, as he himself records, by the apostles, that there is "one God, and one Christ, and one hope, and one faith, and one Church, and one baptism." [1565]Since then we find that in the times of the apostles themselves there were some who had not the one hope, but had the one baptism, the truth is so brought down to us from the fountain itself, that it is clear to us that it is possible that though there is one Church, as there is one hope, and one baptism, they may yet have the one baptism who have not the one Church; just as even in those early times it was possible that men should have the one baptism who had not the one hope. For how had they one hope with the holy and the just, who used to say, "Let us eat and drink, for to-morrow we die," [1566] asserting that there was no resurrection of the dead? And yet they were among the very men to whom the same apostle says, "Was Paul crucified for you? or were you baptized in the name of Paul?" [1567]For he writes most manifestly to them, saying, "How say some among you that there is no resurrection of the dead?" [1568]

[1562] "Docibilis;" and so the passage (2 Tim. ii. 24) is quoted frequently by Augustin. The English version, "apt to teach," is more true to the original, didaktikos.

[1563] Cypr. Ep. lxxiv. 10.

[1564] Cypr. Ep. lxxiv. 10.

[1565] Ib. 11, and Eph. iv. 4-6.

[1566] 1 Cor. xv. 32.

[1567] 1 Cor. i. 13.

[1568] 1 Cor. xv. 12.

Chapter 27.

38. And in that the Church is thus described in the Song of Songs, "A garden enclosed is my sister, my spouse; a spring shut up, a fountain sealed, a well of living water; thy plants are an orchard of pomegranates, with pleasant fruits;" [1569] I dare not understand this save of the holy and just,--not of the covetous, and defrauders, and robbers, and usurers, and drunkards, and the envious, of whom we yet both learn most fully from Cyprian's letters, as I have often shown, and teach ourselves, that they had baptism in common with the just, in common with whom they certainly had not Christian charity. For I would that some one would tell me how they "crept into the garden enclosed and the fountain sealed," of whom Cyprian bears witness that they renounced the world in word and not in deed, and that yet they were within the Church. For if they both are themselves there, and are themselves the bride of Christ, can she then be as she is described "without spot or wrinkle," [1570] and is the fair dove defiled with such a portion of her members? Are these the thorns among which she is a lily, as it is said in the same Song? [1571]So far therefore, as the lily extends, so far does "the garden enclosed and the fountain sealed," namely, through all those just persons who are Jews inwardly in the circumcision of the heart [1572] (for "the king's daughter is all glorious within" [1573]), in whom is the fixed number of the saints predestined before the foundation of the world. But that multitude of thorns, whether in secret or in open separation, is pressing on it from without, above number. "If I would declare them," it is said, "and speak of them, they

are more than can be numbered." [1574]The number, therefore, of the just persons, "who are the called according to His purpose," [1575] of whom it is said, "The Lord knoweth them that are His," [1576] is itself "the garden enclosed, the fountain sealed, a well of living water, the orchard of pomegranates with pleasant fruits." Of this number some live according to the Spirit, and enter on the excellent way of charity; and when they "restore a man that is overtaken in a fault in the spirit of meekness, they consider themselves, lest they also be tempted." [1577]And when it happens that they also are themselves overtaken, the affection of charity is but a little checked, and not extinguished; and again rising up and being kindled afresh, it is restored to its former course. For they know how to say, "My soul melteth for heaviness: strengthen thou me according unto Thy word." [1578]But when "in anything they be otherwise minded, God shall reveal even this unto them," [1579] if they abide in the burning flame of charity, and do not break the bond of peace. But some who are yet carnal, and full of fleshly appetites, are instant in working out their progress; and that they may become fit for heavenly food, they are nourished with the milk of the holy mysteries, they avoid in the fear of God whatever is manifestly corrupt even in the opinion of the world, and they strive most watchfully that they may be less and less delighted with worldly and temporal matters. They observe most constantly the rule of faith which has been sought out with diligence; and if in aught they stray from it, they submit to speedy correction under Catholic authority, although, in Cyprian's words, they be tossed about, by reason of their fleshly appetite, with the various conflicts of phantasies. There are some also who as yet live wickedly, or even lie in heresies or the superstitions of the Gentiles, and yet even then "the Lord knoweth them that are His." For, in that unspeakable foreknowledge of God, many who seem to be without are in reality within, and many who seem to be within yet really are without. Of all those, therefore, who, if I may so say, are inwardly and secretly within, is that "enclosed garden" composed, "the fountain sealed, a well of living water, the orchard of pomegranates, with pleasant fruits." The divinely imparted gifts of these are partly peculiar to themselves, as in this world the charity that never faileth, and in the world to come eternal life; partly they are common with evil and perverse men, as all the other things in which consist the holy mysteries.

[1569] Cant. iv. 12, 13.

[1570] Eph. v. 27.

[1571] Cant. ii. 2.

[1572] Rom. ii. 29.

[1573] Ps. xlv. 13.

[1574] Ps. xl. 5.

[1575] Rom. viii. 28.

[1576] 2 Tim. ii. 19.

[1577] Gal. vi. 1.

[1578] Ps. cxix. 28.

[1579] Phil. iii. 15.

Chapter 28.

39. Hence, therefore, we have now set before us an easier and more simple consideration of that ark of which Noah was the builder and pilot. For Peter says that in the ark of Noah, "few, that is, eight souls, were saved by water. The like figure whereunto even baptism doth also now save us, (not the putting away of the filth of the flesh, but the answer of a good conscience towards God)." [1580] Wherefore, if those appear to men to be baptized in Catholic unity who renounce the world in words only and not in deeds, how do they belong to the mystery of this ark in whom there is not the answer of a good conscience? Or how are they saved by water, who, making a bad use of holy baptism, though they seem to be within, yet persevere to the end of their days in a wicked and abandoned course of life? Or how can they fail to be saved by water, of whom Cyprian himself records that they were in time past simply admitted to the Church with the baptism which they had received in heresy? For the same unity of the ark saved them, in which no one has been saved except by water. For Cyprian himself says, "The Lord is able of His mercy to grant pardon, and not to sever from the gifts of His Church those who, being in all simplicity admitted to the Church, have fallen asleep within her pale." [1581] If not by water, how in the ark? If not in the ark, how in the Church? But if in the Church, certainly in the ark; and if in the ark, certainly by water. It is therefore possible that some who have been baptized without may be considered, through the foreknowledge of God, to have been really baptized within, because within the water begins to be profitable to them unto salvation; nor can they be said to have been otherwise saved in the ark except by water. And again, some who seemed to have been baptized within may be considered, through the same foreknowledge of God, more truly to have been baptized without, since, by

making a bad use of baptism, they die by water, which then happened to no one who was not outside the ark. Certainly it is clear that, when we speak of within and without in relation to the Church, it is the position of the heart that we must consider, not that of the body, since all who are within in heart are saved in the unity of the ark through the same water, through which all who are in heart without, whether they are also in body without or not, die as enemies of unity. As therefore it was not another but the same water that saved those who were placed within the ark, and destroyed those who were left without the ark, so it is not by different baptisms, but by the same, that good Catholics are saved, and bad Catholics or heretics perish. But what the most blessed Cyprian thinks of the Catholic Church, and how the heretics are utterly crushed by his authority; notwithstanding the much I have already said, I have yet determined to set forth by itself, if God will, with somewhat greater fullness and perspicuity, so soon as I shall have first said about his Council what I think is due from me, which, in God's will, I shall attempt in the following book.

[1580] 1 Pet. iii. 20, 21.

[1581] Cypr. Ep. lxxiii. 23.

Book VI.

In which is considered the Council of Carthage, held under the authority and presidency of Cyprian, to determine the question of the baptism of heretics.

Chapter 1.

1. It might perhaps have been sufficient, that after the reasons have been so often repeated, and considered, and discussed

with such variety of treatment, supplemented too, with the addition of proofs from holy Scripture, and the concurrent testimony of so many passages from Cyprian himself, even those who are slow of heart should thus understand, as I believe they do, that the baptism of Christ cannot be rendered void by any perversity on the part of man, whether in administering or receiving it. And when we find that in those times, when the point in question was decided in a manner contrary to ancient custom, after discussions carried on without violation of saving charity and unity, it appeared to some even eminent men who were bishops of Christ, among whom the blessed Cyprian was specially conspicuous, that the baptism of Christ could not exist among heretics or schismatics, this simply arose from their not distinguishing the sacrament from the effect or use of the sacrament; and because its effect and use were not found among heretics in freeing them from their sins and setting their hearts right, the sacrament itself was also thought to be wanting among them. But if we turn our eyes to the multitude of chaff within the Church, since these also who are perverse and lead an abandoned life in unity itself appear to have no power either of giving or retaining remission of sins, seeing that it is not to the wicked but the good sons that it was said, "Whosesoever sins ye remit, they are remitted unto them; and whosesoever sins ye retain, they are retained," [1582] yet that such persons both have, and give, and receive the sacrament of baptism, was sufficiently manifest to the pastors of the Catholic Church dispersed over the whole world, through whom the original custom was afterwards confirmed by the authority of a plenary Council; so that even the sheep which was straying outside, and had received the mark of the Lord from false plunderers outside, if it seek the salvation of Christian unity, is purified from error, is freed from captivity, is healed of its wound, and yet the mark of the Lord is recognized rather than rejected in it; since the mark itself is often impressed both by wolves and on wolves, who seem indeed to be within the fold, but yet are proved by the fruits of their conduct, in which they persevere even to the end, not to belong to that sheep which is one in many; because, according to the foreknowledge of God, as many sheep wander outside, so many wolves lurk treacherously within, among whom the Lord yet knoweth them that are His, which hear only the voice of the Shepherd, even when He calls by the voice of men like the Pharisees, of whom it was said, "Whatsoever they bid you observe that observe and do." [1583]

2. For as the spiritual man, keeping "the end of the commandment," that is, "charity out of a pure heart, and of a good conscience, and of faith unfeigned," [1584] can see some things less clearly out of a body which is yet "corruptible and presseth down the soul," [1585] and is liable to be otherwise minded in some things which God will reveal [1586] to him in His own good time if he abide in the same charity, so in a carnal and perverse man something good and useful may be found, which has its origin not in the man himself, but in some other source. For as in the fruitful branch there is found something which must be purged that it may bring forth more fruit, so also a grape is often found to hang on a cane that is barren and dry or fettered. And so, as it is foolish to love the portions which require purging in the fruitful branch, while he acts wisely who does not reject the sweet fruit wherever it may hang, so, if any one cuts himself off from unity by rebaptizing, simply because it seemed to Cyprian that one ought to baptize again those who came from the heretics, such a man turns aside from what merits praise in that great man, and follows what

requires correction, and does not even attain to the very thing he follows after. For Cyprian, while grievously abhorring, in his zeal for God, all those who severed themselves from unity, thought that thereby they were separated from baptism itself; while these men, thinking it at most a slight offense that they themselves are severed from the unity of Christ, even maintain that His baptism is not in that unity, but issued forth with them. Therefore they are so far from the fruitfulness of Cyprian, as not even to be equal to the parts in him which needed purging.

[1582] John xx. 23.

[1583] Matt. xxiii. 3.

[1584] 1 Tim. i. 5.

[1585] Wisd. ix. 15.

[1586] Phil. iii. 15.

Chapter 2.

3. Again, if any one not having charity, and walking in the abandoned paths of a most wicked life, seems to be within while he really is without, and at the same time does not seek for the repetition of baptism even in the case of heretics, it in no wise helps his barrenness, because he is not rendered fruitful with his own fruit, but laden with that of others. But it is possible that some one may flourish in the root of charity, and may be most rightly minded in the point in which Cyprian was otherwise minded, and yet there may be more that is fruitful in Cyprian than in him, more that requires purging in him than in Cyprian. Not only, therefore, do we not compare bad Catholics with the blessed Cyprian, but even good Catholics we

do not hastily pronounce to be on an equality with him whom our pious mother Church counts among the few rare men of surpassing excellence and grace, although these others may recognize the baptism of Christ even among heretics, while he thought otherwise; so that, by the instance of Cyprian, who saw one point less clearly, and yet remained most firm in the unity of the Church, it might be shown more clearly to heretics what a sacrilegious crime it was to break the bond of peace. For neither were the blind Pharisees, although they sometimes enjoined what was right to be done, to be compared to the Apostle Peter, though he at times enjoined what was not right. But not only is their dryness not to be compared to his greenness, but even the fruit of others may not be deemed equal to his fertility. For no one now compels the Gentiles to judaize, and yet no one now in the Church, however great his progress in goodness, may be compared with the apostleship of Peter. Wherefore, while rendering due reverence, and paying, so far as I can, the fitting honor to the peaceful bishop and glorious martyr Cyprian, I yet venture to say that his view concerning the baptism of schismatics and heretics was contrary to that which was afterwards brought to light by a decision, not of mine, but of the whole Church, confirmed and strengthened by the authority of a plenary Council: just as, while paying the reverence he deserves to Peter, the first of the apostles and most eminent of martyrs, I yet venture to say that he did not do right in compelling the Gentiles to judaize; for this also, I say, not of my own teaching, but according to the wholesome doctrine of the Apostle Paul, retained and preserved through out the whole Church. [1587]

4. Therefore, in discussing the opinion of Cyprian, though myself of far inferior merit to Cyprian, I say that good and bad

alike can have, can give, can receive the sacrament of baptism,--the good, indeed, to their health and profit; the bad to their destruction and ruin,--while the sacrament itself is of equal perfectness in both of them; and that it is of no consequence to its equal perfectness in all, how much worse the man may be that has it among the bad, just as it makes no difference how much better he may be that has it among the good. And accordingly it makes no difference either how much worse he may be that confers it, as it makes no difference how much better he may be; and so it makes no difference how much worse he may be that receives it, as it makes no difference how much better he may be. For the sacrament is equally holy, in virtue of its own excellence, both in those who are unequally just, and in those who are unequally unjust.

[1587] Gal. ii. 14.

Chapter 3.

5. But I think that we have sufficiently shown, both from the canon of Scripture, and from the letters of Cyprian himself, that bad men, while by no means converted to a better mind, can have, and confer, and receive baptism, of whom it is most clear that they do not belong to the holy Church of God, though they seem to be within it, inasmuch as they are covetous, robbers, usurers, envious, evil thinkers, and the like; while she is one dove, [1588] modest and chaste, a bride without spot or wrinkle, [1589] a garden enclosed, a fountain sealed, an orchard of pomegranates with pleasant fruits, [1590] with all similar properties which are attributed to her; and all this can only be understood to be in the good, and holy, and just,--following, that is, not only the operations of the gifts of God, which are common to good and bad alike, but also the

inner bond of charity conspicuous in those who have the Holy Spirit, to whom the Lord says, "Whosoever sins ye remit, they are remitted unto them; and whosoever sins ye retain, they are retained." [1591]

[1588] Cant. vi. 8, 9.

[1589] Eph. v. 27; Cp. Aug. Retract. ii. 18.

[1590] Cant. iv. 12, 13.

[1591] John xx. 23.

Chapter 4.

6. And so it is clear that no good ground is shown herein why the bad man, who has baptism, may not also confer it; and as he has it to destruction, so he may also confer it to destruction,--not because this is the character of the thing conferred, nor of the person conferring, but because it is the character of him on whom it is conferred. For when a bad man confers it on a good man, that is, on one in the bond of unity, converted with a true conversion, the wickedness of him who confers it makes no severance between the good sacrament which is conferred, and the good member of the Church on whom it is conferred. And when his sins are forgiven him on his true conversion to God, they are forgiven by those to whom he is united by his true conversion. For the same Spirit forgives them, which is given to all the saints that cling to one another in love, whether they know one another in the body or not. Similarly when a man's sins are retained, they are assuredly retained by those from whom he, in whom they are retained, separates himself by dissimilarity of life, and by the turning away of a corrupt heart, whether they know him in the body or not.

Chapter 5.

7. Wherefore all bad men are separated in the spirit from the good; but if they are separated in the body also by a manifest dissension, they are made yet worse. But, as it has been said, it makes no difference to the holiness of baptism how much worse the man may be that has it, or how much worse he that confers it: yet he that is separated may confer it, as he that is separated may have it; but as he has it to destruction, so he may confer it to destruction. But he on whom he confers it may receive it to his soul's health, if he, on his part, receive it not in separation; as it has happened to many that, in a catholic spirit, and with heart not alienated from the unity of peace, they have, under some pressure of impending death, turned hastily to some heretic and received from him the baptism of Christ without any share in his perversity, so that, whether dying or restored to life, they by no means remain in communion with those to whom they never passed in heart. But if the recipient himself has received the baptism in separation, he receives it so much the more to his destruction, in proportion to the greatness of the good which he has not received well; and it tends the more to his destruction in his separation, as it would avail the more to the salvation of one in unity. And so, if, reforming himself from his perverseness and turning from his separation, he should come to the Catholic peace, his sins are remitted through the bond of peace and the same baptism under which his sins were retained through the sacrilege of separation, because that is always holy both in the just and the unjust, which is neither increased by the righteousness nor diminished by the unrighteousness of any man.

8. This being the case, what bearing has it on so clear a truth, that many of his fellow-bishops agreed with Cyprian in that

opinion, and advanced their own several opinions on the same side, except that his charity towards the unity of Christ might become more and more conspicuous? For if he had been the only one to hold that opinion, with no one to agree with him, he might have been thought, in remaining, to have shrunk from the sin of schism, because he found no companions in his error; but when so many agreed with him, he showed, by remaining in unity with the rest who thought differently from him, that he preserved the most sacred bond of universal catholicity, not from any fear of isolation, but from the love of peace. Wherefore it might indeed seem now to be superfluous to consider the several opinions of the other bishops also in that Council; but since those who are slow in heart think that no answer has been made at all, if to any passage in any discourse the answer which might be brought to bear on the spot be given not there but somewhere else, it is better that by reading much they should be polished into sharpness, than that by understanding little they should have room left for complaining that the argument has not been fairly conducted.

Chapter 6.

9. First, then, let us record for further consideration the case proposed for decision by Cyprian himself, with which he initiates the proceedings of the Council, and by which he shows a peaceful spirit, abounding in the fruitfulness of Christian charity. "Ye have read," he says, "most beloved colleagues, what Jubaianus, our fellow-bishop, has written to me, consulting my poor ability about the unlawful and profane baptism of heretics, and what I have written back to him, expressing to him the same opinion that I have expressed once and again and often, that heretics coming to the Church ought to be baptized, and sanctified with the baptism of the Church. Another letter also

of Jubaianus has been read to you, in which, agreeably to his sincere and religious devotion, in answer to our epistle, he not only expressed his assent to it, but also gratefully acknowledged that he had received instruction. It remains that we should individually express our opinions on this same subject, judging no one, and removing no one from the right of communion if he should entertain a different opinion. For neither does any one of us set himself up as a bishop of bishops, or by tyrannical terror force his colleagues to the necessity of obeying, since every bishop, in the free use of his liberty and power, has the right of free judgment, and can no more be judged by another than he can himself judge another. But we are all awaiting the judgment of our Lord Jesus Christ who alone has the power both of preferring us in the government of His Church, and of judging of our actions." [1592]

[1592] Conc. Carth., the seventh under Cyprian, A.D. 256. Introduction.

Chapter 7.

10. I have already, I think, argued to the best of my power, in the preceding books, in the interests of Catholic unanimity and counsel, in whose unity these continued as pious members, in reply not only to the letter which Cyprian wrote to Jubaianus, but also to that which he sent to Quintus, and that which, in conjunction with certain of his colleagues, he sent to certain other colleagues, and that which he sent to Pompeius. Wherefore it seems now to be fitting to consider also what the others severally thought, and that with the liberty of which he himself would not deprive us, as he says, "Judging no one, nor removing any from the right of communion if he entertain different opinions." And that he did not say this with the

object of arriving at the hidden thoughts of his colleagues, extracted as it were from their secret lurking-places, but because he really loved peace and unity, is very easily to be seen from other passages of the same sort, where he wrote to individuals as to Jubaianus himself. "These things," he says, "we have written very shortly in answer to you, most beloved brother, according to our poor ability, not preventing any one of the bishops by our writing or judgment, from acting as he thinks right, having a free exercise of his own judgment." [1593]And that it might not seem that any one, because of his entertaining different opinions in this same free exercise of his judgment, should be driven from the society of his brethren, he goes on to say, "We, so far as lies in us, do not strive on behalf of heretics against our colleagues and fellow-bishops, with whom we maintain godly unity and the peace of our Lord;" [1594] and a little later he says, "Charity of spirit, respect for our fraternity, the bond of faith, the harmony of the priesthood, are by us maintained with patience and gentleness." [1595]And so also in the epistle which he wrote to Magnus, when he was asked whether there was any difference in the efficacy of baptism by sprinkling or by immersion, "In this matter," he says, "I am too modest and diffident to prevent any one by my judgment from thinking as he deems right, and acting as he thinks." [1596]By which discourses he clearly shows that these subjects were being handled by them at a time when they were not yet received as decided beyond all question, but were being investigated with great care as being yet unrevealed. We, therefore, maintaining on the subject of the identity of all baptisms what must be acknowledged everywhere to be the custom [1597] of the universal Church, and what is confirmed by the decision of general Councils, [1598] and taking greater confidence also from the words of Cyprian, which allowed me even then to hold opinions differing from his own without forfeiting the right of communion, seeing that greater importance and praise were attached to unity, such as the blessed Cyprian and his colleagues, with whom he held that Council, maintained with those of different opinions, disturbing and overthrowing thereby the seditious calumnies of heretics and schismatics in the name of the Lord Jesus Christ, who, speaking by His apostle, says, "Forbearing one another in love, endeavoring to keep the unity of the Spirit in the bond of peace;" [1599] and again, by the mouth of the same apostle, "If in anything ye be otherwise minded, God shall reveal even this unto you," [1600] --we, I say, propose for consideration and discussion the opinions of the holy bishops, without violating the bond of unity and peace with them, in maintaining which we imitate them so far as we can by the aid of the Lord Himself.

[1593] Cypr. Ep. lxxiii. 26.

[1594] Cypr. Ep. lxxiii. 26.

[1595] Cypr. Ep. lxxiii. 26.

[1596] Cypr. Ep. lxix. 12.

[1597] De baptismi simplicitate ubique agnoscendam consuetudinem. The Benedictines give the reading of some Mss.: "De baptismi simplicitate ubique agnoscenda," etc., "maintaining the custom of the universal Church to acknowledge everywhere the identity of baptism."

[1598] Conciliis universalibus.

[1599] Eph. iv. 2, 3.

[1600] Phil. iii. 15.

Chapter 8.

11. Cæcilius of Bilta [1601] said: "I know of one baptism in the one Church and of none outside the Church. The one will be where there is true hope and sure faith. For so it is written, One faith, one hope, one baptism.' [1602]Not among heretics, where there is no hope and a false faith; where all things are done by a lie; where one possessed of a devil exorcises; the question of the sacrament is asked by one from whose mouth and words proceeds a cancer; the faithless gives faith; the guilty gives pardon for sins and Antichrist baptizes in the name of Christ; one accursed of God blesses; the dead promises life; the unpeaceful gives peace; the blasphemer calls on God; the profane administers the priesthood; the sacrilegious sets up the altar. To all this is added this further evil that the servant of the devil dares to celebrate the eucharist. If this be not so, let those who stand by them prove that all of it is false concerning heretics. See the kind of things to which the Church is compelled to assent, being forced to communicate without baptism or the remission of sins. This, brethren, we ought to shun and avoid, separating ourselves from so great a sin, and holding to the one baptism which is granted to the Church alone." [1603]

12. To this I answer, that all who even within the Church profess that they know God, but deny Him in their deeds, such as are the covetous and envious, and those who, because they hate their brethren, are pronounced to be murderers, not on my testimony, but on that of the holy Apostle John, [1604] --all these are both devoid of hope, because they have a bad conscience; and are faithless, because they do not do what they

have vowed to God; and liars, because they make false professions; and possessed of devils, because they give place in their heart to the devil and his angels; and their words work corruption, since they corrupt good manners by evil communications; and they are infidels, because they laugh at the threats which God utters against such men; and accursed, because they live wickedly; and antichrists, because their lives are opposed to Christ; and cursed of God, since holy Scripture everywhere calls down curses on such men; and dead, because they are without the life of righteousness; and unpeaceful, because by their contrary deeds they are at variance with God's behests; and blasphemous, because by their abandoned acts despite is done to the name of Christian; and profane, because they are spiritually shut out from that inner sanctuary of God; and sacrilegious, because by their evil life they defile the temple of God within themselves; and servants of the devil, because they do service to fraud and covetousness, which is idolatry. That of such a kind are some, nay very many, even within the Church, is testified both by Paul the apostle and by Cyprian the bishop. Why, then, do they baptize? Why also are some, who "renounce the world in words and not in deeds," baptized without being converted from a life like this, and not rebaptized when they are converted? And as to what he says with such indignation, "See the kind of things to which the Church is compelled to assent, being forced to communicate without baptism or the remission of sins," he could never have used such expressions had there not been the other bishops who elsewhere forced men to such things. Whence also it is shown that at that time those men held the truer views who did not depart from the primitive custom, which is since confirmed by the consent of a general Council. [1605]But what does he mean by adding, "This, brethren, we ought to shun and avoid, separating ourselves from so great a sin?" For if he means that he is not to do nor to approve of this, that is another matter; but if he means to condemn and sever from him those that hold the contrary opinion, he is setting himself against the earlier words of Cyprian, "Judging no man, nor depriving any of the right of communion if he differ from us."

[1601] Bilta (Biltha, Vilta) was in Africa Proconsularis. This Cæcilius is probably the same as the one addressed by Cyprian in Ep. lxiii., and who unites with Cyprian and other bishops in letters addressed to others. Epp. iv. (to Pomponius), lvii., lxvii., lxx.

[1602] Eph. iv. 4, 5.

[1603] Conc. Carth. sec. 1.

[1604] 1 John iii. 15.

[1605] Concilii universitate.

Chapter 9.

13. The elder Felix [1606] of Migirpa said: "I think that every one coming from heresy should be baptized. For in vain does any one suppose that he has been baptized there, seeing that there is no baptism save the one true baptism in the Church; for there is one Lord, and one faith, and one Church, in which rests the one baptism, and holiness, and the rest. For the things that are practised without have no power to work salvation."

14. To what Felix of Migirpa said we answer as follows. If the one true baptism did not exist except in the Church, it surely would not exist in those who depart from unity. But it does exist in them, since they do not receive it when they return,

simply because they had not lost it when they departed. But as regards his statement, that "the things that are practised without have no power to work salvation," I agree with him, and think that it is quite true; for it is one thing that baptism should not be there, and another that it should have no power to work salvation. For when men come to the peace of the Catholic Church, then what was in them before they joined it, but did not profit them, begins at once to profit them.

[1606] This section is wanting in the Mss. and in the edition of Amerbach, so that it has been supposed to have been added by Erasmus from Cyprian (Conc. Carth. sec. 2),--the name of Felix (really Primus), which is not found in Cyprian, being derived from the following section of Augustin. So Hartel: Primas a Misgirpa dixit. Migirpa or Misgirpa, was in Zeugitana. This Primus is seemingly identical with the Primus of Cypr. Epp. 67 (following Cæcilius), and 70 (preceding Cæcilius).

Chapter 10.

15. To the declaration of Polycarp of Adrumetum, [1607] that "those who declare the baptism of heretics to be valid, make ours of none effect," we answer, if that is the baptism of heretics which is given by heretics, then that is the baptism of the covetous and murderers which is given by them within the Church. But if this be not their baptism, neither is the other the baptism of heretics; and so it is Christ's, by whomsoever it be given.

[1607] Adrumetum (Hadrumetum) was an ancient Phoenician settlement, made a Roman colony by Trajan, on the coast of the Sinus Neapolitanus, some ninety miles south-east of Carthage, capital of Byzacium. Cyprian writes to Bp. Cornelius, Ep. xlviii., vindicating Polycarp: his name occurs also in the titles of Cypr. Epp. lvii., lxvii. (after Primus), and lxx. (after Cæcilius).

Chapter 11.

16. Novatus of Thamugadis [1608] said: "Though we know that all Scripture gives its testimony respecting saving baptism, yet we ought to express our belief that heretics and schismatics, coming to the Church with the semblance of having been baptized, ought to be baptized in the unfailing fountain; and that therefore, according to the testimony of the Scriptures, and according to the decree of those most holy men, our colleagues, [1609] all schismatics and heretics who are converted to the Church ought to be baptized; and that, moreover, all that seemed to have received ordination should be admitted as simple laymen."

17. Novatus of Thamugadis has stated what he has done, but he has brought forward no proofs by which to show that he ought to have acted as he did. For he has made mention of the testimony of the Scriptures, and the decree of his colleagues, but he has not adduced out of them anything which we could consider.

[1608] Thamugadis (Thamogade), a town in Numidia, on the east side of Mount Aurasius. The whole opinion of Novatus (Conc. Carth. sec. 4), is omitted in the Mss.

[1609] The words in Cyprian are, "secundum decretum collegarum nostrorum sanctissimæ memoriæ virorum." The decree referred to is one of the Council held by Agrippinus.

Chapter 12.

18. Nemesianus of Tubunæ [1610] said: "That the baptism which is given by heretics and schismatics is not true is everywhere declared in the holy Scriptures, inasmuch as their very prelates are false Christs and false prophets, as the Lord declares by the mouth of Solomon, Whoso trusteth in lies, the same feedeth the winds; he also followeth flying birds. For he deserteth the ways of his own vineyard, and hath strayed from the paths of his own field. For he walketh through pathless and dry places, and a land destined to thirst; and he gathereth fruitless weeds in his hands.' [1611]And again, Abstain from strange water, and drink not of a strange fountain, that thou mayest live long, and that years may be added to thy life.' [1612] And in the gospel our Lord Jesus Christ spake with His own voice, saying, Except a man be born of water and of the Spirit, he cannot enter into the kingdom of God.' [1613]This is the Spirit which from the beginning moved upon the face of the waters.' [1614]For neither can the Spirit act without the water, nor the water without the Spirit. Ill, therefore, for themselves do some interpret, saying that by imposition of hands they receive the Holy Ghost, and are received into the Church, when it is manifest that they ought to be born again by both sacraments in the Catholic Church. For then indeed will they be able to become the sons of God, as the apostle says, Endeavoring to keep the unity of the Spirit in the bond of peace. There is one body, and one Spirit, even as ye are called in one hope of your calling; one Lord, one faith, one baptism, one God.' [1615]All this the Catholic Church asserts. And again he says in the gospel, That which is born of the flesh is flesh, and that which is born of the Spirit is spirit; for the Spirit is God, and is born of God.' [1616]Therefore all things whatsoever all heretics and schismatics do are carnal, as the apostle says, Now the works of the flesh are manifest, which

are these: fornication, uncleanness, lasciviousness, idolatry, witchcraft, hatred, variance, emulations, wrath, seditions, heresies, and such like: of the which I tell you before, as I have also told you in time past, that they which do such things shall not inherit the kingdom of God.' [1617] The apostle condemns, equally with all the wicked, those also who cause divisions, that is, schismatics and heretics. Unless therefore they receive that saving baptism which is one, and found only in the Catholic Church, they cannot be saved, but will be condemned with the carnal in the judgment of the Lord."

19. Nemesianus of Tubunæ has advanced many passages of Scripture to prove his point; but he has in fact said much on behalf of the view of the Catholic Church, which we have undertaken to set forth and maintain. Unless, indeed, we must suppose that he does not "trust in what is false" who trusts in the hope of things temporal, as do all covetous men and robbers, and those "who renounce the world in words but not in deeds," of whom Cyprian yet bears witness that such men not only baptize, but even are baptized within the Church. [1618]For they themselves also "follow flying birds," [1619] since they do not attain to what they desire. But not only the heretic, but everyone who leads an evil life "deserteth the ways of his own vineyard, and hath strayed from the paths of his own field. And he walketh through pathless and dry places, and a land destined to thirst; and he gathereth fruitless weeds in his hands;" because all justice is fruitful, and all iniquity is barren. Those, again, who "drink strange water out of a strange fountain," are found not only among heretics, but among all who do not live according to the teaching of God, and do live according to the teaching of the devil. For if he were speaking of baptism, he would not say, "Do not drink of a strange

fountain," but, do not wash thyself in a strange fountain. Again, I do not see at all what aid he gets towards proving his point from the words of our Lord, "Except a man be born of water and of the Spirit, he cannot enter into the kingdom of God." [1620]For it is one thing to say that every one who shall enter into the kingdom of heaven is first born again of water and the Spirit, because except a man be born of water and of the Spirit, he shall not enter into the kingdom of heaven, which is the Lord's saying, and is true; another thing to say that every one who is born of water and the Spirit shall enter into the kingdom of heaven, which is assuredly false. For Simon Magus also was born of water and of the Spirit, [1621] and yet he did not enter into the kingdom of heaven; and this may possibly be the case with heretics as well. Or if only those are born of the Spirit who are changed with a true conversion, all "who renounce the world in word and not in deed" are assuredly not born of the Spirit, but of water only, and yet they are within the Church, according to the testimony of Cyprian. For we must perforce grant one of two things,--either those who renounce the world deceitfully are born of the Spirit, though it is to their destruction, not to salvation, and therefore heretics may be so born; or if what is written, that "the Holy Spirit of discipline will flee deceit," [1622] extends to proving as much as this, that those who renounce the world deceitfully are not born of the Spirit, then a man may be baptized with water, and not born of the Spirit, and Nemesianus says in vain that neither the Spirit can work without the water, nor the water without the Spirit. Indeed it has been already often shown how it is possible that men should have one baptism in common who have not one Church, as it is possible that in the body of the Church herself those who are sanctified by their righteousness, and those who are polluted through their covetousness, may not have the same one Spirit, and yet have the same one baptism. For it is said "one body," that is, the Church, just as it is said "one Spirit" and "one baptism." The other arguments which he has adduced rather favor our position. For he has brought forward a proof from the gospel, in the words, "That which is born of the flesh is flesh, and that which is born of the Spirit is spirit; for the Spirit is God, and born of God;" [1623] and he has advanced the argument that therefore all things that are done by any heretic or schismatic are carnal, as the apostle says, "The works of the flesh are manifest, which are these: fornication, uncleanness;" and so he goes through the list which the apostle there enumerates, amongst which he has reckoned heresies, since "they who do such things shall not inherit the kingdom of God." [1624]Then he goes on to add, that "therefore the apostle condemns with all wicked men those also who cause division, that is, schismatics and heretics." And in this he does well, that when he enumerates the works of the flesh, among which are also heresies, he found and declared that the apostle condemns them all alike. Let him therefore question the holy Cyprian himself, and learn from him how many even within the Church live according to the evil works of the flesh, which the apostle condemns in common with the heresies, and yet these both baptize and are baptized. Why then are heretics alone said to be incapable of possessing baptism, which is possessed by the very partners in their condemnation?

[1610] Tubunæ, a town in Mauritania Cæsariensis. Nemesianus probably same with one of that name in Cypr. Epp. lxii., lxx., lxxvi., lxxvii.

[1611] Prov. ix. 12, LXX., the passage being altogether absent in the Hebrew, and consequently in the English version. Probably in N. Afr. version. The text in Erasmus is somewhat different, and was revised by the Louvain editors to bring it into harmony with the answer of Augustin and the text of Cyprian (Conc. Carth. sec. 5).

[1612] Prov. ix. 18, LXX., possibly N. Afr. version also.

[1613] John iii. 5.

[1614] Gen. i. 2.

[1615] Eph. iv. 3-6.

[1616] Quoniam Spiritus Deus est, et de Deo natus est. These words are found at the end of John iii. 6, in the oldest Latin Ms. (in the Bodleian Library), and their meaning appears to be, as given in the text, that whatsoever is born of the Spirit is spirit, since the Holy Ghost, being God, and born of, or proceeding from God, in virtue of His supreme power makes those to be spirits whom He regenerates. If the meaning had been (as Bishop Fell takes it), that "he who is born of the Spirit is born of God," the neuter "de Deo natum est" would have been required. To refer "Spiritus Deus est," with the Benedictines, to John iv. 24, "God is a Spirit," reverses the grammar and destroys the sense of the passage. The above explanation is taken from the preface to Cyprian by the monk of St. Maur (Maranus), p. xxxvi., quoted by Routh, Rel. Sac. iii. 193.

[1617] Gal. v. 19-21.

[1618] Cypr. Ep. xi. 1.

[1619] Prov. ix. 12, cp. LXX.

[1620] John iii. 5.

[1621] Acts viii. 13.

[1622] Wisd. i. 5.

[1623] John iii. 6.

[1624] Gal. v. 19-21.

Chapter 13.

20. Januarius of Lambæse [1625] said: "Following the authority of the holy Scriptures, I pronounce that all heretics should be baptized, and so admitted into the holy Church." [1626]

21. To him we answer, that, following the authority of the holy Scriptures, a universal Council of the whole world decreed that the baptism of Christ was not to be disavowed even when found among heretics. But if he had brought forward any proof from the Scriptures, we should have shown either that they were not against us, or even that they were for us, as we proceed to do with him who follows.

[1625] Lambæse (Lambese) was one of the chief cities in southern Numidia. This Januarius is not unlikely identical with the first of that name in Cypr. Ep. lxvii., and with the one of Epp. lxii. and lxx. For an opponent of Cyprian in Lambese, see Cypr. Epp. xxxvi. and lix.

[1626] Conc. Carth. sec. 6.

Chapter 14.

22. Lucius of Castra Galbæ [1627] said: "Since the Lord hath said in His gospel, Ye are the salt of the earth: but if the salt have lost his savor, that which is salted from it shall be thenceforth good for nothing, but to be cast out, and to be

trodden under foot of men;' [1628] and seeing that again, after His resurrection, when sending forth His apostles, He commanded them, saying, All power is given unto me in heaven and in earth: go ye therefore, and teach all nations, baptizing them in the name of the Father, and of the Son, and of the Holy Ghost,' [1629] --since then it is plain that heretics, that is, the enemies of Christ, have not the full confession of the sacrament, also that schismatics cannot reason with spiritual wisdom, since they themselves, by withdrawing when they have lost their savor from the Church, which is one, have become contrary to it, [1630] let that be done which is written, The houses of those that are opposed to the law must needs be cleansed;' [1631] and it therefore follows that those who have been polluted by being baptized by men opposed to Christ should first be cleansed, and only then baptized." [1632]

23. Lucius of Castra Galbæ has brought forward a proof from the gospel, in the words of the Lord, "Ye are the salt of the earth: but if the salt have lost his savor, that which is salted from it shall be good for nothing, but to be cast out, and to be trodden under foot of men;" just as though we maintained that men when cast out were of any profit for the salvation either of themselves or of any one else. But those also who, though seeming to be within, are yet of such a kind, not only are without spiritually, but will in the end be separated in the body also. For all such are for nothing. But it does not therefore follow that the sacrament of baptism which is in them is nothing. For even in the very men who are cast out, if they return to their senses and come back, the salvation which had departed from them returns; but the baptism does not return, because it never had departed. And in what the Lord says, "Go therefore, and teach all nations, baptizing them in the name of

the Father, and of the Son, and of the Holy Ghost," He did not permit any to baptize except the good, inasmuch as He did not say to the bad, "Whosoever sins ye remit, they are remitted unto them; and whosoever sins ye retain, they are retained." [1633]How then do the wicked baptize within, who cannot remit sins? How also is it that they baptize the wicked whose hearts are not changed, whose sins are yet upon them, as John says, "He that hateth his brother is in darkness even until now?" [1634]But if the sins of these men are remitted when they join themselves in the close bonds of love to the good and just, through whom sins are remitted in the Church, though they have been baptized by the wicked, so the sins of those also are remitted who come from without and join themselves by the inner bond of peace to the same framework of the body of Christ. Yet the baptism of Christ should be acknowledged in both, and held invalid in none, whether before they are converted, though then it profit them nothing, or after they are converted, that so it may profit them, as he says, "Since they themselves, by withdrawing when they have lost their savor from the Church, which is one, have become contrary to it, let that be done which is written, The houses of those that are opposed to the law must need be cleansed.' And it therefore follows," he goes on to say, "that those who have been polluted by being baptized by men opposed to Christ should first be cleansed, and only then baptized." What then? Are thieves and murderers not contrary to the law, which says, "Thou shalt not kill; thou shalt not steal?" [1635] "They must therefore needs be cleansed." Who will deny it? And yet not only those who are baptized by such within the Church, but also those who, being such themselves, are baptized without being changed in heart, are nevertheless exempt from further baptism when they are so changed. So great is the force of the sacrament of mere baptism, that though we allow that a man who has been baptized and continues to lead an evil life requires to be cleansed, we yet forbid him to be any more baptized.

[1627] Castra Galbæ was most likely in Numidia. Lucius as bishop occurs in Cypr. Epp. lxvii., lxx., lxxvi. and lxxvii., but it is doubtful to which of the four of this name attendant on this council these references may apply.

[1628] Matt. v. 13. "Id quod salietur ex eo, ad nihilum valebit."

[1629] Matt. xxviii. 18, 19.

[1630] Recedendo infatuati contrarii facti sunt. Dr. Routh from a Ms. in his own possession, inserts "et" after "infatuati."-- "have lost their savor and become contrary to the Church." Rel. Sac. iii. p. 194.

[1631] Prov. xiv. 9, cp. LXX.

[1632] Conc. Carth. sec. 7.

[1633] John xx. 23.

[1634] 1 John ii. 9.

[1635] Ex. xx. 13, 15.

Chapter 15.

24. Crescens of Cirta [1636] said: "The letters of our most beloved Cyprian to Jubaianus, and also to Stephen, [1637] having been read in so large an assembly of our most holy brethren in the priesthood, containing as they do so large a body of sacred testimony derived from the Scriptures that give us our God, [1638] that we have every reason to assent to them,

being all united by the grace of God, I give my judgment that all heretics or schismatics who wish to come to the Catholic Church should not enter therein unless they have been first exorcised and baptized; with the obvious exception of those who have been originally baptized in the Catholic Church, these being reconciled and admitted to the penance of the Church by the imposition of hands." [1639]

25. Here we are warned once more to inquire why he says, "Except, of course, those who have been originally baptized in the Catholic Church." Is it because they had not lost what they had before received? Why then could they not also transmit outside the Church what they were able to possess outside? Is it that outside it is unlawfully transmitted? But neither is it lawfully possessed outside, and yet it is possessed; so it is unlawfully given outside, but yet it is given. But what is given to the person returning from heresy who had been baptized inside, is given to the person coming to the Church who had been baptized outside,--that is, that he may have lawfully inside what before he had unlawfully outside. But perhaps some one may ask what was said on this point in the letter of the blessed Cyprian to Stephen, which is mentioned in this judgment, though not in the opening address to the Council,--I suppose because it was not considered necessary. For Crescens stated that the letter itself had been read in the assembly, which I have no doubt was done, if I am not mistaken, as is customary, in order that the bishops, being already assembled, might receive some information at the same time on the subject contained in that letter. For it certainly has no bearing on the present subject; and I am more surprised at Crescens having thought fit to mention it at all, than at its having been passed over in the opening address. But if any one thinks that I have shrunk from

bringing forward something which has been urged in it that is essential to the present point, let him read it and see that what I say is true; or if he finds it otherwise, let him convict me of falsehood. For that letter contains nothing whatsoever about baptism administered among heretics or schismatics, which is the subject of our present argument. [1640]

[1636] Cirta, an inland city of the Massylii in Numidia, was rebuilt by Constantine, and called Constantina.

[1637] See below, on sec. 25.

[1638] Ex Scripturis deificis.

[1639] Conc. Carth. sec. 8.

[1640] There are two letters extant from Cyprian to Stephen, No. 68, respecting Marcianus of Arles, who had joined Novatian, and No. 72, on a Council concerning heretical baptism. It is clear, however, from Ep. lxxiv. 1, that this Council, and consequently the letter to Stephen, was subsequent to the Council under consideration; and consequently Augustin is right in ignoring it, and referring solely to the former. Dr. Routh thinks the words an interpolation, of course before Augustin's time; and they may perhaps have been inserted by some one who had Cyprian's later letter to Stephen before his mind. Rel. Sac. iii. p. 194.

Chapter 16.

26. Nicomedes of Segermi [1641] said: "My judgment is that heretics coming to the Church should be baptized, because they can obtain no remission of sins among sinners outside." [1642]

27. The answer to which is: The judgment of the whole Catholic Church is that heretics, being already baptized with the baptism of Christ, although in heresy, should not be rebaptized on coming to the Church. For if there is no remission of sins among sinners, neither can sinners within the Church remit sins; and yet those who have been baptized by them are not rebaptized.

[1641] Segermi church province of Byzacium. A Nicomedes occurs in Cypr. Epp. lvii., lxvii., lxx.

[1642] Conc. Carth, sec. 9.

Chapter 17.

28. Monnulus of Girba [1643] said: "The truth of our mother, the Catholic Church, hath continued, and still continues among us, brethren, especially in the threefold nature [1644] of baptism, as our Lord says, Go, baptize all nations in the name of the Father, and of the Son, and of the Holy Ghost.' [1645]Since, therefore," he goes on to say, "we know clearly that heretics have neither Father, Son, nor Holy Ghost, they ought, on coming to our mother, the Church, to be truly regenerated and baptized, that the cancer which they had, and the wrath of condemnation, and the destructive energy of error [1646] may be sanctified by the holy and heavenly laver." [1647]

29. To this we answer, That all who are baptized with the baptism that is consecrated in the words of the gospel have the Father, and the Son, and the Holy Ghost in the sacrament alone; but that in heart and in life neither do those have them who live an abandoned and accursed life within.

[1643] Girba, formerly Meninx (Lotophagitis), an island to the south-east of the Lesser Syrtis belonged to church province of Tripolis. For Bp. Monnulus, see Cypr. Ep. lvii.

[1644] In baptismi trinitate. "Quia trina immersione expediebatur, in nomine Patris, Filii, et S. Spiritus."--Bishop Fell.

[1645] Matt. xxviii. 19.

[1646] Erroris offectura. Other readings are "offensa" and "effectura."

[1647] Conc. Carth. sec. 10.

Chapter 18.

30. Secundinus of Cedias [1648] said: "Since our Lord Christ said, He that is not with me is against me,' [1649] and the Apostle John declares those who go out from the Church to be antichrists, [1650] without all doubt the enemies of Christ, and those who are called antichrists, cannot minister the grace of the baptism which gives salvation; and therefore my judgment is that those who take refuge in the Church from the snares of heresy should be baptized by us, who of His condescension are called the friends of God." [1651]

31. The answer to which is, That all are the opponents of Christ, to whom, on their saying, "Lord, have we not in Thy name done many wonderful things?" with all the rest that is there recorded, He shall at the last day answer, "I never knew you: depart from me, ye that work iniquity," [1652] --all which kind of chaff is destined for the fire, if it persevere to the last in its wickedness, whether any part of it fly outside before its winnowing, or whether it seem to be within. If, therefore,

those heretics who come to the Church are to be again baptized, that they may be baptized by the friends of God, are those covetous men, those robbers, murderers, the friends of God, or must those whom they have baptized be baptized afresh?

[1648] Cedias (Cedia) has been identified, but without sufficient reason, with Quidias, or Quiza, in Mauritania Cæsariensis for both places have bishops at the Collation of 411. A Bp. Secundinus is mentioned in Cypr. Epp. lvii., lxvii., but whether these refer to him of Cedias or him of Carpos (ch. 31) cannot be decided.

[1649] Matt. xii. 30.

[1650] 1 John ii. 18.

[1651] Conc. Carth. sec. 11.

[1652] Matt. vii. 22, 23.

Chapter 19.

32. Felix of Bagai [1653] said: "As when the blind leads the blind, both fall into the ditch, [1654] so when a heretic baptizes a heretic, both fall together into death."

33. This is true, but it does not follow that what he adds is true. "And therefore," he says, "the heretic must be baptized and brought to life, lest we who are alive should hold communion with the dead." [1655] Were they not dead who said, "Let us eat and drink, for to-morrow we die?" [1656] for they did not believe in the resurrection of the dead. Those then who were corrupted by their evil communications, and followed them, were not they likewise falling with them into the

pit? And yet among them there were men to whom the apostle was writing as being already baptized; nor would they, therefore, if they were corrected, be baptized afresh. Does not the same apostle say, "To be carnally-minded is death?" [1657] and certainly the covetous, the deceivers, the robbers, in the midst of whom Cyprian himself was groaning, were carnally-minded. What then? Did the dead hurt him who was living in unity? Or who would say, that because such men had or gave the baptism of Christ, that it was therefore violated by their iniquities?

[1653] Bagai, in church province of Numidia. See on I. 5. 7. Among the many of the name of Felix in the letters of Cyprian, lvi., lvii., lxvii; title 1, 6, lxx., lxxvi. bis, lxxvii., lxxix., title and text, it would be unsafe to decide a sure reference to distinguish between this and the other bishops of the same cognomen in this council.

[1654] Matt. xv. 14.

[1655] Conc. Carth. sec. 12.

[1656] 1 Cor. xv. 32.

[1657] Rom. viii. 6.

Chapter 20.

34. Polianus of Mileum [1658] said: "It is right that a heretic should be baptized in the holy Church." [1659]

35. Nothing, indeed, could be expressed more shortly. But I think this too is short: It is right that the baptism of Christ should not be depreciated in the Church of Christ.

[1658] Mileum, Milevis, Mileve, in ecclesiastical province of Numidia, noted as the seat of two Councils 402 A.D. and 416 A.D.; also as the See of Optatus. Polianus is most likely to be identified with the one in Cypr. Epp. lxxvi., lxxix.

[1659] Conc. Cath. sec. 13.

Chapter 21.

36. Theogenes of Hippo Regius [1660] said: "According to the sacrament of the heavenly grace of God which we have received, we believe in the one only baptism which is in the holy Church." [1661]

37. This may be my own judgment also. For it is so balanced, that it contains nothing contrary to the truth. For we also believe in the one only baptism which is in the holy Church. Had he said, indeed, We believe in that which is in the holy Church alone, the same answer must have been made to him as to the rest. But as it is, since he has expressed himself in this wise, "We believe in the one only baptism which is in the holy Church," so that it is asserted that it exists in the holy Church, but not denied that it may be elsewhere as well, whatever his meaning may have been, there is no need to argue against these words. For if I were questioned on the several points, first, whether there was one baptism, I should answer that there was one. Then if I were asked, whether this was in the holy Church, I should answer that it was. In the third place, if it were asked whether I believed in this baptism, I should answer that I did so believe; and consequently I should answer that I believed in the one baptism which is in the holy Church. But if it were asked whether it was found in the holy Church alone, and not among heretics and schismatics, I should answer that, in common with the whole Church, I believed the contrary. But since he did not

insert this in his judgment, I should consider that it was mere wantonness if I added words which I did not find there, for the sake of arguing against them. For if he were to say, There is one water of the river Euphrates, which is in Paradise, no one could gainsay the truth of what he said. But if he were asked whether that water were in Paradise and nowhere else, and were to say that this was so, he would be saying what was false. For, besides Paradise, it is also in those lands into which it flows from that source. But who is rash enough to say that he would have been likely to assert what is false, when it is quite possible that he was asserting what is true? Wherefore the words of this judgment require no contradiction, because they in no wise run counter to the truth.

[1660] Hippo Regius, the see of Augustin himself, in ecclesiastical province of Numidia.

[1661] Conc. Carth. sec. 14.

C.D.H.

Chapter 22.

38. Dativus of Badiæ [1662] said "We, so far as lies within our power, refuse to communicate with a heretic, unless he has been baptized in the Church, and received remission of his sins." [1663]

39. The answer to this is: If your reason for wishing him to be baptized is that he has not received remission of sins, supposing you find a man within the Church who has been baptized, though entertaining hatred towards his brother, since the Lord cannot lie, who says, "If ye forgive not men their trespasses, neither will your Father forgive your trespasses,"

[1664] will you bid such an one, when corrected, to be baptized afresh? Assuredly not; so neither should you bid the heretic. It is clear that we must not pass unnoticed why he did not briefly say, "We do not communicate with a heretic," but added, "so far as lies within our power." For he saw that a greater number agreed with this view, from whose communion, however, he and his friends could not separate themselves, lest unity should be impaired, and so he added, "so far as lies within our power,"--showing beyond all doubt that he did not willingly communicate with those whom he held to be without baptism, but that yet all things were to be endured for the sake of peace and unity; just as was done also by those who thought that Dativus and his party were in the wrong, and who held what afterwards was taught by a fuller declaration of the truth, and urged by ancient custom, which received the stronger confirmation of a later Council; yet in turn, with anxious piety, they showed toleration towards each other, though without violation of Christian charity they entertained different opinions, endeavoring to keep the unity of the Spirit in the bond of peace, [1665] till God should reveal to one of them, were he otherwise minded, even this error of his ways. [1666] And to this I would have those give heed, by whom unity is attacked on the authority of this very Council by which it is declared how much unity should be loved.

[1662] Badiæ (Vada) in ecclesiastical province of Numidia. For Dativus see Cypr. Epp. lxxvi., lxxvii.

[1663] Conc. Carth. sec. 15.

[1664] Matt. vi. 15.

[1665] Eph. iv. 3.

[1666] Phil. iii. 15.

Chapter 23.

40. Successus of Abbir Germaniciana [1667] said: "Heretics may either do nothing or everything. If they can baptize, they can also give the Holy Spirit; but if they cannot give the Holy Spirit, because they do not possess the Holy Spirit, then can they not either spiritually baptize. Therefore we give our judgment that heretics should be baptized." [1668]

41. To this we may answer almost word for word: Murderers may either do nothing or everything. If they can baptize, they can also give the Holy Spirit; but if they cannot give the Holy Spirit, because they do not possess the Holy Spirit, then can they not either spiritually baptize. Therefore we give our judgment that persons baptized by murderers, or murderers themselves who have been baptized without being converted, should, when they have corrected themselves, be baptized. Yet this is not true. For "whosoever hateth his brother is a murderer;" [1669] and Cyprian knew such men within the Church, who certainly baptized. Therefore it is to no purpose that words of this sort are used concerning heretics.

[1667] Abbir Germaniciana was in ecclesiastical province of Zeugitana, or Africa Proconsularis. Successus probably identical with one mentioned in Cypr. Epp. lvii., lxvii., lxx., lxxx.

[1668] Conc. Carth. sec. 16.

[1669] 1 John iii. 15.

Chapter 24.

42. Fortunatus of Thuccabori [1670] said: "Jesus Christ our Lord and God, the Son of God the Father and Creator, built His Church upon a rock, not upon heresy, and gave the power of baptizing to bishops, not to heretics. Wherefore those who are outside the Church, and stand against Christ, scattering His sheep and flock, cannot baptize outside." [1671]

43. He added the word "outside" in order that he might not be answered with a like brevity to Successus. For otherwise he might also have been answered word for word: Jesus Christ our Lord and God, the Son of God the Father and Creator, built His Church upon a rock, not upon iniquity, and gave the power of baptizing to bishops, not to the unrighteous. Wherefore those who do not belong to the rock on which they build, who hear the word of God and do it, [1672] but, living contrary to Christ in hearing the word and not doing it, and hereby building on the sand, in this way scatter His sheep and flock by the example of an abandoned character, cannot baptize. Might not this be said with all the semblance of truth? and yet it is false. For the unrighteous do baptize, since those robbers are unrighteous whom Cyprian maintained to be at unity with himself. [1673]But for this reason, says the Donatist, he adds "outside." Why therefore can they not baptize outside? Is it because they are worse from the very fact that they are outside? But it makes no difference, in respect of the validity of baptism, how much worse the minister may be. For there is not so much difference between bad and worse as between good and bad; and yet, when the bad baptizes, he gives the selfsame sacrament as the good. Therefore, also, when the worse baptizes, he gives the selfsame sacrament as the less bad. Or is it that it is not in respect of man's merit, but of the sacrament of baptism itself, that it cannot be given outside? If

this were so, neither could it be possessed outside, and it would be necessary that a man should be baptized again so often as he left the Church and again returned to it.

44. Further, if we inquire more carefully what is meant by "outside," especially as he himself makes mention of the rock on which the Church is built, are not they in the Church who are on the rock, and they who are not on the rock, not in the Church either? Now, therefore, let us see whether they build their house upon a rock who hear the words of Christ and do them not. The Lord Himself declares the contrary, saying, "Whosoever heareth these sayings of mine, and doeth them, I will liken him unto a wise man, which built his house upon a rock;" and a little later, "Every one that heareth these sayings of mine, and doeth them not, shall be likened unto a foolish man, which built his house upon the sand." [1674]If, therefore, the Church is on a rock, those who are on the sand, because they are outside the rock, are necessarily outside the Church. Let us recollect, therefore, how many Cyprian mentions as placed within who build upon the sand, that is, who hear the words of Christ and do them not. And therefore, because they are on the sand, they are proved to be outside the rock, that is, outside the Church; yet even while they are so situated, and are either not yet or never changed for the better, not only do they baptize and are baptized, but the baptism which they have remains valid in them though they are destined to damnation.

45. Neither can it be said in this place, [1675] Yet who is there that doeth all the words of the Lord which are written in the evangelic sermon itself, [1676] at the end of which He says, that he who heard the said words and did them built upon a rock, and he who heard them and did them not built upon the sand? For, granting that by certain persons all the words are not

accomplished, yet in the same sermon He has appointed the remedy, saying, "Forgive, and ye shall be forgiven." [1677]And after the Lord's prayer had been recorded in detail in the same sermon, He says, "For I say unto you, if ye forgive men their trespasses, your heavenly Father will also forgive you: but if ye forgive not men their trespasses, neither will your Father forgive your trespasses." [1678]Hence also Peter says, "For charity shall cover the multitude of sins;" [1679] which charity they certainly did not have, and on this account they built upon the sand, of whom the same Cyprian says, that within the Church they held conversation, even in the time of the apostles, in unkindly hatred alien from Christian charity; [1680] and therefore they seemed indeed to be within, but really were without, because they were not on that rock by which the Church is signified.

[1670] Thuccabori, Tucca or Terebrinthina, in ecclesiastical province of Africa Proconsularis or Zeugitana. For Bp. Fortunatus, see Cypr. Epp. xlviii., lvi., lvii. (the first), lxvii., lxx.

[1671] Conc. Carth. sec. 17.

[1672] Matt. vii. 24.

[1673] Cypr. Serm. de Laps.

[1674] Matt. vii. 24, 26.

[1675] It is pointed out by the Louvain editors that this passage shows that Augustin considered our Lord's precept to comprehend everything contained in the Sermon on the Mount.

[1676] It is pointed out by the Louvain editors that this passage shows that Augustin considered our Lord's precept to comprehend everything contained in the Sermon on the Mount.

[1677] Luke vi. 37.

[1678] Matt. vi. 14, 15.

[1679] 1 Pet. iv. 8.

[1680] Cypr. Ep. lxxiii. 14.

Chapter 25.

46. Sedatus of Tuburbo [1681] said: "Inasmuch as water, sanctified by the prayer of the priest in the Church, washes away sins, just so much does it multiply sins when infected, as by a cancer, with the words of heretics. Wherefore one must strive, with all such efforts as conduce to peace, that no one who has been infected and tainted by heretical error should refuse to receive the one true baptism, with which whosoever is not baptized shall not inherit the kingdom of heaven." [1682]

47. To this we answer, that if the water is not sanctified, when through want of skill the priest who prays utters some words of error, many, not only of the bad, but of the good brethren in the Church itself, fail to sanctify the water. For the prayers of many are corrected every day on being recited to men of greater learning, and many things are found in them contrary to the Catholic faith. Supposing, then, that it were shown that some persons were baptized when these prayers had been uttered over the water, will they be bidden to be baptized afresh? Why not? Because generally the fault in the prayer is more than counterbalanced by the intent of him who offers it; and those fixed words of the gospel, without which baptism cannot be consecrated, are of such efficacy, that, by their virtue, anything

faulty that is uttered in the prayer contrary to the rule of faith is made of no effect, just as the devil is excluded by the name of Christ. For it is clear that if a heretic utters a faulty prayer, he has no good intent of love whereby that want of skill may be compensated, and therefore he is like any envious or spiteful person in the Catholic Church itself, such as Cyprian proves to exist within the Church. Or one might offer some prayer, as not unfrequently happens, in which he should speak against the rule of faith, since many rush into the use of prayers which are composed not only by unskillful men who love to talk, but even by heretics, and in the simplicity of ignorance, not being able to discern their true character, use them, thinking they are good; and yet what is erroneous in them does not vitiate what is right, but rather it is rendered null thereby, just as in the man of good hope and approved faith, who yet is but a man, if in anything he be otherwise minded, what he holds aright is not thereby vitiated until God reveal to him also that in which he is otherwise minded. [1683]But supposing that the man himself is wicked and perverse, then, if he should offer an upright prayer, in no part contrary to the Catholic faith, it does not follow that because the prayer is right the man himself is also right; and if over some he offer an erroneous prayer, God is present to uphold the words of His gospel, without which the baptism of Christ cannot be consecrated, and He Himself consecrates His sacrament, that in the recipient, either before he is baptized, or when he is baptized, or at some future time when he turns in truth to God, that very sacrament may be profitable to salvation, which, were he not to be converted, would be powerful to his destruction. But who is there who does not know that there is no baptism of Christ, if the words of the gospel in which consists the outward visible sign be not forthcoming? But you will more easily find heretics who do not baptize at all, than any who baptize without those words. And therefore we say, not that every baptism (for in many of the blasphemous rites of idols men are said to be baptized), but that the baptism of Christ, that is, every baptism consecrated in the words of the gospel, is everywhere the same, and cannot be vitiated by any perversity on the part of any men. [1684]

48. We must certainly not lightly pass over in this judgment that he here inserted a clause, and says, "Wherefore we must strive, with all such efforts as conduce to peace, that no one who has been infected," etc. For he had regard to those words of the blessed Cyprian in his opening speech, "Judging no man, nor depriving any of the right of communion if he entertain a different view." See of what power is the love of unity and peace in the good sons of the Church, that they should choose rather to show tolerance towards those whom they called sacrilegious and profane, being admitted, as they thought, without the sacrament of baptism, if they could not correct them as they thought was right, than on their account to break that holy bond, lest on account of the tares the wheat also should be rooted out, [1685] --permitting, so far as rested with them, as in that noblest judgment of Solomon, that the infant body should rather be nourished by the false mother than be cut in pieces. [1686]But this was the opinion both of those who held the truer view about the sacrament of baptism, and of those to whom God, in consideration of their great love, was purposing to reveal any point in which they were otherwise minded.

[1681] Tuburbo (Thuburbo) was in the ecclesiastical province of Zeugitana. Sedatus is not unlikely the same as the one mentioned in Cypr. Epp. iv., lxvii., lxx.

[1682] Conc. Carth sec. 18.

[1683] Phil. iii. 15.

[1684] See above, III. cc. 14, 15.

[1685] Matt. xiii. 29.

[1686] 1 Kings iii. 26.

Chapter 26.

49. Privatianus of Sufetula [1687] said: "He who says that heretics have the power of baptizing should first say who it was that founded heresy. For if heresy is of God, it may have the divine favor; but if it be not of God, how can it either have or confer on any one the grace of God?" [1688]

50. This man may thus be answered word for word: He who says that malicious and envious persons have the power of baptizing, should first say who was the founder of malice and envy. For if malice and envy are of God, they may have the divine favor; but if they are not of God, how can they either have or confer on any one the grace of God? But as these words are in the same way most manifestly false, so are also those which these were uttered to confute. For the malicious and envious baptize, as even Cyprian himself allows, because he bears testimony that they also are within. So therefore even heretics may baptize, because baptism is the sacrament of Christ; but envy and heresy are the works of the devil. Yet though a man possesses them, he does not thereby cause that if he have the sacrament of Christ, it also should itself be reckoned in the number of the devil's works.

[1687] Sufetula was a town in ecclesiastical province of Byzacene, twenty-five miles from Sufes (same province), of which the name is a diminutive. Bp. Privatianus is mentioned in Cypr. Epp. lvi., lvii.

[1688] Conc. Carth. sec. 19.

Chapter 27.

51. Privatus of Sufes [1689] said: "What can be said of the man who approves the baptism of heretics, save that he communicates with heretics?" [1690]

52. To this we answer: It is not the baptism of heretics which we approve in heretics, as it is not the baptism of the covetous, or the treacherous, or deceitful, or of robbers, or of envious men which we approve in them; for all of these are unjust, but Christ is just, whose sacrament existing in them, they do not in its essence violate. Otherwise another man might say: What can be said of the man who approves the baptism of the unjust, save that he communicates with the unjust. And if this objection were brought against the Catholic Church herself, it would be answered just as I have answered the above.

[1689] See n. 6. p. 475.

[1690] Conc. Carth. sec. 20.

Chapter 28.

53. Hortensianus of Lares [1691] said: "How many baptisms there are, let those who uphold or favor heretics determine. We assert one baptism of the Church, which we only know in the Church. Or how can those baptize any one in the name of

Christ whom Christ Himself declares to be His enemies?" [1692]

54. Giving answer to this man in a like tenor of words, we say: Let those who uphold or favor the unrighteous see to it: we recall to the Church when we can the one baptism which we know to be of the Church alone, wherever it be found. Or how can they baptize any one in the name of Christ whom Christ Himself declares to be His enemies? For He says to all the unrighteous, "I never knew you: depart from me, ye that work iniquity;" [1693] and yet, when they baptize, it is not themselves that baptize, but He of whom John says, "The same is He which baptizeth." [1694]

[1691] Lares, in ecclesiastical province of Numidia. Hortensianus is very likely the same as the one in Cypr. Epp. lvii., lxx.

[1692] Conc. Carth. sec. 21.

[1693] Matt. vii. 23.

[1694] John i. 33.

Chapter 29.

55. Cassius of Macomades [1695] said: "Since there cannot be two baptisms, he who grants baptism unto heretics takes it away from himself. I therefore declare my judgment that heretics, those objects for our tears, those masses of corruption, [1696] should be baptized when they begin to come to the Church, and that so being washed by the sacred and divine laver, and enlightened with the light of life, they may be received into the Church,--as being now made not enemies, but peaceful; not strangers, but of the household of the faith of the

Lord; not bastards, [1697] but sons of God; partaking not of error, but of salvation,--with the exception of those who, being believers transplanted from the Church, had gone over to heresy, and that these should be restored by the laying on of hands." [1698]

56. Another might say: Since there cannot be two baptisms, he who grants baptism to the unrighteous takes it away from himself. But even our opponents would join us in resisting such a man when he says that we grant baptism to the unrighteous, which is not of the unrighteous, like their unrighteousness, but of Christ, of whom is righteousness, and whose sacrament, even among the unrighteous, is not unrighteous. What, therefore, they would join us in saying of the unrighteous, that let them say to themselves of heretics. And therefore he should rather have said as follows: I therefore give my judgment that heretics, those objects for our tears, those masses of corruption, should not be baptized when they begin to come to the Church, if they already have the baptism of Christ, but should be corrected from their error. For we may similarly say of the unrighteous, of whom the heretics are a part: I therefore give my judgment that the unrighteous, those objects for our tears, and masses of corruption, if they have been already baptized, should not be baptized again when they begin to come to the Church, that is, to that rock outside which are all who hear the words of Christ and do them not; but being already washed with the sacred and divine laver, and now further enlightened with the light of truth, should be received into the Church no longer as enemies but as peaceful, for the unrighteous have no peace; no longer as strangers, but of the household of the faith of the Lord, for to the unrighteous it is said, "How then art thou turned into the

degenerate plant of a strange vine unto me?" [1699] no longer as bastards, but the sons of God, for the unrighteous are the sons of the devil, partaking not of error but of salvation, for un-righteousness cannot save. And by the Church I mean that rock, that dove, that garden enclosed and fountain sealed, which is recognized only in the wheat, not in the chaff, whether that be scattered far apart by the wind, or appear to be mingled with the corn even till the last winnowing. In vain, therefore, did Cassius add, "With the exception of those who, being believers transplanted from the Church, had gone over to heresy." For if even they themselves had lost baptism by seceding, to themselves also let it be restored; but if they had not lost it, let what was given by them receive due recognition.

[1695] Macomades [in ecclesiastical province of Numidia.] Bp. Cassius is probably to be identified with the one in Cypr. Ep. lxx.

[1696] Flebiles et tabidos. This is otherwise taken of the repentant heretics "Melting with the grief and wretchedness of penitence;" but Bishop Fell points out that the interpretation in the text is supported by an expression in c. 33, 63: Mens hæretica, quæ diuturna tabe polluta est. Routh Rel. Sac. iii. p. 199.

[1697] Adulteros. So all the Mss. of Augustin, though in Cyprian is sometimes found "adulterinos." In classical Latin, however "adulterit" is sometimes used in the sense of "adulterinus." Cassius seems to have had in mind Heb. xii. 8, "Then are ye bastards, and not sons."

[1698] Conc. Carth. sec. 22.

[1699] Jer. ii. 21.

Chapter 30.

57. Another Januarius of Vicus Cæsaris [1700] said: "If error does not obey truth, much more does truth refuse assent to error; and therefore we stand by the Church in which we preside, so that, claiming her baptism for herself alone, we baptize those whom the Church has not baptized." [1701]

58. We answer: Whom the Church baptizes, those that rock baptizes outside which are all they who hear the words of Christ and do them not. Let all, therefore, be baptized again who have been baptized by such. But if this is not done, then, as we recognize the baptism of Christ in these, so should we recognize it in heretics, though we either condemn or correct their unrighteousness and error.

[1700] Vicus Cæsaris, probably of ecclesiastical province of Byzacium. This Bp. Januarius may be the second of that name in Cypr. Ep. lxvii., and is to be distinquished from Bp. Januarius of Lambæse, ch. xiii. 20.

[1701] Conc. Carth. sec. 23.

Chapter 31.

59. Another Secundinus of Carpis [1702] said: "Are heretics Christians or not? If they are Christians, why are they not in the Church of God? If they are not Christians, let them be made so. [1703]Else what will be the reference in the discourse of the Lord, in which He says, He that is not with me is against me; and he that gathereth not with me scattereth abroad?' [1704]Whence it is clear that on strange children and the offspring of Antichrist the Holy Spirit cannot descend by the

laying on of hands alone, since it is clear that heretics have not baptism." [1705]

60. To this we answer: Are the unrighteous Christians or not? If they are Christians, why are they not on that rock on which the Church is built? for they hear the words of Christ and do them not. If they are not Christians, let them be made so. Else what will be the reference in the discourse of our Lord, in which He says, "He that is not with me is against me; and he that gathereth not with me scattereth abroad?" For they scatter His sheep who lead them to the ruin of their lives by a false imitation of the Lord. Whence it is clear that upon strange children (as all the unrighteous are called), and upon the offspring of Antichrist (which all are who oppose themselves to Christ), the Holy Spirit cannot descend by the laying on of hands alone, if there be not added a true conversion of the heart; since it is clear that the unrighteous, so long as they are unrighteous, may indeed have baptism, but cannot have the salvation of which baptism is the sacrament. For let us see whether heretics are described in that psalm where the following words are used of strange children: "Deliver me, O Lord, from the hand of strange children, whose mouth speaketh vanity, and their right hand is a right hand of falsehood: whose sons are like young shoots well established, and their daughters polished after the similitude of the temple. Their garners are full, affording all manner of store; their sheep are fruitful, bringing forth plenteously in their streets; their oxen are strong: there is no breaking down of their fence, no opening of a passage out, no complaining in their streets. Men deemed happy the people that is in such a case; rather blessed is the people whose God is the Lord." [1706]If, therefore, those are strange children who place their happiness in temporal

things, and in the abundance of earthly prosperity, and despise the commandments of the Lord, let us see whether these are not the very same of whom Cyprian so speaks, transforming them also into himself, that he may show that he is speaking of men with whom he held communion in the sacraments: "In not keeping," he says, "the way of the Lord, nor observing the heavenly commandments given us for our salvation. Our Lord did the will of His Father, and we do not do the will of the Lord, being eager about our patrimony or our gains, following after pride, and so forth." [1707] But if these could both have and transmit baptism, why is it denied that it may exist among strange children, whom he yet exhorts, that, by keeping the heavenly commandments conveyed to them through the only-begotten Son, they should deserve to be His brethren and the sons of God?

[1702] Carpis (Carpos) was in ecclesiastical province of Zeugitana. See for Secundinus, note on chap. 18.

[1703] Fiant. Another reading in some Mss. of Cyprian (not found in those of Augustin) is, "quomodo Christianos faciunt," which is less in harmony with the context.

[1704] Matt. xii. 30.

[1705] Conc. Carth. sec. 24.

[1706] Ps. cxliv. 11-15, so LXX. cp. Hieron. Ps. cxliii. 11-15.

[1707] Cypr. Presbyteris et diaconibus fratribus, Ep. xi. 1.

Chapter 32.

61. Victoricus of Thabraca [1708] said: "If heretics may baptize, and give remission of sins, why do we destroy their credit, and call them heretics?" [1709]

62. What if another were to say: If the unrighteous may baptize, and give remission of sins, why do we destroy their credit, and call them unrighteous? The answer which we should give to such an one concerning the unrighteous may also be given to the other concerning heretics,--that is, in the first place, that the baptism with which they baptize is not theirs; and secondly, that it does not follow that whosoever has the baptism of Christ is also certain of the remission of his sins if he has this only in the outward sign, and is not converted with a true conversion of the heart, so that he who gives remission should himself have remission of his sins.

[1708] Thabraca was on the coast of Numidia, in ecclesiastical province of that name, the frontier town towards Zeugitana, at the mouth of the Tucca. The name of a Victoricus occurs in Cypr. Epp. lvii., lxvii.

[1709] Conc. Carth. sec. 25.

Chapter 33.

63. Another Felix of Uthina [1710] said: "No one can doubt, most holy brethren in the priesthood, that human presumption has not so much power as the adorable and venerable majesty of our Lord Jesus Christ. Remembering then the danger, we ought not only to observe this ourselves, but to confirm it by our general consent, that all heretics who come to the bosom of our mother the Church be baptized, that the heretical mind, which has been polluted by long-continued corruption, may be

reformed when cleansed by the sanctification of the laver." [1711]

64. Perhaps the man who has placed the strength of his case for the baptizing of heretics in the cleansing away of the long-continued corruption, would spare those who, having fallen headlong into some heresy, had remained in it a brief space, and presently being corrected, had passed from thence to the Catholic Church. Furthermore, he has himself failed to observe that it might be said that all unrighteous persons who come to that rock, in which is understood the Church, should be baptized, so that the unrighteous mind, which was building outside the rock upon the sand by hearing the words of Christ and not doing them, might be reformed when cleansed by the sanctification of the laver; and yet this is not done if they have been baptized already, even if it be proved that such was their character when they were baptized, that is, that they "renounced the world in words and not in deeds."

[1710] Uthina was in ecclesiastical province of Zeugitana. This Felix is to be distinguished from the bishop of Bagai, ch. 19: A reference to a bishop of Utina is made by Tert. de Monog. ch. xii., but he cannot have been this Felix, as some assume.

[1711] Conc. Carth. sec. 26.

Chapter 34.

65. Quietus of Burug [1712] said: "We who live by faith ought with believing observance to obey what has been before foretold for our instruction. For it is written in Solomon, He that is washed by one dead, what availeth his washing?' [1713]Which assuredly he says of those who are washed by heretics, and of those who wash. For if they who are baptized

among them receive eternal life through the remission of their sins, why do they come to the Church? But if no salvation is received from a dead person, and they therefore, acknowledging their former error, return with penance to the truth, they ought to be sanctified with the one life-giving baptism which is in the Catholic Church." [1714]

66. What it is to be baptized by the dead, we have already, without prejudice to the more careful consideration of the same scripture, sufficiently declared before. [1715]But I would ask why it is that they wish heretics alone to be considered dead, when Paul the apostle has said generally of sin, "The wages of sin is death;" [1716] and again, "To be carnally minded is death." [1717]And when he says that a widow that liveth in pleasure is dead, [1718] how are they not dead "who renounce the world in words and not in deeds"? What, therefore, is the profit of washing in him who is baptized by them, except, indeed, that if he himself also is of the same character, he has the laver indeed, but it does not profit him to salvation? But if he by whom he is baptized is such, but the man who is baptized is turned to the Lord with no false heart, he is not baptized by that dead person, but by that living One of whom it is said, "The same is He which baptizeth." [1719]But to what he says of heretics, that if they who are baptized among them receive eternal life through the remission of their sins, why do they come to the Church? we answer: They come for this reason, that although they have received the baptism of Christ up to the point of the celebration of the sacrament, yet they cannot attain to life eternal save through the charity of unity; just as neither would those envious and malicious ones attain to life eternal, who would not have their sins forgiven them, even if they entertained hatred only against those from whom they

suffered wrong; since the Truth said, "If ye forgive not men their trespasses, neither will your Father forgive your trespasses," [1720] how much less when they were hating those towards whom they were rewarding evil for good? [1721] And yet these men, though "renouncing the world in words and not in deeds," would not be baptized again, if they should afterwards be corrected, but they would be made holy by the one living baptism. And this is indeed in the Catholic Church, but not in it alone, as neither is it in the saints alone who are built upon the rock, and of whom that one dove is composed. [1722]

[1712] Burug (Buruc) or Burca was in ecclesiastical province of Numidia. Quietus may be identical with the one mentioned in Cypr. Ep. lxvii.

[1713] In the English version this is, "He that washeth himself after touching a dead body, if he touch it again, what availeth his washing?"--Ecclus. xxxiv. 25.

[1714] Conc. Carth. sec. 27.

[1715] Contra Parmenianum, II. 10. 22.

[1716] Rom. vi. 23.

[1717] Rom. viii. 6.

[1718] 1 Tim. v. 6.

[1719] John i. 33.

[1720] Matt. vi. 15.

[1721] Ps. xxxv. 12.

[1722] Cant. vi. 9.

Chapter 35.

67. Castus of Sicca [1723] said: He who presumes to follow custom in despite of truth is either envious and evilly disposed towards the brethren to whom the truth is revealed, or else he is ungrateful towards God, by whose inspiration His Church is instructed." [1724]

68. If this man proved that those who differed from him, and held the view that has since been held by the whole world under the sanction of a Christian Council, were following custom so as to despise truth, we should have reason for fearing these words; but seeing that this custom is found both to have had its origin in truth and to have been confirmed by truth, we have nothing to fear in this judgment. And yet, if they were envious or evilly disposed towards the brethren, or ungrateful towards God, see with what kind of men they were willing to hold communion; see what kind of men, holding different opinions from their own, they treated as Cyprian enjoined them at the first, not removing them from the right of communion; see by what kind of men they were not polluted in the preservation of unity; see how greatly the bond of peace was to be loved; see what views they hold who bring charges against us, founded on the Council of bishops, their predecessors, whose example they do not imitate, and by whose example, when the rights of the case are considered, they are condemned. If it was the custom, as this judgment bears witness, that heretics coming to the Church should be received with the baptism which they already had, either this was done rightly, or the evil do not pollute the good in unity. If it was rightly done, why do they accuse the world because they are so

received? But if the evil do not pollute the good in unity, how do they defend themselves against the charge of sacrilegious separation?

[1723] Sicca was in ecclesiastical province of Zeugitana. This is certainly not the Castus of Cypr. de Laps. c. xiii.

[1724] Conc. Carth. sec. 28.

Chapter 36.

69. Eucratius of Theni [1725] said: "Our God and Lord Jesus Christ, teaching the apostles with His own mouth, fully laid down our faith, and the grace of baptism, and the rule of the law of the Church, saying, Go ye, and teach all nations, baptizing them in the name of the Father, and of the Son, and of the Holy Ghost.' [1726] Therefore the false and unrighteous baptism of heretics is to be repudiated by us, and contradicted with all solemnity of witness, seeing that from their mouth issues not life, but poison, not heavenly grace, but blaspheming of the Trinity. And so it is plain that heretics coming to the Church ought to be baptized with perfect and Catholic baptism, that, being purified from the blasphemy of their presumption, they may be reformed by the grace of the Holy Spirit." [1727]

70. Clearly, if the baptism is not consecrated in the name of the Father, and of the Son, and of the Holy Ghost, it should be considered to be of the heretics, and repudiated as unrighteous by us with all solemnity of witness; but if we discern this name in it, we do better to distinguish the words of the gospel from heretical error, and approve what is sound in them, correcting what is faulty.

[1725] Theni was in ecclesiastical province of Byzacene. A Eucratius occurs in Cypr. Ep. ii.

[1726] Matt. xxviii. 19.

[1727] Conc. Carth. sec. 29.

Chapter 37.

71. Libosus of Vaga [1728] said: "The Lord says in the gospel, I am the truth;' [1729] He did not say, I am custom. Therefore, when the truth is made manifest, let custom yield to truth; so that, if even in time past any one did not baptize heretics in the Church, he may now begin to baptize them." [1730]

72. Here he has in no way tried to show how that is the truth to which he says that custom ought to yield. But it is of more importance that he helps us against those who have separated themselves from unity, by confessing that the custom existed, than that he thinks it ought to yield to a truth which he does not show. For the custom is of such a nature, that if it admitted sacrilegious men to the altar of Christ without the cleansing of baptism, and polluted none of the good men who remained in unity, then all who have cut themselves off from the same unity, in which they could not be polluted by the contagion of any evil persons whatsoever, have separated themselves without reason, and have committed the manifest sacrilege of schism. But if all perished in pollution through that custom, from what cavern do they issue without the original truth, and with all the cunning of calumny? If, however, the custom was a right one by which heretics were thus received, let them abandon their madness, let them confess their error; let them come to the Catholic Church, not that they may be

bathed again with the sacrament of baptism, but that they may be cured from the wound of severance.

[1728] Vaga was in ecclesiastical province of Byzacium. The name of a Libosus occurs in Cypr. Ep. lxvii.

[1729] John xiv. 6.

[1730] Conc. Carth. sec. 30.

Chapter 38.

73. Lucius of Thebaste [1731] said: "I declare my judgment that heretics, and blasphemers, and unrighteous men, who with various words pluck away the sacred and adorable words of the Scriptures, should be held accursed, and therefore exorcised and baptized." [1732]

74. I too think that they should be held accursed, but not that therefore they should be exorcised and baptized; for it is their own falsehood which I hold accursed, but Christ's sacrament which I venerate.

[1731] Thebaste (Thebeste) in ecclesiastical province of Numidia. For Lucius, cp. c. 14.

[1732] Conc. Carth. sec. 31.

Chapter 39.

75. Eugenius of Ammedera [1733] said: "I too pronounce this same judgment, that heretics should be baptized." [1734]

76. To him we answer: But this is not the judgment which the Church pronounces, to which also God has now revealed in a plenary Council the point in which ye were then still otherwise

minded, [1735] but because saving charity was in you, ye remained in unity.

[1733] Ammedera, probably in ecclesiastical province of Proconsularis Africa.

[1734] Conc. Carth. sec. 32.

[1735] Phil. iii. 15.

Chapter 40.

77. Also another Felix of Ammacura [1736] said: "I too, following the authority of the holy Scriptures, give my judgment that heretics should be baptized, and with them those also who maintain that they have been baptized among schismatics. For if, according to the warning of Christ, our fountain is sealed to ourselves, [1737] let all the enemies of our Church understand that it cannot belong to others; nor can He who is the Shepherd of our flock give the water unto salvation to two different peoples. And therefore it is clear that neither heretics nor schismatics can receive anything heavenly, who dare to accept from men that are sinners and aliens from the Church. When the giver has no ground to stand upon, surely neither can the receiver derive any profit." [1738]

78. To him we answer, that the holy Scriptures nowhere have enjoined that heretics baptized among heretics should be baptized afresh, but that they have shown in many places that all are aliens from the Church who are not on the rock, nor belong to the members of the dove, and yet that they baptize and are baptized and have the sacrament of salvation without salvation. But how our fountain is like the fountain of Paradise, in that, like it, it flows forth even beyond the bounds

of Paradise, has been sufficiently set forth above; [1739] and that "He who is the Shepherd of our flock cannot give the water unto salvation to two different peoples," that is, to one that is His own, and to another that is alien, I fully agree in admitting. But does it follow that because the water is not unto salvation it is not the identical water? For the water of the deluge was for salvation unto those who were placed within the ark, but it brought death to those without, and yet it was the same water. And many aliens, that is to say, envious persons, whom Cyprian declares and proves from Scripture to be of the party of the devil, seem as it were to be within, and yet, if they were not without the ark, they would not perish by water. For such men are slain by baptism, as the sweet savor of Christ was unto death to those of whom the apostle speaks. [1740] Why then do not either heretics or schismatics receive anything heavenly, just as thorns or tares, like those who were without the ark received indeed the rain from the floods of heaven, but to destruction, not to salvation? And so I do not take the pains to refute what he said in conclusion: "When the giver has no ground to stand upon, surely neither can the receiver derive any profit," since we also say that it does not profit the receivers while they receive it in heresy, consenting with the heretics; and therefore they come to Catholic peace and unity, not that they may receive baptism, but that what they had received may begin to profit them.

[1736] Ammacura (Bamacorra) in ecclesiastical province of Numidia.

[1737] Cant. iv. 12.

[1738] Conc. Carth. sec. 33.

[1739] Ch. 21, 37.

[1740] 2 Cor. ii. 15.

Chapter 41.

79. Also another Januarius of Muzuli [1741] said: "I wonder that, while all acknowledge that there is one baptism, all do not understand the unity of the same baptism. For the Church and heresy are two distinct things. If heretics have baptism we have it not; but if we have it, heretics cannot have it. But there is no doubt that the Church alone possesses the baptism of Christ, since it alone possesses both the favor and the truth of Christ." [1742]

80. Another might equally say, and say with equal want of truth: I wonder that, while all confess there is one baptism, all do not understand the unity of baptism. For righteousness and unrighteousness are two distinct things. If the unrighteous have baptism, the righteous have it not; but if the righteous have it, the unrighteous cannot have it. But there is no doubt that the righteous alone possess the baptism of Christ, since they alone possess both the favor and the truth of Christ. This is certainly false, as they confess themselves. For those envious ones also who are of the party of the devil, though placed within the Church, as Cyprian tells us, and who were well known to the Apostle Paul, had baptism, but did not belong to the members of that dove which is safely sheltered on the rock.

[1741] Muzuli is perhaps the same as Muzuca in ecclesiastical province of Byzacium.

[1742] Conc. Carth. sec. 34.

Chapter 42.

81. Adelphius of Thasbalte [1743] said: "It is surely without cause that they find fault with the truth in false and invidious terms, saying that we rebaptize, since the Church does not rebaptize heretics, but baptizes them." [1744]

82. Truly enough it does not rebaptize them, because it only baptizes those who were not baptized before; and this earlier custom has only been confirmed in a later Council by a more careful perfecting of the truth.

[1743] Thasbalte (Thasvalthe) was in ecclesiastical province of Byzacene. An Adelphius is mentioned in Cypr. Ep. lxvii.

[1744] Conc. Carth. sec. 35.

Chapter 43.

83. Demetrius of the Lesser Leptis [1745] said: "We uphold one baptism, because we claim for the Catholic Church alone what is her own. But those who say that heretics baptize truly and lawfully are themselves the men who make, not two, but many baptisms; for since heresies are many in number, the baptisms, too, will be reckoned according to their number." [1746]

84. To him we answer: If this were so, then would as many baptisms be reckoned as there are works of the flesh, of which the apostle says "that they which do such things shall not inherit the kingdom of God;" [1747] among which are reckoned also heresies; and so many of those very works are tolerated within the Church as though in the chaff, and yet there is one baptism for them all, which is not vitiated by any work of unrighteousness.

[1745] Leptis the Lesser was in ecclesiastical province of Byzacene, the Greater being in that of Tripolis. A Demetrius occurs in Cypr. Epp. lvii., lxx.

[1746] Conc. Carth. sec. 36.

[1747] Gal. v. 21.

Chapter 44.

85. Vincentius of Thibari [1748] said: "We know that heretics are worse than heathens. If they, being converted, wish to come to God, they have assuredly a rule of truth, which the Lord by His divine precept committed to the apostles, saying, Go ye, lay on hands in my name, cast out devils;' [1749] and in another place, Go ye, and teach all nations, baptizing them in the name of the Father, and of the Son, and of the Holy Ghost.' [1750]Therefore, first by the laying on of hands in exorcism, secondly by regeneration in baptism, they may come to the promises of Christ; but my judgment is that in no other way should this be done." [1751]

86. By what rule he asserts that heretics are worse than heathens I do not know, seeing that the Lord says, "If he neglect to hear the Church, let him be unto thee as a heathen man and a publican." [1752]Is a heretic worse even than such? I do not gainsay it. I do not, however, allow that because the man himself is worse than a heathen, that is, than a Gentile and pagan, therefore whatever the sacrament contains that is Christ's is mingled with his vices and character, and perishes through the corruption of such admixture. For if even those who depart from the Church, and become not the followers but the founders of heresies, have been baptized before their secession, they continue to have baptism, although, according

to the above rule, they are worse than heathens; for if on correction they return, they do not receive it, as they certainly would do if they had lost it. It is therefore possible that a man may be worse than a heathen, and yet that the sacrament of Christ may not only be in him, but be not a whit inferior to what it is in a holy and righteous man. For although to the extent of his powers he has not preserved the sacrament, but done it violence in heart and will, yet so far as the sacrament's own nature is concerned, it has remained unhurt in its integrity even in the man who despised and rejected it. Were not the people of Sodom heathens, that is to say, Gentiles? The Jews therefore were worse, to whom the Lord says, "It shall be more tolerable for the land of Sodom in the day of judgment than for thee;" [1753] and to whom the prophet says, "Thou hast justified Sodom," [1754] that is to say, in comparison with thee Sodom is righteous. Shall we, however, maintain that on this account the holy sacraments which existed among the Jews partook of the nature of the Jews themselves,--those sacraments which the Lord Himself also accepted, and sent the lepers whom He had cleansed to fulfill them, [1755] of which when Zacharias was administering them, the angel stood by him, and declared that his prayer had been heard while he was sacrificing in the temple? [1756]These same sacraments were both in the good men of that time, and in those bad men who were worse than are the heathens, seeing that they were ranked before the Sodomites for wickedness, and yet those sacraments were perfect and holy in both.

87. For even if the Gentiles themselves could have anything holy and right in their doctrines, our saints did not condemn it, however much the Gentiles themselves were to be detested for their superstitions and idolatry and pride, and the rest of their

corruptions, and to be punished with judgment from heaven unless they submitted to correction. For when Paul the apostle also was saying something concerning God before the Athenians, he adduced as a proof of what he said, that certain of them had said something to the same effect, [1757] which certainly would not be condemned but recognized in them if they should come to Christ. And the holy Cyprian uses similar evidence against the same heathens; for, speaking of the magi, he says, "The chief of them, however, Hostanes, asserts both that the form of the true God cannot be seen, and also that true angels stand beside His seat. In which Plato also agrees in like manner, and, maintaining the existence of one God, he calls the others angels or demons. Hermes Trismegistus also speaks of one God, and confesses that He is incomprehensible, and past our powers of estimation." [1758]If, therefore, they were to come to the perception of salvation in Christ, it surely would not be said to them, This that ye have is bad, or false; but clearly it would deservedly be said, Though this in you is perfect and true, yet it would profit nothing unless ye came to the grace of Christ. If, therefore, anything that is holy can be found and rightly approved in the very heathens, although the salvation which is of Christ is not yet to be granted to them, we ought not, even though heretics are worse than they, to be moved to the desire of correcting what is bad in them belonging to themselves, without being willing to acknowledge what is good in them of Christ. But we will set forth from a fresh preface to consider the remaining judgments of this Council.

[1748] Thibari, perhaps the same as Tabora, in ecclesiastical province of Mauritania Cæsariensis. A Bp. Vincentius is mentioned in Cypr. Ep. lxvii.

[1749] Mark xvi. 15-18.

[1750] Matt. xxviii. 19.

[1751] Conc. Carth. sec. 37.

[1752] Matt. xviii. 17.

[1753] Matt. xi. 24.

[1754] Ezek. xvi. 51.

[1755] Luke xvii. 14.

[1756] Luke i. 11, 13.

[1757] Acts xvii. 28.

[1758] Cypr. de Idol. Vanitate, c. vi.

Book VII.

In which the remaining judgments of the Council of Carthage are examined.

Chapter 1.

1. Let us not be considered troublesome to our readers, if we discuss the same question often and from different points of view. For although the Holy Catholic Church throughout all nations be fortified by the authority of primitive custom and of a plenary Council against those arguments which throw some darkness over the question about baptism, whether it can be the same among heretics and schismatics that it is in the Catholic Church, yet, since a different opinion has at one time been entertained in the unity of the Church itself, by men who are in no wise to be despised, and especially by Cyprian, whose

authority men endeavor to use against us who are far removed from his charity, we are therefore compelled to make use of the opportunity of examining and considering all that we find on this subject in his Council and letters, in order, as it were, to handle at some considerable length this same question, and to show how it has more truly been the decision of the whole body of the Catholic Church, that heretics or schismatics, who have received baptism already in the body from which they came, should be admitted with it into the communion of the Catholic Church, being corrected in their error and rooted and grounded in the faith, that, so far as concerns the sacrament of baptism, there should not be an addition of something that was wanting, but a turning to profit of what was in them. And the holy Cyprian indeed, now that the corruptible body no longer presseth down the soul, nor the earthly tabernacle presseth down the mind that museth upon many things, [1759] sees with greater clearness that truth to which his charity made him deserving to attain. May he therefore help us by his prayers, while we labor in the mortality of the flesh as in a darksome cloud, that if the Lord so grant it, we may imitate so far as we can the good that was in him. But if he thought otherwise than right on any point, and persuaded certain of his brethren and colleagues to entertain his views in a matter which he now sees clearly through the revelation of Him whom he loved, let us, who are far inferior to his merits, yet following, as our weakness will allow, the authority of the Catholic Church of which he was himself a conspicuous and most noble member, strive our utmost against heretics and schismatics, seeing that they, being cut off from the unity which he maintained, and barren of the love with which he was fruitful, and fallen away from the humility in which he stood, are disavowed and condemned the more by him, in proportion as he knows that they wish to search out his writings for purposes of treachery, and are unwilling to imitate what he did for the maintainance of peace,--like those who, calling themselves Nazarene Christians, and circumcising the foreskin of their flesh after the fashion of the Jews, being heretics by birth in that error from which Peter, when straying from the truth, was called by Paul [1760] persist in the same to the present day. As therefore they have remained in their perversity cut off from the body of the Church, while Peter has been crowned in the primacy of the apostles through the glory of martyrdom, so these men, while Cyprian, through the abundance of his love, has been received into the portion of the saints through the brightness of his passion, are obliged to recognize themselves as exiles from unity, and, in defence of their calumnies, set up a citizen of unity as an opponent against the very home of unity. Let us, therefore, go on to examine the other judgments of that Council after the same fashion.

[1759] Wisd. ix. 15.

[1760] Gal. ii. 11.

Chapter 2.

2. Marcus of Mactaris [1761] said: "It is not to be wondered at if heretics, being enemies and opponents of the truth, claim to themselves what has been entrusted and vouchsafed to other men. What is marvellous is that some of us, traitors to the truth, uphold heretics and oppose Christians; therefore we decree that heretics should be baptized." [1762]

3. To him we answer: It is indeed much more to be wondered at, and deserving of expressions of great praise, that Cyprian and his colleagues had such love for unity that they continued

in unity with those whom they considered to be traitors to the truth, without any apprehension of being polluted by them. For when Marcus said, "It is marvellous that some of us, traitors to the truth, uphold heretics and oppose Christians," it seemed natural that he should add, Therefore we decree that communion should not be held with them. This he did not say; but what he does say is, "Therefore we decree that heretics should be baptized," adhering to what the peaceful Cyprian had enjoined in the first instance, saying, "Judging no man, nor removing any from the right of communion if he entertain a different opinion." While, therefore, the Donatists calumniate us and call us traitors, I should be glad to know, supposing that any Jew or pagan were found, who, after reading the records of that Council should call both us and them, according to their own rules, traitors to the truth, how we should be able to make our joint defense so as to refute and wash away so grave a charge. They give the name of traitors to men whom they were never able in times past to convict of the offense, and whom they cannot now show to be involved in it, being themselves rather shown to be liable to the same charge. But what has this to do with us? What shall we say of them who, by their own showing, are unquestionably traitors? For if we, however falsely, are called traitors, because, as they allege, we took part in the same communion with traitors, we have all taken part with the traitors in question, seeing that in the time of the blessed Cyprian the party of Donatus had not yet separated itself from unity. For the delivery of the sacred books, from which they began to be called traitors, occurred somewhat more than forty years after his martyrdom. If, therefore, we are traitors, because we sprang from traitors, as they believe or pretend, we both of us derive our origin from those other traitors. For there is no room for saying that they did not communicate with these traitors, since they call them men of their own party. In the words of the Council which they are most forward to quote, "Some of us," it declares, "traitors to the truth, uphold heretics." To this is added the testimony of Cyprian, showing clearly that he remained in communion with them, when he says, "Judging no man, nor removing any from the right of communion if he entertain a different opinion." For those who entertained a different opinion were the very persons whom Marcus calls traitors to the truth because they upheld heretics, as he maintains, by receiving them into the Church without baptism. That it was, moreover, the custom that they should be so received, is testified both by Cyprian himself in many passages, and by some bishops in this Council. Whence it is evident that, if heretics have not baptism, the Church of Christ of those days was full of traitors, who upheld them by receiving them in this way. I would urge, therefore, that we plead our cause in common against the charge of treason which they cannot disavow, and therein our special case will be argued against the charge of delivering the books, which they could not prove against us. But let us argue the point as though they had convicted us; and what we shall answer jointly to those who urge against both of us the general treason of our forefathers, that we will answer to these men who urge against us that our forefathers gave up the sacred books. For as we were dead because our forefathers delivered up the books, which caused them to divide themselves from us, so both we and they themselves are dead through the treason of our forefathers, from whom both we and they are sprung. But since they say they live, they hold that that treason does not in any way affect them, therefore neither are we affected by the delivery of the books. And it should be observed that, according to them, the treason is indisputable: while, according to us, there is no truth either in the former charge of treason, because we say that heretics also may have the baptism of Christ; nor in the latter charge of delivering the books, because in that they were themselves beaten. They have therefore no reason for separating themselves by the wicked sin of schism, because, if our forefathers were not guilty of delivering up the books, as we say, there is no charge which can affect us at all; but if they were guilty of the sin, as these men say, then it is just as far from affecting us as the sin of those other traitors is from affecting either us or them. And hence, since there is no charge that can implicate us from the unrighteousness of our forefathers, the charge arising against them from their own schism is manifestly proved.

[1761] Mactaris (Macthari) was in ecclesiastical province of Byzacium. This bishop is probably the Marcus of Cypr. Ep. lxx.

[1762] Conc. Carth. sec. 38.

Chapter 3.

4. Satius of Sicilibba [1763] said: "If heretics receive forgiveness of their sins in their own baptism, it is without reason that they come to the Church. For since it is for sins that men are punished in the day of judgment, heretics have nothing to fear in the judgment of Christ if they have obtained remission of their sins." [1764]

5. This too might also have been our own judgment; but let its author beware in what spirit it was said. For it is expressed in terms of such import, that I should feel no compunction in consenting and subscribing to it in the same spirit in which I too believe that heretics may indeed have the baptism of Christ,

but cannot have the remission of their sins. But he does not say, If heretics baptize or are baptized, but "If heretics," he says, "receive forgiveness of their sins in their own baptism, it is without reason that they come to the Church." For if we were to set in the place of heretics those whom Cyprian knew within the Church as "renouncing the world in words alone and not in deeds," we also might express this same judgment, in just so many words, with the most perfect truth. If those who only seem to be converted receive forgiveness of their sins in their own baptism, it is without reason that they are afterwards led on to a true conversion. For since it is for sins that men are punished in the day of judgment, "those who renounce the world in words and not in deeds" have nothing to fear in the judgment of Christ if they have obtained remission of their sins. But this reasoning is only made perfect by some such context as is formed by the addition of the words. But they ought to fear the judgment of Christ, and to lose no time in being converted in the truth of their hearts; and, when they have done this, it is certainly not necessary that they should be baptized a second time. It was possible, therefore, for them to receive baptism, and either not to receive remission of their sins, or to be burdened again at once with the load of sins which were forgiven them; and so the same is the case also with the heretics.

[1763] Sicilibba was in ecclesiastical province of Zeugitana. In the text of this Council the bishop's name is Sattius, and the name occurs in Cypr. Epp. lvii., lxvii., lxx.

[1764] Con. Carth. sec. 39.

Chapter 4.

6. Victor of Gor [1765] said: "Seeing that sins are forgiven only in the baptism of the Church, he who admits heretics to communion without baptism is guilty of two errors contrary to reason; for, on the one hand, he does not cleanse the heretics, and, on the other, he defiles the Christians." [1766]

7. To this we answer that the baptism of the Church exists even among heretics, though they themselves are not within the Church; just as the water of Paradise was found in the land of Egypt, though that land was not itself in Paradise. We do not therefore admit heretics to communion without baptism; and since they come with their waywardness corrected, we receive not their sins, but the sacraments of Christ. And, in respect of the remission of their sins, we say again here exactly what we said above. And certainly, in regard of what he says at the end of his judgment, declaring that he "is guilty of two errors contrary to reason, seeing that on the one hand he does not cleanse the heretics, and on the other he defiles the Christians," Cyprian himself is the first and the most earnest in repudiating this with the colleagues who agreed with him. For neither did he think that he was defiled, when, on account of the bond of peace, he decreed that it was right to hold communion with such men, when he used the words, "Judging no one, nor removing any from the right of communion if he entertain a different opinion." Or, if heretics defile the Church by being admitted to communion without being baptized, then the whole Church has been defiled in virtue of that custom which has been so often recorded here. And just as those men call us traditors because of our forefathers, in whom they were able to prove nothing of the sort when they laid the charge against them, so, if every man partakes of the character of those with whom he may have held communion, all were then made

heretics. And if every one who asserts this is mad, it must be false that Victor says, when he declares that "he who admits heretics to communion without baptism, not only fails to cleanse the heretics, but pollutes the Christians as well." Or if this be true, they were then not admitted without baptism, but those men had the baptism of Christ, although it was given and received among heretics, who were so admitted in accordance with that custom which these very men acknowledged to exist; and on the same grounds they are even now rightly admitted in the same manner.

[1765] Gor (Gorduba) is variously supposed to be Garra in ecclesiastical province of Mauritania Cæsariensis, or Garriana in ecclesiastical province of Byzacium. The name of a bishop Victor occurs in Cypr. Epp. iv., lvii., lxii., lxvii. In Ep. lxx. the names of three.

[1766] Conc. Carth. sec. 40.

Chapter 5.

8. Aurelius of Utica [1767] said: "Since the apostle says that we ought not to be partakers with the sins of other men, [1768] what else does he do but make himself partaker with the sins of other men, who holds communion with heretics without the baptism of the Church? And therefore I pronounce my judgment that heretics should be baptized, that they may receive remission of their sins, and so communion be allowed to them." [1769]

9. The answer is: Therefore Cyprian and all those bishops were partakers in the sins of other men, inasmuch as they remained in communion with such men, when they removed no one from the right of communion who entertained a

different opinion. Where, then, is the Church? Then, to say nothing for the moment of heretics,--since the words of this judgment are applicable also to other sinners, such as Cyprian saw with lamentation to be in the Church with him, whom, while he confuted them, he yet tolerated,--where is the Church, which, according to these words must be held to have perished from that very moment by the contagion of their sins? But if, as is the most firmly established truth, the Church both has remained and does remain, the partaking of the sins of others, which is forbidden by the apostle, must be considered only to consist in consenting to them. But let heretics be baptized again, that they may receive remission of their sins, if the wayward and the envious are baptized again, who, seeing that "they renounced the world in words and not in deeds," were indeed able to receive baptism, but did not obtain remission of their sins, as the Lord says, "If ye forgive not men their trespasses, neither will your Father forgive your trespasses." [1770]

[1767] Utica, the well-known city in ecclesiastical province of Zeugitana. The Aurelius of Cypr. Epp. xxvii. 4, lvii. and lxvii. (the first) are more likely to be identical with the bishop of Utica, than with the Aurelius of Chullabis, who delivers his opinion the 81st in order.

[1768] 1 Tim. v. 22.

[1769] Conc. Carth. sec. 41.

[1770] Matt. vi. 15.

Chapter 6.

10. Iambus of Germaniciana [1771] said: "Those who approve the baptism of heretics disapprove ours, so as to deny that such as are, I will not say washed, but defiled outside the Church, ought to be baptized within the Church." [1772]

11. To him we answer, that none of our party approves the baptism of heretics, but all the baptism of Christ, even though it be found in heretics who are as it were chaff outside the Church, as it may be found in other unrighteous men who are as chaff within the Church. For if those who are baptized without the Church are not washed, but defiled, assuredly those who are baptized outside the rock on which the Church is built are not washed, but defiled. But all are without the said rock who hear the words of Christ and do them not. Or if it be the case that they are washed indeed in baptism, but yet continue in the defilement of their unrighteousness, from which they were unwilling to be changed for the better, the same is true also of the heretics.

[1771] Germaniciana Nova was in ecclesiastical province of Byzacium, and so called after the German veterans settled there. An Iambus is mentioned as bishop in Cypr. Epp. lvii., lxvii.

[1772] Conc. Carth. sec. 42.

Chapter 7.

12. Lucianus of Rucuma [1773] said: "It is written, And God saw the light that it was good, and God divided the light from the darkness.' [1774]If light and darkness can agree, then can there be something in common between us and heretics. Therefore I give my judgment that heretics should be baptized." [1775]

13. To him the answer is: If light and darkness can agree, then can there be something common between the righteous and unrighteous. Let him therefore declare his judgment that those unrighteous should be baptized afresh whom Cyprian confuted within the Church itself; or let him who can say if those are not unrighteous "who renounce the world in words and not in deeds."

[1773] Rucuma was in ecclesiastical province of Zeugitana. This Lucianus is probably the same with the one mentioned in Cypr. Epp. lvii., lxx.

[1774] Gen. i. 4.

[1775] Conc. Carth. sec. 43.

Chapter 8.

14. Pelagianus of Luperciana [1776] said: "It is written, Either the Lord is God, or Baal is God.' [1777]So now either the Church is the Church, or heresy is the Church. Further, if heresy be not the Church, how can the baptism of the Church exist among heretics?" [1778]

15. To him we may answer as follows: Either Paradise is Paradise, or Egypt is Paradise. Further, if Egypt be not Paradise, how can the water of Paradise be in Egypt? But it will be said to us that it extends even thither by flowing forth from Paradise. In like manner, therefore, baptism extends to heretics. Also we say: Either the rock is the Church, or the sand is the Church. Further, since the sand is not the Church, how can baptism exist with those who build upon the sand by hearing the words of Christ and doing them not? [1779]And yet

it does exist with them; and in like manner also it exists among the heretics.

[1776] The position of Luperciana in unknown.

[1777] See 1 Kings xviii. 21.

[1778] Con. Carth. sec. 44.

[1779] Matt. vii. 24-27.

Chapter 9.

16. Jader of Midila [1780] said: "We know that there is but one baptism in the Catholic Church, and therefore we ought not to admit a heretic unless he has been baptized in our body, lest he should think that he has been baptized outside the Catholic Church." [1781]

17. To him our answer is, that if this were said of those unrighteous men who are outside the rock, it certainly would be falsely said. And so it is therefore also in the case of heretics.

[1780] Midila (Midili) was in ecclesiastical province of Numidia. Jader is Punic name. Occurs as bishop in Cypr. Epp. lxxvi., lxxix.

[1781] Conc. Carth. sec. 45.

Chapter 10.

18. Likewise another Felix of Marazana [1782] said: "There is one faith, one baptism, [1783] but of the Catholic Church, to which alone is given authority to baptize." [1784]

19. What if another were to say as follows: One faith, one baptism, but of the righteous only, to whom alone authority is given to baptize? As these words might be refuted, so also may the judgment of Felix be refuted. Do even the unrighteous who are not [1785] changed in heart in baptism, while "they renounce the world in words and not in deeds" yet belong to the members of the Church? Let them consider whether such a Church is the actual rock, the very dove, the bride herself without spot or wrinkle. [1786]

[1782] Marazana was in ecclesiastical province of Byzacene. On Felix, see Bk. VI. c. 19. note 2.

[1783] Eph. iv. 5.

[1784] Conc. Carth. sec. 46.

[1785] Nec...mutati. "Nec" is restored by the Benedictines from the Mss.

[1786] Eph. v. 27. See Retract. ii. 18, quoted on I. 17, 26.

Chapter 11.

20. Paul of Bobba [1787] said: "I for my part am not moved if some fail to uphold the faith and truth of the Church, seeing that the apostle says For what if some did not believe? shall their unbelief make the faith of God without effect? God forbid: yea let God be true, but every man a liar.' [1788]But if God be true, how can the truth of baptism be in the company of heretics, where God is not?" [1789]

21. To him we answer: What is God among the covetous? And yet baptism exists among them; and so also it exists among heretics. For they among whom God is, are the temple of

God. "But what agreement hath the temple of God with idols?" [1790]Further, Paul considers, and Cyprian agrees with him, that covetousness is idolatry; and Cyprian himself again associates with his colleagues, who were robbers, but yet baptized, with great reward of toleration.

[1787] Bobba (Obba) was in ecclesiastical province of Mauritania Cæsariensis, including Tingitana. A bishop Paul is mentioned in Cypr. Ep. lxvii.

[1788] Rom. iii. 3, 4.

[1789] Conc. Carth. sec. 47.

[1790] 2 Cor. vi. 16.

Chapter 12.

22. Pomponius of Dionysiana [1791] said: "It is manifest that heretics cannot baptize and give remission of sins, seeing that no power is given to them that they should be able either to loose or bind anything on earth." [1792]

23. The answer is: This power is not given to murderers either, that is, to those who hate their brothers. For it was not said to such as these, "whosesoever sins ye remit, they are remitted unto them; and whosesoever sins ye retain, they are retained." [1793]And yet they baptize, and both Paul tolerates them in the same communion of baptism, and Cyprian acknowledges them.

[1791] Dionysiana was in ecclesiastical province of Byzacium. The name of Pomponius occurs in Cypr. Epp. iv., lvii., lxvii., lxx.

[1792] Conc. Carth. sec. 48.

[1793] John xx. 23.

Chapter 13.

24. Venantius of Tinisa [1794] said: "If a husband, going on a journey into foreign countries, had entrusted the guardianship of his wife to a friend, he would surely keep her that was entrusted to his care with the utmost diligence, that her chastity and holiness might not be defiled by any one. Christ our Lord and God, when going to the Father, committed His bride to our care: do we keep her uncorrupt and undefiled, or do we betray her purity and chastity to adulterers and corrupters? For he who makes the baptism of Christ common with heretics betrays the bride of Christ to adulterers." [1795]

25. We answer: What of those who, when they are baptized, turn themselves to the Lord with their lips and not with their heart? do not they possess an adulterous mind? Are not they themselves lovers of the world, which they renounce in words and not in deeds; and they corrupt good manners through evil communications, saying, "Let us eat and drink; for to-morrow we die?" [1796]Did not the discourse of the apostle take heed even against such as these, when he says, "But I fear, lest by any means, as the serpent beguiled Eve through his subtilty, so your minds [also] should be corrupted from the simplicity that is in Christ?" [1797]When, therefore, Cyprian held the baptism of Christ to be in common with such men, did he therefore betray the bride of Christ into the hands of adulterers, or did he not rather recognize the necklace of the Bridegroom even on an adulteress?

[1794] Tinisa (Thinisa) was in ecclesiastical province of Zeugitana. In Cypr. Ep. lxvii. the name Venantius is found.

[1795] Conc. Carth. sec. 49.

[1796] 1 Cor. xv. 33, 32.

[1797] 2 Cor. xi. 3.

Chapter 14.

26. Aymnius [1798] of Ausuaga [1799] said: "We have received one baptism, which same also we administer; but he who says that authority is given to heretics also to baptize, the same makes two baptisms." [1800]

27. To him we answer: Why does not he also make two baptisms who maintains that the unrighteous also can baptize? For although the righteous and unrighteous are in themselves opposed to one another, yet the baptism which the righteous give, such as was Paul, or such as was also Cyprian, is not contrary to the baptism which those unrighteous men were wont to give who hated Paul, whom Cyprian understands to have been not heretics, but bad Catholics; and although the moderation which was found in Cyprian, and the covetousness which was found in his colleagues, are in themselves opposed to one another, yet the baptism which Cyprian used to give was not contrary to the baptism which his colleagues who opposed him used to give, but one and the same with it, because in both cases it is He that baptizes of whom it is said, "The same is He which baptizeth." [1801]

[1798] Ahymmus. See Cypr. Ep. lvi.

[1799] Ausuaga was in ecclesiastical province of Zeugitana.

[1800] Conc. Carth. sec. 50.

[1801] John i. 33.

Chapter 15.

28. Saturninus of Victoriana [1802] said: "If heretics may baptize, they are excused and defended in doing unlawful things; nor do I see why either Christ called them His adversaries, or the apostle called them antichrists." [1803]

29. To him we answer: We say that heretics have no authority to baptize in the same sense in which we say that defrauders have no authority to baptize. For not only to the heretic, but to the sinner, God says, "What hast thou to do to declare my statutes, or that thou shouldest take my covenant in thy mouth?" To the same person He assuredly says, "When thou sawest a thief, then thou consentedst with him." [1804] How much worse, therefore, are those who did not consent with thieves, but themselves were wont to plunder farms with treacherous deceits? Yet Cyprian did not consent with them, though he did tolerate them in the corn-field of the Catholic Church, lest the wheat should be rooted out together with it. And yet at the same time the baptism which they themselves conferred was the very selfsame baptism, because it was not of them, but of Christ. As therefore they, although the baptism of Christ be recognized in them, were yet not excused and defended in doing unlawful things, and Christ rightly called those His adversaries who were destined, by persevering in such things, to hear the doom, "Depart from me, ye that work iniquity," [1805] whence also they are called antichrists, because they are contrary to Christ while they live in opposition to His words, so likewise is it the case with heretics.

[1802] Victoriana was in ecclesiastical province of Byzacium. [The name Saturninus is found in Cypr. Epp. xxi. 4, xxii. 3, xxvii. 1, 11, lvii. ter. lxvii. bis, lxx. quinquies.

[1803] Conc. Carth. sec. 51.

[1804] Ps. l. 16, 18.

[1805] Matt. vii. 23.

Chapter 16.

30. Another Saturninus of Tucca [1806] said: "The Gentiles, although they worship idols, yet acknowledge and confess the supreme God, the Father and Creator. Against Him Marcion blasphemes, and some men do not blush to approve the baptism of Marcion. [1807] How do such priests either maintain or vindicate the priesthood of God, who do not baptize the enemies of God, and hold communion with them while they are thus unbaptized?" [1808]

31. The answer is this: Truly when such terms as this are used, all moderation is passed; nor do they take into consideration that even they themselves hold communion with such men, "judging no one, nor removing any from the right of communion if he entertain a contrary opinion." But Saturninus has used an argument in this very judgment of his, which might furnish materials for his admonition (if he would pay attention to it), that in each man what is wrong should be corrected, and what is right should be approved, since he says, "The Gentiles, although they worship idols, yet acknowledge and confess the supreme God, the Father and Creator." If, then, any Gentile of such a kind should come to God, would he wish to correct and change this point in him, that he acknowledged and confessed

God the Father and Creator? I trow not. But he would amend in him his idolatry, which was an evil in him; and he would give to him the sacraments of Christ, which he did not possess; and anything that was wayward which he found in him he would correct; and anything which had been wanting he would supply. So also in the Marcionist heretic he would acknowledge the perfectness of baptism, he would correct his waywardness, he would teach him Catholic truth.

[1806] Tucca was in ecclesiastical province of Numidia. For Saturninus, see c. 15-28, n. 2.

[1807] He is alluding to Stephen, bishop of Rome, of whom Cyprian says in his Ep. lxxiv. 7 (to Pompeius): "Why has the perverse obstinacy of our brother Stephen burst out to such a point, that he should even contend that sons of God are born of the baptism of Marcion, also of Valentinus and Apelles, and others who blaspheme against God the Father?"

[1808] Conc. Carth. sec. 52.

Chapter 17.

32. Marcellus of Zama [1809] said: "Since sins are remitted only in the baptism of the Church, he who does not baptize a heretic holds communion with a sinner." [1810]

33. What, does he who holds communion with one who does this not hold communion with a sinner? But what else did all of them do, "in judging no one, or removing from the right of communion any one who entertained a different opinion"? Where, then, is the Church? Are those things not an obstacle to those who are patient, and tolerate the tares lest the wheat should be rooted out together with them? I would have them

therefore say, who have committed the sacrilege of schism by separating themselves from the whole world, how it comes that they have in their mouths the judgment of Cyprian, while they do not have in their hearts the patience of Cyprian. But to this Marcellus we have an answer in what has been said above concerning baptism and the remission of sins, explaining how there can be baptism in a man although there be in him no remission of his sins.

[1809] Zama was in ecclesiastical province of Numidia. For Marcellus, see Cypr. Ep. lxvii.

[1810] Conc. Carth. sec. 53.

Chapter 18.

34. Irenæus of Ululi [1811] said: "If the Church does not baptize a heretic, because it is said that he has been baptized already, then heresy is the greater." [1812]

35. The answer is: On the same principle it might be said, If therefore the Church does not baptize the covetous man, because it is said that he has been baptized already, then covetousness is the greater. But this is false, therefore the other is also false.

[1811] Ululi (Ullita, Vallita) in ecclesiastical province of Numidia.

[1812] Conc. Carth. sec. 54.

Chapter 19.

36. Donatus of Cibaliana [1813] said: "I acknowledge one Church, and one baptism that appertains thereto. If there is

any one who says that the grace of baptism exists among heretics, he must first show and prove that the Church exists with them." [1814]

37. To him we answer: If you say that the grace of baptism is identical with baptism, then it exists among heretics; but if baptism is the sacrament or outward sign of grace, while the grace itself is the abolition of sins, then the grace of baptism does not exist with heretics. But so there is one baptism and one Church, just as there is one faith. As therefore the good and bad, not having one hope, can yet have one baptism, so those who have not one common Church can have one common baptism.

[1813] ^ [Cibaliana (Cybaliana), most probably in ecclesiastical province of Africa Proconsularis.] Donatus, as contemporary bishop, occurs in Cypr. Epp. lvii. bis. lxx. bis.

[1814] Conc. Carth. sec. 55.

Chapter 20.

38. Zozimus of Tharassa [1815] said: "When a revelation has been made of the truth, error must give way to truth; inasmuch as Peter also, who before was wont to circumcise, gave way to Paul when he declared the truth." [1816]

39. The answer is: This may also be considered as the expression of our judgment too, and this is just what has been done in respect of this question of baptism. For after that the truth had been more clearly revealed, error gave way to truth, when that most wholesome custom was further confirmed by the authority of a plenary Council. It is well, however, that they so constantly bear in mind that it was possible even for Peter,

the chief of the apostles, to have been at one time minded otherwise than the truth required; which we believe, without any disrespect to Cyprian, to have been the case with him, and that with all our love for Cyprian, for it is not right that he should be loved with greater love than Peter.

[1815] Tharassa was in ecclesiastical province of Numidia.

[1816] Gal ii. 11; Conc. Carth. sec. 56.

Chapter 21.

40. Julianus of Telepte [1817] said: "It is written, A man can receive nothing, except it be given him from heaven;' [1818] if heresy is from heaven, it can give baptism." [1819]

41. Let him hear another also saying: If covetousness is from heaven, it can give baptism. And yet the covetous do confer it; so therefore also may the heretics.

[1817] Telepte (Thelepte) or Thala, was in ecclesiastical province of Byzacium.

[1818] John iii. 27.

[1819] Conc. Carth. sec. 57.

Chapter 22.

42. Faustus of Timida Regia [1820] said: "Let not these persons flatter themselves who favor heretics. He who interferes with the baptism of the Church on behalf of heretics makes them Christians, and us heretics." [1821]

43. To him we answer: If any one were to say that a man who, when he received baptism had not received remission of his

sins, because he entertained hatred towards his brother in his heart, was nevertheless not to be baptized again when he dismissed that hatred from his heart, does such a man interfere with the baptism of the Church on behalf of murderers, or does he make them righteous and us murderers? Let him therefore understand the same also in the case of heretics.

[1820] Timida Regia was in ecclesiastical province of Zeugitana. A Faustus is mentioned in Cypr. Ep. lxvii.

[1821] Conc. Carth. sec. 58.

Chapter 23.

44. Geminius of Furni [1822] said: "Certain of our colleagues may prefer heretics to themselves, they cannot prefer them to us: and therefore what we have once decreed we hold, that we should baptize those who come to us from heretics." [1823]

45. This man also acknowledges most openly that certain of his colleagues entertained opinions contrary to his own: whence again and again the love of unity is confirmed, because they were separated from one another by no schism, till God should reveal to one or other of them anything wherein they were otherwise minded. [1824]But to him our answer is, that his colleagues did not prefer heretics to themselves, but that, as the baptism of Christ is acknowledged in the covetous, in the fraudulent, in robbers, in murderers, so also they acknowledged it in heretics.

[1822] Furni was in ecclesiastical province of Zeugitana. For Geminius as bishop, see Cypr. Ep. lxvii.

[1823] Conc. Carth. sec. 59.

[1824] Phil. iii. 15.

Chapter 24.

46. Rogatianus of Nova [1825] said: "Christ established the Church, the devil heresy: how can the synagogue of Satan have the baptism of Christ?" [1826]

47. To him our answer is: Is it true that because Christ established the well-affected, and the devil the envious, therefore the party of the devil, which is proved to be among the envious, cannot have the baptism of Christ?

[1825] Nova was in ecclesiastical province of Mauritania Cæsariensis. For Rogatianus as bishop, see Cypr. Epp. lvii., lxvii., lxx., bis.

[1826] Conc. Carth. sec. 60.

Chapter 25.

48. Therapius of Bulla [1827] said: "If a man gives up and betrays the baptism of Christ to heretics, what else can he be said to be but a Judas to the Bride of Christ?" [1828]

49. How great a condemnation have we here of all schismatics, who have separated themselves by wicked sacrilege from the inheritance of Christ dispersed throughout the whole world, if Cyprian held communion with such as was the traitor Judas, and yet was not defiled by them; or if he was defiled, then were all made such as Judas; or if they were not, then the evil deeds of those who went before do not belong to those who came after even though they were the offspring of the same communion. Why, therefore, do they cast in our teeth the traditores, against whom they did not prove their charge, and

do not cast in their own teeth Judas, with whom Cyprian and his colleagues held communion? Behold the Council in which these men are wont to boast! We indeed say, that he who approves the baptism of Christ even in heretics, does not betray to heretics the baptism of Christ; just in the same way as he does not betray to murderers the baptism of Christ who approves the baptism of Christ even in murderers: but inasmuch as they profess to prescribe to us from the decrees of this Council what opinions we ought to hold, let them first assent to it themselves. See how therein were compared to the traitor Judas, all who said that heretics, although baptized in heresy, should not be baptized again. Yet with such Cyprian was willing to hold communion, when he said, "Judging no man, nor depriving any of the right of communion if he entertain a contrary opinion." But that there had been men of such a sort in former times within the Church, is made clear by the sentence in which he says: "But some one will say, What, then, shall be done with these men who in times past were admitted into the Church without baptism?" [1829]That such had been the custom of the Church, is testified again and again by the very men who compose this Council. If, therefore, any one who does this "can be said to be nothing else but a Judas to the Bride of Christ," according to the terms in which the judgment of Therapius is couched; but Judas, according to the teaching of the gospel, was a traitor; then all those men held communion with traitors who at that time uttered those very judgments, and before they uttered them they all had become traitors through that custom which at that time was retained by the Church. All, therefore--that is to say, both we and they themselves who were the offspring of that unity--are traitors. But we defend ourselves in two ways: first, because without prejudice to the right of unity, as Cyprian himself declared in his opening speech, we do not assent to the decrees of this Council in which this judgment was pronounced; and secondly, because we hold that the wicked in no way hurt the good in Catholic unity, until at the last the chaff be separated from the wheat. But our opponents, inasmuch as they both shelter themselves as it were under the decrees of this Council, and maintain that the good perish as by a kind of infection from communion with the wicked, have no resource to save them from allowing both that the earlier Christians, whose offspring they are, were traitors, inasmuch as they are convicted by their own Council; and that the deeds of those who went before them do reflect on them, since they throw in our teeth the deeds of our ancestors.

[1827] Bulla (Vulla) was in ecclesiastical province of Africa Proconsularis. For Therapius cp. Cypr. Ep. lxiv. 1.

[1828] Conc. Carth. sec. 61.

[1829] Cypr. Ep. lxxiii. 23.

Chapter 26.

50. Also another Lucius of Membresa [1830] said: "It is written, God heareth not sinners.' [1831]How can he who is a sinner be heard in baptism?" [1832]

51. We answer: How is the covetous man heard, or the robber, and usurer, and murderer? Are they not sinners? And yet Cyprian, while he finds fault with them in the Catholic Church, yet tolerates them.

[1830] Membresa was in ecclesiastical province of Zeugitana. For Lucius, see Bk. VI. c. 38.

[1831] John ix. 31.

[1832] Conc. Carth. sec. 62.

Chapter 27.

52. Also another Felix of Buslaceni [1833] said: "In admitting heretics to the Church without baptism, let no one place custom before reason and truth; for reason and truth always exclude custom." [1834]

53. To him our answer is: You do not show the truth; you confess the existence of the custom. We should therefore do right in maintaining the custom which has since been confirmed by a plenary Council, even if the truth were still concealed, which we believe to have been already made manifest.

[1833] Buslaceni (Cussaceni) is probably Byzacium, the capital of province of Byzacium, since we know that it was also called Bizica Lucana; others place it in Africa Proconsularis. For Felix, cp. Bk. VI. cc. 19 and 23.

[1834] Conc. Carth. sec. 63.

Chapter 28.

54. Another Saturninus of Abitini [1835] said: "If Antichrist can give to any one the grace of Christ, then can heretics also baptize, who are called Antichrists." [1836]

55. What if another were to say, If a murderer can give the grace of Christ, then can they also baptize that hate their brethren who are called murderers? For certainly he would

seem in a way to speak the truth, and yet they can baptize; in like manner, therefore, can the heretics as well.

[1835] Abitini (Avitini) was in ecclesiastical province of Africa Proconsularis. For Saturninus, cp. cc. 15, 16.

[1836] Conc. Carth. sec. 64.

Chapter 29.

56. Quintus of Aggya [1837] said: "He who has a thing can give it; but what can the heretics give, who are well known to have nothing?" [1838]

57. To him our answer is: If, then, any man can give a thing who has it, it is clear that heretics can give baptism: for when they separate from the Church, they have still the sacrament of washing which they had received while in the Church; for when they return they do not again receive it, because they had not lost it when they withdrew from the Church.

[1837] Aggya, probably the same as Aggiva and the Aga in ecclesiastical province of Proconsular Africa. The name Quintas as bishop occurs in Cypr. Epp lvii., lxvii., lxx., lxxi., but this one is of Mauritania, as appears from Epp lxxii. 1, lxxiii. 1.

[1838] Conc. Carth. sec. 65.

Chapter 30.

58. Another Julianus of Marcelliana [1839] said: "If a man can serve two masters, God and mammon, [1840] then baptism also can serve two, the Christian and the heretic." [1841]

59. Truly, if it can serve the self-restrained and the covetous man, the sober and the drunken, the well-affectioned and the

murderer, why should it not also serve the Christian and the heretic?--whom, indeed, it does not really serve; but it ministers to them, and is administered by them, for salvation to those who use it right, and for judgment to such as use it wrong.

[1839] Marcelliana (Gyrnmarcelli) in ecclesiastical province of Numidia.

[1840] Matt. vi. 24.

[1841] Conc. Carth. sec. 66.

Chapter 31.

60. Tenax of Horrea Celiæ [1842] said: "There is one baptism, but of the Church; and where the Church is not, there baptism also cannot be." [1843]

61. To him we answer: How then comes it that it may be where the rock is not, but only sand; seeing that the Church is on the rock, and not on sand?

[1842] Horrea Celiæ (Cæliæ) was a village of ecclesiastical province of Byzacium, ten miles north of Hadrumetum. A Tenax is mentioned as bishop in Cypr. Ep. lxvii.

[1843] Conc. Carth. sec. 67.

Chapter 32.

62. Another Victor of Assuras [1844] said: "It is written, that there is one God and one Christ, one Church and one baptism.' [1845]How then can any one baptize in a place where there is not either God, or Christ, or the Church?" [1846]

63. How can any one baptize either in that sand, where the Church is not, seeing that it is on the rock; nor God and Christ, seeing that there is not there the temple of God and Christ?

[1844] Assuras was in ecclesiastical province of Zeugitana. For Victor, cp. c. 4.

[1845] See Eph. iv. 4-6.

[1846] Conc. Carth. sec. 68.

Chapter 33.

64. Donatulus of Capse [1847] said: "I also have always entertained this opinion, that heretics, who have gained nothing outside the Church, should be baptized when they are converted to the Church." [1848]

65. To this the answer is: They have, indeed, gained nothing outside the Church, but that is nothing towards salvation, not nothing towards the sacrament. For salvation is peculiar to the good; but the sacraments are common to the good and bad alike.

[1847] Capse was in ecclesiastical province of Byzacene. This Donatulus is probably to be identified with the one mentioned Cypr. Ep. lvi.

[1848] Conc. Carth. sec. 69.

Chapter 34.

66. Verulus of Rusiccade [1849] said: "A man that is a heretic cannot give that which he has not; much more is this the case with a schismatic, who has lost what he had." [1850]

67. We have already shown that they still have it, because they do not lose it when they separate themselves. For they do not receive it again when they return: wherefore, if it was thought that they could not give it because they were supposed not to have it, let it now be understood that they can give it, because it is understood that they also have it.

[1849] Rusiccade was at the mouth of the Thapsus, in ecclesiastical province of Numidia.

[1850] Conc. Carth. sec. 70.

Chapter 35.

68. Pudentianus of Cuiculi [1851] said: "My recent ordination to the episcopate induced me, brethren, to wait and hear what my elders would decide. For it is plain that heresies have and can have nothing; and so, if any come from them, it is determined righteously that they should be baptized." [1852]

69. As, therefore, we have already answered those who went before, for whose judgment this man was waiting, so be it understood that we have answered himself.

[1851] Cuiculi was in ecclesiastical province of Numidia.

[1852] Conc. Carth. sec. 71.

Chapter 36.

70. Peter of Hippo Diarrhytus [1853] said: "Since there is one baptism in the Catholic Church, it is clear that a man cannot be baptized outside the Church; and therefore I give my judgment, that those who have been bathed in heresy or in schism ought to be baptized on coming to the Church." [1854]

71. There is one baptism in the Catholic Church, in such a sense that, when any have gone out from it, it does not become two in those who go out, but remains one and the same. What, therefore, is recognized in those who return, should also be recognized in those who received it from men who have separated themselves, since they did not lose it when they went apart into heresy.

[1853] Hippo Diarrhytus (Hippozaritus) was on the coast in ecclesiastical province of Zeugitana. For Petrus, cp. Cypr. Ep. lxvii.

[1854] Conc. Carth. sec. 72.

Chapter 37.

72. Likewise another Lucius of Ausafa [1855] said: "According to the motion of my mind and of the Holy Spirit, since there is one God, the Father of our Lord Jesus Christ, and one Christ, and one hope, one Spirit, one Church, there ought also to be only one baptism. And therefore I say, both that if anything has been set on foot or done among the heretics, that it ought to be rescinded; and also, that they who come out from among the heretics should be baptized in the Church." [1856]

73. Let it therefore be pronounced of no effect that they baptize, who hear the words of God and do them not, when they shall begin to pass from unrighteousness to righteousness, that is, from the sand to the rock. And if this is not done, because what there was in them of Christ was not violated by their unrighteousness, then let this also be understood in the case of heretics: for neither is there the same hope in the unrighteous, so long as they are on the sand, as there is in those who are upon the rock; and yet there is in both the same

baptism, although as it is said that there is one hope, so also is it said that there is one baptism.

[1855] Ausafa was in ecclesiastical province of Zeugitana. For Lucius, cp. Bk. VI. cc. 14 and 38, and Bk. VII. c. 26.

[1856] Conc. Carth. sec. 73.

Chapter 38.

74. Felix of Gurgites [1857] said: "I give my judgment, that, according to the precepts of the holy Scriptures, those who have been unlawfully baptized outside the Church by heretics, if they wish to flee to the Church, should obtain the grace of baptism where it is lawfully given." [1858]

75. Our answer is: Let them indeed begin to have in a lawful manner to salvation what they before had unlawfully to destruction; because each man is justified under the same baptism, when he has turned himself to God with a true heart, as that under which he was condemned, when on receiving it he "renounced the world in words alone, and not in deeds."

[1857] Gurgites was in ecclesiastical province of Byzacium. For Felix, cp. Bk. VI. cc. 19, 33, 40; Bk. VII. cc. 10, 28.

[1858] Conc. Carth. sec. 74.

Chapter 39.

76. Pusillus of Lamasba [1859] said: "I believe that baptism is not unto salvation except within the Catholic Church. Whatsoever is without the Catholic Church is mere pretense." [1860]

77. This indeed is true, that "baptism is not unto salvation except within the Catholic Church." For in itself it can indeed exist outside the Catholic Church as well; but there it is not unto salvation, because there it does not work salvation; just as that sweet savor of Christ is certainly not unto salvation in them that perish, [1861] though from a fault not in itself, but in them. But "whatsoever is without the Catholic Church is mere pretense," yet only in so far as it is not Catholic. But there may be something Catholic outside the Catholic Church, just as the name of Christ could exist outside the congregation of Christ, in which name he who did not follow with the disciples was casting out devils. [1862] For there may be pretense also within the Catholic Church, as is unquestionable in the case of those "who renounce the world in words and not in deeds," and yet the pretense is not Catholic. As, therefore, there is in the Catholic Church something which is not Catholic, so there may be something which is Catholic outside the Catholic Church.

[1859] Lamasba was in ecclesiastical province of Numidia.

[1860] Conc. Carth. sec. 75.

[1861] 2 Cor. ii. 15.

[1862] Mark ix. 38.

Chapter 40.

78. Salvianus of Gazaufala [1863] said: "It is generally known that heretics have nothing; and therefore they come to us, that they may receive what previously they did not have." [1864]

79. Our answer is: On this theory, the very men who founded heresies are not heretics themselves, because they separated themselves from the Church, and certainly they previously had

what they received there. But if it is absurd to say that those are not heretics through whom the rest became heretics, it is therefore possible that a heretic should have what turns to his destruction through his evil use of it.

[1863] Gazaufala (Gazophyla) was in ecclesiastical province of Numidia.

[1864] Conc. Carth. sec. 76.

Chapter 41.

80. Honoratus of Tucca [1865] said: "Since Christ is the truth, we ought to follow the truth rather than custom; that we may sanctify by the baptism of the Church the heretics who come to us, simply because they could receive nothing outside." [1866]

81. This man, too, is a witness to the custom, in which he gives us the greatest assistance, whatever else he may appear to say against us. But this is not the reason why heretics come over to us, because they have received nothing outside, but that what they did receive may begin to be of use to them: for this it could not be outside in any wise.

[1865] Tucca (Thucca) was in ecclesiastical province of Numidia. Honoratus occurs as bishop's name in Cypr. Epp. lvii., lxii., lxvii., lxx. bis. The attempts to distinguish or to identify these are hazardous.

[1866] Conc. Carth. sec. 77.

Chapter 42.

82. Victor of Octavus [1867] said: "As ye yourselves also know, I have not been long appointed a bishop, and therefore I

waited for the counsel of my seniors. This therefore I express as my opinion, that whosoever comes from heresy should undoubtedly be baptized." [1868]

83. What, therefore, has been answered to those for whom he waited, may be taken as the answer also to himself.

[1867] Octavus was in ecclesiastical province of Numidia. For Victor, cp. cc. 4, 32.

[1868] Conc. Carth. sec. 78.

Chapter 43.

84. Clarus of Mascula [1869] said: "The sentence of our Lord Jesus Christ is manifest, when He sent forth His apostles, and gave the power which had been given Him of His Father to them alone, whose successors we are, governing the Church of the Lord with the same power, and baptizing those who believe the faith. And therefore heretics, who, being without, have neither power nor the Church of Christ, cannot baptize any one with His baptism." [1870]

85. Are, then, ill-affectioned murderers successors of the apostles? Why, then, do they baptize? Is it because they are not outside? But they are outside the rock, to which the Lord gave the keys, and on which He said that He would build His Church. [1871]

[1869] Mascula was in ecclesiastical province of Numidia.

[1870] Conc. Carth. Ibid. sec. 79.

[1871] Matt. xvi. 18, 19.

Chapter 44.

86. Secundianus of Thambei [1872] said: "We ought not to deceive heretics by our too great forwardness, that not having been baptized in the Church of our Lord Jesus Christ, and having therefore not received remission of their sins, they may not impute to us, when the day of judgment comes, that we have been the cause of their not being baptized, and not having obtained the indulgence of the grace of God. On which account, since there is one Church and one baptism, when they are converted to us, let them receive together with the Church the baptism also of the Church." [1873]

87. Nay, when they are transferred to the rock, and joined to the society of the Dove, let them receive the remission of their sins, which they could not have outside the rock and outside the Dove, whether they were openly without, like the heretics, or apparently within, like the abandoned Catholics; of whom, however, it is clear that they both have and confer baptism without remission of sins, when even from themselves it is received by men, who, being not changed for the better, honor God with their lips, while their heart is far from Him. [1874]Yet it is true that there is one baptism, just as there is one Dove, though those who are not in the one communion of the Dove may yet have baptism in common.

[1872] Thambei (Thambi, Satambei), was in ecclesiastical province of Byzacium.

[1873] Conc. Carth. sec. 80.

[1874] Isa. xxix. 13.

Chapter 45.

88. Also another Aurelius of Chullabi [1875] said: "The Apostle John has laid down in his epistle the following precept: If there come any unto you, and bring not this doctrine, receive him not into your house, neither bid him God speed: for he that biddeth him God speed is partaker of his evil deeds.' [1876]How can such men be admitted without consideration into the house of God, who are forbidden to be admitted into our private house? Or how can we hold communion with them without the baptism of Christ, when, if we only so much as bid them God speed, we are partakers of their evil deeds?" [1877]

89. In respect of this testimony of John there is no need of further disputation, since it has no reference at all to the question of baptism, which we are at present discussing. For he says, "If any come unto you, and bring not the doctrine of Christ." But heretics leaving the doctrine of their error are converted to the doctrine of Christ, that they may be incorporated with the Church, and may begin to belong to the members of that Dove whose sacrament they previously had; and therefore what previously they lacked belonging to it is given to them, that is to say, peace and charity out of a pure heart, and of a good conscience, and of faith unfeigned. [1878]But what they previously had belonging to the Dove is acknowledged, and received without any depreciation; just as in the adulteress God recognises His gifts, even when she is following her lovers; because when after her fornication is corrected she is turned again to chastity, those gifts are not laid to her charge, but she herself is corrected. [1879]But just as Cyprian might have defended himself if this testimony of John had been cast in his teeth whilst he was holding communion with men like these, so let those against whom it is spoken

make their own defense. For to the question before us, as I said before, it has no reference at all. For John says that we are not to bid God speed to men of strange doctrine; but Paul the apostle says, with even greater vehemence, "If any man that is called a brother be covetous, or a drunkard," or anything of the sort, with such an one no not to eat; [1880] and yet Cyprian used to admit to fellowship, not with his private table, but with the altar of God, his colleagues who were usurers, and treacherous, and fraudulent, and robbers. But in what manner this may be defended has been sufficiently set forth in other books already.

[1875] Chullabi, or Cululi, was in ecclesiastical province of Byzacium. For Aurelius, cp. c. 5.

[1876] 2 John 10, 11.

[1877] Conc. Carth. sec. 81.

[1878] 1 Tim. i. 5.

[1879] Hos. ii.

[1880] 1 Cor. v. 11.

Chapter 46.

90. Litteus [1881] of Gemelli [1882] said: "If the blind lead the blind, both shall fall into the ditch.' [1883]Since, therefore, it is clear that heretics can give no light [1884] to any one, as being blind themselves, therefore their baptism is invalid." [1885]

91. Neither do we say that it is valid for salvation so long as they are heretics, just as it is of no value to those murderers of whom we spoke, so long as they hate their brethren: for they

also themselves are in darkness, and if any one follows them they fall together into the ditch; and yet it does not follow that they either have not baptism or are unable to confer it.

[1881] Some read Licteus; not unlikely the bishop of Cypr. Ep. lxxvi.

[1882] Gemelli was a Roman colony in ecclesiastical province of Numidia.

[1883] Matt xv. 14.

[1884] Illuminare; baptism being often called photismos.

[1885] Conc. Carth. sec. 82.

Chapter 47.

92. Natalis of Oëa [1886] said: "It is not only I myself who am present, but also Pompeius of Sabrati, [1887] and Dioga of Leptis Magna, [1888] who commissioned me to represent their views, being absent indeed in body, but present in spirit, who deliver this same judgment as our colleagues, that heretics cannot have communion with us, unless they have been baptized with the baptism of the Church." [1889]

93. He means, I suppose, that communion which belongs to the society of the Dove; for in the partaking of the sacraments they doubtless held communion with them, judging no man, nor removing any from the right of communion if he held a different opinion. But with whatever reference he spoke, there is no great need for these words being refuted. For certainly a heretic would not be admitted to communion, unless he had been baptized with the baptism of the Church. But it is clear that the baptism of the Church exists even among heretics if it

be consecrated with the words of the gospel; just as the gospel itself belongs to the Church, and has nothing to do with their waywardness, but certainly retains its own holiness.

[1886] Sabrati, Oëa and Leptis Magna were the three cities whose combination gave its name to Tripolis, an ecclesiastical province.

[1887] Sabrati, Oëa and Leptis Magna were the three cities whose combination gave its name to Tripolis, an ecclesiastical province.

[1888] Sabrati, Oëa and Leptis Magna were the three cities whose combination gave its name to Tripolis, an ecclesiastical province.

[1889] Conc. Carth. sec. 83-85.

Chapter 48.

94. Junius of Neapolis [1890] said: "I do not depart from the judgment which we once pronounced, that we should baptize heretics on their coming to the Church." [1891]

95. Since this man has adduced no argument nor proof from the Scriptures, he need not detain us long.

[1890] Neapolis was in ecclesiastical province of Zeugitana. The name Junius as bishop appears in Cypr. Epp. lvii., lxx.

[1891] Conc. Carth. sec. 86.

Chapter 49.

96. Cyprian of Carthage said: "My opinion has been set forth with the greatest fullness in the letter which has been written to

our colleague Jubaianus, [1892] that heretics being called enemies of Christ and antichrists according to the testimony of the gospel and the apostles, should, when they come to the Church, be baptized with the one baptism of the Church, that from enemies they may be made friends, and that from antichrists they may be made Christians." [1893]

97. What need is there of further disputation here, seeing that we have already handled with the utmost care that very epistle to Jubaianus of which he has made mention? And as to what he has said here, let us not forget that it might be said of all unrighteous men who, as he himself bears witness, are in the Catholic Church, and whose power of possessing and of conferring baptism is not questioned by any of us. For they come to the Church, who pass to Christ from the party of the devil, and build upon the rock, and are incorporated with the Dove, and are placed in security in the garden enclosed and fountain sealed; where none of those are found who live contrary to the precepts of Christ, wherever they may seem to be. For in the epistle which he wrote to Magnus, while discussing this very question, he himself warned us at sufficient length, and in no ambiguous terms, of what kind of society we should understand that the Church consists. For he says, in speaking of a certain man, "Let him become an alien and profane, an enemy to the peace and unity of the Lord, not dwelling in the house of God, that is to say, in the Church of Christ, in which none dwell save those who are of one heart and of one mind." [1894]Let those, therefore, who would lay injunctions on us on the authority of Cyprian, pay attention for a time to what we here say. For if only those who are of one heart and of one mind dwell in the Church of Christ, beyond all question those were not dwelling in the Church of Christ,

however much they might appear to be within, who of envy and contention were announcing Christ without charity; by whom he understands, not the heretics and schismatics who are mentioned by the Apostle Paul, [1895] but false brethren holding conversation with him within, who certainly ought not to have baptized, because they were not dwelling in the Church, in which he himself says that none dwell save those who are of one heart and of one mind: unless, indeed, any one be so far removed from the truth as to say that those were of one heart and of one mind who were envious and malevolent, and contentious without charity; and yet they used to baptize: nor did the detestable waywardness which they displayed in any degree violate or diminish from the sacrament of Christ, which was handled and dispensed by them.

[1892] Cypr. Ep. lxxiii.

[1893] Conc. Carth. sec. 87.

[1894] Cypr. Ep. lxix. 5.

[1895] Phil. i. 15, 17.

Chapter 50.

98. It is indeed worth while to consider the whole of the passage in the aforesaid letter to Magnus, which he has put together as follows: "Not dwelling," he says, "in the house of God--that is to say, in the Church of Christ--in which none dwell save those that are of one heart and of one mind, as the Holy Spirit says in the Psalms, speaking of God that maketh men to be of one mind in an house.' [1896] Finally, the very sacrifices of the Lord declare that Christians are united among themselves by a firm and inseparable love for one another. For

when the Lord calls bread, which is compacted together by the union of many grains, His body, [1897] He is signifying one people, whom He bore, compacted into one body; and when He calls wine, which is pressed out from a multitude of branches and clusters and brought together into one, His blood, [1898] He also signifies one flock joined together by the mingling of a multitude united into one." These words of the blessed Cyprian show that he both understood and loved the glory of the house of God, which house he asserted to consist of those who are of one heart and of one mind, proving it by the testimony of the prophets and the meaning of the sacraments, and in which house certainly were not found those envious persons, those malevolent without charity, who nevertheless used to baptize. From whence it is clear that the sacrament of Christ can both be in and be administered by those who are not in the Church of Christ, in which Cyprian himself bears witness that there are none dwelling save those who are of one heart and of one mind. Nor can it indeed be said that they are allowed to baptize so long as they are undetected, seeing that the Apostle Paul did not fail to detect those of whose ministry he bears unquestionable testimony in his epistle, saying that he rejoices that they also were proclaiming Christ. For he says of them, "Whether in pretense or in truth, Christ is preached; and I therein do rejoice, yea, and will rejoice." [1899]

[1896] Ps. lxviii. 6; cp. LXX. and Hieron.

[1897] John vi. 51.

[1898] Matt. xxvi. 26-29.

[1899] Phil. i. 18.

Chapter 51.

99. Taking all these things, therefore, into consideration, I think that I am not rash in saying that there are some in the house of God after such a fashion as not to be themselves the very house of God, which is said to be built upon a rock, [1900] which is called the one dove, [1901] which is styled the beauteous bride without spot or wrinkle, [1902] and a garden enclosed, a fountain sealed, a well of living water, an orchard of pomegranates with pleasant fruits; [1903] which house also received the keys, and the power of binding and loosing. [1904] If any one shall neglect this house when it arrests and corrects him, the Lord says, "Let him be unto thee as an heathen man and a publican." [1905] Of this house it is said, "Lord, I have loved the habitation of Thy house, and the place where Thine honor dwelleth;" [1906] and, "He maketh men to be of one mind in an house;" [1907] and, "I was glad when they said unto me, Let us go into the house of the Lord;" [1908] and, "Blessed are they that dwell in Thy house, O Lord; they will be still praising Thee;" [1909] with countless other passages to the same effect. This house is also called wheat, bringing forth fruit with patience, some thirty-fold, some sixtyfold, and some an hundredfold. [1910] This house is also in vessels of gold and of silver, [1911] and in precious stones and imperishable woods. To this house it is said, "Forbearing one another in love, endeavoring to keep the unity of the Spirit in the bond of peace;" [1912] and, "For the temple of God is holy, which temple ye are." [1913] For this house is composed of those that are good and faithful, and of the holy servants of God dispersed throughout the world, and bound together by the unity of the Spirit, whether they know each other personally or not. But we hold that others are said to be in the house after

such a sort, that they belong not to the substance of the house, nor to the society of fruitful and peaceful justice, but only as the chaff is said to be among the corn; for that they are in the house we cannot deny, when the apostle says, "But in a great house there are not only vessels of gold and of silver, but also of wood and of earth; and some to honor, and some to dishonor." [1914]Of this countless multitude are found to be not only the crowd which within the Church afflicts the hearts of the saints, who are so few in comparison with so vast a host, but also the heresies and schisms which exist in those who have burst the meshes of the net, and may now be said to be rather out of the house than in the house, of whom it is said, "They went out from us, but they were not of us." [1915]For they are more thoroughly separated, now that they are also divided from us in the body, than are those who live within the Church in a carnal and worldly fashion, and are separated from us in the spirit.

[1900] Matt. xvi. 18.

[1901] Cant. vi. 9.

[1902] Eph. v. 27; cp. Retract. ii. 18.

[1903] Cant. iv. 12, 13.

[1904] Matt. xvi. 19.

[1905] Matt. xviii. 17.

[1906] Ps. xxvi. 8.

[1907] Ps. lxviii. 6; cp. LXX. and Hieron.

[1908] Ps. cxxii. 1.

[1909] Ps. lxxxiv. 4.

[1910] Matt. xiii. 23; Luke viii. 15.

[1911] 2 Tim. ii. 20.

[1912] Eph. iv. 2, 3.

[1913] 1 Cor. iii. 17.

[1914] 2 Tim. ii. 20. In Retract. ii. 18, Augustin says that he thinks the meaning of this last passage to be, not as Cyprian took it, Ep. liv. 3, that the vessels of gold and silver are the good, which are to honor; the vessels of wood and earth the wicked, which are to dishonor: but that the material of the vessels refers to the outward appearance of the several members of the Church, and that in each class some will be found to honor, and some to dishonor. This interpretation he derives from Tychonius.

[1915] 1 John ii. 19.

Chapter 52.

100. Of all these several classes, then, no one doubts respecting those first, who are in the house of God in such a sense as themselves to be the house of God, whether they be already spiritual, or as yet only babes nurtured with milk, but still making progress with earnestness of heart, towards that which is spiritual, that such men both have baptism so as to be of profit to themselves, and transmit it to those who follow their example so as to benefit them; but that in its transmission to those who are false, whom the Holy Spirit shuns, though they themselves, so far as lies with them, confer it so as to be of profit, yet the others receive it in vain, since they do not imitate

those from whom they receive it. But they who are in the great house after the fashion of vessels to dishonor, both have baptism without profit to themselves, and transmit it without profit to those who follow their example: those, however, receive it with profit, who are united in heart and character, not to their ministers, but to the holy house of God. But those who are more thoroughly separated, so as to be rather out of the house than in the house, have baptism without any profit to themselves; and, moreover, there is no profit to those who receive it from them, unless they be compelled by urgent necessity to receive it, and their heart in receiving it does not depart from the bond of unity: yet nevertheless they possess it, though the possession be of no avail; and it is received from them, even when it is of no profit to those who so receive it, though, in order that it may become of use, they must depart from their heresy or schism, and cleave to that house of God. And this ought to be done, not only by heretics and schismatics, but also by those who are in the house through communion in the sacraments, yet so as to be outside the house through the perversity of their character. For so the sacrament begins to be of profit even to themselves, which previously was of no avail.

Chapter 53.

101. The question is also commonly raised, whether baptism is to be held valid which is received from one who had not himself received it, if, from some promptings of curiosity, he had chanced to learn how it ought to be conferred; and whether it makes no difference in what spirit the recipient receives it, whether in mockery or in sincerity: if in mockery, whether the difference arises when the mockery is of deceit, as in the Church, or in what is thought to be the Church; or when

it is in jest, as in a play: and which is the more accursed, to receive it deceitfully in the Church, or in heresy or schism without deceit, that is to say, with full sincerity of heart: or whether it be worse to receive it deceitfully in heresy or in good faith in a play, if any one were to be moved by a sudden feeling of religion in the midst of his acting. And yet, if we compare such an one even with him who receives it deceitfully in the Catholic Church itself, I should be surprised if any one were to doubt which of the two should be preferred; for I do not see of what avail the intention of him who gives in truth can be to him who receives deceitfully. But let us consider, in the case of some one also giving it in deceit, when both the given and the recipient are acting deceitfully in the unity of the Catholic Church itself, whether this should rather be acknowledged as baptism, or that which is given in a play, if any one should be found who received it faithfully from a sudden impulse of religion: or whether it be not true that, so far as the men themselves are concerned, there is a very great difference between the believing recipient in a play, and the mocking recipient in the Church; but that in regard to the genuineness of the sacrament there is no difference. For if it makes no difference in respect to the genuineness of the sacrament within the Catholic Church itself, whether certain persons celebrate it in truth or in deceit, so long as both still celebrate the same thing, I cannot see why it should make a difference outside, seeing that he who receives it is not cloaked by his deceit, but he is changed by his religious impulse. Or have those truthful persons among whom it is celebrated more power for the confirmation of the sacrament, than those deceitful men by whom and in whom it is celebrated can exert for its invalidation? And yet, if the deceit be subsequently brought to light, no one seeks a repetition of the sacrament; but the fraud is either punished by excommunication or set right by penitence.

102. But the safe course for us is, not to advance with any rashness of judgment in setting forth a view which has neither been started in any regionary Council of the Catholic Church nor established in a plenary one; but to assert, with all the confidence of a voice that cannot be gainsaid, what has been confirmed by the consent of the universal Church, under the direction of our Lord God and Saviour Jesus Christ. Nevertheless, if any one were to press me--supposing I were duly seated in a Council in which a question were raised on points like these--to declare what my own opinion was, without reference to the previously expressed views of others, whose judgment I would rather follow, if I were under the influence of the same feelings as led me to assert what I have said before, I should have no hesitation in saying that all men possess baptism who have received it in any place, from any sort of men, provided that it were consecrated in the words of the gospel, and received without deceit on their part with some degree of faith; although it would be of no profit to them for the salvation of their souls if they were without charity, by which they might be grafted into the Catholic Church. For "though I have faith," says the apostle, "so that I could remove mountains, but have not charity, I am nothing." [1916]Just as already, from the established decrees of our predecessors, I have no hesitation in saying that all those have baptism who, though they receive it deceitfully, yet receive it in the Church, or where the Church is thought to be by those in whose society it is received, of whom it was said, "They went out from us." [1917] But when there was no society of those who so believed, and when the man who received it did not himself hold such

belief, but the whole thing was done as a farce, or a comedy, or a jest,--if I were asked whether the baptism which was thus conferred should be approved, I should declare my opinion that we ought to pray for the declaration of God's judgment through the medium of some revelation seeking it with united prayer and earnest groanings of suppliant devotion, humbly deferring all the time to the decision of those who were to give their judgment after me, in case they should set forth anything as already known and determined. And, therefore, how much the more must I be considered to have given my opinion now without prejudice to the utterance of more diligent research or authority higher than my own!

[1916] 1 Cor. xiii. 2.

[1917] 1 John ii. 19.

Chapter 54.

103. But now I think that it is fully time for me to bring to their due termination these books also on the subject of baptism, in which our Lord God has shown to us, through the words of the peaceful Bishop Cyprian and his brethren who agreed with him, how great is the love which should be felt for catholic unity; so that even where they were otherwise minded until God should reveal even this to them, [1918] they should rather bear with those who thought differently from themselves, than sever themselves from them by a wicked schism; whereby the mouths of the Donatists are wholly closed, even if we say nothing of the followers of Maximian. For if the wicked pollute the good in unity, then even Cyprian himself already found no Church to which he could be joined. But if the wicked do not infect the good in unity, then the sacrilegious Donatist has no ground to set before himself for separation.

But if baptism is both possessed and transferred by the multitude of others who work the works of the flesh, of which it is said, that "they which do such things shall not inherit the kingdom of God," [1919] then it is possessed and transferred also by heretics, who are numbered among those works; because they could have transferred it had they remained, and did not lose it by their secession. But men of this kind confer it on their fellows as fruitlessly and uselessly as the others who resemble them, inasmuch as they shall not inherit the kingdom of God. And as, when those others are brought into the right path, it is not that baptism begins to be present, having been absent before, but that it begins to profit them, having been already in them; so is it the case with heretics as well. Whence Cyprian and those who thought with him could not impose limits on the Catholic Church, which they would not mutilate. But in that they were otherwise minded we feel no fear, seeing that we too share in their veneration for Peter; yet in that they did not depart from unity we rejoice, seeing that we, like them, are founded on the rock.

[1918] Phil. iii. 15.

[1919] Gal. v. 19-21.

THE THREE BOOKS OF AUGUSTIN, BISHOP OF HIPPO,
IN ANSWER TO THE LETTERS OF PETILIAN, THE DONATIST
[CONTRA LITTERAS PETILIANI DONATISTÆ CORTENSIS, EPISCOPI]
CIRCA A.D. 400.

Written c. 400 A.D., some say 398 A.D., but Augustin places it some time after the treatise on Baptism: Retractt. Bk. ii. xxv. From the same, we gather the following points as to the origin of this treatise: Before A. had finished his books on the Trinity and his word-for-word commentary on Genesis, a reply to a letter which Petilian had addressed to his followers, only a small part of which however had come into A.'s hands, demanded immediate preparation. This constitutes Book First. Subsequently the whole document was obtained, and he was engaged in preparing the second Book, c. 401; but even before the full treatise of Petilian had been secured, the latter had obtained A.'s first book, and afterwards put an epistle abusive of A. in circulation. The answer to this latter is Book Third, c. 402. Petilian was originally an advocate. The opponents charged him with having become a Donatist by compulsion, with assuming the title of Paraclete, and with endeavoring to prevent all access on their part to his writings.

Book I.

Written in the form of a letter addressed to the Catholics, in which the first portion of the letter which Petilian had written to his adherents is examined and refuted.

Augustin, to the well-beloved brethren that belong to the care of our charge, greeting in the Lord:

Chapter 1.

1. Ye know that we have often wished to bring forward into open notoriety, and to confute, not so much from our own arguments as from theirs, the sacrilegious error of the Donatist heretics; whence it came to pass that we wrote letters even to some of their leaders,--not indeed for purposes of communion with them, for of that they had already in times past rendered themselves unworthy by dissenting from the Church; nor yet in terms of reproach, but of a conciliatory character, with the view that, having discussed the question with us which caused them to break off from the holy communion of the whole world, they might, on consideration of the truth, be willing to be corrected, and might not defend the headstrong perversity of their predecessors with a yet more foolish obstinacy, but might be reunited to the Catholic stock, so as to bring forth the fruits of charity. But as it is written, "With those who have hated peace I am more peaceful," [1920] so they rejected my letters, just as they hate the very name of peace, in whose interests they were written. Now, however, as I was in the church of Constantina, Absentius [1921] being present, with my colleague Fortunatus, his bishop, the brethren brought before my notice a letter, which they said that a bishop of the said schism had addressed to his presbyters, as was set forth in the superscription of the letter itself. When I had read it, I was so amazed to find that in his very first words he cut away the very roots of the whole claims of his party to communion, that I was unwilling to believe that it could be the letter of a man who, if fame speaks truly, is especially conspicuous among them for learning and eloquence. But some of those who were present

when I read it, being acquainted with the polish and embellishment of his composition, gradually persuaded me that it was undoubtedly his address. I thought, however, that whoever the author might be, it required refutation, lest the writer should seem to himself, in the company of the inexperienced, to have written something of weight against the Catholic Church.

2. The first point, then, that he lays down in his letter is the statement, "that we find fault with them for the repetition of baptism, while we ourselves pollute our souls with a laver stained with guilt." But to what profit is it that I should reproduce all his insulting terms? For, since it is one thing to strengthen proofs, another thing to meddle with abusive words by way of refutation, let us rather turn our attention to the mode in which he has sought to prove that we do not possess baptism, and that therefore they do not require the repetition of what was already present, but confer what hitherto was wanting. For he says: "What we look for is the conscience of the giver to cleanse that of the recipient." But supposing the conscience of the giver is concealed from view, and perhaps defiled with sin, how will it be able to cleanse the conscience of the recipient, if, as he says, "what we look for is the conscience of the giver to cleanse that of the recipient?" For if he should say that it makes no matter to the recipient what amount of evil may lie concealed from view in the conscience of the giver, perhaps that ignorance may have such a degree of efficacy as this, that a man cannot be defiled by the guilt of the conscience of him from whom he receives baptism, so long as he is unaware of it. Let it then be granted that the guilty conscience of his neighbor cannot defile a man so long as he is unaware of

it, but is it therefore clear that it can further cleanse him from his own guilt?

[1920] Ps. cxx. 7; cf. Hieron.

[1921] Probably Alypius.

Chapter 2.

3. Whence, then, is a man to be cleansed who receives baptism, when the conscience of the giver is polluted without the knowledge of him who is to receive it? Especially when he goes on to say, "For he who receives faith from the faithless receives not faith, but guilt." There stands before us one that is faithless ready to baptize, and he who should be baptized is ignorant of his faithlessness: what think you that he will receive? Faith, or guilt? If you answer faith, then you will grant that it is possible that a man should receive not guilt, but faith, from him that is faithless; and the former saying will be false, that "he who receives faith from the faithless receives not faith, but guilt." For we find that it is possible that a man should receive faith even from one that is faithless, if he be not aware of the faithlessness of the giver. For he does not say, He who receives faith from one that is openly and notoriously faithless; but he says, "He who receives faith from the faithless receives not faith, but guilt;" which certainly is false when a person is baptized by one who hides his faithlessness. But if he shall say, Even when the faithlessness of the baptizer is concealed, the recipient receives not faith from him, but guilt, then let them rebaptize those who are well known to have been baptized by men who in their own body have long concealed a life of guilt, but have eventually been detected, convicted, and condemned.

Chapter 3.

For, so long as they escaped detection, they could not bestow faith on any whom they baptized, but only guilt, if it be true that whosoever receives faith from one that is faithless receives not faith, but guilt. Let them therefore be baptized by the good, that they may be enabled to receive not guilt, but faith.

4. But how, again, shall they have any certainty about the good who are to give them faith, if what we look to is the conscience of the giver, which is unseen by the eyes of the proposed recipient? Therefore, according to their judgment, the salvation of the spirit is made uncertain, so long as in opposition to the holy Scriptures, which say, "It is better to trust in the Lord than to put confidence in man," [1922] and, "Cursed be the man that trusteth in man," [1923] they remove the hope of those who are to be baptized from the Lord their God, and persuade them that it should be placed in man; the practical result of which is, that their salvation becomes not merely uncertain, but actually null and void. For "salvation belongeth unto the Lord," [1924] and "vain is the help of man." [1925]Therefore, whosoever places his trust in man, even in one whom he knows to be just and innocent, is accursed. Whence also the Apostle Paul finds fault with those who said they were of Paul saying, "Was Paul crucified for you? or were ye baptized in the name of Paul?" [1926]

[1922] Ps. cxviii. 8.

[1923] Jer. xvii. 6.

[1924] Ps. iii. 8.

[1925] Ps. lx. 11.

[1926] 1 Cor. i. 13.

Chapter 4.

5. Wherefore, if they were in error, and would have perished had they not been corrected, who wished to be of Paul, what must we suppose to be the hope of those who wished to be of Donatus? For they use their utmost endeavors to prove that the origin, root, and head of the baptized person is none other than the individual by whom he is baptized. The result is, that since it is very often a matter of uncertainty what kind of man the baptizer is, the hope therefore of the baptized being of uncertain origin, of uncertain root, of uncertain head, is of itself uncertain altogether. And since it is possible that the conscience of the giver may be in such a condition as to be accursed and defiled without the knowledge of the recipient, it results that, being of an accursed origin, accursed root, accursed head, the hope of the baptized may prove to be vain and ungrounded. For Petilian expressly states in his epistle, that "everything consists of an origin and root; and if it have not something for a head, it is nothing." And since by the origin and root and head of the baptized person he wishes to be understood the man by whom he is baptized, what good does the unhappy recipient derive from the fact that he does not know how bad a man his baptizer really is? For he does not know that he himself has a bad head, or actually no head at all. And yet what hope can a man have, who, whether he is aware of it or not, has either a very bad head or no head at all? Can we maintain that his very ignorance forms a head, when his baptizer is either a bad head or none at all? Surely any one who thinks this is unmistakeably without a head.

Chapter 5.

6. We ask, therefore, since he says, "He who receives faith from the faithless receives not faith, but guilt," and immediately adds to this the further statement, that "everything consists of an origin and root; and if it have not something for a head, it is nothing;"--we ask, I say, in a case where the faithlessness of the baptizer is undetected: If then, the man whom he baptizes receives faith, and not guilt; if, then, the baptizer is not his origin and root and head, who is it from whom he receives faith? where is the origin from which he springs? where is the root of which he is a shoot? where the head which is his starting-point? Can it be, that when he who is baptized is unaware of the faithlessness of his baptizer, it is then Christ who gives faith, it is then Christ who is the origin and root and head? Alas for human rashness and conceit! Why do you not allow that it is always Christ who gives faith, for the purpose of making a man a Christian by giving it? Why do you not allow that Christ is always the origin of the Christian, that the Christian always plants his root in Christ, that Christ is the head of the Christian? Do we then maintain that, even when spiritual grace is dispensed to those that believe by the hands of a holy and faithful minister, it is still not the minister himself who justifies, but that One of whom it is said, that "He justifieth the ungodly?" [1927]But unless we admit this, either the Apostle Paul was the head and origin of those whom he had planted, or Apollos the root of those whom he had watered, rather than He who had given them faith in believing; whereas the same Paul says, "I have planted, Apollos watered, but God gave the increase: so then neither is he that planteth anything, nor he that watereth, but God that giveth the increase." [1928]Nor was the apostle himself their root, but rather He who says, "I am the vine, ye are the branches." [1929]How, too, could he be their head, when he says, that "we, being many, are one body in

Christ," [1930] and expressly declares in many passages that Christ Himself is the head of the whole body?

[1927] Rom. iv. 5.

[1928] 1 Cor. iii. 6, 7.

[1929] John xv. 5.

[1930] Rom. xii. 5.

Chapter 6.

7. Wherefore, whether a man receive the sacrament of baptism from a faithful or a faithless minister, his whole hope is in Christ, that he fall not under the condemnation that "cursed is he that placeth his hope in man." Otherwise, if each man is born again in spiritual grace of the same sort as he by whom he is baptized, and if when he who baptizes him is manifestly a good man, then he himself gives faith, he is himself the origin and root and head of him who is being born; whilst, when the baptizer is faithless without its being known, then the baptized person receives faith from Christ, then he derives his origin from Christ, then he is rooted in Christ, then he boasts in Christ as his head,--in that case all who are baptized should wish that they might have faithless baptizers, and be ignorant of their faithlessness: for however good their baptizers might have been, Christ is certainly beyond comparison better still; and He will then be the head of the baptized, if the faithlessness of the baptizer shall escape detection.

Chapter 7.

8. But if it is perfect madness to hold such a view (for it is Christ always that justifieth the ungodly, by changing his

ungodliness into Christianity; it is from Christ always that faith is receivcd, Christ is always the origin of the regenerate and the head of the Church), what weight, then, will those words have, which thoughtless readers value by their sound, without inquiring what their inner meaning is? For the man who does not content himself with hearing the words with his ear, but considers the meaning of the phrase, when he hears, "What we look to is the conscience of the giver, that it may cleanse the conscience of the recipient," will answer, The conscience of man is often unknown to me, but I am certain of the mercy of Christ: when he hears, "He who receives faith from the faithless receives not faith, but guilt," will answer, Christ is not faithless, from whom I receive not guilt, but faith: when he hears, "Everything consists of an origin and root; and if it have not something for a head, is nothing," will answer, My origin is Christ, my root is Christ, my head is Christ. When he hears, "Nor does anything well receive second birth, unless it be born again of good seed," he will answer, The seed of which I am born again is the Word of God, which I am warned to hear with attention, even though he through whom I hear it does not himself do what he preaches; according to the words of the Lord, which make me herein safe, "All whatsoever they bid you observe, that observe and do; but do not ye after their works: for they say, and do not." [1931]When he hears, "What perversity must it be, that he who is guilty through his own sins should make another free from guilt!" he will answer, No one makes me free from guilt but He who died for our sins, and rose again for our justification. For I believe, not in the minister by whose hands I am baptized, but in Him who justifieth the ungodly, that my faith may be counted unto me for righteousness. [1932]

[1931] Matt. xxiii. 3.

[1932] Rom. iv. 25, 5.

Chapter 8.

9. When he hears, "Every good tree bringeth good fruit, but a corrupt tree bringeth forth evil fruit: do men gather grapes of thorns?" [1933] and, "A good man out of the good treasure of his heart bringeth forth good things, and an evil man out of the evil treasure bringeth forth evil things;" [1934] he will answer, This therefore is good fruit, that I should be a good tree, that is, a good man, that I should show forth good fruit, that is, good works. But this will be given to me, not by him that planteth, nor by him that watereth, but by God that giveth the increase. For if the good tree be the good baptizer, so that his good fruit should be the man whom he baptizes, then any one who has been baptized by a bad man, even if his wickedness be not manifest, will have no power to be good, for he is sprung from an evil tree. For a good tree is one thing; a tree whose quality is concealed, but yet bad, is another. Or if, when the tree is bad, but hides its badness, then whosoever is baptized by it is born not of it, but of Christ; then they are justified with more perfect holiness who are baptized by the bad who hide their evil nature, than they who are baptized by the manifestly good. [1935]

[1933] Matt. vii. 17, 16.

[1934] Matt. xii. 35.

[1935] See below, Book II. 6, 12.

Chapter 9.

10. Again, when he hears, "He that is washed by one dead, his washing profiteth him nought," [1936] he will answer, "Christ, being raised from the dead, dieth no more; death hath no more dominion over Him:" [1937] of whom it is said, "The same is He which baptizeth with the Holy Ghost." [1938] But they are baptized by the dead, who are baptized in the temples of idols. For even they themselves do not suppose that they receive the sanctification which they look for from their priests, but from their gods; and since these were men, and are dead in such sort as to be now neither upon earth nor in the rest of heaven, [1939] they are truly baptized by the dead: and the same answer will hold good if there be any other way in which these words of holy Scripture may be examined, and profitably discussed and understood. For if in this place I understand a baptizer who is a sinner, the same absurdity will follow, that whosoever has been baptized by an ungodly man, even though his ungodliness be undiscovered, is yet washed in vain, as though baptized by one dead. For he does not say, He that is baptized by one manifestly dead, but absolutely, "by one dead." And if they consider any man to be dead whom they know to be a sinner, but any one in their communion to be alive, even though he manages most adroitly to conceal a life of wickedness, in the first place with accursed pride they claim more for themselves than they ascribe to God, that when a sinner is unveiled to them he should be called dead, but when he is known by God he is held to be alive. In the next place, if that sinner is to be called dead who is known to be such by men, what answer will they make about Optatus, whom they were afraid to condemn though they had long known his wickedness? Why are those who were baptized by him not said to have been baptized by one dead? Did he live because the Count was his faith? [1940] --an elegant and well-turned saying

of some early colleagues of their own, which they themselves are wont to quote with pride, not understanding that at the death of the haughty Goliath it was his own sword by which his head was cut off. [1941]

[1936] So the Donatists commonly quoted Ecclus. xxiv. 25, which is more correctly rendered in our version, "He that washeth himself after touching of a dead body, if he touch it again, what availeth his washing?" Augustin (Retractt. i. 21, 3) says that the misapplication was rendered possible by the omission in many African Mss. of the second clause, "and touches it again." Cp. Hieron, Ecclus. xxxiv. 30.

[1937] Rom. vi. 9.

[1938] John i. 33.

[1939] Cp. Contra Cresconium, Book II. 25-30: "Ita mortui sunt, ut neque super terras, neque in requie sanctorum vivant."

[1940] Benedictines suggest as an emendation "quod Deus illi comes erat," as in II. 23, 53; 37, 88, 103, 237.

[1941] 1 Sam. xvii. 51.

Chapter 10.

11. Lastly, if they are willing to give the name of dead neither to the wicked man whose sin is hidden, nor to him whose sin is manifest, but who has yet not been condemned by them, but only to him whose sin is manifest and condemned, so that whosoever is baptized by him is himself baptized by the dead, and his washing profits him nothing; what are we to say of those whom their own party have condemned "by the unimpeachable voice of a plenary Council," [1942] together

with Maximianus and the others who ordained him,--I mean Felicianus of Musti, and Prætextatus of Assura, of whom I speak in the meantime, who are counted among the twelve ordainers of Maximianus, as erecting an altar in opposition to their altar at which Primianus stands? They surely are reckoned by them among the dead. To this we have the express testimony of the noble decree of that Council of theirs which formerly called forth shouts of unreserved [1943] applause when it was recited among them for the purpose of being decreed, but which would now be received in silence if we should chance to recite it in their ears; whereas they should rather have been slow at first to rejoice in its eloquence, lest they should afterwards come to mourn over it when its credit was destroyed. For in it they speak in the following terms of the followers of Maximianus, who were shut out from their communion: "Seeing that the shipwrecked members of certain men have been dashed by the waves of truth upon the sharp rocks, and after the fashion of the Egyptians, the shores are covered with the bodies of the dying; whose punishment is intensified in death itself, since after their life has been wrung from them by the avenging waters, they fail to find so much as burial." In such gross terms indeed, do they insult those who were guilty of schism from their body, that they call them dead and unburied; but certainly they ought to have wished that they might obtain burial, if it were only that they might not have seen Optatus Gildonianus advancing with a military force, and like a sweeping wave that dashes beyond its fellows, sucking back Felicianus and Prætextatus once again within their pale, out of the multitude of bodies lying unburied on the shore.

[1942] That of Bagai. See on de Bapt. I. 5, 7.

[1943] Ore latissimo acclamaverunt. The Louvain edition has "lætissimo," both here and Contra Crescon. IV. 41, 48.

Chapter 11.

12. Of these I would ask, whether by coming to their sea they were restored to life, or whether they are still dead there? For if still they are none the less corpses, then the laver cannot in any way profit those who are baptized by such dead men. But if they have been restored to life, yet how can the laver profit those whom they baptized before outside, while they were lying without life, if the passage, "He who is baptized by the dead, of what profit is his baptism to him," is to be understood in the way in which they think? For those whom Prætextatus and Felicianus baptized while they were yet in communion with Maximianus are now retained among them, sharing in their communion, without being again baptized, together with the same men who baptized them--I mean Felicianus and Prætextatus: taking occasion by which fact, if it were not that they cherish the beginning of their own obstinacy, instead of considering the certain end of their spiritual salvation, they would certainly be bound to vigilance, and ought to recover the soundness of their senses, so as to breathe again in Catholic peace; if only, laying aside the swelling of their pride, and overcoming the madness of their stubbornness, they would take heed and see what monstrous sacrilege it is to curse the baptism of the foreign churches, which we have learned from the sacred books were planted in primitive times, and to receive the baptism of the followers of Maximianus, whom they have condemned with their own lips.

Chapter 12.

13. But our brethren themselves, the sons of the aforesaid churches, were both ignorant at the time, and still are ignorant, of what has been done so many years ago in Africa: wherefore they at any rate cannot be defiled by the charges which have been brought, on the part of the Donatists, against the Africans, without even knowing whether they were true. But the Donatists having openly separated and divided themselves off, although they are even said to have taken part in the ordination of Primianus, yet condemned the said Primianus, ordained another bishop in opposition to Primianus, baptized outside the communion of Primianus, rebaptized after Primianus, and returned to Primianus with their disciples who had been baptized by themselves outside, and never rebaptized by any one inside. If such a union with the party of Maximianus does not pollute the Donatists, how can the mere report concerning the Africans pollute the foreigners? If the lips meet together without offense in the kiss of peace, which reciprocally condemned each other, why is each man that is condemned by them in the churches very far removed by the intervening sea from their jurisdiction, not saluted with a kiss as a faithful Catholic, but driven forth with a blast of indignation as an impious pagan? And if, in receiving the followers of Maximianus, they made peace in behalf of their own unity, far be it from us to find fault with them, save that they cut their own throats by their decision, that whereas, to preserve unity in their schism, they collect together again what had been parted from themselves, they yet scorn to reunite their schism itself to the true unity of the Church.

Chapter 13.

14. If, in the interests of the unity of the party of Donatus, no one rebaptizes those who were baptized in a wicked schism,

and men, who are guilty of a crime of such enormity as to be compared by them in their Council to those ancient authors of schism whom the earth swallowed up alive, [1944] are either unpunished after separation, or restored again to their position after condemnation; why is it that, in defence of the unity of Christ, which is spread throughout the whole inhabited world, of which it has been predicted that it shall have dominion from sea to sea, and from the river unto the ends of the earth, [1945] --a prediction which seems from actual proof to be in process of fulfillment; why is it that, in defence of this unity, they do not acknowledge the true and universal law of that inheritance which rings forth from the books that are common to us all: "I shall give Thee the heathen for Thine inheritance, and the uttermost parts of the earth for Thy possession?" [1946] In behalf of the unity of Donatus, they are not compelled to call together again what they have scattered abroad, but are warned to hear the cry of the Scriptures: why will they not understand that they meet with such treatment through the mercy of God, that since they brought false charges against the Catholic Church, by contact as it were with which they were unwilling to defile their own excessive sanctity, they should be compelled by the sovereign authority of Optatus Gildonianus to receive again and associate with themselves true offenses of the greatest enormity, condemned by the true voice, as they say, of their own plenary Council? Let them at length perceive how they are filled with the true crimes of their own party, after inventing fictitious crimes wherewith to charge their brethren, when, even if the charges had been true, they ought at length to feel how much should be endured in the cause of peace, and in behalf of Christ's peace to return to a Church which did not condemn crimes undiscovered, if on behalf of the peace of Donatus they were ready to pardon such as were condemned.

[1944] Num. xvi. 31-35.

[1945] Ps. lxxii. 8.

[1946] Ps. ii. 8.

Chapter 14.

15. Therefore, brethren, let it suffice us that they should be admonished and corrected on the one point of their conduct in the matter of the followers of Maximianus. We do not ransack ancient archives, we do not bring to light the contents of time honored libraries, we do not publish our proofs to distant lands; but we bring in, as arbiters betwixt us, all the proofs derived from our ancestors, we spread abroad the witness that cries aloud throughout the world.

Chapter 15.

16. Look at the states of Musti [1947] and Assura: [1948] there are many still remaining in this life and in this province who have severed themselves, and many from whom they have severed themselves; many who have erected an altar, and many against whom that altar has been erected; many who have condemned, and many who have been condemned; who have received, and who have been received; who have been baptized outside, and not baptized again within: if all these things in the cause of unity defile, let the defiled hold their tongues; if these things in the cause of unity do not defile, let them submit to correction, and terminate their strife.

[1947] Musti is in ecclesiastical province of Numidia.

[1948] Assura is in ecclesiastical province of Zeugitana. See Treatise on Baptism, Book VII. c. 32.

Chapter 16.

17. As for the words which follow in his letter, the writer himself could scarcely fail to laugh at them, when, having made an unlearned and lying use of the proof in which he quotes the words of Scripture, "He who is washed by the dead, what profiteth him his washing?" he endeavors to show to us "how far a traditor being still in life may be accounted dead." And then he goes on further to say: "That man is dead who has not been worthy to be born again in true baptism; he is likewise dead who, although born in genuine baptism, has joined himself to a traditor." If, therefore, the followers of Maximianus are not dead, why do the Donatists say, in their plenary Council, that "the shores are covered with their dying bodies?" But if they are dead, whence is there life in the baptism which they gave? Again, if Maximianus is not dead, why is a man baptized again who had been baptized by him? But if he is dead why is not also Felicianus of Musti dead with him, who ordained him, and might have died beyond the sea with some African colleague or another who was a traditor? Or, if he also is himself dead, how is there life with him in your society in those who, having been baptized outside by him who is dead, have never been baptized again within?

Chapter 17.

18. Then he further adds: "Both are without the life of baptism, both he who never had it at all, and he who had it but has lost it." He therefore never had it, whom Felicianus, the follower of Maximianus or Prætextatus, baptized outside; and these men themselves have lost what once they had when, therefore, these were received with their followers, who gave to those whom they baptized what previously they did not have?

and who restored to themselves what they had lost? But they took away with them the form of baptism, but lost the veritable excellence of baptism by their wicked schism. Why do you repudiate the form itself, which is holy at all times and all places, in the Catholics whom you have not heard, whilst you are willing to acknowledge it in the followers of Maximianus whom you have punished?

19. But whatever he seemed to himself to say by way of accusation about the traitor Judas, I see not how it can concern us, who are not proved by them to have betrayed our trust; nor, indeed, if such treason were proved on the part of any who before our time have died in our communion, would that treason in any way defile us by whom it was disavowed, and to whom it was displeasing. For if they themselves are not defiled by offenses condemned by themselves, and afterwards condoned, how much less can we be defiled by what we have disavowed so soon as we have heard of them! However weighty, therefore, his invective against traditors, let him be assured that they are condemned by me in precisely the same terms. But yet I make a distinction; for he accuses one on my side who has long been dead without having been condemned in any investigation made by me. I point to a man adhering closely to his side, who had been condemned by him, or at least had been separated by a sacrilegious schism, and whom he received again with undiminished honor.

Chapter 18.

20. He says: "You who are a most abandoned traditor have come out in the character of a persecutor and murderer of us who keep the law." If the followers of Maximianus kept the law when they separated from you, then we may acknowledge

you as a keeper of the law, when you are separated from the Church spread abroad throughout the world. But if you raise the question of persecutions, I at once reply: If you have suffered anything unjustly, this does not concern those who, though they disapprove of men who act in such a way, [1949] yet endure them for the peace that is in unity, in a manner deserving of all praise. Wherefore you have nothing to bring up against the Lord's wheat, who endure the chaff that is among them till the last winnowing, from whom you never would have separated yourself, had you not shown yourself lighter than chaff by flying away under the blast of temptation before the coming of the Winnower. But not to leave this one example, which the Lord hath thrust back in their teeth, to close the mouths of these men, for their correction if they will show themselves to be wise, but for their confusion if they remain in their folly: if those are more just that suffer persecution than those who inflict it, then those same followers of Maximianus are the more just, whose basilica was utterly overthrown, and who were grievously maltreated by the military following of Optatus, when the mandates of the proconsul, ordering that all of them should be shut out of the basilicas, were manifestly procured by the followers of Primianus. Wherefore, if, when the emperors hated their communion, they ventured on such violent measures for the persecution of the followers of Maximianus, what would they do if they were enabled to work their will by being in communion with kings? And if they did such things as I have mentioned for the correction of the wicked, why are they surprised that Catholic emperors should decree with greater power that they should be worked upon and corrected who endeavor to rebaptize the whole Christian world, when they have no ground for differing from them? seeing that they, themselves bear witness that it is right to bear with wicked men even where they have true charges to bring against them in the cause of peace, since they received those whom they had themselves condemned, acknowledging the honors conferred among themselves, and the baptism administered in schism. Let them at length consider what treatment they deserve at the hands of the Christian powers of the world, who are the enemies of Christian unity throughout the world. If, therefore, correction be bitter, yet let them not fail to be ashamed; lest when they begin to read what they themselves have written, they be overcome with laughter, when they do not find in themselves what they wish to find in others, and fail to recognize [1950] in their own case what they find fault with in their neighbors.

[1949] Qui talia facientes quamvis improbent. A comparison of the explanation of this passage in Contra Crescon. III. 41, 45, shows the probability of Migne's conjecture, "quamvis improbe," "who endure the men that act in such a way, however monstrous their conduct may be."

[1950] Nec in se agnoscunt. The reading of the Louvain edition gives better sense, "Et in se agnoscunt," "and discover in themselves."

Chapter 19.

21. What, then, does he mean by quoting in his letter the words with which our Lord addressed the Jews: "Wherefore, behold, I send unto you prophets, and wise men, and scribes; and some of them ye shall kill and crucify, and some of them shall ye scourge?" [1951] For if by the wise men and the scribes and the prophets they would have themselves be understood, while we were as it were the persecutors of the prophets and wise men, why are they unwilling to speak with us, seeing they

are sent to us? For, indeed, if the man who wrote that epistle which we are at this present moment answering, were to be pressed by us to acknowledge it as his own, stamping its authenticity with his signature, I question much whether he would do it, so thoroughly afraid are they of our possessing any words of theirs. For when we were anxious by some means or other to procure the latter part of this same letter, because those from whom we obtained it were unable to describe the whole of it, no one who was asked for it was willing to give it to us, so soon as they knew that we were making a reply to the portion which we had. Therefore, when they read how the Lord says to the prophet, "Cry aloud, spare not, and write their sins with my pen," [1952] these men who are sent to us as prophets have no fears on this score, but take every precaution that their crying may not be heard by us: which they certainly would not fear if what they spoke of us were true. But their apprehension is not groundless, as it is written in the Psalm, "The mouth of them that speak lies shall be stopped." [1953] For if the reason that they do not receive our baptism be that we are a generation of vipers--to use the expression in his epistle--why did they receive the baptism of the followers of Maximianus, of whom their Council speaks in the following terms: "Because the enfolding of a poisoned womb has long concealed the baneful offspring of a viper's seed, and the moist concretions of conceived iniquity have by slow heat flowed forth into the members of serpents"? Is it not therefore of themselves also that it is said in the same Council, "The poison of asps is under their lips, their mouth is full of cursing and bitterness, their feet are swift to shed blood; destruction and unhappiness is in their ways, and the way of peace have they not known"? [1954]And yet they now hold these men themselves in undiminished honor, and receive within their body those whom these men had baptized without.

[1951] Matt. xxiii. 34.

[1952] Isa. lviii. 1.

[1953] Ps. lxiii. 11.

[1954] Ps. xiv. 5-7, LXX. and Hieron., and probably N. Af. version.

Chapter 20.

22. Wherefore all this about the generation of vipers, and the poison of asps under their lips, and all the other things which they have said against those which have not known the way of peace, are really, if they would but speak the truth, more strictly applicable to themselves, since for the sake of the peace of Donatus they received the baptism of these men, in respect of which they used the expressions quoted above in the wording of the decree of the Council; but the baptism of the Church of Christ dispersed throughout the world, from which peace itself came into Africa, they repudiate, to the sacrilegious wounding of the peace of Christ. Which, therefore, are rather the false prophets, who come in sheep's clothing, while inwardly they are ravening wolves, [1955] --they who either fail to detect the wicked in the Catholic Church, and communicate with them in all innocence, or else for the sake of the peace of unity are bearing with those whom they cannot separate from the threshing-floor of the Lord before the Winnower shall come, or they who do in schism what they censure in the Catholic Church, and receive in their own separation, when manifest to all and condemned by their own voice, what they profess that

they shun in the unity of the Church when it calls for toleration, and does not even certainly exist?

[1955] Matt. vii. 15.

Chapter 21.

23. Lastly, it has been said, as he himself has also quoted, "Ye shall know them by their fruits:" [1956]let us therefore examine into their fruits. You bring up against our predecessors their delivery of the sacred books. This very charge we urge with greater probability against their accusers themselves. And not to carry our search too far, in the same city of Constantina your predecessors ordained Silvanus bishop at the very outset of his schism. He, while he was still a subdeacon, was most unmistakeably entered as a traditor in the archives of the city. [1957]If you on your side bring forward documents against our predecessors, all that we ask is equal terms, that we should either believe both to be true or both to be false. If both are true, you are unquestionably guilty of schism, who have pretended that you avoid offenses in the communion of the whole world, which you had commonly among you in the small fragment of your own sect. But again, if both are false, you are unquestionably guilty of schism, who, on account of the false charges of giving up the sacred books, are staining yourselves with the heinous offence of severance from the Church. But if we have something to urge in accusation while you have nothing, or if our charges are true whilst yours are false, it is no longer matter of discussion how thoroughly your mouths are closed.

[1956] Matt. vii. 16.

[1957] See below, III. 57, 69; 68, 70; and Contra Cresc. III. 29, 33, IV. 56, 66.

Chapter 22.

24. What if the holy and true Church of Christ were to convince and overcome you, even if we held no documents in support of our cause, or only such as were false, while you had possession of some genuine proofs of delivery of the sacred books? what would then remain for you, except that, if you would, you should show your love of peace, or otherwise should hold your tongues? [1958]For whatever, in that case, you might bring forward in evidence, I should be able to say with the greatest ease and the most perfect truth, that then you are bound to prove as much to the full and catholic unity of the Church already spread abroad and established throughout so many nations, to the end that you should remain within, and that those whom you convict should be expelled. And if you have endeavored to do this, certainly you have not been able to make good your proof; and being vanquished or enraged, you have separated yourselves, with all the heinous guilt of sacrilege, from the guiltless men who could not condemn on insufficient proof. But if you have not even endeavored to do this, then with most accursed and unnatural blindness you have cut yourselves off from the wheat of Christ, which grows throughout His whole fields, that is, throughout the whole world, until the end, because you have taken offense at a few tares in Africa.

[1958] "Obmutescatis" is the most probable conjecture of Migne or "obtumescatis," which could only mean, "you should swell with confusion."

Chapter 23.

25. In conclusion, the Testament is said to have been given to the flames by certain men in the time of persecution. Now let its lessons be read, from whatever source it has been brought to light. Certainly in the beginning of the promises of the Testator this is found to have been said to Abraham: "In thy seed shall all the nations of the earth be blessed;" [1959] and this saying is truthfully interpreted by the apostle: "To thy seed," he says, "which is Christ." [1960] No betrayal on the part of any man has made the promises of God of none effect. Hold communion with all the nations of the earth, and then you may boast that you have preserved the Testament from the destruction of the flames. But if you will not do so, which party is the rather to be believed to have insisted on the burning of the Testament, save that which will not assent to its teaching when it is brought to light? For how much more certainly, without any sacrilegious rashness, can he be held to have joined the company of traditors who now persecutes with his tongue the Testament which they are said to have persecuted with the flames! You charge us with the persecution: the true wheat of the Lord answers you, "Either it was done justly, or it was done by the chaff that was among us." What have you to say to this? You object that we have no baptism: the same true wheat of the Lord answers you, that the form of the sacrament even within the Church fails to profit some, as it did no good to Simon Magus when he was baptized, much more it fails to profit those who are without. Yet that baptism remains in them when they depart, is proved from this, that it is not restored to them when they return. Never, therefore, except by the greatest shamelessness, will you be able to cry out against that wheat, or to call them false prophets clad in sheep's clothing, whilst inwardly they are ravening wolves; since either they do not

know the wicked in the unity of the Catholic Church, or for the sake of unity bear with those whom they know.

[1959] Gen. xxii. 18.

[1960] Gal. iii. 16.

Chapter 24.

26. But let us turn to the consideration of your fruits. I pass over the tyrannous exercise of authority in the cities, and especially in the estates of other men; I pass over the madness of the Circumcelliones, and the sacrilegious and profane adoration of the bodies of those who had thrown themselves of their own accord over precipices, the revellings of drunkenness, and the ten years' groaning of the whole of Africa under the cruelty of the one man Optatus Gildonanius: all this I pass over, because there are certain among you who cry out that these things are, and have ever been displeasing to them. But they say that they bore with them in the cause of peace, because they could not put them down; wherein they condemn themselves by their own judgment: for if indeed they felt such love for peace, they never would have rent in twain the bond of unity. For what madness can be greater, than to be willing to abandon peace in the midst of peace itself, and to be anxious to retain it in the midst of discord? Therefore, for the sake of those who pretend that they do not see the evils of this same faction of Donatus, which all men see and blame, ignoring them even to the extent of saying of Optatus himself, "What did he do?" "Who accused him?" "Who convicted him?" "I know nothing," "I saw nothing," "I heard nothing,"--for the sake of these, I say, who pretend that they are ignorant of what is generally notorious, the party of Maximianus has arisen, through whom their eyes are opened, and their mouths are

closed: for they openly sever themselves; they openly erect altar against altar; they are openly in a Council [1961] called sacrilegious and vipers, and swift to shed blood, to be compared with Dathan and Abiram and Korah, and are condemned in cutting terms of abhorrence; and are as openly received again with undiminished honors in company with those whom they have baptized. Such are the fruits of these men, who do all this for the peace of Donatus, that they may clothe themselves in sheep's clothing, and reject the peace of Christ throughout the world that they may be ravening wolves within the fold.

[1961] That of Bagai.

Chapter 25.

27. I think that I have left unanswered none of the statements in the letter of Donatus, so far at least as relates to what I have been able to find in that part of which we are in possession. I should be glad if they would produce the other part as well, in case there should be anything in it which does not admit of refutation. But as for these answers which we have made to him, with the help of God, I admonish your Christian love, that ye not only communicate them to those who seek for them, but also force them on those who show no longing for them. Let them answer anything they will; and if they shrink from sending a reply to us, let them at any rate send letters to their own party, only not forbidding that the contents should be shown to us. For if they do this, they show their fruits most openly, by which they are proved to demonstration to be ravening wolves disguised in sheep's clothing, in that they secretly lay snares for our sheep, and openly shrink from giving any answer to the shepherds. We only lay to their charge the sin of schism, in

which they are all most thoroughly involved,--not the offenses of certain of their party, which some of them declare to be displeasing to themselves. If they, on the other hand, abstain from charging us with the sins of other men, they have nothing they can lay to our charge, and therefore they are wholly unable to defend themselves from the charge of schism; because it is by a wicked severance that they have separated themselves from the threshing-floor of the Lord, and from the innocent company of the corn that is growing throughout the world, on account of charges which either are false, and invented by themselves, or even if true, involve the chaff alone.

Chapter 26.

28. But it is possible that you may expect of me that I should go on to refute what he has introduced about Manichæus. Now, in respect of this, the only thing that offends me is that he has censured a most pestilent and pernicious error--I mean the heresy of the Manichæans--in terms of wholly inadequate severity, if indeed they amount to censure at all, though the Catholic Church has broken down his defenses by the strongest evidence of truth. [1962]For the inheritance of Christ, established in all nations, is secure against heresies which have been shut out from the inheritance; but, as the Lord says, "How can Satan cast out Satan?" [1963] so how can the error of the Donatists have power to overthrow the error of the Manichæans? [1964]

[1962] Veritatis fortissimis documentis Catholica expugnat; and so the Mss. The earlier editors, apparently not understanding the omission of "ecclesia," read "veritas."

[1963] Mark iii. 23.

[1964] See II. 18, 40, 41.

Chapter 27.

29. Wherefore, my beloved brethren, though that error is exposed and overcome in many ways, and dare not oppose the truth on any show of reason whatsoever, but only with the unblushing obstinacy of impudence; yet, not to load your memory with a multitude of proofs, I would have you bear in mind this one action of the followers of Maximianus, confront them with this one fact, thrust this in their teeth, to make them their treacherous tongues, destroy their calumny with this, as it were a three-pronged dart destroying a three-headed monster. They charge us with betrayal of the sacred books; they charge us with persecution; they charge us with false baptism: to all their charges make the same answer about the followers of Maximianus. For they think that the proofs are lost which show that their predecessors gave the sacred volumes to the flames; but this at least they cannot hide, that they have received with unimpaired honors those who were stained with the sacrilege of schism. Also they think that those most violent persecutions are hidden, which they direct against any who oppose them whenever they are able; but whilst spiritual persecution surpasses bodily persecution, they received with undiminished honors the followers of Maximianus, whom they themselves persecuted in the body, and of whom they themselves said, "Their feet are swift to shed blood;" [1965] and this at any rate they cannot hide.

[1965] Ps. xiv. 6, LXX. Hieron., N. Af. version.

Chapter 28.

Finally, they think that the question of baptism is hidden, with which they deceive wretched souls. But whilst they say that none have baptism who were baptized outside the communion of the one Church, they received with undiminished honors the followers of Maximianus, with those whom they baptized in schism outside the Donatist communion, and this at least they cannot hide.

30. "But these things," they say, "bring no pollution in the cause of peace; and it is well to bend to mercy the rigor of extreme severity, that broken branches may be grafted in anew." Accordingly, in this way the whole question is settled, by defeat in them, by the impossibility of defeat for us; for if the name of peace be assumed for even the faintest shadow of defense to justify the bearing with wicked men in schism, then beyond all doubt the violation of true peace itself involves detestable guilt, with nothing to be said in its defence throughout the unity of the world.

Chapter 29.

31. These things, brethren, I would have you retain as the basis of your action and preaching with untiring gentleness: love men, while you destroy errors; take of the truth without pride; strive for the truth without cruelty. Pray for those whom you refute and convince of error. For the prophet prays to God for mercy upon such as these, saying, "Fill their faces with shame, that they may seek Thy name, O Lord." [1966]And this, indeed, the Lord has done already, so as to fill the faces of the followers of Maximianus with shame in the sight of all mankind: it only remains that they should learn how to blush to their soul's health. For so they will be able to seek the name of the Lord, from which they are turned away to their utter

destruction, whilst they exalt their own name in the place of that of Christ. May ye live and persevere in Christ, and be multiplied, and abound in the love of God, and in love towards one another, and towards all men, brethren well beloved.

[1966] Ps. lxxxiii. 16.

Book II. [1967]

In which Augustin replies to all the several statements in the letter of Petilianus, as though disputing with an adversary face to face.

Chapter 1.

1. That we made a full and sufficient answer to the first part of the letter of Petilianus, which was all that we had been able to find, will be remembered by all who were able to read or hear what we replied. But since the whole of it was afterwards found and copied by our brethren, and sent to us with the view that we should answer it as a whole, this task was one which our pen could not escape,--not that he says anything new in it, to which answer has not been already made in many ways and at various times; but still, on account of the brethren of slower comprehension, who, when they read a matter in any place, cannot always refer to everything that has been said upon the same subject, I will comply with those who urge me by all means to reply to every point, and that as though we were carrying on the discussion face to face in the form of a dialogue. I will set down the words of his epistle under his name, and I will give the answer under my own name, as though it had all been taken down by reporters while we were debating. And so there will be no one who can complain either that I have passed anything over, or that they have been unable

to understand it for want of distinction between the parties to the discussion; at the same time that the Donatists themselves, who are unwilling to argue the question in our presence, as is shown by the letters which they have circulated among their party, may thus not fail to find the truth answering them point by point, just as though they were discussing the matter with us face to face.

2. In the very beginning of the letter Petilianus said: "Petilianus, a bishop, to his well-beloved brethren, fellow-priests, and deacons, appointed ministers with us throughout our diocese in the gospel, grace be to you and peace, from God our Father and from the Lord Jesus Christ."

3. Augustin answered: I acknowledge the apostolic greeting. You see who you are that employ it, but see from what source you have learned what you say. For in these terms Paul salutes the Romans, and in the same terms the Corinthians, the Galatians, the Ephesians, the Colossians, the Philippians, the Thessalonians. What madness is it, therefore, to be unwilling to share the salvation of peace with those very Churches in whose epistles you learned its form of salutation?

Chapter 2.

4. Petilianus said: "Those who have polluted their souls with a guilty laver, under the name of baptism, reproach us with baptizing twice,--than whose obscenity, indeed, any kind of filth is more cleanly, seeing that through a perversion of cleanliness they have come to be made fouler by their washing."

5. Augustin answered: We are neither made fouler by our washing, nor cleaner by yours. But when the water of baptism is given to any one in the name of the Father, and of the Son,

and of the Holy Ghost, it is neither ours nor yours, but His of whom it was said to John, "Upon whom thou shalt see the Spirit descending, and remaining on Him, the same is He which baptizeth with the Holy Ghost." [1968]

[1968] John i. 33.

Chapter 3.

6. Petilianus said: "For what we look to is the conscience of the giver, to cleanse that of the recipient."

7. Augustin answered: We therefore need have no anxiety about the conscience of Christ. But if you assert any man to be the giver, be he who he may, there will be no certainty about the cleansing of the recipient, because there is no certainty about the conscience of the giver.

Chapter 4.

8. Petilianus said: "For he who receives faith from the faithless, receives not faith but guilt."

9. Augustin answered: Christ is not faithless, from whom the faithful man receives not guilt but faith. For he believeth on Him that justifieth the ungodly, that his faith may be counted for righteousness. [1969]

[1969] Rom. iv. 5.

Chapter 5.

10. Petilianus said: "For everything consists of an origin and root; and if it have not something for a head, it is nothing: nor does anything well receive second birth, unless it be born again of good seed."

11. Augustin answered: Why will you put yourself forward in the room of Christ, when you will not place yourself under Him? He is the origin, and root, and head of him who is being born, and in Him we feel no fear, as we must in any man, whoever he may be, lest he should prove to be false and of abandoned character, and we should be found to be sprung from an abandoned source, growing from an abandoned root, united to an abandoned head. For what man can feel secure about a man, when it is written, "Cursed be the man that trusteth in man?" [1970]But the seed of which we are born again is the word of God, that is, the gospel. Whence the apostle says, "For in Christ Jesus I have begotten you through the gospel." [1971]And yet he allows even those to preach the gospel who were preaching it not in purity, and rejoices in their preaching; [1972] because, although they were preaching it not in purity, but seeking their own, not the things which are Jesus Christ's, [1973] yet the gospel which they preached was pure. And the Lord had said of certain of like character, "Whatsoever they bid you observe, that observe and do; but do not yet after their works: for they say, and do not." [1974]If, therefore, what is in itself pure is preached in purity, then the preacher himself also, in that he is a partner with the word, has his share in begetting the believer; but if he himself be not regenerate, and yet what he preaches be pure, then the believer is born not from the barrenness of the minister but from the fruitfulness of the word.

[1970] Jer. xvii. 5.

[1971] 1 Cor. iv. 15.

[1972] Phil. i. 17, 18.

[1973] Phil. ii. 21.

[1974] Matt. xxiii. 3.

Chapter 6.

12. Petilianus said: "This being the case, brethren, what perversity must it be, that he who is guilty through his own sins should make another free from guilt, when the Lord Jesus Christ says, Every good tree bringeth forth good fruit, but a corrupt tree bringeth forth evil fruit: do men gather grapes of thorns?' [1975] And again: A good man, out of the good treasure of the heart, bringeth forth good things: and an evil man, out of the evil treasure, bringeth forth evil things.'" [1976]

13. Augustin answered: No man, even though he be not guilty through his own sins, can make his neighbor free from sin, because he is not God. Otherwise, if we were to expect that out of the innocence of the baptizer should be produced the innocence of the baptized, then each will be the more innocent in proportion as he may have found a more innocent person by whom to be baptized; and will himself be the less innocent in proportion as he by whom he is baptized is less innocent. And if the man who baptizes happens to entertain hatred against another man, this will also be imputed to him who is baptized. Why, therefore, does the wretched man hasten to be baptized,-- that his own sins may be forgiven him, or that those of others may be reckoned against him? Is he like a merchant ship, to discharge one burden, and to take on him another? But by the good tree and its good fruit, and the corrupt tree and its evil fruit, we are wont to understand men and their works, as is consequently shown in those other words which you also quoted: "A good man, out of the good treasure of his heart, bringeth forth good things: and an evil man, out of the evil treasure, bringeth forth evil things." But when a man preaches

the word of God, or administers the sacraments of God, he does not, if he is a bad man, preach or minister out of his own treasure; but he will be counted among those of whom it is said, "Whatsoever they bid you observe, that observe and do; but do not ye after their works:" for they bid you observe what is God's, but their works are their own. For if it is as you say, that is, if the fruit of those who baptize consist in the baptized persons themselves, you declare a great woe against Africa, if a young Optatus has sprung up for every one that Optatus baptized.

[1975] Matt. vii. 17, 16.

[1976] Matt. xii. 35.

Chapter 7.

14. Petilianus said: "And again, He who is baptized by one that is dead, his washing profiteth him nothing.' [1977]He did not mean that the baptizer was a corpse, a lifeless body, the remains of a man ready for burial, but one lacking the Spirit of God, who is compared to a dead body, as He declares to a disciple in another place, according to the witness of the gospel. For His disciple says, Lord, suffer me first to go and bury my father. But Jesus said unto him, Follow me, and let the dead bury their dead.' [1978]The father of the disciple was not baptized. He declared him as a pagan to belong to the company of pagans; unless he said this of the unbelieving, The dead cannot bury the dead. He was dead, therefore, not as smitten by some death, but as smitten even during life. For he who so lives as to be doomed to eternal death is tortured by a death in life. To be baptized, therefore, by the dead, is to have received not life but death. We must therefore consider and declare how far the traditor is to be accounted dead while yet

alive. He is dead who has not deserved to be born again with a true baptism; he is likewise dead who, having been born again with a true baptism, has become involved with a traditor. Both are wanting in the life of baptism,--both he who never had it at all, and he who had it and has lost it. For the Lord Jesus Christ says, There shall come to that man seven spirits more wicked than the former one, and the last state of that man shall be worse than the first.'" [1979]

15. Augustin answered: Seek with greater care to know in what sense the words which you have quoted from Scripture in proof of your position were really uttered, and how they should be understood. For that all unrighteous persons are wont to be called dead in a mystical sense is clear enough; but Christ, to whom true baptism belongs, which you say is false because of the faults of men, is alive, sitting at the right hand of the Father, and He will not die any more through any infirmity of the flesh: death will no more have dominion over Him. [1980]And they who are baptized with His baptism are not baptized by one who is dead. And if it so happen that certain ministers, being deceitful workers, seeking their own, not the things which are Jesus Christ's, proclaiming the gospel not in purity, and preaching Christ of contention and envy, are to be called dead because of their unrighteousness, yet the sacrament of the living God does not die even in one that is dead. For that Simon was dead who was baptized by Philip in Samaria, who wished to purchase the gift of God for money; but the baptism which he had lived in him still to work his punishment. [1981]

16. But how false the statement is which you make, that "both are wanting in the life of baptism, both he who never had it at all, and he who had it and has lost it," you may see from this, that in the case of those who apostatize after having been

baptized, and who return through penitence, baptism is not restored to them, as it would be restored if it were lost. In what manner, indeed, do your dead men baptize according to your interpretation? Must we not reckon the drunken among the dead (to say nothing of the rest, and to mention only what is well known and of daily experience among all), seeing that the apostle says of the widow, "But she that liveth in pleasure is dead while she liveth?" [1982]In the next place, in that Council of yours, in which you condemned Maximianus with his advisers or his ministers, have you forgotten with what eloquence you said, "Even after the manner of the Egyptians, the shores are full of the bodies of the dying, on whom the weightier punishment falls in death itself, in that, after their life has been wrung from them by the avenging waters, they have not found so much as burial?" And yet you yourselves may see whether or no one of them, Felicianus, has been brought to life again; yet he has with him within the communion of your body those whom he baptized outside. As therefore he is baptized by One that is alive, who is clothed with the baptism of the living Christ, so he is baptized by the dead who is wrapped in the baptism of the dead Saturn, or any one like him; that we may set forth in the meanwhile, with what brevity we may, in what sense the words which you have quoted may be understood without any cavilling on the part of any one of us. For, in the sense in which they are received by you, you make no effort to explain them, but only strive to entangle us together with yourselves.

[1977] Ecclus. xxxiv. 25; see on I. 9, 10.

[1978] Matt. viii. 21, 22.

[1979] Matt. xii. 45.

[1980] Rom. vi. 9.

[1981] Acts viii. 13, 18, 19.

[1982] 1 Tim. v. 6.

Chapter 8.

17. Petilianus said: "We must consider, I say, and declare how far the treacherous traditor is to be accounted dead while yet in life. Judas was an apostle when he betrayed Christ; and the same man was already dead, having spiritually lost the office of an apostle, being destined afterwards to die by hanging himself, as it is written: I have sinned,' says he, in that I have betrayed the innocent blood; and he departed, and went and hanged himself.' [1983]The traitor perished by the rope: he left the rope for others like himself, of whom the Lord Christ cried aloud to the Father, Father, those that Thou gavest me I have kept, and none of them is lost, but the son of perdition; that the Scripture might be fulfilled.' [1984] For David of old had passed this sentence on him who was to betray Christ to the unbelievers: Let another take his office. Let his children be fatherless, and his wife a widow.' [1985]See how mighty is the spirit of the prophets, that it was able to see all future things as though they were present, so that a traitor who was to be born hereafter should be condemned many centuries before. Finally, that the said sentence should be completed, the holy Matthias received the bishopric of that lost apostle. Let no one be so dull, no one so faithless, as to dispute this: Matthias won for himself a victory, not a wrong, in that he carried off the spoils of the traitor from the victory of the Lord Christ. Why then, after this, do you claim to yourself a bishopric as the heir of a worse traitor? Judas betrayed Christ in the flesh to the unbelievers; you in the spirit madly betrayed the holy gospel to

the flames of sacrilege. Judas betrayed the Lawgiver to the unbelievers; you, as it were, betraying all that he had left, gave up the law of God to be destroyed by men. Whilst, had you loved the law, like the youthful Maccabees, you would have welcomed death for the sake of the laws of God (if indeed that can be said to be death to men which makes them immortal because they died for the Lord); for of those brethren we learn that one replied to the sacrilegious tyrant with these words of faith: Thou like a fury takest us out of this present life; but the King of the world (who reigns for ever, and of His kingdom there shall be no end) shall raise us up who have died for His laws, unto everlasting life.' [1986]If you were to burn with fire the testament of a dead man, would you not be punished as the falsifier of a will? What therefore is likely to become of you who have burned the most holy law of our God and Judge? Judas repented of his deed even in death; you not only do not repent, but stand forth as a persecutor and butcher of us who keep the law, whilst you are the most wicked of traditors."

18. Augustin answered: See what a difference there is between your calumnious words and our truthful assertions. Listen for a little while. See how you have exaggerated the sin of delivering up the sacred books, comparing us in most odious terms, like some sophistical inventor of charges, with the traitor Judas. But when I shall have answered you on this point with the utmost brevity,--I did not do what you assert; I did not deliver up the sacred books; your charge is false; you will never be able to prove it,--will not all that smoke of mighty words presently vanish away? Or will you perchance endeavor to prove the truth of what you say? This, then, you should do first; and then you might rise against us, as against men who were already

convicted, with whatever mass of invective you might choose. Here is one absurdity: behold again a second.

19. You yourself, when speaking of the foretelling of the condemnation of Judas, used these expressions: "See how mighty is the spirit of the prophets, that it was able to see all future things as though they were present, so that a traitor who was to be born hereafter should be condemned many centuries before;" and yet you did not see that in the same sure prophecy, and certain and unshaken truth, in which it was foretold that one of the disciples should hereafter betray the Christ; it was also foretold that the whole world should hereafter believe in Christ. Why did you pay attention in the prophecy to the man who betrayed Christ, and in the same place give no heed to the world for which Christ was betrayed? Who betrayed Christ? Judas. To whom did he betray Him? To the Jews. What did the Jews do to Him? "They pierced my hands and my feet," says the Psalmist. "I may tell all my bones: they look and stare upon me. They part my garments among them, and cast lots upon my vesture." [1987]Of what importance, then, that is which is bought at such a price, I would have you read a little later in the psalm itself: "All the ends of the world shall remember and turn unto the Lord; and all the kindreds of the nations shall worship before Thee. For the kingdom is the Lord's; and He is the governor among the nations." [1988]But who is able to suffice for the quotation of all the other innumerable prophetic passages which bear witness to the world that is destined to believe? Yet you quote a prophecy because you see in it the man who sold Christ: you do not see in it the possession which Christ bought by being sold. Here is the second absurdity: behold again the third.

20. Among the many other expressions in your invective, you said: "If you were to burn with fire the testament of a dead man, would you not be punished as the falsifier of a will? What therefore is likely to become of you who have burned the most holy law of our God and Judge?" In these words you have paid no attention to what certainly ought to have moved you, to the question of how it might be that we should burn the testament, and yet stand fast in the inheritance which was described in that testament; but it is marvellous that you have preserved the testament and lost the inheritance. Is it not written in that testament, "Ask of me, and I shall give thee the heathen for thine inheritance, and the uttermost parts of the earth for thy possession"? [1989]Take part in this inheritance, and you may bring what charges you will against me about the testament. For what madness is it, that while you shrank from committing the testament to the flames, you should yet strive against the words of the testator! We, on the other hand, though we hold in our hands the records of the Church and of the State, in which we read that those who ordained a rival bishop [1990] in opposition to Cæcilianus were rather the betrayers of the sacred books, yet do not on this account insult you, or pursue you with invectives, or mourn over the ashes of the sacred pages in your hands, or contrast the burning torments of the Maccabees with the sacrilege of your fear, saying, "You should deliver your own limbs to the flames rather than the utterances of God." For we are unwilling to be so absurd as to excite an empty uproar against you on account of the deeds of others, which you either know nothing of, or else repudiate. But in that we see you separated from the communion of the whole world (a sin both of the greatest magnitude, and manifest to all mankind, and common to you all), if I were desirous of exaggerating, I should find time failing me sooner than words. And if you

should seek to defend yourself on this charge, it could only be by bringing accusations against the whole world, of such a kind that, if they could be maintained, you would simply be furnishing matter for further accusation against yourself; if they could not be maintained, there is in them no defence for you. Why therefore do you puff yourself up against me about the betrayal of the sacred books, which concerns neither you nor me if we abide by the agreement not to charge each other with the sins of other men: and which, if that agreement does not stand, affects you rather than me? And, yet, even without any violation of that agreement, I think I may say with perfect justice that he should be deemed a partner with him who delivered up Christ who has not delivered himself up to Christ in company with the whole world. "Then," says the apostle, "then are ye Abraham's seed, and heirs according to the promise." [1991]And again he says, "Heirs of God, and joint-heirs with Christ." [1992]And the same apostle shows that the seed of Abraham belongs to all nations from the promise which was given to Abraham, "In thy seed shall all the nations of the earth be blessed." [1993]Wherefore I consider that I am only making a fair demand in asking that we should for a moment consider the testament of God, which has already long been opened, and that we should consider every one to be himself an heir of the traitor whom we do not find to be a joint-heir with Him whom he betrayed; that every one should belong to him who sold Christ who denies that Christ has bought the whole world. For when He showed Himself after His resurrection to His disciples, and gave His limbs to those who doubted, that they should handle them, He says this to them, "For thus it is written, and thus it behoved Christ to suffer, and to rise again from the dead the third day: and that repentance and remission of sins should be preached in His name among all nations, beginning at Jerusalem." [1994]See from what an inheritance you estrange yourselves! see what an Heir you resist! Can it really be that a man would spare Christ if He were walking here on earth who speaks against Him while He sits in heaven? Do you not yet understand that whatever you allege against us you allege against His words? A Christian world is promised and believed in: the promise is fulfilled, and it is denied. Consider, I entreat of you, what you ought to suffer for such impiety. And yet, if I know not what you have suffered,--if I have not seen it, have not wrought it,--then do you to-day, who do not suffer the violence of my persecution, render to me an account of your separation. But you are likely to say over and over again what, unless you prove it, can affect no one, and if you prove it, has no bearing upon me.

[1983] Matt. xxvii. 4, 5.

[1984] John xvii. 12.

[1985] Ps. cix. 8, 9.

[1986] 2 Macc. vii. 9. The words in brackets are not in the original Greek.

[1987] Ps. xxii. 16-18.

[1988] Ps. xxii. 27, 28.

[1989] Ps. ii. 8.

[1990] Majorinus, ordained by the Numidian bishops in 311 A.D.

[1991] Gal. iii. 29.

[1992] Rom. viii. 17.

[1993] Gen. xxii. 18.

[1994] Luke xxiv. 46, 47.

Chapter 9.

21. Petilianus said: "Hemmed in, therefore, by these offenses, you cannot be a true bishop."

22. Augustin answered: By what offenses? What have you shown? What have you proved? And if you have proved charges on the part of I know not whom, what has that to do with the seed of Abraham, in which all the nations of the earth are blessed?

Chapter 10.

23. Petilianus said: "Did the apostle persecute any one? or did Christ betray any one?"

24. Augustin answered: I might indeed say that Satan himself was worse than all wicked men; and yet the apostle delivered a man over to him for the destruction of the flesh, that his spirit might be saved in the day of the Lord Jesus. [1995]And in the same way he delivered over others, of whom he says, "Whom I have delivered unto Satan, that they may learn not to blaspheme." [1996]And the Lord Christ drove out the impious merchants from the temple with scourges; in which connection we also find advanced the testimony of Scripture, where it says, "The zeal of Thine house hath eaten me up." [1997]So that we do find the apostle delivering over to condemnation, and Christ a persecutor. All this I might say, and put you into no small heat and perturbation, so that you would be compelled to inquire, not into the complaints of those who suffer, but into the intention of those who cause the suffering. But do not

trouble yourself about this; I do not say this. But I do say that it has nothing to do with the seed of Abraham, which is in all nations, if anything has been done to you which ought not to have been done, perhaps by the chaff among the harvest of the Lord, which in spite of this is found among all nations. Do you therefore render an account of your separation. But first, consider what kind of men you have among you, with whom you would not wish to be reproached; and see how unjustly you act, when you cast in our teeth the acts of other men, even if you proved what you assert. Therefore it will be found that there is no ground for your separation.

[1995] 1 Cor. v. 5.

[1996] 1 Tim. i. 20.

[1997] John ii. 15-17.

Chapter 11.

25. Petilianus said: "Yet some will be found to say, We are not the sons of a traditor. Any one is the son of that man whose deeds he imitates. For those are most assuredly sons, and at the same time bear a strong resemblance to their parents, who are born in the likeness of their parents, not only as being of their flesh and blood, but in respect of their characters and deeds."

26. Augustin answered: A little while ago you were saying nothing contrary to us, now you even begin to say something in our favor. For this proposition of yours binds you to as much as this, that if you shall fail to-day to convict us, with whom you are arguing, of being traditors and murderers, and anything else with which you charge us, you will then be wholly

powerless to hurt us by any charge of the kind which you may prove against those who have gone before us. For we cannot be the sons of those to whose deeds our actions bear no resemblance. And see to what you have committed yourself. If you should be so successful as to convict some man, even of our own times, and living with us, of any guilt of the kind, that is in no way to the prejudice of all the nations of the earth who are blessed in the seed of Abraham, by separating yourself from whom you are found to be guilty of sacrilege. Accordingly, unless (as is altogether impossible) you are acquainted with all men that exist throughout the world, and have not only made yourself familiar with all their characters and deeds, but have also proved that they are as bad as you describe, you have no ground for reproaching all the world, which is among the saints, with parentage of I know not what description, to whom you prove that they are like. Nor will it help you at all, even if you are able to show that those who are not of the same character take the holy sacraments in common with those who are. In the first place, because you ought yourselves to look at those with whom you celebrate those sacraments, to whom you give them, from whom you receive them, and whom you would be unwilling to have cast up against you as a reproach. And again, if all those are the sons of Judas, who was the devil among the apostles, who imitate his deeds, why do we not call those of the sons of the apostles who make such men partakers, not in their own deeds, but in the sacraments of the Lord, as the apostles partook of the supper of the Lord in company with that traitor? and in this way they are very different from you, who cast in the teeth of men who are striving for the preservation of unity the very thing that you do to the rending asunder of unity.

Chapter 12.

27. Petilianus said: "The Lord Jesus said to the Jews concerning Himself, If I do not the works of my Father, believe me not.'" [1998]

28. Augustin answered: I have already answered above, This is both true, and makes for us against you.

[1998] John x. 37.

Chapter 13.

29. Petilianus said: Over and over again He reproaches the false speakers and liars in such terms as these: Ye are the children of the devil, for he also was a slanderer from the beginning, and abode not in the truth.'"

30. Augustin answered: We are not wont to say, "He was a slanderer," but "He was a murderer." [1999]But we ask how it was that the devil was a murderer from the beginning; and we find that he slew the first man, not by drawing a sword, nor by applying to him any bodily violence, but by persuading him to sin, and thus driving him from the happiness of Paradise. What, then, was Paradise is now represented by the Church. Therefore those are the sons of the devil who slay men by withdrawing them from the Church. But as by the words of God we know what was the situation of Paradise, so now by the words of Christ we have learned where the Church is to be found: "Throughout all nations," He says, "beginning at Jerusalem." Whosoever, therefore, separates a man from that complete whole to place him in any single part, is proved to be a son of the devil and a murderer. But see, further, what is the application of the expression which you yourself employed in

saying of the devil, "He was a slanderer, and abode not in the truth." For you bring an accusation against the whole world on account of the sins of others, though even those others themselves you were more able to accuse than to convict; and you abode not in the truth of Christ. For He says that the Church is "throughout all nations, beginning at Jerusalem;" but ye say that it is in the party of Donatus.

[1999] John viii. 44.

Chapter 14.

31. Petilianus said: "In the third place, also, He calls the madness of persecutors in like manner by this name, Ye generation of vipers, how can ye escape the damnation of hell? Wherefore, behold, I send unto you prophets, and wise men, and scribes; and some of them ye shall kill and crucify; and some of them shall ye scourge in your synagogues, and persecute them from city to city: that upon you may come all the righteous blood shed upon the earth, from the blood of righteous Abel unto the blood of Zacharias, son of Barachias, whom ye slew between the temple and the altar.' [2000]Are they then really the sons of vipers according to the flesh, and not rather serpents in mind, and three-tongued malice, and deadliness of touch, and burning with the spirit of poison? They have truly become vipers, who by their bites have vomited forth death against the innocent people."

32. Augustin answered: If I were to say that this is said of men of character like unto yourselves, you would reply, "Prove it." What then, have you proved it? Or if you think that it is proved by the mere fact of its being uttered, there is no need to repeat the same words. Pronounce the same judgment against yourselves as coming from us to you. See you not that I too

have proved it, if this amounts to proof? And yet I would have you learn what is really meant by proof. For indeed I do not even seek for evidence from without to enable me to prove you vipers. For be well assured that this very fact marks in you the nature of vipers, that you have not in your mouth the foundation of truth, but the poison of slanderous abuse, as it is written, "The poison of asps is under their lips." [2001]And because this might be said indiscriminately by any one against any one, as though it were asked, Under whose lips? he immediately adds, "Their mouth is full of cursing and bitterness." [2002]When, therefore, you say such things as this against men dispersed throughout the whole world, of whom you know nothing whatsoever, and many of whom have never heard the name either of Cæcilianus or of Donatus, and when you do not hear them answering amid silence, Nothing of what you say has reference to us; we never saw it; we never did it; we are totally at a loss to understand what you are saying,--seeing that you desire nothing else than to say what you are entirely powerless to prove, how can you help allowing that your mouth is full of cursing and bitterness? See, therefore, whether you can possibly show that you are not vipers, [2003] unless you show that all Christians throughout all nations of the world are traditors, and murderers, and anything but Christians. Nay, in very truth, even though you should be able to know and set before us the lives and deeds of every individual man throughout the world, yet before you can do that, seeing that you act as you do without any consideration, your mouth is that of a viper, your mouth is full of cursing and bitterness. Show to us now, if you can, what prophet, what wise man, what scribe we have slain, or crucified, or scourged in our synagogues. Look how much labor you have expended without in any way being able to prove that Donatus and Marculus

[2004] were prophets, or wise men, or scribes, because, in fact, they were nothing of the sort. But even if you could prove as much as this, what progress would you have made towards proving that they had been killed by us, when even we ourselves did not so much as know them? and how much less the whole world, whom you calumniate with poisonous mouth? [2005]Or whence will you be able to prove that we have a spirit like that of those who murdered them, when you actually cannot show that they were murdered by any one at all? Look carefully to all these points, see whether you can prove any single one of them either about the whole world, or to the satisfaction of the whole world,--in your persevering calumnies against which you show that the charges are true in you, which you falsely propagate against the world.

33. Further, even if we should desire to prove you to be slayers of the prophets, it would be too long a task to collect the evidence through all the several instances of the slaughter which your infuriated leaders of the Circumcelliones, and the actual crowd of men inflamed by wine and madness, not only have committed since the beginning of your schism, but even continue to commit at the present time. To take the case nearest at hand. Let the divine utterances be produced, which are commonly in the hands of both of us. Let us consider those to be murderers of the prophets whom we find contradicting the words of the prophets. What more learned definition could be given? What could admit of speedier proof? You would be acting less cruelly in piercing the bodies of the prophets with a sword, than in endeavoring to destroy the words of the prophets with your tongue. The prophet says, "All the ends of the world shall remember and turn unto the Lord." [2006]Behold and see how this is being done, how it is

being fulfilled. But you not only close your ears in disbelief against what is said, but you even thrust out your tongues in madness to speak against what is already being done. Abraham heard the promise, "In thy seed shall all the nations of the earth be blessed," [2007] and "he believed, and it was counted unto him for righteousness." [2008]You see the fact accomplished, and you cry out against it; and you will not that it should be counted unto you for unrighteousness, as it fairly would be counted, even if your refusal to believe was not on the accomplishment, but only on the utterance of the prophecy. Nay, not only are you not willing that it should be counted unto you for unrighteousness, but even what you suffer as the punishment of this impiety you would fain have counted unto you for righteousness. Or if your conduct is not a persecution of the prophets, because your instrument is not the sword but the tongue, what was the reason of its being said under divine inspiration, "The sons of men, whose teeth are spears and arrows, and their tongue a sharp sword"? [2009]But what time would suffice me to collect from all the prophets all the testimonies to the Church dispersed throughout the world, all of which you endeavor to destroy and render nought by contradicting them? But you are caught; for "their sound is gone out into all lands, and their words to the end of the world." [2010]I will, however, advance this one saying from the mouth of the Lord, who is the Witness of witnesses. "All things must be fulfilled," He says, "which were written in the law of Moses, and in the prophets, and in the Psalms, concerning me." And what these were let us hear from Himself: "Then opened He their understanding, that they might understand the Scriptures, and said unto them, Thus it is written, and thus it behoved Christ to suffer, and to rise from the dead the third day: and that repentance and remission of sins should be preached in His name among all nations, beginning at Jerusalem." [2011]See what it is that is written in the law of Moses, and in the prophets, and in the Psalms, concerning the Lord. See what the Lord Himself revealed about Himself and about the Church, making Himself manifest, uttering promises about the Church. But for you, see that you resist such manifest proofs as these, and as you cannot destroy them, endeavor to pervert them, what would you do, if you were to come across the bodies of the prophets, when you rage so madly against the utterances of the prophets, as not even to hearken to the Lord when He is fulfilling, and making manifest, and expounding the prophets? For do you not, to the utmost of your power, strive to slay the Lord Himself, since even to Himself you will not yield?

[2000] Matt. xxiii. 33-35.

[2001] Ps. xiv. 5, LXX, cp. Hieron.

[2002] Ps. xiv. 6, LXX. cp. Hieron.

[2003] A suggested reading is, "nos esse viperas."

[2004] These both with others are celebrated in the martyrology of the Donatists, see IIII. Idas Martii Sermo de Passione SS. Donati et Advocati, c. 340; Passio Marculi sacerdotis Donatistæ qui sub Macario interfectus a Donatistis pro Martyre habebatur (Dec. 25, a. 348), and others. See Du Pin Monumenta vetera ad Donatistarum Historiam pertinentia, in his edition of Optatus.

[2005] See below, c. 20, 46: and Contra Crescon. III. 49, 54.

[2006] Ps. xxii. 27.

[2007] Gen. xxii. 18.

[2008] Rom. iv. 3.

[2009] Ps. lvii. 4.

[2010] Ps. xix. 4.

[2011] Luke xxiv. 44-47.

Chapter 15.

34. Petilianus said: "David also spoke of you as persecutors in the following terms: Their throat is an open sepulchre; with their tongues have they deceived; the poison of asps is under their lips. Their mouth is full of cursing and bitterness; their feet are swift to shed blood. Destruction and unhappiness is in their ways, and the way of peace have they not known: there is no fear of God before their eyes. Have all the workers of wickedness no knowledge, who eat up my people as they eat bread?'" [2012]

35. Augustin answered: Their throat is an open sepulchre, whence they breathe out death by lies. For "the mouth that belieth slayeth the soul." [2013]But if nothing is more true than that which Christ said, that His Church should be throughout all nations, beginning at Jerusalem, then there is nothing more false than that which you say, that it is in the party of Donatus. But the tongues which have deceived are the tongues of those who, whilst they are acquainted with their own deeds, not only say that they are just men, but that they are justifiers of men, which is said of One only "that justifieth the ungodly," [2014] and that because "He is just and the justifier." [2015]As regards the poison of asps, and the mouth full of cursing and bitterness, we have said enough already. But you have yourselves said that the followers of Maximianus had feet swift

to shed blood, as is testified by the sentence of your plenary Council, so often quoted in the records of the proconsular province and of the state. But they, so far as we hear, never killed any one in the body. You evidently, therefore, understood that the blood of the soul was shed in spiritual murder by the sword of schism, which you condemned in Maximianus. See then if your feet are not swift to shed blood, when you cut off men from the unity of the whole world, if you were right in saying it of the followers of Maximianus, because they cut off some from the party of Donatus. Are we again without the knowledge of the way of peace, who study to preserve the unity of the Spirit in the bond of peace? and yet do you possess that knowledge, who resist the discourse which Christ held with His disciples after His resurrection, of so peaceful a nature that He began it with the greeting, "Peace be unto you;" [2016] and that so strenuously that you are proved to be saying nothing less to Him than this, "What Thou saidst of the unity of all nations is false; what we say of the offense of all nations is true"? Who would say such things as this if they had the fear of God before their eyes? See, therefore, if in daily saying things like this you are not trying to destroy the people of God dispersed throughout the world, eating them up as it were bread.

[2012] Ps. xiv. 5-8, cp. LXX. and Hieron., the last verse only being in the Hebrew.

[2013] Wisd. i. 11.

[2014] Rom. iv. 5.

[2015] Rom. iii. 26.

[2016] John xx. 19, 21.

Chapter 16.

36. Petilianus said: "The Lord Christ also warns us, saying, Beware of false prophets, which come unto you in sheep's clothing, but inwardly they are ravening wolves; and ye shall not know them by their fruits.'" [2017]

37. Augustin answered: If I were to inquire of you by what fruits you know us to be ravening wolves, you are sure to answer by charging us with the sins of other men, and these such as were never proved against those who are said to have been guilty of them. But if you should ask of me by what fruits we know you rather to be ravening wolves, I bring against you the charge of schism, which you will deny, but which I will straightway go on to prove; for, as a matter of fact, you do not communicate with all the nations of the earth, nor with those Churches which were founded by the labor of the apostles. Hereupon you will say, "I do not communicate with traditors and murderers." The seed of Abraham answers you, "These are those charges which you made, which are either not true, or have no reference to me." But these I set aside for the present; do you meanwhile show me the Church. Now that voice will sound in my ears which the Lord showed was to be avoided in the false prophets who made a show of their several parties, and strove to estrange men from the Catholic Church, "Lo, here is Christ, or there." But do you think that the true sheep of Christ are so utterly destitute of sense, who are told, "Believe it not," [2018] that they will hearken to the wolf when he says, "Lo, here is Christ," and will not hearken to the Shepherd when He says, "Throughout all nations, beginning at Jerusalem?"

[2017] Matt. vii. 15, 16.

[2018] Matt. xxiv. 23.

Chapter 17.

38. Petilianus said: "Thus, thus, thou wicked persecutor, under whatsoever cloak of righteousness thou hast concealed thyself, under whatsoever name of peace thou wagest war with kisses, under whatsoever title of unity thou endeavorest to ensnare the race of men--thou, who up to this time art cheating and deceiving, thou art the true son of the devil, showing thy parentage by thy character."

39. Augustin answered: Consider in reply that these things have been said by us against you; and that you may know to which of us they are more appropriate, call to mind what I have said before.

Chapter 18.

40. Petilianus said: "Nor is it, after all, so strange that you assume to yourself the name of bishop without authority. This is the true custom of the devil, to choose in preference a mode of deceiving by which he usurps to himself a word of holy meaning, as the apostle declares to us: And no marvel,' he says: for Satan himself is transformed into an angel of light. Therefore it is no great thing if his ministers also be transformed as the ministers of righteousness.' [2019]Nor is it therefore a marvel if you falsely call yourself a bishop. For even those fallen angels, lovers of the maidens of the world, who were corrupted by the corruption of their flesh, though, from having stripped themselves of divine excellence, they have ceased to be angels, yet retain the name of angels, and always esteem themselves as angels, though, being released from the service of God, they have passed from the likeness of their character into the army of the devil, as the great God declares, My spirit shall not always strive with man, for that he also is

flesh.' [2020]To those guilty ones and to you the Lord Christ will say, Depart from me, ye cursed, into everlasting fire, prepared for the devil and his angels.' [2021]If there were no evil angels, the devil would have no angels; of whom the apostle says, that in the judgment of the resurrection they shall be condemned by the saints: Know ye not,' says he, that we shall judge angels?' [2022]If they were true angels, men would not have authority to judge the angels of God. So too those sixty apostles, who, when the twelve were left alone with the Lord Christ, departed in apostasy from the faith, are so far yet considered among wretched men to be apostles, that from them Manichæus and the rest entangle many souls in many devilish sects which they destroyed [2023] that they might take them in their snares. For indeed the fallen Manichæus, if fallen he was, is not to be reckoned among those sixty, if it be that we can find his name as an apostle among the twelve, or if he was ordained by the voice of Christ when Matthias was elected into the place of the traitor Judas, or another thirteenth like Paul, who calls himself the last [2024] of the apostles, expressly that any one who was later than himself might not be held to be an apostle. For these are his words: For I am the last of the apostles, that am not meet to be called an apostle, because I persecuted the Church of God.' [2025] And do not flatter yourselves in this: he was a Jew that had done this. You too, as Gentiles, may work destruction upon us. For you carry on war without license, against whom we may not fight in turn. For you desire to live when you have murdered us; but our victory is either to escape or to be slain."

41. Augustin answered: See how you have quoted the testimony of holy Scripture, or how you have understood it, when it has no bearing at all upon the present point at issue.

For all that you have brought forward was simply said to prove that there are false bishops, just as there are false angels and false apostles. Now we too know quite well that there are false angels and false apostles, and false bishops, and, as the true apostle says, false brethren also; [2026] but, seeing that charges such as yours may be brought by either side against the other, what is required is a certain degree of proof, and not mere empty words. But if you would see to which of us the charge of falseness more truly applies, recall to mind what we have said before, and you will see it there set forth, that we may not become tedious to our readers by repeating the same thing over and over again. And yet how is the Church dispersed throughout the world affected either by what you may have found to say about its chaff, which is mixed with it throughout the whole world; or by what you said of Manichæus and the other devilish sects? For if the wheat is not affected by anything which is said even about the chaff which is still mingled with it, how much less are the members of Christ dispersed throughout the whole world affected by monstrosities [2027] which have been so long and so openly separated from it? [2028]

[2019] 2 Cor. xi. 14, 15.

[2020] Gen. vi. 3.

[2021] Matt. xxv. 41.

[2022] 1 Cor. vi. 3.

[2023] "Perdiderunt," which the Benedictines think may be a confusion for "perierunt."

[2024] Novissimus.

[2025] 1 Cor. xv. 9.

[2026] 2 Cor. xi. 26.

[2027] Portenta.

[2028] Down to this point Augustin had already answered Petilianus in the First Book, as he says himself below, III. 50, 61.

Chapter 19.

42. Petilianus said: "The Lord Jesus Christ commands us, saying, When they persecute you in this city, flee ye into another; and if they persecute you in that, flee yet into a third; for verily I say unto you, ye shall not have gone over the cities of Israel, till the Son of man be come.' [2029]If He gives us this warning in the case of Jews and pagans, you who call yourself a Christian ought not to imitate the dreadful deeds of the Gentiles. Or do you serve God in such wise that we should be murdered at your hands? You do err, you do err, if you are wretched enough to entertain such a belief as this. For God does not have butchers for His priests."

43. Augustin answered: To flee from one state to another from the face of persecution has not been enjoined as precept or permission on heretics or schismatics, such as you are; but it was enjoined on the preachers of the gospel, whom you resist. And this we may easily prove in this wise: you are now in your own cities, and no man persecutes you. You must therefore come forth, and give an account of your separation. For it cannot be maintained that, as the weakness of the flesh is excused when it yields before the violence of persecution, so truth also ought to yield to falsehood. Furthermore, if you are

suffering persecution, why do you not retire from the cities in which you are, that you may fulfill the instructions which you quote out of the gospel? But if you are not suffering persecution, why are you unwilling to reply to us? Or if the fact be that you are afraid lest, when you should have made reply, you then should suffer persecution, in that case how are you following the example of those preachers to whom it was said, "Behold, I send you forth as sheep in the midst of wolves?" To whom it was also further said "Fear not them which kill the body, but are not able to kill the soul." [2030]And how do you escape the charge of acting contrary to the injunction of the Apostle Peter, who says, "Be ready always to give an answer to every man that asketh you a reason of the faith and hope that is in you?" [2031] And, lastly, wherefore are you ever eager to annoy the Catholic Churches by the most violent disturbances, whenever it is in your power, as is proved by innumerable instances of simple fact? But you say that you must defend your places, and that you resist with cudgels and massacres and with whatever else you can. Wherefore in such a case did you not hearken to the voice of the Lord, when He says, "But I say unto you, that ye resist not evil"? [2032]Or, allowing that it is possible that in some cases it should be right for violent men to be resisted by bodily force, and that it does not violate the precept which we receive from the Lord, "But I say unto you, that ye resist not evil," why may it not also be that a pious man should eject an impious man, or a just man him that is unjust, in the exercise of duly and lawfully constituted authority, from seats which are unlawfully usurped, or retained to the despite of God? For you would not say that the false prophets suffered persecution at the hands of Elijah, in the same sense that Elijah suffered persecution from the wickedest of kings? [2033]Or that because the Lord was scourged by His persecutors, therefore those whom He Himself drove out of the temple with scourges are to be put in comparison with His sufferings? It remains, therefore, that we should acknowledge that there is no other question requiring solution, except whether you have been pious or impious in separating yourselves from the communion of the whole world. For if it shall be found that you have acted impiously, you would not be surprised if there should be no lack of ministers of God by whom you might be scourged, seeing that you suffer persecution not from us, but as it is written, from their own abominations. [2034]

[2029] Matt. x. 23.

[2030] Matt. x. 16, 28.

[2031] 1 Pet. iii. 15.

[2032] Matt. v. 39.

[2033] 1 Kings xviii.

[2034] Wisd. xii. 23.

Chapter 20.

44. Petilianus said: "The Lord Christ cries again from heaven to Paul, Saul, Saul, why persecutest thou me? It is hard for thee to kick against the pricks.' [2035]He was then called Saul, that he might afterwards receive his true name in baptism. But for you it is not hard so often to persecute Christ in the persons of His priests, though the Lord Himself cries out, Touch not mine anointed.' [2036]Reckon up all the deaths of the saints, and so often have you murdered Christ, who lives in each of them. [2037]Lastly, if you are not guilty of sacrilege, then a saint cannot be a murderer."

45. Augustin answered: Defend yourselves from the charge of the persecution which those men suffered at the hands of your party who separated themselves from you with the followers of Maximianus, and therein you will find our defence. For if you say that you committed no such deeds, we simply read to you the records of the pro-consular province and the state. If you say that you were right in persecuting them, why are you unwilling to suffer the like yourselves? If you say, "But we caused no schism," then let this be inquired into, and, till it is decided whether it be so or not, let no one make accusation against persecutors. If you say that even schismatics ought not to have suffered persecution, I ask whether it is also the case that they ought not to have been driven out of the basilicas, in which they lay snares for the leading astray of the weak, even though it were done by duly constituted authorities? If you say that this also should not have been done, first restore the basilicas to the followers of Maximianus, and then discuss the point with us. If you say that it was right, then see what they ought to suffer at the hands of duly constituted authority, who, in resisting it, "resist the ordinance of God." Wherefore the apostle expressly says, "For he beareth not the sword in vain: for he is the minister of God, a revenger to execute wrath on him that doeth evil." [2038]But even if this had been discovered after the truth had been searched out with all diligence, that not even after public trial ought schismatics to undergo any punishment, or be driven from the positions which they have occupied, for their treachery and deceit; and if you should say that you are vexed that the followers of Maximianus should have suffered such conduct at the hands of some of you,--why does not the wheat of the Lord cry out with the more freedom from the whole field of the Lord, that is, from the world, and say, Neither are we at all affected by what the tares and the

chaff amongst us do, seeing that it is contrary to our wish? If you confess that it is sufficient to clear you of responsibility, that all the evil that is done by men of your party is done in opposition to your wishes, why then have you separated yourselves? For if your reason for not separating from the unrighteous among the party of Donatus is that each man bears his own burden, why have you separated yourselves from those throughout the world whom you think, or profess to think, to be unrighteous? Is it that you might all share equally in bearing the burden of schism?

46. And when we ask of you which of your party you can prove to have been slain by us, I indeed can remember no law issued by the emperors to the effect that you should be put to death. Those indeed whose deaths you quote most frequently to bring us into odium, Marculus and Donatus, present a great question,--whether they threw themselves down a precipice, as your teaching does not hesitate to encourage by examples of daily occurrence, or whether they were thrown down by the true command of some authority. For if it is a thing incredible that the leaders of the Circumcelliones should have wrought upon themselves a death in accordance with their custom, how much more incredible it is that the Roman authorities should have been able to condemn them to a punishment at variance with custom! Accordingly, in considering this matter, which you think excessive in its hatefulness, supposing what you say is true, what is there in it which bears upon the Lord's wheat? Let the chaff which flew away outside accuse the chaff which yet remained within for it is not possible that it should all be separated till the winnowing at the last day. But if what you say is false, what wonder is it if, when the chaff is carried away as it were by a light blast of dissension, it even attacks the wheat of

the Lord with false accusations? Wherefore, on the consideration of all such odious accusations, the wheat of Christ, which is ordered to grow together with the tares throughout the field, that is, throughout the whole world, makes this answer to you with a free and fearless voice: If you cannot prove what you say, it has no application to any one; and if you prove it, it yet does not apply to me. The result of which is, that whosoever has separated himself from the unity of the wheat on account of the offenses chargeable against the tares, or against the chaff, is unable to defend himself from the charge of murder which is involved in the mere offense of dissension and schism, as the Scripture says, "Whoso hateth his brother is a murderer." [2039]

[2035] Acts ix. 4, 5.

[2036] Ps. cv. 15.

[2037] Vivacem Christum.

[2038] Rom. xiii. 2, 4.

[2039] 1 John iii. 15.

Chapter 21.

47. Petilianus said: "Accordingly, as we have said, the Lord Christ cried, Saul, Saul, why persecutest thou me? It is hard for thee to kick against the pricks. And he said, Who art Thou, Lord? And the Lord said, I am Christ of Nazareth, whom thou persecutest. And he, trembling and astonished, said, Lord, what wilt Thou have me to do? And the Lord said unto him, Arise, and go into the city, and it shall be told thee what thou must do.' And so presently it goes on, But Saul arose from the earth; and when his eyes were opened, he saw no man.' See

here how blindness, coming in punishment of madness, obscures the light in the eyes of the persecutor, not to be again expelled except by baptism! Let us see, therefore, what he did in the city. Ananias,' it is said, entered into the house to Saul, and putting his hands on him, said, Brother Saul, the Lord, even Jesus, that appeared unto thee in the way as thou camest, hath sent me, that thou mightest receive thy sight, and be filled with the Holy Ghost. And immediately there fell from his eyes as it had been scales; and he received sight forthwith, and arose, and was baptized.' [2040]Seeing therefore that Paul, being freed by baptism from the offense of persecution, received again his eyesight freed from guilt, why will not you, a persecutor and traditor, blinded by false baptism be baptized by those whom you persecute?"

48. Augustin answered: You do not prove that I, whom you wish to baptize afresh, am either a persecutor or a traditor. And if you prove this charge against any one, yet the persecutor and traditor is not to be baptized afresh, if he had been baptized already with the baptism of Christ. For the reason why it was necessary that Paul should be baptized was that he had never been washed in any baptism of the kind. Therefore what you have chosen to insert about Paul has no point of resemblance with the case which you are arguing with us. But if you had not inserted this, you would have found no place for your childish declamation, "See how blindness comes in punishment of madness, not to be again expelled except by baptism!" For with how much more force might one exclaim against you, See how blindness comes in punishment of madness, which, finding its similitude in Simon, not in Paul, is not expelled from you even when you have received baptism? For if persecutors ought to be baptized by those whom they

persecute, then let Primianus be baptized by the followers of Maximianus, whom he persecuted with the utmost eagerness.

[2040] Acts ix. 4-18.

Chapter 22.

49. Petilianus said: "It may be urged that Christ said to His apostles, as you are constantly quoting against us, He that is washed needeth not save to wash his feet, but is clean every whit.' Now if you discuss those words in all their fullness, you are bound by what immediately follows. For this is what He said, in His very words: He that is washed needeth not save to wash his feet, but is clean every whit: and ye are clean, but not all. But this he said on account of Judas, who should betray Him; therefore said He, Ye are not all clean.' [2041]Whosoever, therefore, has incurred the guilt of treason, has forfeited, like you, his baptism. Again, after that the betrayer of Christ had himself been condemned, He thus more fully confirmed His words to the eleven apostles: Now are ye clean through the word which I have spoken unto you. Abide in me, and I in you.' [2042]And again He said to these same eleven, Peace I leave with you, my peace I give unto you.' [2043]Seeing, then, that these things were said to the eleven apostles, when the traitor, as we have seen, had been condemned, you likewise, being traditors, are similarly without both peace and baptism."

50. Augustin answered: If therefore every traditor has forfeited his baptism, it will follow that every one who, having been baptized by you, has afterwards become a traditor, ought to be baptized afresh. And if you do not do this, you yourselves sufficiently prove the falseness of the saying, "Whosoever therefore has incurred the guilt of treason, has forfeited, like you, his baptism." For if he has forfeited it, let him return and

receive it again; but if he returns and does not receive it, it is clear that he had not forfeited it. Again, if the reason why it was said to the apostles, "Now are ye clean," and "My peace I give unto you," was that the traitor had already left the room, then was not that supper of so great a sacrament clean and able to give peace, which He distributed to all before his going out? And if you venture to say this with your eyes closed against the truth, what can we do save exclaim the more, See how blindness comes in punishment of the madness of those who wish to be, as the apostle says, "teachers of the law, understanding neither what they say, nor whereof they affirm?" [2044]And yet, unless blindness came in the way of their pertinacity, it was not a very difficult matter that you should understand and see that the Lord did not say in the presence of Judas, Ye are not yet clean, but "Now are ye clean." He added, however, "But not all," because there was one there who was not clean; yet if he had been polluting the others by his presence, it would not have been declared to them, "Now are ye clean," but, as I said before, Ye are not yet clean. But, after Judas had gone out, He said to them, "Now are ye clean," and did not add the words, But not all, because he had now departed in whose presence indeed, as had been said to them, they were already clean, but not all, because there was one there unclean. Wherefore in these words the Lord rather declared that in the one company of men receiving the same sacraments, the uncleanness of some members cannot hurt the clean. Certainly, if you think that there are among us men like Judas, you might apply to us the words, "Ye are clean, but not all." But this is not what you say; but you say that because of the presence of some who are unclean, therefore we are all unclean. This the Lord did not say to the disciples in the presence of

Judas, and therefore whoever says this has not learned from the good Master what He says.

[2041] John xiii. 10, 11.

[2042] John xv. 3, 4.

[2043] John xiv. 27.

[2044] 1 Tim. i. 7.

Chapter 23.

51. Petilianus said: "But if you say that we give baptism twice over, truly it is rather you who do this, who slay men who have been baptized; and this we do not say because you baptize them, but because you cause each one of them, by the act of slaying him, to be baptized in his own blood. For the baptism of water or of the Spirit is as it were doubled when the blood of the martyr is wrung from him. And so our Saviour also Himself, after being baptized in the first instance by John, declared that He must be baptized again, not this time with water nor with the Spirit, but with the baptism of blood, the cross of suffering, as it is written, Two disciples, the sons of Zebedee, came unto Him, saying, Lord, when thou comest into thy kingdom grant that we may sit, one on Thy right hand, and the other on Thy left hand. But Jesus said unto them, Ye ask a difficult thing: can ye drink of the cup that I drink of, and be baptized with the baptism that I am baptized with? They said unto Him, We are able. And He said unto them, Ye can indeed drink of the cup that I drink of; and with the baptism that I am baptized withal shall ye be baptized,' [2045] and so forth. If these are two baptisms, you commend us by your malice, we must needs confess. For when you kill our bodies, then we do

celebrate a second baptism; but it is that we are baptized with our baptism and with blood, like Christ. Blush, blush, ye persecutors. Ye make martyrs like unto Christ, who are sprinkled with the baptism of blood after the water of the genuine baptism."

52. Augustin answered: In the first place, we reply without delay that we do not kill you, but you kill yourselves by a true death, when you cut yourselves off from the living root of unity. In the next place, if all who are killed are baptized in their own blood, then all robbers, all unrighteous, impious, accursed men, who are put to death by the sentence of the law, are to be considered martyrs, because they are baptized in their own blood. But if only those are baptized in their own blood who are put to death for righteousness' sake, since theirs is the kingdom of heaven, [2046] you have already seen that the first question is why you suffer, and only afterwards should we ask what you suffer. Why therefore do you puff out your cheeks before you have shown the righteousness of your deeds? Why, does your tongue resound before your character is approved? If you have made a schism, you are impious; if you are impious, you die as one guilty of sacrilege, when you are punished for impiety; if you die as one guilty of sacrilege, how are you baptized in your blood? Or do you say, I have not made a schism? Let us then inquire into this. Why do you make an outcry before you prove your case?

53. Or do you say, Even if I am guilty of sacrilege, I ought not to be slain by you? It is one question as to the enormity of my action, which you never prove with any truth, another as to the baptism of your blood, from whence you derive your boast. For I never killed you, nor do you prove that you are killed by any one. Nor even if you were to prove it would it in any way

affect me, whoever it was that killed you, whether he did it justly in virtue of power lawfully given by the Lord, or committed the crime of murder, like the chaff of the Lord's harvest, through some evil desire; just as you are in no way concerned with him who in recent times, with an intolerable tyranny, attended even by a company of soldiers, not because he feared any one, but that he might be feared by all, oppressed widows, destroyed pupils, betrayed the patrimonies of other men, annulled the marriages of other men, contrived the sale of the property of the innocent, divided the price of the property when sold with its mourning owners. I should seem to be saying all this out of the invention of my own head, if it were not sufficiently obvious of whom I speak without the mention of his name. [2047]And if all this is undoubtedly true, then just as you are not concerned with this, so neither are we concerned with anything you say, even though it were true. But if that colleague of yours, being really a just and innocent man, is maligned by a lying tale, then should we also learn in no way to give credit to reports, which have been spread abroad of innocent men, as though they had delivered up the sacred books, or murdered any of their fellow-men. To this we may add, that I refer to a man who lived with you, whose birthday you were wont to celebrate with such large assemblies, with whom you joined in the kiss of peace in the sacraments, in whose hands you placed the Eucharist, to whom in turn you extended your hands to receive it from his ministering, whose ears, when they were deaf amid the groanings of all Africa, you durst not offend by free speech; for paying to whom, even indirectly, a most witty compliment, by saying that in the Count [2048] he had a god for his companion, some one of your party was extolled to the skies. But you reproach us with the deeds of men with whom we never lived, whose faces we never saw, in whose lifetime we were either boys, or perhaps as yet not even born. What is the meaning, then, of your great unfairness and perversity, that you should wish to impose on us the burdens of those whom we never knew, whilst you will not bear the burdens of your friends? The divine Scriptures exclaim: "When thou sawest a thief, then thou consentedst with him." [2049]If he whom you saw did not pollute you, why do you reproach me with one whom I could not have seen? Or do you say, I did not consent with him, because his deeds were displeasing to me? But, at any rate, you went up to the altar of God with him. Come now, if you would defend yourself, make a distinction between your two positions, and say that it is one thing to consent together for sin, as the two elders consented together when they laid a plot against the chastity of Susannah, and another thing to receive the sacrament of the Lord in company with a thief, as the apostles received even that first supper in company with Judas. I am all in favor of your defense. But why do you not consider how much more easily, in the course of your defense, you have acquitted all the nations and boundaries of the earth, throughout which the inheritance of Christ is dispersed? For if it was possible for you to see a thief, and to share the sacraments with the thief whom you saw, and yet not to share his sin, how much less was it possible for the remotest nations of the earth to have anything in common with the sins of African traditors and persecutors, supposing your charges and assertions to be true, even though they held the sacraments in common with them? Or do you say, I saw in him the bishop, I did not see in him the thief? Say what you will. I allow this defense also, and in this the world is acquitted of the charges which you brought against it. For if it was permitted you to ignore the character of a man whom you knew, why is the whole world not allowed to be ignorant of those it never knew, unless, indeed, the Donatists are allowed to be ignorant of what they do not wish to know, while the nations of the earth may not be ignorant of what they cannot know?

54. Or do you say, Theft is one thing, delivery of the sacred books or persecution is another? I grant there is a difference, nor is it worth while now to show wherein that difference consists. But listen to the summary of the argument. If he could not make you a thief, because his thieving was displeasing in your sight, who can make men traditors or murderers to whom such treachery or murder is abhorrent? First, then, confess that you share in all the evil of Optatus, whom you knew, and even so reproach me with any evil which was found in those whom I knew not. And do not say to me, But my charges are serious, yours but trifling. You must first acknowledge them, however trifling they may be in your case, not before I on my side confess the charges against me, but before I can allow you to say these serious things about me at all. Did Optatus, whom you knew make you a thief by being your colleague, or not? Answer me one or the other. If you say he did not, I ask why he did not,--because he was not a thief himself? or because you do not know it? or because you disapprove of it? If you say, Because he himself was not a thief, much more ought we not to believe that those with whom you reproach us were of such a character as you assert. For if we must not believe of Optatus what both Christians and pagans and Jews, ay, and what both our party and yours assert, how much less should we believe what you assert of any one? But if you say, Because you do not know it, all the nations of the earth answer you, Much more do we not know of all that you reproach us with in these men. But if you say, Because you

disapproved of it, they answer you with the same voice, Although you have never proved the truth of what you say, yet acts like these are viewed by us with disapproval. But if you say, Lo, Optatus, whom I knew, made me a thief because he was my colleague, and I was in the habit of going to the altar with him when he committed those deeds; but I do not greatly heed it, because the fault was trivial, but your party made you a traditor and a murderer,--I answer that I do not allow that I too am made a traditor and a murderer by the sins of other men, just because you confess that you are made a thief by the sin of another man; for it must be remembered that you are proved a thief, not by our judgment, but by your own confession. For we say that every man must bear his own burden, as the apostle is our witness. [2050]But you, of your own accord, have taken the burden of Optatus on your own shoulders, not because you committed the theft, or consented to it, but because you declared your conviction that what another did applied to you. For, as the apostle says, when speaking of food, "I know, and am persuaded by the Lord Jesus, that there is nothing unclean of itself: but to him that esteemeth anything to be unclean, to him it is unclean;" [2051] by the same rule, it may be said that the sins of others cannot implicate those who disapprove of them; but if any one thinks that they affect him, then he is affected by them. Wherefore you do not convict us of being traditors or murderers, even though you were to prove something of the sort against those who share the sacraments with us; but the guilt of theft is fastened on you, even if you disapprove of everything that Optatus did, not in virtue of our accusation, but by your own decision. And that you may not think this a trivial fault, read what the apostle says, "Nor shall thieves inherit the kingdom of God." [2052]But those who shall not inherit the kingdom of God will certainly not be on His right hand among those whom it shall be said, "Come, ye blessed of my Father, inherit the kingdom prepared for you from the foundation of the world." If they are not there, where will they be except on the left hand? Therefore among those to whom it shall be said, "Depart from me, ye cursed, into everlasting fire, prepared for the devil and his angels." [2053]In vain, therefore, do you indulge in your security, thinking it a trivial fault which separates you from the kingdom of God, and sends you into everlasting fire. How much better will you do to betake yourself to true confusion, saying, Every one of us shall bear his own burden, and the winnowing fan at the last day shall separate the chaff from the wheat!

55. But it is evident that you are afraid of its being forthwith said to you, "Why then, whilst you attempt to place on some men's backs the burdens of their neighbors, have you dared to separate yourselves from the Lord's corn, dispersed throughout the world, before the winnowing at the last day?" Accordingly, you who disapprove of the deeds of your party, whilst you are taking precautions against being charged with the schism which you all have made, are involving yourselves also in their sins which you did not commit; and while the shrewd Petilianus is afraid of my being able to say that am I not such as he thinks Cæcilianus was, he is obliged to confess that he himself is such as he knows Optatus to have been. Or are you not such as the common voice of Africa proclaims him to have been? Then neither are we such as those with whom you reproach us are either suspected to have been by your mistake, or calumniously asserted to have been by your madness, or proved to have been by the truth. Much less is the wheat of the Lord in all the nations of the earth of such a character, seeing that it never heard the names of those of whom you speak. There is

therefore no reason why you should perish in such sin of separation and such sacrilege of schism. And yet, if you are made to suffer for this great impiety by the judgment of God, you say that you are even baptized in your blood; so that you are not content with feeling no remorse for your division, but you must even glory in your punishment.

[2045] Mark x. 35-39.

[2046] Matt. v. 10.

[2047] Optatus Gildonianus is the person to whom he refers.

[2048] Gildo, from subservience to whom Optatus received the name Gildonianus, was "Comes Africæ." The play on the meanings of "Comes," in the expression "quod Comitem haberet Deum," is incapable of direct translation. Cp. 37, 88; 103, 237.

[2049] Ps. l. 18.

[2050] Gal. vi. 5.

[2051] Rom. xiv. 14.

[2052] 1 Cor. vi. 10.

[2053] Matt. xxv. 34, 41.

Chapter 24.

56. Petilianus said: "But you will answer that you abide by the same declaration, He that is once washed needeth not save to wash his feet.' [2054]Now the once' is once that has authority, once that is confirmed by the truth."

57. Augustin answered: Baptism in the name of the Father and of the Son and of the Holy Ghost [2055] has Christ for its authority, not any man, whoever he may be; and Christ is the truth, not any man.

[2054] John xiii. 10.

[2055] Matt. xxviii. 19.

Chapter 25.

58. Petilianus said: "For when you in your guilt perform what is false, I do not celebrate baptism twice, which you have never celebrated once."

59. Augustin answered: In the first place, you do not convict us of guilt. And if a guilty man baptizes with a false baptism, then none of those have true baptism who are baptized by men in your party, that are, I do not say openly, but even secretly guilty. For if he who gives baptism gives something that is God's, if he is already guilty in the sight of God, how can he be giving something that is God's if a guilty man cannot give true baptism? But in reality you wait till he is guilty in your sight as well, as though what he proposes to confer were something that belonged to you.

Chapter 26.

60. Petilianus said: "For if you mix what is false with what is true, falsehood often imitates the truth by treading in its steps. Just in the same way a picture imitates the true man of nature, depicting with its colors the false resemblance of truth. And in the same way, too, the brilliancy of a mirror catches the countenance, so as to represent the eyes of him who gazes on it. In this way it presents to each comer his own countenance,

so that the very features of the comer meet themselves in turn; and of such virtue is the falsehood of a clear mirror, that the very eyes which see themselves recognize themselves as though in some one else. And even when a shadow stands before it, it doubles the reflection, dividing its unity in great part through a falsehood. Must we then hold that anything is true, because a lying representation is given of it? But it is one thing to paint a man, another to give birth to one. For does any one represent fictitious children to a man who wishes for an heir? or would any one look for true heirs in the falsehood of a picture? Truly it is a proof of madness to fall in love with a picture, letting go one's hold of what is true."

61. Augustin answered: Are you then really not ashamed to call the baptism of Christ a lie, even when it is found in the most false of men? Far be it from any one to suppose that the wheat of the Lord, which has been commanded to grow among the tares throughout the whole field, that is, throughout the whole of this world, until the harvest, that is, until the end of the world, [2056] can have perished in consequence of your evil words. Nay, even among the very tares themselves, which are commanded not to be gathered, but to be tolerated even to the end, and among the very chaff, which shall only be separated from the wheat by the winnowing at the last day, [2057] does any one dare to say that any baptism is false which is given and received in the name of the Father, and of the Son, and of the Holy Ghost? Would you say that those whom you depose from their office, whether as your colleagues or your fellow-priests, on the testimony of women whom they have seduced (since examples of this kind are not wanting anywhere), were false or true before their crime was proved against them? You will certainly answer, False. Why then were they able both to

have and to give true baptism? Why did not their falseness as men corrupt in them the truth of God? Is it not most truly written, "For the Holy Spirit of discipline will flee deceit?" [2058]Seeing then that the Holy Spirit fled from them, how came it that the truth of baptism was in them, except because what the Holy Spirit fled from was the falseness of man, not the truth of the sacrament? Further, if even the deceitful have the true baptism, how do they have it who possess it in truthfulness? Whence you ought to observe that it is rather your conversation which is colored with childish pigments; and accordingly, he who neglects the living Word to take pleasure in such coloring is himself loving the picture in the place of the reality.

[2056] Matt. xiii. 24-30, 36-43.

[2057] Matt. iii. 12.

[2058] Wisd. i. 5.

Chapter 27.

62. Petilianus said: "It will be urged against us, that the Apostle Paul said, One Lord, one faith, one baptism.' [2059]We profess that there is only one; for it is certain that those who declare that there are two are mad."

63. Augustin replied: These words of yours are arguments against yourselves; but in your madness you are not aware of it. For the men who say there are two baptisms are those who declare their opinion that the just and the unjust have different baptisms; whereas it belongs neither to one party nor the other, but in both of them is one, being Christ's, although they

themselves are not one: and yet the baptism, which is one, the just have to salvation, the unjust to their destruction.

[2059] Eph. iv. 5.

Chapter 28.

64. Petilianus said: "But yet, if I may be allowed the comparison, it is certain that the sun appears double to the insane, although it only be that a dark blue cloud often meets it, and its discolored surface, being struck by the brightness, while the rays of the sun are reflected from it, seems to send forth as it were rays of its own. So in the same way in the faith of baptism, it is one thing to seek for reflections, another to recognize the truth."

65. Augustin answered: What are you saying, if I may ask? When a dark blue cloud reflects the rays of the sun with which it is struck, is it only to the insane, and not to all who look on it, that there appear to be two suns? But when it appears so to the insane as such, it appears to them alone. But if I may say so without being troublesome, I would have you take care lest saying such things and talking in such a way should be itself a sign of madness. I suppose, however, that what you meant to say was this,--that the just had the truth of baptism, the unjust only its reflection. And if this be so, I venture to say that the reflection was found in that man of our party, [2060] to whom not God, but a certain Count, [2061] was God; but that the truth was either in you or in him who uttered the witty saying against Optatus, when he said that "in the Count he had a god for his companion." [2062] And distinguish between those who were baptized by either of these, and in the one party approve the true baptism, in the others exclude the reflection, and introduce the truth.

[2060] Optatus.

[2061] Gildo.

[2062] See above, on 23, 53.

Chapter 29.

66. Petilianus said: "But to pass rapidly through these minor points: can he be said to lay down the law who is not a magistrate of the court? or is what he lays down to be considered law, when in the character of a private person he disturbs public rights? Is it not rather the case that he not only involves himself in guilt, but is held to be a forger, and that which he composes a forgery?"

67. Augustin answered: What if your private person, whom you deem a forger, were to set forth to any one the law of the emperor? Would not the man, when he had compared it with the law of those who have the genuine law, and found it to be identically the same, lay aside all care about the source from which he had obtained it, and consider only what he had obtained? For what the forger gives is false when he gives it of his own falseness; but when something true is given by any person, even though he be a forger, yet, although the giver be not truthful, the gift is notwithstanding true.

Chapter 30.

68. Petilianus said: "Or if any one chance to recollect the chants of a priest, is he therefore to be deemed a priest, because with sacrilegious mouth he publishes the strain of a priest?"

69. Augustin answered: In this question you are speaking just as though we were at present inquiring what constituted a true

priest, not what constituted true baptism. For that a man should be a true priest, it is requisite that he should be clothed not with the sacrament alone, but with righteousness, as it is written, "Let thy priests be clothed with righteousness." [2063]But if a man be a priest in virtue of the sacrament alone, as was the high priest Caiaphas, the persecutor of the one most true Priest, then even though he himself be not truthful, yet what he gives is true, if he gives not what is his own but what is God's; as it is said of Caiaphas himself, "This spake he not of himself: but being high priest that year, he prophesied." [2064]And yet, to use the same simile which you employed yourself: if you were to hear even from any one that was profane the prayer of the priest couched in the words suitable to the mysteries of the gospel, can you possibly say to him, Your prayer is not true, though he himself may be not only no true priest, but not a priest at all? seeing that the Apostle Paul said that certain testimony of I know not what Cretan prophet was true, though he was not reckoned among the prophets of God for he says, "One of themselves, even a prophet of their own, said the Cretians are always liars, evil beasts, slow bellies: this witness is true." [2065]If, therefore, the apostle even himself bore witness to the testimony of some obscure prophet of a foreign race, because he found it to be true, why do not we, when we find in any one what belongs to Christ, and is true even though the man with whom it may be found be deceitful and perverse, why do not we in such a case make a distinction between the fault which is found in the man, and the truth which he has not of his own but of God's? and why do we not say, This sacrament is true, as Paul said, "This witness is true"? Does it at all follow that we say, The man himself also is truthful, because we say, This sacrament is true? Just as I would ask whether the apostle counted that prophet among the prophets of the Lord, because he confirmed the truth of what he found to be true in him. Likewise the same apostle, when he was at Athens, perceived a certain altar among the altars of the false gods, on which was this inscription, "To the unknown God." And this testimony he made use of to build them up in Christ, to the extent of quoting the inscription in his sermon, and adding, "Whom, therefore, ye ignorantly worship, Him declare I unto you." Did he, because he found that altar among the altars of idols, or set up by sacrilegious hands, therefore condemn or reject what he found in it that was true? or did he, because of the truth which he found upon it, therefore persuade them that they ought also to follow the sacrilegious practices of the pagans? Surely he did neither of the two; but presently, when, as he judged fitting, he wished to introduce to their knowledge the Lord Himself unknown to them, but known to him, he says among other things, that "He is not far from every one of us: for in Him we live, and move, and have our being; as certain also of your own poets have said." [2066]Can it be said that here also, because he found among the sacrilegious, the evidence of truth, he either approved their wickedness because of the evidence, or condemned the evidence because of their wickedness? But it is unavoidable that you should be always in the wrong, so long as you do despite to the sacraments of God because of the faults of men, or think that we take upon ourselves the sacrilege even of your schism, for the sake of the sacraments of God, to which we are unwilling to do despite in you.

[2063] Ps. cxxxii. 9.

[2064] John xi. 51.

[2065] Tit. i. 12, 13.

[2066] Acts xvii. 23, 27, 28.

Chapter 31.

70. Petilianus said: "For there is no power but of God," [2067] none in any man of power; as the Lord Jesus Christ answered Pontius Pilate, Thou couldest have no power at all against me, except it were given thee from above.' [2068]And again, in the words of John, A man can receive nothing, except it be given him from heaven.' [2069]Tell us, therefore, traditor, when you received the power of imitating the mysteries."

71. Augustin answered: Tell us rather thyself when the power of baptizing was lost by the whole world through which is dispersed the inheritance of Christ, and by all that multitude of nations in which the apostles founded the Churches. You will never be able to tell us,--not only because you have calumniated them, and do not prove them to be traditors, but because, even if you did prove this, yet no guilt on the part of any evil-doers, whether they be unsuspected, or deceitful, or be tolerated as the tares or as the chaff, can possibly overthrow the promises, so that all the nations of the earth should not be blessed in the seed of Abraham; in which promises you deprive them of their share when you will not have the communion of unity with all nations of the earth.

[2067] Rom. xiii. 1.

[2068] John xix. 11.

[2069] John iii. 27.

Chapter 32.

72. Petilianus said: "For although there is only one baptism, yet it is consecrated in three several grades. John gave water without the name of the Trinity, as he declared himself, saying, I indeed baptize you with water unto repentance: but He that cometh after me is mightier than I, whose shoes I am not worthy to bear; He shall baptize you with the Holy Ghost, and with fire.' [2070] Christ gave the Holy Spirit, as it is written, He breathed on them, and saith unto them, Receive ye the Holy Ghost,' [2071] And the Comforter Himself came on the apostles as a fire burning with rustling flames. O true divinity, which seemed to blaze, not to burn! as it is written, And suddenly there came a sound from heaven as of a rushing mighty wind, and it filled all the house where the apostles were sitting. And there appeared unto them cloven tongues, like as of fire, and it sat upon each of them. And they were all filled with the Holy Ghost, and began to speak with other tongues, as the Spirit gave them utterance.' [2072] But you, O persecutor, have not even the water of repentance, seeing that you hold the power not of the murdered John, but of the murderer Herod. You therefore, O traditor, have not the Holy Spirit of Christ; for Christ did not betray others to death, but was Himself betrayed. For you, therefore, the fire in the spirit in Hades is full of life,-- that fire which, surging with hungry tongues of flame, will be able to burn your limbs to all eternity without consuming them, as it is written of the punishment of the guilty in hell, Neither shall their fire be quenched.'" [2073]

73. Augustin answered: You are the calumnious slanderer, not the truthful arguer. Will you not at length cease to make assertions of a kind which, if you do not prove them, can apply to nobody; and even if you prove them, certainly cannot apply to the unity of the whole world, which is in the saints as in the

wheat of God? If we too were pleased to return calumnies for calumnies, we too might possibly be able to give vent to eloquent slanderers. We too might use the expression, "With rustling flames;" but to me an expression never sounds in any way eloquent which is inappropriate in its use. We too might say, "Surging with hungry tongues of flame;" but we do not wish that the tongues of flame in our writings, when they are read by any one in his senses, should be judged hungry for want of the sap of weightiness, or that the reader himself, while he finds in them no food of useful sentiments, should be left to suffer from the hunger of excessive emptiness. See, I declare that your Circumcelliones are burning, not with rustling but with headlong flames. If you answer, What is that to us? why do not you, when you reproach with any one whom you will, not listen in turn to our answer, We too know nothing of it? If you answer, You do not prove the fact, why may not the whole world answer you in turn, Neither do you prove it? Let us agree, therefore, if you please, that you should not charge us with the guilt of the wicked men whom you consider to belong to us, and that we should abstain from similar charges against you. So you will see, by this just agreement, confirmed and ratified, that you have no charge which you can bring against the seed of Abraham, as found in all the nations of the earth. But I find without difficulty a grievous charge to bring against you: Why have you impiously separated yourselves from the seed of Abraham, which is in all nations of the earth? Against this charge you certainly have no means whereby you may defend yourselves. For we each of us clear ourselves of the sins of other men; but this, that you do not hold communion with all the nations of the earth, which are blessed in the seed of Abraham, is a very grievous crime, of which not some but all of you are guilty.

74. And yet you know, as you prove by your quotation, that the Holy Spirit descended in such wise, that those who were then filled with it spake with divers tongues: what was the meaning of that sign and prodigy? Why then is the Holy Spirit given now in such wise, that no one to whom it is given speaks with divers tongues, except because that miracle then prefigured that all nations of the earth should believe, and that thus the gospel should be found to be in every tongue? Just as it was foretold in the psalm so long before: "There is no speech nor language where their voice is not heard." This was said with reference to those men who were destined, after receiving the Holy Spirit, to speak with every kind of tongue. But because this passage itself signified that the gospel should be found hereafter in all nations and languages, and that the body of Christ should sound forth throughout all the world in every tongue, therefore he goes on to say, "Their sound is gone out throughout all the earth, and their words to the ends of the world." Hence it is that the true Church is hidden from no one. And hence comes that which the Lord Himself says in the gospel, "A city that is set on a hill cannot be hid." [2074]And therefore David continues in the same psalm, "In the sun hath He placed His tabernacle," that is, in the open light of day; as we read in the Book of Kings, "For thou didst it secretly; but I will do this thing before all Israel, and before the sun." [2075]And He Himself is "as a bridegroom coming out of His chamber, and rejoiceth as a giant to run His race. His going forth is from the end of heaven:" here you have the coming of the Lord in the flesh. "And His circuit unto the ends of it:" here you have His resurrection and ascension. "And there is nothing hid from the heat thereof:" [2076]here you have the coming of the Holy Spirit, whom He sent in tongues of fire, that He might make manifest the glowing heat of charity, which

he certainly cannot have who does not keep the unity of the Spirit in the bond of peace with the Church, which is throughout all languages.

75. Next, however, with regard to your statement that there is indeed one baptism, [2077] but that it is consecrated in three several grades, and to your having distributed the three forms of it to three persons after such fashion, that you ascribe the water to John, the Holy Spirit to the Lord Jesus Christ, and, in the third place, the fire to the Comforter sent down from above,--consider for a moment in how great an error you are involved. For you were brought to entertain such an opinion simply from the words of John: "I indeed baptize you with water: but He that cometh after me is mightier than I: He shall baptize you with the Holy Ghost, and with fire." [2078]Nor were you willing to take into consideration that the three things are not attributed to three persons taken one by one,--water to John, the Holy Spirit to Christ, fire to the Comforter,--but that the three should rather be referred to two persons--one of them to John, the other two to our Lord. For neither is it said, I indeed baptize you with water: but He that cometh after me is mightier than I, whose shoes I am not worthy to bear: He shall baptize you with the Holy Ghost: and the Comforter, who is to come after Him, He shall baptize you with fire; but "I indeed," He says, "with water: but He that cometh after me with the Holy Ghost, and with fire." One he attributes to himself, two to Him that cometh after him. You see, therefore, how you have been deceived in the number. Listen further. You said that there was one baptism consecrated in three stages--water, the Holy Spirit, and fire; and you assigned three persons to the three stages severally--John to the water, Christ to the Spirit, the Comforter to the fire. If, therefore, the water

of John bears reference to the same baptism which is commended as being one, it was not right that those should have been baptized a second time by the command of the Apostle Paul whom he found to have been baptized by John. For they already had water, belonging, as you say, to the same baptism; so that it remained that they should receive the Holy Spirit and fire, because these were wanting in the baptism of John, that their baptism might be completed, being consecrated, as you assert, in three stages. But since they were ordered to be baptized by the authority of an apostle, it is sufficiently made manifest that that water with which John baptized had no reference to the baptism of Christ, but belonged to another dispensation suited to the exigencies of the times.

76. Lastly, when you wished to prove that the Holy Spirit was given by Christ, and had brought forward as a proof from the gospel, that Jesus on rising from the dead breathed into the face of His disciples, saying, "Receive ye the Holy Ghost;" [2079] and when you wished to prove that that last fire which was named in connection with baptism was found in the tongues of fire which were displayed on the coming of the Holy Ghost, how came it into your head to say, "And the Comforter Himself came upon the apostles as a fire burning with rustling flames," as though there were one Holy Spirit whom He gave by breathing on the face of His disciples, and another who, after His ascension, came on the apostles? Are we to suppose, therefore, that there are two Holy Spirits? Who will be found so utterly mad as to assert this? Christ therefore Himself gave the same Holy Spirit, whether by breathing on the face of the disciples, or by sending Him down from heaven on the day of Pentecost, with undoubted commendation of His holy

sacrament. Accordingly it was not that Christ gave the Holy Spirit, and the Comforter gave the fire, that the saying might be fulfilled, "With the Holy Spirit, and with fire;" but the same Christ Himself gave the Holy Spirit in both cases, making it manifest while He was yet on earth by His breathing, and when He was ascended into heaven by the tongues of flame. For that you may know that the words of John, "He shall baptize you with the Holy Ghost," were not fulfilled at the time when He breathed on His disciples face, so that they should require to be baptized, when the Comforter should come, not with the Spirit any longer, but with fire, I would have you remember the most outspoken words of Scripture, and see what the Lord Himself said to them when He ascended into heaven: "John truly baptized you with water; but ye shall be baptized with the Holy Ghost, whom ye shall receive not many days hence at Pentecost." [2080]What could be plainer than this testimony? But according to your interpretation, what He should have said was this: John verily baptized you with water; but ye were baptized with the Holy Spirit when I breathed on your faces; and next in due order shall ye be baptized with fire, which ye shall receive not many days hence;--in order that by this means the three stages should be completed, in which you say that the one baptism was consecrated. And so it proves to be the case that you are still ignorant of the meaning of the words, "He shall baptize you with the Holy Ghost, and with fire;" and you are rash enough to be williing to teach what you do not know yourselves.

[2070] Matt. iii. 11.

[2071] John xx. 22.

[2072] Acts ii. 2-4.

[2073] Isa. lxvi. 24.

[2074] Matt. v. 14.

[2075] 2 Sam. xii. 12.

[2076] Ps. xix. 3-6, cp. Hieron.

[2077] Eph. iv. 5.

[2078] Matt. iii. 11.

[2079] John xx. 22.

[2080] Acts i. 5.

Chapter 33.

77. Petilianus said: "But that I may thoroughly investigate the baptism in the name of the Trinity, the Lord Christ said to His apostles: Go ye, and baptize the nations, in the name of the Father, and of the Son, and of the Holy Ghost; teaching them to observe all things whatsoever I command you.' [2081]Whom do you teach, traditor? Him whom you condemn? Whom do you teach, traditor? Him whom you slay? Once more, whom do you teach? Him whom you have made a murderer? How then do you baptize in the name of the Trinity? You cannot call God your Father. For when the Lord Christ said, Blessed are the peacemakers, for they shall be called the children of God,' [2082] you who have not peace of soul cannot have God for your Father. Or how, again, can you baptize in the name of the Son, who betray that Son Himself, who do not imitate the Son of God in any of His sufferings or crosses? Or how, again, can you baptize in the name of the Holy Ghost, when the Holy Ghost came only on those apostles who were not guilty of

treason? Seeing, therefore, that God is not your Father, neither are you truly born again with the water of baptism. No one of you is born perfectly. You in your impiety have neither father nor mother. Seeing, then, that you are of such a kind, ought I not to baptize you, even though you wash yourselves a thousand times, after the similitude of the Jews, who as it were baptize the flesh?"

78. Augustin answered: certainly you had proposed thoroughly to investigate the baptism in the name of the Trinity, and you had set us to listen with much attention; but following, as it would seem, what is the easiest course to you, how soon have you returned to your customary abuse! This you carry out with genuine fluency. For you set before yourself what victims you please, against whom to inveigh with whatsoever bitterness you please: in the midst of which last latitude of discourse you are driven into the greatest straits if any one does but use the little word, Prove it. For this is what is said to you by the seed of Abraham; and since in him all nations of the earth are blessed, they care but little when they are cursed by you. But yet, since you are treating of baptism, which you consider to be true when it is found in a just man, but false when it is found in the unjust, see how I too, if I were to investigate baptism in the name of the Trinity, according to your rule, might say, with great fullness, as it seems to me, that he has not God for his father who in a Count has God for his companion, [2083] nor believes that any is his Christ, save him for whose sake he has endured suffering; and that he has not the Holy Ghost who burned the wretched Africa in so very different a fashion with tongues of fire. How then can they have baptism, or how can they administer it in the name of the Father, and of the Son, and of the Holy Ghost? Surely you must now perceive that

baptism can exist in an unrighteous man, and be administered by an unrighteous man, and that no unrighteous baptism, but such as is just and true,--not because it belongs to the unrighteous man, but because it is of God. And herein I am uttering no calumny against you, as you never cease to do, on some pretense or other, against the whole world; and, what is even more intolerable, you do not even bring any proof about the very points on which you found your calumnies. But I know not how this can possibly be endured, because you not only bring calumnies against holy men about unrighteous men, but you even bring a charge against the holy baptism itself, which must needs be holy in any man, however unrighteous he may be, from a comparison with the infection arising from the sins of wicked men, so that you say that baptism partakes of the character of him by whom it is possessed, or administered, or received. Furthermore, if a man partakes of the character of him in whose company he approaches sacred mysteries, and if the sacraments themselves partake of the character of the men in whom they are, holy men may well be satisfied to find consolation in the thought that they only fare like holy baptism itself in hearing false accusations from your lips. But it would be well for you to see how you are condemned out of your own mouths, if both the sober among you are counted as drunken from the infection of the drunken in your ranks, and the merciful among you become robbers from the infection of the robbers, and whatever evil is found among you in the persons of wicked men is perforce shared by those who are not wicked; and if baptism itself is unclean in all of you who are unclean, and if it is of different kinds according to the varying character of uncleanness itself, as it must be if it is perforce of the same character as the man by whom it is possessed or administered. These suppositions most undoubtedly are false, and accordingly they in no wise injure us, when you bring them forward against us without looking back upon yourselves. But they do injure you, because, when you bring them forward falsely, they do not fall on us; but since you imagine them to be true, they recoil upon yourselves.

[2081] Matt. xxviii. 19, 20.

[2082] Matt. v. 9.

[2083] See above, 23, 53.

Chapter 34.

79. Petilianus said: "For if the apostles were allowed to baptize those whom John had washed with the baptism of repentance, shall it not likewise be allowed to me to baptize men guilty of sacrilege like yourselves?"

80. Augustin answered: Where then is what you said above, that there was not one baptism of John and another of Christ, but that there was one baptism, consecrated in three stages, of which three stages John gave the water, Christ the Spirit, and the Comforter the fire? Why then did the apostles repeat the water in the case of those to whom John had already administered water belonging to the one baptism which is consecrated in three stages? Surely you must see how necessary it is that every one should understand the meaning of what he is discussing.

Chapter 35.

81. Petilianus said: "Nor indeed will it be possible that the Holy Spirit should be implanted in the heart of any one by the

laying on of the hands of the priest, unless the water of a pure conscience has gone before to give him birth."

82. Augustin answered: In these few words of yours two errors are involved; and one of them, indeed, has no great bearing on the question which is being discussed between us, but yet it helps to convict you of want of skill. For the Holy Spirit came upon a hundred and twenty men, without the laying on of any person's hands, and again upon Cornelius the centurion and those who were with him, even before they were baptized. [2084]But the second error in these words of yours entirely overthrows your whole case. For you say that the water of a pure conscience must necessarily precede to give new birth, before the Holy Spirit can follow on it. Accordingly, either all the water consecrated in the name of the Father, and of the Son, and of the Holy Ghost, is water of a pure conscience, not for the merits of those by whom it is administered, or by whom it is received, but in virtue of the stainless merits of Him who instituted this baptism; or else if only a pure conscience on the part both of the ministrant and the recipient can produce the water of a pure conscience, what do you make of those whom you find to have been baptized by men who bore a conscience stained with as yet undiscovered guilt, especially if there exist among the said baptized persons any one that should confess that he at the time when he was baptized had a bad conscience, in that he might possbily have desired to use that opportunity for the accomplishment of some sinful act? When, therefore, it shall be made clear to you that neither the man who administered baptism, nor the man who received it, had a pure conscience, will you give your judgment that he ought to be baptized afresh? You will assuredly neither say nor do anything of the sort. The purity

therefore of baptism is entirely unconnected with the purity or impurity of the conscience either of the giver or the recipient. Will you therefore dare to say that the deceiver, or the robber, or the oppressor of the fatherless and widows, or the sunderer of marriages, or the betrayer, the seller, the divider of the patrimony of other men, [2085] was a man of pure conscience? Or will you further dare to say that those were men of pure conscience, whom it is hard to imagine wanting in such times, men who made interest with the man I have described, that they might be baptized, not for the sake of Christ, nor for the sake of eternal life, but to conciliate earthly friendships, and to satisfy earthly desires? Further, if you do not venture to say that these were men of pure conscience, then if you find any of their number who have been baptized, give to them the water of a pure conscience, which they as yet have not received; and if you will not do this, then leave off casting in our teeth a matter which you do not understand, lest you should be forced to answer in reply to us about a matter which you know full well.

[2084] Acts i. 15, ii. 4, x. 44.

[2085] Optatus Gildonianus.

Chapter 36.

83. Petilianus said: "Which Holy Spirit certainly cannot come on you, who have not been washed even with the baptism of repentance; but the water of the traditor, which most truly needs to be repented of, does but work pollution."

84. Augustin answered: As a matter of fact, not only do you not prove us to be traditors, but neither did your fathers prove that our fathers were guilty of that sin; though, even if that had been proved, the consequence would have been that they

would not be our fathers, according to your earlier assertion, seeing that we had not followed their deeds: yet neither should we on their account be severed from the companionship of unity, and from the seed of Abraham, in which all nations of the earth are blessed. [2086]However, if the water of Christ be one thing, and the water of the traditor another, because Christ was not a traditor, why should not the water of Christ be one thing, and the water of a robber another, since certainly Christ was not a robber? Do you therefore baptize again after baptism by your robber, and I will baptize again after the traditor, who is neither mine nor yours; or, if one must believe the documents which are produced, who is both mine and yours; or, if we are to believe the communion of the whole world rather than the party of Donatus, who is not mine, but yours. But, by a better and a sounder judgment, because it is according to the words of the apostle, every one of us shall bear his own burden; [2087] nor is either that robber yours, if you are not yourselves robbers; nor does any traditor belong to any one either of us or you, who is not himself a traditor. And yet we are Catholics, who, following the spirit of that judgment, do not desert the unity of the Church; but you are heretics, who, on account of charges, whether true or false, which you have brought against certain men, are unwilling to maintain Christian charity with the seed of Abraham.

[2086] Gen. xxii. 18.

[2087] Gal. vi. 5.

Chapter 37.

85. Petilianus said: "But that the truth of this may be made manifest from the apostles, we are taught by their actions, as it is written: It came to pass that while Apollos was at Corinth,

Paul, having passed through the upper coasts, came to Ephesus; and finding certain disciples, he said unto them, Have ye received the Holy Ghost since ye believed? And they said unto him, We have not so much as heard whether there be any Holy Ghost. And he said unto them, Unto what then were ye baptized? And they said, Unto John's baptism. Then said Paul, John verily baptized with the baptism of repentance, saying unto the people, that they should believe on Him which should come after him, that is, on Christ Jesus. When they heard this, they were baptized in the name of the Lord Jesus. And when Paul had laid his hands upon them, the Holy Ghost came on them; and they spake with tongues, and prophesied. And all the men were about twelve.' [2088] If, therefore, they were baptized that they might receive the Holy Ghost, why do not you, if you wish to receive the Holy Ghost, take measures to obtain a true renewing, after your falsehoods? And if we do ill in urging this, why do you seek after us? or at any rate, if it is an offense, condemn Paul in the first instance; the Paul who certainly washed off what had already existed, whereas we in you give baptism which as yet does not exist. For you do not, as we have often said before, wash with a true baptism; but you bring on men an ill repute by your empty name of a false baptism."

86. Augustin answered: "We bring no accusation against Paul, who gave to men the baptism of Christ because they had not the baptism of Christ, but the baptism of John, according to their own reply; for, being asked, Unto what were ye baptized? they answered, Unto John's baptism; which has nothing to do with the baptism of Christ, and is neither a part of it nor a step towards it. Otherwise, either at that time the water of the baptism of Christ was renewed a second time, or if the baptism

of Christ was then made perfect by the two waters, the baptism is less perfect which is given now, because it is not given with the water which was given at the hands of John. But either one of these opinions it is impious and sacrilegious to entertain. Therefore Paul gave the baptism of Christ to those who had not the baptism of Christ, but only the baptism of John.

87. But why the baptism of John, which is not necessary now, was necessary at that time, I have explained elsewhere; and the question has no bearing on the point at issue between us at the present time, except so far as that it may appear that the baptism of John was one thing, the baptism of Christ another,-- just as that baptism was a different thing with which the apostle says that our fathers were baptized in the cloud and in the sea, when they passed through the Red Sea under the guidance of Moses. [2089]For the law and the prophets up to the time of John the Baptist had sacraments which foreshadowed things to come; but the sacraments of our time bear testimony that that has come already which the former sacraments foretold should come. John therefore was a foreteller of Christ nearer to Him in time than all who went before him. And because all the righteous men and prophets of former times desired to see the fulfillment of what, through the revelation of the Spirit, they foresaw would come to pass,--whence also the Lord Himself says, "That many prophets and righteous men have desired to see those things which ye see, and have not seen them; and to hear those things which ye hear, and have not heard them," [2090] --therefore it was said of John that he was more than a prophet, and that among all that were born of women there was none greater than he; [2091] because to the righteous men who went before him it was only granted to foretell the coming of Christ, but to John it was given both to foretell Him in His

absence and to behold His presence, so that it should be found that to him was made manifest what the others had desired. And therefore the sacrament of his baptism is still connected with the foretelling of Christ's coming, though as of something very soon to be fulfilled, seeing that up to his time there were still foretellings of the first coming of our Lord, of which coming we have now announcements, but no longer predictions. But the Lord, teaching the way of humility, condescended to make use of the sacraments which He found here in reference to the foretelling of His coming, not in order to assist the operation of His cleansing, but as an example for our piety, that so He might show to us with what reverence we ought to receive those sacraments which bear witness that He is already come, when He did not disdain to make use of those which foreshadowed His coming in the future. And John, therefore, though the nearest to Christ in point of time, and within one year of the same age with Him, yet, while he was baptizing, went before the way of Christ who was still to come; for which reason it was said of him, "Behold, I send my messenger before Thy face, which shall prepare Thy way before Thee." [2092]And he himself preached, saying, "There cometh one mightier than I after me." [2093]In like manner, therefore, the circumcision on the eighth day, which was given to the patriarchs, foretold our justification, to the putting away of carnal lusts through the resurrection of our Lord, which took place after the seventh day, which is the Sabbath-day, on the eighth, that is, the Lord's day, which fell on the third day after His burial; yet the infant Christ received the same circumcision of the flesh, with its prophetic signification. And as the Passover, which was celebrated by the Jews with the slaying of a lamb, prefigured the passion of our Lord and His departure from this world to the Father, yet the same Lord celebrated the same Passover with His disciples, when they reminded Him of it, saying, Where wilt Thou that we prepare for Thee to eat the Passover? [2094] so too He Himself also received the baptism of John, which formed a part of the latest foretelling of His coming. But as the Jews' circumcision of the flesh is one thing, and the ceremony which we observe on the eighth day after persons are baptized is another; [2095] and the Passover which the Jews still celebrate with the slaying of a lamb is one thing, [2096] and that which we receive in the body and blood of our Lord is another,--so the baptism of John was one thing, the baptism of Christ is another. For by the former series of rites the latter were foretold as destined to arrive; by these latter the others are declared to be fulfilled. And even though Christ received the others, yet are they not necessary for us, who have received the Lord Himself who was foretold in them. But when the coming of our Lord was as yet recent, it was necessary for any one who had received the former that he should be imbued with the latter also; but it was wholly needless that any one who had been so imbued should be compelled to go back to the former rites.

88. Wherefore do not seek to raise confusion out of the baptism of John, the source and intention of which was either such as I have here set forth; or if any other better explanation of it can be given, this much still is clear, that the baptism of John and the baptism of Christ are two distinct and separate things, and that the former was expressly called the baptism of John, as is clear both from the answer of those men whose case you quoted, and from the words of our Lord Himself, when he says, "The baptism of John, whence was it? from heaven, or of men?" [2097]But the latter is never called the baptism of Cæcilianus, or of Donatus, or of Augustin, or of Petilianus, but

the baptism of Christ. For if you think that we are shameless, because we will not allow that any one should be baptized after baptism from us, although we see that men were baptized again who had received the baptism of John, who certainly is incomparably greater than ourselves, will you maintain that John and Optatus were of equal dignity? The thing appears ridiculous. And yet I fancy that you do not hold them to be equals, but consider Optatus the greater of the two. For the apostle baptized after baptism by John: you venture to baptize no one after baptism by Optatus. Was it because Optatus was in unity with you? I know not with what heart a theory like this can be maintained, if the friend of the Count, [2098] who had in the Count a god for his companion, is said to have been in unity, and the friend of the Bridegroom to have been excluded from it. But if John was preeminently in unity, and far more excellent and greater than all of us and all of you, and yet the Apostle Paul baptized after him, why do you then not baptize after Optatus? Unless indeed it be that your blindness brings you into such a strait that you should say that Optatus had the power of giving the Holy Spirit, and that John had not! And if you do not say this, for fear of being ridiculed for your madness even by the insane themselves, what answer will you be able to make when you are asked why men should have required to be baptized after receiving baptism from John, while no one needs to be baptized after receiving it from Optatus, unless it be that the former were baptized with the baptism of John, while, whenever any one is baptized with the baptism of Christ, whether he be baptized by Paul or by Optatus, there is no difference in the nature of his baptism, though there is so great a difference between Paul and Optatus? Return then, O ye transgressors, to a right mind, [2099] and do not seek to weigh the sacraments of God by considerations of the characters and deeds of men. For the sacraments are holy through Him to whom they belong; but when taken in hand worthily, they bring reward, when unworthily, judgment. And although the men are not one who take in hand the sacrament of God worthily or unworthily, yet that which is taken in hand, whether worthily or unworthily, is the same; so that it does not become better or worse in itself, but only turns to the life or death of those who handle it in either case. And in respect of what you said, that "in those whom Paul baptized after they had received the baptism of John, he washed off what had already existed," you certainly would not have said it had you taken a moment to consider what you were saying. For if the baptism of John required washing off, it must, beyond all doubt, have had some foulness in it. Why then should I press you further? Recollect or read, and see whence John received it, so shall you see against whom you have uttered that blasphemy; and when you have discovered this, your heart will surely be beaten, if a rein be not set on your tongue.

89. To come next to what you think you say against us with so much point: "If we do ill in urging this, why do you seek after us?" cannot you even yet call to mind that only those are sought after who have perished? Or is the incapacity for seeing this an element in your ruin? For the sheep might say to the shepherd with equal absurdity, If I do wrong in straying from the flock, why do you search after me? not understanding that the very reason why it is being sought is because it thinks there is no need for seeking it. But who is there that seeks for you, either through His Scriptures, or by catholic and conciliatory voices, or by the scourgings of temporal afflictions, save only Him who dispenses that mercy to you in all things? We therefore seek you that we may find you; for we love you that you should have

life, with the same intensity with which we hate your error, that it might be destroyed which seeks to ruin you, so long as it is not itself involved in your destruction. And would to God that we might seek you in such a manner as even to find, and be able to say with rejoicing of each one of you, "He was dead, and is alive again; he was lost, and is found!" [2100]

[2088] Acts xix. 1-7.

[2089] 1 Cor. x. 1, 2.

[2090] Matt. xiii. 17.

[2091] Matt. xi. 9, 11.

[2092] Mark i. 2; cp. Mal. iii. 1.

[2093] Mark i. 7.

[2094] Matt. xxvi. 17.

[2095] In his treatise on the Sermon on the Mount, Book I. iv. 12, Augustin again compares the "celebratio octavarum feriarum quas in regeneratione novi hominis celebramus" with the circumcision on the eighth day; and in Serm. 376, c. ii. 2, he says that the heads of the infants were uncovered on the eighth day, as a token of liberty. Cp. Bingham, Orig. Sacr. XII. iv. 3.

[2096] Augustin apparently supposed that the sacrifice of the paschal lamb was still observed among the Jews of the dispersion; cp. Retract. I. x. 2. It was, however, forbidden them to sacrifice the Passover except in the place which the Lord should choose to place His name there; and hence the Jews, though they observe the other paschal solemnities, abstain from the sacrifice of the lamb.

[2097] Matt. xxi. 25.

[2098] Gildo; see above, 23, 53.

[2099] Isa. xlvi. 8.

[2100] Luke xv. 32.

Chapter 38.

90. Petilianus said: "If you declare that you hold the Catholic Church, the word catholic' is merely the Greek equivalent for entire or whole. But it is clear that you are not in the whole, because you have gone aside into the part."

91. Augustin answered: I too indeed have attained to a very slight knowledge of the Greek language, scarcely to be called knowledge at all, yet I am not shameless in saying that I know that holon means not "one," but "the whole;" and that kath' holon means "according to the whole:" whence the Catholic Church received its name, according to the saying of the Lord, "It is not for you to know the times, which the Father hath put in His own power. But ye shall receive power, after that the Holy Ghost is come upon you: and ye shall be witnesses unto me both in Jerusalem, and in Judea, and in Samaria, and even in the whole earth." [2101]Here you have the origin of the name "Catholic." But you are so bent upon running with your eyes shut against the mountain which grew out of a small stone, according to the prophecy of Daniel, and filled the whole earth, [2102] that you actually tell us that we have gone aside into a part, and are not in the whole among those whose communion is spread throughout the whole earth. But just in the same way as, supposing you were to say that I was Petilianus, I should not be able to find any method of refuting you unless I were to

laugh at you as being in jest, or mourn over you as being mad, so in the present case I see that I have no other choice but this; and since I do not believe that you are in jest, you see what alternative remains.

[2101] Acts i. 7, 8.

[2102] Dan. ii. 35.

Chapter 39.

92. Petilianus said: "But there is no fellowship of darkness with light, nor any fellowship of bitterness with the sweet of honey; there is no fellowship of life with death, of innocence with guilt, of water with blood; the lees have no fellowship with oil though they are related to it as being its dregs, but everything that is reprobate will flow away. It is the very sink of iniquity; according to the saying of John, They went out from us, but they were not of us; for if they had been of us, they would no doubt have continued with us.' [2103]There is no gold among their pollution: all that is precious has been purged away. For it is written, As gold is tried in the furnace, so also are the just tried by the harassing of tribulation.' [2104]Cruelty is not a part of gentleness, nor religion a part of sacrilege; nor can the party of Macarius [2105] in any way be part of us, because he pollutes the likeness of our rite. For the enemy's line, which fills up an enemy's name, is no part of the force to which it is opposed; but if it is truly to be called a part, it will find a suitable motto in the judgment of Solomon, Let their part be cut off from the earth.'" [2106]

93. Augustin answered: What is it but sheer madness to utter these taunts without proving anything? You look at the tares throughout the world, and pay no heed to the wheat, although

both have been bidden to grow together throughout the whole of it. You look at the seed sown by the wicked one, which shall be separated in the time of harvest, [2107] and you pay no heed to the seed of Abraham, in which all nations of the earth shall be blessed. [2108]Just as though you were already a purged mass, and virgin honey, and refined oil, and pure gold, or rather the very similitude of a whited wall. For, to say nothing of your other faults, do the drunken form a portion of the sober, or are the covetous reckoned among the portion of the wise? If men of gentle temper appropriate the term of light, where shall the madness of the Circumcelliones be esteemed to be, excepting in the darkness? Why then is baptism, given by men like these, held valid among you, and the same baptism of Christ not held valid, by whatsoever men it may be administered throughout the world? You see, in fact, that you are separated from the communion of the whole world in so far as this, that you are not indeed all drunk, nor all of you covetous, nor all men of violence, but that you are all heretics, and, in virtue of this, are all impious and all sacrilegious.

94. But as to your saying that the whole world that rejoices in Christian communion is the party of Macarius, who with any remnant of sanity in his brain could make such a statement? But because we say that you are of the party of Donatus, you therefore seek for a man of whose party you may say we are; and, being in a great strait, you mention the name of some obscure person, who, if he is known in Africa, is certainly unknown in any other quarter of the globe. And therefore hearken to the answer made to you by all the seed of Abraham from every corner of the earth: Of that Macarius, to whose party you assert us to belong, we know absolutely nothing. Can you reply in turn that you know nothing of Donatus? But even

if we were to say that you are the party of Optatus, which of you can say that he is unacquainted with Optatus, unless in the sense that he does not know him personally, as perhaps he does not know Donatus either? But you acknowledge that you rejoice in the name of Donatus, do you also take any pleasure in the name of Optatus? What then can the name of Donatus profit you, when all of you alike are polluted by Optatus? What advantage can you derive from the sobriety of Donatus, when you are defiled by the drunkenness of the Circumcelliones? What, according to your views, are you profited by the innocence of Donatus, when you are stained by the rapacity of Optatus? For this is your mistake, that you think that the unrighteousness of a man has more power in infecting his neighbor than the righteousness of a man has in purifying those around him. Therefore, if two share in common the sacraments of God, the one a just man, the other an unrighteous one, but so that neither the former should imitate the unrighteousness of the latter, nor the latter the righteousness of the former, you say that the result is not that both are made just, but that both are made unrighteous; so that also that holy thing, which both receive in common, becomes unclean and loses its original holiness. When does unrighteousness find for herself such advocates as these, through whose madness she is esteemed victorious? How comes it then that, in the midst of such mistaken perversity, you congratulate yourselves upon the name of Donatus, when it shows not that Petilianus deserves to be what Donatus is, but that Donatus is compelled to be what Optatus is? But let the house of Israel say, "God is my portion for ever;" [2109] let the seed of Abraham say in all nations "The Lord is the portion of mine inheritance." [2110] For they know how to speak through the gospel of the glory of the blessed God. For you, too, through the sacrament which is in you, like

Caiaphas the persecutor of the Lord, prophesy without being aware of it. [2111] For what in Greek is expressed by the word Macharios is in our language simply "Blessed;" and in this way certainly we are of the party of Macarius, the Blessed One. For what is more blessed than Christ, of whose party we are, after whom all the ends of the earth are called, and to whom they all are turned, and in whose sight all the countries of the nations worship? Therefore the party of this Macarius, that is to say, of this Blessed One, feels no apprehension at your last curse, distorted from the words of Solomon, lest it should perish from the earth. For what is said by him of the impious you endeavor to apply to the inheritance of Christ, and you strive to prove that this has been achieved with inexpressible impiety; for when he was speaking of the impious, he says, "Let their portion perish from off the earth." [2112] But when you say, with reference to the words of Scripture, "I shall give Thee the heathen for Thine inheritance," [2113] and "all the ends of the world shall remember and turn unto the Lord," [2114] that the promise contained in them has already perished from the earth, you are seeking to turn against the inheritance of Christ what was foretold about the lot of the impious; but so long as the inheritance of Christ endures and increases, you are perishing in saying such things. For you are not in every case prophesying through the sacrament of God, since in this case you are merely uttering evil wishes through your own madness. But the prophecy of the true prophets is more powerful than the evil speaking of the false prophets.

[2103] 1 John ii. 19.

[2104] Apparently from Wisd. iii. 6.

[2105] Macarius acted as imperial commissioner with Paulus, c. 348, to settle the disputes between Donatists and Catholics, but only to the further exasperation of the former, who accused him of intrusion and murder, and thereafter called their opponents Macarians.

[2106] Prov. ii. 22.

[2107] Matt. xiii. 24-30.

[2108] Gen. xxii. 18.

[2109] Ps. lxxiii. 26.

[2110] Ps. xvi. 5.

[2111] John xi. 51.

[2112] Prov. ii. 22.

[2113] Ps. ii. 8.

[2114] Ps. xxii. 27.

Chapter 40.

95. Petilianus said: "Paul the apostle also bids us, Be ye not unequally yoked with unbelievers: for what fellowship hath righteousness with unrighteousness? and what communion hath light with darkness? and what concord hath Christ with Belial? or what part hath he that believeth with an infidel?'" [2115]

96. Augustin answered: I recognize the words of the apostle; but how they can help you I cannot see at all. For which of us says that there is any fellowship between righteousness and

unrighteousness, even though the righteous and the unrighteous, as in the case of Judas and Peter, should be alike partakers of the sacraments? For from one and the same holy thing Judas received judgment to himself and Peter salvation, just as you received the sacrament with Optatus, and, if you were unlike him, were not therefore partakers in his robberies. Or is robbery not unrighteousness? Who would be mad enough to assert that? What fellowship was there, then, on the part of your righteousness with his unrighteousness, when you approached together to the same altar?

[2115] 2 Cor. vi. 14, 15.

Chapter 41.

97. Petilianus said: "And, again, he taught us that schisms should not arise, in the following terms: Now this I say, that every one of you saith, I am of Paul, and I of Apollos, and I of Cephas, and I of Christ. Is Christ divided? was Paul crucified for you? or were ye baptized in the name of Paul?'" [2116]

98. Augustin answered: Remember all of you who read this, it was Petilianus who quoted these words from the apostle. For who could have believed that he would have brought forward words which tell so much for us against himself?

[2116] 1 Cor. i. 12, 13.

Chapter 42.

99. Petilianus said: "If Paul uttered these words to the unlearned and to the righteous, I say this to you who are unrighteous, Is Christ divided, that you should separate yourselves from the Church?"

100. Augustin answered: I am afraid lest any one should think that in this work of mine the writer has made a mistake, and has written the heading Petilianus said, when he ought to have written Augustin answered. But I see what your object is: you wished, as it were, to preoccupy the ground, lest we should bring those words in testimony against you. But what have you really done, except to cause them to be quoted twice? If, therefore, you are so much pleased with hearing the words which make against you, as to render it necessary that they should be repeated, hear, I pray you, these words as coming from me, Petilianus: Is Christ divided, that you should separate yourselves from the Church?

Chapter 43.

101. Petilianus said: "Can it be that the traitor Judas hung himself for you, or did he imbue you with his character, that, following his deeds, you should seize on the treasures of the Church, and sell for money to the powers of this world us who are the heirs of Christ?"

102. Augustin answered: Judas did not die for us, but Christ, to whom the Church dispersed throughout the world says, "So shall I have wherewith to answer him that reproacheth me: for I trust in Thy word." [2117] When, therefore, I hear the words of the Lord, saying, "Ye shall be witnesses unto me both in Jerusalem, and in all Judea, and in Samaria, and even in the whole earth," [2118] and through the voice of His prophet, "Their sound is gone out through all the earth, and their words into the ends of the world," [2119] no bodily admixture of evil ever is able to disturb me, if I know how to say, "Be surety for Thy servant for good: let not the proud oppress me." [2120] I do not, therefore, concern myself about a vain calumniation

when I have a substantial promise. But if you complain about matters or places appertaining to the Church, which you used once to hold, and hold no longer, then the Jews also may say that they are righteous, and reproach us with unrighteousness, because the Christians now occupy the place in which of old they impiously reigned. What then is there unfitting, if, according to a similar will of the Lord, the Catholics now hold the things which formerly the heretics used to have? For against all such men as this, that is to say, against all impious and unrighteous men, those words of the Lord have force, "The kingdom of God shall be taken from you, and be given to a nation bringing forth the fruits thereof;" [2121] or is it written in vain, "The righteous shall eat of the labors of the impious"? [2122]Wherefore you ought rather to be amazed that you still possess something, than that there is something which you have lost. But neither need you wonder even at this, for it is by degrees that the whitened wall falls down. Yet look back at the followers of Maximianus, see what places they possessed, and by whose agency and under whose attacks they were driven from them, and do you venture, if you can, to say that to suffer things like these is righteousness, while to do them is unrighteousness. In the first place, because you did the deed, and they suffered them; and secondly, because, according to the rule of this righteousness, you are found to be inferior. For they were driven from the ancient palaces by Catholic emperors acting through judges, while you are not even driven forth by the mandates of the emperors themselves from the basilicas of unity. For what reason is this, save that you are of less merit, not only than the rest of your colleagues, but even than those very men whom you assuredly condemned as guilty of sacrilege by the mouth of your plenary Council?

[2117] Ps. cxix. 42.

[2118] Acts i. 8.

[2119] Ps. xix. 4.

[2120] Ps. cxix. 122.

[2121] Matt. xxi. 43.

[2122] Ps. cv. 44.

Chapter 44.

103. Petilianus said: "For we, as it is written, when we are baptized, put on Christ who was betrayed; [2123] you, when you are infected, put on Judas the betrayer."

104. Augustin answered: I also might say, You when you are infected put on Optatus the betrayer, the robber, the oppressor, the separater of husband and wife; but far be it from me that the desire of returning an evil word should provoke me into any falsehood: for neither do you put on Optatus, nor we Judas. Therefore, if each one who comes to us shall answer to our questions that he has been baptized in the name of Optatus, he shall be baptized in the name of Christ; and if you baptized any that came from us and said that they had been baptized in the name of the traitor Judas, in that case we have no fault to find with what you have done. But if they had been baptized in the name of Christ, do you not see what an error you commit in thinking that the sacraments of God can undergo change through any changeableness of human sins, or be polluted by defilement in the life of any man?

[2123] Gal. iii. 27.

Chapter 45.

105. Petilianus said: "But if these are the parties, the name of member of a party is no prejudice against us. For there are two ways, the one narrow, in which we walk; the other is for the impious, wherein they shall perish. And yet, though the designations be alike, there is a great difference in the reality, that the way of righteousness should not be defiled by fellowship in a name. "

106. Augustin answered: You have been afraid of the comparison of your numbers with the multitude throughout the world; and therefore, in order to win praise for the scantiness of your party, you have sought to bring in the comparison of yourself walking in the narrow path. Would to God that you had betaken yourself not to its praise, but to the path itself! Truly you would have seen that there was the same scantiness in the Church of all nations; but that the righteous are said to be few in comparison with the multitude of the unrighteous, just as, in comparison with the chaff, there may be said to be few grains of corn in the most abundant crop, and yet these very grains of themselves, when brought into a heap, fill the barn. For the followers of Maximianus themselves will surpass you in this scantiness of number, if you think that righteousness consists in this, as well as in the persecution involved in the loss of places which they held.

Chapter 46.

107. Petilianus said: "In the first Psalm David separates the blessed from the impious, not indeed making them into parties, but excluding all the impious from holiness. Blessed is the man that walketh not in the counsel of the ungodly, nor standeth in the way of sinners.' Let him who had strayed from the path of

righteousness, so that he should perish, return to it again. Nor sitteth in the seat of the scornful.' [2124]When he gives this warning, O ye miserable men, why do you sit in that seat? But his delight is in the law of the Lord; and in His law doth he meditate day and night. And he shall be like a tree planted by the rivers of water, that bringeth forth his fruit in his season: his leaf also shall not wither; and whatsoever he doeth shall prosper. The ungodly are not so: but are like the chaff which the wind driveth away.' He blindeth their eyes, so that they should not see. Therefore the ungodly shall not stand in the judgment, nor sinners in the congregation of the righteous. For the Lord knoweth the way of the righteous: but the way of the ungodly shall perish.'" [2125]

108. Augustin answered: Who is there in the Scriptures that would not distinguish between these two classes of men? But you slanderously charge the corn with the offenses of the chaff; and being yourselves mere chaff, you boast yourselves to be the only corn. But the true prophets declare that both these classes have been mingled together throughout the whole world, that is, throughout the whole corn-field of the Lord, until the winnowing which is to take place on the day of judgment. But I advise you to read that first Psalm in the Greek version, and then you will not venture to reproach the whole world with being of the party of Macarius; because you will perhaps come to understand of what Macarius there is a party among all the saints, who throughout all nations are blessed in the seed of Abraham. For what stands in our language as "Blessed is the man," is in Greek Macharios aner. But that Macarius who offends you, if he is a bad man, neither belongs to this division, nor is to its prejudice. But if he is a good man, let him prove

his own work, that he may have glory in himself alone, and not in another. [2126]

[2124] Et super cathedram pestilentiæ, cp. Hieron.

[2125] Ps. i.

[2126] Gal. vi. 4.

Chapter 47.

109. Petilianus said: "But the same Psalmist has sung the praises of our baptism. The Lord is my shepherd, I shall not want. He maketh me to lie down in the green pastures: He leadeth me beside the still waters. He restoreth my soul: He leadeth me in the paths of righteousness for His name's sake. Yea, though I walk through the valley of the shadow of death,'--though the persecutor, he means, should slay me,--I will fear no evil: for Thou art with me; Thy rod and Thy staff comfort me.' It was by this that it conquered Goliath, being armed with the anointing oil. Thou hast prepared a table before me in the presence of mine enemies: Thou anointest my head with oil; my cup runneth over. Surely goodness and mercy shall follow me all the days of my life; and I will dwell in the house of the Lord for ever.'" [2127]

110. Augustin answered: This psalm speaks of those who receive baptism aright, and use as holy what is so holy. For those words have no reference even to Simon Magus, who yet received the same holy baptism; and because he would not use it in a holy way, he did not therefore pollute it, or show that in such cases it should be repeated. But since you have made mention of Goliath, listen to the psalm which treats of Goliath himself, and see that he is portrayed in a new song; for there it

is said, "I will sing a new song unto Thee, O God: upon a psaltery, and an instrument of ten strings, will I sing praise unto Thee." [2128]And see whether he belongs to this song who refuses to communicate with the whole earth. For elsewhere it is said, "O sing unto the Lord a new song; sing unto the Lord, all the earth." [2129]Therefore the whole earth, with whom you are not in unity, sings the new song. And these too are the words of the whole earth, "The Lord is my shepherd, I shall not want," etc. These are not the words of the tares, though they be endured until the harvest in the same crop. They are not the words of the chaff, but of the wheat, although they are nourished by one and the same rain, and are threshed out on the same threshing-floor at the same time, till they shall be separated the one from the other by the winnowing at the last day. And yet these both assuredly have the same baptism, though they are not the same themselves. But if your party also were the Church of God, you would certainly confess that this psalm has no application to the infuriated bands of the Circumcelliones. Or if they too themselves are led through the paths of righteousness, why do you deny that they are your associates, when you are reproached with them, although, for the most part, you console yourselves for the scantiness of your section, not by the rod and staff of the Lord, but by the cudgels of the Circumcelliones, with which you think that you are safe even against the Roman laws,--to bring oneself into collision with which is surely nothing less than to walk through the valley of the shadow of death? But he with whom the Lord is, fears no evils. Surely, however, you will not venture to say that the words which are sung in this song belong even to those infuriated men, and yet you not only acknowledge, but ostentatiously set forth the fact that they have baptism. These words, therefore, are not used by any who are not refreshed by the holy water, as are all the righteous men of God; not by those who are brought to destruction by using it, as was that magician when baptized by Philip: and yet the water itself in both kinds of men is the same, and of the same degree of sanctity. These words are not used except by those who will belong to the right hand; but yet both sheep and goats feed in the same pasture under one Shepherd, until they shall be separated, that they may receive their due reward. These words are not used except by those who, like Peter, receive life from the table of the Lord, not judgment, as did Judas; and yet the supper was itself the same to both, but it was not of the same profit to both, because they were not one. These words are not used except by those who, by being anointed with the sacred oil, are blessed in spirit also, as was David; not merely consecrated in the body only, as was Saul: and yet, as they had both received the same outward sign, it was not the sacrament, but the personal merit that was different in the two cases. These words are not used except by those who, with converted heart, receive the cup of the Lord unto eternal life; not by those who eat and drink damnation to themselves, as the apostle says: [2130]and yet, though they are not one, the cup which they receive is one, exerting its power on the martyrs that they should obtain a heavenly reward, not on the Circumcelliones, that they should mark precipices with death. Remember, therefore, that the characters of bad men in no wise interfere with the virtue of the sacraments, so that their holiness should either be destroyed, or even diminished; but that they injure the unrighteous men themselves, that they should have them as witnesses of their damnation, not as aids to health. For beyond all doubt you should have taken into consideration the actual concluding words of this psalm, and have understood that, on account of those who forsake the faith after they have been baptized, it cannot be said by all who receive holy baptism that "I will dwell in the house of the Lord for ever:" and yet, whether they abide in the faith, or whether they have fallen away, though they themselves are not one, their baptism is one, and though they themselves are not both holy, yet the baptism in both is holy; because even apostates, if they return, are not baptized as though they had lost the sacrament, but undergo humiliation, because they have done a despite to it which remains in them.

[2127] Ps. xxiii.

[2128] Ps. cxliv. 9.

[2129] Ps. xcvi. 1.

[2130] 1 Cor. xi. 29.

Chapter 48.

111. Petilianus said: "Yet that you should not call yourselves holy, in the first place, I declare that no one has holiness who has not led a life of innocence."

112. Augustin answered: Show us the tribunal where you have been enthroned as judge, that the whole world should stand for trial before you, and with what eyes you have inspected and discussed, I do not say the consciences, but even the acts of all men, that you should say that the whole world has lost its innocence. He who was carried up as far as the third heaven says, "Yea, I judge not mine own self;" [2131] and do you venture to pronounce sentence on the whole world, throughout which the inheritance of Christ is spread abroad? In the next place, if what you have said appears to you to be sufficiently certain, that "no one has holiness who has not led a life of

innocence," I would ask you, if Saul had not the holiness of the sacrament, what was in him that David reverenced? But if he had innocence, why did he persecute the innocent? For it was on account of the sanctity of his anointing that David honored him while alive, and avenged him after he was dead; and because he cut off so much as a scrap from his garment, he trembled with a panic-stricken heart. Here you see that Saul had not innocence, and yet he had holiness,--not the personal holiness of a holy life (for that no one can have without innocence), but the holiness of the sacrament of God, which is holy even in unrighteous men.

[2131] 1 Cor. iv. 3.

Chapter 49.

113. Petilianus said: "For, granting that you faithless ones are acquainted with the law, without any prejudice to the law itself, I may say so much as this, the devil knows it too. For in the case of righteous Job he answered the Lord God concerning the law as though he were himself righteous, as it is written, "And the Lord said unto Satan, Hast thou considered my servant Job, that there is none like him in the earth, a man without malice, a true worshipper of God abstaining from every evil; and still he holdeth fast his integrity, although thou movedst me against him, to destroy him without cause?" [2132]And Satan answered the Lord, Skin for skin, yea, all that a man hath will he give for his life. Behold he speaks in legal phrase, even when he is striving against the law. And a second time he endeavored thus to tempt the Lord Christ with his discourse, as it is written, The devil taketh Jesus into the holy city, and setteth Him on a pinnacle of the temple, and saith unto Him, If thou be the Son of God, cast thyself down: for it

is written, He shall give His angels charge concerning thee; and in their hands they shall bear thee up, lest at any time thou dash thy foot against a stone. Jesus said unto him, It is written again, Thou shall not tempt the Lord thy God.' [2133] You know the law, I say, as did the devil, who is conquered in his endeavors, and blushes in his deeds."

114. Augustin answered: I might indeed ask of you in what law the words are written which the devil used when he was uttering calumnies against the holy man Job, if the position which I am set to prove were this, that you yourself are unacquainted with the law which you assert the devil to have known, but as this is not the question at issue between us, I pass it by. But you have endeavored in such sort to prove that the devil is skilled in the law, as though we maintained that all who know the law are just. Accordingly, I do not see in what manner you are assisted by what you have chosen to quote concerning the devil,--unless, indeed, it may be that we should be thereby reminded how you imitate the devil himself. For as he brought forward the words of the law against the Author of the law, so you also out of the words of the law bring accusation against men whom you do not know, that you may resist the promises of God which are made in that very self-same law. Then I should be glad if you would tell me in whose honor do those confessors of yours achieve their martyrdom, when they throw themselves over precipices,--in honor of Christ, who thrust the devil from Him when he made a like suggestion, or rather in honor of the devil himself, who suggested such a deed to Christ? There are two especially vile and customary deaths resorted to by those who kill themselves,--hanging and the precipice. You assuredly said in the earlier part of this epistle, "The traitor hung himself: he left

this death to all who are like him." This has no application whatever to us; for we refuse to reverence with the name of martyr any who have strangled themselves. With how much greater show of reason might we say against you, That master of all traitors, the devil, wished to persuade Christ to throw Himself headlong down, and was repulsed! What, therefore, must we say of those whom he persuaded with success? What, indeed, except that they are the enemies of Christ, the friends of the devil, the disciples of the seducer, the fellow-disciples of the traitor? For both have learned to kill themselves from the same master,--Judas by hanging himself, the others by throwing themselves over precipices.

[2132] Job ii. 3, 4.

[2133] Matt. iv. 5-7.

Chapter 50.

115. Petilianus said: "But that we may destroy your arguments one by one, if you call yourselves by the name of priests, it was said by the Lord God, through the mouth of His prophet, The vengeance of the Lord is upon the false priests.'"

116. Augustin answered: Seek rather what you may say with truth, not whence you may derive abusive words; and what you may teach, not what reproaches you may cast in our teeth.

Chapter 51.

117. Petilianus said: "If you wretched men claim for yourselves a seat, as we said before, you assuredly have that one of which the prophet and psalmist David speaks as being the seat of the scornful. [2134]For to you it is rightly left, seeing that the holy cannot sit therein."

118. Augustin answered: Here again you do not see that this is no kind of argument, but empty abuse. For this is what I said a little while ago, You utter the words of the law, but take no heed against whom you utter them; just as the devil uttered the words of the law, but failed to perceive to whom he uttered them. He wished to thrust down our Head, who was presently to ascend on high; but you wish to reduce to a small fraction the body of that same Head which is dispersed throughout the entire world. Certainly you yourself said a little time before that we know the law, and speak in legal terms, but blush in our deeds. Thus much indeed you say without a proof of anything; but even though you were to prove it of some men, you would not be entitled to assert it of these others. However, if all men throughout all the world were of the character which you most vainly charge them with, what has the chair done to you of the Roman Church, in which Peter sat, and which Anastasius fills to-day; or the chair of the Church of Jerusalem, in which James once sat, and in which John sits today, with which we are united in catholic unity, and from which you have severed yourselves by your mad fury? Why do you call the apostolic chair a seat of the scornful? If it is on account of the men whom you believe to use the words of the law without performing it, do you find that our Lord Jesus Christ was moved by the Pharisees, of whom He says, "They say, and do not," to do any despite to the seat in which they sat? Did He not commend the seat of Moses, and maintain the honor of the seat, while He convicted those that sat in it? For He says, "They sit in Moses' seat: all therefore whatsoever they bid you observe, that observe and do; but do not ye after their works: for they say, and do not." [2135]If you were to think of these things, you would not, on account of men whom you calumniate, do despite to the apostolic seat, in which you have

no share. But what else is conduct like yours but ignorance of what to say, combined with want of power to abstain from evil-speaking?

[2134] Ps. i. 1.

[2135] Matt. xxiii. 2, 3.

Chapter 52.

119. Petilianus said: "If you suppose that you can offer sacrifice, God Himself thus speaks of you as most abandoned sinners: The wicked man,' He says, that sacrificeth a calf is as if he cut off a dog's neck; and he that offereth an oblation, as if he offered swine's blood.' [2136]Recognize herein your sacrifice, who have already poured out human blood. And again He says, Their sacrifices shall be unto them as the bread of mourners; all that eat thereof shall be polluted.'" [2137]

120. Augustin answered: We say that in the case of every man the sacrifice that is offered partakes of the character of him who approaches to offer it, or approaches to partake of it; and that those eat of the sacrifices of such men, who in approaching to them partake of the character of those who offer them. Therefore, if a bad man offer sacrifice to God, and a good man receive it at his hands, the sacrifice is to each man of such character as he himself has shown himself to be, since we find it also written that "unto the pure all things are pure." [2138]In accordance with this true and catholic judgment, you too are free from pollution by the sacrifice of Optatus, if you disapproved of his deeds. For certainly his bread was the bread of mourners, seeing that all Africa was mourning under his iniquities. But the evil involved in the schism of all your party makes this bread of mourners common to you all. For,

according to the judgment of your Council, Felicianus of Musti was a shedder of man's blood. For you said, in condemning them, [2139] "Their feet are swift to shed blood." [2140]See therefore what kind of sacrifice he offers whom you hold to be a priest, when you have yourselves convicted him of sacrilege. And if you think that this is in no way to your prejudice, I would ask you how the emptiness of your calumnies can be to the prejudice of the whole world?

[2136] Isa. lxvi. 3.

[2137] Hos. ix. 4.

[2138] Tit. i. 15.

[2139] In the Council of Bagai.

[2140] Ps. xiv. 3, cp. LXX. and Hieron.

Chapter 53.

121. Petilianus said: "If you make prayer to God, or utter supplication, it profits you absolutely nothing whatsoever. For your blood-stained conscience makes your feeble prayers of no effect; because the Lord God regards purity of conscience more than the words of supplication, according to the saying of the Lord Christ, Not every one that saith unto me, Lord, Lord, shall enter into the kingdom of heaven; but he that doeth the will of my Father which is in heaven.' [2141]The will of God unquestionably is good, for therefore we pray as follows in the holy prayer, Thy will be done in earth, as it is in heaven,' [2142] that, as His will is good, so it may confer on us whatever may be good. You therefore do not do the will of God, because you do what is evil every day."

122. Augustin answered: If we on our side were to utter against you all that you assert against us, would not any one who heard us consider that we were rather insane litigants than Christian disputants, if he himself were in his senses? We do not, therefore, render for railing. For it is not fitting that the servant of the Lord should strive; but he should be gentle unto all men, willing to learn, in meekness instructing those that oppose themselves. [2143]If, therefore, we reproach you with those who daily do what is evil among you, we are guilty of striving unbefittingly, accusing one for the sins of another. But if we admonish you, that as you are unwilling that these things should be brought against yourselves, so you should abstain from bringing against us the sins of other men, we then in meekness are instructing you, solely in the hope that some time you will return to a better mind.

[2141] Matt. vii. 21.

[2142] Matt. vi. 10.

[2143] 2 Tim. ii. 24, 25.

Chapter 54.

123. Petilianus said: "But if it should so happen, though whether it be so I cannot say, that you cast out devils, neither will this in you do any good; because the devils themselves yield neither to your faith nor to your merits, but are driven out in the name of the Lord Jesus Christ."

124. Augustin answered: God be thanked that you have at length confessed that the invocation of the name of Christ may be of profit for the salvation of others, even though it be invoked by sinners! Hence, therefore, you may understand that

when the name of Christ is invoked, the sins of one man do not stand in the way of the salvation of another. But to determine in what manner we invoke the name of Christ, we require not your judgment, but the judgment of Christ Himself who is invoked by us; for He alone can know in what spirit He is invoked. Yet from His own words we are assured that He is invoked to their salvation by all nations, who are blessed in the seed of Abraham.

Chapter 55.

125. Petilianus said: "Even though you do very virtuous actions, and perform miraculous works, yet on account of your wickedness the Lord does not know you; even so, according to the words of the Lord Himself, Many will say to me in that day, Lord, Lord, have we not prophesied in Thy name? and in Thy name have cast out devils? and in Thy name done many wonderful works? And then will I profess unto them, I never knew you; depart from me, ye that work iniquity.'" [2144]

126. Augustin answered: We acknowledge the word of the Lord. Hence also the apostle says, "Though I have all faith, so that I could remove mountains, and have not charity, I am nothing." [2145]Here therefore we must inquire who it is that has charity: you will find that it is no one else but those who are lovers of unity. For as to the driving out of devils, and as to the working of miracles, seeing that very many do not do such things who yet belong to the kingdom of God, and very many do them who do not belong to it, neither our party nor your party have any cause for boasting, if any of them chance to have this power, since the Lord did not think it right that even the apostles, who could truly do such things both to profit and salvation, should boast in things like this, when He says to

them, "In this rejoice not, that the spirits are subject unto you; but rather rejoice, because your names are written in heaven." [2146]Wherefore all those things which you have advanced from the writings of the gospel I also might repeat to you, if I saw you working the powerful acts of signs and miracles; and so might you repeat them to me, if you saw me doing things of a like sort. Let us not, therefore, say one to another what may equally be said on the other side as well; and, putting aside all quibbles, since we are inquiring where the Church of Christ is to be found, let us listen to the words of Christ Himself, who redeemed it with His own blood: "Ye shall be witnesses unto me both in Jerusalem, and in all Judea, and in Samaria, and even in the whole earth." [2147]You see then who it is with whom a man refuses to communicate who will not communicate with this Church, which is spread throughout all the world, if at least you hear whose words these are. For what is a greater proof of madness than to hold communion with the sacraments of the Lord, and to refuse to hold communion with the words of the Lord? Such men at any rate are likely to say, In Thy name have we eaten and drunken, and to hear the words, "I never knew you," [2148] seeing that they eat His body and drink His blood in the sacrament, and do not recognize in the gospel His members which are spread abroad throughout the earth, and therefore are not themselves counted among them in the judgment.

[2144] Matt. vii. 22, 23.

[2145] 1 Cor. xiii. 2.

[2146] Luke x. 20.

[2147] Acts i. 8.

[2148] Matt. vii. 22, 23.

Chapter 56.

127. Petilianus said: "But even if, as you yourselves suppose, you are following the law of the Lord in purity, let us nevertheless consider the question of the most holy law itself in a legal form. The Apostle Paul says, The law is good, if a man use it lawfully.' [2149]What then does the law say? Thou shalt not kill.' What Cain the murderer did once, you have often done in slaying your brethren."

128. Augustin answered: We do not wish to be like you: for there are not wanting words which might be uttered, as you too utter these; and known also, for you do not know these; and set forth in the conduct of a life, as these are not set forth by you.

[2149] 1 Tim. i. 8.

Chapter 57.

129. Petilianus said: "It is written, Thou shalt not commit adultery.' Each one of you, even though he be chaste in his body, yet in spirit is an adulterer, because he pollutes his holiness."

130. Augustin answered: These words also might be spoken with truth against certain both of our number and of yours; but if their deeds are condemned by us and you alike, they belong to neither us nor you. But you wish that what you say against certain men, without proving it even in their especial case, should be taken just as if you had established it,--not in the case of some who have fallen away from the seed of Abraham, but in reference to all the nations of the earth who are blessed in the seed of Abraham.

Chapter 58.

131. Petilianus said: "It is written, Thou shalt not bear false witness against thy neighbor.' When you falsely declare to the kings of this world that we hold your opinions, do you not make up a falsehood?"

132. Augustin answered: If those are not our opinions which you hold, neither were they your opinions which you received from the followers of Maximianus. But if they were therefore yours, because they were guilty of a sacrilegious schism in not communicating with the party of Donatus, take heed what ground you occupy, and with whose inheritance you refuse communion, and consider what answer you can make, not to the kings of this world, but to Christ your King. Of Him it is said, "He shall have dominion also from sea to sea, and from the river unto the ends of the earth." [2150]From what river does it mean, save that where He was baptized, and where the dove descended on Him, that mighty token of charity and unity? But you refuse communion with this unity, and occupy as yet the place of unity; and you bring us into disfavor with the kings of this world in making use of the edicts of the proconsul to expel your schismatics from the place of the party of Donatus. These are not mere words flying at random through the empty void: the men are still alive, the states bear witness to the fact, the archives of the proconsuls and of the several towns are quoted in evidence of it. Let then the voice of calumny be at length silent, which would bring up against the whole earth the kings of this world, through whose proconsuls you, yourselves a fragment, would not spare the fragment which was separated from you. When then we say that you hold our opinions, we are not shown to be bearing false witness, unless you can show that we are not in the Church of

Christ, which indeed you never cease alleging, but never will be able to establish; nay, in real truth, when you say this, you are bringing a charge of false witness no longer against us, but against the Lord Himself. For we are in the Church which was foretold by His own testimony, and where He bore witness to His witnesses, saying, "Ye shall be witnesses unto me both in Jerusalem and in all Judea, and in Samaria, and even in the whole earth." But you show yourselves to be false witnesses not only from this, that you resist this truth, but also in the very trial in which you joined issue with the schism of Maximianus. For if you were acting according to the law of Christ, how much more consistently do certain Christian emperors frame ordinances in accordance with it, if even pagan proconsuls can follow its behests in passing judgment? But if you thought that even the laws of an earthly empire were to be summoned to your aid, we do not blame you for this. It is what Paul did when he bore witness before his adversaries that he was a Roman citizen. [2151] But I would ask by what earthly laws it is ordained that the followers of Maximianus should be driven from their place? You will find no law whatever to this effect. But, in point of fact, you have chosen to expel them under laws which have been passed against heretics, and against yourselves among their number. You, as though by superior strength, have prevailed against the weak. Whence they, being wholly powerless, say that they are innocent, like the wolf in the power of the lion. Yet surely you could not use laws which were passed against yourselves as instruments against others, except by the aid of false witness. For if those laws are founded on truth, then do you come down from the position which you occupy; but if on falsehood, why did you use them to drive others from the Church? But how if they both are founded on truth, and could not be used by you for the expulsion of others except with the aid of falsehood? For that the judges might submit to their authority, they were willing to expel heretics from the Church, from which they ought first to have expelled yourselves; but you declared yourselves to be Catholics, that you might escape the severity of the laws which you employed to oppress others. It is for you to determine what you appear to yourselves among yourselves; at any rate, under those laws you are not Catholics. Why then have you either made them false, if they are true, by your false witness, or made use of them, if they are false, for the oppression of others?

[2150] Ps. lxxii. 8.

[2151] Acts xxii. 25.

Chapter 59.

133. Petilianus said: "It is written, Thou shalt not covet anything that is thy neighbor's.' [2152]You plunder what is ours, that you may have it for your own."

134. Augustin answered: All things of which unity was in possession belong to none other than ourselves, who remain in unity, not in accordance with the calumnies of men, but with the words of Christ, in whom all the nations of the whole earth are blessed. Nor do we separate ourselves from the society of the wheat, on account of the unrighteous men whom we cannot separate from the wheat of the Lord before the winnowing at the judgment; and if there are any things which you who are cut off begin already to possess, we do not, because the Lord has given to us what has been taken away from you, therefore covet our neighbors' goods, seeing that they have been made ours by the authority of Him to whom all things belong; and they are rightly ours, for you were wont to

use them for purposes of schism, but we use them for the promotion of unity. Otherwise your party might reproach even the first people of God with coveting their neighbors' goods, seeing that they were driven forth before their face by the power of God, because they used the land amiss; and the Jews in turn themselves, from whom the kingdom was taken away, according to the words of the Lord, and given to a nation bringing forth the fruits thereof, [2153] may bring a charge against that nation, of coveting their neighbors' goods, because the Church of Christ is in possession where the persecutors of Christ were wont to reign. And, after all, when it has been said to yourselves, You are coveting the goods of other men, because you have driven out from the basilicas the followers of Maximianus, you are at a loss to find any answer that you can make.

[2152] Ex. xx. 13-17.

[2153] Matt. xxi. 43.

Chapter 60.

135. Petilianus said: "Under what law, then, do you make out that you are Christians, seeing that you do what is contrary to the law?"

136. Augustin answered: You are anxious for strife, and not for argument.

Chapter 61.

137. Petilianus said: "But the Lord Christ says, Whosoever shall do and teach them, the same shall be called the greatest in the kingdom of heaven.' But He condemns you wretched men as follows: Whosoever shall break one of these

commandments, he shalt be called the least in the kingdom of heaven.'"

138. Augustin answered: When you happen to quote the testimony of Scripture as other than it really is, and it does not bear on the question which is at issue between us, I am not greatly concerned; but when it interferes with the matter on hand, unless it is quoted truly, then I think that you have no right to find fault if I remind you how the passage really stands. For you must be aware that the verse which you quoted is not as you quoted it, but rather thus: "Whosoever shall break one of these least commandments, and shall teach men so, he shall be called the least in the kingdom of heaven; but whosoever shall do and teach them, the same shall be called great in the kingdom of heaven." And immediately He continues, "For I say unto you, That except your righteousness shall exceed the righteousness of the scribes and Pharisees, ye shall in no case enter into the kingdom of heaven." [2154]For elsewhere He shows and proves of the Pharisees that they say and do not. It is these, therefore, to whom He is referring also here, when He said, "Whosoever shall break one of these commandments, and shall teach men so,"--that is, shall teach in words what he has violated in deeds; whose righteousness He says that our righteousness must excel, in that we must both keep the commandments and teach men so. And yet not even on account of those Pharisees, with whom you compare us,--not from any motives of prudence, but from malice,--did our Lord enjoin that the seat of Moses should be deserted, which seat He doubtless meant to be a figure of His own; for He said indeed that they who sat in Moses' seat were ever saying and not doing, but warns the people to do what they say, and not to do what they do, [2155] lest the chair, with all its holiness, should

be deserted, and the unity of the flock divided through the faithlessness of the shepherds.

[2154] Matt. v. 19, 20.

[2155] Matt. xxiii. 2, 3.

Chapter 62.

139. Petilianus said: "And again it is written, Every sin which a man shall sin is without the body; but he that sinneth in the Holy Spirit, it shall not be forgiven him, neither in this world, neither in the world to come.'"

140. Augustin answered: This too is not written as you have quoted it, and see how far it has led you astray. The apostle, writing to the Corinthians, says, "Every sin that a man doeth is without the body; but he that committeth fornication sinneth against his own body." [2156] But this is one thing, and that is another which the Lord said in the gospel: "All manner of sin and blasphemy shall be forgiven unto men: but whosoever speaketh against the Holy Ghost, it shall not be forgiven him, neither in this world, neither in the world to come." [2157]But you have begun a sentence from the writing of the apostle, and ended it as though it were one from the gospel, which I fancy you have done not with any intention to deceive, but through mistake; for neither passage has any bearing on the matter in hand. And why you have said this, and in what sense you have said it, I am wholly unable to perceive, unless it be that, whereas you had said above that all were condemned by the Lord who had broken any one of His commandments, you have considered since how many there are in your party who break not one but many of them; and lest an objection should be brought against you on that score, you have sought, by way

of surpassing the difficulty, to bring in a distinction of sins, whereby it might be seen that it is one thing to break a commandment in respect of which pardon may easily be obtained, another thing to sin against the Holy Ghost, which shall receive no forgiveness, either in this world or in the world to come. In your dread, therefore, of infection from sin, you were unwilling to pass this over in silence; and again, in your dread of a question too deep for your powers, you wish to touch cursorily on it in passing, in such a state of agitation, that, just as men who are setting about a task in haste, and consequent confusion, are wont to fasten their dress or shoes awry, so you have not thought fit either to see what belongs to what, or in what context or what sense the passage which you quote occurs. But what is the nature of that sin which shall not be forgiven, either in this world or in the world to come, you are so far from knowing, that, though you believe that we are actually living in it, you yet promise us forgiveness of it through your baptism. And yet how could this be possible, if the sin be of such a nature that it cannot be forgiven, either in this world or in the world to come?

[2156] 1 Cor. vi. 18.

[2157] Matt. xii. 31, 32.

Chapter 63.

141. Petilianus said: "But wherein do you fulfill the commandments of God? The Lord Christ said, Blessed are the poor in spirit; for theirs is the kingdom of heaven.' But you by your malice in persecution breathe forth the riches of madness."

142. Augustin answered: Address that rather to your own Circumcelliones.

Chapter 64.

143. Petilianus said: "Blessed are the meek: for they shall inherit the earth.' You therefore, not being meek, have lost both heaven and earth alike."

144. Augustin answered: Again and again you may hear the Lord saying, "Ye shall be witnesses unto me both in Jerusalem, and in all Judea, and in Samaria, and even in the whole earth." [2158]How is it, then, that those men have not lost heaven and earth, who, in order to avoid communicating with all the nations of the earth, despise the words of Him that sitteth in heaven? For, in proof of your meekness, it is not your words but the cudgels of the Circumcelliones which should be examined. You will say, What has that to do with us? Just as though we were making the remark with any other object except to extract that answer from you. For the reason that your schism is a valid charge against you is that you do not allow that you are chargeable with another's sin, whereas you have separated from us for no other reason but that you charge us with the sins of other men.

[2158] Acts i. 8.

Chapter 65.

145. Petilianus said: "Blessed are they that mourn: for they shall be comforted.' You, our butchers, are the cause of mourning in others: you do not mourn yourselves."

146. Augustin answered: Consider for a short space to how many, and with what intensity, the cry of "Praises be to God,"

proceeding from your armed men, has caused others to mourn. [2159]Do you say again, What is that to us? Then I too will rejoin again your own words, What is that to us? What is it to all the nations of the earth? What is it to those who praise the name of the Lord from the rising of the sun to the setting of the same? What is it to all the earth, which sings a new song? What is it to the seed of Abraham, in which all the nations of the earth are blessed? [2160]And so the sacrilege of your schism is chargeable on you, just because the evil deeds of your companions are not chargeable on you; and because you are from this that the deeds of those on whose account you separated from the world, even if you proved your charges to be true, do not involve the world in sin.

[2159] The older editions have, "Quam multum et quantum luctum dederint Deo" (Erasmus alone ideo) laudes amatorum vestrorum:" "How much and how great grief have the praises of your lovers caused to God?" The Benedictines restored the reading translated above ("Quam multis...Deo laudes armatorum vestrorum"), Deo laudes being the cry of the Circumcelliones. Cp. Aug. in Ps. cxxxii. 6: "A quibus plus timetur Deo laudes quam fremitus leonis;" and ib.: "Deo laudes vestrum plorant homines."

[2160] Gen. xxii. 18.

Chapter 66.

147. Petilianus said: "Blessed are they which do hunger and thirst after righteousness: for they shall be filled.' To you it seems to be righteousness that you thirst after our blood."

148. Augustin answered: What shall I say unto thee, O man, except that thou art calumnious? The unity of Christ, indeed, is

hungering and thirsting after all of you; and I would that it might swallow you up, for then would you be no longer heretics.

Chapter 67.

149. Petilianus said: "Blessed are the merciful: for they shall obtain mercy.' But how shall I call you merciful when you inflict punishment on the righteous? Shall I not rather call you a most unrighteous communion, so long as you pollute souls?"

150. Augustin answered: You have proved neither point,-- neither that you yourselves are righteous, nor that we inflict punishment on even the unrighteous; and yet, even as false flattery is generally cruel, so just correction is ever merciful. For whence is that which you do not understand: "Let the righteous smite me, it shall be a kindness; and let him reprove me"? For while he says this of the severity of merciful correction, the Psalmist immediately went on to say of the gentleness of destructive flattery, "But the oil of sinners shall not break my head." [2161]Do you therefore consider whither you are called, and from what you are summoned away. For how do you know what feelings he entertains towards you whom you suppose to be cruel? But whatever be his feelings, every one must bear his own burden both with us and with you. But I would have you cast away the burden of schism which you all of you are bearing, that you may bear your good burdens in unity; and I would bid you mercifully correct, if you should have the power, all those who are bearing evil burdens; and, if this be beyond your power, I would bid you bear with them in peace.

[2161] Ps. cxli. 5, LXX., cf. Hieron.

Chapter 68.

151. Petilianus said: "Blessed are the pure in heart: for they shall see God.' When will you see God, who are possessed with blindness in the impure malice of your hearts?"

152. Augustin answered: Wherefore say you this? Can it be that we reproach all nations with the dark and hidden things which are declared by men, and do not choose to understand the manifest sayings which God spake in olden time of all the nations of the earth? This is indeed great blindness of heart; and if you do not recognize it in yourselves, that is even greater blindness.

Chapter 69.

153. Petilianus said: "Blessed are the peacemakers; for they shall be called the children of God.' [2162]You make a pretence of peace by your wickedness, and seek unity by war."

154. Augustin answered: We do not make a pretense of peace by wickedness, but we preach peace out of the gospel; and if you were at peace with it, you would be at peace also with us. The risen Lord, when presenting Himself to the disciples, not only that they should gaze on Him with their eyes, but also that they should handle Him with their hands, began His discourse to them with the words, "Peace be unto you." And how this peace itself was to be maintained, He disclosed to them in the words which followed. For "then opened He their understanding, that they might understand the Scriptures, and said unto them, Thus is it written, and thus it behoved Christ to suffer, and to rise from the dead the third day; and that repentance and remission of sins should be preached in His name among all nations, beginning at Jerusalem." [2163]If you

will keep peace with these words, you will not be at variance with us. For if we seek unity by war, our war could not be praised in more glorious terms, seeing that it is written, "Thou shall love thy neighbor as thyself." [2164]And again it is written, "No man ever yet hated his own flesh." [2165]And yet the flesh lusteth against the spirit, and the spirit against the flesh. [2166] But if no man ever yet hated his own flesh, and yet a man lusteth against his own flesh, here you have unity sought by war, that the body, being subject to correction, may be brought under submission. But what the spirit does against the flesh, waging war with it, not in hatred but in love, this those who are spiritual do against those who are carnal, that they may do towards them what they do towards themselves, because they love their neighbors as neighbors indeed. But the war which the spiritual wage is that correction which is in love: their sword is the word of God. To such a war they are aroused by the trumpet of the apostle sounding with a mighty force: "Preach the word; be instant in season, out of season; reprove, rebuke, exhort, with all long-suffering and doctrine." [2167]See then that we act not with the sword, but with the word. But you answer what is not true, while you accuse us falsely. You do not correct your own faults, and you bring against us those of other men. Christ bears true witness concerning the nations of the earth; you, in opposition to Christ, bear false witness against the nations of the earth. If we were to believe you rather than Christ, you would call us peacemakers; because we believe Christ rather than you, we are said to make a pretense of peace by our wickedness. And while you say and do such things as this, you have the further impudence to quote the words, "Blessed are the peacemakers; for they shall be called the children of God."

[2162] Matt. v. 3-9.

[2163] Luke xxiv. 36, 45-47.

[2164] Matt. xxii. 39.

[2165] Eph. v. 29.

[2166] Gal. v. 17.

[2167] 2 Tim. iv. 2.

Chapter 70.

155. Petilianus said: "Though the Apostle Paul says, I therefore, the prisoner of the Lord, beseech you, brethren, that ye walk worthy of the vocation wherewith ye are called, with all lowliness and meekness, with long-suffering, forbearing one another in love; endeavoring to keep the unity of the Spirit in the bond of peace.'" [2168]

156. Augustin answered: If you would not only say these words, but hearken to them as well, you would put up even with known evils for the sake of peace, instead of inventing new ones for the sake of quarreling, if it were only because you subsequently learned, for the sake of the peace of Donatus, to put up with the most flagrant and notorious wickedness of Optatus. What madness is this that you display? Those who are known are borne with, that a fragment may not be further split up; those of whom nothing is known are defamed, that they themselves may not remain in the undivided whole.

[2168] Eph. iv. 1-3.

Chapter 71.

157. Petilianus said: "To you the prophet says, Peace, peace; and where is there peace?'" [2169]

158. Augustin answered: It is you that say this to us, not the prophet. We therefore answer you: If you ask where peace is to be found, open your eyes, and see of whom it is said, "He maketh wars to cease in all the world." [2170] If you ask where peace is to be found, open your eyes to see that city which cannot be hidden, because it is built upon a hill; open your eyes to see the mountain itself, and let Daniel show it to you, growing out of a small stone, and filling the whole earth. [2171] But when the prophet says to you, "Peace, peace; and where is there peace?" what will you show? Will you show the party of Donatus, unknown to the countless nations to whom Christ is known? It is surely not the city which cannot be hid; and whence is this, except that it is not founded on the mountain? "For He is our peace, who hath made both one," [2172] --not Donatus, who has made one into two.

[2169] Jer. viii. 11.

[2170] Ps. xlvi. 9.

[2171] Dan. ii. 35.

[2172] Eph. ii. 14.

Chapter 72.

159. Petilianus said: "Blessed are they which are persecuted for righteousness' sake; for theirs is the kingdom of heaven.' [2173] You are not blessed; but you make martyrs to be blessed, with whose souls the heavens are filled, and the earth has flourished with their memory. You therefore do not honor them yourselves, but you provide us with objects of honor."

160. Augustin answered: The plain fact is, that if it had not been said, "Blessed are they which are persecuted for righteousness' sake," but had been said instead, Blessed are they who throw themselves over precipices, then heaven would have been filled with your martyrs. Of a truth we see many flowers on the earth blooming from their bodies; but, as the saying goes, the flower is dust and ashes.

[2173] Matt. v. 10.

Chapter 73.

161. Petilianus said: "Since then you are not blessed by falsifying the commands of God, the Lord Christ condemns you by His divine decrees: Woe unto you, scribes and Pharisees, hypocrites! for ye shut up the kingdom of heaven against men: for ye neither go in yourselves, neither suffer ye them that are entering to go in. Woe unto you, scribes and Pharisees, hypocrites! for ye compass sea and land to make one proselyte; and when he is made, ye make him twofold more the child of hell than yourselves. Woe unto you, scribes and Pharisees, hypocrites! for ye pay tithe of mint, and anise, and cummin, and have omitted the weightier matters of the law, judgment, mercy, and faith: these ought ye to have done, and not to leave the other undone. Ye blind guides, which strain at a gnat, and swallow a camel. Woe unto you, scribes and Pharisees, hypocrites! for ye are like unto whited sepulchres, which indeed appear beautiful outwardly, but are within full of dead men's bones, and of all uncleanness. Even so ye also outwardly appear righteous unto men, but within ye are full of hypocrisy and iniquity.'" [2174]

162. Augustin answered: Tell me whether you have said anything which may not equally be said against you in turn by

any slanderous and evil-speaking tongue. But from what has been said by me before, any one who wishes may find out that these things may be said against you, not by way of empty abuse, but with the support of truthful testimony. As, however, the opportunity is presented to us we must not pass this by. There is no doubt that to the ancient people of God circumcision stood in the place of baptism. I ask, therefore, putting the case that the Pharisees against whom those words you quote are spoken, had made some proselyte, who, if he were to imitate them, would, as it is said, become twofold more the child of hell than themselves, supposing that he were to be converted, and desire to imitate Simeon, or Zacharias, or Nathanael, would it be necessary that he should be circumcised again by them? And if it is absurd to put this case why, although in empty fashion and with empty sounds you compare us to men like this, do you nevertheless baptize after us? But if you are really men like this, how much better and how much more in accordance with truth do we act in not baptizing after you, as neither was it right that those whom I have mentioned should be circumcised after the worst of Pharisees! Furthermore, when such men sit in the seat of Moses, for which the Lord preserved its due honor, why do you blaspheme the apostolic chair on account of men whom, justly or unjustly, you compare with these?

[2174] Matt. xxiii. 13, 15, 23, 24, 27, 28.

Chapter 74.

163. Petilianus said: "But these things do not alarm us Christians; for of the evil deeds which you are destined to commit we have before a warning given us by the Lord Christ. Behold,' He says, I send you forth as sheep in the midst of

wolves.' [2175]You fill up the measure of the madness of wolves, who either lay or are preparing to lay snares against the Churches in precisely the same way in which wolves, with their mouths wide open against the fold, even with destructive eagerness, breathe forth panting anger from their jaws, suffused with blood."

164. Augustin answered: I should be glad to utter the same sentiment against you, but not in the words which you have used: they are too inappropriate, or rather mad. But what was required was, that you should show that we were wolves and that you were sheep, not by the emptiest of evil-speaking, but by some distinct proofs. For when I too have said, We are sheep, and you are wolves, do you think that there is any difference caused by the fact that you express the idea in swelling words? But listen whilst I prove what I assert. For the Lord says in the gospel, as you know full well, whether you please it or not, "My sheep hear my voice, and follow me." [2176]There are many sayings of the Lord on different subjects; but supposing, for example, that any one were in doubt whether the same Lord had risen in the body, and His words were to be quoted where He says, "Handle me, and see; for a spirit hath not flesh and bones, as ye see me have;"--if even after this he should be unwilling to acquiesce in the belief that His body had risen from the dead, surely such a man could not be reckoned among the sheep of the Lord, because he would not hear His voice. And so too now, when the question between us is, Where is the Church? whilst we quote the words that follow in the same passage of the gospel, where, after His resurrection, He gave His body even to be handled by those who were in doubt, in which He showed the future wide extent of the Church, saying, "Thus it is written, and thus it behoved

Christ to suffer, and to rise from the dead the third day; and that repentance and remission of sins should be preached in His name throughout all nations, beginning at Jerusalem;" [2177] whereas you will not communicate with all nations, in whom these words have been fulfilled, how are you the sheep of this Shepherd, whose words you not only do not obey when you have heard them, but even fight against them? And so we show to you from this that you are not sheep. But listen further whence we show you that, on the contrary, you are wolves. For necessarily, when it is shown by His own words where the Church is to be found, it is also clear where we must look for the fold of Christ. Whenever, therefore, any sheep separate themselves from this fold, which is expressly pointed out and shown to us by the unmistakeable declaration of the Lord,--and that, I will not say because of charges falsely brought, but on account of charges brought, as no one can deny, with great uncertainty against their fellow-men, and consequently slay those sheep which they have torn and alienated from the life of unity and Christian love--is it not evident that they are ravening wolves? But it will be said that these very men themselves praise and preach the Lord Christ. They are therefore those of whom He says Himself, "They come unto you in sheep's clothing, but inwardly they are ravening wolves. By their fruits ye shall know them." [2178]The sheep's clothing is seen in the praises of Christ; the fruits of their wolfish nature in their slanderous teeth.

[2175] Matt. x. 16.

[2176] John x. 27.

[2177] Luke xxiv. 39, 46, 47.

[2178] Matt. vii. 15, 16.

Chapter 75.

165. Petilianus said: "O wretched traditors! Thus indeed it was fitting that Scripture should be fulfilled. But in you I grieve for this, that you have shown yourselves worthy to fulfill the part of wickedness."

166. Augustin answered: I might rather say, O wretched traditors! if I were minded, or rather if justice urged me to cast up against all of you the deeds of some among your number. But as regards what bears on all of you, O wretched heretics, I on my part will quote the remainder of your words; for it is written, "There must be also heresies among you, that they which are approved may be made manifest among you." [2179]Therefore "it was fitting thus that Scripture should be fulfilled. But in you I grieve for this, that you have shown yourselves worthy to fulfill the part of wickedness."

[2179] 1 Cor. xi. 19.

Chapter 76.

167. Petilianus said: "But to us the Lord Christ, in opposition to your deadly commands, commanded simple patience and harmlessness. For what says He? A new commandment I give unto you, That ye love one another; as I have loved you, that ye also love one another.' And again, By this shall all men know that ye are my disciples, if ye have love one to another.'" [2180]

168. Augustin answered: If you did not transfer these words, so widely differing from your character, to the surface of your talk, how could you be covering yourselves with sheep's clothing?

[2180] John xiii. 34, 35.

Chapter 77.

169. Petilianus said: "Paul also, the apostle, whilst he was suffering fearful persecutions at the hands of all nations, endured even more grievous troubles at the hands of false brethren, as he bears witness of himself, being oftentimes afflicted: In perils by the heathen, in perils by mine own countrymen, in perils among false brethren.' [2181]And again he says, Be ye followers of me, even as I also am of Christ.' [2182]When, therefore, false brethren like yourselves assault us, we imitate the patience of our master Paul under our dangers."

170. Augustin answered: Certainly those of whom you speak are false brethren, of whom the apostle thus complains in another place, where he is extolling the natural sincerity of Timothy: "I have no man," he says, "like-minded, who will naturally care for your state. For all seek their own, not the things which are Jesus Christ's." [2183] Undoubtedly he was speaking of those who were with him at the time when he was writing that epistle; for it could not be that all Christians in every quarter of the earth were seeking their own, and not the things which were Jesus Christ's. It was of those, therefore, as I said, who were with him at the time when he was writing the words which you have quoted, that he uttered this lamentation. For who else was it to whom he referred, when he says in another place, "Without were fightings, within were fears," [2184] except those whom he feared all the more intensely because they were within? If, therefore, you would imitate Paul, you would be tolerant of false brethren within, not a slanderer of the innocent without.

[2181] 2 Cor. xi. 26.

[2182] 1 Cor. xi. 1.

[2183] Phil. ii. 20, 21.

[2184] 2 Cor. vii. 5.

Chapter 78.

171. Petilianus said: "For what kind of faith is that which is in you which is devoid of charity? when Paul himself says, Though I speak with the tongues of men, and have the knowledge of angels, and have not charity, I am become as sounding brass, or a tinkling cymbal. And though I have the gift of prophecy, and understand all mysteries, and all knowledge; and though I have all faith, so that I could remove mountains, and have not charity, I am nothing. And though I bestow all my goods to feed the poor, and though I give my body to be burned, and have not charity, it profiteth me nothing.'"

172. Augustin answered: This is what I said just now, that you were desirous to be clad in sheep's clothing, that, if possible, the sheep might feel your bite before it had any consciousness of your approach. Is it not that praise of charity in which you indulge that commonly proves your calumny in the clearest light of truth? Will you bring it about that those arms shall be no longer ours, because you endeavor to appropriate them first? Furthermore, these arms are endowed with life: from whatever quarter they are launched, they recognize whom they should destroy. If they have been sent forth from our hands, they will fix themselves in you; if they are aimed by you, they recoil upon yourselves. For in these apostolic words, which commend the excellence of charity, we are wont to show to you how profitless it is to man that he should be in possession of faith or of the sacraments, when he has not charity, that, when you come to Catholic unity, you may understand what it is that

is conferred on you, and how great a thing it is of which you were at least to some extent in want; for Christian charity cannot be preserved except in the unity of the Church: and that so you may see that without it you are nothing, even though you may be in possession of baptism and faith, and through this latter may be able even to remove mountains. But if this is your opinion as well, let us not repudiate and reject in you either the sacraments of God which we know, or faith itself, but let us hold fast charity, without which we are nothing even with the sacraments and with faith. But we hold fast charity if we cling to unity; while we cling to unity, if we do not make a fictitious unity in a party by our own words, but recognize it in a united whole through the words of Christ.

Chapter 79.

173. Petilianus said: "And again, Charity suffereth long, and is kind; charity envieth not; charity vaunteth not itself, is not puffed up, doth not behave itself unseemly, seeketh not her own.' But you seek what belongs to other men. Is not easily provoked, thinketh no evil; rejoiceth not in iniquity, but rejoiceth in the truth; beareth all things, endureth all things. Charity never faileth.' [2185]This is to say, in short, Charity does not persecute, does not inflame emperors to take away the lives of other men; does not plunder other men's goods; does not go on to murder men whom it has spoiled."

174. Augustin answered: How often must I tell you the same thing? If you do not prove these charges, they tell against no one in the world; and if you prove them, they have no bearing upon us; just as those things have no bearing upon you which are daily done by the furious deeds of the insane, by the luxury of the drunken, by the blindness of the suicides, by the tyranny

of robbers. For who can fail to see that what I say is true? But now if charity were in you, it would rejoice in the truth. For how neatly it is said under covering of the sheep's clothing, "Charity beareth all things, endureth all things!" but when you come to the test, the wolf's teeth cannot be concealed. For when, in obedience to the words of Scripture, "forbearing one another in love, endeavoring to keep the unity of the Spirit in the bond of peace," [2186] charity would compel you, even if you knew of any evils within the Church, I do not say to consent to them, but yet to tolerate them if you could not prevent them, lest, on account of the wicked who are to be separated by the winnowing-fan at the last day, you should at the present time sever the bond of peace by breaking off from the society of good men, you, resisting her influence, and being cast out by the wind of levity, charge the wheat with being chaff, and declare that what you invent of the wicked holds good through the force of contagion even in the righteous. And when the Lord has said, "The field is the world, the harvest is the end of the world," though He said of the wheat and of the tares, "Let both grow together until the harvest," [2187] you endeavor by your words to bring about a belief that the wheat has perished throughout the main portion of the field, and only continued to exist in your little corner,--being desirous that Christ should be proved a liar, but you the man of truth. And you speak, indeed, against your own conscience; for no one who in any way looks truly at the gospel will venture in his heart to say that in all the many nations throughout which is heard the response of Amen, and among whom Alleluia is sung almost with one single voice, no Christians are to be found. And yet, that it may not appear that the party of Donatus, which does not communicate with the several nations of the world, is involved in error, if any angel from heaven, who could see the whole world, were to declare that outside your communion good and innocent men were nowhere to be found, there is little doubt that you would rejoice over the iniquity of the human race, and boast of having told the truth before you had received assurance of it. How then is there in you that charity which rejoices not in iniquity? But be not deceived. Throughout the field, that is, throughout the world, there will be found the wheat of the Lord growing till the end of the world. Christ has said this: Christ is truth. Let charity be in you, and let it rejoice in the truth. Though an angel from heaven preach unto you another gospel contrary to His gospel, let him be accursed. [2188]

[2185] 1 Cor. xiii. 1-8.

[2186] Eph. iv. 2, 3.

[2187] Matt. xiii. 38, 39, 30.

[2188] Gal. i. 8.

Chapter 80.

175. Petilianus said: "Lastly, what is the justification of persecution? I ask you, you wretched men, if it so be that you think that your sin rests on any authority of law."

176. Augustin answered: He who sins, sins not on the authority of the law, but against the authority of the law. But since you ask what is the justification of persecution, I ask you in turn whose voice it is that says in the psalm, "Whoso privily slandereth his neighbor, him will I cut off." [2189]Seek therefore the reason or the measure of the persecution, and do not display your gross ignorance by finding fault in general terms with those who persecute the unrighteous.

[2189] Ps. ci. 5.

Chapter 81.

177. Petilianus said: "But I answer you, on the other hand, that Jesus Christ never persecuted any one. And when the apostle found fault with certain parties, and suggested that He should have recourse to persecution (He Himself having come to create faith by inviting men to Him, rather than by compelling them), those apostles say, Many lay on hands in Thy name, and are not with us:' but Jesus said, Let them alone; if they are not against you, they are on your side.'"

178. Augustin answered: You say truly that you will bring forth out of your store with greater abundance things which are not written in the Scriptures. For if you wish to bring forth proofs from holy Scripture, will you bring forth even those which you cannot find therein? But it is in your own power to multiply your lies according to your will. For where is what you quoted written? or when was that either suggested to our Lord, or answered by our Lord? "Many lay on hands in Thy name, and are not with us," are words that no one of the disciples ever uttered to the Son of God; and therefore neither could the answer have been made by Him, "Let them alone: if they are not against you, they are on your side." But there is something somewhat like it which we really do read in the gospel,--that a suggestion was made to the Lord about a certain man who was casting out devils in His name, but did not follow Him with His disciples; and in that case the Lord does say, "Forbid him not: for he that is not against us is for us." [2190]But this has nothing to do with pointing out parties whom the Lord is supposed to have spared. And if you have been deceived by an apparent resemblance of sentiment, this is not a lie, but merely

human infirmity. But if you wished to cast a mist of falsehood over those who are unskilled in holy Scripture, then may you be pricked to the heart, and covered with confusion and corrected. Yet there is a point which we would urge in respect of this very man of whom the suggestion was made to our Lord. For even as at that time, beyond the communion of the disciples, the holiness of Christ was yet of the greatest efficacy, even so now, beyond the communion of the Church, the holiness of the sacraments is of avail. For neither is baptism consecrated save in the name of the Father, and of the Son, and of the Holy Ghost. But who will be so utterly insane as to declare that the name of the Son may be of avail even beyond the communion of the Church, but that this is not possible with the names of the Father and of the Holy Ghost? or that it may be of avail in healing a man, but not in consecrating baptism? But it is manifest that outside the communion of the Church, and the most holy bond of unity, and the most excellent gift of charity, neither he by whom the devil is cast out nor he who is baptized obtains eternal life; just as those do not obtain it, who through communion in the sacraments seem indeed to be within, and through the depravity of their character are understood to be without. But that Christ persecuted even with bodily chastisement those whom He drove with scourges from the temple, we have already said above.

[2190] Luke ix. 49, 50.

Chapter 82.

179. Petilianus said: "But the holy apostle said this: 'In any way, whatsoever it may be,' he says, let Christ be preached.'"

180. Augustin answered: You speak against yourself; but yet, since you speak on the side of truth, if you love it, let what you

say be counted for you. For I ask of you of whom it was that the Apostle Paul said this? Let us, if you please, trace this a little further back. "Some," he says, "preach Christ even of envy and strife; and some also of good will, some of love, knowing that I am set for the defense of the gospel. But some indeed preach Christ even of contention, not sincerely, supposing to add affliction to my bonds. What then? notwithstanding every way, whether in pretense, or in truth, Christ is preached; and I therein do rejoice, yea, and will rejoice." [2191]We see that they preached what was in itself holy, and pure, and true, but yet not in a pure manner, but of envy and contention, without charity, without purity. Certainty a short time ago you appeared to be urging the praises of charity as against us, according to the witness of the apostle, that where there is no charity, whatever there is is of no avail; and yet you see that in those there is no charity, and there was with them the preaching of Christ, of which the apostle says here that he rejoices. For it is not that he rejoices in what is evil in them, but in what is good in the name of Jesus Christ. In him assuredly there was the charity which "rejoiceth not in iniquity, but rejoiceth in the truth." [2192]The envy, moreover, which was in them is an evil proceeding from the devil, for by this he has both killed and cast down. Where then were these wicked men whom the apostle thus condemns, and in whom there was so much that was good to cause him to rejoice? Were they within, or without? Choose which you will. If they were within, then Paul knew them, and yet they did not pollute him. And so you would not be polluted in the unity of the whole world by those of whom you make certain charges, whether these be true, or falsehoods invented by yourselves. Wherefore do you separate yourself? Why do you destroy yourself by the criminal sacrilege of schism? But if they were without, then you see that even in those who were without, and who certainly cannot belong to everlasting life, since they have not charity, and do not abide in unity, there is yet found the holiness of the name of Christ, so that the apostle joyfully confirms their teaching, on account of the intrinsic holiness of the name, although he repudiates them. We are right, therefore, in not doing wrong to the actual name, when those come to us who were without; but we correct the individuals, while we do honor to the name. Do you therefore take heed, and see how wickedly you act in the case of those whose acts as it seems you condemn, by treating as naught the sacrament of the name of Christ, which is holy in them. And you, indeed, as is shown by your words, think that those men of whom the apostle spoke were outside the limits of the Church. Therefore, when you fear persecution from the Catholics, of which you speak in order to create odium against us, you have confirmed in heretics the name of Christ to which you do despite by rebaptizing.

[2191] Phil. i. 15-18.

[2192] 1 Cor. xiii. 6.

Chapter 83.

181. Petilianus said: "If then there are not some to whom all this power of faith is found to be in opposition, on what principle do you persecute, so as to compel men to defile themselves:?"

182. Augustin answered: We neither persecute you, except so far as truth persecutes falsehood; nor has it anything to do with us if any one has persecuted you in other ways, just as it has nothing to do with you if any of your party do likewise; nor do

we compel you to defile yourselves, but we persuade you to be cured.

Chapter 84.

183. Petilianus said: "But if authority had been given by some law for persons to be compelled to what is good, you yourselves, unhappy men, ought to have been compelled by us to embrace the purest faith. But far be it, far be it from our conscience to compel any one to embrace our faith."

184. Augustin answered: No one is indeed to be compelled to embrace the faith against his will; but by the severity, or one might rather say, by the mercy of God, it is common for treachery to be chastised with the scourge of tribulation. Is it the case, because the best morals are chosen by freedom of will, that therefore the worst morals are not punished by integrity of law? But yet discipline to punish an evil manner of living is out of the question, except where principles of good living which had been learned have come to be despised. If any laws, therefore, have been enacted against you, you are not thereby forced to do well, but are only prevented from doing ill. [2193]For no one can do well unless he has deliberately chosen, and unless he has loved what is in free will; but the fear of punishment, even if it does not share in the pleasures of a good conscience, at any rate keeps the evil desire from escaping beyond the bounds of thought. Who are they, however, that have enacted adverse laws by which your audacity could be repressed? Are they not those of whom the apostle says that "they bear not the sword in vain; for they are the ministers of God, revengers to execute wrath upon them that do evil?" [2194]The whole question therefore is, whether you are not doing ill, who are charged by the whole world with the sacrilege

of so great a schism. And yet, neglecting the discussion of this question, you talk on irrelevant matters; and while you live as robbers, you boast that you die as martyrs. [2195]And, through fear either of the laws themselves, or of the odium which you might incur, or else because you are unequal to the task of resisting, I do not say so many men, but so many Catholic nations, you even glory in your gentleness, that you do not compel any to join your party. According to your way of talking, the hawk, when he has been prevented by flight from carrying off the fowls, might call himself a dove. For when have you ever had the power without using it? And hence you show how you would do more if you only could. When Julian, envying the peace of Christ, restored to you the churches which belonged to unity, who could tell of all the massacres which were committed by you, when the very devils rejoiced with you at the opening of their temples? In the war with Firmus and his party, let Mauritania Cæsariensis itself be asked to tell us what the Moor Rogatus [2196] suffered at your hands. In the time of Gildo, because one of your colleagues [2197] was his intimate friend, let the followers of Maximianus be our witnesses to their sufferings. For if one might appeal to Felicianus himself, who is now with you, on his oath, whether Optatus did not compel him against his will to return to your communion, he would not dare to open his lips, especially if the people of Musti could behold his face, who were witnesses to everything that was done. But let them, as I have said, be witnesses to what they have suffered at the hands of those with whom they acted in such wise towards Rogatus. The Catholic Church herself, though strengthened by the assistance of Catholic princes ruling by land and sea, was savagely attacked by hostile troops in arms under Optatus. It was this that first made it necessary to urge before the vicar Seranus that the law should be put in force against you which imposes a fine of ten pounds of gold, which none of you have ever paid to this very day, and yet you charge us with cruelty. But where could you find a milder course of proceeding, than that crimes of such magnitude on your part should be punished by the imposition of a pecuniary fine? Or who could enumerate all the deeds which you commit in the places which you hold, of your own sovereign will and pleasure, each one as he can, without any friendship on the part of judges or any others in authority? Who is there of our party, among the inhabitants of our towns, who has not either learned something of this sort from those who came before him, or experienced it for himself? Is it not the case that at Hippo, where I am, there are not wanting some who remember that your leader Faustinus gave orders, in the time of his supreme power, in consequence of the scanty numbers of the Catholics in the place, that no one should bake their bread for them, insomuch that a baker, who was the tenant of one of our deacons, threw away the bread of his landlord unbaked, and though he was not sentenced to exile under any law, he cut him off from all share in the necessaries of life not only in a Roman state, [2198] but even in his own country, and not only in his own country, but in his own house? Why, even lately, as I myself recall with mourning to this day, did not Crispinus of Calama, one of your party, having bought a property, and that only copy-hold, [2199] boldly and unhesitatingly immerse in the waters of a second baptism no less than eighty souls, murmuring with miserable groans under the sole influence of terror; and this in a farm belonging to the Catholic emperors, by whose laws you were forbidden even to be in any Roman city? [2200]But what else was it, save such deeds as these of yours, that made it necessary for the very laws to be passed of which you complain? The laws, indeed, are very far from being proportionate to your offenses; but, such as they are, you may thank yourselves for their existence. Indeed, should we not certainly be driven on all sides from the country by the furious attacks of your Circumcelliones, who fight under your command in furious troops, unless we held you as hostages in the towns, who might well be unwilling to endure under any circumstances the mere gaze of the people, and the censure of all honorable men. from very shame, if not from fear? Do not therefore say, "Far be it, far be it from our conscience, to force any one to embrace our faith." For you do it when you can; and when you do not do it, it is because you are unable, either from fear of the laws or the odium which would accompany it, or because of the numbers of those who would resist.

[2193] See below, 95, 217, and c. Gaudentium, I. 25, 28 sqq.

[2194] Rom. xiii. 4.

[2195] Augustin speaks of the Moor Rogatus, bishop of Cartenna in ecclesiastical province of Mauritania Cæsariensis in his ninety-third epistle, to Vincentius, c. iii. 11. We learn from the eighty-seventh epistle, to Emeritus, sec. 10, that the followers of Rogatus called the other Donatists Firmiani, because they had been subjected to much cruelty at their hands under the authority of Firmus.

[2196] Cp. note 3, p. 556.

[2197] Optatus of Thaumugade (Thamogade), the friend of Gildo.

[2198] Augustin mentions again in his thirty-fifth epistle, to Eusebius, sec. 3, that Hippo had received the Roman citizenship. His argument is that, even if not a native of the place, the deacon should have been safe from molestation wherever Roman laws prevailed.

[2199] Emphyteuticam. The land, therefore, was held under the emperors, and less absolutely in the power of the owner than if it had been freehold.

[2200] Augustin remonstrates with Crispinus on the point, Epist. lxvi.

Chapter 85.

185. Petilianus said: "For the Lord Christ says, No man can come to me, except the Father which hath sent me draw him.' [2201] But why do we not permit each several person to follow his free will, since the Lord God Himself has given free will to men, showing to them, however, the way of righteousness, lest any one by chance should perish from ignorance of it? For He said, I have placed before thee good and evil. I have set fire and water before thee; choose which thou wilt.' From which choice, you wretched men, you have chosen for yourselves not water, but rather fire. But yet,' He says, choose the good, that thou mayest live.' [2202]You who will not choose the good, have, by your own sentence, declared that you do not wish to live."

186. Augustin answered: If I were to propose to you the question how God the Father draws men to the Son, when He has left them to themselves in freedom of action, you would perhaps find it difficult of solution. For how does He draw them to Him if He leaves them to themselves, so that each should choose what he pleases? And yet both these facts are true; but this is a truth which few have intellect enough to

penetrate. As therefore it is possible that, after leaving men to themselves in free will, the Father should yet draw them to the Son, so is it also possible that those warnings which are given by the correction of the laws do not take away free will. For whenever a man suffers anything that is harsh and unpleasing, he is warned to consider why it is that he is suffering, so that, if he shall discover that he is suffering in the cause of justice, he may choose the good that consists in the very act of suffering as he does in the cause of justice; but if he sees that it is unrighteousness for which he suffers, he may be induced, from the consideration that he is suffering and being tormented most fruitlessly, to change his purpose for the better, and may at the same time escape both the fruitless annoyance and the unrighteousness itself, which is likely to prove yet more hurtful and pernicious in the mischief it produces. And so you, when kings make any enactments against you, should consider that you are receiving a warning to consider why this is being done to you. For if it is for righteousness' sake, then are they truly your persecutors; but you are the blessed ones, who, being persecuted for righteousness' sake, shall inherit the kingdom of heaven: [2203]but if it is because of the iniquity of your schism, what are they more than your correctors; while you, like all the others who are guilty of various crimes, and pay the penalty appointed by the law, are undoubtedly unhappy both in this world and in that which is to come? No one, therefore, takes away from you your free will. But I would urge you diligently to consider which you would rather choose,--whether to live corrected in peace, or, by persevering in malice, to undergo real punishment under the false name of martyrdom. But I am addressing you just as though you were suffering something proportionate to your sin, whereas you are committing sins of such enormity and reigning in such impunity. You are so furious, that you cause more terror than a war trumpet with your cry of "Praise to God;" so full of calumny, that even when you throw yourselves over precipices without any provocation, you impute it to our persecutions.

187. He says also, like the kindest of teachers, "You who will not choose the good, have, by your own sentence, declared that you do not wish to live." According to this, if we were to believe your accusations, we should live in kindness; but because we believe the promises of God, we declare by our own sentence that we do not wish to live. You remember well, it seems to me, what the apostles answered to the Jews when they were desired to abstain from preaching Christ. This therefore we also say, that you should answer us whether we ought rather to obey God or man. [2204]Traditors, offerers of incense, persecutors: these are the words of men against men. Christ remained only in the love of Donatus: these are the words of men extolling the glory of a man under the name of Christ, that the glory of Christ Himself may be diminished. For it is written, "In the multitude of people is the king's honor: but in the want of people is the destruction of the prince:" [2205]these, therefore, are the words of men. But those words in the gospel, "It behoved Christ to suffer, and to rise from the dead the third day; and that repentance and remission of sins should be preached in His name among all nations, beginning at Jerusalem," [2206] are the words of Christ, showing forth the glory which He received from His Father in the wideness of His kingdom. When we have heard them both, we choose in preference the communion of the Church, and prefer the words of Christ to the words of men. I ask, who is there that can say that we have chosen what is evil, except one who shall say that Christ taught what was evil?

[2201] John vi. 44.

[2202] Ecclus. xv. 16, 17.

[2203] Matt. v. 10; 1 Pet. ii. 20.

[2204] Acts v. 29.

[2205] Prov. xiv. 28.

[2206] Luke xxiv. 46, 47.

Chapter 86.

188. Petilianus said: "Is it then the case that God has ordered the massacre even of schismatics? and if He were to issue such an order at all, you ought to be slain by some barbarians and Scythians, not by Christians."

189. Augustin answered: Let your Circumcelliones remain quiet, and let me entreat you not to terrify us about barbarians. But as to whether we or you are schismatics, let the question be put neither to you nor to me, but to Christ, that He may show where His Church is to be found. Read the gospel then, and there you find the answer, "In Jerusalem, and in all Judea, and in Samaria and even in the whole earth." [2207]If any one, therefore, is not found within the Church, let not any further question be put to him, but let him either be corrected or converted, or else, being detected, let him not complain.

[2207] Acts i. 8.

Chapter 87.

190. Petilianus said: "For neither has the Lord God at any time rejoiced in human blood, seeing that He was even willing

that Cain, the murderer of his brother, should continue to exist in his murderer's life."

191. Augustin answered: If God was unwilling that death should be inflicted on him who slew his brother, preferring that he should continue to exist in his murderer's life, see whether this be not the cause why, seeing that the heart of the king is in the hand of God, whereby he has himself enacted many laws for your correction and reproof, yet no law of the king has commanded that you should be put to death, perhaps with this very object, that any one of you who persists in the obstinate self-will of his sacrilegious madness should be tortured with the punishment of the fratricide Cain, that is to say, with the life of a murderer. For we read that many were slain in mercy by Moses the servant of the Lord; for in that he prayed thus in intercession to the Lord for their wicked sacrilege, saying, "O Lord, if Thou wilt forgive their sin--; and if not, blot me, I pray thee, out of the book which Thou hast written," [2208] his unspeakable charity and mercy are plainly shown. Could it be, then, that he was suddenly changed to cruelty, when, on descending from the mount, he ordered so many thousands to be slain? Consider, therefore, whether it may not be a sign of greater anger on the part of God, that, whilst so many laws have been enacted against you, you have not been ordered by any emperor to be put to death. Or do you think that you are not to be compared to that fratricide? Hearken to the Lord speaking through His prophet: "From the rising of the sun, even unto the going down of the same, my name shall be great among the Gentiles; and in every place incense shall be offered unto my name, and a pure offering; for my name shall be great among the heathen, saith the Lord of hosts." [2209]On this brother's sacrifice you show that you look with malignant eyes,

over and above the respect which God pays to it; and if ye have ever heard that "from the rising of the sun, unto the going down of the same, the Lord's name is to be praised," [2210] which is that living sacrifice of which it is said, "Offer unto God thanksgiving," [2211] then will your countenance fall like that of yonder murderer. But inasmuch as you cannot kill the whole world, you are involved in the same guilt by your mere hatred, according to the words of John, "Whosoever hateth his brother is a murderer." [2212] And I would that any innocent brother might rather fall into the hands of your Circumcelliones, to be murdered by their weapons, than be subjected to the poison of your tongue and rebaptized.

[2208] Ex. xxxii. 28-32.

[2209] Mal. i. 11.

[2210] Ps. cxiii. 3.

[2211] Ps. l. 14.

[2212] 1 John iii. 15.

Chapter 88.

192. Petilianus said: "We advise you, therefore, if so be that you will hear it willingly, and even though you do not willingly receive it, yet we warn you that the Lord Christ instituted for Christians, not any form of slaying, but one of dying only. For if He loved men who thus delight in battle, He would not have consented to be slain for us."

193. Augustin answered: Would that your martyrs would follow the form that He prescribed! they would not throw themselves over precipices, which He refused to do at the

bidding of the devil. [2213]But when you persecute our ancestors with false witness even now that they are dead, whence have you received this form? In that you endeavor to stain us with the crimes of men we never knew, while you are unwilling that the most notorious misdeeds of your own party should be reckoned against you, whence have you received this form? But we are too much yielding to our own conceit if we find fault about ourselves, when we see that you utter false testimony against the Lord Himself, since He Himself both promised and made manifest that His Church should extend throughout all nations, and you maintain the contrary. This form, therefore, you did not receive even from the Jewish persecutors themselves, for they persecuted His body while He was walking on the earth: you persecute His gospel as He is seated in heaven. Which gospel endured more meekly the flames of furious kings than it can possibly endure your tongues; for while they blazed, unity remained, and this it cannot do amid your words. They who desired that the word of God should perish in the flames did not believe that it could be despised if read. They would not, therefore, set their flames to work upon the gospel, if you would let them use your tongues against the gospel. In the earlier persecution the gospel of Christ was sought by some in their rage, it was betrayed by others in their fear; it was burned by some in their rage, it was hidden by others in their love; it was attacked, but none were found to speak against its truth. The more accursed share of persecution was reserved for you when the persecution of the heathen was exhausted. Those who persecuted the name of Christ believed in Christ: now those who are honored for the name of Christ are found to speak against His truth.

[2213] Matt. iv. 6, 7.

Chapter 89.

194. Petilianus said: "Here you have the fullest possible proof that a Christian may take no part in the destruction of another. But the first establishing of this principle was in the case of Peter, as it is written, Simon Peter having a sword, drew it, and smote the high priest's servant, and cut off his right ear. Then said Jesus unto Peter, Put up thy sword into the sheath. For all they that take the sword shall perish with the sword.'" [2214]

195. Augustin answered: Why then do you not restrain the weapons of the Circumcelliones with such words as these? Should you think that you were going beyond the words of the gospel if you should say, All they that take the cudgel shall perish with the cudgel? Withhold not then your pardon, if our ancestors were unable to restrain the men by whom you complain that Marculus was thrown down a precipice; for neither is it written in the gospel, He that useth to throw men down a precipice shall be cast therefrom. And would that, as your charges are either false or out of date, so the cudgels of those friends of yours would cease! And yet, perhaps, you take it ill that, if not by force of law, at any rate in words, we take away their armor from your legions in saying that they manifest their rage with sticks alone. For that was the ancient fashion of their wickedness, but now they have advanced too far. For amid their drunken revellings, and amid the free license of assembling together, wandering in the streets, jesting, drinking, passing the whole night in company with women who have no husbands, they have learned not only to brandish cudgels, but to wield swords and whirl slings. But why should I not say to them (God knows with what feelings I say it and with what feelings they receive it!), Madmen, the sword of Peter, though drawn from motives not yet free from fleshly impurity, was yet

drawn in defence of the body of Christ against the body of His persecutor, but your arms are portioned out against the cause of Christ; but the body of which He is the head, that is, His Church, extends throughout all nations. He Himself has said this, and has ascended into heaven, whither the fury of the Jews could not follow Him; and it is your fury which attacks His members in the body, which on His ascension He commended to our care. In defense of those members all men rage against you, all men resist you, as many as being in the Catholic Church, and possessing as yet but little faith, are influenced by the same motives as Peter was when he drew his sword in the name of Christ. But there is a great difference between your persecution and theirs. You are like the servant of the Jews' high priest; for in the service of your princes you arm yourselves against the Catholic Church, that is, against the body of Christ. But they are such as Peter then was, fighting even with the strength of their bodies for the body of Christ, that is, the Church. But if they are bidden to be still, as Peter then was bidden, how much more should you be warned that, laying aside the madness of heresy, you should join the unity of those members for which they so fight? But, being wounded by such men as these, you hate us also; and, as though you had lost your right ears, you do not hear the voice of Christ as He sits at the right hand of the Father. But to whom shall I address myself, or how shall I address myself to them, seeing that in them I find no time wherein to speak? for even early in the morning they are reeking with wine, drunk, it may be already in the day, it may be still from overnight. Moreover, they utter threats, and not they only, but their own bishops utter threats concerning them, being ready to deny that what they have done has any bearing on them. May the Lord grant to us a song of degrees, in which we may say, "When I am with those who hate peace, I am peaceful. When I would speak with them, they are wont to fight me without cause." [2215]For thus says the body of Christ, which throughout the whole world is assailed by heretics, by some here, by others there, and by all alike wherever they may be. [2216]

[2214] John xviii. 10, 11; Matt. xxvi. 52.

[2215] Ps. cxx. 6, 7, cp. Hieron.

[2216] See Contr. Cresc. l. III. c. 67, l. IV. cc. 60, 61.

Chapter 90.

196. Petilianus said: "Therefore I say, He ordained that we should undergo death for the faith, which each man should do for the communion of the Church. For Christianity makes progress by the deaths of its followers. For if death were feared by the faithful, no man would be found to live with perfect faith. For the Lord Christ says, Except a corn of wheat fall into the ground and die, it abideth alone: but if it die, it bringeth forth much fruit.'" [2217]

197. Augustin answered: I should be glad to know which of your party it was who first threw himself over a precipice. For truly that grain of corn was fruitful from which so great a crop of similar suicides has sprung. Tell me, when you make mention of the words of the Lord, that He says a grain of wheat shall die and bring forth much fruit, why do you envy the real fruit, which has most truly [2218] sprung up throughout the whole world, and bring up against it all the charges of the tares or chaff which you have ever either heard of or invented?

[2217] John xii. 24.

[2218] Veracissime. Another reading is "feracissime," "most abundantly."

Chapter 91.

198. Petilianus said: "But you scatter thorns and tares, not seeds of corn so that you ought to be burned together with them at the last judgment. We do not utter curses; but every thorny conscience is bound under this penalty by the sentence which God has pronounced."

199. Augustin answered: Surely, when you mention tares, it might bring to your minds the thought of wheat as well; for both have been commanded to grow together in the field until the harvest. But you fix the eye of malice fiercely on the tares, and maintain, in opposition to the express declaration of Christ, that they alone have grown throughout the earth, with the exception of Africa alone.

Chapter 92.

200. Petilianus said: "Where is the saying of the Lord Christ, Whosoever shall smite thee on the right cheek, turn to him the other also'? [2219]Where is the patience which He displayed when they spat upon His face, who Himself with His most holy spittle opened the eyes of the blind? Where is the saying of the Apostle Paul, If a man smite you in the face?' Where is that other saying of the same apostle, In stripes above measure, in prisons more frequent, in deaths oft'? [2220]He makes mention of the sufferings which he underwent, not of the deeds which he performed. It had been enough for the Christian faith that these things should be done by the Jews: why do you, wretched men, do these others in addition?"

201. Augustin answered: Is it then really so, that when men smite you on the one cheek, you turn to them the other? This is not the report that your furious bands won for you by wandering everywhere throughout the whole of Africa with dreadful wickedness. I would fain have it that men should make a bargain with you, that, in accordance with the old law, you should seek but "an eye for an eye, a tooth for a tooth," [2221] instead of bringing out cudgels in return for the words which greet your ears.

[2219] Matt. v. 39.

[2220] 2 Cor. xi. 20, 23.

[2221] Deut. xix. 21.

Chapter 93.

202. Petilianus said: "But what have you to do with the kings of this world, in whom Christianity has never found anything save envy towards her? And to teach you shortly the truth of what I say, A king persecuted the brethren of the Maccabees. [2222]A king also condemned the three children to the sanctifying flames, being ignorant what he did, seeing that he himself was fighting against God. [2223] A king sought the life of the infant Saviour. [2224]A king exposed Daniel, as he thought, to be eaten by wild beasts. [2225]And the Lord Christ Himself was slain by a king's most wicked judge. [2226] Hence it is that the apostle cries out, We speak wisdom among them that are perfect; yet not the wisdom of this world, nor of the princes of this world, that come to nought: but we speak the wisdom of God in a mystery, which was hidden, which God ordained before the world unto our glory; which none of the princes of this world knew: for had they known it, they would

not have crucified the Lord of glory.' [2227] But grant that this was said of the heathen kings of old. Yet you, rulers of this present age, because you desire to be Christians, do not allow men to be Christians, seeing that, when they are believing in all honesty of heart, you draw them by the defilement and mist of your falsehood wholly over to your wickedness, that with their arms, which were provided against the enemies of the state, they should assail the Christians, and should think that, at your instigation, they are doing the work of Christ if they kill us whom you hate, according to the saying of the Lord Christ: The time cometh,' He says, that whosoever killeth you will think that he doeth God service.' [2228] It makes no matter therefore to you, false teachers, whether the kings of this world desire to be heathens, which God forbid, or Christians, so long as you cease not in your efforts to arm them against the family of Christ. But do you not know, or rather, have you not read, that the guilt of one who instigates a murder is greater than the guilt of him who carries it out? Jezebel had excited the king her husband to the murder of a poor and righteous man, yet husband and wife alike perished by an equal punishment. [2229] Nor indeed is your mode of urging on kings different from that by which the subtle persuasion of women has often urged kings on to guilt. For the wife of Herod earned and obtained the boon by means of her daughter, that the head of John should be brought to table in a charger. [2230] Similarly the Jews forced on Pontius Pilate that he should crucify the Lord Jesus, whose blood Pilate prayed might remain in vengeance upon them and on their children. [2231] So therefore you also overwhelm yourselves with our blood by your sin. For it does not follow that because it is the hand of the judge that strikes the blow, your calumnies therefore are not rather guilty of the deed. For the prophet David says, speaking in the person of Christ, Why do the heathen rage, and the people imagine a vain thing? The kings of the earth set themselves, and the rulers take counsel together, against the Lord, and against His Anointed, saying, Let us break their bands asunder, and cast away their cords from us. He that sitteth in the heavens shall laugh: the Lord shall have them in derision. Then shall He speak unto them in His wrath, and vex them in His sore displeasure. Yet have I set my King upon my holy hill of Zion. I will declare the decree: the Lord hath said unto me, Thou art my Son; this day have I begotten Thee. Ask of me, and I shall give Thee the heathen for Thine inheritance, and the uttermost parts of the earth for Thy possession. Thou shalt rule them with a rod of iron; Thou shalt dash them in pieces like a potter's vessel.' And he warned the kings themselves in the following precepts, that they should not, like ignorant men devoid of understanding, seek to persecute the Christians, lest they should themselves be destroyed,--which precepts I would that we could teach them, seeing that they are ignorant of them; or, at least, that you would show them to them, as doubtless you would do if you desired that they should live; or, at any rate, if neither of the other courses be allowed, that your malice would have permitted them to read them for themselves. The first Psalm of David would certainly have persuaded them that they should live and reign as Christians; but meanwhile you deceive them, so long as they entrust themselves to you. For you represent to them things that are evil, and you hide from them what is good. Let them then at length read this, which they should have read already long ago. For what does he say, Be wise now therefore, O ye kings; be instructed, ye judges of the earth. Serve the Lord with fear, and rejoice with trembling. Lay hold of instruction lest the Lord be angry, and ye perish from the right way. Since how quickly has His wrath kindled over you? Blessed are all they that put their trust in Him.' [2232]You urge on emperors, I say, with your persuasions, even as Pilate, whom, as we showed above, the Jews urged on, though he himself cried aloud, as he washed his hands before them all, I am innocent of the blood of this just person,' [2233] --as though a person could be clear from the guilt of a sin who had himself committed it. But, to say nothing of ancient examples, observe, from instances taken from your own party, how very many of your emperors and judges have perished in persecuting us. To pass over Nero, who was the first to persecute the Christians, Domitian perished almost in the same way as Nero, as also did Trajan, Geta, [2234] Decius, Valerian, Diocletian; Maximian also perished, at whose command that men should burn incense to their gods, burning the sacred volumes, Marcellinus indeed first, but after him also Mensurius of Carthage, and Cæcilianus, escaped death from the sacrilegious flames, surviving like some ashes or cinders from the burning. For the consciousness of the guilt of burning incense involved you all, as many as agreed with Mensurius. Macarius perished, Ursacius [2235] perished, and all your counts perished in like manner by the vengeance of God. For Ursacius was slain in a battle with the barbarians, after which birds of prey with their savage talons, and the greedy teeth of dogs with their biting, tore him limb from limb. Was not he too a murderer at your suggestion, who, like king Ahab, whom we showed to have been persuaded by a woman, slew a poor and righteous man? [2236]So you too do not cease to murder us, who are just and poor (poor, that is, in worldly wealth; for in the grace of God no one of us is poor). For even if you do not murder a man with your hands, you do not cease to do so with your butcherous tongues. For it is written, Death and life are in the power of the tongue.' [2237]All, therefore, who have been murdered, you, the instigator of the deed, have slain. Nor indeed does the hand of the butcher glow save at the instigation of your tongue; and that terrible heat of the breast is inflamed by your words to take the blood of others,--blood that shall take a just vengeance upon him who shed it."

203. Augustin answered: If I were to answer adequately, and as I ought, to this passage, which has been exaggerated and arranged at such length by you, where you speak in invidious terms against us concerning the kings of this world, I am much afraid that you would accuse me too of having wished to excite the anger of kings against you. And yet, whilst you are borne after your own fashion by the violence of this invective against all Catholics, you certainly do not pass me by. I will endeavor, however, to show, if I can, that it is rather you who have been guilty of this offense by speaking as you have done, than myself by answering as I shall do. And first of all, see how you yourself oppose your self; for certainly you prefaced the passage which you quoted with the words, "What have you to do with the kings of this world, in whom Christianity has never found anything save envy towards her?" In these words you certainly cut off from us all access to the kings of this world. And a little later you say, "And he warned the kings themselves in the following precepts, that they should not, like ignorant men devoid of understanding, seek to persecute the Christians, lest they should be themselves destroyed,--which precepts I would that we could teach them, seeing that they are ignorant of them; or, at least, that you would show them to them, as doubtless you would do if you desired that they should live." In what way then do you wish us to be the instructors of kings? And indeed those of our body who have any friendship with Christian kings commit no sin if they make a right use of that friendship; but if

any are elated by it, they yet sin far less grievously than you. For what had you, who thus reproach us,--what had you to do with a heathen king, and what is worse, with Julian, the apostate and enemy of the name of Christ, to whom, when you were begging that the basilicas should be restored to you as though they were your own, you ascribed this meed of praise, "that in him justice alone was found to have a place"?--in which words (for I believe that you understand the Latin tongue) both the idolatry and the apostasy of Julian are styled justice. I hold in my hands the petition which your ancestors presented; the memorial [2238] which embodied their request; the chronicles, where they made their representation. Watch and attend. To the enemy of Christ, to the apostate, the antagonist of Christians, the servant of the devil, that friend, that representative, that Pontius of yours, made supplication in such words as these: "Go to then, and say to us, What have you to do with the kings of this world?" that as deaf men you may read to the deaf nations what you as well as they refuse to hear;" Thou beholdest the mote that is in thy brother's eye, but considerest not the beam that is in thine own eye." [2239]

204. "What," say you, "have you to do with the kings of this world, in whom Christianity has never found anything save envy towards her?" Having said this, you endeavored to reckon up what kings the righteous had found to be their enemies, and did not consider how many more might be enumerated who have proved their friends. The patriarch Abraham was both most friendly treated, and presented with a token of friendship, by a king who had been warned from heaven not to defile his wife. [2240]Isaac his son likewise found a king most friendly to him. [2241]Jacob, being received with honor by a king in Egypt, went so far as to bless him. [2242]What shall I say of his son

Joseph, who, after the tribulation of a prison, in which his chastity was tried as gold is tried in the fire, being raised by Pharaoh to great honors, [2243] even swore by the life of Pharaoh, [2244] --not as though puffed up with vain conceit, but being not unmindful of his kindness. The daughter of a king adopted Moses. [2245]David took refuge with a king of another race, compelled thereto by the unrighteousness of the king of Israel. [2246]Elijah ran before the chariot of a most wicked king,--not by the king's command, but from his own loyalty. [2247] Elisha thought it good to offer of his own accord to the woman who had sheltered him anything that she might wish to have obtained from the king through his intercession. [2248]But I will come to the actual times when the people of God were in captivity, in which, to use a mild expression, a strange forgetfulness came over you. For, wishing to prove that Christianity has never found anything in kings saving envy towards her, you made mention of the three children and Daniel, who suffered at the hands of persecuting kings, and you could not derive instruction from circumstances not occurring near, but in the very same passages, viz., from the conduct of the king himself after the miracle of the flames which did no hurt, whether as shown in praising and setting forth the name of God, or in honoring the three children themselves, or from the esteem in which the king held Daniel, and the gifts with which he honored him, nothing loth to receive them, when he, rendering the honor that was due to the king's power, as sufficiently appears from his own words, did not hesitate to use the gift with which he was endowed by God, in interpreting the king's dream. And when, in consequence, the king was compelled by the men who envied the holy prophet, and heaped calumnies upon him with sacrilegious madness, most unwillingly to cast him into the den of lions, sadly though he did it, yet he had the conviction that he would be safe through the help and protection of his God. Accordingly, when Daniel, by the miraculous repression of the lions' rage, had been preserved unhurt, when the friendly voice of the king spoke first to him, in accents of anxiety, he himself replied with benediction from the den, "O king, live for ever!" [2249]How came it that, when your argument was turning on the very same subject, when you were yourself quoting the examples of the servants of God in whose case these things were done, you either failed to see, or were unwilling to see, or seeing and knowing, were silent, in a manner which I know not how you will defend, about those instances of friendship felt by kings for the saints? But if it were not that, as a defender of the basest cause, you are hindered by the desire of building up falsehood, and thereby turned away either as unwilling or as ignorant from the light of truth, there can be no doubt that you could, without any difficulty, recall some good kings as well as some bad ones, and some friendly to the saints as well as some unfriendly. And we cannot but wonder that your Circumcelliones thus throw themselves from precipices. Who was running after you, I pray? What Macarius, what soldier was pursuing you? Certainly none of our party thrust you into this abyss of falsehood. Why then did you thus run headlong with your eyes shut, so that when you said, "What have you to do with the kings of this world?" you did not add, In whom Christianity has often found envy towards herself, instead of boldly venturing to say, "In whom Christianity has never found anything save envy towards her?" Was it really true that you neither thought yourself, nor considered that those who read your writings would think, how many instances of kings there were that went against your views? Does he not know what he says?

205. Or do you think that, because those whom I have mentioned belonged to olden times, therefore they form no argument against you, because you did not say, In whom righteousness has never found anything save envy towards her, but "In whom Christianity has never found anything saving envy towards her,"--meaning, perhaps, that it should be understood that they began to show envy towards the righteous from the time when they began to bear the name of Christians? What then is the meaning of those examples from olden times, by which you even more imprudently wished to prove what you had so imprudently ventured to assert? For was it not before Christ was born in the world that the Maccabees, and the three children, and Daniel, did and suffered what you told of them? And again, why was it, as I asked just now, that you offered a petition to Julian, the undoubted foe of Christianity? Why did you seek to recover the basilicas from him? Why did you declare that only righteousness found a place with him? If it is the foe of Christianity that hears such things as these, what then are they from whom he hears them? But it should be observed that Constantine, who was certainly no foe to the name of Christian, but rather rendered glorious by it, being mindful of the hope which he maintained in Christ, and deciding most justly on behalf of His unity, was not worthy to be acknowledged by you, even when you yourselves appealed to him. Both these were emperors in Christian times, but yet not both of them were Christians. But if both of them were foes of Christianity, why did you thus appeal to one of them? why did you thus present a petition to the other? For on your ancestors making their petition, Constantine had given an episcopal judgment both at Rome and at Arles; and yet the first of them you accused before him, from the other you appealed to him. But if, as is the case, one of them had believed in

Christ, the other had apostatized from Christ, why is the Christian despised while furthering the interests of unity, the apostate praised while favoring deceit? Constantine ordered that the basilicas should be taken from you, Julian that they should be restored. Do you wish to know which of these actions is conducive to Christian peace? The one was done by a man who had believed in Christ, the other by one who had abandoned Christ. O how you would wish that you could say, It was indeed ill done that supplication should so be made to Julian, but what has that to do with us? But if you were to say this, the Catholic Church would also conquer in these same words, whose saints dispersed throughout the world are much less concerned with what you say of those towards whom you feel as you may be disposed to feel. But it is beyond your power to say, It was ill done that supplication should so be made to Julian. Your throat is closed; your tongue is checked by an authority close at home. It was Pontius that did it. Pontius presented the petition; Pontius declared that the apostate was most righteous; Pontius set forth that only righteousness found a place with the apostate. That Pontius made a petition to him in these words, we have the express evidence of Julian himself, mentioning him by name, without any disguise. Your representations still exist. It is no uncertain rumor, but public documents that bear witness to the fact. Can it be, that because the apostate made some concession to your prayer, to the detriment of the unity of Christ, you therefore find truth in what was said, that only righteousness found a place with him? but because Christian emperors decide against your wishes, since this appears to them most likely to contribute to the unity of Christ, therefore they are called the foes of Christianity? Such folly may all heretics display; and may they regain wisdom, so that they should be no longer heretics.

206. And when is that fulfilled, you will say, which the Lord declares, "The time cometh, that whosoever killeth you will think that he doeth God service"? [2250]At any rate neither can this be said of the heathen, who persecuted Christians, not for the sake of God, but for the sake of their idols. You do not see that if this had been said of these emperors who rejoice in the name of Christian, their chief command would certainly have been this, that you should have been put to death; and this command they never gave at all. But the men of your party, by opposing the laws in hostile fashion, bring deserved punishment on themselves; and their own voluntary deaths, so long as they think that they bring odium on us, they consider in no wise ruinous to themselves. But if they think that that saying of Christ refers to kings who honor the name of Christ, let them ask what the Catholic Church suffered in the East, when, Valens the Arian was emperor. There indeed I might find what I should understand to be sufficient fulfillment of the saying of the Lord, "The time cometh, that whosoever killeth you will think that he doeth God service," that heretics should not claim, as conducing to their especial glory, the injunctions issued against their errors by Catholic emperors. But we remember that that time was fulfilled after the ascension of our Lord, of which holy Scripture is known by all to be a witness. The Jews thought that they were doing a service to God when they put the apostles to death. Among those who thought that they were showing service to God was even our Saul, though not ours as yet; so that among his causes for confidence which were past and to be forgotten, he enumerates the following: "An Hebrew," he says, "of the Hebrews; as touching the law, a Pharisee; concerning zeal, persecuting the Church." [2251]Here was one who thought that he did God service when he did what presently he suffered himself. For forty Jews bound

themselves by an oath that they would slay him, when he caused that this should be made known to the tribune, so that under the protection of a guard of armed men he escaped their snares. [2252]But there was no one yet to say to him, What have you to do (not with kings, but) with tribunes and the arms of kings? There was no one to say to him, Dare you seek protection at the hand of soldiers, when your Lord was dragged by them to undergo His sufferings? There were as yet no instances of madness such as yours; but there were already examples being prepared, which should be sufficient for their refutation.

207. Moreover, with what terrible force did you venture to set forth and utter the following: "But to say nothing of ancient examples, observe, from instances taken from your own party, how very many of your emperors and judges have perished in persecuting us." When I read this in your letter, I waited with the most earnest expectation to see what you were going to say, and whom you were going to enumerate, when, lo and behold! as though passing them over; you began to quote to me Nero, Domitian, Trajan, Geta, Decius, Valerian, Diocletian, Maximian. I acknowledge that there were more; but you have altogether forgotten against whom you are arguing. Were not all of these pagans, persecuting generally the Christian name on behalf of their idols? Be vigilant, then; for the men whom you mention were not of our communion. They were persecuting the whole aggregate of unity itself, from which we as you think, or you, as Christ teaches, have gone forth. But you had proposed to show that our emperors and judges had perished in consequence of persecuting you. Or is it that you yourself do not require that we should reckon these, because, in mentioning them, you passed them over, saying, "To pass over

Nero;" and with this reservation did you mean to run through all the rest? What then was the use of their being quoted, if they had nothing to do with the matter? But what has it to do with me? I now join with you in leaving these. Next, let that larger number which you promised to us be produced, unless, indeed, it may be that they cannot be found, inasmuch as you said that they had perished.

208. For now you go on to make mention of the bishops whom you are wont to accuse of having delivered up the sacred books, concerning whom we on our part are wont to answer: Either you fail in your proof, and so it concerns no one at all; or you succeed and then it still has no concern with us. For they have borne their own burden, whether it be good or bad; and we indeed believe that it was good. But of whatever character it was, yet it was their own; just as your bad men have borne their own burden, and neither you theirs nor they yours. But the common and most evil burden of you all is schism. This we have already often said before. Show us, therefore, not the names of bishops, but the names of our emperors and judges, who have perished in persecuting you. For this, is what you had proposed, this is what you had promised, this is what you had caused us most eagerly to expect. "Hear," he says, "Macarius perished, Ursacius perished, and all your counts perished in like manner, by the vengeance of God." You have mentioned only two by name, and neither of them was emperor. Who would be satisfied with this, I ask? Are you not utterly dissatisfied with yourself? You promise that you will mention a vast number of emperors and judges of our party who perished in persecuting you; and then, without a word of emperors, you mention two who were either judges or counts. For as to what you add, "And all your counts perished in like

manner by the vengeance of God," it has nothing to do with the matter. For on this principle you might some time ago have closed your argument, without mentioning the name of any one at all. Why then have you not made mention of our emperors, that is to say, of emperors of our communion? Were you afraid that you should be indicted for high treason? Where is the fortitude that marks the Circumcelliones? And further, what do you mean by introducing those whom you mentioned above in such numbers? They might with more right say to you, Why did you seek us out? For they did nothing to assist your cause, and yet you mentioned them by name. What kind of man, then, must you be, who fear to mention those by name, who, as you say, have perished? At any rate, you might mention more of the judges and counts, of whom you seem to feel no fear. But yet you stopped at Macarius and Ursacius. Are these two whom you mention the vast number of whom you spoke? Are you thinking of the lesson which we learned as boys? For if you were to ask of me what number two is, singular or plural, what could I answer, except that it was plural? But even so I am still not without the means of reply. I take away Macarius from your list; for you certainly have not told us how he perished. Or do you maintain that any one who persecutes you, unless he be immortal on the face of this earth, is to be deemed when he dies to have died because of you? What if Constantine had not lived to enjoy so long a reign, and such prolonged prosperity, who was the first to pass many decrees against your errors? And what if Julian, who gave you back the basilicas, had not been so speedily snatched away from life? [2253]In that case, when would you make an end of talking such nonsense as you do, seeing that even now you are unwilling to hold your tongues? And yet neither do we say that Julian died so soon because he gave back the basilicas to you.

For we might be equally prolix with you in this, but we are unwilling to be equally foolish. Well, then, as I had begun to say, from these two we will take away Macarius. For when you had mentioned the names of two, Macarius and Ursacius, you repeated the name of Ursacius with the view of showing us how he deserved his death; and you said, "For Ursacius was slain in a battle with the barbarians, after which birds of prey with their savage talons, and the greedy teeth of dogs with their biting, tore him limb from limb." Whence it is quite clear, since it is your custom to excite greater odium against us on account of Macarius, insomuch that you call us not Ursacians but Macarians, that you would have been sure to say by far the most concerning him, had you been able to say anything of the sort about his death. Of these two, therefore, when you used the plural number, if you take away Macarius, there remains Ursacius alone, a proper name of the singular number. Where is therefore the fulfillment of your threatening and tremendous promise of so many who should support your argument?

209. By this time all men who are in any degree acquainted with the meaning of words must understand, it seems to me, how ridiculous it is that, when you had said, "Macarius perished, Ursacius perished, and all your counts perished in like manner, by the vengeance of God," as though men were calling upon you to prove the fact, whereas, in reality, neither hearer nor reader was calling on you for anything further whatsoever, you immediately strung together a long argument in order to prove that all our counts perished in like manner by the vengeance of God. "For Ursacius," you say, "was slain in a battle with the barbarians, after which birds of prey with their savage talons, and the greedy teeth of dogs with their biting, tore him limb from limb." In the same way, any one else, who

was similarly ignorant of the meaning of what he says, might assert that all your bishops perished in prison by the vengeance of God; and when asked how he could prove this fact, he might at once add, For Optatus, having been accused of belonging to the company of Gildo, was put to death in a similar way. Frivolous charges such as these we are compelled to listen to, to consider, to refute; only we are apprehensive for the weak, lest, from the greater slowness of their intellect, they should fall speedily into your toils. But Ursacius, of whom you speak, if it be the case that he lived a good life, and really died as you assert, will receive consolation from the promise of God, who says, "Surely your blood of your lives will I require; at the hand of every beast will I require it." [2254]

210. But as to the calumnious charges which you bring against us, saying that by us the wrath of the kings of the world is excited against you, so long as we do not teach them the lesson of holy Scripture, but rather suggest our own desire of war, I do not imagine that you are so absolutely deaf to the eloquence of the sacred books themselves as that you should not rather fear that they should be acquainted with it. But whether you so will or no, they gain entrance to the Church; and even if we hold our tongues, they give heed to the readers; and, to say nothing of the rest, they especially listen with the most marked attention to that very psalm which you quoted. For you said that we do not teach them, nor, so far as we can help it, allow them to become acquainted with the words of Scripture: "Be wise now therefore, O ye kings; be instructed ye judges of the earth. Serve the Lord with fear and rejoice with trembling. Take hold of instruction lest the Lord be angry, [2255] etc. Believe that even this is sung, and that they hear it. But, at any rate, they hear what is written above in the same psalm, which you, unless

I am mistaken, were only unwilling to pass over, for fear you should be understood to be afraid. They hear therefore this as well "The Lord hath said unto me, Thou art my Son; this day have I begotten Thee. Ask of me, and I shall give Thee the heathen for Thine inheritance, and the uttermost parts of the earth for Thy possession." [2256]On hearing which, they cannot but marvel that some should be found to speak against this inheritance of Christ, endeavoring to reduce it to a little corner of the earth; and in their marvel they perhaps ask, on account of what they hear in what follows, "Serve the Lord with fear," wherein they can serve Him, in so far as they are kings. For all men ought to serve God,--in one sense, in virtue of the condition common to them all, in that they are men; in another sense, in virtue of their several gifts, whereby this man has one function on the earth, and that man has another. For no man, as a private individual, could command that idols should be taken from the earth, which it was so long ago foretold should come to pass. [2257]Accordingly, when we take into consideration the social condition of the human race, we find that kings, in the very fact that they are kings, have a service which they can render to the Lord in a manner which is impossible for any who have not the power of kings.

211. When, therefore, they think over what you quote, they hear also what you yourself quoted concerning the three children, and hear it with circumstances of marvellous solemnity. For that same Scripture is most of all sung in the Church at a time when the very festal nature of the season excites additional fervor even in those who, during the rest of the year, are more given to be sluggish. What then do you think must be the feelings of Christian emperors, when they hear of the three children being cast into the burning fiery

furnace because they were unwilling to consent to the wickedness of worshipping the image of the king, [2258] unless you suppose that they consider that the pious liberty of the saints cannot be overcome either by the power of kings, or by any enormity of punishment, and that they rejoice that they are not of the number of those kings who used to punish men that despised idols as though they were guilty of sacrilege? But, further, when they hear in what follows that the same king, terrified by the marvellous sight of, not only the three children, but the very flames performing service unto God, himself too began to serve God in fear, and to rejoice with reverence, and to lay hold of instruction, do they not understand that the reason that this was recorded, and set forth with such publicity, was that an example might be set both before the servants of God, to prevent them from committing sacrilege in obedience to kings, and before kings themselves, that they should show themselves religious by belief in God? Being willing, therefore, on their part, from the admonition of the very psalm which you yourself inserted in your writings, both to be wise, and to receive instruction, and to serve God with fear and to rejoice unto Him with reverence, and to lay hold of instruction, with what attention do they listen to what that king said afterwards! For he said that he would make a decree for all the people over whom he ruled, that whosoever should speak blasphemy against the God of Shadrach, Meshach, and Abednego should perish, and their house be utterly destroyed. And if they know that he made this decree that blasphemy should not be uttered against the God who tempered the force of the fire, and liberated the three children, they surely go on to consider what decrees they ought to make in their kingdom, that the same God who has granted remission of sins, and given freedom to the whole earth, should not be treated with scorn among the faithful in their realm.

212. See therefore, when Christian kings make any decree against you in defence of Catholic unity, that it be not the case that with your lips you are accusing them of being unlearned, as it were, in holy Scripture, while in your hearts you are grieving that they are so well acquainted with its teaching. For who could put up with the sacrilegious and hateful fallacy which you advance in the case of one and the same Daniel, to find fault with kings because he was cast into the den of lions, and to refuse praise to kings in that he was raised to exalted honor, seeing that, even when he was cast into the den of lions, the king himself was more inclined to believe that he would be safe than that he would be destroyed, and, in anxiety for him, refused to eat his food? And then do you dare to say to Christians, "What have you to do with the kings of the world?" because Daniel suffered persecution at a king's hands, and yet not look back upon the same Daniel faithfully interpreting dreams to kings, calling a king lord, receiving gifts and honors from a king? And so again do you dare, in the case of the aforesaid three children, to excite the flames of odium against kings, because, when they refused to worship the statue, they were cast into the flames, while at the same time you hold your tongue, and say nothing about their being thus extolled and honored by the king? Granted that the king was a persecutor when he cast Daniel into the lions' den; but when, on receiving him safely out again, in his joy and congratulations he cast in his enemies to be torn in pieces and devoured by the same lions, what was he then,--a persecutor, or not? [2259]I call on you to answer me. For if he was, why did not Daniel himself resist him, as he might so easily have done in virtue of his great

friendship for him, while yet you bid us restrain kings from persecuting men? But if he was not a persecutor, because he avenged with prompt justice the outrage committed against a holy man, what kind of vengeance, I would ask, must be exacted from kings for indignities offered to the sacraments of Christ, if the limbs of the prophet required such a vengeance because they were exposed to danger? Again, I acknowledge that the king, as indeed is manifest, was a persecutor when he cast the three children into the furnace because they refused to worship his image; but I ask whether he was still a persecutor when he set forth the decree that all who should blaspheme against the one true God should be destroyed, and their whole house laid waste? For if he was a persecutor, why do you answer Amen to the words of a persecutor? [2260]But if he was not a persecutor, why do you call those persecutors who deter you from the madness of blasphemy? For if they compel you to worship an idol, then they are like the impious king, and you are like the three children; but if they are preventing you from fighting against Christ, it is you who are impious if you attempt to do this. But what they may be if they forbid this with terrible threats, I do not presume to say. Do you find some other name for them, if you will not call them pious emperors.

213. If I had been the person to bring forward these examples of Daniel and the three children, you would perhaps resist, and declare that they ought not to have been brought from those times in illustration of our days; but God be thanked that you yourself brought them forward, to prove the point, it is true, which you desired to establish, but you see that their force was rather in favor of what you least would wish to prove. Perhaps you will say that this proceeds from no deceit of yours, but from the fallibility of human nature. Would that this were true!

Amend it, then You will not lose in reputation nay, it marks unquestionably the higher mind to extinguish the fire of animosity by a frank confession, than merely to escape the mist of falsehood by acuteness of the understanding.

[2222] 2 Mac. vii.

[2223] Dan. iii.

[2224] Matt. ii. 16.

[2225] Dan. vi.

[2226] Matt. xxvii. 26.

[2227] 1 Cor. ii. 6-8.

[2228] John xvi. 2.

[2229] 1 Kings xxi.

[2230] Matt. xiv. 8, 9.

[2231] Matt. xxvii. 24-26.

[2232] Ps. ii., cp. Hieron.

[2233] Matt. xxvii. 24.

[2234] Some editions have Varius in the place of Geta, referring to Aurelius Antoninus Heliogabalus, of whom Lampridius asserts that he derived the name of Varius from the doubtfulness of his parentage. Aelii Lampridii Antoninus Heliogabalus, in S.S. Historiæ Augustæ. The Mss. agree, however, in the reading "Geta," which was a name of the second son of Severus, the brother of Caracalla.

[2235] Optatus defends the cause of Macarius at great length in his third book against Parmenianus. Of Ursacius he says in the same place: "You are offended at the times of a certain Leontius, of Ursacius, Macarius and others." And Augustin, in his third book against Cresconius, c. 20, introduces an objection of the Donatists against himself: "But so soon as Silvanus, bishop of Cirta, had refused to communicate with Ursacius and Zenophilus the persecutors, he was driven into exile." Usuardus, deceived by a false story made up by the Donatists, enters in his Martyrology, that a pseudo-martyr Donatus suffered on the 1st of March, under Ursacius and Marcellinus, to this effect: "On the same day of the holy martyr Donatus, who suffered under Ursacius the judge (or dux), and the tribune Marcellinus."

[2236] 1 Kings xxi.

[2237] Prov. xviii. 21.

[2238] Constitutio quam impetraverunt. Some editions have "quam dederunt Constantio;" but there is no place for Constantius in this history of the Donatists, nor was any boon either sought or obtained from him in their name. The Louvain editors therefore restored "constitutio," which is the reading of the Gallic Mss.

[2239] Matt. vii. 3.

[2240] Gen. xx.

[2241] Gen. xxvi. 11.

[2242] Gen. xlvii.

[2243] Gen. xxxix., xli.

[2244] Gen. xlii. 15.

[2245] Ex. ii. 10.

[2246] 1 Sam. xxvii.

[2247] 1 Kings xviii. 44-46.

[2248] 2 Kings iv. 13.

[2249] Dan. iii.-vi.

[2250] John xvi. 2.

[2251] Phil. iii. 5, 6.

[2252] Acts xxiii. 12-33.

[2253] The reign of Constantine lasted about thirty-two years, from 306 to 337 A.D. Julian succeeded Constantius, and reigned one year and seven months, dying at the age of thirty, in a war against the Persians, in 363 A.D.

[2254] Gen. ix. 5.

[2255] Ps. ii. 10-12.

[2256] Ps. ii. 7, 8.

[2257] Isa. ii. 18; Zech. xiii. 2.

[2258] Simulacri; and so the Mss. The older editions have "adorandi simulacra;" but the singular is more forcible in its special reference to the image on the plain of Dura. Dan. iii.

[2259] Dan. ii.-vi.

[2260] This is illustrated by the words of Augustin, Epist. 105, ad Donatistas, c. I. 7: "Do ye not know that the words of the king were: I thought it good to show the signs and wonders that the high God hath wrought toward me. How great are His signs! and how mighty are His wonders! His kingdom is an everlasting kingdom, and His dominion from generation to generation' (Dan. iv. 2, 3)? Do you not, when you hear this, answer Amen, and by saying this in a loud voice, place your seal on the king's decree by a holy and solemn act?" In the Gothic liturgy this declaration was made on Easter Eve (when the third chapter of Daniel is still read in the Roman Church), and the people answered "Amen."

Chapter 94.

214. Petilianus said: "Where is the law of God? where is your Christianity, if you not only commit murders and put men to death, but also order such things to be done?"

215. Augustin answered: In reply to this, see what the fellow-heirs of Christ say throughout the world. We neither commit murders, and put men to death, nor order such things to be done; and you are raging much more madly than those who do such things, in that you put such things into the minds of men in opposition to the hopes of everlasting life.

Chapter 95.

216. Petilianus said: "If you wish that we should be your friends, why do you drag us to you against our will? But if you wish that we should be your foes, why do you kill your foes?"

217. Augustin answered: We neither drag you to us against your will, nor do we kill our foes; but whatever we do in our

dealings with you, though we may do it contrary to your inclination, yet we do it from our love to you, that you may voluntarily correct yourselves, and live an amended life. For no one lives against his will; and yet a boy, in order to learn this lesson of his own free will, [2261] is beaten contrary to his inclination, and that often by the very man that is most dear to him. And this, indeed, is what the kings would desire to say to you if they were to strike you, for to this end their power has been ordained of God. But you cry out even when they are not striking you.

[2261] Nam nemo vivit invitus; et tamen puer ut hoc volens discat, invitus vapulat. Perhaps a better reading is, "Nam nemo vult invitus; et tamen puer ut volens discat," etc., leaving out "hoc," which is wanting in the Fleury Mss.: "No one wishes against his will; and yet a boy, wishing to learn, is beaten against his will."

Chapter 96.

218. Petilianus said: "But what reason is there, or what inconsistency of emptiness, in desiring communion with us so eagerly, when all the time you call us by the false title of heretics?"

219. Augustin answered: If we so eagerly desired communion with heretics, we should not be anxious that you should be converted from the error of heresy; but when the very object of our negotiations with you is that you should cease to be heretics, how are we eagerly desiring communion with heretics? For, in fact, it is dissension and division that make you heretics; but peace and unity make men Catholics. When, then, you come over from your heresy to us, you cease to be what we hate, and begin to be what we love.

Chapter 97.

220. Petilianus said: "Choose, in short, which of the two alternatives you prefer. If innocence is on your side, why do you persecute us with the sword? Or if you call us guilty, why do you, who are yourselves innocent, seek for our company?"

221. Augustin answered: O most ingenious dilemma, or rather most foolish verbosity! Is it not usual for the choice of two alternatives to be offered to an antagonist, when it is impossible that he should adopt both? For if you should offer me the choice of the two propositions, that I should say either that we were innocent, or that we were guilty; or, again, of the other pair of propositions, viz., those concerning you, I could not escape choosing either one or the other. But as it is, you offer me the choice of these two, whether we are innocent or you are guilty, and wish me to say which of these two I choose for my reply. But I refuse to make a choice; for I assert them both, that we are innocent, and that you are guilty. I say that we are innocent of the false and calumnious accusations which you bring against us, so far as any of us, being in the Catholic Church, can say with a safe conscience that we have neither given up the sacred books, nor taken part in the worship of idols, nor murdered any man, nor been guilty of any of the other crimes which you allege against us; and that any who may have committed any such offenses, which, however, you have not proved in any case, have thereby shut the doors of the kingdom of heaven, not against us, but against themselves; "for every man shall bear his own burden." [2262]Here you have your answer on the first head. And I further say that you are all guilty and accursed,--not some of you owing to the sins of others, which are wrought among you by certain of your number, and are censured by certain others, but all of you by

the sin of schism; from which most heinous sacrilege no one of you can say that he is free, so long as he refuses to hold communion with the unity of all nations, unless, indeed, he be compelled to say that Christ has told a lie concerning the Church which is spread abroad among all nations, beginning at Jerusalem. [2263]And so you have my second answer. See how I have made you two replies, of which you were desirous that we should be reduced to choose the one. At any rate, you should have taken notice that both assertions might be made by us; and certainly, if this was what you wished, you should have asked it as a favor of us that we should choose one or the other, when you saw that it was in our power to choose both.

222. But "if innocence is on your side, why do you persecute us with the sword?" Look back for a moment on your troops, which are not now armed after the ancient fashion of their fathers only with cudgels, but have further added to their equipment axes and lances and swords, and determine for yourselves to which of us the question best belongs, "Why do you persecute us with the sword?" "Or if you call us guilty," say you, "why do you, who are yourselves innocent, seek for our company?" Here I answer very briefly. The reason why you, being guilty, are sought after by the innocent, is that you may cease to be guilty, and begin to be innocent. Here then I have chosen both of the alternatives concerning us, and answered both of those concerning you, only do you in turn choose one of the two. Are you innocent or guilty? Here you cannot choose to make the two assertions, and yet choose both, if so it pleases you. For at any rate you cannot be innocent in reference to the same circumstances in respect of which you are guilty. If therefore you are innocent do not be surprised that you are invited to be at peace with your brethren; but if you are

guilty, do not be surprised that you are sought for punishment by kings. But since of these two alternatives you assume one for yourselves, and the other is alleged of you by us,--for you assume to yourselves innocence and it is alleged of you by us that you are living impiously,--hear again once more what I shall say on either head. If you are innocent, why do you speak against the testimony of Christ? But if you are guilty, why do you not fly for refuge to His mercy? For His testimony, on the one hand, is to the unity of the world, and His mercy, on the other, is in brotherly love.

[2262] Gal. vi. 5.

[2263] Luke xxiv. 47.

Chapter 98.

223. Petilianus said: "Lastly, as we have often said before, how great is your presumption, that you should speak as you presume to do of kings, when David says, It is better to trust in the Lord than to put confidence in man: it is better to trust in the Lord than to put confidence in princes?'" [2264]

224. Augustin answered: We put no confidence in man, but, so far as we can, we warn men to place their trust in the Lord; nor do we put confidence in princes, but, so far as we can, we warn princes to put confidence in the Lord. And though we may seek aid from princes to promote the advantage of the Church, yet do we not put confidence in them. For neither did the apostle himself put confidence in that tribune, in the sense in which the Psalmist talks of putting confidence in princes, from whom he obtained for himself that an escort of armed men should be assigned to him; nor did he put confidence in the armed men, by whose protection he escaped the snares of

the wicked ones, in any such sense as that of the Psalmist where he speaks of putting confidence in men. [2265]But neither do we find fault with you yourselves, because you sought from the emperor that the basilicas should be restored to you, as though you had put your trust in Julian the prince; but we find fault with you, that you have despaired of the witness of Christ, from whose unity you have separated the basilicas themselves. For you received them at the bidding of an enemy of Christ, that in them you should despise the commands of Christ, whilst you find force and truth in what Julian ordained, saying, "This, moreover, on the petition of Rogatianus, Pontius, Cassianus, and other bishops, not without an intermixture of clergy, is added to complete the whole, that those proceedings which were taken to their prejudice wrongly and without authority being all annulled, everything should be restored to its former position;" and yet you find nothing that has either force or truth in what Christ ordained, saying, "Ye shall be witnesses unto me both in Jerusalem, and in all Judea, and in Samaria, and even in the whole earth." [2266]We entreat you, let yourselves be reformed. Return to this most manifest unity of the whole world; and let all things be restored to their former position, not in accordance with the words of the apostate Julian, but in accordance with the words of our Saviour Christ. Have pity on your own soul. We are not now comparing Constantine and Julian in order to show how different they are. We are not saying, If you have not placed confidence in a man and in a prince, when you said to a pagan and apostate emperor, that "in him justice only found a place," seeing that the party of Donatus has universally employed the prayers and the rescript in which those words occur, as is proved by the records of the audience; much less ought we to be accused by you, as though we put our confidence in any man or prince, if without any blasphemous flattery we obtained any request from Constantine or from the other Christian emperors; or if they themselves, without our asking for it, but remembering the account which they shall render to the Lord, under whose words they tremble when they hear what you yourself have quoted, "Be wise now therefore, O ye kings," etc., and many other sayings of the sort, make any ordinance of their own accord in support of the unity of the Catholic Church. But I say nothing about Constantine. It is Christ and Julian that we contrast before you; nay, more than this, it is God and man, the Son of God and the son of hell, the Saviour of our souls and the destroyer of his own. Why do you maintain the rescript of Julian in the occupation of the basilicas, and yet not maintain the gospel of Christ in embracing the peace of the Church? We too cry out, "Let all things that have been done amiss be restored to their ancient condition." The gospel of Christ is of greater antiquity than the rescript of Julian; the unity of Christ is of greater antiquity than the party of Donatus; the prayers of the Church to the Lord on behalf of the unity of the Church are of greater antiquity than the prayers of Rogatianus, and Pontius, and Cassianus, to Julian on behalf of the party of Donatus. Are proceedings wrongly taken when kings forbid division? and are they not wrongly taken when bishops divide unity? Is that wrong action when kings minister to the witness of Christ in defence of the Church? and is it not wrong action when bishops contradict the witness of Christ in order to deny the Church? We entreat you, therefore, that the words of Julian himself, to whom you thus made supplication, may be listened to, not in opposition to the gospel, but in accordance with the gospel, and that "all things which have been done amiss may be restored to their former condition."

[2264] Ps. cxviii. 8, 9.

[2265] Acts xxiii. 12-33.

[2266] Acts i. 8.

Chapter 99.

225. Petilianus said: "On you, yes you, you wretched men, I call, who, being dismayed with the fear of persecution, whilst you seek to save your riches, not your souls, love not so much the faithless faith of the traitors, as the wickedness of the very men whose protection you have won unto yourselves,--just in the same way as sailors, shipwrecked in the waves, plunge into the waves by which they must be overwhelmed, and in the great danger of their lives seek unmistakeably the very object of their dread; just as the madness of a tyrant, that he may be free from apprehension of any person whatsoever, desires to be feared, though this is fraught with peril to himself: so, so you fly for refuge to the citadel of wickedness, being willing to look on the loss or punishment of the innocent if you may escape fear for yourselves. If you consider that you escape danger when you plunge into ruin, truly also it is a faith that merits condemnation to observe the faith of a robber. Lastly, it is trafficking in a madman's gains to lose your own souls in order not to lose your wealth. For the Lord Christ says, If a man shall gain the whole world, and lose his own soul, what shall a man give in exchange for his soul?'" [2267]

226. Augustin answered: That exhortation of yours would be useful, I cannot but acknowledge, if any one were to employ it in a good cause. It is undoubtedly well that you have tried to deter men from preferring their riches to their souls. But I would have you, who have heard these words, listen also for a

time to us; for we also say this, but listen in what sense. If kings threaten to take away your riches, because you are not Jews according to the flesh, or because you do not worship idols or devils, or because you are not carried about into any heresies, but abide in Catholic unity, then choose rather that your riches should perish, that you perish not yourselves; but be careful to prefer neither anything else, nor the life of this world itself, to eternal salvation, which is in Christ. But if kings threaten you with loss or condemnation, simply on the ground that you are heretics, such things are terrifying you not in cruelty, but in mercy; and your determination not to fear is a sign not of bravery, but of obstinacy. Hear then the words of Peter, where he says, "What glory is it, if, when ye be buffeted for your faults, ye take it patiently?" [2268] so that herein you have neither consolation upon earth, nor in the world to come life everlasting; but you have here the miseries of the unfortunate, and there the hell of heretics. Do you see, therefore, my brother, with whom I am now arguing, that you ought first to show whether you hold the truth, and then to exhort men that in upholding it they should be ready to give up all the blessings which they possess in this present world? And so, when you do not show this, because you cannot,--not that the talent is wanting, but because the cause is bad,--why do you hasten by your exhortations to make men both beggars and ignorant, both in want and wandering from the truth, in rags and contentions, household drudges and heretics, both losing their temporal goods in this world, and finding eternal evils in the judgment of Christ? But the cautious son, who, while he stands in dread of his father's rod, keeps away from the lair of the serpent, escapes both blows and destruction; whereas he who despises the pains of discipline, when set in rivalry with his own pernicious will, is both beaten and destroyed. Do you not now understand, O learned man, that he who has resigned all earthly goods in order to maintain the peace of Christ, possesses God; whereas he who has lost even a very few coins in behalf of the party of Donatus is devoid of heart?

[2267] Matt. xvi. 26.

[2268] 1 Pet. ii. 20.

Chapter 100.

227. Petilianus said: "But we who are poor in spirit [2269] are not apprehensive for our wealth, but rather feel a dread of wealth. We, as having nothing, and yet possessing all things,' [2270] look on our soul as our wealth, and by our punishments and blood purchase to ourselves the everlasting riches of heaven. So again the same Lord says, Whosoever shall lose his substance, shall find it again an hundred fold.'"

228. Augustin answered: It is not beside the purpose to inquire into the true meaning of this passage also. For where my purpose is not interfered with by any mistake which you make, or any false impression which you convey in quoting from the Scriptures, I do not concern myself about the matter. It is not then written, "Whosoever shall lose his substance," but "Whosoever shall lose his life for my sake." [2271] And the passage about substance is not, "Whosoever shall lose," but "Every one that hath forsaken;" [2272] and that not only with reference to substance of money, but many other things besides. But you meanwhile have not lost your substance; but whether you have forsaken it, in that you so boast of poverty, I cannot say. And if by any chance my colleague Fortunatus may know this, being in the same city with you, he never told me, because I had never asked him. However, even if you had done

this, you have yet yourself quoted the testimony of the apostle against yourself in this very epistle which you have written: "Though I bestow all my goods to feed the poor, and though I give my body to be burned, and have not charity, it profiteth me nothing." [2273]For if you had charity, you would not bring charges against the whole world, which knows nothing of you, and of which you know no more,--no, not even such charges as are founded on the proved offenses of the Africans. If you had charity, you would not picture to yourself a false unity in your calumnies, but you would learn to recognize the unity that is most clearly set forth in the words of the Lord: "even in the whole earth." [2274]But if you did not do this, why do you boast as though you had done it? Are you really so filled with fear of riches, that, having nothing, you possess all things? Tell that to your colleague Crispinus, who lately bought a farm near our city of Hippo, that he might there plunge men into the lowest abyss. [2275]Whence I too know this all too well. You perhaps are not aware of it, and therefore shout out in security, "We stand in fear of riches." And hence I am surprised that that cry of yours has been allowed to pass Crispinus, so as to reach us. For between Constantina, where you are, and Hippo, where I am, lies Calama, where he is, nearer indeed to our side, but still between us. I wonder, therefore, how it was that he did not first intercept this cry, and strike it back so that it should not reach to our ears; and that he did not, in opposition to you, recite in much more copious phrase a eulogy on riches. For he not only stands in no fear of riches, but he actually loves them. And certainly, before you utter anything about the rest, you should rehearse such views to him. If he makes no corrections, then we have our answer ready. But for yourself, if it be true that you are poor, you have with you my brother Fortunatus. You will be more likely with such sentiments to please him, who is my colleague, than Crispinus, who is your own.

[2269] Matt. v. 3.

[2270] 2 Cor. vi. 10.

[2271] Matt. xvi. 25.

[2272] Matt. xix. 29.

[2273] 1 Cor. xiii. 3.

[2274] Acts i. 8.

[2275] See above, c. 84.

Chapter 101.

229. Petilianus said: "Inasmuch as we live in the fear of God, we have no fear of the punishments and executions which you wreak with the sword; but the only thing which we avoid is that by your most wicked communion you destroy men's souls, according to the saying of the Lord Himself: Fear not them which kill the body, but are not able to kill the soul; but rather fear Him which is able to destroy both soul and body in hell.'" [2276]

230. Augustin answered: You do the destruction which you speak of, not with a visible sword, but with that of which it is said, "The sons of men, whose teeth are spears and arrows, and their tongue a sharp sword." [2277] For with this sword of accusation and calumny against the world of which you are wholly ignorant, you destroy the souls of those who lack experience. But if you find fault with a most wicked communion, as you term it, I would bid you presently, not with

my words, but with your own, to ascend, descend, enter, turn yourself about, change sides, be such as was Optatus. But if you return to your senses, and shall find that you are not such as he, not because he refused to partake of the sacraments with you, but because you took offense at what he did, then you will acquit the world of crimes which do not belong to it, and you will find yourself involved in the sin of schism.

[2276] Matt. x. 28.

[2277] Ps. lvii. 4.

Chapter 102.

231. Petilianus said: "You, therefore, who prefer rather to be washed with the most false of baptisms than to be regenerate, not only do not lay aside your sins, but also load your souls with the offenses of criminals. For as the water of the guilty has been abandoned by the Holy Spirit, so it is clearly filled full of the offenses of the traditors. To any wretched man, then, who is baptized by one of this sort, we would say, If you have wished to be free from falsehood, you are really drenched with falsity. If you desired to shut out the sins of the flesh, you will, as the conscience of the guilty comes upon you, be partakers likewise of their guilt. If you wished to extinguish the flames of avarice, you are drenched with deceit, you are drenched with wickedness, you are drenched also with madness. Lastly, if you believe that faith is identical in the giver and the receiver, you are drenched with the blood of a brother by him who slays a man. And so it comes to pass that you, who had come to baptism free from sin, return from baptism guilty of the sin of murder."

232. Augustin answered: I should like to come to argument with those who shouted assent when they either heard or read those words of yours. For such men have not ears in their hearts, but their heart in their ears. Yet let them read again and again, and consider, and find out for themselves, not what the sound of those words is, but what they mean. First of all, to sift the meaning of the last clause, "So it comes to pass," you say, "that you who had come to baptism free from sin, return from baptism guilty of the sin of murder:" tell me, to begin with, who there is that comes to baptism free from sin, with the single exception of Him who came to be baptized, not that His iniquity should be purged away, but that an example of humility might be given us? For what shall be forgiven to one free from sin? Or are you indeed endowed with such an eloquence, that you can show to us some innocence which yet committeth sin? Do you not hear the words of Scripture saying, "No one is clean from sin in Thy sight, not even the infant whose life is but of a single day upon the earth?" [2278]For whence else is it that one hastens even with infants to seek remission of their sins? Do you not hear the words of another Scripture, "In sin did my mother conceive me?" [2279]In the next place, if a man returns a murderer, who had come without the guilt of murder, merely because he receives baptism at a murderer's hands, then all they who returned from receiving baptism at the hands of Optatus were made partakers with Optatus. Go now, and see with what face you cast in our teeth that we excite the wrath of kings against you. Are you not afraid that as many satellites of Gildo will be sought for among you, as there are men who may have been baptized by Optatus? Do you see at length how that sentence of yours, like an empty bladder, has rattled not only with a meaningless sound, but on your own head?

233. To go on to the other earlier arguments which you have set before us to be refuted, they are of such a nature that we must needs allow that every one returns from baptism endued with the character of him by whom he is baptized; but God forbid that those whom you baptize should return from you infected with the same madness as possesses you when you make such a statement! And what a dainty sound there was in your words, "You are drenched with deceit, you are drenched with wickedness, you are drenched also with madness!" Surely you would never pour forth words like this unless you were, not drenched, but filled even to repletion with madness. Is it then true, to say nothing of the rest, that all who come untainted with covetousness to receive baptism at the hands of your covetous colleagues, or the priests of your party, return guilty of covetousness, and that those who run in soberness to the whirlpool of intoxication to be baptized return in drunkenness? If you entertain and teach such views as this, you will have the effrontery even to quote, as making against us, the passage which you advanced some little time ago: "It is better to trust in the Lord than to put confidence in man. It is better to trust in the Lord than to put confidence in princes." [2280]What is the meaning of your teaching, I would ask, save only this, that we should put our confidence not in the Lord, but in man, when you say that the baptized person is made to resemble him who has baptized him? And since you assume this as the fundamental principle of your baptism, are men to place their trust in you? and are those to place their trust in princes who were disposed to place it in the Lord? Truly I would bid them hearken not to you, but rather to those proofs which you have urged against ourselves, ay, and to words more awful yet; for not only is it written, "It is better to trust in the

Lord than to put confidence in man," but also, "Cursed be the man that trusteth in man." [2281]

[2278] Job xiv. 4, 5; cp. LXX.

[2279] Ps. li. 5.

[2280] Ps. cxviii. 8, 9.

[2281] Jer. xvii. 5.

Chapter 103.

234. Petilianus said: "Imitate indeed the prophets, who feared to have their holy souls deceived with false baptism. For Jeremiah says of old that among impious men water is as one that lies. Water,' he says, that lies has not faith.'"

235. Augustin answered: Any one that hears these words, without being acquainted with the Scriptures, and who does not believe that you are either so far astray as not to know what you are saying, or deceiving in such wise that he whom you have deceived should not know what he says, would believe that the prophet Jeremiah, wishing to be baptized, had taken precautions not to be baptized by impious men, and had used these words with this intent. For what was your object in saying, previous to your quotation of this passage, "Imitate indeed the prophets, who feared to have their holy souls deceived with false baptism?" Just as though, in the days of Jeremiah, any one were washed with the sacrament of baptism, except so far as the Pharisees almost every moment bathed themselves, and their couches and cups and platters, with the washings which the Lord condemned, as we read in the gospel. [2282]How then could Jeremiah have said this, as though he desired to be baptized, and sought to avoid being baptized by

impious men? He said it, then, when he was complaining of a faithless people, by the corruption of whose morals he was vexed, not wishing to associate with their deeds; and yet he did not separate himself bodily from their congregation, nor seek other sacraments than those which the people received as suitable to that time, according to the law of Moses. To this people, therefore, in their evil mode of life, he gave the name of "a wound," with which the heart of the righteous man was grievously smitten, whether speaking thus of himself, or foreshadowing in himself what he foresaw would come to pass. For he speaks as follows: "O Lord, remember me, and visit me; make clear my innocence before those who persecute me in no spirit of long-suffering: know that for Thy sake I have suffered rebuke from those that scorn Thy words. Make their portion complete; and Thy word shall be unto me the joy and rejoicing of mine heart: for I am called by Thy name, O Lord God of hosts. I sat not in the assembly of the mockers, but was afraid of the presence of Thy hand; I sat alone, because I was filled with bitterness. Why do those who make me sad prevail against me? My wound is grievous; whence shall I be healed? It is become unto me as lying water, that has no faith." [2283]In all this it is manifest what the prophet wished to be understood, but manifest only to those who do not wish to distort to their own perverse cause the meaning of what they read. For Jeremiah says that his wound has become unto him as lying water, which cannot inspire faith; but he wished that by his wound those should be understood who made him sad by the evil conduct of their lives. Whence also the apostle says, "Without were fightings, within were fears;" [2284] and again, "Who is weak, and I am not weak? who is offended, and I burn not?" [2285]And because he had no hopes that they could be reformed, therefore he said, "Whence shall I be healed?" as though his own pain must needs continue so long as those among whom he was compelled to live continued what they were. But that a people is commonly understood under the appellation of water is shown in the Apocalypse, where we understand "many waters" to mean "many peoples," not by any conjecture of our own, but by an express explanation in the place itself. [2286]Abstain then from blaspheming the sacrament of baptism from any misunderstanding, or rather error, even when found in a man of most abandoned character; for not even in the lying Simon was the baptism which he received a lying water, [2287] nor do all the liars of your party administer a lying water when they baptize in the name of the Trinity. For neither do they begin to be liars only when they are betrayed and convicted, and so forced to acknowledge their misdeeds; but rather they were already liars, when, being adulterers and accursed, they pretended to be chaste and innocent.

[2282] Mark vii. 4.

[2283] Jer. xv. 15-18; cp. LXX.

[2284] 2 Cor. vii. 5.

[2285] 2 Cor. xi. 29.

[2286] Rev. xvii. 15.

[2287] Acts viii. 13.

Chapter 104.

236. Petilianus said: "David also said, 'The oil of the sinner shall not anoint my head.' Who is it, therefore, that he calls a

sinner? Is it I who suffer your violence, or you who persecute the innocent?"

237. Augustin answered: As representing the body of Christ, which is the Church of the living God, the pillar and mainstay of the truth, dispersed throughout the world, on account of the gospel which was preached, according to the words of the apostle, "to every creature which is under heaven:" [2288]as representing the whole world, of which David, whose words you cannot understand, has said, "The world also is stablished, that it cannot be moved;" [2289] whereas you contend that it not only has been moved, but has been utterly destroyed: as representing this, I answer, I do not persecute the innocent. But David said, "The oil of the sinner," not of the traditor; not of him who offers incense, not of the persecutor, but "of the sinner." What then will you make of your interpretation? See first whether you are not yourself a sinner. It is nothing to the point if you should say, I am not a traditor, I am not an offerer of incense, I am not a persecutor. I myself, by the grace of God, am none of these, nor is the world, which cannot be moved. But say, if you dare, I am not a sinner. For David says, "The oil of the sinner." For so long as any sin, however light, be found in you, what ground have you for maintaining that you are not concerned in the expression that is used, "The oil of the sinner"? For I would ask whether you use the Lord's prayer in your devotions? For if you do not use that prayer, which our Lord taught His disciples for their use, where have you learned another, proportioned to your merits, as exceeding the merits of the apostles? But if you pray, as our great Master deigned to teach us, how do you say, "Forgive us our trespasses, as we forgive them that trespass against us?" For in this petition we are not referring to those sins which have

already been forgiven us in baptism. Therefore these words in the prayer either exclude you from being a petitioner to God, or else they make it manifest that you too are a sinner. Let those then come and kiss your head who have been baptized by you, whose heads have perished through your oil. But see to yourself, both what you are and what you think about yourself. Is it really true that Optatus, whom pagans, Jews, Christians, men of our party, men of your party, all proclaim throughout the whole of Africa to have been a thief, a traitor, an oppressor, a contriver of schism; not a friend, not a client, but a tool of him [2290] whom one of your party declared to have been his count, companion, and god,--is it true that he was not a sinner in any conceivable interpretation of the term? What then will they do whose heads were anointed by one guilty of a capital offense? Do not those very men kiss your heads, on whose heads you pass so serious a judgment by this interpretation which you place upon the passage? Truly I would bid you bring them forth, and admonish them to heal themselves. Or is it rather your heads which should be healed, who run so grievously astray? What then, you will ask, did David really say: Why do you ask me: rather ask himself. He answers you in the verse above: "The righteous shall smite me in kindness, and shall reprove me; but let not the oil of the sinner anoint my head." [2291] What could be plainer? what more manifest? I had rather, he says, be healed by a rebuke administered in kindness, than be deceived and led astray by smooth flattery, coming on me as an ointment on my head. The self-same sentiment is found elsewhere in Scripture under other words: "Better are the wounds of a friend than the proffered kisses of an enemy." [2292]

[2288] Col. i. 23.

[2289] Ps. xciii. 1.

[2290] Gildo.

[2291] Ps. cxli. 5; cp. LXX and Hieron.

[2292] Prov. xxvii. 6; cp. LXX. and Hieron.

Chapter 105.

238. Petilianus said: "But he thus praises the ointment of concord among brethren: Behold how good and how pleasant it is for brethren to dwell together in unity! It is like the precious ointment upon the head, that ran down upon the beard, even Aaron's beard; that went down to the skirts of his garments; as the dew of Hermon, and as the dew that descended upon the mountains of Zion: for there the Lord commanded the blessing, even life for evermore.' [2293]Thus, he says, is unity anointed, even as the priests are anointed."

239. Augustin answered: What you say is true. For that priesthood in the body of Christ had an anointing, and its salvation is secured by the bond of unity. For indeed Christ Himself derives His name from chrism, that is, from anointing. Him the Hebrews call the Messiah, which word is closely akin to the Phoenician language, as is the case with very many other Hebrew words, if not with almost all. [2294] What then is meant by the head in that priesthood, what by the beard, what by the skirts of the garments? So far as the Lord enables me to understand, the head is none other than the Saviour of the body, of whom the apostle says, "And He is the head of the body, the Church." [2295]By the beard is not unsuitably understood fortitude. Therefore, on those who show themselves to be brave in His Church, and cling to the light of

His countenance, to preach the truth without fear, there descends from Christ Himself, as from the head, a sacred ointment, that is to say, the sanctification of the Spirit. By the skirts of the garments we are here given to understand that which is at the top of the garments, through which the head of Him who gives the clothing enters. By this are signified those who are perfected in faith within the Church. For in the skirts is perfection. And I presume you must remember what was said to a certain rich man: "If thou wilt be perfect, go and sell that thou hast, and give to the poor, and thou shall have treasure in heaven; and come and follow me." [2296] He indeed went away sorrowful, slighting what was perfect, choosing what was imperfect. But does it follow that there were wanting those who were so made perfect by such a surrender of earthly things, that the ointment of unity descended upon them, as from the head upon the skirts of the garments? For, putting aside the apostles, and those who were immediately associated with those leaders and teachers of the Church, whom we understand to be represented with greater dignity and more conspicuous fortitude in the beard, read in the Acts of the Apostles, and see those who "brought the prices of the things that were sold, and laid them down at the apostles' feet. Neither said any of them that aught of the things which he possessed was his own: but they had all things common: and distribution was made unto every man according as he had need. And the multitude of them that believed were of one heart and of one soul." [2297]I doubt not that you are aware that it is so written. Recognize, therefore, how good and how pleasant it is for brethren to dwell together in unity. Recognize the beard of Aaron; recognize the skirts of the spiritual garments. Search the Scriptures themselves, and see where those things began to be done; you will find that it was in

Jerusalem. From this skirt of the garment is woven together the whole fabric of unity throughout all nations. By this the Head entered into the garment, that Christ should be clothed with all the variety of the several nations of the earth, because in this skirt of the garment appeared the actual variety of tongues. Why, therefore, is the Head itself, whence that ointment of unity descended, that is, the spiritual fragrance of brotherly love,--why, I say, is the Head itself exposed to your resistance, while it testifies and declares that "repentance and remission of sins should be preached in His name among all nations, beginning at Jerusalem"? [2298]And by this ointment you wish the sacrament of chrism to be understood, which is indeed holy as among the class of visible signs, like baptism itself, but yet can exist even among the worst of men, wasting their life in the works of the flesh, and never destined to possess the kingdom of heaven, and having therefore nothing to do either with the beard of Aaron, or with the skirts of his garments, or with any fabric of priestly clothing. For where do you intend to place what the apostle enumerates as "the manifest works of the flesh, which," he says, "are these: fornication, uncleanness, lasciviousness, idolatry, poisonings, hatred, variance, emulations, wrath, strife, heresies, envyings, drunkenness, revellings, and such like: of the which I tell you before, as I have also told you in time past, that they which do such things shall not inherit the kingdom of God?" [2299]I put aside fornications, which are committed in secret; interpret uncleanness as you please, I am willing to put it aside as well. Let us put on one side also poisons, since no one is openly a compounder or giver of poisons. I put aside also heresies, since you will have it so. I am in doubt whether I ought to put aside idolatry, since the apostle classes with it covetousness, which is openly rife among you. However, setting aside all these, are there none among you lascivious, none covetous, none open in their indulgence of enmities, none fond of strife, or fond of emulation, wrathful, given to seditions, envious, drunken, wasting their time in revellings? Are none of such a character anointed among you? Do none die well known among you to be given to such things, or openly indulging in them? If you say there are none, I would have you consider whether you do not come under the description yourself, since you are manifestly telling lies in the desire for strife. But if you are yourself severed from men of this sort, not by bodily separation, but by dissimilarity of life, and if you behold with lamentation crowds like these around your altars, what shall we say, since they are anointed with holy oil, and yet, as the apostle assures us with the clearness of truth, shall not inherit the kingdom of God? Must we do such impious despite to the beard of Aaron and to the skirts of his garments, as to suppose that they are to be placed there? Far be that from us. Separate therefore the visible holy sacrament, which can exist both in the good and in the bad,--in the former for their reward, in the latter for judgment; separate it from the invisible unction of charity, which is the peculiar property of the good. Separate them, separate them, ay, and may God separate you from the party of Donatus, and call you back again into the Catholic Church, whence you were torn by them while yet a catechumen, to be bound by them in the bond of a deadly distinction. Now are ye not in the mountains of Zion, the dew of Hermon on the mountains of Zion, in whatever sense that be received by you; for you are not in the city upon a hill, which has this as its sure sign, that it cannot be hid. It is known therefore unto all nations. But the party of Donatus is unknown to the majority of nations, therefore is it not the true city.

[2293] Ps. cxxxiii.

[2294] Compare Tract. xv. 27 in Joannem: "Messiah was anointed. The Greek for anointed' is Christ,' the Hebrew Messiah; whence also in Phoenician we have Messe' for anoint.' For these languages, the Hebrew, Phoenician and Syrian, are closely cognate, as well as geographically bordering on each other." See also Max Müller's Lectures on the Science of Language, series I. Lect. VIII. "The ancient language of Phoenicia, to judge from inscriptions, was most closely allied to Hebrew."

[2295] Col. i. 18.

[2296] Matt. xix. 21.

[2297] Acts iv. 32-35.

[2298] Luke xxiv. 47.

[2299] Gal. v. 19-21.

Chapter 106.

240. Petilianus said: "Woe unto you, therefore, who, by doing violence to what is holy, cut away the bond of unity; whereas the prophet says, If the people shall sin, the priest shall pray for them: but if the priest shall sin, who will pray for him?'"

241. Augustin answered: I seemed too a little while ago, when we were disputing about the oil of the sinner, to anoint your forehead, in order that you might say, if you dared, whether you yourself were not a sinner. You have had the hardihood to say as much. What a portentous sin! For in that you assert yourself to be a priest, what else have you maintained by

quoting this testimony of the prophet, save that you are wholly without sin? For if you have sin, who is there that shall pray for you, according to your understanding of the words? For thus you blazon yourselves among the wretched people, quoting from the prophet: "If the people shall sin, the priest shall pray for them: but if the priest shall sin, who will pray for him? [2300] to the intent that they may believe you to be without sin, and entrust the wiping away their sins to your prayers. Truly ye are great men, exalted above your fellows, heavenly, godlike, angels indeed rather than men, who pray for the people, and will not have the people pray for you! Are you more righteous than Paul, more perfect than that great apostle, who was wont to commend himself to the prayers of those whom he taught? "Continue," he says, "in prayer, and watch in the same with thanksgiving; withal praying also for us, that God would open unto us a door of utterance, to speak the mystery of Christ, for which I am also in bonds; that I may make it manifest, as I ought to speak." [2301]See how prayer is made for an apostle, which you would have not made for a bishop. Do you perceive of how devilish a nature your pride is? Prayer is made for an apostle, that he may make manifest the mystery of Christ as he ought to speak. Accordingly, if you had a pious people under you, you ought to have exhorted them to pray for you, that you might not give utterance as you ought not. Are you more righteous than the evangelist John, who says, "If we say that we have no sin, we deceive ourselves, and the truth is not in us?" [2302] Finally, are you more righteous than Daniel, whom you yourself quoted in this very epistle, going so far as to say, "The most righteous king cast forth Daniel, as he supposed, to be devoured by wild beasts?"--a thing which he never did suppose, since he said to Daniel himself, in the most friendly spirit, as the context of the lesson shows, "Thy God, whom thou servest continually, He will deliver thee." [2303]But on this subject we have already said much. With regard to the question now before us, viz., that Daniel was most righteous, it is proved not by your testimony, though that might be sufficient for me in the argument which I hold with you, but by the testimony of the Spirit of God, speaking also by the mouth of Ezekiel, where he named three men of most eminent righteousness, Noah, Daniel, and Job, who, he said, were the only men that could be saved from a certain excessive wrath of God, which was hanging over all the rest. [2304]A man, therefore, of the highest righteousness, one of three conspicuous for righteousness, prays, and says, "While I was speaking, and praying, and confessing my sin, and the sin of my people Israel, and presenting my supplication before the Lord my God." [2305]And you say that you are without sin, because forsooth you are a priest; and if the people sin, you pray for them: but if you sin, who shall pray for you? For clearly by the impiety of such arrogance you show yourself to be unworthy of the mediation of that Priest whom the prophet would have to be understood in these words, which you do not understand. For now that no one may ask why this was said, I will explain it so far as by God's grace I shall be able. God was preparing the minds of men, by His prophet, to desire a Priest of such a sort that none should pray for Him. He was Himself prefigured in the times of the first people and the first temple, in which all things were figures for our ensample. Therefore the high priest used to enter alone into the holy of holies, that he might make supplication for the people, which did not enter with the priest into that inner sanctuary; [2306] just as our High Priest is entered into the secret places of the heavens, into that truer holy of holies, whilst we for whom He prays are still placed here. [2307]It is with this reference that the prophet says, "If the people shall sin, the priest shall pray for them: but if the priest shall sin, who will pray for him?" Seek therefore a priest of such a kind that he cannot sin, nor need that one should pray for him. And for this reason prayer is made for the apostles by the people; [2308] but for that Priest who is the Master and Lord of the apostles is prayer not made. Hear John confessing this, and saying, "My little children, these things write I unto you, that ye sin not. And if any man sin, we have an Advocate with the Father, Jesus Christ the righteous, and He is the propitiation for our sins." [2309]"We have," he says; and "for our sins." I pray you, learn humility, that you may not fall, or rather, that in time you may arise again. For had you not already fallen, you never would have used such words.

[2300] Apparently misquoted from 1 Sam. ii. 25.

[2301] Col. iv. 2-4.

[2302] 1 John i. 8.

[2303] Dan. vi. 16.

[2304] Ezek. xiv. 14.

[2305] Dan. ix. 20.

[2306] Lev. xvi.; Heb. ix. 7.

[2307] Lev. xvi.; Heb. ix. 7.

[2308] 2 Cor. i. 11.

[2309] 1 John ii. 1, 2.

Chapter 107.

242. Petilianus said: "And that none who is a layman may claim to be free from sin, they are all bound by this prohibition: Be not partakers of other men's sins.'"

243. Augustin answered: You are mistaken toto cælo, as the saying is, by reason of your pride, whilst, by reason of your humility, you are unwilling to communicate with the whole world. For, in the first place, this was not spoken to a layman; and, in the second place, you are wholly ignorant in what sense it was spoken. The apostle, writing to Timothy, gives this warning to none other than Timothy himself, to whom he says in another place, "Neglect not the gift that is in thee, which was given thee by prophecy, with the laying on of the hands of the presbytery." [2310]And by many other proofs it is made clear that he was not a layman. But in that he says, "Be not partaker of other men's sins," [2311] he means, Be not partaker voluntarily, or with consent. And hence he immediately subjoins directions how he shall obey the injunction, saying, "Keep thyself pure." For neither was Paul himself partaker of other men's sins, because he endured false brethren, over whom he groans, in bodily unity; nor did the apostles who preceded him partake of the thievery and crime of Judas, because they partook of the holy supper with him when he had already sold his Lord, and been pointed out as the traitor by that Lord.

[2310] 1 Tim. iv. 14.

[2311] 1 Tim. v. 22.

Chapter 108.

244. Petilianus said: "By this sentence, again, the apostle places in the same category those who have fellowship in the

consciousness of evil. Worthy of death,' he says, are both those who do such things, and those who consent with those that do them.'" [2312]

245. Augustin answered: I care not in what manner you have used these words, they are true. And this is the substance of the teaching of the Catholic Church, that there is a great difference between those who consent because they take pleasure in such things, and those who tolerate while they dislike them. The former make themselves chaff, while they follow the barrenness of the chaff; the latter are the grain. Let them wait for Christ, who bears the winnowing-fan, that they may be separated from the chaff.

[2312] Rom. i. 32.

Chapter 109.

246. Petilianus said: "Come therefore to the Church, all ye people, and flee the company of traditors, if you would not also perish with them. For that you may the more readily know that, while they are themselves guilty, they yet entertain an excellent opinion of our faith, let me inform you that I baptize their polluted ones; they, though may God never grant them such an opportunity, receive those who are made mine by baptism,--which certainly they would not do if they recognized any defects in our baptism. See therefore how holy that is which we give, when even our sacrilegious enemy fears to destroy it."

247. Augustin answered: Against this error I have said much already, both in this work and elsewhere. But since you think that in this sentence you have so strong a confirmation of your vain opinions, that you deemed it right to end your epistle with

these words, that they might remain as it were the fresher in the minds of your readers, I think it well to make a short reply. We recognize in heretics that baptism, which belongs not to the heretics but to Christ, in such sort as in fornicators, in unclean persons or effeminate, in idolaters, in poisoners, in those who retain enmity, in those who are fond of contention, in the credulous, in the proud, given to seditions, in the envious, in drunkards, in revellers; and in men like these we hold valid the baptism which is not theirs but Christ's. For men like these, and among them are included heretics also, none, as the apostle says, shall inherit the kingdom of heaven. [2313]Nor are they to be considered as being in the body of Christ, which is the Church, simply because they are materially partakers of the sacraments. For the sacraments indeed are holy, even in such men as these, and shall be of force in them to greater condemnation, because they handle and partake of them unworthily. But the men themselves are not within the constitution of the Church, which increases in the increase of God in its members through connection and contact with Christ. For that Church is founded on a rock, as the Lord says, "Upon this rock I will build my Church." [2314]But they build on the sand, as the same Lord says, "Every one that heareth these sayings of mine, and doeth them not, shall be likened unto a foolish man, which built his house upon the sand." [2315]But that you may not suppose that the Church which is upon a rock is in one part only of the earth, and does not extend even to its furthest boundaries, hear her voice groaning from the psalm, amid the evils of her pilgrimage. For she says, "From the end of the earth have I cried unto Thee; when my heart was distressed Thou didst lift me up upon the rock; Thou hast led me, Thou, my hope, hast become a tower of courage from the face of the enemy." [2316]See how she cries from the end of the earth. She is not therefore in Africa alone, nor only among the Africans, who send a bishop from Africa to Rome to a few Montenses, [2317] and into Spain to the house of one lady. [2318]See how she is exalted on a rock. All, therefore, are not to be deemed to be in her which build upon the sand, that is, which hear the words of Christ and do them not, even though both among us and among you they have and transmit the sacrament of baptism. See how her hope is in God the Father, the Son, and the Holy Ghost,--not in Peter or in Paul, still less in Donatus or Petilianus. What we fear, therefore, to destroy, is not yours, but Christ's; and it is holy of itself, even in sacrilegious hands. For we cannot receive those who come from you, unless we destroy in them whatsoever appertains to you. For we destroy the treachery of the deserter, not the stamp of the sovereign. Accordingly, do you yourself consider and annul what you said: "I," say you, "baptize their polluted ones; they, though may God never grant them such an opportunity, receive those who are made mine by baptism." For you do not baptize men who are infected, but you rebaptize them, so as to infect them with the fraud of your error. But we do not receive men who are made yours by baptism; but we destroy that error of yours whereby they are made yours, and we receive the baptism of Christ, by which they are baptized. Therefore it is not without significance that you introduce the words, "Though may God never grant them such an opportunity." For you said, "They, though may God never grant them such an opportunity, receive those who are made mine by baptism." For while you in your fear that we may receive your followers desire to be understood, "may God never give them the opportunity of receiving such as are mine," I suppose that, without knowing what it meant, you said, "May God never make them mine that you should receive them." For we pray that those may not be really yours who come over at the present moment to the Catholic Church. Nor do they come over so as to be ours by right of baptism, but by fellowship with us, and that with us they may belong to Christ, in virtue of their baptism.

[2313] Gal. v. 19-21.

[2314] Matt. xvi. 18.

[2315] Matt. vii. 26.

[2316] Ps. lxi. 2, 3.

[2317] That the Donatists were called at Rome Montenses, is observed by Augustin, de Hæresibus, c. lxix., and Epist. liii. 2; and before him by Optatus, Book II. c. iv. That they were also called Cutzupitani, or Cutzupitæ, we learn from the same epistle, and from his treatise de Unitate Ecclesiæ, c. iii. 6.

[2318] Lucilla.

[1967] Written probably in the beginning of 401 A.D. Some say in 402.

Book III.

In this book Augustin refutes the second letter [2319] which Petilianus wrote to him after having seen the first of Augustin's earlier books. This letter had been full of violent language; and Augustin rather shows that the arguments of Petilianus had been deficient and irrelevant, than brings forward arguments in support of his own statements.

Chapter 1.

1. Being able to read, Petilianus, I have read your letter, in which you have shown with sufficient clearness that, in supporting the party of Donatus against the Catholic Church, you have neither been able to say anything to the purpose, nor been allowed to hold your tongue. What violent emotions did you endure, what a storm of feelings surged within your heart, on reading the answer which I made, with all possible brevity and clearness, to that portion of your letter which alone at that time had come into my hands! For you saw that the truth which we maintain and defend was confirmed with such strength of argument, and illustrated with such abundant light, that you could not find anything which could be said against it, whereby the charges which we make might be refuted. You observed, also, that the attention of many who had read it was fixed on you, since they desired to know what you would say, what you would do, how you would escape from the difficulty, how you would make your way out of the strait in which the word of God had encompassed you. Hereupon you, when you ought to have shown contempt for the opinion of the foolish ones, and to have gone on to adopt sound and truthful sentiments, preferred rather to do what Scripture has foretold of men like you: "Thou hast loved evil more than good, and lying rather than to speak righteousness." [2320]Just as if I in turn were willing to recompense unto you railing for railing; in which case, what should we be but two evil speakers, so that those who read our words would either preserve their self-respect by throwing us aside with abhorrence, or eagerly devour what we wrote to gratify their malice? For my own part, since I answer every one, whether in writing or by word of mouth, even when I have been attacked with insulting accusations, in such language as the Lord puts in my mouth, restraining and crushing the stings of empty indignation in the interests of my

hearer or reader, I do not strive to prove myself superior to my adversary by abusing him, but rather to be a source of health in him by convicting him of his error.

2. For if those who take into consideration what you have written have any feelings whatsoever, how did it serve you in the cause which is at issue between us respecting the Catholic communion and the party of Donatus, that, leaving a matter which was in a certain sense of public interest, you should have been led by private animosity to attack the life of an individual with malicious revilings, just as though that individual were the question in debate? Did you think so badly, I do not say of Christians, but of the whole human race, as not to suppose that your writings might come into the hands of some prudent men, who would lay aside all thoughts of individuals like us, and inquire rather into the question which was at issue between us, and pay heed, not to who and what we were, but to what we might be able to advance in defense of the truth or against error? You should have paid respect to these men's judgment, you should have guarded yourself against their censure, lest they should think that you could find nothing to say, unless you set before yourself some one whom you might abuse by any means within your power. But one may see by the thoughtlessness and foolishness of some men, who listen eagerly to the quarrels of any learned disputants, that while they take notice of the eloquence wherewith you lavish your abuse, they do not perceive with what truth you are refuted. At the same time, I think your object partly was that I might be driven, by the necessity of defending myself, to desert the very cause which I had undertaken; and that so, while men's attention was turned to the words of opponents who were engaged not in disputation, but in quarrelling, the truth might be obscured,

which you are so afraid should come to light and be well known among men. What therefore was I to do in opposing such a design as this, except to keep strictly to my subject, neglecting rather my own defense, praying withal that no personal calumny may lead me to withdraw from it? I will exalt the house of my God, whose honor I have loved, with the tribute of a faithful servant's voice, but myself I will humiliate and hold of no account. "I had rather be a door-keeper in the house of my God, than to dwell in the tents of heretics." [2321]I will therefore turn my discourse from you, Petilianus, for a time, and direct it rather to those whom you have endeavored to turn away from me by your revilings, as though my endeavor rather were that men should be converted unto me, and not rather with me unto God.

[2320] Ps. lii. 3.

[2321] Ps. lxxxiv. 10.

Chapter 2.

3. Hear therefore, all ye who have read his revilings, what Petilianus has vented against me with more anger than consideration. To begin with, I will address you in the words of the apostle, which certainly are true, whatever I myself may be: "Let a man so account of us as of the ministers of Christ, and stewards of the mysteries of God. Moreover, it is required in stewards, that a man be found faithful. But with me it is a very small thing that I should be judged of you, or of man's judgment: yea, I judge not mine own self." With regard to what immediately follows, although I do not venture to apply to myself the words, "For I am conscious of nothing in myself," [2322] yet I say confidently in the sight of God, that I am conscious in myself of none of those charges which Petilianus

has brought against my life since the time when I was baptized in Christ; "yet am I not hereby justified, but He that judgeth me is the Lord. Therefore judge nothing before the time, until the Lord come, who both will bring to light the hidden things of darkness, and will make manifest the counsels of the hearts; and then shall every man have praise of God. And these things, brethren, I have in a figure transferred to myself; that ye might learn in us not to think of men above that which is written, that no one of you be puffed up for one against another." [2323]"Therefore let no man glory in men: for all things are yours; and ye are Christ's; and Christ is God's." [2324]Again I say, "Let no man glory in men;" nay, oftentimes I repeat it, "Let no man glory in men." If you perceive anything in us which is deserving of praise, refer it all to His praise, from whom is every good gift and every perfect gift; for it is "from above, and cometh down from the Father of lights, with whom is no variableness, neither shadow of turning." [2325]For what have we which we did not receive? and if we have received it, let us not boast as though we had not received it. [2326] And in all these things which you know to be good in us, be ye our followers, at any rate, if we are Christ's; [2327] but if, on the other hand, you either suspect, or believe, or see that any evil is in us, hold fast to that saying of the Lord's, in which you may safely resolve not to desert His Church because of men's ill deeds. Whatsoever we bid you observe, that observe and do; but whatsoever evil works you think or know to be in us, those do ye not. [2328]For this is not the time for me to justify myself before you, when I have undertaken, neglecting all considerations of self, to recommend to you what is for your salvation, that no one should make his boast of men. For "cursed be the man that trusteth in man." [2329]So long as this precept of the Lord and His apostle be adhered to and observed, the cause which I serve will be victorious, even if I myself, as my enemy would fain have thought, am faint and oppressed in my own cause. For if you cling most firmly to what I urge on you with all my might, that every one is cursed who places his trust in man, so that none should make his boast of man, then you will in no wise desert the threshing-floor of the Lord on account of the chaff which either is now being dispersed beneath the blast of the wind of pride, or will be separated by the final winnowing; [2330] nor will you fly from the great house on account of the vessels made to dishonor; [2331] nor will you quit the net through the breaches made in it because of the bad fish which are to be separated on the shore; [2332] nor will you leave the good pastures of unity, because of the goats which are to be placed on the left when the Good Shepherd shall divide the flock; [2333] nor will you separate yourselves by an impious secession, because of the mixture of the tares, from the society of that good wheat, whose source is that grain that dies and is multiplied thereby, and that grows together throughout the world until the harvest. For the field is the world,--not only Africa; and the harvest is the end of the world, [2334] --not the era of Donatus.

[2322] Nihil enim mihi conscius sum.

[2323] 1 Cor. iv. 1-6.

[2324] 1 Cor. iii. 21, 23.

[2325] Jas. i. 17.

[2326] 1 Cor. iv. 7.

[2327] 1 Cor. iv. 16.

[2328] Matt. xxiii. 3.

[2329] Jer. xvii. 5.

[2330] Matt. iii. 12.

[2331] 2 Tim. ii. 20.

[2332] Matt. xiii. 47, 48.

[2333] Matt. xxv. 32, 33.

[2334] Matt. xiii. 24-40.

Chapter 3.

4. These comparisons of the gospel you doubtless recognize. Nor can we suppose them given for any other purpose, except that no one should make his boast in man, and that no one should be puffed up for one against another, or divided one against another, saying, "I am of Paul," when certainly Paul was not crucified for you, nor were you baptized in the name of Paul, much less in that of Cæcilianus, or of any one of us, [2335] that you may learn, that so long as the chaff is being bruised with the corn, so long as the bad fishes swim together with the good in the nets of the Lord, till the time of separation shall come, it is your duty rather to endure the admixture of the bad out of consideration for the good, than to violate the principle of brotherly love towards the good from any consideration of the bad. For this admixture is not for eternity, but for time alone; nor is it spiritual, but corporal. And in this the angels will not be liable to err, when they shall collect the bad from the midst of the good, and commit them to the burning fiery furnace. For the Lord knoweth those which are His. And if a man cannot depart bodily from those who practise iniquity so long as time shall last, at any rate, let every one that nameth the name of Christ depart from iniquity itself.

[2336]For in the meantime he may separate himself from the wicked in life, and in morals, and in heart and will, and in the same respects depart from his society; and separation such as this should always be maintained. But let the separation in the body be waited for till the end of time, faithfully, patiently, bravely. In consideration of which expectation it is said, "Wait on the Lord; be of good courage, and He shall strengthen thine heart; wait, I say, upon the Lord." [2337]For the greatest palm of toleration is won by those who, among false brethren that have crept in unawares, seeking their own, and not the things of Jesus Christ, yet show that they on their part seek not to disturb the love which is not their own, but Jesus Christ's, by any turbulent or rash dissension, nor to break the unity of the Lord's net, in which are gathered together fish of every kind; till it is drawn to the shore, that is, till the end of time, by any wicked strife fostered in the spirit of pride: whilst each might think himself to be something, being really nothing, and so might lead himself astray, and wish that sufficient reason might be found for the separation of Christian peoples in the judgment of himself or of his friends, who declare that they know beyond all question certain wicked men unworthy of communion in the sacraments of the Christian religion: though whatever it may be that they know of them, they cannot persuade the universal Church, which, as it was foretold, is spread abroad throughout all nations, to give credit to their tale. And when they refuse communion with these men, as men whose character they know, they desert the unity of the Church; whereas they ought rather, if there really were in them that charity which endureth all things, themselves to bear what they know in one nation, lest they should separate themselves from the good whom they were unable throughout all nations to fill with the teaching of evil alien to them. Whence even, without discussing the case, in which they are convicted by the weightiest proofs of having uttered calumnies against the innocent, they are believed with greater probability to have invented false charges of giving up the sacred books, when they are found to have themselves committed the far more heinous crime of wicked division in the Church. For even, if whatever imputations they have cast of giving up the sacred books were true, yet they in no wise ought to have abandoned the society of Christians, who are commended by holy Scripture even to the ends of the world, on considerations which they have been familiar with, while these men showed that they were not acquainted with them.

[2335] 1 Cor. i. 12, 13.

[2336] 2 Tim. ii. 19.

[2337] Ps. xxvii. 14.

Chapter 4.

5. Nor would I therefore be understood to urge that ecclesiastical discipline should be set at naught, and that every one should be allowed to do exactly as he pleased, without any check, without a kind of healing chastisement, a lenity which should inspire fear, the severity of love. For then what will become of the precept of the apostle, "Warn them that are unruly, comfort the feeble-minded, support the weak, be patient toward all men; see that none render evil for evil unto any man?" [2338]At any rate, when he added these last words, "See that none render evil for evil unto any man," he showed with sufficient clearness that there is no rendering of evil for evil when one chastises those that are unruly, even though for the fault of unruliness be administered the punishment of

chastising. The punishment of chastising therefore is not an evil, though the fault be an evil. For indeed it is the steel, not of an enemy inflicting a wound, but of a surgeon performing an operation. Things like this are done within the Church, and that spirit of gentleness within its pale burns with zeal towards God, lest the chaste virgin which is espoused to one husband, even Christ, should in any of her members be corrupted from the simplicity which is in Christ, as Eve was beguiled by the subtilty of the serpent. [2339]Notwithstanding, far be it from the servants of the father of the family that they should be unmindful of the precept of their Lord, and be so inflamed with the fire of holy indignation against the multitude of the tares, that while they seek to gather them in bundles before the time, the wheat should be rooted up together with them. And of this sin these men would be held to be guilty, even though they showed that those were true charges which they brought against the traditors whom they accused; because they separated themselves in a spirit of impious presumption, not only from the wicked, whose society they professed to be avoiding, but also from the good and faithful in all nations of the world, to whom they could not prove the truth of what they said they knew; and with themselves they drew away into the same destruction many others over whom they had some slight authority, and who were not wise enough to understand that the unity of the Church dispersed throughout the world was on no account to be forsaken for other men's sins. So that, even though they themselves knew that they were pressing true charges against certain of their neighbors, yet in this way a weak brother, for whom Christ died, was perishing through their knowledge; [2340] whilst, being offended at other men's sins, he was destroying in himself the blessing of peace which he had with the good brethren, who partly had never heard such charges, partly had shrunk from giving hasty credence to what was neither discussed nor proved, partly, in the peaceful spirit of humility, had left these charges, whatsoever they might be, to the cognizance of the judges of the Church, to whom the whole matter had been referred, across the sea.

[2338] 1 Thess. v. 14, 15.

[2339] 2 Cor. xi. 2, 3.

[2340] 1 Cor. viii. 11.

Chapter 5.

6. Do you, therefore, holy scions of our one Catholic mother, beware with all the watchfulness of which you are capable, in due submission to the Lord, of the example of crime and error such as this. With however great light of learning and of reputation he may shine, however much he may boast himself to be a precious stone, who endeavors to lead you after him, remember always that that brave woman who alone is lovely only to her husband, whom holy Scripture portrays to us in the last chapter of the Book of Proverbs, is more precious than any precious stones. Let no one say, I will follow such an one, for it was even he that made me a Christian; or, I will follow such an one, for it was even he that baptized me. For "neither is he that planteth anything, neither he that watereth, but God that giveth the increase." [2341]And "God is love; and he that dwelleth in love, dwelleth in God, and God in him." [2342]No one also that preaches the name of Christ, and handles or administers the sacrament of Christ, is to be followed in opposition to the unity of Christ. "Let every man prove his own work; and then shall he have rejoicing in himself alone, and not in another. For every man shall bear his own burden,"

[2343] --the burden, that is, of rendering an account; for "every one of shall give an account of himself. Let us not therefore judge one another any more." [2344]For, so far as relates to the burdens of mutual love, "bear ye one another's burdens, and so fulfill the law of Christ. For if a man think himself to be something, when he is nothing, he deceiveth himself." [2345]Let us therefore "forbear one another in love, endeavoring to keep the unity of the Spirit in the bond of peace;" [2346] for no one who gathers outside that peace is gathering with Christ; but "he that gathering not with Him scattereth abroad." [2347]

[2341] 1 Cor. iii. 7.

[2342] 1 John iv. 16.

[2343] Gal. vi. 4, 5.

[2344] Rom. xiv. 12, 13.

[2345] Gal. vi. 2, 3.

[2346] Eph. iv. 2, 3.

[2347] Matt. xii. 30.

Chapter 6.

7. Furthermore, whether concerning Christ, or concerning His Church, or any other matter whatsoever which is connected with your faith and life, to say nothing of ourselves, who are by no means to be compared with him who said, "Though we," at any rate, as he went on to say, "Though an angel from heaven preach any other gospel unto you than that which" ye have received in the lawful and evangelical Scripture, "let him be

accursed." [2348]While carrying out this principle of action in our dealings with you, and with all whom we desire to gain in Christ, and, amongst other things, while preaching the holy Church which we read of as promised in the epistles of God, and see to be fulfilled according to the promises in all nations of the world, we have earned, not the rendering of thanks, but the flames of hatred, from those whom we desire to have attracted into His most peaceful bosom; as though we had bound them fast in that party for which they cannot find any defense that they should make; or as though we so long before had given injunctions to prophets and apostles that they should insert in their books no proofs by which it might be shown that the party of Donatus was the Church of Christ. And we indeed, dear brethren, when we hear false charges brought against us by those whom we have offended by preaching the eloquence of truth, and confuting the vanity of error, have, as you know, the most abundant consolation. For if, in the matters which they lay to my charge, the testimony of my conscience does not stand against me in the sight of God, where no mortal eye can reach, not only ought I not to be cast down, but I should even rejoice and be exceeding glad, for great is my reward in heaven. [2349]For in fact I ought to consider, not how bitter, but how false is what I hear, and how true He is in defense of whose name I am exposed to it, and to whom it is said, "Thy name is as ointment poured forth." [2350]And deservedly does it smell sweet in all nations, though those who speak evil of us endeavor to confine its fragrance within one corner of Africa. Why therefore should we take amiss that we are reviled by men who thus detract from the glory of Christ, whose party and schism find offense in what was foretold so long before of His ascent into the heavens, and of the pouring forth of His name, as of the savor of ointment:

"Be Thou exalted, O God, above the heavens: let Thy glory be above all the earth"? [2351]

[2348] Gal. i. 8.

[2349] Matt. v. 12.

[2350] Cant. i. 3.

[2351] Ps. lvii. 11.

Chapter 7.

8. Whilst we bear the testimony of God to this and the like effect against the vain speaking of men, we are forced to undergo bitter insults from the enemies of the glory of Christ. Let them say what they will, whilst He exhorts us, saying, "Blessed are they which are persecuted for righteousness' sake: for theirs is the kingdom of heaven. Blessed are ye, when men shall revile you, and persecute you, and shall say all manner of evil against you falsely for my sake." What He says in the first instance, "for righteousness' sake," He has repeated in the words that He uses afterwards, "for my sake;" seeing that He "is made unto us wisdom, and righteousness, and sanctification, and redemption, that, according as it is written, He that glorieth, let him glory in the Lord." [2352]And when He says, "Rejoice, and be exceeding glad, for great is your reward in heaven," [2353] if I hold in a good conscience what is said "for righteousness' sake," and "for my sake," whosoever willfully detracts from my reputation is against his will contributing to my reward. For neither did He only instruct me by His word, without also confirming me by His example. Follow the faith of the holy Scriptures, and you will find that Christ rose from the dead, ascended into heaven, sitteth at the right hand of the

Father. Follow the charges brought by His enemies, and you will presently believe that He was stolen from the sepulchre by His disciples. Why then should we, while defending His house to the best of the abilities given us by God, expect to meet with any other treatment from His enemies? "If they have called the Master of the house Beelzebub, how much more shall they call them of His household?" [2354]If, therefore, we suffer, we shall also reign with Him. But if it be not only the wrath of the accuser that strikes the ear, but also the truth of the accusation that stings the conscience, what does it profit me if the whole world were to exalt me with perpetual praise? So neither the eulogy of him who praises has power to heal a guilty conscience, nor does the insult of him, who reviles wound the good conscience. Nor, however, is your hope which is in the Lord deceived, even though we chance to be in secret what our enemies wish us to be thought; for you have not placed your hope in us, nor have you ever heard from us any doctrine of the kind. You therefore are safe, whatever we may be, who have learned to say, "I have trusted in the Lord; therefore I shall not slide;" [2355] and "In God have I put my trust: I will not be afraid what man can do unto me." [2356]And to those who endeavor to lead you astray to the earthly heights of proud men, you know how to answer, "In the Lord put I my trust: how say ye to my soul, Flee as a bird to your mountain?" [2357]

[2352] 1 Cor. i. 30, 31.

[2353] Matt. v. 10-12.

[2354] Matt. x. 25.

[2355] Ps. xxvi. 1.

[2356] Ps. lvi. 11.

[2357] Ps. xi. 1.

Chapter 8.

9. Nor is it only you that are safe, whatever we may be, because you are satisfied with the very truth of Christ which is in us, in so far as it is preached through us, and everywhere throughout the world, and because, listening to it willingly, so far as it is set forth by the humble ministry of our tongue, you also think well and kindly of us,--for so your hope is in Him whom we preach to you out of His loving-kindness, which extends over you,-- but further, all of you, who also received the sacrament of holy baptism from our ministering, may well rejoice in the same security, seeing that you were baptized, not into us, but into Christ. You did not therefore put on us, but Christ; nor did I ask you whether you were converted unto me, but unto the living God; nor whether you believed in me, but in the Father, the Son, and the Holy Ghost. But if you answered my question with truthful hearts, you were placed in a state of salvation, not by the putting away of the filth of the flesh, but by the answer of a good conscience towards God; [2358] not by a fellow-servant, but by the Lord; not by the herald, but by the judge. For it is not true, as Petilianus inconsiderately said, that "the conscience of the giver," or, as he added "the conscience of him who gives in holiness is what we look for to wash the conscience of the recipient." For when something is given that is of God, it is given in holiness, even by a conscience which is not holy. And certainly it is beyond the power of the recipient to discern whether the said conscience is holy or not holy; but that which is given he can discern with clearness. That which is known to Him who is ever holy is received with perfect safety, whatever be the character of the minister at whose hands it is received. For unless the words which are spoken from Moses'

seat were necessarily holy, He that is the Truth would never have said, "Whatsoever they bid you observe, that observe and do." But if the men who uttered holy words were themselves holy, He would not have said, "Do not ye after their works: for they say, and do not." [2359]For it is true that in no way do men gather grapes of thorns, because grapes never spring from the root of a thorn; but when the shoot of the vine has entwined itself in a thorn hedge, the fruit which hangs upon it is not therefore looked upon with dread, but the thorn is avoided, while the grape is plucked.

[2358] 1 Pet. iii. 21.

[2359] Matt. xxiii. 2, 3.

Chapter 9.

10. Therefore, as I have often said before, and am desirous to bring home to you, whatsoever we may be, you are safe, who have God for your Father and His Church for your mother. For although the goats may feed in company with the sheep, yet they shall not stand on the right hand; although the chaff may be bruised together with the wheat, it shall not be gathered into the barn; although the bad fish may swim in company with the good within the Lord's nets, they shall not be gathered into vessels. Let no man make his boast even in a good man: let no man shun the good gifts of God even in a bad man.

Chapter 10.

11. Let these things suffice you, my beloved Christian brethren of the Catholic Church, so far as the present business is concerned; and if you hold fast to this in Catholic affection, so long as you are one sure flock of the one Shepherd, I am not

too much concerned with the abuse that any enemy may lavish on me, your partner in the flock, or, at any rate, your watch-dog, so long as he compels me to bark rather in your defense than in my own. And yet, if it were necessary for the cause that I should enter on my own defense, I should do so with the greatest brevity and the greatest ease, joining freely with all men in condemning and bearing witness against the whole period of my life before I received the baptism of Christ, so far as relates to my evil passions and my errors, lest, in defending that period, I should seem to be seeking my own glory, not His, who by His grace delivered me even from myself. Wherefore, when I hear that life of mine abused, in whatever spirit he may be acting who abuses it, I am not so thankless as to be grieved. However much he finds fault with any vice of mine, I praise him in the same degree as my physician. Why then should I disturb myself about defending those past and obsolete evils in my life, in respect of which, though Petilianus has said much that is false, he has yet left more that is true unsaid? But concerning that period of my life which is subsequent to my baptism, to you who know me I speak unnecessarily in telling of those things which might be known to all mankind; but those who know me not ought not to act with such unfairness towards me as to believe Petilianus rather than you concerning me. For if one should not give credence to the panegyrics of a friend, neither should one believe the detraction of an enemy. There remain, therefore, those things which are hidden in a man, in which conscience alone can bear testimony, which cannot be a witness before men. Herein Petilianus says that I am a Manichæan, speaking of the conscience of another man; I, speaking of my own conscience, aver that I am not. Choose which of us you had sooner believe. Notwithstanding, since there is not any need even of this short and easy defense on my part, where the question at issue is not concerning the merits of any individual, whoever he may be, but concerning the truth [2360] of the whole Church, I have more also to say to any of you, who, being of the party of Donatus, have read the evil words which Petilianus has written about me, which I should not have heard from him if I had had no care about the loss of your salvation; but then I should have been wanting in the bowels of Christian love.

[2360] Some editors have "unitate," but Amerbach and the Mss. "veritate;" and this is supported by c. 24, 28 below: "De ecclesiæ vel baptismi veritate;" and c. 13, 22 of the treatise de Unico Baptismo: "Ambulantibus in ecclesiæ veritate."

Chapter 11.

12. What wonder is it then, if, when I draw in the grain that has been shaken forth from the threshing-floor of the Lord, together with the soil and chaff, I suffer injury from the dust that rebounds against me; or that, when I am diligently seeking after the lost sheep of my Lord, I am torn by the briars of thorny tongues? I entreat you, lay aside for a time all considerations of party feeling, and judge with some degree of fairness between Petilianus and myself. I am desirous that you should be acquainted with the cause of the Church; he, that you should be familiar with mine. For what other reason than because he dares not bid you disbelieve my witnesses, whom I am constantly citing in the cause of the Church,--for they are prophets and apostles, and Christ Himself, the Lord of prophets and apostles,--whereas you easily give him credit in whatever he may choose to say concerning me, a man against a man, and one, moreover, of your own party against a stranger to you? And should I adduce any witnesses to my life, however

important the thing he might say would be, it would not be believed by them, and of this Petilianus would quickly persuade you; especially when any one would bring forward a plea for me. Since he is an enemy of the Donatist party, in virtue of this fact he would also continually be considered your enemy. Petilianus therefore reigns supreme. Whenever he aims any abuse at me, of whatever character it may be, you all applaud and shout assent. This cause he has found wherein the victory is possible for him, but only with you for judges. He will seek for neither proof nor witness; for all that he has to prove in his words is this, that he lavishes most copious abuse on one whom you most cordially hate. For whereas, when the testimony of divine Scripture is quoted in such abundance and in such express terms in favor of the Catholic Church, he remains silent amidst your grief, he has chosen for himself a subject on which he may speak amidst applause from you; and though really conquered, yet, pretending that he stands unmoved, he may make statements concerning me like this, and even worse than this. It is enough for me, [2361] in respect of the cause which I am now pleading, that whatsoever I may be found to be, yet the Church for which I speak unconquered.

[2361] Ubi vobis faventibus loquatur, et victus verum simulans statum, talia vel etiam sceleratiori dictat in me. Mihi sat est ad rem, etc. Morel (Elem. Crit. pp. 326-328) suggests as an improvement. "Ubi vobis faventibus loquatur et victus. Verum si millies tantum talia vel etiam sceleratiora dicat in me, mihi sat est", etc.,-- "on which he may speak amidst applause from you, even when beaten. But if he were to make a thousand times as many statements concerning me," etc.

Chapter 12.

13. For I am a man of the threshing-floor of Christ: if a bad man, then part of the chaff; if good, then of the grain. The winnowing-fan of this threshing-floor is not the tongue of Petilianus; and hereby, whatever evil he may have uttered, even with truth, against the chaff of this threshing-floor, this in no way prejudices its grain. But whereinsoever he has cast any revilings or calumnies against the grain itself, its faith is tried on earth, and its reward increased in the heavens. For where men are holy servants of the Lord, and are fighting with holiness for God, not against Petilianus, or any flesh and blood like him, but against principalities and powers, and the rulers of the darkness of this world, [2362] such as are all enemies of the truth, to whom I would that we could say, "Ye were sometime darkness, but now are ye light in the Lord," [2363] --where the servants of God, I say, are waging such a war as this, then all the calumnious revilings that are uttered by their enemies, which cause an evil report among the malicious and those that are rash in believing, are weapons on the left hand: it is with such as these that even the devil is defeated. For when we are tried by good report, whether we resist the exaltation of ourselves to pride, and are tried by evil report, whether we love even those very enemies by whom it is invented against us, then we overcome the devil by the armor of righteousness on the right hand and on the left. For when the apostle had used the expression, "By the armor of righteousness on the right hand and on the left," he at once goes on to say, as if in explanation of the terms, "By honor and dishonor, by evil report and good report," [2364] and so forth,--reckoning honor and good report among the armor on the right hand, dishonor and evil report among that upon the left.

[2362] Eph. vi. 12.

[2363] Eph. v. 8.

[2364] 2 Cor. vi. 7, 8.

Chapter 13.

14. If, therefore, I am a servant of the Lord, and a soldier that is not reprobate, with whatever eloquence Petilianus stands forth reviling me, ought I in any way to be annoyed that he has been appointed for me as a most accomplished craftsman of the armor on the left? It is necessary that I should fight in this armor as skillfully as possible in defence of my Lord, and should smite with it the enemy against whom I wage an unseen fight, who in all cunning strives and endeavors, with the most perverse and ancient craftiness, that this should lead me to hate Petilianus, and so be unable to fulfill the command which Christ has given, that we should "love our enemies." [2365]But from this may I be saved by the mercy of Him who loved me, and gave Himself for me, so that, as He hung upon the cross, He said, "Father, forgive them; for they know not what they do;" [2366] and so taught me to say of Petilianus and all other enemies of mine like him "Father, forgive them; for they know not what they do.'

[2365] Luke vi. 35.

[2366] Luke xxiii. 34.

Chapter 14.

15. Furthermore, if I have obtained from you, in accordance with my earnest endeavors, that, laying aside from your minds all prejudice of party, you should be impartial judges between Petilianus and myself, I will show to you that he has not replied to what I wrote, that you may understand that he has been

compelled by lack of truth to abandon the dispute, and also see what revilings he has allowed himself to utter against the man who so conducted it that he had no reply to make. And yet what I am going to say displays itself with such manifest clearness, that, even though your minds were estranged from me by party prejudice and personal hatred, yet, if you would only read what is written on both sides, you could not but confess among yourselves, in your inmost hearts, that I have spoken truth.

16. For, in replying to the former part of his writings, which then alone had come into my hands, without taking any notice of his wordy and sacrilegious revilings, where he says, "Let those men cast in our teeth our twice-repeated baptism, who, under the name of baptism, have polluted their souls with a guilty washing; whom I hold to be so obscene that no manner of filth is less clean than they; whose lot it has been, by a perversion of cleanliness, to be defiled by the water wherein they washed;" I thought that what follows was worthy of discussion and refutation, where he says, "For what we look for is the conscience of the giver, that the conscience of the recipient may thereby be cleansed;" and I asked what means were to be found for cleansing one who receives baptism when the conscience of the giver is polluted, without the knowledge of him who is to receive the sacrament at his hands. [2367]

[2367] See above, Book I. c. 1, 2.

Chapter 15.

17. Read now the most profuse revilings which he has poured forth whilst puffed up with indignation against me, and see whether he has given me any answer, when I ask what means are to be found for cleansing one who receives baptism when

the conscience of the giver is polluted, without the knowledge of him who receives the sacrament at his hands. I beg of you to search minutely, to examine every page, to reckon every line, to ponder every word, to sift the meaning of each syllable, and tell me, if you can discover it, where he has made answer to the question, What means are to be found for cleansing the conscience of the recipient who is unaware that the conscience of the giver is polluted?

18. For how did it bear upon the point that he added a phrase which he said was suppressed by me, maintaining that he had written in the following terms: "The conscience of him who gives in holiness is what we look for to cleanse the conscience of the recipient?" For to prove to you that it was not suppressed by me, its addition in no way hinders my inquiry, or makes up the deficiency which was found in him. For in the face of those very words I ask again, and I beg of you to see whether he has given any answer, If "the conscience of him who gives in holiness is what we look for to cleanse the conscience of the recipient," what means are to be found for cleansing the conscience of the recipient when the conscience of the giver is stained with guilt, without the knowledge of him who is to receive the sacrament at his hands? I insist upon an answer being given to this. Do not allow that any one should be prejudiced by revilings irrelevant to the matter in hand. If the conscience of him who gives in holiness is what we look for,--observe that I do not say "the conscience of him who gives," but that I added the words, "of him who gives in holiness,"--if the conscience, then, of him who gives in holiness is what we look for, what means are to be found for cleansing one who receives baptism when the conscience of the giver is

polluted, without the knowledge of him who is to receive the sacrament at his hands?

Chapter 16.

19. Let him go now, and with panting lungs and swollen throat find fault with me as a mere dialectician. Nay, let him summon, not me, but the science of dialectics itself, to the bar of popular opinion as a forger of lies, and let him open his mouth to its widest against it, with all the noisiest uproar of a special pleader. Let him say whatever he pleases before the inexperienced, that so the learned may be moved to wrath, while the ignorant are deceived. Let him call me, in virtue of my rhetoric, by the name of the orator Tertullus, by whom Paul was accused; [2368] and let him give himself the name of Advocate, [2369] in virtue of the pleading in which he boasts his former power, and for this reason delude himself with the notion that he is, or rather was, a namesake of the Holy Ghost. Let him, with all my heart, exaggerate the foulness of the Manichæans, and endeavor to divert it on to me by his barking. Let him quote all the exploits of those who have been condemned, whether known or unknown to me; and let him turn into the calumnious imputation of a prejudged crime, by some new right entirely his own, the fact that a former friend of mine there named me in my absence to the better securing of his own defense. Let him read the titles that have been placed upon my letters by himself or by his friends, as suited their pleasure, and boast that he has, as it were, involved me hopelessly in their expressions. When I acknowledge certain eulogies of bread, uttered in all simplicity and merriment, let him take away my character with the absurd imputations of poisonous baseness and madness. And let him entertain so bad an opinion of your understanding, as to imagine that he can be

believed when he declares that pernicious love-charms were given to a woman, not only with the knowledge, but actually with the complicity [2370] of her husband. What the man who was afterwards to ordain me bishop [2371] wrote about me in anger, while I was as yet a priest, he may freely seek to use as evidence against me. That the same man sought and obtained forgiveness from a holy Council for the wrong he thus had done me, he is equally at liberty to ignore as being in my favor,--being either so ignorant or so forgetful of Christian gentleness, and the commandment of the gospel, that he brings as an accusation against a brother what is wholly unknown to that brother himself, as he humbly entreats that pardon may in kindness be extended to him.

[2368] Acts xxiv. 1.

[2369] Paracletus.

[2370] "Favente," which is wanting in the Mss., was inserted in the margin by Erasmus, as being needed to complete the sense.

[2371] Megalius, bishop of Calama, primate of Numidia, was the bishop who ordained Augustin, as we find in c. viii. of his life by Possidius. Augustin makes further reply to the same calumny, which was gathered from a letter of Megalius, in Contra Cresconium, Book III. c. 80, 92, and Book IV. c. 64, 78, 79.

Chapter 17.

20. Let him further go on, in his discourse of many but manifestly empty words, to matters of which he is wholly ignorant, or in which rather he abuses the ignorance of the mass of those who hear him, and from the confession of a

certain woman, that she had called herself a catechumen of the Manichæans, being already a full member of the Catholic Church, let him say or write what he pleases concerning their baptism,--not knowing, or pretending not to know, that the name of catechumen is not bestowed among them upon persons to denote that they are at some future time to be baptized, but that this name is given to such as are also called Hearers, on the supposition that they cannot observe what are considered the higher and greater commandments, which are observed by those whom they think right to distinguish and honor by the name of Elect. Let him also maintain with wonderful rashness, either as himself deceived or as seeking to deceive, that I was a presbyter among the Manichæans. Let him set forth and refute, in whatever sense seems good to him, the words of the third book of my Confessions, which, both in themselves, and from much that I have said before and since, are perfectly clear to all who read them. Lastly, let him triumph in my stealing his words, because I have suppressed two of them, as though the victory were his upon their restoration.

Chapter 18.

21. Certainly in all these things, as you can learn or refresh your memory by reading his letter, he has given free scope to the impulse of his tongue, with all the license of boasting which he chose to use, but nowhere has he told us where means are to be found for cleansing the conscience of the recipient, when that of the giver has been stained with sin without his knowing it. But amid all his noise, and after all his noise, serious as it is, too terrible as he himself supposes it to be, I deliberately, as it is said, and to the purpose, [2372] ask this question once again: If the conscience of him who gives in holiness is what we look for, what means are to be found for cleansing one who receives

baptism without knowing that the conscience of the giver is stained with sin? And throughout his whole epistle I find nothing said in answer to this question.

[2372] Lente, ut dicitur, et bene. Morel (Element. Crit. pp. 140, 141) suggests as an amendment, "lene," as suiting better with "lente."

Chapter 19.

22. For perhaps some one of you will say to me, All these things which he said against you he wished to have force for this purpose, that he might take away your character, and through you the character of those with whom you hold communion, that neither they themselves, nor those whom you endeavor to bring over to your communion, may hold you to be of any further importance. But, in deciding whether he has given no answer to the words of your epistle, we must look at them in the light of the passage in which he proposed them for consideration. Let us then do so: let us look at his writings in the light of that very passage. Passing over, therefore, the passage in which I sought to introduce my subject to the reader, and to ignore those few prefatory words of his, which were rather insulting than revelant to the subject under discussion, I go on to say, "He says, What we look for is the conscience of the giver, to cleanse that of the recipient.' But supposing the conscience of the giver is concealed from view, and perhaps defiled with sin, how will it be able to cleanse the conscience of the recipient, if, as he says, what we look for is the conscience of the giver, to cleanse that of the recipient?' For if he should say that it makes no matter to the recipient what amount of evil may be concealed from view in the conscience of the giver, perhaps that ignorance may have such

a degree of efficacy as this, that a man cannot be defiled by the guilt of the conscience of him from whom he receives baptism, so long as he is unaware of it. Let it then be granted that the guilty conscience of his neighbor cannot defile a man so long as he is unaware of it; but is it therefore clear that it can further cleanse him from his own guilt? Whence then is a man to be cleansed who receives baptism, when the conscience of the giver is polluted without the knowledge of him who is to receive it, especially when he goes on to say, For he who receives faith from the faithless receives not faith but guilt?'" [2373]

[2373] See Book I. c. 1, 2, c. 2, 3.

Chapter 20.

23. All these statements in my letter Petilianus set before himself for refutation. Let us see, therefore, whether he has refuted them; whether he has made any answer to them at all. For I add the words which he calumniously accuses me of having suppressed, and, having done so, I ask him again the same question in an even shorter form; for by adding these two words he has helped me much in shortening this proposition. If the conscience of him who gives in holiness is what we look for to cleanse that of the recipient, and if he who has received his faith wittingly from one that is faithless, receives not faith but guilt, where shall we find means to cleanse the conscience of the recipient, when he has not known that the conscience of the giver is stained with guilt, and when he receives his faith unwittingly from one that is faithless? I ask, where shall we find means to cleanse it? Let him tell us; let him not pass off into another subject; let him not cast a mist over the eyes of the inexperienced. To end with, at any rate, after many tortuous

circumlocutions have been interposed and thoroughly worked out, let him at last tell us where we shall find means to cleanse the conscience of the recipient when the stains of guilt in the conscience of the faithless baptizer are concealed from view, if the conscience of him who gives in holiness is what we look for to cleanse that of the recipient, and if he who has received his faith wittingly from one that is faithless, receives not faith but guilt? For the man in question receives it from a faithless man who has not the conscience of one who gives in holiness, but a conscience stained with guilt, and veiled from view. Where then shall we find means to cleanse his conscience? whence then does he receive his faith? For if he is neither then cleansed, nor then receives faith, when the faithlessness and guilt of the baptizer are concealed, why, when these are afterwards brought to light and condemned, is he not then baptized afresh, that he may be cleansed and receive faith? But if, while the faithlessness and guilt of the other are concealed, he is cleansed and does receive faith, whence does he obtain his cleansing, whence does he receive faith, when there is not the conscience of one that gives in holiness to cleanse the conscience of the recipient? Let him tell us this; let him make reply to this: Whence does he obtain his cleansing, whence does he receive faith, if the conscience of him that gives in holiness is what we look for to cleanse the conscience of the recipient, seeing that this does not exist, when the baptizer conceals his character of faithlessness and guilt? To this no answer has been made whatever.

Chapter 21.

24. But see, when he is reduced to straits in the argument, he again makes an attack on me full of mist and wind, that the calm clearness of the truth may be obscured; and through the

extremity of his want he becomes full of resources, shown not in saying what is true, but in unbought empty revilings. Hold fast, with the keenest attention and utmost perseverance, what he ought to answer,--that is, where means may be found for cleansing the conscience of the recipient when the stains in that of the giver are concealed,--lest possibly the blast of his eloquence should wrest this from your hands, and you in turn should be carried away by the dark tempest of his turgid discourse, so as wholly to fail in seeing whence he has digressed, and to what point he should return; and see where the man can wander, whilst he cannot stand in the matter which he has undertaken. For see how much he says, through having nothing that he ought to say. He says "that I slide in slippery places, but am held up; that I neither destroy nor confirm the objections that I make; that I devise uncertain things in the place of certainty; that I do not permit my readers to believe what is true, but cause them to look with increased suspicion on what is doubtful." He says "that I have the accursed talents of the Academic philosopher Carneades." [2374]He endeavors to insinuate what the Academics think of the falseness or the falsehood of human sensation, showing in this also that he is wholly without knowledge of what he says. He declares that "it is said by them that snow is black, whereas it is white; and that silver is black; and that a tower is round, or free from projections, when it is really angular; that an oar is broken in the water, while it is whole." [2375] And all this because, when he had said that "the conscience of him that gives," or "of him that gives in holiness, is what we look for to cleanse the conscience of the recipient," I said in reply, What if the conscience of the giver be hidden from sight, and possibly be stained with guilt? Here you have his black snow, and black silver, and his tower round instead of angular, and the oar in the water broken while yet whole, in that I suggested a state of the case which might be conceived, and could not really exist, that the conscience of the giver might be hidden from view, and possibly might be stained with guilt!

25. Then he continues in the same strain, and cries out: "What is that what if? what is that possibly? except the uncertain and wavering hesitation of one who doubts, of whom your poet says'--

What if I now return to those who say, What if the sky should fall?'" [2376]

Does he mean that when I said, What if the conscience of the giver be hidden from sight, and possibly be stained with guilt? that it is much the same as if I had said, What if the sky should fall? There certainly is the phrase What if, because it is possible that it may be hidden from view, and it is possible that it may not. For when it is not known what the giver is thinking of, or what crime he has committed, then his conscience is certainly hidden from the view of the recipient; but when his sin is plainly manifest, then it is not hidden. I used the expression, And possibly may be stained with guilt, because it is possible that it may be hidden from view and yet be pure; and again, it is possible that it may be hidden from view and be stained with guilt. This is the meaning of the What if; this the meaning of the Possibly. Is this at all like "What if the sky should fall?" O how often have men been convicted, how often have they confessed themselves that they had consciences stained with guilt and adultery, whilst men were unwittingly baptized by them after they were degraded by the sin subsequently brought to light, and yet the sky did not fall! What have we here to do with Pilus and Furius, [2377] who defended the cause of injustice against justice? What have we here to do with the atheist Diagoras, [2378] who denied that there was any God, so that he would seem to be the man of whom the prophet spoke beforehand, "The fool hath said in his heart there is no God?" [2379] What have we here to do with these? Why were their names brought in, except that they might make a diversion in favor of a man who had nothing to say? that while he is at any rate saying something, though needlessly, about these, the matter in hand may seem to be progressing, and an answer may be supposed to be made to a question which remains without an answer?

[2374] Lactantius, Divin. Instit. Book V. c. xv., tells us of the talents of Carneades, recording that when he was sent on an embassy to Rome by the Athenians, he spoke there first in defense of justice, and then on the following day in opposition to it; and that he was in the habit of speaking with such force on either side, as to be able to refute any arguments advanced by anybody else.

[2375] Ter. Heaut. act. IV. scen. iii. vers. 41.

[2376] Ter. Heaut. act. IV. scen. iii. vers. 41.

[2377] In de Civ. Dei, Book II. c. xxi., Augustin mentions L. Furius Philus, one of the interlocutors in Cicero's Laelius, as maintaining this same view. From the similarity of the name, it has been thought that here Furius and Pilus are only one man.

[2378] The Mss. here and below have Protagoras. Both were atheists, according to Cicero, Nat. Deor. I. i. 2, and Lactantius Divin. Instit. I. c. ii.; de Ira Dei, c. ix.

[2379] Ps. xiv. 1.

Chapter 22.

26. Lastly, if these two or three words, What if, and Possibly, are so absolutely intolerable, that on their account we should have aroused from their long sleep the Academics, and Carneades, and Pilus, and Furius, and Diagoras, and black snow, and the falling of the sky, and everything else that is equally senseless and absurd, let them be removed from our argument. For, as a matter of fact, it is by no means impossible to express what we desire to say without them. There is quite sufficient for our purpose in what is found a little later, and has been introduced by himself from my letter: "By what means then is he to be cleansed who receives baptism when the conscience of the giver is polluted, and that without the knowledge of him who is to receive the sacrament?" [2380]Do you acknowledge that here there is no What if, no Possibly? Well then, let an answer be given. Give close heed, lest he be found to answer this in what follows. "But," says he, "I bind you in your cavilling to the faith of believing, that you may not wander further from it. Why do you turn away your life from errors by arguments of folly? Why do you disturb the system of belief in respect of matters without reason? By this one word I bind and convince you." It was Petilianus that said this, not I. These words are from the letter of Petilianus; but from that letter, to which I just now added the two words which he accuses me of having suppressed, showing that, notwithstanding their addition, the pertinency of my question, to which he makes no answer, remains with greater brevity and simplicity. It is beyond dispute that these two words are, In holiness, and Wittingly: so that it should not be, "The conscience of him who gives," but "The conscience of him who gives in holiness;" and that it should not be, "He who has

received his faith from one that is faithless," but "He who has wittingly received his faith from one that is faithless." And yet I had not really suppressed these words; but I had not found them in the copy which was placed in my hands. It is possible enough that it was incorrect; nor indeed is it wholly beyond the possibility of belief that even by this suggestion Academic grudge should be roused against me, and that it should be asserted that, in declaring the copy to be incorrect, I had said much the same sort of thing as if I had declared that snow was black. For why should I repay in kind his rash suggestion, and say that, though he pretends that I suppressed the words, he really added them afterwards himself, since the copy, which is not angry, can confirm that mark of incorrectness, without any abusive rashness on my part?

[2380] See Book I. c. 2, 3.

Chapter 23.

27. And, in the first place, with regard to that first expression, "Of him who gives in holiness," it does not interfere in the least with my inquiry, by which he is so much distressed, whether I use the expression, "If the conscience of him that gives is what we look for," or the fuller phrase, "If the conscience of him that gives in holiness is what we look for, to cleanse the conscience of the recipient," by what means then is he to be cleansed who receives baptism if the conscience of the giver is polluted, without the knowledge of him who is to receive the sacrament? And with regard to the other word that is added, "wittingly," so that the sentence should not run, "He who has received his faith from one that is faithless," but "He who has wittingly received his faith from one that is faithless, receives not faith but guilt," I confess that I had said some things as

though the word were absent, but I can easily afford to do without them; for they caused more hindrance to the facility of my argument than they gave assistance to its power. For how much more readily, how much more plainly and shortly, can I put the question thus: "If the conscience of him who gives in holiness is what we look for to cleanse the conscience of the recipient," and "if he who has wittingly received his faith from one that is faithless receives not faith but guilt," by what means is he cleansed, from whom the stain on the conscience of him who gives, but not in holiness, is hidden? and whence does he receive true faith, who is baptized unwittingly by one that is faithless? Let it be declared whence this shall be, and then the whole theory of baptism will be disclosed; then all that is matter of investigation will be brought to light,--but only if it be declared, not if the time be consumed in evil-speaking.

Chapter 24.

28. Whatever, therefore, he finds in these two words,--whether he brings calumnious accusations about their suppression, or boasts of their being added,--you perceive that it in no way hinders my question, to which he can find no answer that he can make; and therefore, not wishing to remain silent, he takes the opportunity of making an attack upon my character,-- retiring, I should have said, from the discussion, except that he had never entered on it. For just as though the question were about me, and not about the truth of the Church, or of baptism, therefore he says that I, by suppressing these two words, have argued as though it were no stumblingblock in the way of my conscience, that I have ignored what he calls the sacrilegious conscience of him who polluted me. But if this were so, the addition of the word "wittingly," which is thus introduced, would be in my favor, and its suppression would

tell against me. For if I had wished that my defense should be urged on the ground that I should be supposed to have been unacquainted with the conscience of the man that baptized me, then I would accept Petilianus as having spoken in my behalf, since he does not say in general terms, "He that has received his faith from one that is faithless," but "He that has wittingly received his faith from one that is faithless, receives not faith but guilt;" so that hence I might boast that I had received not guilt, but faith, since I could say I did not receive it wittingly from one that was faithless, but was unacquainted with the conscience of him that gave it. See, therefore, and reckon carefully, if you can, what an amount of superfluous words he wastes on the one phrase, "I was unacquainted with" which he declares that I have used; whereas I never used it at all,--partly because the question under discussion was not concerning me, so that I should need to use it; partly because no fault was apparent in him that baptized me, so that I should be forced to say in my defense that I had been unacquainted with his conscience.

Chapter 25.

29. And yet Petilianus, to avoid answering what I have said, sets before himself what I have not, and draws men's attention away from the consideration of his debt, lest they should exact the answer which he ought to make. He constantly introduces the expressions, "I have been unacquainted with," "I say," and makes answer, "But if you were unacquainted with;" and, as though convicting me, so that it should be out of my power to say, "I was unacquainted with," he quotes Mensurius, Cæcilianus, Macarius, Taurinus, Romanus, and declares that "they had acted in opposition to the Church of God, as I could not fail to know, seeing that I am an African, and already well

advanced in years," whereas, so far as I hear, Mensurius died in the unity of the communion of the Church, before the faction of Donatus separated itself therefrom; whilst I had read the history of Cæcilianus, that they themselves had referred his case to Constantine, and that he had been once and again acquitted by the judges whom that emperor had appointed to try the matter, and again a third time by the sovereign himself, when they appealed to him. But whatever Macarius and Taurinus and Romanus did, either in their judicial or executive functions, in behalf of unity as against their pertinacious madness, it is beyond doubt that it was all done in accordance with the laws, which these same persons made it unavoidable should be passed and put in force, by referring the case of Cæcilianus to the judgment of the emperor.

30. Among many other things which are wholly irrelevant, he says that "I was so hard hit by the decision of the proconsul Messianus, that I was forced to fly from Africa." And in consequence of this falsehood (to which, if he was not the author of it, he certainly lent malicious ears when others maliciously invented it), how many other falsehoods had he the hardihood not only to utter, but actually to write with wondrous rashness, seeing that I went to Milan before the consulship of Banto, and that, in pursuance of the profession of rhetorician which I then followed, I recited a panegyric in his honor as consul on the first of January, in the presence of a vast assembly of men; and after that journey I only returned to Africa after the death of the tyrant Maximus: whereas the proconsul Messianus heard the case of the Manichæans after the consulship of Banto, as the day of the chronicles inserted by Petilianus himself sufficiently shows. And if it were necessary to prove this for the satisfaction of those who are in

doubt, or believe the contrary, I could produce many men, illustrious in their generation, as most sufficient witnesses to all that period of my life.

Chapter 26.

31. But why do we make inquiry into these points? Why do we both suffer and cause unnecessary delay? Are we likely to find out by such a course as this what means we are to use for cleansing the conscience of the recipient, who does not know that the conscience of the giver is stained with guilt: whence the man is to receive faith who is unwittingly baptized by one that is faithless?--the question which Petilianus had proposed to himself to answer in my epistle, then going on to say anything else he pleased except what the matter in hand required. How often has he said, "If ignorant you were,"--as though I had said, what I never did say, that I was unacquainted with the conscience of him who baptized me. And he seemed to have no other object in all that his evil-speaking mouth poured forth, except that he should appear to prove that I had not been ignorant of the misdeeds of those among whom I was baptized, and with whom I was associated in communion, understanding fully, it would seem, that ignorance did not convict me of guilt. See then that if I were ignorant, as he has repeated so often, beyond all doubt I should be innocent of all these crimes. Whence therefore should I be cleansed, who am unacquainted with the conscience of him who gives but not in holiness, so that I may be least ensnared by his offenses? Whence then should I receive faith, seeing that I was baptized unwittingly by one that was faithless? For he has not repeated "If ignorant you were" so often without purpose, but simply to prevent my being reputed innocent, esteeming beyond all doubt that no man's innocence is violated if he unwittingly receives his faith

from one that is faithless, and is not acquainted with the stains on the conscience of him that gives, but not in holiness. Let him say, therefore, by what means such men are to be cleansed, whence they are to receive not guilt but faith. But let him not deceive you. Let him not, while uttering much, say nothing; or rather, let him not say much while saying nothing. Next, to urge a point which occurs to me, and must not be passed over,--if I am guilty because I have not been ignorant, to use his own phraseology, and I am proved not to have been ignorant, because I am an African, and already advanced in years, let him grant that the youths of other nations throughout the world are not guilty, who had no opportunity either from their race, or from that age you bring against me, of knowing the points that are laid to our charge, be they true, or be they false; and yet they, if they have fallen into your hands, are rebaptized without any considerations of such a kind.

Chapter 27.

32. But this is not what we are now inquiring. Let him rather answer (what he wanders off into the most irrelevant matters in order to avoid answering) by what means the conscience of the recipient is cleansed who is unacquainted with the stain on the conscience of the giver, if the conscience of one that gives in holiness is what we look for to cleanse the conscience of the recipient? and from what source he receive faith who is unwittingly baptized by one that is faithless, if he that has wittingly received his faith from one that is faithless receives not faith but guilt? Omitting, therefore, his revilings, which he has cast at me without any sound consideration, let us still notice that he does not say what we demand in what follows. But I should like to look at the garrulous mode in which he has set this forth, as though he were sure to overwhelm us with

confusion. "But let us return," he says, "to that argument of your fancy, whereby you seem to have represented to yourself in a form of words the persons you baptize. For since you do not see the truth, it would have been more seemly to have imagined what was probable." These words of his own, Petilianus put forth by way of preface, being about to state the words that I had used. Then he went on to quote: "Behold, you say, the faithless man stands ready to baptize, but he who is to be baptized knows nothing of his faithlessness." [2381]He has not quoted the whole of my proposition and question; and presently he begins to ask me in his turn, saying, "Who is the man, and from what corner has he started up, that you propose to us? Why do you seem to see a man who is the produce of your imagination, in order to avoid seeing one whom you are bound to see, and to examine and test most carefully? But since I see that you are unacquainted with the order of the sacrament, I tell you this as shortly as I can: you were bound both to examine your baptizer, and to be examined by him." What is it, then, that we were waiting for? That he should tell us by what means the conscience of the recipient is to be cleansed, who is unacquainted with the stain on the conscience of him that gives but not in holiness, and whence the man is to receive not guilt but faith, who has received baptism unwittingly from one that is faithless. All that we have heard is that the baptizer ought most diligently to be examined by him who wishes to receive not guilt but faith, that the latter may make himself acquainted with the conscience of him that gives in holiness, which is to cleanse the conscience of the recipient. For the man that has failed to make this examination, and has unwittingly received baptism from one that is faithless, from the very fact that he did not make the examination, and therefore did not know of the stain on the conscience of the giver, was incapacitated from receiving faith instead of guilt. Why therefore did he add what he made so much of adding,-- the word wittingly, which he calumniously accused me of having suppressed? For in his unwillingness that the sentence should run, "He who has received his faith from one that is faithless, receives not faith but guilt," he seems to have left some hope to the man that acts unwittingly. But now, when he is asked whence that man is to receive faith who is baptized unwittingly by one that is faithless, he has answered that he ought to have examined his baptizer; so that, beyond all doubt, he refuses the wretched man permission even to be ignorant, by not finding out from what source he may receive faith, unless he has placed his trust in the man that is baptizing him.

[2381] See Book I. c. 2, 3.

Chapter 28.

33. This is what we look upon with horror in your party; this is what the sentence of God condemns, crying out with the utmost truth and the utmost clearness, "Cursed is every one that trusteth in man." [2382]This is what is most openly forbidden by holy humility and apostolic love, as Paul declares, "Let no man glory in men." [2383] This is the reason that the attack of empty calumnies and of the bitterest invectives grows even fiercer against us, that when human authority is as it were overthrown, there may remain no ground of hope for those to whom we administer the word and sacrament of God in accordance with the dispensation entrusted unto us. We make answer to them: How long do you rest your support on man? The venerable society of the Catholic Church makes answer to them: "Truly my soul waiteth upon God: from Him cometh my salvation. He only is my God and my helper; I shall not be

moved." [2384]For what other reason have they had for removing from the house of God, except that they pretended that they could not endure those vessels made to dishonor, from which the house shall not be free until the day of judgment? whereas all the time they rather appear, by their deeds and by the records of the time, to have themselves been vessels of this kind, while they threw the imputation in the teeth of others; of which said vessels made unto dishonor, in order that no one should on their account remove in confusion of mind from the great house, which alone belongs to the great Father of our family, the servant of God, one who was good and faithful, or was capable of receiving faith in baptism, as I have shown above, expressly says, "Truly my soul waiteth upon God" (on God, you see, and not on man): "from Him cometh my salvation" (not from man). But Petilianus would refuse to ascribe to God the cleansing and purifying of a man, even when the stain upon the conscience of him who gives, but not in holiness, is hidden from view, and any one receives his faith unwittingly from one that is faithless. "I tell you this," he says, "as shortly as I can: you were bound both to examine your baptizer, and to be examined by him."

[2382] Jer. xvii. 5.

[2383] 1 Cor. iii. 21.

[2384] Ps. lxii. 1, 2; cp. Hieron.

Chapter 29.

34. I entreat of you, pay attention to this: I ask where the means shall be found for cleansing the conscience of the recipient, when he is not acquainted with the stain upon the conscience of him that gives but not in holiness, if the

conscience of him that gives in holiness is waited for to cleanse the conscience of the recipient? and from what source he is to receive faith, who is unwittingly baptized by one that is faithless, if, whosoever has received his faith wittingly from one that is faithless, receives not faith but guilt? and he answers me, that both the baptizer and the baptized should be subjected to examination. And for the proof of this point, out of which no question arises, he adduces the example of John, in that he was examined by those who asked him who he claimed to be, [2385] and that he also in turn examined those to whom he says, "O generation of vipers, who hath warned you to flee from the wrath to come?" [2386] What has this to do with the subject? What has this to do with the question under discussion? God had vouchsafed to John the testimony of most eminent holiness of life, confirmed by the previous witness of the noblest prophecy, both when he was conceived, and when he was born. But the Jews put their question, already believing him to be a saint, to find out which of the saints he maintained himself to be, or whether he was himself the saint of saints, that is, Christ Jesus. So much favor indeed was shown to him, that credence would at once have been given to whatever he might have said about himself. If, therefore, we are to follow this precedent in declaring that each several baptizer is now to be examined, then each must also be believed, whatever he may say of himself. But who is there that is made up of deceit, whom we know that the Holy Spirit flees from, in accordance with the Scripture, [2387] who would not wish the best to be believed of him, or who would hesitate to bring this about by the use of any words within his reach? Accordingly, when he shall have been asked who he is, and shall have answered that he is the faithful dispenser of God's ordinances, and that his conscience is not polluted with the stain of any crime, will this be the whole examination, or will there be a further more careful investigation into his character and life? Assuredly there will. But it is not written that this was done by those who in the desert of Jordan asked John who he was.

[2385] John i. 22.

[2386] Matt. iii. 7.

[2387] Wisd. i. 5.

Chapter 30.

35. Accordingly this precedent is wholly without bearing on the matter in hand. We might rather say that the declaration of the apostle sufficiently inculcates this care, when he says, "Let these also first be proved; then let them use the office of a deacon, being found blameless." [2388]And since this is done anxiously and habitually in both parties, by almost all concerned, how comes it that so many are found to be reprobates subsequently to the time of having undertaken this ministry, except that, on the one hand, human care is often deceived, and, on the other hand, those who have begun well occasionally deteriorate? And since things of this sort happen so frequently as to allow no man to hide them or to forget them, what is the reason that Petilianus now teaches us insultingly, in a few words, that the baptizer ought to be examined by the candidate for baptism, since our question is, by what means the conscience of the recipient is to be cleansed, when the stain on the conscience of him that gives, but not in holiness, has been concealed from view, if the conscience of one that gives in holiness is what we look for to cleanse the conscience of the recipient. "Since I see," he says, "that you are

unacquainted with the order of the sacrament, I tell you this as shortly as I can: you were bound both to examine your baptizer, and to be examined by him." What an answer to make! He is surrounded in so many places by such a multitude of men that have been baptized by ministers who, having in the first instance seemed righteous and chaste, have subsequently been convicted and degraded in consequence of the disclosure of their faults: and he thinks that he is avoiding the force of this question, in which we ask by what means the conscience of the recipient is to be cleansed, when he is unacquainted with the stain upon the conscience of him that gives but not in holiness, if the conscience of one that gives in holiness is what we look for to cleanse the conscience of the recipient,--he thinks, I say, that he is avoiding the force of this question, by saying shortly that the baptizer ought to be examined. Nothing is more unfortunate than not to be consistent with truth, by which every one is so shut in, that he cannot find a means of escape. We ask from whom he is to receive faith who is baptized by one that is faithless? The answer is, "He ought to have examined his baptizer." Is it therefore the case that, since he does not examine him, and so even unwittingly receives his faith from one that is faithless, he receives not faith but guilt? Why then are those men not baptized afresh, who are found to have been baptized by men that are detected and convicted reprobates, while their true character was yet concealed?

[2388] 1 Tim. iii. 10.

Chapter. 31.

36. "And where," he says, "is the word that I added, wittingly?so that I did not say, He that has received his faith from one that is faithless; but, He that has received his faith

wittingly from one that is faithless, receives not faith but guilt." He therefore who received his faith unwittingly from one that was faithless, received not guilt but faith; and accordingly I ask from what source he has received it? And being thus placed in a strait, he answers, "He ought to have examined him." Granted that he ought to have done so; but, as a matter of fact, he did not, or he was not able: what is your verdict about him? Was he cleansed, or was he not? If he was cleansed, I ask from what source? For the polluted conscience of him that gave but not in holiness, with which he was unacquainted, could not cleanse him. But if he was not cleansed, command that he be so now. You give no such orders, therefore he was cleansed. Tell me by what means? Do you at any rate tell me what Petilianus has failed to tell. For I propose to you the very same words which he was unable to answer. "Behold the faithless man stands ready to baptize; but he who is to be baptized knows nothing of his faithlessness: what do you think that he will receive--faith, or guilt?" [2389]This is sufficient as a constant form of question: answer, or search diligently to find what he has answered. You will find abuse that has already been convicted. He finds fault with me, as though in derision, maintaining that I ought to suggest what is probable for consideration, since I cannot see the truth. For, repeating my words, and cutting my sentence in two, he says, "Behold, you say, the faithless man stands ready to baptize; but he who is to be baptized knows nothing of his faithlessness." Then he goes on to ask, "Who is the man, and from what corner has he started up, that you propose to us?" Just as though there were some one or two individuals, and such cases were not constantly occurring everywhere on either side! Why does he ask of me who the man in question is, and from what corner he has started up, instead of looking round, and seeing that the churches are few and far between, whether in cities or in country districts, which do not contain men detected in crimes, and degraded from the ministry? While their true character was concealed, while they wished to be thought good, though really bad, and to be reputed chaste, though really guilty of adultery, so long they were involved in deceit; and so the Holy Spirit, according to the Scripture, was fleeing from them. [2390]It is from the crowd, therefore, of these men who hitherto concealed their character that the faithless man whom I suggested started up. Why does he ask me whence he started up, shutting his eyes to all this crowd, from which sufficient noise arises to satisfy the blind, if we take into consideration none but those who might have been convicted and degraded from their office?

[2389] Book I. cc. 1, 2, 2, 3.

[2390] Wisd. i. 5.

Chapter 32.

37. What shall we say of what he himself advanced in his epistle, that "Quodvultdeus, having been convicted of two adulteries, and cast out from among you, was received by those of our party?" [2391]What then (I would speak without prejudice to this man, who proved his case to be a good one, or at least persuaded men that it was so), when such men among you, being as yet undetected, administer baptism, what is received at their hands,--faith, or guilt? Surely not faith, because they have not the conscience of one who gives in holiness to cleanse the conscience of the recipient. But yet not guilt either, in virtue of that added word: "For he that has received his faith wittingly from one that is faithless, receives not faith but guilt." But when men were baptized by those of

whom I speak, they were surely ignorant what sort of men they were. Furthermore, not receiving faith from their baptizers, who had not the conscience of one that gives in holiness, and not receiving guilt, because they were baptized not knowing but in ignorance of their faults, they therefore remained without faith and without guilt. They are not, therefore, in the number of men of such abandoned character. But neither can they be in the number of the faithful, because, as they could not receive guilt, so neither could they receive faith from their baptizers. But we see that they are reputed by you in the number of the faithful, and that no one of you declares his opinion that they ought to be baptized, but all of you hold valid the baptism which they have already received. They have therefore received faith; and yet they have not received it from those who had not the conscience of one that gives in holiness, to cleanse the conscience of the recipient. Whence then did they receive it? This is the point from which I make my effort; this is the question that I press most earnestly; to this I do most urgently demand an answer.

[2391] The Council of Carthage, held on the 13th of September, 401, passed a decree (canon 2) in favor of receiving the clergy of the Donatists with full recognition of their orders.

Chapter 33.

38. See now how Petilianus, to avoid answering this question, or to avoid being proved to be incapable of answering it, wanders off vainly into irrelevant matter in abuse of us, accusing us and proving nothing; and when he chances to make an endeavor to resist, with something like a show of fighting for his cause, he is everywhere overcome with the greatest ease. But yet he nowhere gives an answer of any kind to this one

question which we ask: If the conscience of one that gives in holiness is what we look for to cleanse the conscience of the recipient, by what means is he to be cleansed who received baptism while the conscience of the giver was polluted, without the knowledge of him who was to receive it? for in these words, which he quoted from my epistle, he set me forth as asking a question, while he showed himself as giving no answer. For after saying what I have just now recited, and when, on being brought into a great strait on every side, he had been compelled to say that the baptizer ought to be examined by the candidate for baptism, and the candidate in turn by the baptizer; and when he had tried to fortify this statement by the example of John, in hopes that he might find auditors either of the greatest negligence or of the greatest ignorance, he then went on to advance other testimonies of Scripture wholly irrelevant to the matter in hand, as the saying of the eunuch to Philip, "See, here is water; what doth hinder me to be baptized?" [2392] "inasmuch as he knew," says he, "that those of abandoned character were prevented;" arguing that the reason why Philip did not forbid him to be baptized was because he had proved, in his reading of the Scriptures, how far he believed in Christ,-- as though he had prohibited Simon Magus. And again, he urges that the prophets were afraid of being deceived by false baptism, and that therefore Isaiah said, "Lying water that has not faith," [2393] as though showing that water among faithless men is lying; whereas it is not Isaiah but Jeremiah that says this of lying men, calling the people in a figure water, as is most clearly shown in the Apocalypse. [2394] And again, he quotes as words of David, "Let not the oil of the sinner anoint my head," when David has been speaking of the flattery of the smooth speaker deceiving with false praise, so as to lead the head of the man praised to wax great with pride. And this meaning is made manifest by the words immediately preceding in the same psalm. For he says, "Let the righteous smite me, it shall be a kindness; and let him reprove me: but the oil of the sinner shall not break my head." [2395] What can be clearer than this sentence? what more manifest? For he declares that he had rather be reproved in kindness with the sharp correction of the righteous, so that he may be healed, than anointed with the soft speaking of the flatterer, so as to be puffed up with pride.

[2392] Acts viii. 36.

[2393] Jer. xv. 18. See Book II. c. 102, 234, 235.

[2394] Rev. xvii. 15.

[2395] Ps. cxli. 5. See Book II. c. 103, 236, 237.

Chapter 34.

39. Petilianus quotes also the warning of the Apostle John, that we should not believe every spirit, but try the spirits whether they are of God, [2396] as though this care should be bestowed in order that the wheat should be separated from the chaff in this present world before its time, and not rather for fear that the wheat should be deceived by the chaff; or as though, even if the lying spirit should have said something that was true, it was to be denied, because the spirit whom we should abominate had said it. But if any one thinks this, he is mad enough to contend that Peter ought not to have said, "Thou art the Christ, the Son of the living God," [2397] because the devils had already said something to the same effect. [2398]Seeing, therefore, that the baptism of Christ, whether administered by an unrighteous or a righteous man, is nothing but the baptism of Christ what a cautious man and faithful Christian should do

is to avoid the unrighteousness of man, not to condemn the sacraments of God.

40. Assuredly in all these things Petilianus gives no answer to the question, If the conscience of one that gives in holiness is what we look for to cleanse the conscience of the recipient, by what means is he to be cleansed who receives baptism, when the conscience of the giver is polluted without the knowledge of the proposed recipient? A certain Cyprian, a colleague of his from Thubursicubur, was caught in a brothel with a woman of most abandoned character, and was brought before Primianus of Carthage, and condemned. Now, when this man baptized before he was detected and condemned, it is manifest that he had not the conscience of one that gives in holiness, so as to cleanse the conscience of the recipient. By what means then have they been cleansed who at this day, after he has been condemned, are certainly not washed again? It was not necessary to name the man save only to prevent Petilianus from repeating, "Who is the man, and from what corner has he started up, that you propose to us?" Why did not your party examine that baptizer, as John, in the opinion of Petilianus, was examined? Or was the real fact this, that they examined him so far as man can examine man, but were unable to find him out, as he long lay hid with cunning falseness?

[2396] 1 John iv. 1.

[2397] Matt. xvi. 16.

[2398] Matt. viii. 29; Mark i. 24; Luke viii. 28.

Chapter 35.

Was the water administered by this man not lying? or is the oil of the fornicator not the oil of the sinner? or must we hold what the Catholic Church says, and what is true, that that water and that oil are not his by whom they were administered, but His whose name was then invoked? Why did they who were baptized by that hypocrite, whose sins were concealed, fail to try the spirit, to prove that it was not of God? For the Holy Spirit of discipline was even then fleeing from the hypocrite. [2399]Was it that He was fleeing from him, but at the same time not deserting His sacraments, though ministered by him? Lastly, since you do not deny that those men have been already cleansed, whom you take no care to have cleansed now that he is condemned, see whether, after shedding over the subject so many mists in so many different ways, Petilianus, after all, in any place gives any answer to the question by what means these men have been cleansed, if what we look for to cleanse the conscience of the recipient is the conscience of one that gives in holiness, such as the man who was secretly unclean could not have had.

41. Making then, no answer to this which is so urgently asked of him, and, in the next place, even seeking for himself a latitude of speech, he says, "since both prophets and apostles have been cautious enough to fear these things, with what face do you say that the baptism of the sinner is holy to those who believe with a good conscience?" Just as though I or any Catholic maintained that that baptism was of the sinner which is administered or received with a sinner to officiate, instead of being His in virtue of belief in whose name the candidate is baptized! Then he goes off to an invective against the traitor Judas, saying against him whatever he can, quoting the testimony of the prophets uttered concerning him so long a

time before, as though he would steep the Church of Christ dispersed throughout the world, whose cause is involved in this discussion, in the impiety of the traitor Judas,--not considering what this very thing should have recalled to his mind, that we ought no more to doubt that that is the Church of Christ which is spread abroad throughout the world, since this was prophesied with truth so many years before, than we ought to doubt that it was necessary that Christ should be betrayed by one of His disciples, because this was prophesied in like manner.

[2399] Wisd. i. 5.

Chapter 36.

42. But after this, when Petilianus came to that objection of ours, that they allowed the baptism of the followers of Maximianus, whom they had condemned, [2400] --although in the statement of this question he thought it right to use his own words rather than mine; for neither do we assert that the baptism of sinners is of profit to us, seeing that we maintain it to belong not only to no sinners, but to no men whatsoever, in that we are satisfied that it is Christ's alone,--having put the question in this form, he says, "Yet you obstinately aver that it is right that the baptism of sinners should be of profit to you, because we too, according to your statement, maintained the baptism of criminals whom we justly condemned." When he came to this question, as I said before, even all the show of fight which he had made deserted him. He could not find any way to go, any means of escape, any path by which, either through subtle watching or bold enterprise, he could either secretly steal away, or sally forth by force. "Although this," he says, "I will demonstrate in my second book, how great the

difference is between those of our party and those of yours whom you call innocent, yet, in the meantime, first extricate yourselves from the offenses with which you are acquainted in your colleagues, and then seek out the mode of dealing with those whom we cast out." Would any one, any man upon the earth, give an answer like this, save one who is setting himself against the truth, against which he cannot find any answer that can be made? Accordingly, if we too were to use the same words: In the meantime, first extricate yourselves from the offenses with which you are acquainted in your colleagues, and then bring up against us any charge connected with those whom you hold to be wicked amongst us,--what is the result? Have we both won the victory, or are we both defeated? Nay, rather He has gained the victory for His Church and in His Church, who has taught us in His Scriptures that no man should glory in men, and that he that glorieth should glory in the Lord. [2401]For behold in our case who assert with the eloquence of truth that the man who believes is not justified by him by whom he is baptized, but by Him of whom it is written, "To him that believeth on Him that justifieth the ungodly, his faith is counted for righteousness," [2402] since we do not glory in men, and strive, when we glory, to glory in the Lord in virtue of His own gift, how wholly safe are we, whatever fault or charge Petilianus may have been able to prove concerning certain men of our communion! For among us, whatever wicked men are either wholly undetected, or, being known to certain persons, are yet tolerated for the sake of the bond of unity and peace, in consideration of other good men to whom their wickedness is unknown, and before whom they could not be convicted, in order that the wheat may not be rooted up together with the tares, yet they so bear the burden of their own wickedness, that no one shares it with them except those who are pleased with their unrighteousness. Nor indeed have we any apprehension that those whom they baptize cannot be justified, since they believe in Him that justifieth the ungodly that their faith may be counted for righteousness. [2403]

[2400] See Book I. cc. 10, 11, 11, 12.

[2401] 1 Cor. iii. 21, and i. 31.

[2402] Rom. iv. 5.

[2403] Rom. iv. 5.

Chapter 37.

43. Furthermore, according to our tenets, neither he of whom Petilianus said that he was cast forth by us for the sin of the men of Sodom, another being appointed in his place, and that afterwards he was actually restored to our college,--talking all the time without knowing what he was saying,--nor he whom he declares to have been penitent among you, in whatever degree their respective cases do or do not admit of any defense, can neither of them prejudice the Church, which is spread abroad throughout all nations, and increases in the world until the harvest. For if they were really wicked members of it that you accuse, then they were already not in it, but among the chaff; but if they are good, while you defame their character with unrighteous accusations, they are themselves being tried like gold, while you burn after the similitude of chaff. Yet the sins of other men do not defile the Church, which is spread abroad throughout the whole world, according to most faithful prophesies, waiting for the end of the world as for its shore, on which, when it is landed, it will be freed from the bad fish, in company with which the inconvenience of nature might be

borne without sin within the same nets of the Lord, so long as it was not right to be impatiently separated from them. Nor yet is the discipline of the Church on this account neglected by constant and diligent and prudent ministers of Christ, in whose province crimes are in such wise brought to light that they cannot be defended on any plea of probability. Innumerable proofs of this may be found in those who have been bishops or clergy of the second degree of orders, and now, being degraded, have either gone abroad into other lands through shame, or have gone over to you yourselves or to other heresies, or are known in their own districts; of whom there is so great a multitude dispersed throughout the earth, that if Petilianus, bridling for a time his rashness in speaking, had taken them into consideration, he would never have fallen into so manifestly false and groundless a misconception, as to think that we ought to join in what he says: None of you is free from guilt, where no one that is guilty is condemned.

Chapter 38.

44. For, to pass over others dwelling in different quarters of the earth,--for you will scarcely find any place in which this kind of men is not represented, from whom it may appear that overseers and ministers are wont to be condemned even in the Catholic Church,--we need not look far to find the example of Honorius of Milevis. But take the case of Splendonius, whom Petilianus ordained priest after he had been condemned in the Catholic Church, and rebaptized by himself, whose condemnation in Gaul, communicated to us by our brethren, our colleague Fortunatus caused to be publicly read in Constantina, and whom the same Petilianus afterwards cast forth on experience of his abominable deceit. From the case of this Splendonius, when was there a time when he might not

have been reminded after what fashion wicked men are degraded from their office even in the Catholic Church? I wonder on what precipice of rashness his heart was resting when he dictated those words in which he ventured to say, "No one of you is free from guilt, where no one that is guilty is condemned." Wherefore the wicked, being bodily intermingled with the good, but spiritually separated from them in the Catholic Church, both when they are undetected through the infirmity of human nature, and when they are condemned from considerations of discipline, in every case bear their own burden. And in this way those are free from danger who are baptized by them with the baptism of Christ, if they keep free from share in their sins either by imitation or consent; seeing that in like manner, if they were baptized by the best of men, they would not be justified except by Him that justifieth the ungodly: since to those that believe on Him that justifieth the ungodly their faith is counted for righteousness.

Chapter 39.

45. But as for you, when the case of the followers of Maximianus is brought up against you, who, after being condemned by the sentence of a Council of 310 bishops; [2404] after being utterly defeated in the same Council, quoted in the records of so many proconsuls, in the chronicles of so many municipal towns; after being driven forth from the basilicas of which they were in possession, by the order of the judges, enforced by the troops of the several cities, were yet again received with all honor by you, together with those whom they had baptized outside the pale of your communion, without any question respecting their baptism,--when confronted, I say, with their case, you can find no reply to make. Indeed, you are vanquished by an expressed opinion, not indeed true, but

proceeding from yourselves, by which you maintain that men perish for the faults of others in the same communion of the sacraments, and that each man's character is determined by that of the man by whom he is baptized,--that he is guilty if his baptizer is guilty, innocent if he is innocent. But if these views are true, there can be no doubt that, to say nothing of innumerable others, you are destroyed by the sins of the followers of Maximianus, whose guilt your party, in so large a Council, has exaggerated even to the proportions of the sin of those whom the earth swallowed up alive. But if the faults of the followers of Maximianus have not destroyed you, then are these opinions false which you entertain; and much less have certain indefinite unproved faults of the Africans been able to destroy the entire world. And accordingly, as the apostle says, "Every man shall bear his own burden;" [2405] and the baptism of Christ is no one's except Christ's; and it is to no purpose that Petilianus promises that he will take as the subject of his second book the charges which we bring concerning the followers of Maximianus, entertaining too low an opinion of men's intellects, as though they do not perceive that he has nothing to say.

[2404] That of Bagai.

[2405] Gal. vi. 5.

Chapter 40.

46. For if the baptism which Prætextatus and Felicianus administered in the communion of Maximianus was their own, why was it received by you in those whom they baptized as though it were the baptism of Christ? But if it is truly the baptism of Christ, as indeed it is, and yet could not profit those who had received it with the guilt of schism, what do you say

that you could have granted to those whom you have received into your body with the same baptism, except that, now that the offense of their accursed division is wiped out by the bond of peace, they should not be compelled to receive the sacrament of the holy laver as though they had it not, but that, as what they had was before for their destruction, so it should now begin to be of profit to them? Or if this is not granted to them in your communion, because it could not possibly be that it should be granted to schismatics among schismatics, it is at any rate granted to you in the Catholic communion, not that you should receive baptism as though it were lacking in you, but that the baptism which you have actually received should be of profit to you. For all the sacraments of Christ, if not combined with the love which belongs to the unity of Christ, are possessed not unto salvation, but unto judgment. But since it is not a true verdict, but your verdict, "that through the baptism of certain traditors the baptism of Christ has perished from the world in general," it is with good reason that you cannot find any answer to make respecting the recognition of the baptism of the followers of Maximianus.

47. See therefore, and remember with the most watchful care, how Petilianus has made no answer to that very question, which he proposes to himself in such terms as to seem to make it a starting-point from which to say something. For the former question he has dismissed altogether, and has not wished to speak of it to us, because I suppose it was beyond his power; nor is he at any time, up to the very end of his volume, going to say anything about it, though he quoted it from the first part of my epistle as though it were a matter calling for refutation. For even though he has added the two words which he accused me of having suppressed, as though they were the

strongest bulwarks of his position, he yet lies wholly defenseless, unable to find any answer to make when he is asked, If the conscience of one that gives in holiness is what we look for to cleanse the conscience of the recipient, where are we to find means for cleansing the conscience of the man who is unacquainted with the conscience of him gives, but not in holiness? and if it be the case that any one who has received his faith from one that is faithless, receives not faith but guilt, from what source is he to receive not guilt but faith, who is unwittingly baptized by one that is faithless? To this question it has long been manifest from what he says that he has made no answer.

48. In the next place, he has gone on, with calumnious mouth, to abuse monasteries and monks, finding fault also with me, as having been the founder of this kind of life. [2406]And what this kind of life really is he does not know at all, or rather, though it is perfectly well known throughout all the world, he pretends that he is unacquainted with it. Then, asserting that I had said that Christ was the baptizer, he has also added certain words from my epistle as though I had set this forth as my own sentiment, when I had really quoted it as his and yours, and it was inveighed against with most copious harshness, as if it were I who had said these things against myself, when what he reprehended was not mine, but his and your sentiment, as I will presently show clearly to the best of my ability. [2407]Then he has endeavored to show us, in many unnecessary words, that Christ does not baptize, but that baptism is administered in His name, at once in the name of the Father, and of the Son, and of the Holy Ghost; of which Trinity itself he has said, either because it was what he wished, or because it was all that he could say, that "Christ is the centre of the Trinity." In the next

place, he has taken occasion of the names of the sorcerers Simon and Barjesus to vent against us what insults he thought fit. Then he goes on, keeping in guarded suspense the case of Optatus of Thamugas, that he might not be steeped in the odium that arose from it, denying that neither he or his party could have passed judgment upon him, and actually intimating in respect of him, that he was crushed in consequence of suggestions from myself.

[2406] See Possidius' Life of St. Augustin, cc. v.-xi.

[2407] See c. 45, 54.

Chapter 41.

49. Lastly, he has ended his epistle with an exhortation and warning to his own party, that they should not be deceived by us, and with a lamentation over those of our party, that we had made them worse than they had been before. Having therefore carefully considered and discussed these points, as appears with sufficient clearness from the words of the epistle which he wrote, Petilianus has made no answer at all to the position which I advanced to begin with in my epistle, when I asked, Supposing it to be true, as he asserts, that the conscience of one that gives--or rather, to add what he considers so great a support to his argument--that the conscience of one that gives in holiness is what we look for to cleanse the conscience of the recipient, by what means he who receives baptism is to be cleansed, when, if the conscience of the giver is polluted, it is without the knowledge of the proposed recipient? Whence it is not surprising that a man resisting in the cause of falsehood, pressed hard in the straits of the truth that contradicts it, should have chosen rather to gasp forth mad abuse, than to walk in the path of that truth which cannot be overcome.

50. And now I would beg of you to pay especial attention to the next few words, that I may show you clearly what he has been afraid of in not answering this, and that I may bring into the light what he has endeavored to shroud in obscurity. It certainly was in his power, when we asked by what means he is to be cleansed, who receives baptism when the conscience of the giver is polluted without the knowledge of the proposed recipient, to answer with the greatest ease, From our Lord God; and at any rate to say with the utmost confidence, God wholly cleanses the conscience of the recipient, when he is unacquainted with the stain upon the conscience of him that gives but not in holiness. But when a man had already been compelled by the tenets of your sect to rest the cleansing of the recipient on the conscience of the giver, in that he had said, "For the conscience of him that gives," or "of him that gives in holiness, is looked for to cleanse the conscience of the recipient," he was naturally afraid lest any one should seem to be better baptized by a wicked man who concealed his wickedness, than by one that was genuinely and manifestly good; for in the former case his cleansing would depend not on the conscience of one that gave in holiness, but on the most excellent holiness of God Himself. With this apprehension, therefore, that he might not be involved in so great an absurdity, or rather madness, as not to know where he could make his escape, he was unwilling to say by what means the conscience of the recipient should be cleansed, when he does not know of the stain upon the conscience of him that gives but not in holiness; and he thought it better, by making a general confusion with his quarrelsome uproar, to conceal what was asked of him, than to give a reply to his question, which should at once discomfit him; never, however, thinking that our letter could be read by men of such good understanding, or that

his would be read by those who had read ours as well, to which he has professed to make an answer.

Chapter 42.

51. For what I just now said is put with the greatest clearness in that very epistle of mine, in answering which he has said nothing; and I would beg of you to listen for a few moments to what he there has done. And although you are partisans of his, and hate us, yet, if you can, bear it with equanimity. For in his former epistle, to the first portion of which--the only portion which had then come into our hands--I had in the first instance made my reply, he had so rested the hope that is found in baptism in the baptizer, as to say, "For everything consists of an origin and root; and if anything has not a head, it is nothing." Since then Petilianus had said this, not wishing anything to be understood by the origin and root and head of baptizing a man, except the man by whom he might be baptized, I made a comment, and said "We ask, therefore, in a case where the faithlessness of the baptizer is undetected, if then the man whom he baptizes receives faith and not guilt? if then the baptizer is not his origin and root and head, who is it from whom he receives faith? where is the origin from which he springs? where is the root of which he is a shoot? where the head which is his starting-point? Can it be that, when he who is baptized is unaware of the faithlessness of his baptizer, it is then Christ who is the origin and root and head?" This therefore I say and exclaim now also, as I did there as well: "Alas for human rashness and conceit! Why do you not allow that it is always Christ who gives faith, for the purpose of making a man a Christian by giving it? Why do you not allow that Christ is always the origin of the Christian, that the Christian always plants his root in Christ, that Christ is the

Head of the Christian? Will it then be urged that, even where spiritual grace is dispensed to those that believe by the hands of a holy and faithful minister, it is still not the minister himself who justifies, but that One of whom it is said, He justifieth the ungodly'? [2408]But unless we admit this, either the Apostle Paul was the head and origin of those whom he had planted, or Apollos the root of those whom he had watered, rather than He who had given them faith in briefing; whereas the same Paul says, I have planted, Apollos watered; but God gave the increase. So that neither is he that planteth anything, neither he that watereth; but God that giveth the increase.' [2409]Nor was the apostle himself their root, but rather He who says, I am the vine, ye are the branches.' [2410]How, too, could he be their head, when he says that we, being many, are one body in Christ,' [2411] and expressly declares in many passages that Christ Himself is the Head of the whole body? Wherefore, whether a man receives the sacrament of baptism from a faithful or a faithless minister his whole hope is in Christ, that he fall not under the condemnation, that Cursed is he that placeth his hope in man!'" [2412]

[2408] Rom. iv. 5.

[2409] 1 Cor. iii. 6, 7.

[2410] John xv. 5.

[2411] Rom. xii. 5.

[2412] Book I. c. 5, 6.

Chapter 43.

52. These things, I think, I put with clearness and truth in my former epistle, when I made answer to Petilianus. These things

I have also now quoted, intimating and commending to you the truth that our faith rests on something else altogether than man, and that we believe that the Lord Christ is the cleanser and the justifier of men that believe in Him that justifieth the ungodly, that their faith may be counted unto them for righteousness, whether the man who administers the baptism be righteous, or such an impious and deceitful man as the Holy Spirit flees. Then I went on to point out what absurdity would follow were it otherwise, and I said, as I say now: "Otherwise, if each man is born again in spiritual grace of the same sort as he by whom he is baptized, and if, when he who baptizes him is manifestly a good man, then he himself gives faith, he is himself the origin and root and head of him who is being born; whilst, when the baptizer is faithless without its being known, then the baptized person receives faith from Christ, then derives his origin from Christ, then he is rooted in Christ then he boasts in Christ as his head; in that case all who are baptized should wish that they might have faithless baptizers, and be ignorant of their faithlessness. For however good their baptizers might have been, Christ is certainly beyond comparison better still, and He will then be the Head of the baptized if the faithlessness of the baptizer shall escape detection. But if it be perfect madness to hold such a view (for it is Christ always that justifieth the ungodly, by changing his ungodliness into Christianity; it is from Christ always that faith is received; Christ is always the origin of the regenerate, and the Head of the Church), what weight then will those words have, which thoughtless readers value by their sound, without inquiring what their inner meaning is?" [2413]This much I said at that time; this is written in my epistle.

[2413] Book I. c. 6, 7.

Chapter 44.

53. Then a little after, as he had said, "This being so, brethren, what perversity must that be, that he who is guilty by reason of his own faults should make another free from guilt, whereas the Lord Jesus Christ says, Every good tree bringeth forth good fruit, but a corrupt tree bringeth forth evil fruit: do men gather grapes of thorns?' [2414] and again, A good man, out of the good treasure of the heart, bringeth forth good things: and an evil man, out of the evil treasure, bringeth forth evil things,'" [2415] --by which words Petilianus showed with sufficient clearness, that the man who baptizes is to be looked on as the tree, and he who is baptized as the fruit: to this I had answered, If the good tree is the good baptizer, and his good fruit he whom he has baptized, then any one who has been baptized by a bad man, even if his wickedness be not manifest, cannot by any possibility be good, for he is sprung from an evil tree. For a good tree is one thing; a tree whose quality is concealed, but yet bad, is another. What else did I wish to be understood by those words, except what I had stated a little above, that the tree and its fruit do not represent him that baptizes and him that is baptized; but that the man ought to be received as signified by the tree, his works and his life by the fruit, which are always good in the good man, and evil in the evil man, lest this absurdity should follow, that a man should be bad when baptized by a bad man, even though his wickedness were concealed, being, as it were, the fruit of a tree whose quality was unknown, but yet bad? To which he has answered nothing whatsoever.

[2414] Matt. vii. 17, 16.

[2415] Matt. xii. 35.

Chapter 45.

54. But that neither he nor any one of you might say that, when any one of concealed bad character is the baptizer, then he whom he baptizes is not his fruit, but the fruit of Christ, I went on immediately to point out what a foolish error is consequent also on that opinion; and I repeated, though in other words, what I had said shortly before: If, when the quality of the tree is concealed, but evil, any one who may have been baptized by it is born, not of it but of Christ, then they are justified with greater holiness who are baptized by wicked men, whose wickedness is concealed, than they who are baptized by men that are genuinely and manifestly good. [2416] Petilianus then, being hemmed in by these embarrassing straits, said nothing about the earlier part on which these remarks depended, and in his answer so quoted his absurd consequence of his error as though I had stated it as my own opinion, whereas it was really stated in order that he might perceive the amount of evil consequent on his opinion, and so be forced to alter it. Imposing, therefore, this deceit on those who hear and read his words, and never for a moment supposing that what we have written could be read, he begins a vehement and petulant invective against me, as though I had thought that all who are baptized ought to wish that they might have as their baptizers men who are faithless, without knowing this themselves, since, however good the men might be whom they had to baptize them, Christ is incomparably better, who will then be the head of the person baptized, if the faithless baptizer conceal his true character. As though, too, I had thought that those were justified with greater holiness who are baptized by evil men, whose character is concealed, than those who are baptized by men that are genuinely and manifestly good; when

this marvellous piece of madness was only mentioned by me as following necessarily on the opinion of those who think with Petilianus, that a man, when baptized, bears the same relation to his baptizer as fruit does to the tree from which it springs,--good fruit springing from a good tree, evil fruit from an evil tree,--seeing that they, when they are bidden by me to answer whose fruit they think a man that is baptized to be when he is baptized by one of secretly bad character, since they do not venture to rebaptize him, are compelled to answer, that then he is not the fruit of that man of secretly bad character, but that he is the fruit of Christ. And so they are followed by a consequence contrary to their inclination, which none but a madman would entertain,--that if a man is the fruit of his baptizer when he is baptized by one that is genuinely and manifestly good, but when he is baptized by one of secretly bad character, he is then not his fruit, but the fruit of Christ,--it cannot but follow that they are justified with greater holiness who are baptized by men of secretly bad character, than those who are baptized by men who are genuinely and manifestly good.

[2416] See Book I. cc. 7, 8, 8, 9.

Chapter 46.

55. Now, seeing that when Petilianus attributes this to me as though it were my opinion, he makes it an occasion for a serious and vehement invective against me, he at any rate shows, by the very force of his indignation, how great a sin it is in his opinion to entertain such views; and, accordingly, whatever he has wished it to appear that he said against me for holding this opinion will be found to have been really said against himself, who is proved to entertain the view. For he

shows herein by how great force on the side of truth he is overcome, when he cannot find any other door of escape except to pretend that it was I who entertained the views which really are his own. Just as if those whom the apostle confutes for maintaining that there was no resurrection from the dead, were to wish to bring an accusation against the same apostle, on the ground that he said, "Then is Christ not risen," and to maintain that the preaching of the apostle was vain, and the faith of those who believed in it was also vain, and that false witnesses were found against God in those who had said that He raised up Christ from the dead. This is what Petilianus wished to do to me, never expecting that any one could read what I had written, which he could not answer, though very anxious that men should believe him to have answered it. But just as, if any one had done this to the apostle, the whole calumnious accusation would have recoiled on the head of those who made it so soon as the entire passage in his epistle was read, and the preceding words restored, on which any one who reads them must perceive that those which I have quoted depend, in the same way, so soon as the preceding words of my epistle are restored, the accusation which Petilianus brings against me is cast back with all the greater force upon his own head, from which he had striven to remove it.

56. For the apostle, in confuting those who denied that there was any resurrection of the dead, corrects their view by showing the absurdity which follows those who entertain this view, however loth they may be to admit the consequence, in order that, while they shrink in abhorrence from what is impious to say, they may correct what they have ventured to believe. His argument continues thus: "But if there be no resurrection of the dead, then is Christ not risen: and if Christ

be not risen, then is our preaching vain, and your faith is also vain. Yea, and we are found false witnesses of God: because we have testified of God that He raised up Christ; whom He raised not up, if so be that the dead rise not." [2417]In order that, while they fear to say that Christ had not risen, with the other wicked and accursed conclusions which follow from such a statement, they may correct what they said in a spirit of folly and infidelity, that there is no resurrection of the dead. If, therefore, you take away what stands at the head of this argument, "If there be no resurrection of the dead," the rest is spoken amiss, and yet must be ascribed to the apostle. But if you restore the supposition on which the rest depends, and place as the hypothesis from which you start, "There is no resurrection of the dead," then the conclusion will follow rightly, "Then is Christ not risen, and our preaching is vain, and your faith is also vain," with all the rest that is appended to it. And all these statements of the apostle are wise and good, since whatever evil they have in them is to be imputed to those who denied the resurrection of the dead. In the same manner also, in my epistle, take away my supposition, If every one is born again in spiritual grace of the same character as he by whom he is baptized, and if, when the man who baptizes is genuinely and manifestly good, he does of himself give faith, he is the origin and root and head of him who is being born again; but when the baptizer is a wicked man, and undetected in his wickedness, then each man who is baptized receives his faith from Christ, derives his origin from Christ, is rooted in Christ, makes his boast in Christ as his Head:--take away, I say, this hypothesis, on which all that follows depends, and there remains a saying of the worst description which must fairly be ascribed to me, viz., that all who are baptized should desire that they should have faithless men to baptize them, and be ignorant of their faithlessness. For however good men they may have to baptize them, Christ is incomparably better who will then be the Head of the baptized, if the baptizer be a faithless man, but undetected. [2418] But let the statements that you make be restored, and then it will forthwith be found that this which depends upon it and follows in close connection from it is not my sentiment, and that any evil which it contains is retorted on the opinion which you maintain. In like manner, take away the supposition, If the good baptizer is the good tree, so that he whom he has baptized is his good fruit, and if, when the character of an evil tree is concealed, then any one that has been baptized by it is born, not of it, but of Christ,--take away this hypothesis, which you were compelled to confess had its origin in your sect and in the letter of Petilianus, and the mad conclusion which follows from it will be mine, to be ascribed to me alone, then they are justified with greater holiness who are baptized by undetected evil men, than they who are baptized by men that are genuinely and manifestly good. [2419]But restore the hypothesis on which this depends, and you will at once see both that I have been right in making this statement for your correction, and that all that with good reason displeases you in this opinion has recoiled upon your own head.

[2417] 1 Cor. xv. 13-15.

[2418] See Book I. c. 6, 7.

[2419] See Book I. c. 8, 9.

Chapter 47.

57. Furthermore, in like manner as those who denied the resurrection of the dead could in no way defend themselves from the evil consequences which the apostle proved to follow

from their premises, in order to refute their error, saying, "Then is not Christ raised," with the other conclusions of similar atrocity, unless they changed their opinions, and acknowledged that there was a resurrection of the dead; so is it necessary that you should change your opinion, and cease to rest on man the hope of those who are baptized, if you do not wish to have imputed to you what we say for your refutation and correction, that they are justified with greater holiness who are baptized by undetected evil men than those that are baptized by men that are genuinely and manifestly good. For if you make your first assertion, see what I say, unless some one shall suppress this a second time, and make out that I have entertained the opinion which I quote for your refutation and correction. See what I lay down as my premiss, from which hangs the statement which I shall subsequently make: If you rest the hope of those who are to be baptized on the man by whom they are baptized, and if you maintain, as Petilianus wrote, that the man who baptizes is the origin and root and head of him that is baptized; if you receive as the good tree the good man who baptizes, and as his good fruit the man who has been baptized by him; then you put it into our heads to ask from what origin he springs, from what root he shoots up, to what head he is joined, from what tree he is born, who is baptized by an undetected bad man? For to this inquiry, belongs also the following, to which I have over and over again maintained that Petilianus has given no reply: By what means is a man to be cleansed who receives baptism while he is ignorant of the stain upon the conscience of him that gives but not in holiness? for this conscience of him that gives, or of him that gives in holiness, Petilianus wishes to be the origin, root, head, seed, tree from which the sanctification of the baptized has its existence,--springs, begins, sprouts forth, is born.

Chapter 48.

58. When we ask, therefore, by what means the man is to be cleansed whom you do not baptize again in your communion, even when it has been made clear that he has been baptized by some one who, on account of some concealed iniquity, did not at the time possess the conscience of one that gives in holiness, what answer do you intend to make, except that he is cleansed by Christ or by God, although, indeed, Christ is Himself God over all, blessed for ever, [2420] or by the Holy Spirit since He too is Himself God, because this Trinity of Persons is one God? Whence Peter, after saying to a man, "Thou hast dared to lie to the Holy Ghost," immediately went on to add what was the nature of the Holy Ghost, saying, "Thou hast not lied unto men, but unto God." [2421]Lastly, even if you were to say that he was cleansed and purified by an angel when he is unacquainted with the pollution in the conscience of him that gives but not in holiness, take notice that it is said of the saints, when they shall have risen to eternal life, that they shall then be equal to the angels of God. [2422]Any one, therefore, that is cleansed even by an angel is cleansed with greater holiness than if he were cleansed by any kind of conscience of man. Why then are you unwilling that it should be said to you, If cleaning is wrought by the hands of a man when he is genuinely and manifestly good; but when the man is evil, but undetected in his wickedness, then since he has not the conscience of one that gives in holiness, it is no longer he, but God, or an angel, that cleanses; therefore they who are baptized by undetected evil men are justified with greater holiness than those who are baptized by men that are genuinely and manifestly good? And if this opinion is displeasing to you, as in reality it ought to be displeasing to every one, then take away the source from which

it springs, correct the premiss to which it is indissolubly bound; for if these do not precede as hypotheses, the other will not follow as a consequence.

[2420] Rom. ix. 5.

[2421] Acts v. 3, 4.

[2422] Matt. xxii. 30.

Chapter 49.

59. Do not therefore any longer say, "The conscience of one that gives in holiness is what we look for to cleanse the conscience of the recipient," lest you be asked, When a stain on the conscience of the giver is concealed, who cleanses the conscience of the recipient? And when you shall have answered, Either God or an angel (since there is no other answer which you possibly can make), then should follow a consequence whereby you would be confounded: Those then are justified with greater holiness who are baptized by undetected evil men, so as to be cleansed by God or by an angel, than those who are baptized by men who are genuinely and manifestly good, who cannot be compared with God or with the angels. But prevail upon yourselves to say what is said by Truth and by the Catholic Church, that not only when the minister of baptism is evil, but also when he is holy and good, hope is still not to be placed in man, but in Him that justifieth the ungodly, in whom if any man believe, his faith is counted for righteousness. [2423]For when we say, Christ baptizes, we do not mean by a visible ministry, as Petilianus believes, or would have men think that he believes, to be our meaning, but by a hidden grace, by a hidden power in the Holy Spirit as it is said of Him by John the Baptist, "The same is He which

baptizeth with the Holy Ghost." [2424]Nor has He, as Petilianus says, now ceased to baptize; but He still does it, not by any ministry of the body, but by the invisible working of His majesty. For in that we say, He Himself baptizes, we do not mean, He Himself holds and dips in the water the bodies of the believers; but He Himself invisibly cleanses, and that He does to the whole Church without exception. Nor, indeed, may we refuse to believe the words of the Apostle Paul who says concerning Him, "Husbands, love your wives, even as Christ also loved the Church, and gave Himself for it, that He might sanctify and cleanse it with the washing of water by the word." [2425]Here you see that Christ sanctifies; here you see that Christ also Himself washes, Himself purifies with the self-same washing of water by the word, wherein the ministers are seen to do their work in the body. Let no one, therefore, claim unto himself what is of God. The hope of men is only sure when it is fixed on Him who cannot deceive, since "Cursed be every one that trusteth in man," [2426] and "Blessed is that man that maketh the Lord His trust." [2427] For the faithful steward shall receive as his reward eternal life; but the unfaithful steward, when he dispenses his lord's provisions to his fellow-servants, must in no wise be conceived to make the provisions useless by his own unfaithfulness. For the Lord says, "Whatsoever they bid you observe, that observe and do; but do not ye after their works." [2428]And this is therefore the injunction that is given us against evil stewards, that the good things of God should be received at their hands, but that we should beware of their own evil life, by reason of its unlikeness to what they thus dispense.

[2423] Rom. iv. 5.

[2424] John i. 33.

[2425] Eph. v. 25, 26.

[2426] Jer. xvii. 5.

[2427] Ps. xl. 4.

[2428] Matt. xxiii. 3.

Chapter 50.

60. But if it is clear that Petilianus has made no answer to those first words of my epistle, and that, when he has endeavored to make an answer, he has shown all the more clearly how incapable he was of answering, what shall I say in respect of those portions of my writings which he has not even attempted to answer, on which he has not touched at all? And yet if any one shall be willing to review their character, having in his possession both my writings and those of Petilianus, I think he will understand by what confirmation they are supported. And that I may show you this as shortly as I can, I would beg you to call to mind the proofs that were advanced from holy Scripture, or refresh your memory by reading both what he has brought forward as against me, and what I have brought forward in my answer as against you, and see how I have shown that the passages which he has brought forward are antagonistic not to me, but rather to yourselves; whilst he has altogether failed to touch those which I brought forward as especially necessary, and in that one passage of the apostle which he has endeavored to make use of as though it favored him, you will see how he found himself without the means of making his escape.

61. For the portion of this epistle which he wrote to his adherents--from the beginning down to the passage in which he says, "This is the commandment of the Lord to us, When they

persecute you in this city, flee ye into another;' [2429] and if they persecute you in that also, flee ye to a third"--came first into my hands, and to it I made a reply; and when this reply of ours had fallen, in turn, into his hands, he wrote in answer to it this which I am now refuting, showing that he has made no reply to mine. In that first portion, therefore, of his writings to which I first replied, these are the passages of Scripture which he conceives to be opposed to us: "Every good tree bringeth forth good fruit, but a corrupt tree bringeth forth evil fruit. Do men gather grapes of thorns?" [2430] And again: "A good man, out of the good treasure of his heart, bringeth forth good things: and an evil man, out of the evil treasure, bringeth forth evil things." [2431] And again: "When a man is baptized by one that is dead, his washing profiteth him nothing." [2432] From these passages he is anxious to show that the man who is baptized is made to partake of the character of him by whom he is baptized; I on the other hand, have shown in what sense these passages should be received, and that they could in no wise aid his view. But as for the other expressions which he has used against evil and accursed men, I have sufficiently shown that they are applicable to the Lord's wheat, dispersed, as was foretold and promised, throughout the world, and that they might rather be used by us against you. Examine them again, and you will find it so.

62. But the passages which I have advanced to assert the truth of the Catholic Church, are the following: As regards the question of baptism, that our being born again, cleansed, justified by the grace of God, should not be ascribed to the man who administered the sacrament, I quoted these: "It is better to trust in the Lord than to put confidence in man:" [2433] and "Cursed be every one that trusteth in man;" [2434]

and that, "Salvation belongeth unto the Lord;" [2435] and that, "Vain is the help of man;" [2436] and that, "Neither is he that planteth anything, neither he that watereth, but God that giveth the increase;" [2437] and that He in whom men believe justifieth the ungodly, that his faith may be counted to him for righteousness. [2438] But in behalf of the unity of the Church itself, which is spread abroad throughout all the world, with which you do not hold communion, I urged that the following passages were prophesied of Christ: that "He shall have dominion also from sea to sea, and from the river unto the ends of the earth;" [2439] and, "I shall give Thee the heathen for Thine inheritance, and the uttermost parts of the earth for Thy possession;" [2440] and that the covenant of God made with Abraham may be quoted in behalf of our, that is, of the Catholic communion, in which it is written, "In thy seed shall all nations of the earth be blessed;" [2441] which seed the apostle interprets, saying, "And to thy seed, which is Christ." [2442]Whence it is evident that in Christ not only Africans or Africa, but all the nations through which the Catholic Church is spread abroad, should receive the blessing which was promised so long before. And that the chaff is to be with the wheat even to the time of the last winnowing, that no one may excuse the sacrilege of his own separation from the Church by calumnious accusations of other men's offenses, if he shall have left or deserted the communion of all nations; and to show that the society of Christians may not be divided on account of evil ministers, that is, evil rulers in the Church, I further quoted the passage, "All whatsoever they bid you observe, that observe and do; but do not ye after their works; for they say and do not." [2443]With regard to these passages of holy Scripture which I advanced to prove my points, he neither showed how they ought to be otherwise interpreted, so as to prove that they neither made for us nor against you, nor was he willing to touch them in any way. Nay, his whole object was could it have been achieved, that by the tumultuous outpouring of his abuse, it might never occur to any one at all, who after reading my epistle might have been willing to read his as well, that these things had been said by me.

[2429] Matt. x. 23.

[2430] Matt. vii. 17, 16.

[2431] Matt. xii. 35.

[2432] Ecclus. xxxiv. 25. See Book I. c. 9, 10.

[2433] Ps. cxviii. 8.

[2434] Jer. xvii. 5.

[2435] Ps. iii. 8.

[2436] Ps. lx. 11.

[2437] 1 Cor. iii. 7.

[2438] Rom. iv. 5.

[2439] Ps. lxxii. 8.

[2440] Ps. ii. 8.

[2441] Gen. xxii. 18.

[2442] Gal. iii. 16.

[2443] Matt. xxiii. 3.

Chapter 51.

63. Next, listen for a short time to the kind of way in which he has tried to use, in his own behalf, the passages which I had advanced from the writings of the Apostle Paul. "For you asserted," he says, "that the Apostle Paul finds fault with those who used to say that they were of the Apostle Paul, saying, Was Paul crucified for you? or were ye baptized in the name of Paul?' [2444]Wherefore, if they were in error, and would have perished had they not been corrected, because they wished to be of Paul, what hope can there possibly be for those who have wished to be of Donatus? For this is their sole object, that the origin, and root, and head of him that is baptized should be none other than he by whom he is baptized." [2445]These words, and this confirmation from the writings of the apostle, he has quoted from my epistle, and he has proposed to himself the task of refuting them. Go on then, I beg of you, to see how he has fulfilled the task. For he says, "This assertion is meaningless, and inflated, and childish, and foolish, and something very far from a true exposition of our faith. For you would only be right in asserting this, if we were to say, We have been baptized in the name of Donatus, or Donatus was crucified for us, or we have been baptized in our own name. But since such things as this neither have been said nor are said by us,--seeing that we follow the formula of the holy Trinity,--it is clear that you are mad to bring such accusations against us. Or if you think that we have been baptized in the name of Donatus, or in our own name, you are miserably deceived, and at the same time confess in your sacrilege that you on your part defile your wretched selves in the name of Cæcilianus." This is the answer which Petilianus has made to those arguments of mine, not supposing--or rather making a noise that no one might suppose--that he has made no answer at all which could bear in any way upon the question which is under discussion.

For who could fail to see that this witness of the apostle has been adduced by us with all the more propriety, in that you do not say that you were baptized in the name of Donatus, or that Donatus was crucified for you, and yet separate yourselves from the communion of the Catholic Church out of respect to the party of Donatus; as also those whom Paul was rebuking certainly did not say that they had been baptized in the name of Paul, or that Paul has been crucified for them, and yet they were making a schism in the name of Paul. As therefore in their case, for whom Christ, not Paul, was crucified, and who were baptized in the name of Christ, not of Paul, and who yet said, "I am of Paul," the rebuke is used with all the more propriety, "Was Paul crucified for you? or were ye baptized in the name of Paul?" to make them cling to Him who was crucified for them, and in whose name they were baptized, and not be guilty of division in the name of Paul; so in your case, also, the rebuke, Was Donatus crucified for you? or were ye baptized in the name of Donatus? is used all the more appositely, because you do not say, We were baptized in the name of Donatus, and yet desire to be of the party of Donatus. For you know that it was Christ who was crucified for you, and Christ in whose name you were baptized; and yet, out of respect to the name and party of Donatus, you show such obstinacy in fighting against the unity of Christ, who was crucified for you, and in whose name you were baptized.

[2444] 1 Cor. i. 13.

[2445] See Book I. cc. 3, 4, 4, 5.

Chapter 52.

64. But if you wish to see that the object of Petilianus in his writings really was to prove "that the origin, and root, and head

of him that is baptized is none other than he by whom he is baptized," and that this has not been asserted by me without meaning, or childishly, or foolishly, review the beginning of the epistle itself to which I made my reply, or rather pay careful attention to me as I quote it. "The conscience," he says, "of one that gives in holiness is what we look for to cleanse the conscience of the recipient; for he who has received his faith from one that is faithless, receives not faith but guilt." And as though some one had said to him, Whence do you derive your proof of this? he goes on to say, "For everything has its existence from a source and root; and if anything has not a head, it is nothing; nor does anything well confer a new birth, unless it be born again of good seed. And this being so, brethren, what perversity must it be to maintain that he who is guilty by reason of his own offenses should make another free from guilt; whereas our Lord Jesus Christ says, A good tree bringeth forth good fruit: do men gather grapes of thorns?' And again, A good man, out of the good treasure of his heart, bringeth forth good things; and an evil man, out of the evil treasure, bringeth forth evil things.' And again, When a man is baptized by one that is dead, his washing profiteth him nothing.'" You see to what end all these things tend, viz., that the conscience of him that gives in holiness (lest any one, by receiving his faith from one that is faithless, should receive not faith but guilt) should be itself the origin, and root, and head, and seed of him that is baptized. For, wishing to prove that the conscience of one that gives in holiness is what we look for to cleanse the conscience of the recipient, and that he receives not faith but guilt, who wittingly receives his faith from one that is faithless, he has added immediately afterwards, "For everything has its existence from a source and root; and if anything has not a head, it is nothing; nor does anything well confer a new birth, unless it be born again of good seed." And for fear that any one should be so dull as still not to understand that in each case he is speaking of the man by whom a person is baptized, he explains this afterwards, and says, "This being so, brethren, what perversity must it be to maintain that he who is guilty by reason of his own offenses should make another free from guilt; whereas our Lord Jesus Christ says, A good tree bringeth forth good fruit: do men gather grapes of thorns?'" And lest, by some incredible stupidity of understanding, the hearer or seer should be blind enough not to see that he is speaking of the man that baptizes, he adds another passage, where he actually specifies the man. "And again," he says, "A good man, out of the good treasure of his heart, bringeth forth good things; and an evil man, out of the evil treasure, bringeth forth evil things;' and again, When a man is baptized by one that is dead, his washing profiteth him nothing,'" Certainly it is now plain, certainly he needs no longer any interpreter, or disputant, or demonstrator, to show that the object of his party is to prove that the origin, and root, and head of him that is baptized is none other than he by whom he is baptized. And yet, being overwhelmed by the force of truth, and as though forgetful of what he had said before, Petilianus acknowledges afterwards to me that Christ is the origin and root of them that are regenerate, and the Head of the Church, and not any one that may happen to be the dispenser and minister of baptism. For having said that the apostles used to baptize in the name of Christ, and set forth Christ as the foundation of their faith, to make men Christians, and being fain to prove this, too, by passages and examples from holy Scripture, just as though we were denying it, he says, "Where is now that voice, from which issued the noise of those minute and constant petty questionings, wherein, in the spirit of envy and self-conceit, you uttered many involved sayings about Christ, and for Christ, and in Christ, in opposition to the rashness and haughtiness of men? Lo, Christ is the origin, Christ is the head, Christ is the root of the Christian." When, therefore, I heard this, what could I do but give thanks to Christ, who had compelled the man to make confession? All those things, therefore, are false which he said in the beginning of his epistle, when he wished to persuade us that the conscience of one that gives in holiness must be looked for to cleanse the conscience of the recipient; and that when one has wittingly received his faith from one that is faithless he receives not faith but guilt. For, wishing as it were to show clearly how much rested in the man that baptizes, he had added what he seems to think most weighty proofs, saying "For everything has its existence from a source and root; and if anything has not a head, it is nothing." But afterwards, when he says what we also say, "Lo, Christ is the origin, Christ is the head, Christ is the root of the Christian," he wipes out what he had said before, "that the conscience of one that gives in holiness is the origin, and root, and head of the recipient." The truth, therefore, has prevailed, so that the man who is desirous to receive the baptism of Christ should not rest his hope upon the man who administers the sacrament, but should approach in all security to Christ Himself, as to the source which is not changed, to the root which is not plucked up, to the head which is not cast down.

Chapter 53.

65. Then who is there that could fail to perceive from what a vein of conceit it proceeds, that in explaining as it were the declaration of the apostle, he says, "He who said, I planted, Apollos watered, but God gave the increase,' surely meant nothing else than this, that I made a man a catechumen in

Christ, Apollo baptized him; God confirmed what we had done?'" Why then did not Petilianus add what the apostle added, and I especially took pains to quote, "So then neither is he that planteth anything, neither he that watereth; but God that giveth the increase"? [2446]And if he be willing to interpret this on the same principle as what he has set down above, it follows beyond all doubt, that neither is he that baptizeth anything but God that giveth the increase. For what matter does it make in reference to the question now before us, in what sense it has been said, "I planted, Apollos watered,"--whether it is really to be taken as equivalent to his saying, "I made a catechumen, Apollos baptized him;" or whether there be any other truer and more congruous understanding of it?--for in the mean time, according to his own interpretation of the words, neither is he that makes the catechumen anything, neither he that baptizes, but God that gives the increase. But there is a great difference between confirming what another does, and doing anything oneself. For He who gives the increase does not confirm a tree or a vine, but creates it. For by that increase it comes to pass that even a piece of wood planted in the ground produces and establishes a root; by that increase it comes to pass that a seed cast into the earth puts forth a shoot. But why should we make a longer dissertation on this point? It is enough that, according to Petilianus himself neither he that maketh a catechumen, nor he that baptizes, is anything, but God that gives the increase. But when would Petilianus say this, so that we should understand that he meant, Neither is Donatus of Carthage anything, neither Januarius, neither Petilianus? When would the swelling of his pride permit him to say this, which now causes the man to think himself to be something, when he is nothing, deceiving himself? [2447]

[2446] 1 Cor. iii. 6, 7.

[2447] Gal. vi. 3.

Chapter 54.

66. Finally, again, a little afterwards, when he resolved and was firmly purposed, as it were, to reconsider once more the words of the apostle which he had brought up against him, he was unwilling to set down this that I had said, preferring something else in which by some means or other the swelling of human pride might find means to breathe. "For to reconsider," he says, "those words of the apostle, on which you founded an argument against us; he said, What is Apollos, what is Paul, save only ministers of Him in whom ye have believed?' [2448]What else for example, does he say to all of us than this, What is Donatus of Carthage, what is Januarius, what is Petilianus, save only ministers of Him in whom ye have believed?" I did not bring forward this passage of the apostle, but I did bring forward that which he has been unwilling to quote, "Neither he that planteth is anything, neither he that watereth; but God that giveth the increase." But Petilianus was willing to insert those words of the apostle, in which he asks what is Paul, and what is Apollos, and answers that "They are ministers of Him in whom ye have believed." This the muscles of the heretic's neck could bear; but he was wholly unable to endure the other, in which the apostle did not ask and answer what he was, but said that he was nothing. But now I am willing to ask whether it be true that the minister of Christ is nothing. Who will say so much as this? In what sense, therefore, is it true that "Neither is he that planteth anything, neither he that watereth, but God that giveth the increase," except that he who is something in one point of view may be

nothing in another? For ministering and dispensing the word and sacrament he is something, but for purifying and justifying he is nothing, seeing that this is not accomplished in the inner man, except by Him by whom the whole man was created, and who while He remained God was made man,--by Him, that is, of whom it was said, "Purifying their hearts by faith;" [2449] and "To him that believeth on Him that justifieth the ungodly." [2450] And this testimony Petilianus has been willing to set forth in my words, whilst in his own he has neither handled it nor even touched it.

[2448] Ministri ejus cui credidistis. See 1 Cor. iii. 4, 5.

[2449] Acts xv. 9.

[2450] Rom. iv. 5.

Chapter 55.

67. A minister, therefore, that is a dispenser of the word and sacrament of the gospel, if he is a good man, becomes a fellow-partner in the working of the gospel; but if he is a bad man, he does not therefore cease to be a dispenser of the gospel. For if he is good, he does it of his own free will; but if he is a bad man,--that is, one who seeks his own and not the things of Jesus Christ,--he does it unwillingly, for the sake of other things which he is seeking after. See, however, what the same apostle has said: "For if I do this thing willingly," he says, "I have a reward; but if against my will, a dispensation of the gospel is committed unto me;" [2451] as though he were to say, If I, being good, announce what is good, I attain unto it also myself; but if, being evil, I announce it, yet I announce what is good. For has he in any way said, If I do it against my will, then shall I not be a dispenser of the gospel? Peter and the other disciples

announce the good tidings, as being good themselves. Judas did it against his will, but yet, when he was sent, he announced it in common with the rest. They have a reward; to him a dispensation of the gospel was committed. But they who received the gospel at the mouth of all those witnesses, could not be cleansed and justified by him that planted, or by him that watered, but by Him alone that gives the increase. For neither are we going to say that Judas did not baptize, seeing that he was still among the disciples when that which is written was being accomplished, "Jesus Himself baptized not, but His disciples." [2452]Are we to suppose that, because he had not betrayed Christ, therefore he who had the bag, and bare what was put therein, [2453] was still enabled to dispense grace without prejudice to those who received it, though he could not be an upright guardian of the money entrusted to his care? Or if he did not baptize, at any rate we must acknowledge that he preached the gospel. But if you consider this a trifling function, and of no importance, see what you must think of the Apostle Paul himself, who said, "For Christ sent me not to baptize, but to preach the gospel." [2454]To this we may add, that according to this, Apollos begins to be more important, who watered by baptizing, than Paul, who planted by preaching the gospel, though Paul claims to himself the relation of father towards the Corinthians in virtue of this very act, and does not grant this title to those who came to them after him. For he says, "Though ye have ten thousand instructors in Christ, yet have ye not many fathers; for in Christ Jesus I have begotten you through the gospel." [2455]He says, "I have begotten you" to the same men to whom he says in another place, "I thank God that I baptized none of you but Crispus and Gaius, and I baptized also the household of Stephanus." [2456]He had begotten them, therefore, not through himself, but through the gospel. And even though he had been seeking his own, and not the things of Jesus Christ, and had been doing this unwillingly, so as to receive no reward for himself, yet he would have been dispensing the treasure of the Lord; and this, though evil himself, he would not have been making evil or useless to those who received it well.

[2451] 1 Cor. ix. 17.

[2452] John iv. 2.

[2453] John xii. 6.

[2454] 1 Cor. i. 17.

[2455] 1 Cor. iv. 15.

[2456] 1 Cor. i. 14, 16.

Chapter 56.

68. And if this is rightly said of the gospel, with how much greater certainty should it be said of baptism, which belongs to the gospel in such wise, that without it no one can reach the kingdom of heaven, and with it only if to the sacrament be added righteousness? For He who said, "Except a man be born of water and of the Spirit, he cannot enter into the kingdom of God," [2457] said Himself also, "Except your righteousness shall exceed the righteousness of the scribes and Pharisees, ye shall in no case enter into the kingdom of heaven." [2458] The form of the sacrament is given through baptism, the form of righteousness through the gospel. Neither one without the other leads to the kingdom of heaven. Yet even men of inferior learning can baptize perfectly, but to preach the gospel perfectly is a task of much greater difficulty and rarity.

Therefore the teacher of the Gentiles, that was superior in excellence to the majority, was sent to preach the gospel, not to baptize; because the latter could be done by many, the former only by a few, of whom he was chief. And yet we read that he said in certain places, "My gospel;" [2459] but he never called baptism either his, or any one's else by whom it was administered. For that baptism alone which John gave is called John's baptism. [2460]This that man received as the special pledge of his ministry, that the preparatory sacrament of washing should even be called by the name of him by whom it was administered; whereas the baptism which the disciples of Christ administered was never called by the name of any one of them, that it should be understood to be His alone of whom it is said, "Christ loved the Church, and gave Himself for it, that He might sanctify and cleanse it with the washing of water by the word." [2461]If, therefore, the gospel, which is Christ's, but so that a minister also may call it his in virtue of his office of administering it, can be received by a man even at the hands of an evil minister without danger to himself, if he does according to what he says, and not after the example of what he does, how much more may any one who comes in good faith to Christ receive without fear of contagion from an evil minister the baptism of Christ, which none of the apostles so administered as to dare to call it his own?

[2457] John iii. 5.

[2458] Matt. v. 20.

[2459] 2 Tim. ii. 8.

[2460] Acts xix. 3.

[2461] Eph. v. 25, 26.

Chapter 57.

69. Furthermore, if, while I have continued without intermission to prove how entirely the passages of Scripture which Petilianus has quoted against us have failed to hurt our cause, he himself has in some cases not touched at all what I have quoted, and partly, when he has endeavored to handle them, has shown that the only thing that he could do was to fail in finding an escape from them, you require no long exhortation or advice in order to see what you ought to maintain, and what you should avoid. But it may be that this has been the kind of show that he has made in dealing with the testimony of holy Scripture, but that he has not been without force in the case of the documentary evidence found in the records of the schism itself. Let us then see in the case of these too, though it is superfluous to inquire into them after testimony from the word of God, what he has quoted, or what he has proved. For, after pouring forth a violent invective against traditors, and quoting loudly many passages against them from the holy books themselves, he yet said nothing which could prove his opponents to be traditors. But I quoted the case of Silvanus of Cirta, who held his own see some little time before himself, who was expressly declared in the Municipal Chronicles to have been a traditor while he was yet a sub-deacon. Against this fact he did not venture to whisper a syllable. And yet you cannot fail to see how strong the pressure was which must have been urging him to reply that he might show a man, who was his predecessor, not only one of his party, but a partner, so to speak, in his see, to have been innocent of the crime of delivering up the sacred books, especially as you rest the whole strength of your cause on the fact that you give the name of traditor to all whom you either

pretend or believe to have been the successors of traditors in the path of their communion. Although, then, the very exigencies of your cause would seem to compel him to undertake the defence of a citizen even of Russicadia, or Calama, or any other city of your party, whom I should declare to be a traditor, on the authority of the Municipal Chronicles, yet he did not open his mouth even in defense of his own predecessor. For what reason, except that he could not find any mist dark enough to deceive the minds of even the slowest and sleepiest of men? For what could he have said, except that the charges brought against Silvanus were false? But we quote the words of the Chronicles, both as to the date of the fact, and as to the time of the information laid before Zenophilus the ex-consul. [2462]And how could he resist this evidence, being encompassed on every side by the most excellent cause of the Catholics, while yours was bad as bad could be? For which reason I quote these words from my epistle to which he would fain be thought to have replied in this which I am now refuting, that you may see for yourselves how impregnable the position must be against which he has been able to find no safer weapon than silence.

[2462] See Book III. c. Cresconium, cc. 27, 28, 31, 32.

Chapter 58.

70. For when he quoted a passage from the gospel as making against us, where our Lord says, "They will come to you in sheep's clothing, but inwardly they are ravening wolves; ye shall know them by their fruits," [2463] --I answered and said, "Then let us consider their fruits;" and then I at once went on to add the following words: "You bring up against them their delivery of the sacred books. This very charge we urge with greater

probability, against their accusers themselves. And not to carry our search too far: in the same city of Constantina, your predecessors ordained Silvanus bishop at the very outset of his schism. He, while he was still a sub-deacon, was most unmistakably entered as a traditor in the archives of the city. If you, on your side, bring forward documents against our predecessors, all that we ask is equal terms, that we should either believe both to be true, or both to be false. If both are true, you are unquestionably guilty of schism, who have pretended that you avoid offenses in the communion of the whole world, though these were common among you in your own fragmentary sect. But again, if both are false, you are unquestionably guilty of schism, who, on account of the false charges of traditors, are staining yourselves with the heinous offense of severance from the Church. But if we have something to urge in accusation, while you have nothing, or if our charges are true, while yours are false, it is no longer matter of discussion how thoroughly your mouths are closed. What if the holy and true Church of Christ were to convince and overcome you, even if we held no documents in support of our cause, or only such as were false, while you had possession of some genuine proof of delivery of the sacred books, what would then remain for you, except that, if you would, you should show your love of peace, or otherwise should hold your tongues? For whatever in that case you might bring forward in evidence, I should be able to say with the greatest ease and with the most perfect truth, that then you are bound to prove as much to the full and Catholic unity of the Church, already spread abroad and established throughout so many nations, to the end that you should remain within, and that those whom you convict should be expelled. And if you have endeavored to do this, certainly you have not been able to make good your proof; and, being vanquished or enraged, you have separated yourselves, with all the heinous guilt of sacrilege, from the guiltless men who could not condemn on insufficient proof. But if you have not even endeavored to do this, then with most accursed and unnatural blindness you have cut yourselves off from the wheat of Christ, which grows throughout His whole fields, that is, throughout the whole world until the end, because you have taken offense at a few tares in Africa." [2464]To this, which I have quoted from my former epistle, Petilianus has made no answer whatsoever. And, at all events, you see that in these few words is comprised the whole question which is at issue between us. For what should he endeavor to say, when, whatever course he chose, he was sure to be debated?

71. For when documents are brought forward relating to the traditors, both by us against the men of your party, and by you against the men of our party, (if indeed any really are brought forward on your side, for to this very day we are left in total ignorance of them; nor indeed can we believe that Petilianus would have omitted to insert them in his letter, seeing that he has taken so much pain to secure the quotation and insertion of those portions of the Chronicles which bear on the matter in opposition to me),--but still, as I began to say, if such documents are brought forward both by us and by you, documents of whose existence we are wholly ignorant to this very day,--surely you must acknowledge that either both are true, or both false, or ours true and yours false, or yours true and ours false; for there is no further alternative that can be suggested.

[2463] Matt. vii. 15, 16.

[2464] See Book I. cc. 21, 22, 23, 24.

Chapter 59.

But according to all these four hypotheses, the truth is on the side of the communion of the Catholic Church. For if both are true, then you certainly should not have deserted the communion of the whole world on account of men such as you too had among yourselves. But if both are false, you should have guarded against the guilt of most accursed division, which had not even any pretext to allege of any delivery of the sacred books. If ours are true and yours are false, you have long been without anything to say for yourselves. If yours are true and ours are false, we have been liable to be deceived, in common with the whole world, not about the truth of the faith, but about the unrighteousness of men. For the seed of Abraham, dispersed throughout the world, was bound to pay attention, not to what you said you knew, but to what you proved to the judges. Whence have we any knowledge of what was done by those men who were accused by your ancestors, even if the allegations made against them were true, so long as they were held to be not true but false, either by the judges who took cognizance of the case, or at least by the general body of the Church dispersed throughout the world, which was only bound to pay heed to the sentence of the judges? God does not necessarily pardon any human guilt that others in the weakness of human judgment fail to discover; yet I maintain that no one is rightly deemed guilty for having believed a man to be innocent who was not convicted. How then do you prove the world to be guilty, merely because it did not know what possibly was really guilt in the Africans,--its ignorance arising either from the fact that no one reported the sin to it, or from its having given credence, in respect of the information which was given, rather to the judges who took cognizance of the case, than to the murmurers who were defeated? So far then, Petilianus deserves all praise, in that, when he saw that on this point I was absolutely impregnable, he passed it by in silence. Yet he does not deserve praise for his attempts to obscure in a mist of words other points which were equally impregnable, which yet he thought could be obscured; or for having put me in the place of his cause, when the cause left him nothing to say; while even about myself he could say nothing except what was either altogether false, or undeserving of any blame, or without any bearing whatsoever upon me. But, in the meantime, are you, whom I have made judges between Petilianus and myself, possessed of discrimination enough to decide in any degree between what is true and what is false, between what is mere empty swelling and what is solid, between what is troubled and what is calm, between inflammation and soundness, between divine predictions and human assumptions, between bringing an accusation and establishing it, between proofs and fictions, between pleading a cause and leading one away from it? If you have such power of discrimination, well and good; but if you have it not, we shall not repent of having bestowed our pains on you, for even though your heart be not converted unto peace, yet our peace shall return unto ourselves.

[2319] Possidius, in the third chapter of his Indiculus, designates this third book as "One book against the second letter of the same." Cp. Aug. Retractt. Bk. II. c. xxv.

ST. AUGUSTIN:
A TREATISE CONCERNING THE CORRECTION OF THE DONATISTS, OR EPISTLE CLXXXV
[DE CORRECTIONE DONATISTARUM, LIBER SEU EPISTOLA CLXXXV.]
CIRCA A.D. 417 [2465]

A Letter of Augustin [2466] to Boniface, who, as we learn from Epistle 220, was Tribune, and afterwards Count in Africa. In it Augustin shows that the heresy of the Donatists has nothing in common with that of Arius; and points out the moderation with which it was possible to recall the heretics to the communion of the Church through awe of the imperial laws. He adds remarks concerning the savage conduct of the Donatists and Circumcelliones, concluding with a discussion of the unpardonable nature of the sin against the Holy Ghost. [2467]

[2465] Written c. 417.

[2466] In Book 11. c. xlviii of his Retractations, Augustin says: "About the same time" (as that at which he wrote his treatise De Gestis Pelagii, i.e., about the year 417), "I wrote also a treatise De Correctione Donatistarum, for the sake of those who were not willing that the Donatists should be subjected to the correction of the imperial laws." This treatise begins with the words "Laudo, et gratulor, et admiror." This letter in the old editions was No. 50,--the letter which is now No. 4 in the appendix (Benedictine) being formerly No. 185.

[2467] He handles the same thought in Ep. 93.

Chapter 1.

1. I must express my satisfaction, and congratulations, and admiration, my son Boniface, [2468] in that, amid all the cares of wars and arms, you are eagerly anxious to know concerning the things that are of God. From hence it is clear that in you it is actually a part of your military valor to serve in truth the faith which is in Christ. To place, therefore, briefly before your Grace the difference between the errors of the Arians and the Donatists, the Arians say that the Father, the Son, and the Holy Ghost are different in substance; whereas the Donatists do not say this, but acknowledge the unity of substance in the Trinity. And if some even of them have said that the Son was inferior to the Father, yet they have not denied that He is of the same substance; whilst the greater part of them declare that they hold entirely the same belief regarding the Father and the Son and the Holy Ghost as is held by the Catholic Church. Nor is this the actual question in dispute with them; but they carry on their unhappy strife solely on the question of communion, and in the perversity of their error maintain rebellious hostility against the unity of Christ. But sometimes, as we have heard, some of them, wishing to conciliate the Goths, since they see that they are not without a certain amount of power, profess to entertain the same belief as they. But they are refuted by the authority of their own leaders; for Donatus himself, of whose party they boast themselves to be, is never said to have held this belief.

2. Let not, however, things like these disturb thee, my beloved son. For it is foretold to us that there must needs be heresies and stumbling-blocks, that we may be instructed among our enemies; and that so both our faith and our love may be the more approved,--our faith, namely, that we should not be deceived by them; and our love, that we should take the utmost pains we can to correct the erring ones themselves; not only

watching that they should do no injury to the weak, and that they should be delivered from their wicked error, but also praying for them, that God would open their understanding, and that they might comprehend the Scriptures. For in the sacred books, where the Lord Christ is made manifest, there is also His Church declared; but they, with wondrous blindness, while they would know nothing of Christ Himself save what is revealed in the Scriptures, yet form their notion of His Church from the vanity of human falsehood, instead of learning what it is on the authority of the sacred books.

3. They recognize Christ together with us in that which is written, "They pierced my hands and my feet. They can tell all my bones: they look and stare upon me. They part my garments among them, and cast lots upon my vesture;" and yet they refuse to recognize the Church in that which follows shortly after: "All the ends of the world shall remember, and turn unto the Lord; and all the kindreds of the nations shall worship before Thee. For the kingdom is the Lord's; and He is the Governor among the nations." [2469]They recognize Christ together with us in that which is written, "The Lord hath said unto me, Thou art my Son, this day have I begotten Thee;" and they will not recognize the Church in that which follows: "Ask of me, and I shall give Thee the heathen for Thine inheritance, and the uttermost parts of the earth for Thy possession." [2470]They recognize Christ together with us in that which the Lord Himself says in the gospel, "Thus it behoved Christ to suffer, and to rise from the dead the third day;" and they will not recognize the Church in that which follows: "And that repentance and remission of sins should be preached in His name among all nations, beginning at Jerusalem." [2471]And the testimonies in the sacred books are without number, all of

which it has not been necessary for me to crowd together into this book. And in all of them, as the Lord Christ is made manifest, whether in accordance with His Godhead, in which He is equal to the Father, so that, "In the beginning was the Word, and; the Word was with God, and the Word was God;" or according to the humility of the flesh which He took upon Him, whereby "the Word was made flesh and dwelt among us;" [2472] so is His Church made manifest, not in Africa alone, as they most impudently venture in the madness of their vanity to assert, but spread abroad throughout the world.

4. For they prefer to the testimonies of Holy Writ their own contentions, because, in the case of Cæcilianus, formerly a bishop of the Church of Carthage, against whom they brought charges which they were and are unable to substantiate, they separated themselves from the Catholic Church,--that is, from the unity of all nations. Although, even if the charges had been true which were brought by them against Cæcilianus, and could at length be proved to us, yet, though we might pronounce an anathema upon him even in the grave, [2473] we are still bound not for the sake of any man to leave the Church, which rests for its foundation on divine witness, and is not the figment of litigious opinions, seeing that it is better to trust in the Lord than to put confidence in man. [2474]For we cannot allow that if Cæcilianus had erred,--a supposition which I make without prejudice to his integrity,--Christ should therefore have forfeited His inheritance. It is easy for a man to believe of his fellow-men either what is true or what is false; but it marks abandoned impudence to desire to condemn the communion of the whole world on account of charges alleged against a man, of which you cannot establish the truth in the face of the world.

5. Whether Cæcilianus was ordained by men who had delivered up the sacred books, I do not know. I did not see it, I heard it only from his enemies. It is not declared to me in the law of God, or in the utterances of the prophets, or in the holy poetry of the Psalms, or in the writings of any one of Christ's apostles, or in the eloquence of Christ Himself. But the evidence of all the several scriptures with one accord proclaims the Church spread abroad throughout the world, with which the faction of Donatus does not hold communion. The law of God declared, "In thy seed shall all the nations of the earth be blessed." [2475]The Lord said by the mouth of His prophet, "From the rising of the sun, even unto the going down of the same, a pure sacrifice shall be offered unto my name: for my name shall be great among the heathen." [2476]The Lord said through the Psalmist, "He shall have dominion also from sea to sea, and from the river unto the ends of the earth." [2477]The Lord said by His apostle, "The gospel is come unto you, as it is in all the world, and bringeth forth fruit." [2478]The Son of God said with His own mouth, "Ye shall be witnesses unto me, both in Jerusalem, and in all Judea, and in Samaria, and even unto the uttermost part of the earth." [2479]Cæcilianus, the bishop of the Church of Carthage, is accused with the contentiousness of men; the Church of Christ, established among all nations, is recommended by the voice of God. Mere piety, truth, and love forbid us to receive against Cæcilianus the testimony of men whom we do not find in the Church, which has the testimony of God; for those who do not follow the testimony of God have forfeited the weight which otherwise would attach to their testimony as men.

[2468] The correspondence between Augustin and Boniface is limited to Epp. 185, 189 and 220. The sixteen smaller letters are spurious. For note to Boniface and translations of 189 and 220, see vol. I of this series pp. 552 and 573.

[2469] Ps. xxii. 16-18, 27, 28.

[2470] Ps. ii. 7, 8.

[2471] Luke xxiv. 46, 47.

[2472] John i. 1, 4.

[2473] This epistle was produced in the fifth conference of the fifth ecumenical Synod (553), when the point was under debate whether Theodorus of Mopsuesta could be condemned after his death.

[2474] Ps. cxviii. 8.

[2475] Gen. xxvi. 4.

[2476] Mal. i. 11.

[2477] Ps. lxxii. 8.

[2478] Col. i. 6.

[2479] Acts i. 8.

Chapter 2.

6. I would add, moreover, that they themselves, by making it the subject of an accusation, referred the case of Cæcilianus to the decision of the Emperor Constantine; and that, even after the bishops had pronounced their judgment, [2480] finding that they could not crush Cæcilianus, they brought him in person before the above-named emperor for trial, in the most determined spirit of persecution. And so they were themselves

the first to do what they censure in us, in order that they may deceive the unlearned, saying that Christians ought not to demand any assistance from Christian emperors against the enemies of Christ. And this, too, they did not dare to deny in the conference which we held at the same time in Carthage: nay, they even venture to make it a matter of boasting that their fathers had laid a criminal indictment against Cæcilianus before the emperor; adding furthermore a lie, to the effect that they had there worsted him, and procured his condemnation. How then can they be otherwise than persecutors, seeing that when they persecuted Cæcilianus by their accusations, and were overcome by him, they sought to claim false glory for themselves by a most shameless life; not only considering it no reproach, but glorying in it as conducive to their praise, if they could prove that Cæcilianus had been condemned on the accusation of their fathers? But in regard to the manner in which they were overcome at every turn in the conference itself, seeing that the records are exceedingly voluminous, and it would be a serious matter to have them read to you while you are occupied in other matters that are essential to the peace of Rome, perhaps it may be possible to have a digest [2481] of them read to you, which I believe to be in the possession of my brother and fellow-bishop Optatus; or if he has not a copy, he might easily procure one from the church at Sitifa; for I can well believe that even that volume will prove wearisome enough to you from its lengthiness, amid the burden of your many cares.

7. For the Donatists met with the same fate as the accusers of the holy Daniel. [2482]For as the lions were turned against them, so the laws by which they had proposed to crush an innocent victim were turned against the Donatists; save that,

through the mercy of Christ, the laws which seemed to be opposed to them are in reality their truest friends; for through their operation many of them have been, and are daily being reformed, and return God thanks that they are reformed, and delivered from their ruinous madness. And those who used to hate are now filled with love; and now that they have recovered their right minds, they congratulate themselves that these most wholesome laws were brought to bear against them, with as much fervency as in their madness they detested them; and are filled with the same spirit of ardent love towards those who yet remain as ourselves, desiring that we should strive in like manner that those with whom they had been like to perish might be saved. For both the physician is irksome to the raging madman, and a father to his undisciplined son,--the former because of the restraint, the latter because of the chastisement which he inflicts; yet both are acting in love. But if they were to neglect their charge, and allow them to perish, this mistaken kindness would more truly be accounted cruelty. For if the horse and mule, which have no understanding, resist with all the force of bites and kicks the efforts of the men who treat their wounds in order to cure them; and yet the men, though they are often exposed to danger from their teeth and heels, and sometimes meet with actual hurt, nevertheless do not desert them till they restore them to health through the pain and annoyance which the healing process gives,--how much more should man refuse to desert his fellow-man, or brother to desert his brother, lest he should perish everlastingly, being himself now able to comprehend the vastness of the boon accorded to himself in his reformation, at the very time that he complained of suffering persecution?

8. As then the apostle says, "As we have therefore opportunity, let us do good unto all men, not being weary in well-doing," [2483] so let all be called to salvation, let all be recalled from the path of destruction,--those who may, by the sermons of Catholic preachers; those who may, by the edicts of Catholic princes; some through those who obey the warnings of God, some through those who obey the emperor's commands. For, moreover, when emperors enact bad laws on the side of falsehood, as against the truth, those who hold a right faith are approved, and, if they persevere, are crowned; but when the emperors enact good laws on behalf of the truth against falsehood, then those who rage against them are put in fear, and those who understand are reformed. Whosoever, therefore, refuses to obey the laws of the emperors which are enacted against the truth of God, wins for himself a great reward; but whosoever refuses to obey the laws of the emperors which are enacted in behalf of truth, wins for himself great condemnation. For in the times, too, of the prophets, the kings who, in dealing with the people of God, did not prohibit nor annul the ordinances which were issued contrary to God's commands, are all of them censured; and those who did prohibit and annul them are praised as deserving more than other men. And king Nebuchadnezzar, when he was a servant of idols, enacted an impious law that a certain idol should be worshipped; but those who refused to obey his impious command acted piously and faithfully. And the very same king, when converted by a miracle from God, enacted a pious and praiseworthy law on behalf of the truth, that every one who should speak anything amiss against the true God, the God of Shadrach, Meshach, and Abednego, should perish utterly, with all his house. [2484]If any persons disobeyed this law, and justly suffered the penalty imposed, they might have said what these

men say, that they were righteous because they suffered persecution through the law enacted by the king: and this they certainly would have said, had they been as mad as these who make divisions between the members of Christ, and spurn the sacraments of Christ, and take credit for being persecuted, because they are prevented from doing such things by the laws which the emperors have passed to preserve the unity of Christ and boast falsely of their innocence, and seek from men the glory of martyrdom, which they cannot receive from our Lord.

9. But true martyrs are such as those of whom the Lord says, "Blessed are they which are persecuted for righteousness' sake." [2485]It is not, therefore, those who suffer persecution for their unrighteousness, and for the divisions which they impiously introduce into Christian unity, but those who suffer for righteousness' sake, that are truly martyrs. For Hagar also suffered persecution at the hands of Sarah; [2486] and in that case she who persecuted was righteous, and she unrighteous who suffered persecution. Are we to compare with this persecution which Hagar suffered the case of holy David, who was persecuted by unrighteous Saul? [2487]Surely there is in essential difference, not in respect of his suffering, but because he suffered for righteousness' sake. And the Lord Himself was crucified with two thieves; [2488] but those who were joined in their suffering were separated by the difference of its cause. Accordingly, in the psalm, we must interpret of the true martyrs, who wish to be distinguished from false martyrs, the verse in which it is said, "Judge me, O Lord, and distinguish [2489] my cause from an ungodly nation." [2490]He does not say, Distinguish my punishment, but "Distinguish my cause." For the punishment of the impious may be the same; but the cause of the martyrs is always different. To whose mouth also

the words are suitable, "They persecute me wrongfully; help Thou me;" [2491] in which the Psalmist claimed to have a right to be helped in righteousness, because his adversaries persecuted him wrongfully; for if they had been right in persecuting him, he would have deserved not help, but correction.

10. But if they think that no one can be justified in using violence,--as they said in the course of the conference that the true Church must necessarily be the one which suffers persecution, not the one inflicting it,--in that case I no longer urge what I observed above; because, if the matter stand as they maintain that it does, then Cæcilianus must have belonged to the true Church, seeing that their fathers persecuted him, by pressing his accusation even to the tribunal of the emperor himself. For we maintain that he belonged to the true Church, not merely because he suffered persecution, but because he suffered it for righteousness' sake; but that they were alienated from the Church, not merely because they persecuted, but because they did so in unrighteousness. This, then, is our position. But if they make no inquiry into the causes for which each person inflicts persecution, or for which he suffers it, but think that it is a sufficient sign of a true Christian that he does not inflict persecution, but suffers it, then beyond all question they include Cæcilianus in that definition, who did not inflict, but suffered persecution; and they equally exclude their own fathers from the definition, for they inflicted, but did not suffer it.

11. But this, I say, I forbear to urge. Yet one point I must press: If the true Church is the one which actually suffers persecution, not the one which inflicts it, let them ask the apostle of what Church Sarah was a type, when she inflicted

persecution on her hand-maid. For he declares that the free mother of us all, the heavenly Jerusalem, that is to say, the true Church of God, was prefigured in that woman who cruelly entreated her hand-maid. [2492]But if we investigate the story further, we shall find that the handmaid rather persecuted Sarah by her haughtiness, than Sarah the handmaid by her severity: for the handmaid was doing wrong to her mistress; the mistress only imposed on her a proper discipline in her haughtiness. Again I ask, if good and holy men never inflict persecution upon any one, but only suffer it, whose words they think that those are in the psalm where we read, "I have pursued mine enemies, and overtaken them; neither did I turn again till they were consumed?" [2493]If, therefore, we wish either to declare or to recognize the truth, there is a persecution of unrighteousness, which the impious inflict upon the Church of Christ; and there is a righteous persecution, which the Church of Christ inflicts upon the impious. She therefore is blessed in suffering persecution for righteousness' sake; but they are miserable, suffering persecution for unrighteousness. Moreover, she persecutes in the spirit of love, they in the spirit of wrath; she that she may correct, they that they may overthrow: she that she may recall from error, they that they may drive headlong into error. Finally, she persecutes her enemies and arrests them, until they become weary in their vain opinions, so that they should make advance in the truth; but they, returning evil for good, because we take measures for their good, to secure their eternal salvation, endeavor even to strip us of our temporal safety, being so in love with murder, that they commit it on their own persons, when they cannot find victims in any others. For in proportion as the Christian charity of the Church endeavors to deliver them from that destruction, so that none of them should die, so their madness endeavors either to slay us, that they may feed the lust of their own cruelty, or even to kill themselves, that they may not seem to have lost the power of putting men to death.

[2480] In the Councils at Rome and Arles.

[2481] This digest will be found in the 9th volume of Benedictine edition of Augustin's Works. Breviculus collationis cum Donatistis, p. 371 sqq., reproduced in Migne 613, sqq.

[2482] Dan. vi. 24.

[2483] Gal. vi. 9, 10.

[2484] Dan. iii. 5, 29.

[2485] Matt v. 1.

[2486] Gen. xvi. 6.

[2487] 1 Sam. xviii., xix., etc.

[2488] Luke xxiii. 33.

[2489] Discerne causam meam. The Eng. Vers. has, "plead my cause against an ungodly nation."

[2490] Ps. xliii. 1.

[2491] Ps. cxix. 86.

[2492] Gal. iv. 22-31.

[2493] Ps. xviii. 37.

Chapter 3.

12. But those who are unacquainted with their habits think that they only kill themselves now that all the mass of the people are freed from the fearful madness of their usurped dominion, in virtue of the laws which have been passed for the preservation of unity. But those who know what they were accustomed to do before the passing of the laws, do not wonder at their deaths, but call to mind their character; and especially how vast crowds of them used to come in procession to the most frequented ceremonies of the pagans, while the worship of idols still continued,--not with the view of breaking the idols, but that they might be put to death by those who worshipped them. For if they had sought to break the idols under the sanction of legitimate authority, they might, in case of anything happening to them, have had some shadow of a claim to be considered martyrs; but their only object in coming was, that while the idols remained uninjured, they themselves might meet with death. For it was the general custom of the strongest youths among the worshippers of idols, for each of them to offer in sacrifice to the idols themselves any victims that he might have slain. Some went so far as to offer themselves for slaughter to any travellers whom they met with arms, using violent threats that they would murder them if they failed to meet with death at their hands. Sometimes, too, they extorted with violence from any passing judge that they should be put to death by the executioners, or by the officer of his court. And hence we have a story, that a certain judge played a trick upon them, by ordering them to be bound and led away, as though for execution, and so escaped their violence, without injury to himself or them. Again, it was their daily sport to kill themselves, by throwing themselves over precipices, or into the water, or into the fire. For the devil taught them these three modes of suicide, so that, when they wished to die, and could

not find any one whom they could terrify into slaying them with his sword, they threw themselves over the rocks, or committed themselves to the fire or the eddying pool. But who can be thought to have taught them this, having gained possession of their hearts, but he who actually suggested to our Saviour Himself as a duty sanctioned by the law, that He should throw Himself down from a pinnacle of the temple? [2494] And his suggestion they would surely have thrust far from them, had they carried Christ, as their Master, in their hearts. But since they have rather given place within them to the devil, they either perish like the herd of swine, whom the legion of devils drove down from the hill-side into the sea, [2495] or, being rescued from that destruction, and gathered together in the loving bosom of our Catholic Mother, they are delivered just as the boy was delivered by our Lord, whom his father brought to be healed of the devil, saying that ofttimes he was wont to fall into the fire, and oft into the water. [2496]

13. Whence it appears that great mercy is shown towards them, when by the force of those very imperial laws they are in the first instance rescued against their will from that sect in which, through the teaching of lying devils, they learned those evil doctrines, so that afterwards they might be made whole in the Catholic Church, becoming accustomed to the good teaching and example which they find in it. For many of the men whom we now admire in the unity of Christ, for the pious fervor of their faith, and for their charity, give thanks to God with great joy that they are no longer in that error which led them to mistake those evil things for good,--which thanks they would not now be offering willingly, had they not first, even against their will, been severed from that impious association. And what are we to say of those who confess to us, as some do

every day, that even in the olden days they had long been wishing to be Catholics; but they were living among men among whom those who wished to be Catholics could not be so through the infirmity of fear, seeing that if any one there said a single word in favor of the Catholic Church, he and his house were utterly destroyed at once? Who is mad enough to deny that it was right that assistance should have been given through the imperial decrees, that they might be delivered from so great an evil, whilst those whom they used to fear are compelled in turn to fear, and are either themselves corrected through the same terror, or, at any rate, whilst they pretend to be corrected, they abstain from further persecution of those who really are, to whom they formerly were objects of continual dread?

14. But if they have chosen to destroy themselves, in order to prevent the deliverance of those who had a right to be delivered, and have sought in this way to alarm the pious hearts of the deliverers, so that in their apprehension that some few abandoned men might perish, they should allow others to lose the opportunity of deliverance from destruction, who were either already unwilling to perish, or might have been saved from it by the employment of compulsion; what is in this case the function of Christian charity, especially when we consider that those who utter threats of their own violent and voluntary deaths are very few in number in comparison with the nations that are to be delivered? What then is the function of brotherly love? Does it, because it fears the shortlived fires of the furnace for a few, therefore abandon all to the eternal fires of hell? and does it leave so many, who are either already desirous, or hereafter are not strong enough to pass to life eternal, to perish everlastingly, while taking precautions that some few should not perish by their own hand, who are only living to be

a hindrance in the way of the salvation of others, whom they will not permit to live in accordance with the doctrines of Christ, in the hopes that some day or other they may teach them too to hasten their death by their own hand, in the manner which now causes them themselves to be a terror to their neighbors, in accordance with the custom inculcated by their devilish tenets? or does it rather save all whom it can, even though those whom it cannot save should perish in their own infatuation? For it ardently desires that all should live, but it more especially labors that not all should die. But thanks be to the Lord, that both amongst us--not indeed everywhere, but in the great majority of places--and also in the other parts of Africa, the peace of the Catholic Church both has gained and is gaining ground, without any of these madmen being killed. But those deplorable deeds are done in places where there is an utterly furious and useless set of men, who were given to such deeds even in the days of old.

[2494] Luke iv. 9.

[2495] Mark v. 13.

[2496] Matt. xvii. 14.

Chapter 4.

15. And indeed, before those laws were put in force by the emperors of the Catholic faith, the doctrine of the peace and unity of Christ was beginning by degrees to gain ground, and men were coming over to it even from the faction of Donatus, in proportion as each learned more, and became more willing, and more master of his own actions; although, at the same time, among the Donatists herds of abandoned men were disturbing the peace of the innocent for one reason or another

in the spirit of the most reckless madness. What master was there who was not compelled to live in dread of his own servant, if he had put himself under the guardianship of the Donatists? Who dared even threaten one who sought his ruin with punishment? Who dared to exact payment of a debt from one who consumed his stores, or from any debtor whatsoever, that sought their assistance or protection? Under the threat of beating, and burning, and immediate death, all documents compromising the worst of slaves were destroyed, that they might depart in freedom. Notes of hand that had been extracted from debtors were returned to them. Any one who had shown a contempt for their hard words were compelled by harder blows to do what they desired. The houses of innocent persons who had offended them were either razed to the ground or burned. Certain heads of families of honorable parentage, and brought up with a good education were carried away half dead after their deeds of violence, or bound to the mill, and compelled by blows to turn it round, after the fashion of the meanest beasts of burden. For what assistance from the laws rendered by the civil powers was ever of any avail against them? What official ever ventured so much as to breathe in their presence? What agents ever exacted payment of a debt which they had been unwilling to discharge? Who ever endeavored to avenge those who were put to death in their massacres? Except, indeed, that their own madness took revenge on them, when some, by provoking against themselves the swords of men, whom they obliged to kill them under fear of instant death, others by throwing themselves over sundry precipices, others by waters, others by fire, gave themselves over on the several occasions to a voluntary death, and gave up their lives as offerings to the dead by punishments inflicted with their own hands upon themselves.

16. These deeds were looked upon with horror by many who were firmly rooted in the same superstitious heresy; and accordingly, when they supposed that it was sufficient to establish their innocence that they were ill contented with such conduct, it was urged against them by the Catholics: If these evil deeds do not pollute your innocence, how then do you maintain that the whole Christian world has been polluted by the alleged sin of Cæcilianus, which are either altogether calumnies, or at least not proved against him? How come you, by a deed of gross impiety, to separate yourselves from the unity of the Catholic Church, as from the threshing-floor of the Lord, which must needs contain, up to the time of the final winnowing, both corn which is to be stored in the garner, and chaff that is to be burned up with fire? [2497]And thus some were so convinced by argument as to come over to the unity of the Catholic Church, being prepared even to meet the hostility of abandoned men; whilst the greater number, though equally convinced, and though desirous to do the same, yet dared not make enemies of these men, who were so unbridled in their violence, seeing that some who had come over to us experienced the greatest cruelty at their hands.

17. To this we may add, that in Carthage itself some of the bishops of the same party, making a schism among themselves, and dividing the party of Donatus among the lower orders of the Carthaginian people, ordained as bishop against bishop a certain deacon named Maximianus, who could not brook the control of his own diocesan. And as this displeased the greater part of them, they condemned the aforesaid Maximinus, with twelve others who had been present at his ordination, but gave the rest that were associated in the same schism a chance of returning to their communion on an appointed day. But

afterwards some of these twelve, and certain others of those who had had the time of grace allowed to them, but had only returned after the day appointed, were received by them without degradation from their orders; and they did not venture to baptize a second time those whom the condemned ministers had baptized outside the pale of their communion. This action of theirs at once made strongly against them in favor of the Catholic party, so that their mouths were wholly closed. And on the matter being diligently spread abroad, as was only right, in order to cure men's souls of the evils of schism, and when it was shown in every possible direction by the sermons and discussions of the Catholic divines, that to maintain the peace of Donatus they had not only received back those whom they had condemned, with full recognition of their orders, but had even been afraid to declare that baptism to be void which had been administered outside their Church by men whom they had condemned or even suspended; whilst, in violation of the peace of Christ, they cast in the teeth of all the world the stain conveyed by contact with some sinners, it matters little with whom, and declared baptism to be consequently void which had been administered even in the very Churches whence the gospel itself had come to Africa;--seeing all this, very many began to be confounded, and blushing before what they saw to be mostly manifest truth, they submitted to correction in greater numbers than was their wont; and men began to breathe with a somewhat freer sense of liberty from their cruelty, and that to a considerably greater extent in every direction.

18. Then indeed they blazed forth with such fury, and were so excited by the goadings of hatred, that scarcely any churches of our communion could be safe against their treachery and

violence and most undisguised robberies; scarcely any road secure by which men could travel to preach the peace of the Catholic Church in opposition to their madness, and convict the rashness of their folly by the clear enunciation of the truth. They went so far, besides, in proposing hard terms of reconciliation, not only to the laity or to any of the clergy, but even in a measure to certain of the Catholic bishops. For the only alternative offered was to hold their tongues about the truth, or to endure their savage fury. But if they did not speak about the truth, not only was it impossible for any one to be delivered by their silence, but many were even sure to be destroyed by their submitting to be led astray; while if, by their preaching the truth, the rage of the Donatists was again provoked to vent its madness, though some would be delivered, and those who were already on our side would be strengthened, yet the weak would again be deterred by fear from following the truth. When the Church, therefore, was reduced to these straits in its affliction, any one who thinks that anything was to be endured, rather than that the assistance of God, to be rendered through the agency of Christian emperors, should be sought, does not sufficiently observe that no good account could possibly be rendered for neglect of this precaution.

[2497] Matt. iii. 12.

Chapter 5.

19. But as to the argument of those men who are unwilling that their impious deeds should be checked by the enactment of righteous laws, when they say that the apostles never sought such measures from the kings of the earth, they do not consider the different character of that age, and that everything comes in

its own season. For what emperor had as yet believed in Christ, so as to serve Him in the cause of piety by enacting laws against impiety, when as yet the declaration of the prophet was only in the course of its fulfillment, "Why do the heathen rage, and the people imagine a vain thing? The kings of the earth set themselves, and their rulers take counsel together, against the Lord, and against His Anointed;" and there was as yet no sign of that which is spoken a little later in the same psalm: "Be wise now, therefore, O ye kings; be instructed, ye judges of the earth. Serve the Lord with fear, and rejoice with trembling." [2498]How then are kings to serve the Lord with fear, except by preventing and chastising with religious severity all those acts which are done in opposition to the commandments of the Lord? For a man serves God in one way in that he is man, in another way in that he is also king. In that he is man, he serves Him by living faithfully; but in that he is also king, he serves Him by enforcing with suitable rigor such laws as ordain what is righteous, and punish what is the reverse. Even as Hezekiah served Him, by destroying the groves and the temples of the idols, and the high places which had been built in violation of the commandments of God; [2499] or even as Josiah served Him, by doing the same things in his turn; [2500] or as the king of the Ninevites served Him, by compelling all the men of his city to make satisfaction to the Lord; [2501] or as Darius served Him, by giving the idol into the power of Daniel to be broken, and by casting his enemies into the den of lions; [2502] or as Nebuchadnezzar served Him, of whom I have spoken before, by issuing a terrible law to prevent any of his subjects from blaspheming God. [2503]In this way, therefore, kings can serve the Lord, even in so far as they are kings, when they do in His service what they could not do were they not kings.

20. Seeing, then, that the kings of the earth were not yet serving the Lord in the time of the apostles, but were still imagining vain things against the Lord and against His Anointed, that all might be fulfilled which was spoken by the prophets, it must be granted that at that time acts of impiety could not possibly be prevented by the laws, but were rather performed under their sanction. For the order of events was then so rolling on, that even the Jews were killing those who preached Christ, thinking that they did God service in so doing, just as Christ had foretold, [2504] and the heathen were raging against the Christians, and the patience of the martyrs was overcoming them all. But so soon as the fulfillment began of what is written in a later psalm, "All kings shall fall down before Him; all nations shall serve Him," [2505] what sober-minded man could say to the kings, "Let not any thought trouble you within your kingdom as to who restrains or attacks the Church of your Lord; deem it not a matter in which you should be concerned, which of your subjects may choose to be religious or sacrilegious," seeing that you cannot say to them, "Deem it no concern of yours which of your subjects may choose to be chaste, or which unchaste?" For why, when free-will is given by God to man, should adulteries be punished by the laws, and sacrilege allowed? Is it a lighter matter that a soul should not keep faith with God, than that a woman should be faithless to her husband? Or if those faults which are committed not in contempt but in ignorance of religious truth are to be visited with lighter punishment, are they therefore to be neglected altogether?

[2498] Ps. ii. 1, 2, 10, 11.

[2499] 2 Kings xviii. 4.

[2500] 2 Kings xxiii. 4, 5.

[2501] Jonah iii. 6-9.

[2502] Bel and Drag. vv. 22, 42.

[2503] Dan. iii. 29.

[2504] John xvi. 2.

[2505] Ps. lxxii. 11.

Chapter 6.

21. It is indeed better (as no one ever could deny) that men should be led to worship God by teaching, than that they should be driven to it by fear of punishment or pain; but it does not follow that because the former course produces the better men, therefore those who do not yield to it should be neglected. For many have found advantage (as we have proved, and are daily proving by actual experiment), in being first compelled by fear or pain, so that they might afterwards be influenced by teaching, or might follow out in act what they had already learned in word. Some, indeed, set before us the sentiments of a certain secular author, who said,

"'Tis well, I ween, by shame the young to train,

And dread of meanness, rather than by pain." [2506]

This is unquestionably true. But while those are better who are guided aright by love, those are certainly more numerous who are corrected by fear. For, to answer these persons out of their own author, we find him saying in another place,

"Unless by pain and suffering thou art taught,

Thou canst not guide thyself aright in aught." [2507]

But, moreover, holy Scripture has both said concerning the former better class, "There is no fear in love; but perfect love casteth out fear;" [2508] and also concerning the latter lower class, which furnishes the majority, "A servant will not be corrected by words; for though he understand, he will not answer." [2509]In saying, "He will not be corrected by words," he did not order him to be left to himself, but implied an admonition as to the means whereby he ought to be corrected; otherwise he would not have said, "He will not be corrected by words," but without any qualification, "He will not be corrected." For in another place he says that not only the servant, but also the undisdained son, must be corrected with stripes, and that with great fruits as the result; for he says, "Thou shall beat him with the rod, and shall deliver his soul from hell;" [2510] and elsewhere he says, "He that spareth the rod hateth his son." [2511]For, give us a man who with right faith and true understanding can say with all the energy of his heart, "My soul thirsteth for God, for the living God: when shall I come and appear before God?" [2512] and for such an one there is no need of the terror of hell, to say nothing of temporal punishments or imperial laws, seeing that with him it is so indispensable a blessing to cleave unto the Lord, that he not only dreads being parted from that happiness as a heavy punishment, but can scarcely even bear delay in its attainment. But yet, before the good sons can say they have "a desire to depart, and to be with Christ," [2513] many must first be recalled to their Lord by the stripes of temporal scourging, like evil slaves, and in some degree like good-for-nothing fugitives.

22. For who can possibly love us more than Christ, who laid down His life for His sheep? [2514]And yet, after calling Peter

and the other apostles by His words alone, when He came to summon Paul, who was before called Saul, subsequently the powerful builder of His Church, but originally its cruel persecutor, He not only constrained him with His voice, but even dashed him to the earth with His power; and that He might forcibly bring one who was raging amid the darkness of infidelity to desire the light of the heart, He first struck him with physical blindness of the eyes. If that punishment had not been inflicted, he would not afterwards have been healed by it; and since he had been wont to see nothing with his eyes open, if they had remained unharmed, the Scripture would not tell us that at the imposition of Ananias' hands, in order that their sight might be restored, there fell from them as it had been scales, by which the sight had been obscured. [2515]Where is what the Donatists were wont to cry: Man is at liberty to believe or not believe? Towards whom did Christ use violence? Whom did He compel? Here they have the Apostle Paul. Let them recognize in his case Christ first compelling, and afterwards teaching; first striking, and afterwards consoling. For it is wonderful how he who entered the service of the gospel in the first instance under the compulsion of bodily punishment, afterwards labored more in the gospel than all they who were called by word only; [2516] and he who was compelled by the greater influence of fear to love, displayed that perfect love which casts out fear.

23. Why, therefore, should not the Church use force in compelling her lost sons to return, if the lost sons compelled others to their destruction? Although even men who have not been compelled, but only led astray, are received by their loving mother with more affection if they are recalled to her bosom through the enforcement of terrible but salutary laws, and are

the objects of far more deep congratulation than those whom she had never lost. Is it not a part of the care of the shepherd, when any sheep have left the flock, even though not violently forced away, but led astray by tender words and coaxing blandishments, to bring them back to the fold of his master when he has found them, by the fear or even the pain of the whip, if they show symptoms of resistance; especially since, if they multiply with growing abundance among the fugitive slaves and robbers, he has the more right in that the mark of the master is recognized on them, which is not outraged in those whom we receive but do not rebaptize? For the wandering of the sheep is to be corrected in such wise that the mark of the Redeemer should not be destroyed on it. For even if any one is marked with the royal stamp by a deserter who is marked with it himself, and the two receive forgiveness, [2517] and the one returns to his service, and the other begins to be in the service in which he had no part before, that mark is not effaced in either of the two, but rather it is recognized in both of them, and approved with the honor which is due to it because it is the king's. Since then they cannot show that the destination is bad to which they are compelled, they maintain that they ought to be compelled by force even to what is good. But we have shown that Paul was compelled by Christ; therefore the Church, in trying to compel the Donatists, is following the example of her Lord, though in the first instance she waited in the hopes of needing to compel no one, that the prediction of the prophet might be fulfilled concerning the faith of kings and peoples.

24. For in this sense also we may interpret without absurdity the declaration of the blessed Apostle Paul, when he says, "Having in a readiness to revenge all disobedience, when your

obedience is fulfilled." [2518]Whence also the Lord Himself bids the guests in the first instance to be invited to His great supper, and afterwards compelled; for on His servants making answer to Him, "Lord, it is done as Thou hast commanded, and yet there is room," He said to them, "Go out into the highways and hedges, and compel them to come in." [2519] In those, therefore, who were first brought in with gentleness, the former obedience is fulfilled; but in those who were compelled, the disobedience is avenged. For what else is the meaning of "Compel them to come in," after it had previously said, "Bring in," and the answer had been made, "Lord, it is done as Thou commanded, and yet there is room"? If He had wished it to be understood that they were to be compelled by the terrifying force of miracles, many divine miracles were rather wrought in the sight of those who were first called, especially in the sight of the Jews, of whom it was said, "The Jews require a sign;" [2520] and, moreover, among the Gentiles themselves the gospel was so commended by miracles in the time of the apostles, that had these been the means by which they were ordered to be compelled, we might rather have had good grounds for supposing, as I said before, that it was the earlier guests who were compelled. Wherefore, if the power which the Church has received by divine appointment in its due season, through the religious character and the faith of kings, be the instrument by which those who are found in the highways and hedges--that is, in heresies and schisms--are compelled to come in, then let them not find fault with being compelled, but consider whether they be so compelled. The supper of the Lord is the unity of the body of Christ, not only in the sacrament of the altar, but also in the bond of peace. Of the Donatists themselves, indeed, we can say that they compel no man to any good thing;

for whomsoever they compel, they compel to nothing else but evil.

[2506] Ter. Adelph. act 1. sc. i. 32, 33.

[2507] This is not found in the extant plays of Terence.

[2508] 1 John iv. 18.

[2509] Prov. xxix. 19.

[2510] Prov. xxiii. 14.

[2511] Prov. xiii. 24.

[2512] Ps. xlii. 2.

[2513] Phil. i. 23.

[2514] John x. 15.

[2515] Acts ix. 1-18.

[2516] 1 Cor. xv. 10.

[2517] Accipiant: sc. the baptizer and the baptized; and so the Mss. The common reading is "accipiat."

[2518] 2 Cor. x. 6.

[2519] Luke xiv. 22, 23.

[2520] 1 Cor. i. 22.

Chapter 7.

25. However, before those laws were sent into Africa by which men are compelled to come in to the sacred Supper, it seemed

to certain of the brethren, of whom I was one, that although the madness of the Donatists was raging in every direction, yet we should not ask of the emperors to ordain that heresy should absolutely cease to be, by sanctioning a punishment to be inflicted on all who wished to live in it; but that they should rather content themselves with ordaining that those who either preached the Catholic truth with their voice, or established it by their study, should no longer be exposed to the furious violence of the heretics. And this they thought might in some measure be effected, if they would take the law which Theodosius, of pious memory, enacted generally against heretics of all kinds, to the effect that any heretical bishop or clergyman, being found in any place, should be fined ten pounds of gold, and confirm it in more express terms against the Donatists, who denied that they were heretics; but with such reservations, that the fine should not be inflicted upon all of them, but only in those districts where the Catholic Church suffered any violence from their clergy, or from the Circumcelliones, or at the hands of any of their people; so that after a formal complaint had been made by the Catholics who had suffered the violence, the bishops or other ministers should forthwith be obliged, under the commission given to the officers, to pay the fine. For we thought that in this way, if they were terrified and no longer dared do anything of the sort, the Catholic truth might be freely taught and held under such conditions, that while no one was compelled to it, any one might follow it who was anxious to do so without intimidation, so that we might not have false and pretended Catholics. And although a different view was held by other brethren, who either were more advanced in years, or had experience of many states and places where we saw the true Catholic Church firmly established, which had, however, been planted and confirmed by God's great goodness at a time when men were compelled to come in to the Catholic communion by the laws of previous emperors, yet we carried our point, to the effect that the measure which I have described above should be sought in preference from the emperors: it was decreed in our council, [2521] and envoys were sent to the court of the Count.

26. But God in His great mercy, knowing how necessary was the terror inspired by these laws, and a kind of medicinal inconvenience for the cold and wicked hearts of many men, and for that hardness of heart which cannot be softened by words, but yet admits of softening through the agency of some little severity of discipline, brought it about that our envoys could not obtain what they had undertaken to ask. For our arrival had already been anticipated by the serious complaints of certain bishops from other districts, who had suffered much ill-treatment at the hands of the Donatists themselves, and had been thrust out from their sees; and, in particular, the attempt to murder Maximianus, the Catholic bishop of the Church of Bagai, under circumstances of incredible atrocity, had caused measures to be taken which left our deputation nothing to do. For a law had already been published, that the heresy of the Donatists, being of so savage a description that mercy towards it really involved greater cruelty than its very madness wrought, should for the future be prevented not only from being violent, but from existing with impunity at all; but yet no capital punishment was imposed upon it, that even in dealing with those who were unworthy, Christian gentleness might be observed, but a pecuniary fine was ordained, and sentence of exile was pronounced against their bishops or ministers.

27. With regard to the aforesaid bishop of Bagai, in consequence of his claim being allowed in the ordinary courts, after each party had been heard in turn, in a basilica [2522] of

which the Donatists had taken possession, as being the property of the Catholics, they rushed upon him as he was standing at the altar, with fearful violence and cruel fury, beat him savagely with cudgels and weapons of every kind, and at last with the very boards of the broken altar. They also wounded him with a dagger in the groin so severely, that the effusion of blood would have soon put an end to his life, had not their further cruelty proved of service for its preservation; for, as they were dragging him along the ground thus severely wounded, the dust forced into the spouting vein stanched the blood, whose effusion was rapidly on the way to cause his death. Then, when they had at length abandoned him, some of our party tried to carry him off with psalms; but his enemies, inflamed with even greater rage, tore him from the hands of those who were carrying him, inflicting grievous punishment on the Catholics, whom they put to flight, being far superior to them in numbers, and easily inspiring terror by their violence. Finally, they threw him into a certain elevated tower, thinking that he was by this time dead, though in fact he still breathed. Lighting then on a soft heap of earth, and being espied by the light of a lamp by some men who were passing by at night, he was recognized and picked up, and being carried to a religious house, by dint of great care, was restored in a few days from his state of almost hopeless danger. Rumor, however, had carried the tidings even across the sea that he had been killed by the violence of the Donatists; and when afterwards he himself went abroad, and was most unexpectedly seen to be alive, he showed, by the number, the severity, and the freshness of his wounds, how fully rumor had been justified in bringing tidings of his death.

28. He sought assistance, therefore, from the Christian emperor, not so much with any desire of revenging himself, as with the view of defending the Church entrusted to his charge. And if he had omitted to do this, he would have deserved not to be praised for his forbearance, but to be blamed for negligence. For neither was the Apostle Paul taking precautions on behalf of his own transitory life, but for the Church of God when he caused the plot of those who had conspired to slay him to be made known to the Roman captain, the effect of which was that he was conducted by an escort of armed soldiers to the place where they proposed to send him, that he might escape the ambush of his foes. [2523]Nor did he for a moment hesitate to invoke the protection of the Roman laws, proclaiming that he was a Roman citizen, who at that time could not be scourged; [2524] and again, that he might not be delivered to the Jews who sought to kill him, he appealed to Cæsar, [2525] --a Roman emperor, indeed, but not a Christian. And by this he showed sufficiently plainly what was afterwards to be the duty of the ministers of Christ, when in the midst of the dangers of the Church they found the emperors Christians. And hence therefore, it came about that a religious and pious emperor, when such matters were brought to his knowledge, thought it well, by the enactment of most pious laws, entirely to correct the error of this great impiety, and to bring those who bore the standards of Christ against the cause of Christ into the unity of the Catholic Church, even by terror and compulsion, rather than merely to take away their power of doing violence, and to leave them the freedom of going astray, and perishing in their error.

29. Presently, when the laws themselves arrived in Africa, in the first place those who were already seeking an opportunity

for doing so, or were afraid of the raging madness of the Donatists, or were previously deterred by a feeling of unwillingness to offend their friends, at once came over to the Church. Many, too, who were only restrained by the force of custom handed down in their homes from their parents, but had never before considered what was the groundwork of the heresy itself,--had never, indeed, wished to investigate and contemplate its nature,--beginning now to use their observation, and finding nothing in it that could compensate for such serious loss as they were called upon to suffer, became Catholics without any difficulty; for, having been made careless by security, they were now instructed by anxiety. But when all these had set the example, it was followed by many who were less qualified of themselves to understand what was the difference between the error of the Donatists and Catholic truth.

30. Accordingly, when the great masses of the people had been received by the true mother with rejoicing into her bosom, there remained outside cruel crowds, persevering with unhappy animosity in that madness. Even of these the greater number communicated in feigned reconciliation, and others escaped notice from the scantiness of their numbers. But those who feigned conformity, becoming by degrees accustomed to our communion, and hearing the preaching of the truth, especially after the conference and disputation which took place between us and their bishops at Carthage, were to a great extent brought to a right belief. Yet in certain places, where a more obstinate and implacable body prevailed, whom the smaller number that entertained better views about communion with us could not resist, or where the masses were under the influence of a few more powerful leaders, whom they followed in a wrong

direction, our difficulties continued somewhat longer. Of these places there are a few in which trouble still exists, in the course of which the Catholics, and especially the bishops and clergy, have suffered many terrible hardships, which it would take too long to go through in detail, seeing that some of them had their eyes put out, and one bishop his hands and tongue cut off, while some were actually murdered. I say nothing of massacres of the most cruel description, and robberies of houses, committed in nocturnal burglaries, with the burning not only of private houses, but even of churches,--some being found abandoned enough to cast the sacred books into the flames.

31. But we were consoled for the suffering inflicted on us by these evils, by the fruit which resulted from them. For wherever such deeds were committed by unbelievers, there Christian unity has advanced with greater fervency and perfection, and the Lord is praised with greater earnestness for having deigned to grant that His servants might win their brethren by their sufferings, and might gather together into the peace of eternal salvation through His blood His sheep who were dispersed abroad in deadly error. The Lord is powerful and full of compassion, to whom we daily pray that He will give repentance to the rest as well, that they may recover themselves out of the snare of the devil, by whom they are taken captive at his will, [2526] though now they only seek materials for calumniating us, and returning to us evil for good; because they have not the knowledge to make them understand what feelings and love we continue to have towards them, and how we are anxious, in accordance with the injunction of the Lord, given to His pastors by the mouth of the prophet Ezekiel, to bring again that which was driven away, and to seek that which was lost. [2527]

[2521] That of Carthage, held June 26 (more correctly, probably June 15th or 16th), 401.

[2522] The basilica of Fundus Calvianensis. See C. Crescon. iii. c. 43.

[2523] Acts xxiii. 17-32.

[2524] Acts xxii. 25.

[2525] Acts xxv. 11.

[2526] 2 Tim. ii. 26.

[2527] Ezek. xxxiv. 4.

Chapter 8.

32. But they, as we have sometimes said before in other places, do not charge themselves with what they do to us; while, on the other hand, they charge us with what they do to themselves. For which of our party is there who would desire, I do not say that one of them should perish, but should even lose any of his possessions? But if the house of David could not earn peace on any other terms except that Absalom his son should have been slain in the war which he was waging against his father, although he had most carefully given strict injunctions to his followers that they should use their utmost endeavors to preserve him alive and safe, that his paternal affection might be able to pardon him on his repentance, what remained for him except to weep for the son that he had lost, and to console himself in his sorrow by reflecting on the acquisition of peace for his kingdom? [2528]The same, then, is the case with the Catholic Church, our mother; for when war is waged against her by men who are certainly different from sons, since it must

be acknowledged that from the great tree, which by the spreading of its branches is extended over all the world, this little branch in Africa is broken off, whilst she is willing in her love to give them birth, that they may return to the root, without which they cannot have the true life, at the same time if she collects the remainder in so large a number by the loss of some, she soothes and cures the sorrow of her maternal heart by the thoughts of the deliverance of such mighty nations; especially when she considers that those who are lost perish by a death which they brought upon themselves, and not, like Absalom, by the fortune of war. And if you were to see the joy of those who are delivered in the peace of Christ, their crowded assemblies, their eager zeal, the gladsomeness with which they flock together, both to hear and sing hymns, and to be instructed in the word of God; the great grief with which many of them recall to mind their former error, the joy with which they come to the consideration of the truth which they have learned, with the indignation and detestation which they feel towards their lying teachers, now that they have found out what falsehoods they disseminated concerning our sacraments; and how many of them, moreover, acknowledge that they long ago desired to be Catholics, but dared not take the step in the midst of men of such violence,--if, I say, you were to see the congregations of these nations delivered from such perdition, then you would say that it would have been the extreme of cruelty, if in the fear that certain desperate men, in number not to be compared with the multitudes of those who were rescued, might be burned in fires which they voluntarily kindled for themselves, these others had been left to be lost for ever, and to be tortured in fires which shall not be quenched.

33. For if two men were dwelling together in one house, which we knew with absolute certainty to be upon the point of falling down, and they were unwillingly to believe us when we warned them of the danger, and persisted in remaining in the house; if it were in our power to rescue them, even against their will, and we were afterwards to show them the ruin threatening their house, so that they should not dare to return again within its reach, I think that if we abstained from doing it, we should well deserve the charge of cruelty. And further, if one of them should say to us, Since you have entered the house to save our lives, I shall forthwith kill myself; while the other was not indeed willing to come forth from the house, nor to be rescued, but yet had not the hardihood to kill himself: which alternative should we choose,--to leave both of them to be overwhelmed in the ruin, or that, while one at any rate was delivered by our merciful efforts, the other should perish by no fault of ours, but rather by his own? No one is so unhappy as not to find it easy enough to deride what should be done in such a case. And I have proposed the question of two individuals,--one, that is to say, who is lost, and one who is delivered; what then must we think of the case where some few are lost, and an innumerable multitude of nations are delivered? For there are actually not so many persons who thus perish of their own free will, as there are estates, villages, streets, fortresses, municipal towns, cities, that are delivered by the laws under consideration from that fatal and eternal destruction.

34. But if we were to consider the matter under discussion with yet greater care, I think that if there were a large number of persons in the house which was going to fall, and any single one of them could be saved, and when we endeavored to effect his rescue, the others were to kill themselves by jumping out of

the windows, we should console ourselves in our grief for the loss of the rest by the thoughts of the safety of the one; and we should not allow all to perish without a single rescue, in the fear lest the remainder should destroy themselves. What then should we think of the work of mercy to which we ought to apply ourselves, in order that men may attain eternal life and escape eternal punishment, if true reason and benevolence compel us to give such aid to men, in order to secure for them a safety which is not only temporal, but very short,--for the brief space of their life on earth?

[2528] 2 Sam. xviii., xxii.

Chapter 9.

35. As to the charge that they bring against us, that we covet and plunder their possessions, I would that they would become Catholics, and possess in peace and love with us, not only what they call theirs, but also what confessedly belongs to us. But they are so blinded with the desire of uttering calumnies, that they do not observe how inconsistent their statements are with one another. At any rate, they assert, and seem to make it a subject of most invidious complaint among themselves, that we constrain them to come in to our communion by the violent authority of the laws,--which we certainly should not do by any means, if we wished to gain possession of their property. What avaricious man ever wished for another to share his possessions? Who that was inflamed with the desire of empire, or elated by the pride of its possession, ever wished to have a partner? Let them at any rate look on those very men who once belonged to them, but now are our brethren joined to us by the bond of fraternal affection, and see how they hold not only what they used to have, but also what was ours, which

they did not have before; which yet, if we are living as poor in fellowship with poor, belongs to us and them alike; whilst, if we possess of our private means enough for our wants, it is no longer ours, inasmuch as we do not commit so infamous an act of usurpation as to claim for our own the property of the poor, for whom we are in some sense the trustees.

36. Everything, therefore, that was held in the name of the churches of the party of Donatus, was ordered by the Christian emperors, in their pious laws, to pass to the Catholic Church, with the possession of the buildings themselves. [2529]Seeing, then, that there are with us poor members of those said churches who used to be maintained by these same paltry possessions, let them rather cease themselves to covet what belongs to others whilst they remain outside, and so let them enter within the bond of unity, that we may all alike administer, not only the property which they call their own, but also with it what is asserted to be ours. For it is written "All are yours; and ye are Christ's; and Christ is God's." [2530]Under Him as our Head, let us all be one in His one body; and in all such matters as you speak of, let us follow the example which is recorded in the Acts of the Apostles: "They were of one heart and of one soul: neither said any of them that aught of the things which he possessed was his own; but they had all things common." [2531]Let us love what we sing: "Behold, how good and how pleasant it is for brethren to dwell together in unity!" [2532] that so they may know, by their own experience, with what perfect truth their mother, the Catholic Church, calls out to them what the blessed apostle writes to the Corinthians: "I seek not yours, but you." [2533]

37. But if we consider what is said in the Book of Wisdom, "Therefore the righteous spoiled the ungodly;" [2534] and also

what is said in the Proverbs, "The wealth of the sinner is laid up for the just;" [2535] then we shall see that the question is not, who are in possession of the property of the heretics? but who are in the society of the just? We know, indeed, that the Donatists arrogate to themselves such a store of justice, that they boast not only that they possess it, but that they also bestow it upon other men. For they say that any one whom they have baptized is justified by them, after which there is nothing left for them but to say to the person who is baptized by them that he must needs believe on him who has administered the sacrament; for why should he not do so, when the apostle says, "To him that believeth on Him that justifieth the ungodly, his faith is counted for righteousness?" [2536]Let him believe, therefore, upon the man by whom he is baptized, if it be none else that justifies him, that his faith may be counted for righteousness. But I think that even they themselves would look with horror on themselves, if they ventured for a moment to entertain such thoughts as these. For there is none that is just and able to justify, save God alone. But the same might be said of them that the apostle says of the Jews, that "being ignorant of God's righteousness, and going about to establish their own righteousness, they have not submitted themselves unto the righteousness of God." [2537]

38. But far be it from us that any one of our number should call himself in such wise just, that he should either go about to establish his own righteousness, as though it were conferred upon him by himself, whereas it is said to him, "For what hast thou that thou didst not receive?" [2538] or venture to boast himself as being without sin in this world, as the Donatists themselves declared in our conference that they were members of a Church which has already neither spot nor wrinkle, nor any

such thing, [2539] --not knowing that this is only fulfilled in those individuals who depart out of this body immediately after baptism, or after the forgiveness of sins, for which we make petition in our prayers; but that for the Church, as a whole, the time will not come when it shall be altogether without spot or wrinkle, or any such thing, till the day when we shall hear the words, "O death, where is thy sting? O grave, where is thy victory? The sting of death is sin." [2540]

39. But in this life, when the corruptible body presseth down the soul, [2541] if their Church is already of such a character as they maintain, they would not utter unto God the prayer which our Lord has taught us to employ: "Forgive us our debts." [2542]For since all sins have been remitted in baptism, why does the Church make this petition, if already, even in this life, it has neither spot nor wrinkle, nor any such thing? They would also have a fight to despise the warning of the Apostle John, when he cries out in his epistle, "If we say that we have no sin, we deceive ourselves, and the truth is not in us. But if we confess our sins, He is faithful and just to forgive us our sins, and to cleanse us from all unrighteousness." [2543]On account of this hope, the universal Church utters the petition, "Forgive us our debts," that when He sees that we are not vainglorious, but ready to confess our sins, He may cleanse us from all unrighteousness, and that so the Lord Jesus Christ may show to Himself in that day a glorious Church, not having spot or wrinkle, or any such thing, which now He cleanses with the washing of water in the word: because, on the one hand, there is nothing that remains behind in baptism to hinder the forgiveness of every bygone sin (so long, that is, as baptism is not received to no effect without the Church, but is either administered within the Church, or, at least, if it has been

already administered without, the recipient does not remain outside with it); and, on the other hand, whatever pollution of sin, of whatsoever kind, is contracted through the weakness of human nature by those who live here after baptism, is cleansed away in virtue of the same laver's efficacy. For neither is it of any avail for one who has not been baptized to say, "Forgive us our debts."

40. Accordingly, He so now cleanses His Church by the washing of water in the word, that He may hereafter show it to Himself as not having spot, or wrinkle, or any such thing,-- altogether beautiful, that is to say, and in absolute perfection, when death shall be "swallowed up in victory." [2544]Now, therefore, in so far as the life is flourishing within us that proceeds from our being born of God, living by faith, so far we are righteous; but in so far as we drag along with us the traces of our mortal nature as derived from Adam, so far we cannot be free from sin. For there is truth both in the statement that "whosoever is born of God doth not commit sin," [2545] and also in the former statement, that "if we say that we have no sin, we deceive ourselves, and the truth is not in us." [2546]The Lord Jesus, therefore, is both righteous and able to justify; but we are justified freely by no other grace than His. [2547]For there is nothing that justifieth save His body, which is the Church; and therefore, if the body of Christ bears off the spoils of the unrighteous, and the riches of the unrighteous are laid up in store as treasures for the body of Christ, the unrighteous ought not therefore to remain outside, but rather to enter within, that so they may be justified.

41. Whence also we may be sure that what is written concerning the day of judgment, "Then shall the righteous man stand in great boldness before the face of such as have afflicted

him, and made no account of his labors," [2548] is not to be taken in such a sense as that the Canaanite shall stand before the face of Israel, though Israel made no account of the labors of the Canaanite; but only as that Naboth shall stand before the face of Ahab, since Ahab made no account of the labors of Naboth, since the Canaanite was unrighteous, while Naboth was a righteous man. In the same way the heathen shall not stand before the face of the Christian, who made no account of his labors, when the temples of the idols were plundered and destroyed; but the Christian shall stand before the face of the heathen, who made no account of his labors, when the bodies of the martyrs were laid low in death. In the same way, therefore, the heretic shall not stand in the face of the Catholic, who made no account of his labors, when the laws of the Catholic emperors were put in force; but the Catholic shall stand in the face of the heretic, who made no account of his labors when the madness of the ungodly Circumcelliones was allowed to have its way. For the passage of Scripture decides the question in itself, seeing that it does not say, Then shall men stand, but "Then shall the righteous stand;" and they shall stand "in great boldness" because they stand in the power of a good conscience.

42. But in this world no one is righteous by his own righteousness,--that is, as though it were wrought by himself and for himself; but as the apostle says, "According as God hath dealt to every man the measure of faith." But then he goes on to add the following: "For as we have many members in one body, and all members have not the same office; so we, being many, are one body in Christ." [2549]And according to this doctrine, no one can be righteous so long as he is separated from the unity of this body. For in the same manner as if a

limb be cut off from the body of a living man, it cannot any longer retain the spirit of life; so the man who is cut off from the body of Christ, who is righteous, can in no wise retain the spirit of righteousness, even if he retain the form of membership which he received when in the body. Let them therefore come into the framework of this body, and so possess their own labors, not through the lust of lordship, but through the godliness of using them aright. But we, as has been said before, cleanse our wills from the pollution of this concupiscence, even in the judgment of any enemy you please to name as judge, seeing that we use our utmost efforts in entreating the very men of whose labors we avail ourselves to enjoy with us, within the society of the Catholic Church, the fruits both of their labors and of our own.

[2529] Cod. Theod. Lib. xvi. tit. v., de Hæreticis, 52.

[2530] 1 Cor. iii. 22, 23.

[2531] Acts iv. 32.

[2532] Ps. cxxxiii. 1.

[2533] 2 Cor. xii. 14.

[2534] Wisd. x. 20.

[2535] Prov. xiii. 22.

[2536] Rom. iv. 5.

[2537] Rom. x. 3.

[2538] 1 Cor. iv. 7.

[2539] Eph. v. 27.

[2540] 1 Cor. xv. 55, 56.

[2541] Wisd. ix. 15.

[2542] Matt. vi. 12.

[2543] 1 John i. 8, 9.

[2544] 1 Cor. xv. 54.

[2545] 1 John iii. 9.

[2546] 1 John i. 8.

[2547] Rom. iii. 24.

[2548] Wisd. v. 1.

[2549] Rom. xii. 3-5.

Chapter 10.

43. But this, they say, is the very thing which disquiets us,--If we are unrighteous, wherefore do you seek our company? To which question we answer, We seek the company of you who are unrighteous, that you may not remain unrighteous; we seek for you who are lost, that we may rejoice over you as soon as you are found, saying, This our brother was dead, and is alive again; and was lost, and is found. [2550]Why, then, he says, do you not baptize me, that you might wash me from my sins? I reply: Because I do not do despite to the stamp of the monarch, when I correct the ill-doing of a deserter. Why, he says, do I not even do penance in your body? Nay truly, except you have done penance, you cannot be saved; for how shall you rejoice that you have been reformed, unless you first grieve that you had been astray? What, then, he says, do we receive with

you, when we come over to your side? I answer, You do not indeed receive baptism, which was able to exist in you outside the framework of the body of Christ, although it could not profit you; but you receive the unity of the Spirit in the bond of peace [2551] without which no one can see God; and you receive charity, which, as it is written, "shall cover the multitude of sins." [2552]And in regard to this great blessing, without which we have the apostle's testimony that neither the tongues of men or of angels, nor the understanding of all mysteries, nor the gift of prophecy, nor faith so great as to be able to remove mountains, nor the bestowal of all one's goods to feed the poor, nor giving one's body to be burned, can profit anything; [2553] if, I say, you think this mighty blessing to be worthless or of trifling value, you are deservedly but miserably astray; and deservedly you must necessarily perish, unless you come over to Catholic unity.

44. If, then, they say, it is necessary that we should repent of having been outside, and hostile to the Church, if we would gain salvation, how comes it that after the repentance which you exact from us we still continue to be clergy, or it may be even bishops in your body? This would not be the case, as indeed, in simple truth, we must confess it should not be the case, were it not that the evil is cured by the compensating power of peace itself. But let them give themselves this lesson, and most especially let those feel sorrow in their hearts, who are lying in this deep death of severance from the Church, that they may recover their life even by this sort of wound inflicted on our Catholic mother Church. For when the bough that has been cut off is grafted in, a new wound is made in the tree, to admit of its reception, that life may be given to the branch which was perishing for lack of the life that is furnished by the

root. But when the newly-received branch has become identified with the stock in which it is received, the result is both vigor and fruit; but if they do not become identified, the engrafted bough withers, but the life of the tree continues unimpaired. For there is further a mode of grafting of such a kind, that without cutting away any branch that is within, the branch that is foreign to the tree is inserted, not indeed without a wound, but with the slightest possible wound inflicted on the tree. In like manner, then, when they come to the root which exists in the Catholic Church, without being deprived of any position which belongs to them as clergy or bishops after ever so deep repentance of their error, there is a kind of wound inflicted as it were upon the bark of the mother tree, breaking in upon the strictness of her discipline; but since neither he that planteth is anything, neither he that watereth, [2554] so soon as by prayers poured forth to the mercy of God peace is secured through the union of the engrafted boughs with the parent stock, charity then covers the multitude of sins.

45. For although it was made an ordinance in the Church, that no one who had been called upon to do penance for any offense should be admired into holy orders, or return to or continue in the body of the clergy, [2555] this was done not to cause despair of any indulgence being granted, but merely to maintain a rigorous discipline; otherwise an argument will be raised against the keys that were given to the Church, of which we have the testimony of Scripture: "Whatsoever thou shall loose on earth shall be loosed in heaven." [2556]But lest it should so happen that, after the detection of offenses, a heart swelling with the hope of ecclesiastical preferment might do penance in a spirit of pride, it was determined, with great severity, that after doing penance for any mortal sin, no one

should be admitted to the number of the clergy, in order that, when all hope of temporal preferment was done away, the medicine of humility might be endowed with greater strength and truth. For even the holy David did penance for deadly sin, and yet was not degraded from his office. And we know that the blessed Peter, after shedding the bitterest of tears, repented that he had denied his Lord, and yet remained an apostle. But we must not therefore be induced to think that the care of those in later times was in any way superfluous, who, when there was no risk of endangering salvation, added something to humiliation, in order that the salvation might be more thoroughly protected,--having, I suppose, experienced a feigned repentance on the part of some who were influenced by the desire of the power attaching to office. For experience in many diseases necessarily brings in the invention of many remedies. But in cases of this kind, when, owing to the serious ruptures of dissensions in the Church, it is no longer a question of danger to this or that particular individual, but whole nations are lying in ruin, it is right to yield a little from our severity, that true charity may give her aid in healing the more serious evils.

46. Let them therefore feel bitter grief for their detestable error of the past, as Peter did for his fear that led him into falsehood, and let them come to the true Church of Christ, that is, to the Catholic Church our mother; let them be in it clergy, let them be bishops unto its profit, as they have been hitherto in enmity against it. We feel no jealousy towards them, nay, we embrace them; we wish, we advise, we even compel those to come in whom we find in the highways and hedges, although we fail as yet in persuading some of them that we are seeking not their property, but themselves. The Apostle Peter, when he denied his Savior, and wept, and did not cease to be an apostle, had

not as yet received the Holy Spirit that was promised; but much more have these men not received Him, when, being severed from the framework of the body, which is alone enlivened by the Holy Spirit, they have usurped the sacraments of the Church outside the Church and in hostility to the Church, and have fought against us in a kind of civil war, with our own arms and our own standards raised in opposition to us. Let them come; let peace be concluded in the virtue of Jerusalem, which virtue is Christian charity,--to which holy city it is said, "Peace be in thy virtue, and plenteousness within thy palaces." [2557] Let them not exalt themselves against the solicitude of their mother, which she both has entertained and does entertain with the object of gathering within her bosom themselves, and all the mighty nations whom they are, or recently were, deceiving; at them not be puffed up with pride, that she receives them in such wise; let them not attribute to the evil of their own exaltation the good which she on her part does in order to make peace.

47. So it has been her wont to come to the aid of multitudes who were perishing through schisms and heresies. This displeased Lucifer, [2558] when it was carried out in receiving and healing those who had perished beneath the poison of the Arian heresy; and, being displeased at it, he fell into the darkness of schism, losing the light of Christian charity. In accordance with this principle the Church of Africa has recognized the Donatists from the very beginning, obeying herein the decree of the bishops who gave sentence in the Church at Rome between Cæcilianus and the party of Donatus; and having condemned one bishop named Donatus, [2559] who was proved to have been the author of the schism, they determined that the others should be received, after correction,

with full recognition of their orders even if they had been ordained outside the Church,--not that they could have the Holy Spirit even outside the unity of the body of Christ, but, in the first place, for the sake of those whom it was possible they might deceive while they remained outside, and prevent from obtaining that gift; and, secondly, that their own weakness also being mercifully received within, might thus be rendered capable of cure, no obstinacy any longer standing in the way to close their eyes against the evidence of truth. For what other intention could have given rise to their own conduct, when they received with full recognition of their orders the followers of Maximianus, whom they had condemned as guilty of sacrilegious schism, as their council [2560] shows, and to fill whose places they had already ordained other men, when they saw that the people did not depart from their company, that all might not be involved in ruin? And on what other ground did they neither speak against nor question the validity of the baptism which had been administered outside by men whom they had condemned? Why, then, do they wonder, why do they complain, and make it the subject of their calumnies, that we receive them in such wise to promote the true peace of Christ, while yet they do not remember what they themselves have done to promote the false peace of Donatus, which is opposed to Christ? For if this act of theirs be borne in mind, and intelligently used in argument against them, they will have no answer whatsoever that they can make.

[2550] Luke xv. 32.

[2551] Eph. iv. 3.

[2552] 1 Pet. iv. 8.

[2553] 1 Cor. xiii. 1-3.

[2554] 1 Cor. iii. 7.

[2555] Pope Innocent I., in his 6th Epistle to Agapitus, Macedonius, and Maurianus, bishops of Apulia, writes to the effect that "canons had been passed at Nicæa, excluding penitents from even the lowest orders of the ministry" (can. 10).

[2556] Matt. xvi. 19.

[2557] Ps. cxxii. 7; cp. Hieron.

[2558] Bishop of Calaris. Cp. De Agone Christiano, c. xxx. 32.

[2559] The Bishop of Casæ Nigræ.

[2560] The Council of Bagai.

Chapter 11.

48. But as to what they say, arguing as follows: If we have sinned against the Holy Ghost, in that we have treated your baptism with contempt, why is it that you seek us, seeing that we cannot possibly receive remission of this sin, as the Lord says, "Whosoever speaketh against the Holy Ghost, it shall not be forgiven him, neither in this world, neither in the world to come?" [2561] --they do not perceive that according to their interpretation of the passage none can be delivered. For who is there that does not speak against the Holy Ghost and sin against him, whether we take the case of one who is not yet a Christian, or of one who shares in the heresy of Arius, or of Eunomius, or of Macedonius, who all say that He is a creature; or of Photinus, who denies that He has any substance at all, saying that there is only one God, the Father; or of any of the other heretics, whom it would now take too long a time to

mention in detail? Are none, therefore, of these to be delivered? Or if the Jews themselves, against whom the Lord directed His reproach, were to believe in Him, would they not be allowed to be baptized? for the Saviour does not say, Shall be forgiven in baptism: but "Shall not be forgiven, neither in this world, neither in the world to come."

49. Let them understand, therefore, that it is not every sin, but only some sin, against the Holy Ghost which is incapable of forgiveness. For just as when our Lord said, "If I had not come and spoken unto them, they had not had sin," [2562] it is clear that He did not wish it to be understood that they would have been free from all sin, since they were filled with many grievous sins, but that they would have been free from some special sin, the absence of which would have left them in a position to receive remission of all the sins which yet remained in them, viz., the sin of not believing in Him when He came to them; for they could not have had this sin, had He not come. In like manner, also, when He said, "Whosoever sinneth against the Holy Ghost,"or, "Whosoever speaketh against the Holy Ghost;" it is clear that He does not refer to every sin of whatsoever kind against the Holy Ghost, in word or deed, but would have us understand some special and peculiar sin. But this is the hardness of heart even to the end of this life, which leads a man to refuse to accept remission of his sins in the unity of the body of Christ, to which life is given by the Holy Ghost. For when He had said to His disciples "Receive the Holy Ghost," immediately added, Whosesoever sins ye remit, they are remitted unto them; and whosesoever sins ye retain, they are retained." [2563] Whosoever therefore has resisted or fought against this gift of the grace of God, or has been estranged from it in any way whatever to the end of this mortal

life, shall not receive the remission of that sin, either in this world, or in the world to come, seeing that it is so great a sin that in it is included every sin; but it cannot be proved to have been committed by any one, till he has passed away from life. But so long as he lives here, "the goodness of God," as the apostle says, "is leading him to repentance;" but if he deliberately, with the utmost perseverance in iniquity, as the apostle adds in the succeeding verse, "after his hardness and impenitent heart, treasures up unto himself wrath against the day of wrath and revelation of the righteous judgment of God," [2564] he shall not receive forgiveness, neither in this world, neither in that which is to come.

50. But those with whom we are arguing, or about whom we are arguing, are not to be despaired of, for they are yet in the body; but they cannot seek the Holy Spirit, except in the body of Christ, of which they possess the outward sign outside the Church, but they do not possess the actual reality itself within the Church of which that is the outward sign, and therefore they eat and drink damnation to themselves. [2565]For there is but one bread which is the sacrament of unity, seeing that, as the apostle says, "We, being many, are one bread, and one body." [2566]Furthermore, the Catholic Church alone is the body of Christ, of which He is the Head and Saviour of His body. [2567]Outside this body the Holy Spirit giveth life to no one seeing that, as the apostle says himself, "The love of God is shed abroad in our hearts by the Holy Ghost which is given unto us;" [2568] but he is not a partaker of the divine love who is the enemy of unity. Therefore they have not the Holy Ghost who are outside the Church; for it is written of them, "They separate themselves being sensual, having not the Spirit." [2569]But neither does he receive it who is insincerely in the

Church, since this is also the intent of what is written: "For the Holy Spirit of discipline will flee deceit." [2570]If any one, therefore, wishes to receive the Holy Spirit, let him beware of continuing in alienation from the Church, let him beware of entering it in the spirit of dissimulation; or if he has already entered it in such wise, let him beware of persisting in such dissimulation, in order that he may truly and indeed become united with the tree of life.

51. I have despatched to you a somewhat lengthy epistle, which may prove burdensome among your many occupations. If, therefore, it may be read to you even in portions, the Lord will grant you understanding, that you may have some answer which you can make for the correction and healing of those men who are commended to you as to a faithful son by our mother the Church, that you may correct and heal them, by the aid of the Lord wherever you can, and howsoever you can, either by speaking and replying to them in your own person, or by bringing them into communication with the doctors of the Church.

[2561] Matt. xii. 32.

[2562] John xv. 22.

[2563] John xx. 22, 23.

[2564] Rom. ii. 4, 5.

[2565] 1 Cor. xi. 29.

[2566] 1 Cor. x. 17.

[2567] Eph. v. 23.

[2568] Rom. v. 5.

[2569] Jude 19.

[2570] Wisd. i. 5.

Writings of St. Augustine Against the Donatists

Made in the USA
Middletown, DE
27 December 2018